W9-ARV-529

INTERNATIONAL
FOLK DANCING U.S.A.

Also by Betty Casey
THE COMPLETE BOOK OF SQUARE DANCING
(and Round Dancing)

INTERNATIONAL FOLK DANCING U.S.A.

By BETTY CASEY

FOREWORD BY MIRIAM GRAY

University of North Texas Press
Denton, Texas

TO ALL FOLK DANCERS EVERYWHERE

Copyright © 2000 by Betty Casey

All Rights Reserved
Printed in the United States of America
First paperback edition

Permissions
University of North Texas Press
PO Box 311336
Denton, Texas 76203
(904) 565-2142

ISBN 1-57441-118-7

Foreword

It has been a distinct privilege to peruse the final draft of this amazing compendium of international folk dances being performed and taught in the United States today. It was indeed an honor to be consulted in the honing process of *International Folk Dancing U.S.A.* and to have the opportunity to write a foreword.

The book is a tremendous achievement, a resource book par excellence, an encyclopedic treasure trove of folk dance information from the people and the countries who have done the most to influence the growth of international folk dancing in the United States, nurturing it to full flowering in so many regions. More than sixty authors, teachers, leaders, and folk dancers have contributed their thoughts, their knowledge, and their unique historical perspective.

I commend the perceptive judgment and persuasive talents of author-compiler Betty Casey for having elicited contributions from such an impressive array of greats in the folk dance field—a list that reads like a who's who of folk dance in America.

The extensive background essays on the history and characteristics of the twenty-seven nationalities represented provide fascinating and instructive reading, in addition to the rich collection of dances emanating from each country. These dances come complete with descriptions, music and record notes, styling suggestions, and sources (i.e., where they came from and how they arrived here). The United States is represented by contras, rounds, and squares. A special section gives hints on teaching children various dances selected for their suitability in matching the abilities and interests of young people; these same dances might serve as an effective core for a beginning class of any age. There are dances galore, many from countries frequently ignored in other folk dance books.

Leaders—whether you are associated with local folk dance clubs, large urban community centers, or recreation departments—this book is for you! Authors, dance students, international folk dancers, researchers, teachers (amateur and professional)—in fact, anyone who likes to dance or to read about dance—this book is for you, too! Every library, personal and public, should own a copy.

You may never need to buy another folk dance book—unless you want *detailed* instructions on the various methods of teaching folk dancing. The one thing this book is *not* is a manual of teaching methods.

However, ideas, hints, and suggestions from an assortment of folk dance leaders on how to teach and perform particular dances pervade these pages. A wealth of teaching materials resides herein.

If you would like to know about some of the most highly rated performing groups in international folk dancing, they are described here. If you want to know about folk dance camps that have imparted leadership, knowledge, and skill to their happy participants over a long period and are still functioning, read on. If you are of a historical bent, enjoyable and informative sketches on the pioneers of folk dancing in America are included for your edification.

If you are research-minded, this invaluable resource is a veritable storehouse of costume, culture, history, nationality, character, and style into which dance researchers can delve with satisfaction and enjoyment for weeks or even months. The section entitled "Folk Dances from Many Lands" contains absorbing accounts of the dance life of every country represented, ranging from poetic sensing of the national dance temperament to elaborate detailing of indigenous steps and styles. If, for instance, you need a *different* sort of dance from a country unknown to you for use with a scout troop, you can find it in this section.

This may be the folk dance book to end all folk dance books. It tells you everything you always wanted to know about folk dancing but are almost sorry you asked. More than two years in preparation, *International Folk Dancing U.S.A.* reflects every minute in its careful and organized presentation. It is worth every penny of the purchase price. May every reader enjoy this treasure as much as I have. Happy reading, provocative studying, joyous dancing! "To dance is to live."—Snoopy

Miriam Gray

(Dr. Miriam Gray, dance educator and professor emerita of health, physical education, recreation, and dance at Illinois State University, also authored the following selections in this book: "American Alliance for Health, Physical Education, Recreation, and Dance" [AAHPERD] and "National Dance Association." A résumé of her long experience and significant leadership in the folk dance field follows the AAHPERD article in Part III.)

John and Betty Casey beside The-Dance-Along, *the trailer used while researching this book.*

Dear Folk Dance Enthusiast,

Folk dancing is alive and thriving in America and I'm documenting it in this major reference book.

Since December 1976 I've seen folk dancing firsthand, from Texas to Alaska and from California to New York. My husband, John, and I spent three exciting summer months on a 10,344-mile research trip consisting of "gourmet" dancing in our travel trailer, *The-Dance-Along*. The research travel totaled 25,374 miles (trailer, plane, car) and covered a span of two years and four months. Everywhere, special folk dance camps were filled and had long waiting lists.

From a Texan-Mexican fiesta and a North Carolina-Israeli camp to a Wisconsin-Scandinavian fest and a California-International potpourri, we thrilled to joyous dancing in the wake of dedicated, nationally recognized teachers and administrators from near and far. I interviewed many outstanding authorities in person and by telephone.

No two approaches are alike. The programs, teachers, and dancers are as different as the many trees and shrubs that make up a great forest. Yet, overall, the branches bend and sway and reach out toward each other to touch and mingle and make up an impressive and significant contribution to America's folk dance scene.

Since the various aspects of folk dance activity are so unstructured and personal, the story can only be told by the folk dancers and their leaders. Therefore, many of these individuals contributed to this book by providing dance lists, instructions, and by writing overviews of the folk dance activities in the country or area represented by their dance specialties. Some I observed teaching or performing administrative duties. Others made suggestions and generously provided research materials and stunning action photographs. The names of those individuals who have made specific contributions are listed in the section entitled "Many, Many Thanks."

The inclusion in this book, as well as subsequent printings and editions, of materials furnished by individuals from their personal files or writings does not in any way curtail or prohibit those contributing to this volume from using such materials in any way they see fit. All rights to individually owned or copyrighted material used here is the property of the original owner.

Thus, I have collected a great deal of material depicting folk dance mores across the land. Yet even though this is the most comprehensive folk dance reference book currently available, it can only offer a sampling of this vast, many-faceted activity.

Sections describing the contributions of outstanding national leaders and teachers were, for the most part, written by personal acquaintances. They reflect not only the deeds but also the esteem felt for these dedicated individuals.

My research revealed that there is wide divergence in the practice and promotion of folk dance ideologies—and even some heated disputes. No effort was made to referee or even to ferret out both (or several) sides of a given controversy. Nor have I attempted to standardize, edit, or influence the selection of representative instructional and background material generously submitted by individual outstanding folk dance leaders from many different areas. Some are effusive writers while others are quite terse; some give explicit dance directions while others are more casual. This is their story and the material selected for inclusion is presented the way they see it.

This volume represents a collective report on international folk dancing activities as practiced in some places in the United States. Conversely, recognition for persons and programs not included (due to lack of space or knowledge), will have to provide material for another writing.

Since international folk dancing is a relatively new activity in this country, many of the pioneers who stimulated its development are still with us. Therefore, we are able to record and preserve their priceless reports and recollections and give recognition to their valuable contributions to the folk dance heritage of America.

My own interest and experience in folk dancing is far-reaching and enthusiastic. I studied with the late Dr. Lloyd "Pappy" Shaw in the United States, with Mrs. Francisca Aquino in the Philippines, and with other individuals in the United States, Europe, Asia, and Africa during my twenty years as a foreign-service wife. I've contributed to cultural exchange dance programs from Tangier and Hongkong to Manila and Munich.

I hope this book will help promote and perpetuate international folk dancing in the United States.

Happy dancing,

Betty Casey

Betty Casey

MANY, MANY THANKS

Valuable contributions from many folk dance authorities and enthusiasts have made possible the wide range of international folk dancing activities presented in this book. I am humbly grateful for the co-operation, contributions, suggestions, and supportive encouragement so generously given. Space limitations preclude a long list of thanks, but I would like to express special thanks to as many individuals as possible. I apologize to those not listed, but do appreciate every single bit of assistance given. None are in any way responsible for errors or mistakes that unknowingly might have crept into the text.

Foremost among those to whom I offer deep and sincere appreciation is Vytautas (Vyts) Beliajus. This giant among folk dance authorities, known nationwide as "Mr. Folk Dance U.S.A.," has been my mainstay, my guide, my mentor, my consultant, and my wise counselor. He has unsparingly shared information from his vast storehouse of folk dance knowledge and from the files of that renowned folk dance magazine, *Viltis,* of which he is publisher and editor. This information has included history, dance details, photographs, articles, names of leaders and camps, as well as addresses. Vyts has read and edited much of the copy for this book. Most importantly, he has provided encouragement and moral support on various occasions when the research problems I faced were tough and discouraging. He has authored the following sections in this book: "The Changing Scene in the Folk Dance Field"; "Publications for Folk Dancers"; and "Lithuanian Folk Dancing."

A valuable contribution was made by Dr. Miriam Gray, an outstanding folk dance educator and author-

ity. For this major service and assistance I extend to her my heartfelt thanks.

Dr. William (Bill) and Gladys Chamberlain, former members of Chang's dance group in San Francisco, have been especially supportive and helpful by providing material from their files, posing for pictures, and serving as sounding boards as the book progressed.

I appreciate Fred Berk's valuable contributions, "From Words to Movement" and "Israeli Folk Dancing," and recall with pleasure his (and the staff's) friendly reception at the Blue Star Folk Dance Camp. Mary Bee Jensen's graciousness and contribution of material at Brigham Young University was enjoyable and informative. Her contribution on Vyts Beliajus and a section, with pictures, on the Brigham Young University International Folk Dancers enhance this book. "How To Build a Folk Dance Group" and "Dance Floor Manners" by Dean Linscott present authoritative guidelines. I also appreciate the selection, with accompanying pictures, of the Linscott's Kopachka Dancers. "Records for Folk Dancers, Then and Now" by Ed Kremers, and "Round Dancing" by Henry (Buzz) Glass provide important historical insights; Buzz also chronicled the contribution made to folk dancing by Lucile Czarnowski.

Millie von Konsky, another outstanding authority, made suggestions and provided photographs and an important section on "Folk Dancing for Children." She was most helpful in checking the Lexicon. Working as a consultant during a two-week stay in our home, Dick Oakes, an all-around international folk dance instructor, helped in checking the many dance instructions and the Lexicon definitions. He devised the clever system of using a larger and smaller raised capital letter (R^L) to indicate that a step can be done with either the right or left foot; he also assisted with photo illustrations and provided the material for "Yugoslavian Folk Dancing."

I also wish to thank the following people who contributed essays on the historical background of folk dancing by writing about outstanding pioneers in this field: Elsie Canterbury wrote about Dick Crum; Kirby Todd discussed Paul and Gretel Dunsing; Madeline Uraneck described Jane Farwell and Folklore Village Farm; Dorothy Kvalnes and others wrote about Madelynne Greene; and Carole Howard discussed the various achievements of Michael and Mary Ann Herman, Lloyd and Dorothy Shaw, and Grace Laura Ryan.

I greatly appreciate the free accommodations generously provided by Herman Popkins at Blue Star Camp and his contribution about the camp. Other contributors on camps and organizations include: Mel Diamond—Buffalo Gap Camp; Genevieve Shimer and Joan Carr—Country Dance and Song Society; Vi Dexheimer and Perle Bleadon—Folk Dance Federation of California; Elma McFarland—Idyllwild Folk Dance Workshop; M. G. Karsner—Kentucky Dance Institute; D. J. Obee—Lloyd Shaw Foundation; Paul Kermiet—Lighted Lantern; Mary E. Fish—Oglebay Institute; Christine Helwig—Pinewoods Camp; Valerie Staigh—San Diego State University Folk Dance Conference; Bernard Kaiman—Tennessee Octoberfest Folk Dance Camp; Bobby Gilotti—Texas Folk Dance Camp; and Walter Grothe—University of the Pacific Folk Dance Camp.

I especially appreciate the contributions of the following folk dance specialists and researchers (not previously mentioned) who shared historical overviews, dance instructions, and photos relating to the region of their particular expertise: Tom Bozigian—Armenia; Yves Moreau—Bulgaria; Anatol Joukowsky—Czechoslovakia; May Gadd—England; Louise and Germain Hebert—France; Gretel (and the late Paul) Dunsing and Morry Gelman—Germany and Austria; Athan Karras—Greece; Kálmán and Judith Magyar—Hungary; Margie L. Tiritelli, Ireland; Elba F. Gurzau—Italy, plus pictures of the Italian Folk Dance Group; Alura Flores de Angeles—Mexico; Kate McGowan and Ibrahim Farrah—Orient, plus photos; Libertad V. Fajardo and Celia Martinez (daughter of Francisca Reyes Aquino, who granted permission to use material written by her mother)—Philippines; Alfred Sokolnicki—Poland, plus photos of the Mazur Polish Dancers of Milwaukee; Eugenia Popescu-Judetz—Romania; Vincent Evanchuk—Russia and the Ukraine; Sharron Deny—Scandinavia; Kate McGowan and Bora Ozkok—Turkey; and Don Armstrong—United States (contras).

I thank Nelda Drury for information and pictures of the San Antonio College Folk Dancers; Leon McGuffin for the use of his files; Diki Shields for pictures of the Jasna Planina Folk Ensemble; and Ron Houston for his suggestions, research material, and for agreeing to pose with his dancers. I am grateful to the following dancers who also posed for pictures: Marci Goldstein, Jan DeWitt and Gary T. Gavlick, Shirley McGraw, Don Stroud, Lori Lynch, and Gail Sears.

I acknowledge the use made of the many research magazines, books, and pamphlets listed in the bibliography and especially appreciate the assistance and cooperation of Max Horn, associate editor of Let's Dance magazine; Paul Pritchard, editor of Folk Dance Scene; Raymond Olson, president of the Folk Dance Federation of California, and his wife, Phyllis; and Arthur C. Brooks, exchange editor of the Northwest Folkdancer.

Sincere appreciation is extended to Walter Kolar, director of the Duquesne University Tamburitzans,

for his co-operation in providing many outstanding photographs; and to the Aman Folk Ensemble for supplying excellent photographs. I also wish to thank the following for other photographs gratefully included: Country Dance and Song Society of America, The Milwaukee Journal, Lee Marshall, Sofia Press, Henry L. Bloom, Robert H. Chevalier, A. C. Smith, James F. Bartlett, Edward Mankus, Taylor Publishing Co., Tadeus Kozielec, Van W. Frazier, Nelson R. Smith, Wendt Studio, and Fuzzy Swayze.

In addition thanks go to the many teachers and organizations who permitted me to attend their sessions in order to observe and report on teaching techniques, dance trends, and student reactions.

My editor, Louise Gault, who conceived the idea for this book, deserves credit, and I thank Evelyn Jaeggli and her staff at the Butt-Holdsworth Memorial library for locating many books for me. I also salute my typist, Kay Satchell, who has cheerfully and faithfully deciphered my scribbled notes.

The one person to whom I owe the greatest debt of gratitude is my husband, John. He not only wrote the article "Sound Systems for Folk Dancing" and laid out the illustrations but has also served as my chauffeur for some twenty thousand research miles. He good-naturedly endured the writing clutter stacked on the dining room table, desk, card table, bookshelves, and sometimes scattered across the floor; carefully photocopied several thousand pages; and has been generally supportive and patient. To him, to those listed here, and to hundreds of others who have contributed to this volume I say, "Many, Many Thanks."

PURPOSE

This book provides, in one volume, a selected collection of instructional and historical reference materials designed to be useful and informative to the folk dance enthusiast, whether teacher, leader, or dancer.

It includes a concise Lexicon of folk dance terms, steps, and movements, as well as a large collection of dances with accompanying instructions. The dances were chosen by top authorities from among those dances being performed in the United States by international folk dance groups. The sections entitled "Dance Descriptions," "Lexicon of Folk Dance Definitions," and "From Words to Movement" provide a helpful guide to performing them.

The book also recognizes the efforts of a handful of national leaders and organizations whose pioneering labors of love have served as a catalytic force in making the dances available for enjoyment by many; it gives an indication of how and where they are being danced across the land.

Contents

I
FOLK DANCE BEGINNINGS

Folk Dancing: Primitive to Modern

"Every dance is and gives ecstasy." —Curt Sachs

Dance movements and rituals have been an instinctive part of mankind's mode of expression since antiquity. Rock paintings created by primitive man thousands of years ago in the region now known as France depict people dancing. Contemporary dances seem to have counterparts among those stone age types.

The original dances are not known, but they can be approximated by comparing traits of human nature. All people walk, run, crouch, and hold out their hands to signify compassion or supplication. Primitive peoples formed circles and moved clockwise, as does modern man. They stepped, stamped, and kicked just as we do today. Irresistible forces propelled mankind toward developing this means of expression.

Curt Sachs, in his *World History of the Dance,* proclaims: "In the ecstasy of the dance man bridges the chasm between this and the other world, to the realm of demons, spirits, and God. Captivated and entranced he bursts his chains and trembling feels himself in tune with all the world" (p. 4).

Whether or not one feels comfortable with this aesthetic premise, the fact remains that down through the ages people have disciplined themselves to practicing the rhythmical movements associated with dancing. At this very moment, celebrants around the world are swinging, swaying, and stepping; dancers will polka and waltz into the future, touching a heel and toe and gliding to three-quarter time.

Dance is not only a physical activity, it is interwoven in the social interaction between an individual and a group engaged in a social activity. All types of human emotions and experiences have been acknowledged or celebrated by dancing rituals. Man's first dances were a form of worship of such natural forces as the sun, the moon, animals, thunder, and rain. Primitive man danced to please and implore the mysterious forces influencing various aspects of his life, including fertility, birth, harvest, sickness, and death. Thus, dances have expressed joy, sorrow, and reverence. While some dances acknowledged occasions of healing, others celebrated the consecration of maidens at puberty, circumcision, courtship, marriage, combat, victory, and peace. Types of dances include convulsive dances, leaping dances, slapping dances, gliding dances, phallic dances, kneeling dances, whirling dances, and sitting dances.

With the approach of the winter solstice, a time of terrible fear, men jumped and stomped on the earth to reawaken it or to call back the dead; sometimes they wore bells and beat drums. Medicine dances assured a return to good health; black magic or voodoo dances were aimed at putting a curse on an enemy; rain dances and fertility dances sought to gain the favor of the gods; and war and hunting dances, performed exclusively by men, served to build up courage.

At first, man imitated nature. Then, in an effort to influence nature, sun rituals were initiated in areas where climatic conditions were unstable and summers short. In Europe, a common practice was for the men to dance around bonfires. Because women's menstrual periods were linked with phases of the moon, their dances often imitated the waxing and waning of the moon.

Original dance forms have been influenced down through the years by environmental and geographic factors. Heavy clothing, necessitated by a cold climate, imposed restrictions on movement, whereas lighter clothing allowed more freedom of movement, thus influencing the choreography of the dances. Some movements were designed to display ornamental dress, others to exhibit the thinly clad bodies of the dancers.

With the development of such work utensils as ploughs, scythes, baskets, and hoes, dance movements came to represent the activities of ploughing, cutting, winnowing, and stacking grain. They also depicted the gathering of grapes and the making of wine, as well as other occupational pursuits. Erotic movements, culminating with the man embracing the woman and carrying her off, were interwoven in early wedding and fertility dances. Then, with the establishment of a code of social behavior, the man knelt with dignity before the lady.

Music accompanying dances depended on the resources at hand: a hollow log to serve as a drum; dried seeds in gourds for counterrhythms; or a piece of split bamboo to blow a tune through. The unique tones produced often influenced the movements and style of the dances. But, above all, the details of regional dances reflected the particular temperament, individuality, and prevailing concerns of the dancers, in addition to current styles popular at any given time.

Dancing has not developed in sophistication at the

same rate in all areas of the world. Even in today's electronic and space-age culture, there are isolated areas of the world where primitive, ritualistic dancing still prevails. Technologically sophisticated societies have attained a refined level of choreography.

Some dances, such as the hornpipe (a solo jig performed to bagpipes), developed as a result of particular circumstances. British sailors, who lacked partners while at sea, developed the dance out of necessity. It was performed to bagpipes because these instruments were small and portable enough to be taken along on the ships.

Like primitive man before him, the ancients who lived prior to the Middle Ages believed in the magic power of dancing. The sword and Maypole dances of Europe are relics of ancient tree-worshiping rituals practiced by the first settlers in the enormous forests that once flourished there. Tree worship has been commonly represented by dancing among the primitive tribes of Australia.

Dances performed by Hungarian shepherds depict the hunting and killing of the boar. Dance movements of the Slavic woodsmen sometimes include the action of tree chopping.

Dancing was a formal part of the Christian service and liturgy until the twelfth century A.D., at which time the early theologians, feeling that dancing was distracting and too often suggestive of impious and worldly ideas, began to root it out of the holy ritual. The Protestant church put a damper on dancing for a while, then the revival started. Down through the centuries, it has proved impossible to prevent people from dancing.

As civilization developed in Europe and became more sophisticated, simple folk dances changed accordingly, becoming more social in character. As travel between countries increased, there was a resultant intermingling of dance forms formerly kept more or less in their original form by virtue of geographic isolation.

Dancing masters borrowed elements of folk dances and refined them for the enjoyment of the court. This brought entire villages into contact with court fashions and furthered the exchange of dance styles. Peasants emulated court dances, while waltzes and polkas took the continent by storm.

The minuet, for instance, originated as a romantic, folkloric peasant dance and attained a splendid stylized dignity in the courts of France during the reign of Louis XIV. At the beginning of the eighteenth century, English country dances, disdained by the elite, were adopted by the French in the form of a "round for eight" and became known as *contre danse française*. The special French name given these dances for eight was *cotillon*. It was supposedly related to the French term meaning petticoat, *cotillon*, found in a tune popular at the time: "Ma commère, quand je danse / Mon cotillon va-t-il bien?" ("My dear, when I dance / Does my petticoat show?")

Under this name, the cotillon returned to England and became popular in other European countries. From there it made its way, accompanied by many others, to the formal halls of George Washington's America, and on to the frontiers of the West. There the name was anglicized to cotillion.

Remnants of early dance rituals are evident in the folk dances of today. But since these dances are performed for social or recreational reasons—and in the modern setting of the space age and television, radio, and electronic recording devices—the style, form, and content of these dances have changed. Primitive dances blended, merged, separated, and re-emerged in their modern forms as they attained new horizons and new homelands.

What Is International Folk Dancing?

". . . Dances are the earth castings . . . the thumb prints of the character . . ."
—Agnes de Mille

Folk dancing is an irrepressible expression of the human need for emotional and physical satisfactions gained through rhythmical body movements. Today folk dancing is thought of as traditional ritualistic and recreational dance forms, anonymous in origin and handed down from generation to generation in specific areas of the world.

Folk dances are as varied and unique as the worldwide ethnic groups that perform them, from Nome to Nairobi, from Munich to Manila, deep in humid jungles, on balmy seashores, across windswept plains, or atop snow-capped mountains. They are the basis for all dance forms—primitive, social, and classical.

Folk dances can be merry and spontaneous or mel-

ancholy and measured. Many of the original movements were imitative or symbolic, representing the actions of or reactions to nature, people, birds, and
animals. Some folk dances are overlaid with foreign
influences, reflecting cultures introduced by invaders
and conquerors. The resulting choreography portrays
the unique life-styles of different peoples—their religions, customs, geography, history, and feelings. Folk
dancing is more than just a cultural profile of a given
people. Their music, costumes, and background combine with rhythms, moods, and patterns to form a
total picture.

Folk dances are always composed of selections from
a common reservoir containing: quick or slow steps
and leaps; lively or languorous arm, leg, and body
movements; and simple or syncopated rhythms. Although the steps are often the same, the differences
in tempo, costume, and performance make the dances
distinctively different from each other.

Although they are closely related, there is a difference between ethnic and folk dancing. In his book
entitled *The Teaching of Ethnic Dance* Anatol Joukowsky makes the following distinction: "Ethnic dance
is one done by the people in the original place, in
living form, today or yesterday. It is transferred or
transported to a new place without any change and
is performed as it was originally. The music is done
without adaptation. . . . Ethnic dance . . . transfers
the culture and knowledge of a people to present and
future generations. Folk dance, as we use this term,
describes a dance which initially was an ethnic dance
but which has undergone some change through the
years" (p. 1).

Dick Crum wrote the following concerning the
dances involved in these changes in an article for *Let's
Dance* magazine: "They are things of beauty, and as
such, they are now being preserved rather like other
things are being preserved in museums. You ARE
able to enjoy *Turopoljski Drmeš*. It's dead now; no
one does it in Turopolje, except the little group that
drags it out every couple (of) months and performs
it at a festival. We can share in that dance as a me-
mento of times past and enjoy it for its beauty . . ."

In the United States there are many different communities where people with specific ethnic backgrounds gather to perpetuate the customs and folk
dances of their particular native lands. Frequently the
dances are only perfomed on special holidays or celebrations or as staged performances. This type of dancing has come to be known as "ethnic folk dancing."

On the other hand, international folk dancers are
a conglomerate of people of no particular ethnic background who share a love for the dances of many nations. Members of international folk dance groups in
the United States study and perform dances of native
and foreign origin in order to understand a variety
of cultures. Serious performers of these dances try to
imitate and preserve the original costumes, customs,
and subtle interpretive choreography and styling that
reflect the unique cultures and temperaments that give
the dances their individuality. Folk dances are often
performed for the enjoyment of spectators during international festivals and pageants.

Yet through the years many symbolic gestures and
movements associated with these dances have faded
and sometimes more than one version of a dance has
evolved. The dances are often performed mainly for
social and recreational enjoyment, with varying degrees of emphasis on costuming or styling.

Some foreign dances have been altered to such an
extent that they have become a traditional part of
the American scene and are labeled American dances,
as are others originally choreographed in this country.
These include some American contra dances, square
dances, and round dances.

The contras have remained closest to the original
forms, while square dancing has undergone so much
Americanization and modernization that it has become
known worldwide as an American folk dance. Rounds,
danced by couples to cued instructions, are associated
with the widespread square dance activity; many have
been choreographed in this country.

Although both round dancing and square dancing
have their own organizations, selected dances from
each category are an integral part of international folk
dancing activities in varying degrees. The term *international folk dancing* is somewhat ambiguous and diffuse
since there are no sharp demarcations between the
ethnic categories of dances and those who practice
them.

Selection of a particular program to be followed
by individual folk dance groups varies widely, sometimes involving many selections from many countries;
at other times limited to dances from only a few countries. It depends, to a large extent, on the availability
and enthusiasm of informed leadership and the personal preferences of the leader and the dancers.

International folk dancing is the performance of
folk dances from far and near by an ethnic potpourri
of people in America in order to better understand various cultures and enjoy the emotional and physical satisfactions gained through rhythmical body movements.

Folk Dancing: U.S.A.

A sizable number of international folk dances representing many countries have made their way across land and sea and international borders to the United States. Without planned direction or conscious choice, certain dances have been introduced to delight folk dance enthusiasts by proud natives, by spellbound travelers bringing instructions back with them, and by educators sharing their academic research in order to promote a better understanding of international cultures.

These dances have permeated the American folk scene just like the immigrants whose life-styles they represent. Many of the folk dances came to these shores in the minds and hearts of settlers who brought the culture of their mother country with them—their food, languages, and dances. Close-knit ethnic communities practiced and perpetuated these dances in time-honored fashion at weddings, christenings, and on important holidays—and they still do.

The settlers brought their fandangos, polkas, hornpipes, and quadrilles. Stage performers also introduced many dances that were later copied. In 1794 the first American dancer of note, John Durang, made his stage debut in Philadelphia. Durang's Hornpipe, a dance he choreographed and sometimes performed on a tightrope, is still popular in some folk dance circles today.

The early history of folk dancing was mainly associated with ethnic groups and folk festivals, featuring performances for spectators rather than participants. Some nationalities did not readily share their dances with others, preferring to save them for special occasions of their own. Other dances, especially those from Europe, were taught to society groups by dancing masters. In the larger cities they introduced the latest contra dance, allemande, minuet, waltz or galop at grand balls. The cotillion was a favorite of George Washington. Some dances survived as they were originally taught, while parts of others were combined or remodeled by adding an extra hop here, a twirl there, or by fitting the steps to the available music.

Regional and ethnic dances came to have wide appeal and ceased to be limited to those with hereditary ties to their countries of origin. Large numbers of folk dance hobbyists of no predominant ethnic origin discovered that they didn't have to be Czechoslovakian to enjoy Czech dances or Irish to find pleasure in Irish reels. Popular folk dance activities have now become a thriving enterprise, expanding and attracting

thousands of happy participants each day. Those individuals who perform a variety of dances from other lands reflect the melting pot of our times. Although it isn't quite accurate from a terminological standpoint (they include ballroom as well as court dances), they are known as international folk dancers [IFD].

Although this mixture of dances is a very popular form of recreation today, the development of IFD in the United States has been and still remains fragmented and diverse. Autonomous pockets of activity ranging from intense to casual are scattered across the land. Groups meet in community centers, YMCAs and YWCAs, settlement houses, international institutes, church and grange halls, gyms, at camps, on tennis courts—wherever there's space for folks to join hands for a hora or choose partners for the hambo. Some groups are locally and regionally organized into clubs and associations, while members of other groups travel far, both nationally and internationally, to attend folk dance camps and seminars directed by authoritative leaders.

Dance in education has come a long way since the twenties. In one small town in western Michigan the subject was so suspect that the course had to be labeled "floor patterns"; and at one Texas university folk dances were called "folk games." Now folk dancing is a popular subject regularly taught on many campuses.

Every night of the week there are folk dance sessions and classes devoted to dances from many lands in places such as New York City, Chicago, Detroit, Los Angeles, and San Francisco; several times each month these activities take place in villages and small towns across the nation. In most instances, the folk dance clubs and classes operate independently of each other, no two being alike. They select from the myriad folk dances performed in countries around the world. Some specialize in only one ethnic type of dancing such as Israeli horas, or Scottish reels or Serbian kolos. Some choose dances from two or three countries while others include dances from a broad spectrum of nationalities, depending on the versatility and knowledge of the instructor. There are some professional folk dance teachers. However, most sessions are financed by minimal fees and teachers often donate their time and effort or are paid according to the size of the group.

The establishment of folk dance coffeehouses proved to be a significant factor in some cities. The Intersection, one of the first such establishments still in operation, opened in 1967 in Los Angeles with the avowed purpose of providing an international center for folk dance activities; a minimal fee was charged for lessons and membership.

There is no central organization for IFD in the United States, although there are some cohesive state and regional federations and associations. The Folk Dance Federation of California, composed of South and North sections, is the most highly organized group, with several hundred member clubs following more or less standardized programming. The Country Dance and Song Society of America with offices in New York, specializes in early English and American country dancing and has some fifty member societies in several states.

There are a few other state and regional IFD organizations. Many schools, colleges, and universities offer folk dance classes of varying degress of intensity; some sponsor Folk Dance Performing Groups. They, too, operate autonomously. Folk dance groups maintain loose contact with each other through classes taught by traveling teachers who introduce dances and provide instruction for them by way of syllabuses at camps, seminars, and festivals.

Scores of dedicated folk dance leaders have served in their own communities for years, their influence being confined to one or two groups. Other teachers and leaders have shared their expertise in larger regional areas. The efforts of a few individual dance leaders and authorities have had far-reaching effects nationwide; a few organizations and institutions have made significant contributions to the overall picture. In the seventies a proliferation of commercially oriented teachers inundated the country with new material. Some of the latter is made up of authentic ethnic steps and music; much is based on new choreography set to ethnically related music, producing hybrid types of dances.

How did this unorganized, disconnected activity grow to such massive proportions? Who is responsible for its development? How did it develop? One might answer that it grew inch by inch as a result of the devoted efforts of leaders with vision, stamina, and the courage to promote it. The present popularity of folk dancing developed slowly, with a pocket of interest here and a bubble of activity there. The need of people everywhere to express enjoyment through dance surfaced in many places, though not always with the same degree of intensity or frequency.

The embryonic formation of folk dancing as a recognizable entity actually took shape in the early 1900s and continued its erratic development to present levels. It would be impossible for any one person, or even a group of persons, to delineate and detail specific stages, chronologically or otherwise, in the development of international folk dancing in the United States. Unrelated programs conducted at the same time but in different geographic and ethnic areas only became significant in the overall picture when later programs pooled them together. In fact, one book could not possibly give adequate recognition to every person who

has made a significant contribution. Yet there are a handful of special individuals whose names come up time and again in discussions of national folk dance history. Many of them published folk dance books, some of which are now out-of-print.

Some made their contribution by opening the door to folk dance programs in schools while others made outstanding contributions through organized recreational organizations or camps. Several made significant contributions through their work with performing groups. A few affected folk dance activity simply as a consequence of their superb enthusiasm and personal charisma in promoting folk dance events.

Teachers of international folk dancing developed expertise in the dance styles and steps of many countries in order to share their knowledge with students. They taught Swedish polskas, Israeli yemenites, Mexican zapateados, and Scottish pas de basques.

International folk dancing is a relatively new activity in America. Several of the early leaders have died, some made their mark and moved on to other interests, but quite a few are still at the forefront of folk dance presentations. In 1909 Elizabeth Burchenal published *Folk Dances and Singing Games* in conjunction with the folk dance movement she had initiated in New York in 1900. Mary Wood Hinman's efforts stimulated educational interest in the Chicago area. Lloyd (Pappy) Shaw's concern for a constant program of wholesome activity for his high school students, first expressed in the 1920s, developed during his thirty-five years with the Cheyenne Mountain School, near Colorado Springs, and had a national impact on academic courses devoted to folk dancing and recreational folk dancing. In 1927 May Gadd joined the work of the twelve-year-old American Branch of the English Folk Dance Societies in New York.

During the thirties and forties, interest accelerated and an exchange of instructors among various organizations and schools helped create a national movement. By 1940 Vyts Beliajus—who started teaching in the Chicago Park District during the thirties—had taught at over two hundred institutions of higher learning. About the same time, Paul and Gretel Dunsing were developing combined gymnastic and folk dance interests in Chicago. With her professional knowledge of folk dance, Lucile Czarnowski, an instructor at the University of California at Berkeley, laid the groundwork for the establishment of the Folk Dance Federation of California in 1942; she devised a form of dance instruction now largely used nationwide.

Sarah Gertrude Knott founded the National Folk Dance Festival in St. Louis in 1934; folk dancing in the schools took another step forward in 1937 when Grace Laura Ryan helped establish a subject minor degree program in education at Central Michigan University. In the 1930s Ralph Page of New Hampshire became one of the first full-time professional callers and started his square and folk dance camps in the 1950s.

During the thirties, Mary Ann and Michael Herman began teaching folk dances from many countries to groups representing many ethnic backgrounds. They programmed audience participation for dances presented at the New York World's Fair in 1940, established Folk Dance House in New York City, and in 1950 took over Jane Farwell's Maine camp. No one has gained more recognition for promoting play party games and recreational dances through national leadership laboratories than Jane Farwell, who began her activities in the 1940s in the ethnic neighborhoods of New York City. The early camps she started in Maine, Texas, West Virginia, and Wisconsin established a significant pattern that is still popular among folk dance camps. By 1945 New York City reported ten thousand registered folk dancers, while northern California claimed five thousand. In between, hundreds were attending folk dances as casually as going to the movies.

Madelynne Greene was labeled "folk dancer's guiding light" in California. She contributed to the establishment of the Mendocino Folklore Camp and the Folk Dance Federation of California and is credited with introducing twenty-eight international dances to American audiences. Since the late 1950s, Balkan dancing has been given impetus through the original research and efforts of Dick Crum, a spin-off from his work as a choreographer for the Tamburitzans of Duquesne University.

The essays in Part II describe the activities of these great folk dance leaders. Most of the essays were written by personal friends. Thus, we gain insight from many quarters and are not limited to one viewpoint. The essays are presented in alphabetical order according to the last names of the folk dance leaders.

Part III describes folk dance camps and organizations that have gained national recognition or have been in operation for more than twenty-five years. These are likewise listed in alphabetical order.

II
PIONEER FOLK DANCE LEADERS

Vytautas Beliajus

by Mary Bee Jensen

"Vyts" Beliajus, a native of Lithuania, is Mr. Folk Dance of the United States. "Where in the world is Lithuania?" Vyts was asked when he first came to this country. He pledged to "acquaint them dum foreigners with Lithuania," a pledge he has fulfilled.

This is Vyts' year [1972]. We can find no more deserving person than our Vyts. Within a matter of months he has been honored on very special occasions. At the twentieth anniversary of the San Francisco Kolo Festival he was honored for being the first person to introduce kolo dancing for general public dancing. The popular annual San Francisco Kolo Festival was started in 1952 by John Filcich and friends to help Vyts, who was hospitalized at the time.

Vyts has popularized folk dancing by teaching thousands the dances of Lithuania and by publishing *Viltis*, a popular folklore magazine. Since 1944 *Viltis* has been America's foremost folklore magazine, with Vyts as the founder and editor. Personally and through the

Vytautas (Vyts) Finadar Beliajus

media of *Viltis*, Vyts has made an outstanding contribution in the folk dance field and has contributed to the cultural enrichment of America.

Yet this outstanding American suffered many hardships in his early days in America. Fourteen-year-old Vyts arrived in America on September 3, 1923, accompanying his eighty-five-year-old grandmother on a visit to see her children, who had immigrated to America. Vyts did not speak English or understand American customs; the tall lad learning English among first graders was embarrassed and wanted to go back home. It was necessary for Vyts to work; he attended night school for a time, but it was difficult. He had to give up school, but he never gave up his desire for learning and broadening his knowledge.

Actually, Vyts is self-taught in many ways. As you become better acquainted with him, you discover that he has a fantastic storehouse of knowledge. He attended operas, symphonies, Shakespearean and other stage plays, and musicals; he visited museums and art galleries; and he read on every subject—literary novels, biographies, and histories. Between reading and crossword puzzles he learned to spell.

When young, Vyts was greatly impressed with Jules Verne's book *Around the World in Eighty Days*. It introduced him to a multitude of strange countries whose customs were unlike those he knew. He yearned to make friends with their inhabitants.

In Chicago he had an exciting opportunity to meet others from many nations. He first became interested in Mexican culture and folk dances, then soon began to include Italian and Hindu dances in his repertoire. He spent ten years learning and performing solo Hindu dances.

To Vyts, the more nationalities he became acquainted with the greater was his thirst to meet still more. He became deeply involved in Hasidic dancing and spent hour after hour dancing the hora with Jewish teen-agers. He was the only person in the Chicago area to authentically interpret the Hasidic style of dance. For two successive years he was engaged by the main Zionist organization for their annual fundraising spectacles held at the Civic Opera Theater. He danced to the singing of Richard Tucker, a member of New York's Metropolitan Opera, and brought down the house when the heartstrings of the audience were touched by his portrayal of a rabbi's aesthetic dance. He feels this would have turned into a career if poor health had not precipitated a move to the warmer clime of San Diego.

Vyts started teaching folk dancing in 1930, organized the first Lithuanian Folk Dance Club in the world in 1933, and was hired by the Chicago Park District to teach folk dancing. Vyts was one of the first traveling folk dance teachers in the country.

By 1940 he'd taught at over two hundred universities, colleges, and institutions and had sparked nationwide interest in folk dancing.

There are many "firsts" in Vyts' earlier life. He cosponsored the first large-scale folk dance festival for the Chicago Park District, held at Soldiers Field, Sept. 7, 1936. He organized the first kolo club to perform for nonethnic groups. His Lithuanian dancers were the first to perform kolos with the Duquesne University Tamburitzans in 1938. He presented the first folk ballets where genuine folk dances, songs, and customs were combined. He presented the first Hindu folk ballet and the first outdoor folkloric spectacle portraying a Lithuanian harvest and St. John's tradition, witnessed by thousands at Mark White Square and Marquette Park. He presented the first International Folk Festival in the South at Fairhope, Alabama, in the spring of 1943, instituted the first folk dance Kafana, and organized the first Israeli group in St. Louis, Missouri, in 1947.

What is Vyts' philosophy of dance? In the preface to the first volume of his book *Dance and Be Merry*, we read: "Folk dances have always been creations of the people. Peasants spent their leisure hours in folk dancing, finding in it the social pleasure otherwise almost entirely denied them. Among the people subject to cultural and economic limitations, the dances remained as the great pleasures of their lives, the only activity in which they could forget their burdens and feel something of the joy of life. Gradually, folk dancing became a thing of the past. . . . now they are looking back to dances of their ancestors to find in them true beauty and lasting pleasure. . . . folk dancing will survive regardless of how often it is overshadowed by passing fads."

He published *Lore* (1936–39), the first folklore magazine devoted to the folk dance, and he supervised a Folkraft album of Lithuanian dance music. He is mentioned in the *Lithuanian Encyclopedia, Best Known Lithuanians in the United States, History of Lithuanians in Chicago,* and is written up in *Arte Lituano,* published in Columbia, South America. Other books he has written include *Dance and Be Merry* (vol. II), *The Dance of Lietuva, Merrily Dance, Let's Be Merry, Linksmi Būkim* and *Ona.*

Vyts founded the now popular folklore magazine *Viltis* (meaning hope) in Fairhope, Alabama, probably the greatest contribution of his life. *Viltis* started as a mimeographed service letter to men in uniform in 1942 and evolved into its current form, published regularly since September 1944. For folklore activities, recipes for foreign foods, and dance descriptions *Viltis* is my guide. (*Viltis* is now available on microfilm from Xerox's University Microfilms, Serials Dept., 300, N. Zeeb Rd., Ann Arbor, Mich. 48106; parts of it are available through Microfilming Corporation, 21 Harristown Road, Glen Rock, N.J. 07452; it is distributed worldwide.) One column is called "Among Our Friends." How many friends Vyts Beliajus must have all over the world! As he writes, they become such personal friends that we almost share them with him.

It is difficult to tell you all of the contributions that Vyts has made in the field of dance and in the field of international friendship and understanding. Vyts' generosity, kindness, modesty, and dedication is amazing to me. To attend our twelfth Annual Christmas Around the World Concert, he took the bus over the Rockies in snowstorms that made me wonder if he would make it. This is our Vyts. He's wanted to share his talents with the world and he has done it graciously.

In response to a request from the embassy in Denmark for an American performing group at their International Folk Festival in Varda, Vyts recommended the International Folk Dancers from Brigham Young University. It was the first of many trips and performances for the BYU dancers.

Mr. Vyts Beliajus, Mr. Folk Dance of the United States, you have made a contribution to the world of dance that will live forever.

(The foregoing remarks were condensed from an introductory speech delivered in Houston, Texas, by Mary Bee Jensen, associate professor, in the College of Physical Education at Brigham Young University. On this occasion the National Dance Association of the American Alliance for Health, Physical Education, and Recreation [AAHPER] presented Mr. Beliajus with the 1972 Heritage Award.

Mary Bee Jensen is nationally and internationally known in the education and dance fields. She has received many awards and has been responsible for much recognition accruing to Utah and Brigham Young University. Mary Bee is founder and director of the International Folk Dancers of BYU. She has coauthored two books with Clayne Jensen, *Square Dancing* and *Folk Dancing,* and has written several other books and pamphlets. In 1974 Outstanding Educators of America selected Mrs. Jensen for special recognition and the Utah Association for Health, Physical Education and Recreation [UAHPER] presented her with an honor award. She has been a past vice-president of UAHPER and chairman of the Dance Forms Section of the Dance Division of AAHPER. For several years Mary Bee has been the official representative of the United States to the Confederation of International Folk Festivals. This organization was originally created in 1974, with folk dance leaders from twenty-five nations, including countries from behind the iron curtain, for the purpose of promoting world understanding through folk dancing. It is an official affiliate of UNESCO. She founded the BYU International Folk Dancers (see the section entitled "Brigham Young University International Folk Dancers"). There is a Performing Arts Company in this group consisting of from twenty-four to thirty-two dancers who tour twice a year within the United States. Every summer a select group of twelve couples tour Europe, Israel, and even behind the iron curtain. The BYU group is one of the most highly acclaimed folk dance groups within the United States. A photograph of Mary Bee Jensen appears on page 305).

Elizabeth Burchenal

by Betty Casey

Many dance leaders have been keenly aware of the great wealth of folklore lying dormant in countries throughout the world. In the United States, one of the foremost and earliest leaders was Elizabeth Burchenal, who, at the beginning of this century, traveled extensively and recorded music and folk dance patterns. Her research resulted in a series of fifteen folk dance books that became *de rigueur* in physical education classes for many years.

She made a great contribution to the growth of folk dancing in America's schools. She established folk dance playground programs and taught many leaders over a period of several decades. A far-reaching aesthetic folk dance movement began in New York City in 1909 when Miss Burchenal, an accomplished folk dancer who learned the dances through personal contact with people from various countries and from visits abroad, published a collection of dances in her book *Folk Dances and Singing Games*.

The following passage was written by Dr. Luther H. Gulick for the original edition of *Folk Dances and Singing Games:* "Herself a skilled technical teacher, she has entered into the spirit of the dances—some of which are relatively unformed, and even uncouth, others highly technical in form and meaning—and selected those dances which were most obviously fitting to American conditions, and worked with distinguished success to introduce them, under difficult conditions of American life. Miss Burchenal has done a great service to the cause in acting as Chairman of the Committee on Folk Dancing of the Playground Association of America. Her report to the Committee included a list of selected dances suitable for grass playgrounds, for playgrounds with earth surfaces, for indoor playgrounds, for small children, for larger boys and girls, as well as for adults. It is one of the most important documents in connection with the practical conduct of the folk dance movement in America."

Lucile Czarnowski, in a review of another book, *Folk Dances of Germany,* said that it was the result of many years of research. It was begun in Austria in 1928 and continued in 1933 and 1934 through two successive fellowship grants by the Oberlaender Trust, an integral part of the Carl Schurz Memorial Foundation, which had as its purpose the furthering of cultural relations between American and German-speaking peoples. In addition, Miss Burchenal acknowledged the co-operation and active assistance of eminent German scholars in the areas of folk arts and folklore while she was pursuing her work in Germany.

Most of the dances in this collection were noted on the spot by Miss Burchenal as she took part in folk celebrations and festivals in homes, farms, and villages of rural Germany. Likewise, many of the dance melodies were recorded firsthand; others were contained in manuscript collections of folk dance melodies. The collection of fifty-three folk dance melodies by Kammermusiker Friedrich Richter was of special significance and was mentioned in her acknowledgments. The musical accompaniments for the dances in this book were arranged and edited by Emma Howells Burchenal.

"Like all of Elizabeth Burchenal's dance descriptions, they are clear, direct and easy to follow, with diagrams to prevent the inexperienced from going astray."

"*Folk Dances of Germany* included many full-page pictures of the people performing these dances in their native setting in regional folk costumes. The pictures are of such clarity and size as to permit details of pattern, decoration, and costume accessories to be noted accurately."

Dr. Luther H. Gulick was one of the founders of the American Folk Dance Society in 1916, of which Miss Burchenal was president and director. Under the Society's auspices, a continuous educational program promoting the use of folk dancing and the appreciation of folk arts in general has been carried out throughout the country. The Society was reorganized in 1929 to serve as the United States section of the International Commission on Folk Arts.

Dick Crum

by Elsie Canterbury and Betty Casey

Dick Crum is nationally recognized as an authority on the Balkan folk arts. His field of expertise includes Bulgarian, Greek, and Romanian dances, as well as those of many ethnic groups in Yugoslavia.

A perennial favorite among folk dancers, Dick Crum has been active in Balkan dance since 1951. Thus far he has made seven trips to the Balkan countries, doing fieldwork as well as formal research with all types of groups, from village dancers to exhibition ensemble choreographers.

For twenty years Dick was associated with the Duquesne University Tamburitzans, first as a dancer and then as choreographer and technical adviser. He has taught Balkan dance at all the major folk dance camps in the United States and Canada and has held innumerable master classes at colleges and universities.

The library of the Tamburitzan Cultural Center vividly reflects the effort that Dick expended to assemble a fine collection of Yugoslavian publications and costumes. Dick is not only a scholar of Slavic Folk Art, a superb dancer, and a dynamic instructor but also an accomplished linguist. He speaks no less than ten languages.

Dick is interested in the ethnographic, choreographic, and recreational aspects of folk dancing. He has recorded dances as they are performed by native folk dancers, choreographed dances for stage and for nondancing audiences, and adapted American and Canadian folk dances for recreation, physical education, and just plain fun.

Among the most popular and enduring dances Dick has introduced to American folk dancers are Šetnja, Čačak, Orijent, Kriči Kriči Tiček, and Godečki Čačak. In addition, he has been a consultant for the recording of ethnic dance music on the Folk Dancer, Xopo, and Du-Tam labels. Dick works as an editor for the Los Angeles firm of Agnew Tech-Tran, a foreign-language service agency.

(The following interview with Dick Crum, conducted by Elsie Canterbury, gives some insights into his philosophy.)

"Rewarding experiences? Oh, I don't know. It's all rewarding. I like teaching. You could say that I find all teaching rewarding. I've always liked to teach, whether languages, dancing, or whatever. It feels natural; it's what I like to do."

He leaned back in his chair, shifted his shoulders. "But, yes, I have thought of one thing. I was teaching at a festival; I forget where. And there were these two women, folkdancers, once old friends. But they hadn't spoken to each other for . . . was it a dozen years? Anyhow, it was about some dance. Each had her own view of the 'right way.' And you know? They both were right. So that's what I did; I got them to see it, that they were both right. And they spoke. They sat down together, side by side; I saw them do that. Yes, I guess you could say that that was a rewarding experience."

We were eating wild blackberry pie for lunch in a little cafe in the Cascade foothills. Across the table Dick's eyes were hidden in the shadow of his sweat-blackened deckhand's cap. Limp hair, wet-black from the morning's hard work, was starting to dry to its natural auburn shade.

We had been talking of his years of touring, here and abroad, with the Tamburitzans, of his career(s) in work with languages, including a spell during World War II involving Far Eastern tongues, and his present translating and editing job, which he is finding much to his taste. To my question he responded that he has no Farsi and is weak in Tagalog.

As he talked, I kept seeing him as he had been that morning, teaching a fast, elusive Šumadija dance. With startling economy, he had been very quick to see precisely which movements needed re-emphasis.

Dick Crum. Photo by A. C. Smith

Somehow, the entire large circle of advanced Balkan dancers came out of that brief session in semicontrol of the dance.

A running counterpart to his economic teaching was the humorous barbs he kept tossing about "colorful ethnic natives" and such. These were a clue to his basic characteristic: the humanity that underlies all his thinking and feeling, along with a sharp detestation of hokum in any form.

He reached for the festival syllabus. "Just look at this, the design on the cover. Beautiful. What a job that girl did! The care she took."

Right. And in his comment I saw more clearly what he himself was: a man who sees the individual, the real person who made the cover. Dick Crum, the perceptive teacher who takes pains to kid us out of our predilection for romanticizing and dehumanizing the individual, who persists in making us see that the "colorful ethnic native" is an individual, sharing our common humanity.

He continued, "You could spend your life trying to be Bulgarian, but you'd never make it. No way. The thing is, you've got to get to know who you are, with no romanticizing, no fantasy. Because, to begin with, all you can ever be is your own real self. Then, after you get that clear, you can go ahead and have fun with folk dance and a lot of other things."

In folk dance across the country Dick sees changes, a new climate of feeling that is moving people toward openness, away from divisiveness and toward acknowledging and accepting our shared humanity, a climate that he welcomes and hopes will soon predominate.

"All dancing together," he said, "just like one big village."

Yes, I thought, I'll settle for your picture. It is a large-scale view of one of its main shapers: Dick Crum, in every sense a together guy.

(This interview material originally appeared in the *Northwest Folkdancer* (Oct. 1975, vol. XX, no. 9) and is used here with permission.)

Lucile K. Czarnowski

by Henry (Buzz) Glass

Lucile Czarnowski, one of the early presidents of the Folk Dance Federation of California, presided at the initial festival joining the Southern Federation to the North, held at Ojai, California. To the diverse dancers of the time Lucile brought a new element. We were novices and enthusiasts and she was the skilled expert. She shared completely and enthusiastically her wide professional knowledge of dance and, in particular, folk dance. She had a knowledge of music, the components of dance, the analysis of patterns and steps, as well as authentic styles and dance. She brought this high standard with her and thus influenced all who came in contact with her. She would never compromise her integrity.

Lucile was the first chairman of the research committee of the Folk Dance Federation of California, which she headed for some five years. Serving on this committee were Mildred Buehler, Alice Jameyson (who wrote a book on *Old Time Ballroom Dances* of old California), Harmer Davis of the engineering school at the University of California, and yours truly. My wife did all the typing. We met almost every week for many years, at Lucile's office on the University of California campus, working for the Federation. The components of the early volumes of *Dances from Near and Far* were to serve nationally and internationally as a base for dance descriptions. For example, *Dance A While* used this format as well as others. Those of us who attended learned from Lucile a technique of writing up dances that still continues to be utilized by those on the present research committee.

Miss Czarnowski began as an elementary school teacher in San Diego. She later earned a bachelor's degree from the University of California. She received a master's degree in dance while a dance major at the University of Wisconsin under Margaret H'Doubler.

Lucile gave a lecture on dance in The United States at the World Conference in Sweden. She was decorated by the Swedish king for her activities in folk dance. In 1939 she received the Lingiad Gold Medal and Diploma. Later she made a trip to Canada to study with Ukrainian émigrés. She shared this material with California dancers. She studied English Old-Time Dancing in Canada with one of the masters in this field. Thus, she presented the Royal Empress Tango and other dances to Californians.

Lucile is the author of *Dances of Early California Days* (Palo Alto: Pacific Books, 1950). Bomar also recorded these dances in an album entitled "Dances of Early California Days." She did a great deal of research in compiling her book and was able to keep alive a part of the heritage of California. As a result of her sincerity and stature, she was able to make genuine contacts unique to her. Unfortunately, Californians may know the forty-seven variations of the dances of Zeroland, but they essentially do not know the early California dances. ¡Qué lástima! Lucile also wrote *Folk Dance Teaching Cues* and, with Jack

McKay, coauthored *How to Teach Folk and Square Dance.*

For many years, Lucile served as an associate professor of physical education at the University of California at Berkeley. She taught folk dance and modern dance, as well as theory courses related to dance. Her reputation was well known, she knew leaders across the nation, who recognized her as a giant in the field. She knew Burchenal, Shambaugh, Gadd, and many others. Many of her students became outstanding leaders in the dance movement and received their impetus from Lucile. For example, Larry and Ruth Miller are active members of the present research committee. Bill and Gretchen Castner were her students. At one time Bill was president of the Folk Dance Federation and was one of America's great square dance callers. In 1968 Lucile was honored with the National Dance Association's Heritage Award at the St. Louis National Convention of the American Alliance for Health, Physical Education and Recreation.

(See section on Round Dancing for biographical data on Henry [Buzz] Glass.)

Paul and Gretel Dunsing

Paul and Gretel Dunsing

by Kirby Todd

It was May 1974, and as the students heard about the master dance classes taught by the visiting Dunsings in one of the university dance studios, the crowds kept getting bigger and bigger. The party that night in one of the gyms was packed with a laughing, swirling festival mass. It was the last full day the late Paul Dunsing was to teach in a remarkably full life of rhythm, dance, and love of people.

As a schoolboy in Berlin, Germany, Paul developed interests in rhythmic gymnastics, swimming, canoeing, and track and field. His first dance training was in a private school at the age of sixteen, when he was introduced to rheinlander, polka, fox trot, and other ballroom dances. He later received a German State Certificate for teaching rhythmic gymnastics and folk dance. It was at a folk dance that he met Gretel Benthin, who immediately told a friend that "she liked that boy." When she came to the United States in 1925 for a two-year visit, they corresponded frequently. Finally, through the simple expedient of staking him to a ticket, Gretel persuaded Paul to come to America. They were married in 1927, starting one of the most famous American folk dance teams of the century. Gretel had danced with her family as soon as she could walk, and received further training in folk dance and rhythmic gymnastics in school as a child.

For several years Paul worked in the paper business but continued gymnastics and folk dance after work as a recreational interest. With their group, the Dunsings attended many dance weekends and meets with active folk dance groups in the Chicago area. They introduced the idea of a "motion choir," a movement group co-ordinated with complementary musical background.

After receiving a B.S. in physical education from George Williams College, Paul served as athletic director at the college for one year. He earned an M.A. in education from Northwestern University while working with a soldiers' rehabilitation program conducted by the Mental Health Service of Illinois. During the summers of 1945–48, he served as director of recreation for the George Williams College camps on Lake Geneva. Shortly afterward, Paul was invited to become assistant professor of physical education at George Williams College, with Gretel as his assistant. Her background in folk dancing, sports, gymnastics, and music was an invaluable aid to the excellence of a rhythm program that developed at that college.

In the ensuing years there was scarcely a dance camp, an institute, or a workshop of note that the Dunsings did not attend as participants or as staff members. Numerous responsibilities came their way to serve as leaders for modern gymnastics workshops.

For ten years they gave workshops and demonstrations in their special fields for the American Alliance for Health, Physical Education and Recreation, the

Illinois Association for Health, Physical Education and Recreation, and district meetings for teacher in-service training. In 1962 they were presented with a certificate of recognition for twenty-five years of service to IAHPER.

In this country and abroad, thousands of dancers have benefited from the use of the materials, techniques, methods of instruction, and infectious enthusiasm of the "Dancing Dunsings." Wherever they went, they were asked to return.

The Dunsings conducted weekend workshops in almost every large city in the United States. Even after retirement from George Williams College in 1970, they vigorously continued to work for beautiful dancing on college campuses, at conventions, or wherever dance teachers and leaders assembled.

One of their lifelong dreams was realized in the summer of 1964 when the Dunsings took the George Williams College Folk Dancers on a fifteen-week tour of Europe with sixty full-length performances, plus dozens of other appearances at schools, churches, and villages. Before leaving on the tour, the group raised money by giving delightful programs in the Chicago area, including a memorable one for the Folk Valley Dancers in Marseilles, Illinois.

Wherever Paul and Gretel Dunsing took their young dancers, audiences were impressed by the fresh, wholesome vitality of American youth. The dancers were deliberately trained through the mutual love and respect the Dunsings had for each other and [for] each member of the group until this became an instinctive quality of their lives.

Paul assumed the leading role in teaching groups wherever they happened to be. Gretel, constantly alert, refreshed his memory on a dance; gave a styling tip; adjusted the tempo of the music; [and] slipped quickly to the center to demonstrate and correct a movement problem. Their team teaching was a continual interplay of spirit and mind. Paul liked his men dancers and students to use strong, virile movements; Gretel helped their women counterparts display grace and femininity. Neither would countenance ladies dancing in shorts or slacks, but encouraged the use of traditional folk costumes of various countries.

The Dunsings came to love the national dance of their adopted country—the square dance—with its roots deep in the colonial and pioneer culture of the American people. The appreciation gained from the playing and teaching of recorder music aroused a keen appreciation for live fiddle music in them.

The American invention of the caller intrigued Paul, and he learned to call the figures for his groups. Both of them deplored the rapid proliferation of terms and figures that kept the American national dance from being truly simple and folk, and discouraged many

from enjoying an important part of their heritage. So they continued to teach and enjoy the simple square dances that were time-tested and true, earning grateful appreciation from thousands of fellow citizens who wanted to dance for fun and recreation.

In 1936 Paul published a book called *German Folk Dances* (Vol. I); in 1946 both Dunsings published *Dance Lightly;* and in 1952 *Golden Bridge* had their editorial supervision. Teachers and dance leaders of the 1940s were given a great treasure of materials when the Methodist Church issued a series of records called The World of Fun, with the Michael Herman Orchestra. Favorite German dances were described and supervised by the Dunsings. These recordings were later reissued by RCA Victor and become standard equipment in music and physical education departments. Other recordings on [the] Rondo [label] followed.

Gretel Dunsing has not ceased the life work that she and Paul began. Their love affair continues. Her home in Florida is a mecca for dancers, leaders, and friends from all over the world. She travels all over America and Europe by bus and train to teach recorder sessions or German and Austrian folk dances. She has been on the staff at the Lighted Lantern in Colorado and at Berea College in Kentucky, as well as instructing at workshops and folk parties on the East Coast and in the South. She continues to exhort higher standards for music and dance, for an excellence that is a way of life.

(The foregoing material was excerpted from an article that originally appeared in the *Journal of Physical Education and Recreation* and is used here with permission. Kirby Todd is retired from the Department of Health, Physical Education, Recreation and Dance at Illinois State University.)

Jane Farwell

by Madeline Uraneck and Betty Casey

Jane Farwell was an outstanding pioneer in promoting and establishing international folk dancing in the United States and other countries and is still active. Her specialties are play-party games and recreational dance. Her Folklore Village Farm has been the recipient of several national and state grants for the promotion of folk art and folk music activities. The University of Wisconsin in Platteville offered credit for a regional folklore study conducted there and the Smithsonian Institution in Washington, D.C., directs visiting folk dancers and musicians programs there.

Jane Farwell. Photo by L. Roger Turner, Wisconsin State Journal

Jane Farwell has many notable accomplishments to her credit. She served in Eruope as recreation specialist for the United States Army and Air Force, as well as for German youth groups. Under the sponsorship of the Japanese State Department Ministry of Education, Asahi Press, and the national YMCA of Japan, she was selected as one of a team of four folk dance leaders to conduct a six-week series of European, American, and Mexican folk dance workshops in twenty-three cities throughout Japan for twenty-three thousand participants.

In the United States she established and directed national leadership laboratories in Maine, South Dakota, and New Mexico, as well as folk dance camps in Maine, Texas, and Wisconsin; she has been a guest staff member for many others.

This energetic leader has served as recreation specialist and instructor across America for universities, rural and city recreation commissions, 4-H groups, YMCAs, the Girl Scouts, youth hostels, church groups, folk weddings, and the National Recreation Association.

Outstanding performing groups consisting of chil-dren and adult dancers have come under her organizational leadership and training. These include the Folklore Village Dancers, Wakefield Dancers, the Folklore Village Orchestra in Wisconsin, and the Oglebay Folk Dancers in West Virginia.

Her research specialties include European and Japanese folklore, customs, and folk dancing, as well as regional folk costumes of northern Europe. Additional specialties include Ukrainian egg dyeing, Norwegian rosemaling, batik, silkscreening, block printing, sculpture, and oil and watercolor painting.

Booklets Jane Farwell has authored include *My Heart Sings* and *Folk Dances for Fun.*

(The following tribute to Jane Farwell and Folklore Village Farm was written by Madeline Uraneck.)

Jane Farwell epitomizes a folk person who somehow strayed into a modern world. Her thinking is intuitive; her organizing nondirective; her relationships warm, caring; her rapport immediate. In her twinkling eyes you see how young she really is.

With wonder and fondness people speak of her ability to walk into any group "cold" and within minutes have nondancers not only dancing but laughing, mixing, creating nonsensical atmospheres or re-creating age-old folk traditions. Her teaching repertoire is committed to simple dances, and her life to being a catalyst—introducing folks who are convinced they have two left feet to the joys and simplicity of folk dancing, and creating in rooms full of strangers a feeling of community and belonging.

Graduating with a self-designed major in rural recreation from Ohio's Antioch College, she got her first taste of folk dance from Russian and Greek groups in Hell's Kitchen, 1940s ethnic neighborhoods in New York City. As a freelance recreation specialist, she logged thousands of miles in the Midwest, Southwest, and Appalachian states, leaving in her wake the nation's first folk dance camps and recreation leadership laboratories.

Left behind wherever she went were new additions to the "Jane Farwell legend"—anecdotes of her mischief, generosity, and reputation for going to ridiculous lengths to see that food, atmosphere, and traditions were re-created authentically: real, lighted candles on Christmas trees; freshly ironed tablecloths and centerpieces at each meal; early-morning forays into the woods to find fresh greens for Maypole garlanding.

Jane's philosophy emphasizes the importance of each person's personal contribution and involvement. She wrote in her Folklore Village [Farm] brochure:

"In today's transient, insecure world of constant change, roots are hard to put down, and in one's work life seldom gives a complete sense of worth as a person. . . . Our human yearnings for roots and worth can often be eased by identifying with traditional celebrations, the re-creation of which can give life greater meaning."

After [spending] twelve years in Germany, Jane returned to her own birthplace, the Farwell family farm near Ridgeway, Wisconsin. There, in 1967, she established a longtime dream, a folk arts center she named Folklore Village Farm.

A traveler on the graveled country roads in search of Folklore Village Farm finds not a village but merely an eighty-four-year-old schoolhouse, decorated with German and Norwegian folk paintings, two modest bunkhouses, and a washhouse. As he stands there amidst the quiet fields of corn and alfalfa, he could hardly suspect Jane Farwell has made this tiny place into a center for weekend festivals, visiting European dance groups and internationally known folk dance instructors, candlelit midnight processions and late nights filled with vibrating fiddle music. Probably more fun and laughter per square foot have been packed into Jane Farwell's schoolhouse than any other schoolhouse in the country.

Local teens come on Tuesday nights, children on Thursday afternoons, whole families for monthly family days, and from a wide radius, every Saturday night, people come for a potluck supper by candlelight, followed by a gay evening of old-fashioned games, informal dancing, skits, and storytelling.

The heart of her Folklore Village [Farm] year, though, lies in eight seasonal festivals, delightful fantasies based on such ancient traditions as the English May, Scandinavian Midsummer, or German Harvest, which last over a whole weekend and attract people of all ages and from many surrounding states. The annual Christmas Festival, first held in 1947, is a veritable explosion of Christmas folklore, magic, and sparkling traditions from many countries. It lasts five days and draws families, who return year after year, from all over the United States, attracted by this noncommercial celebration of a tradition-rich holiday.

With her creative marriage of folk dance instruction in the context of customs and the sense of community this dancing sprang from in the old countries, Jane Farwell has imaginatively touched the lives of thousands of people. Through Folklore Village Farm she leaves not only legend but growing numbers of young people who have learned, shared, and contributed to the Farm, and who themselves now share in passing on this remarkable philosophy of folk dance.

(Madeline Uraneck and her husband, Phil Martin, have served as members of the dance teaching staff at Folklore Village Farm for several years. Phil is a fiddler and has written music for several of the dances. They were married at the Farm in a gala three-day Polish wedding of peasant-style toasting, feasting, and dancing in a circus tent adorned with milkweed and wild cucumber. They studied folk dancing in Sweden.)

May Gadd

by Joan Carr and Betty Casey

In 1927 Miss May Gadd was sent to New York by the English Folk Dance and Song Society [EFDSS] of her native England to assist with a summer dance session for the twelve-year-old organization then called the American Branch of EFDSS. This diminutive dynamo has been here ever since. She is the foremost American authority on English country dancing and Appalachian square dancing.

After reorganization in 1937, the name was changed to the English Folk Dance and Song Society of America. Later restructuring resulted in another name

May Gadd. Photo by Pach Bros.

change to the Country Dance and Song Society of America. Miss Gadd, in her role as national director, spearheaded a move to expand the Society's activity to include eighty chapters in seventeen states, the District of Columbia, and Canada. The Society even has its own Pinewoods Camp deep in the green forests at Plymouth, Massachusetts. (For additional information see the sections entitled "Country Dance and Song Society" and "Pinewoods Camp" in Part III.)

Up until 1976 May was still dancing. Although a young man demonstrated and taught the vigorous steps of the Shetland Reel in the church recreation room in New York in 1976, it was the silver-haired dumpling of a woman that May Gadd had become at age eighty-six who kept the dancers in her group in line with a pert directive nod of her head.

"Here, as in England," she told the author with her charming British accent, "the Society presents its material, not as a museum piece, but with the knowledge that while its roots are firmly in the past, true tradition has always adapted it to current needs of recreational expression."

"In fact," Miss Gadd wrote in a report, "during the first twenty-five years of its existence there was a growing recognition of the importance of the American aspect of the Society's program." The tremendous collection of southern Appalachian songs and dances gathered by Cecil Sharp—founder of the revival movement and first leader of EFDSS—between 1916 and 1918 led to further research in which May Gadd participated. This collection demonstrated that a tradition of folk music and dance exists all over America, and that the English and American traditions are so closely interwoven that they cannot be separated without loss to both.

It was the dance called the Old Mole that started this folk dance enthusiast on her life's work. When she first saw it in a London theater in 1915, she said, "That's what I want to do," and promptly joined EFDSS. It was founded in England in 1911 for the purpose of reviving traditional dances in danger of becoming extinct.

Over the years she taught at least a thousand dances and "loved every minute of it." The dances included some of her favorites: the Morpeth Rant; a polka from Northumberland; and Step Stately, a seventeenth-century dance. Agnes De Mille, who often consulted with her, used the latter in *Brigadoon*. Miss de Mille also consulted her in 1943 when choreographing the popular *Oklahoma!* as well as such productions as *Rodeo*.

"She's an absolutely wonderful person and real professional," said Miss de Mille. "I've seen her get seven hundred people moving in correct circles in an armory in three minutes." (New York *Times,* March 19, 1973)

The group Miss Gadd first saw performing had been trained by Cecil Sharp. The war had already begun, but in 1915 Miss Gadd went to Sharp's summer camp. She began as both a physical education and dancing teacher but soon taught only dancing.

"Our Society stands for group dancing," explained the enthusiastic teacher. "The principle of our Society is that it is an old thing you are doing, but you adapt it to the present time."

The dances have little fancy footwork. Their attraction lies in complex patterns the dancers must follow as they weave and circle. Folksy names such as Hole In the Wall, Parson's Farewell, and Mr. Isaac's Maggot identify the patterns. There are some couple dances and many group dances set up in longways, square sets, sets of three or five couples or, as in Walpole Cottage, double circles.

The Morris dances, originally performed by young men of a village at spring celebrations, are an important part of the repertoire. They are danced with tapping sticks, waving handkerchiefs, and jingling bells.

"We are fortunate in our heritage of dance music and songs and make every effort to use live musicians rather than recorded music," said Miss Gadd. They rely heavily on the famous Playford collection of seventeenth-century dance melodies and the wealth of EFDSS publications of traditional Scottish, Irish, and English dance and song tunes, as well as American contributions, particularly from the southern highlands and New England area. "Our music program falls into four main categories," she continued, "folk singing, guitar and dulcimer, recorder and viola, and music relating to the dance itself."

Under her guidance, classes of instruction were set up at the national society's summer school, the Boston center's June Weekend at Pinewoods Camp, and in New York and elsewhere during the winter months. Other centers are located in Berea, Kentucky, and Brasstown, North Carolina. "The continuing interchange of singers and musicians and dancers over the years between England and America has been a vital factor in the life of the CDSS," she concluded.

May Gadd and her lifelong passion for country dancing have left an indelible mark on, and have made a tremendous contribution to, the folk dance scene in the United States. (Miss Gadd died on January 27, 1979, in her eighty-ninth year.)

Madelynne Greene

by Eric Barker, Walter Grothe, Dorothy Kvalnes, and Winnie Faria

Madelynne Greene was one of the beloved early California folk dance leaders. After her death, the April 1970 issue of *Let's Dance* magazine was dedicated to her memory. The following material, excerpted from that issue, pays tribute to her outstanding achievements.

Eric Barker wrote a poem in her memory that runs ". . . I think of you, a dancer / With the faith of a firewalker, / Suspended seemingly in air, / Or balanced upon the invisible / Tightrope of a tribal dance / That you brought home / From somewhere beyond the seventh sea . . ."

Walter Grothe wrote: "It was in the early days of folk dancing in California, and the Federation had just been organized, when I met Madelynne . . . I admired her and have never lost that admiration. I was president of the Berkeley Folk Dancers at that time, and Madelynne just started her Festival Workshop (later [called] International Dance Theater). She asked me to become a charter member and I was highly flattered. The workshop was being organized for the purpose of learning new dances, exhibiting them at monthly Federation festivals and then teaching them right there to the participants. Our first two dances thusly exhibited and introduced were Road to the Isles and Meitschi Putz Di. As the movement grew, and Madelynne's fame spread, the Festival Workshop was asked to almost every festival for the presentation of a new dance. One of the great successes was the Neapolitan Tarantella, exhibited at the festival on the grounds of the new San Francisco State College before the buildings went up. The workshop met weekly and worked hard under Madelynne's guidance. Her ability to teach and her patience were unbelievable. She inspired us all with such enthusiasm, we would have done anything for her. Then, as the movement grew, Madelynne became more and more in demand—as a leader of an exhibition group, as a teacher, as a person.

"And then the summer camps came into existence; first Stockton and then many others. Of course, Madelynne was a must! She has served on the faculty of more camps, East and West, than any other teacher, and the only ones she missed were when she was in Europe studying and gathering new material. Then came the highlight in her life. She started her own camp. It was called Madelynne Greene's Mendocino

Madelynne Greene

Folklore Camp. She patterned it by taking the best features of all the camps she had attended, and the result was a terrific success right from the start."

In another article, Dorothy Kvalnes wrote: "We have many fine teachers in the Federation, but Madelynne has always been tops with me! These are the qualities which have endeared her to me: warm friendliness and a delightful sense of humor; skill at seeing where you made mistakes, and helping you out of them; her special care of the human ego; her skill as an artist, teacher, organizer; her talent for dancing, comedy, pantomime and for putting on a good show; her special skill of attracting good people around her who begged to help; her driving philosophy of 'The Show Must Go On!'

"Her concern for people's feelings made us love her. There is no way of adding up what she did for folk dancing, not only in California, but in other parts of the U.S.A. and Canada.

"No matter how she felt, she gave you a cheery smile and encouragement, and listened to your troubles or had the needed humorous comment. She was a devoted daughter who cared for her mother all her life. Married to poet Eric Barker, she remained devoted to him although their work made it necessary for them to live apart. She [took] great pride in Eric's work.

"For many years we had had long talks about the kind of folklore camp she wished to establish. We discussed how my knowledge of music and pedagogy might be used to help dance teachers. This resulted, finally, in the Mendocino Folklore Camp, which has steadily increased in enrollment since 1962. It was always a joy each year, at the opening of the camp, to watch all hands falling in line to help get the camp underway. Usually there were more willing workers than jobs available. Each year the experience of camp offered more enrichment in the things learned, the friendships formed, and the general good fun.

"She was instrumental in the formation of the Folk Dance Federation of California and the teachers' institutes sponsored by that organization. This one activity assured the spread of the folk dance movement in California. She taught Chang's folk dancers in San Francisco, Berkeley Folk Dancers and Garfield Folk Dancers in Berkeley, and at Stanford University. [Other places where she taught included the] College of Arts and Crafts in Oakland, [the] college of [the] Pacific in Stockton, Santa Barbara Folk Dance Conference, and Idyllwild. She also taught at special workshops in other parts of the U.S.A., notably at Michael and Mary Ann Herman's camp in Maine."

The following reflections are from Winnie Faria: "Folk dancing really got an impetus when, in 1942, Madelynne Greene discovered folk dancing for Chang's International Folk Dancers, in San Francisco, and decided it was more fun than ballet. Soon she became Chang's advanced teacher and the guiding light of the folk dance movement, both of which she continued to be all during her life. Those of us who knew her cannot think of folk dancing apart from a thought of her. Even those who did not know her are aware of her influence.

"Those who had the pleasure of studying under Madelynne admired her for her unending enthusiasm; her extensive knowledge of other cultures and peoples, and of dance styling, together with her knack of getting it across to her students; her amazing ability to break down a step or pattern until it seemed so easy; her great vitality and glow; her ever-cheerful smile and manner; her great interest in and love for people; her thirst for knowledge; her artistry, including beautiful choreography; her infinite beauty of character; and the incredible grace and sensitivity of her every movement and expression."

Dorothy Tamburini, a California folk dance authority, credited Mrs. Greene with introducing twenty-eight international dances in the United States, including dances from Spain, Mallorca, Portugal, France, China, Hawaii, the Ukraine, and the Canary Islands.

Mary Ann and Michael Herman

by Carole Howard

Mary Ann Bodnar came dancing her way into the world in 1912, born into a ghetto neighborhood in New York City, where her neighbors were of many nationalities and religions. Most of them were freshly [e]migrated from the Old World. "I was lucky enough to have been born among the privileged crowd, for I lived in a ghetto where there were all kinds of ethnic communities. We went to their weddings, social gatherings, wakes, and christenings. And we did their dances and sang their songs."

Her early life was spent in the Ukrainian neighborhood school, and then she went on to attend James Monroe High School. She took courses in a variety of colleges in the New York area but never finished her degree. "Dance was always an important part of our home life. Just going to a Ukrainian school made us all aware of the importance of our heritage through its folk customs. I used to be a performer in our Ukrainian folk group, then I started to teach those dances in places like the YWCA."

During her career of teaching and dancing around the city, Mary Ann Bodnar met a young violinist, Michael Herman, and in due course they were married. "My career as a folk dance teacher was really launched when I married Michael, who was first a musician, then became a folklorist and folk dance teacher. He had attended Western Reserve University in Cleveland, Ohio, and had started his teaching career at the New School for Social Research in 1933; then later he was at International House and the International Institute in New York City."

In the early third of the twentieth century, folk dancing was done primarily by ethnic groups alone. The Irish did their own Irish dancing, the Swedes did their Swedish dancing, and there was little teaching done on an international scale. Most of the dances done by physical education teachers were of the Anglo-Saxon countries. Michael Herman remembered: "In the early days no one went out of their neighborhood to dance with another nationality group. People then felt that their dances should only be for themselves, and that no other group should be able to learn them. They guarded their dances as a private thing."

The folk dance movement got its greatest impetus in 1940 at the New York World's Fair:

"They had this huge place with thousands of people dancing! Everyone that wandered by would want to dance because this wonderful music was pouring out! Before they knew it, someone had them dashing around in a Russian Troika, or an American Shoo Fly, or something else. People came back just for the dance part of the World's Fair. It was evident that everyone there wanted to continue this wonderful thing, going somewhere to dance the world's dances. That is how we could see the idea of a folk dance house way back in 1940."

The Hermans at first rented out the Ukrainian National Home, then the Polish National Home and the German National Home for their first teaching classes, but they yearned for a place of their own where they could carry on everything related to folk dancing. "So we got a little building on 16th [Street] and 6th Avenue, and in it we housed our costume collection and our reference library. We had adult recreational folk dancing as well as a marvelous teenage program on Saturday afternoons at the height of the hippie era. Can you imagine having teenage kids with the classic long hair and sandals dancing for nearly five hours straight!"

The Hermans' folk center enlarged to include family folk dancing on Sundays, workshops on weekends, when they brought in specialists in other countries' dances, and teacher-training workshops. "Michael and I were concerned with the lack of good teachers who possessed good techniques that would want to make people folk dance. It seemed as if the physical education teachers in the schools were not selecting the right dances. They didn't pick the materials that were suitable for children, nor did they infuse them with any joy! They were even *grading* them on their dancing! That is to say that everyone in a village danced equally well. In my opinion, they should just be able to move and enjoy it!"

There was never anything quite like Folk Dance House at 108 West Sixteenth Street, New York City, New York. It was a full-time learning center for folk arts of all the nations. Dancing was its primary activity, but that always led to the folk music, perhaps the language, the history, the costuming, the cuisine, and the craft arts. "It was a seven-day week, 24-hour round-the-clock job. We found that we had helped preserve many dances that would have died. The nationality groups that were hesitant to share their dances before the '40s were now willing to do so. Many times they would teach us the dance to teach just because our English was better, but most of the time they insisted on teaching their own material, feeling no one else could do it quite as well as they. Also, in other countries, because of the wars, people didn't dance that much, nor did they dance in the reconstruc-

tion period between. And then came the heavy input of American music during and after the wars on everyone's radio, and they all wanted to do jazz and jitterbug. So if it wasn't for folk dance groups in this country, many, many dances would have passed away.

"As a matter of fact, this may surprise you, that in many cases ethnic groups get re-enthused about their own dances because they see other people doing them better. In our own community we have a Scottish dance group that is 98% Jewish, probably the only Scottish group that closes on Yom Kippur! And we had another Scottish group that didn't dance too well, but they were real Scots. When they came to our Scottish festival, and they saw the non-Scots-Jewish group dance their dances. WOW! They went home and really practiced then."

In the earlier years of Folk Dance House there was very little recorded music to which to dance. Those were the infant days of the recording companies as well. Michael relates: "Since there were no records for most of the dances, live music was used. I played the violin, Mary Ann was on the piano, Walter Erikksoon and Svend Tollefson were on the accordion, Walter Andreasen on bass, and Frances Witowski on the clarinet made the festivals memorable events."

Folk Dance House attracted people from all walks of life. Michael continued: "People like Gene Kelly, Burl Ives, Peter Lorre, and Damon Runyon mixed in with the dancing crowd. Runyon even wrote up the experience in his daily newspaper column. Burl Ives, without a beard in those days, used to sing during intermissions while the dancers sat around him on the floor."

The Friday-night sessions expanded into three nights a week and the size of the year-end festival grew and grew. Larger quarters had to be found, and Hunter College was the place for one of them. "The authorities were so overwhelmed by the size of the crowd that they refused to let us use it again unless we limited the size of the group, which we couldn't do very well. The festival finally settled for several years in the huge gym of the Needle Trades High School, where classes were also held during the week. There, one year, the Grand March of folk dancers by states revealed 28 states represented, with one group coming all the way from Minnesota."

The Hermans always insisted on quality music for their teaching. They acted as consultants to RCA Victor, using their own folk orchestra in many of the dances, when RCA published their graded Educational Dance Series for the public schools. This has remained a vital teaching tool for the majority of recreation and physical education departments throughout the United States. The Methodist Church Board of Education also used the Hermans as consultants when they did a similar series, The World of Fun. Michael remembers: "The Methodists were very wary of the name 'folk dance' and wanted their recreational dance series to be 'play-party games' to avoid the name of 'dance' in their series. The Methodists! Religious attitude didn't permit dancing, so we had to be very careful with our arrangements and dance instructions. But, after a while, they became a little more relaxed and they started to call them dances, too."

The Michael Herman Orchestra is featured, as are many authentic folk orchestras, on their Folk Dancer record series. With their insistence upon fine music, these records are a beautiful addition to any teacher's collection. Michael said: "Sometime during the forties, we discovered a marvelous orchestra, the Banat Tamburitzans, consisting of musicians who played the Kolos of Yugoslavia in a pure, unadulterated way. We quickly recorded them. As this was before tape was invented, where one could splice errors away, many a 'take' had to be done as they were nervous about recording, and many a bottle of 'slivovitsa' consumed to get a good recording done. The highlight of the festivals at that time was when the Banat Tamburitzan orchestra would come into the middle of the circle to play the Malo Kolo. This dance consists of only the basic kolo step done over and over again, but as the orchestra moves about and stops in front of a segment of the circle, dancers exert themselves into doing all kinds of show-off steps and variations. Orchestra and dancers responded to each other in one of those rare moments of folk dance rapport that we hope every dancer can experience in his lifetime. Sometimes the Malo Kolo would last 30 minutes, but no one minded. Dancers also quickly learned that, while a record lasted three minutes, the orchestra was going to play each kolo just as long as they did for their own native dances, which meant at least ten minutes for each kolo! And, since they usually played at least three kolos in a set, dancers really learned what it was like to dance in the native style."

Through all this frenzied activity, Mary Ann continued her teacher-workshops in cities all over the United States. Her boundless energy, enthusiasm, and inimitable New York wit and accent kept her in demand on college campuses and at professional institutes, conventions and community centers.

The evening sessions grew to five a week, led by the Hermans or members of their staff or by various nationality leaders invited in to teach. Once each month they had two-day workshops given [over] to the study of the dances, foods, and costuming of a particular ethnic group. At the end of each year, the Hermans sponsored a festival to give newcomers a chance to observe the dancing of New York's myriad ethnic groups. Michael relates: "Now folk dancing began to grow in earnest. Leaders began to look to Folk Dance House for new material, teaching hints, records and information on starting a group. There was a need for teacher and dancer to get together, to ask questions. So we conceived the idea of a year's-end workshop which was incorporated into the Festival programs. Dick Crum was among the first of the workshop leaders, and it was his inspired leadership that gave the Balkan dances the real push they needed. He brought more than dance into the movement, with his culture corners on rhythms, music, costumes, foods and folklore. The Festival and Workshop became a launching pad to bring the attention of the leaders to other talents as yet unknown, including people like Ann and Andor Czompo, Cavit Congoz, David Rosenberg, the Taylors, Yves Moreau, Michel Cartier, Ralph Page, David Henry, Steve Glazer and many more. And what a thrill to bring the nationally known Madelynne Greene all the way from San Francisco for some of the festivals. And to have Henry Lash for nationality meals!"

In 1956 the United States State Department sent the Hermans, Jane Farwell, Ralph Page, and Nelda Drury on a six-week, twenty-one-city tour of Japan, teaching forty-six dances of sixteen nations. This was done in conjunction with the Japanese Ministry of Education. Michael remembered: "Morale of the Japanese people was at an all-time low. They felt badly about the war [WW II] . . . But they discovered that, through folk dancing, just by being in a circle and holding hands made them feel closer. It also helped break down the time-honored concept of the woman always following the man. We had a tremendous response wherever we went, and the Japanese people couldn't seem to get enough of folk dancing. We felt it definitely helped build the morale of those Japanese young people. And, then, for the first time ever, Columbia Records and RCA Victor worked together to transcribe our folk dance series into a Japanese series. The translation of the dance directions was a monumental task, but it started international folk dancing, which was nonexistent in Japan until after World War II and our visit."

Mary Ann's methods of teaching continued to break the traditionalist concepts. She made up her own words, used her body to twist around in grotesque shapes as to what you "shouldn't do," shortened teaching sequences to nearly nothing, and continued to establish herself as a master teacher. "Some of the keys in getting to know people are: just begin by holding hands. And let everyone know which foot we are starting on. Keep it simple. Folk dancing can also be quite sexy, you know . . . in a nice way. There are so many ways you can dance with each other. Take the polka step, for instance. There are so many ways a Polish man would do the polka, different from a Scot, and different from a German, who does it different from a Norwegian. And that's the whole fun and joy of folk dancing. You move your body in so many different ways . . . not just one way. And then you find within yourself a release of the spirit. Sometimes you find a new way to express yourself. It is difficult for [a man] to move [his] hands gracefully in different styles. [He] feel[s] so uncomfortable. But when he does, wow! It's great! And it makes the dance feel better. He's experienced something. He doesn't have to sit and meditate nor see a psychiatrist. He's got everything going for him, like the movement of the folk dance. It will break down inhibitions, but I don't like to have people use folk dancing as therapy. Because a lot of people think that folk dancing is only for looks. Or there's something wrong with you if you folk dance. We need to educate people to see things with a different eye. When we hear strange music or see a strange costume, we can't make funny 'cracks.' It offends and hurts people. After all, how would we feel if foreign people did that to some of our American songs and dances and ways of life? So we need to educate newspapers, TV, and movies to present folk material, either singing or dancing or whatever, in its true form."

The folk dance camp concept was started in 1938–39 by Jane Farwell, a noted recreation specialist who believed that one should be able to enjoy a total folk "happening," i.e., that dance, the costumes, the crafts, the cuisine should all blend into one and the same experience. This was much more easily achieved when everyone was in the same place for more than one evening, such as a camp where they could stay for a week or a weekend. Jane went to New York to ask the Hermans if they would help teach dances at a "sort of a camp" in Oglebay Park, West Virginia. So, following the successes there, they taught with her in Mount Horeb, Wisconsin; Lovell, Maine; Florida; and Bridgton, Maine, the site of the current folk dance camp that is world renowned.

Michael remembered the folk dance camp in Florida, where it was so hot and humid: "We tried to do only slow dances like Alexandrovsky so the campers wouldn't wear out so easily. But one day we taught the Doudlebska Polka, which is very vigorous, and one Polish gentleman was so delighted to know the polka . . . at last . . . that upon his and others' insistence, that dance was done 95% of the hot, humid camp time in Florida. It was fantastic!"

Mary Ann always took care to teach her dances, maintaining the true ethnic style and tradition: "I've always believed folk dancing is a social occasion, not a class. People should get together to sing the songs, dance the dances, listen to the music, and dine to-gether. It's a time to relax and have a good time." Mary Ann continued to inspire teachers in the camps with her nontraditional manner of teaching, along with her humorous demonstrations.

She took her philosophy of folk art to the Maine Folk Dance Camp at Bridgton, Maine, in 1950, after Jane Farwell left and she and Michael took over. The camp is a total experience in various ethnic cultures. The great dance teachers flock there from all over the world to serve on their teaching staff. Set in the midst of tall pines and myriad lakes, a peculiar, wonderful magic happens there every week. "Nowadays, everyone is starting to folk dance. What is so nice about it is that we get all walks of life represented here at Pioneer Lodge. This is a very rare kind of thing because most of our activities tend to have a class structure. But folk dance attracts all kinds of people. It is not unusual to have a very wealthy businessman in the same class with a very poor clam-digger, a truck driver, a lawyer, a doctor, the unemployed, a maid. They all meld together and have a very joyous experience."

The Hermans at the present time divide their year into summers at the Maine camp, where Mary Ann is primarily responsible for its functioning, and the other nine months of the year teaching in New York City. The old site of the Folk Dance House in New York City was demolished, and they currently meet in the Armenian Church, 35th [Street] and 2nd Avenue, New York, and St. Margaret's Church, 192nd Street, Flushing, New York. They are looking forward to a permanent place where they will be able to house their massive collection of records, costumes, and books.

Mary Ann and Michael have coauthored *Folk Dances for All, Folk Dance Syllabus,* many articles for *DANCE Magazine,* innumerable pamphlets and brochures on folk dancing, plus they have written syllabi for every festival, workshop, and week at summer camp: "The syllabi issued for all of these festivals and workshops for the past 30 years constitute an amazing assortment of dance directions, making a valuable addition to a folk dancer's library."

The Hermans have trained and presented a variety of exhibition groups who have performed all over the metropolitan New York area, in churches and schools, the Cooper Union, the Museum of Natural History, and at various concert halls throughout the years from 1940 until the present date.

Both have been asked to serve on a consultant basis in the New York area in the matter of dance. Mary Ann has just recently been asked to work on the prestigious *Dance Encyclopedia* as the expert in folk dance. "When the great Moiseyev came to the United States with his folk-ballet group, he came to New York and asked us to teach him the Virginia Reel as an encore number. I happen to understand Russian, and so we were going along nicely, when the ballet master said, 'Dance sloppily.' Moiseyev corrected him immediately by saying, 'It is not sloppily, sir, it is casually.' He caught the difference right away. So they came to the lowly folk dancers for a lesson! They used the Virginia Reel at the end of every show the troup performed that season, and it was very thrilling. As you remember, when he first came with his troup to the U.S.A., it was during the Cold War, and diplomatic relations were very strained. He only wanted to stay twenty minutes in our little dance hall, but the troup stayed 2½ hours! The first time he came to learn, and he took notes, but the second time they came he, the great Moiseyev, danced along with us, his dancers, and his musicians."

Mary Ann received an award for her outstanding contributions to the field of folk dance from San Antonio College, San Antonio, Texas. Her status among teachers is undisputedly the best. Everyone is constantly amazed at her vast knowledge of not only the dance but everything that is associated with it. She has steeped herself in folk traditions, costumes and music. Experienced teachers wonder at her uncanny ability to break down difficult dances into simple forms. Her dynamic enthusiasm and her delightful sense of humor make every class a memorable experience. "It is important to make people happy . . . to give them a certain amount of confidence so they'll enjoy the dance. It is a very uniting kind of thing. Anyone can learn to folk dance. Plus it is a very good form of activity for anybody. I am glad that more people are finding all its values. Just the simple process of holding hands and working together, dancing together to create a new movement you've never done before is something special. You can have a very slow Greek dance or a Balkan dance that is not difficult at all. It may just be a slow walking dance, but the beautiful music plays, and you hold hands with people on both sides of you, and you are within yourself, within your own thoughts, feeling that wonderful release of spirit."

Mary Ann has always felt that the teacher should make the dance look easy to her pupils. In doing this, she never makes the new dancer seem threatened. She throws away all the traditionalist manner of teaching and vocabulary, varies her voice inflections, uses her body as a teaching tool, and sprinkles the total lesson with Eastern humor. Teachers marvel at how she has erased professional vocabulary and substituted ordinary terms. "Let's teach kids how to dance, not to do a dance. So many dances are related. Let's go back to the basics. Don't be worried about how many dances you know, but how well you can dance. I think the whole situation has changed very much in physical education. Up until now most children were turned off by the type of dances they were taught and by the methods. But I've found many physical educators and recreation people who are realizing the whole value of this wonderful activity. They are going to dance camps and classes and are studying with a lot of teachers who have this feeling in spirit, so they are bringing the joy back into their teaching. You'll find that more and more boys are dancing, and so are the men. I know that a lot of athletic coaches are realizing that their baseball, football, and basketball teams could be better if they could folk dance. I think ballet is too rigid, but the movements of folk dancing would certainly make them better athletes."

There is no doubt in any dance teacher's mind that the direction and philosophies of folk dance in America today originate in two places in the East Coast: from inside the wooden frame building labeled Dance Hall, nestled among the tall pines of Maine, and from a tiny Armenian church in New York City. The driving force behind all this, is, of course, the short, pixyish, greying little dynamo, Mary Ann Bodnar Herman, the woman who has put joy back into the folk dance movement and who has written her own chapter in success and achievement. "We don't feel everybody should play tennis and golf, and that everybody should folk dance. But we know that it is an activity that is easy to take up. You don't need equipment nor a uniform . . . just a room and a record player. And something magical will happen when you reach out to hold

Carole A. Howard

hands with people on both sides of you in that circle and you all move to the music. I call it instant friendship."

(The foregoing excerpts, used here with permission, are from an article that first appeared as part of a field study submitted by Carole Howard in partial fulfillment of the requirements for the degree of Specialist in Physical Education at Central Michigan University.

Carole Howard, associate professor of physical education at Central Michigan University, Mt. Pleasant, Michigan, has taught at CMU for eight years in the field of recreational dance. Prior to this, she taught physical education for six years in the Michigan public schools. She earned her B.S. degree at CMU, her M.A. degree at Western Michigan, and recently completed her Specialist Degree in Physical Education at CMU. She is an instructor for the Lloyd Shaw Foundation, directs the university demonstration team, the CMU Country Dancers, has coauthored a 16mm color film, "Anishinabe, Four Dances," and has produced a long-playing record entitled "Authentic Chippewa Dances."

In 1974 she was awarded the prestigious title "Associate Woman Professor of the Year, CMU." She taught in the Honors Program, competed in the Fred Astaire Midwest Competition, created two television program series for children, and received Faculty and University Achievement awards in 1974 and 1976. She recently authored a book on social dance. Mrs. Howard belongs to AAHPER, MAHPER, and the National Dance Therapy Association.)

tucky, St. Petersburg, Denver, Syracuse, Milwaukee, Knoxville, and Vienna, Virginia.

The National Folk Festival has as its primary objective the bringing together of folk dance groups from various sections of the United States, each displaying a characteristic and unique folk expression, in the hope that this national event will give added encouragement to regional festivals, and that continued participation in such festivals will keep alive the fine traditional customs associated with the founding of this nation. In addition to serving as a record of the social life of early America—as well as a later America—the festival provides a basic cultural leisure-time activity program and presents material that may inspire future artistic creations. As a result of the interplay of distinctive folk songs, music, dances, myths, and folk stories of different races, a better understanding and a greater degree of tolerance should hopefully result in a stronger sense of national unity. The program includes presentations of folk music, folk plays, folk dances, legends, superstitions, and exhibits of folk arts and crafts.

Special program divisions have included the following events representing many states: American Indian music and dances; Spanish-American and Mexican customs, music, and dances; French folk songs and music; German music, dances, and customs; British-American folk music, dances, games, and instrumental music. Others included: square dances; traditional religious music; Army, Navy, and Coast Guard songs and music; town crier; ring-games, play-party and singing games; fiddle, harmonica, dulcimer, and band

Sarah Gertrude Knott

by Betty Casey

"Sarah Gertrude Knott . . . is founder of the National Folk Festival Association and one of the great leaders in the preservation of American folk culture."—*Folk Dance Scene*

"Sarah Gertrude Knott has done for international (formerly ethnic) folk festivals more than any person . . ."—Vyts Beliajus.

The first National Folk Festival Association, Inc. [NFFA] (now the National Council for the Traditional Arts, Inc.) event was held in St. Louis in 1934. Subsequent festivals, held annually except for 1945, 1956, 1962, and 1970, were located in Chattanooga, Dallas, Chicago, Washington, D.C., Philadelphia, Cleveland, St. Louis, Oklahoma City, Nashville, Covington, Ken-

Sarah Gertrude Knott. Photo by Harris and Ewing

tunes; and cowboy songs and customs. Additional activities included: lumberjack music and songs; sea chanteys; sacred harp songs; Negro spirituals, work songs, blues, legends, lining-hymns; folk plays (based on folklore), traditional Spanish-American plays; legends and folk tales; ancient Polynesian dances; and newer American ethnic dances and music.

The original idea and general plan for the NFFA came from Sarah Gertrude Knott, then director of the Dramatic League of St. Louis. However, according to Miss Knott, much of the credit for the development of the plan must go to scholars and practitioners who knew the folk music, songs, and dances of the country. Outstanding educational-cultural leaders' ideas went into the creation of the NFFA plan.

The three folklorists who helped most in the creation of the original plan were the late Dr. George Pullen Jackson, of Vanderbilt University, the late Dr. Arthur L. Campa, then at the University of Tennessee, and Dr. Ben Botkin, then at the University of Oklahoma. They helped form the National Advisory Council and lay the overall foundation that has lasted until now. Dr. Jackson transcribed and joined together the many disparate ideas that Miss Knott had gleaned from innumerable letters and face-to-face interviews with scholars and practitioners.

By the end of the first eight years of the NFFA, there was evidence of an awakening of interest among the newer American folk groups in a number of states that had not previously existed. These groups were asked to participate in the National Folk Festival program. Special interest was aroused as World War II approached. It was even more evident after servicemen returned from the fields of war, where many had served in the native lands of their ancestors. They were included with increasing frequency on National Folk Festival programs; the older American groups were always featured since these groups predominated in most states.

In an article published in the *Paducah Sun-Democrat* and *Folk Dance Scene* (Summer 1977, p. 19) Miss Knott wrote: "Cultural tracks of our earlier colonists are growing more dim. They are becoming harder to trace each year. Revival should be started while there is still a pattern to go by, while there is substance in the cultural roots.

"There is more to a folk song than the tune—more to a folk dance than its form (movement). In these traditional expressions are recorded the social life of early America and the growing, changing, later America. They reflect the living history of our country— the struggles and joys we have had together in establishing a nation. Through them we glimpse the life of the native lands from whence our people came.

"Folk songs, dances, legends, and other simple forms of recreation were needed in pioneer America to offset monotony and loneliness as it grew from a land of wilderness and plains to one of the world powers. They are needed now to help us hold our balance in [a] civilization that is much more complex and confusing than our fathers found here. Our cultural and social life will be less rich if we lose them. As they have served in the past and are used in the present, so will the future need them. They should not be blown away with a changing civilization!

"From the very beginning of the National Folk Festival Association [NCTA]" explained Miss Knott, "and in the smaller festivals associated with it, we felt that the natural artist, trained only in tradition's school, ranks right along with the best of the more sophisticated artists and their highly elaborated and developed artistic creations.

"What we mean by 'artist' is the natural or untaught folk singer or player of a typical folk instrument such as a fiddle, banjo, dulcimer, harmonica, or other early American instrument. We mean a group of folk dancers—doing the Kentucky running set or the southern Appalachian style of dances inherited from the British Isles ancestors . . . We mean a group of ethnic dancers—French, German, Lithuanian, Negro, Polish, Spanish-American—just dancing as they do when their people get together on any holiday or family gathering."

Archie Green wrote as follows in the Journal of the Johnny Edwards Memorial Foundation (Vol. XI, Spring 1975): "To write about the NFFA is to portray Sarah Gertrude Knott, now retired at Princeton, Kentucky, where she is writing her autobiography. I begin with her college years in the 1920s at the University of North Carolina. Studying with Frederick Koch, she became a member of The Carolina Playmakers, a group of campus actors and writers staging regional folk dramas. The term 'folk drama' used by Koch and his students meant new scripts about the folk rather than traditional forms such as British mummers plays . . . "

In 1929 Miss Knott took a professional position in St. Louis as director of the Dramatic League and founder of the Strolling Players. Throughout the early depression years she worked with unemployed Negro groups in presenting dramatic skits utilizing their own experiences and employing their impromptu old-time singing. As a recreation worker in a polyglot city, she also encountered many immigrants from Europe and learned something of their traditions. From April 29 through May 2, 1934, she put together her first folk festival in St. Louis' Kiel Municipal Auditorium, involving about three hundred participants from fourteen states. The *Post-Dispatch* lauded her achievement and reported the event in detail.

We can use the *Post-Dispatch* article to record a few highlights of the first NFFA festival. "The cast of performers was impressive and varied, including Mary Austin (New Mexico), J. Frank Dobie (Texas), Helen Harkness Flanders (Vermont), Zora Hurston (Florida), George Pullen Jackson (Tennessee), and Jilson Setters (Kentucky)." Our present term for festival seminars is workshops. In 1934 Miss Knott termed these "educational programs." The Russell Sage Foundation brought 750 examples of handicrafts to the Kiel Municipal Auditorium, many from mountain colleges. While some students demonstrated weaving, carving, and similar skills, other student members of the Carolina Playmakers offered three folk dramas: "Quare Medicine," "On Dixon's Porch," and "Job's Kinfolk," a then current play on textile mill life in Winston-Salem.

Miss Knott's second festival was held in Chattanooga, Tennessee, from May 14 to 18, 1935. The roll call of participants ranged from anthracite coal miners deeply steeped in a specialized occupational tradition to drama students from the then experimental and liberal Black Mountain College.

Not only did Miss Knott cast her net wide in gathering performers but also in assembling collectors. Among those invited were Arthur Campa, George Korson, Romaine Lowdermilk, Bascom Lamar Lunsford, May Kennedy McCord, Jean Thomas, and William Troxell. Although Miss Knott had not incorporated her association by 1935, she had already persuaded various celebrities to lend their names to her enterprise. The Festival's president and vice-president were, respectively, Paul Green, the North Carolina playwright, and Constance Rourke, a perceptive critic of American culture.

When Sarah Gertrude Knott retired in 1971, the NFFA was kept alive largely by federal grants from the National Endowment for the Arts and the National Park Service. The Board of Directors of the National Folk Festival Association, Inc., voted to change the name of the organization to the National Council for the Traditional Arts, Inc. [NCTA]. The name change took effect January 1, 1978. The National Folk Festival name will be retained for the festival at the Wolf Trap Farm Park for the Performing Arts in Vienna, Virginia, near Washington, D.C., as well as for succeeding festivals. It has been used since 1934.

Dr. Charles L. Perdue, Jr., said, "The reason for the name change is a very simple one: it was confusing. Persons hearing it automatically assumed that the only business of the organization was the Wolf Trap festival. This has never been true and it became particularly burdensome at a time when the organization is extending its work to new areas." Dr. Perdue is the current president of the NCTA and is a member of the program committee for the National Folk Festival.

Ralph Page

by Betty Casey

Ralph Page has been called "a true living legend" and "dean of the contra dance." "I called my first square dance December 5, 1930," Page recalls, "when the man who was to call failed to show up. I'd never called a dance before in my life and had to take the full evening of squares and contras. Oh, what a disaster!" An uncle told him he wasn't doing anything right, but if he was going to call he had to learn how in order not to "bring shame" on the family. The uncle, a fiddler, played for the would-be caller in practice sessions and called attention to mistakes by tapping him on the ear with his bow. "Wow," says Page, "by gosh, you get hit on the ear and you'll learn how to call."

He became one of the country's first full-time professional callers in 1938 and called at the New York World's Fair the next year. According to Richard Nevell *(A Time to Dance):* "By 1938 Page and his orchestra were busy four and five nights a week working in the Monadnock region of southern New Hampshire. He was quickly building a reputation as the best caller of the old contra dances, as well as quadrilles and squares. 'We had a full orchestra, ten full men. . . . You always have to have a cornet and a clarinet, and the fiddle, bass, viol, piano, drums. We had saxophones. We were playing in big dance halls for this area . . . accommodating five or six hundred people, sometimes a thousand people . . . and [if] you take five hundred people walking across a floor, you've got to have more than just one fiddle or you ain't going to be heard!' The dance revival was in full swing by this time and had spread to the cities of the Northeast as well." Vyts Beliajus, writing in *Viltis* magazine, said: "He single-handedly kept alive, popularized and spread the New England forms . . . he is a typical New Englander with a delightful sense of humor."

Together with Beth Tolman, a staff member of the magazine *Yankee,* published in Dublin, New Hampshire, Page wrote a series of articles about country dancing activity. The articles, which appeared between 1935 and 1937, were collected and published in *The Country Dance Book* in 1937 (the book was reissued in 1976). In it Ralph states: "We, villagers and visitors, young and old, dance the country dances every Saturday night in the old town hall. Why? Because we've always danced them—for 170 years. We'd rather shake down a Hull's Victory, or pop a large specimen through to the measures of "Pop Goes the Weasel," than do all our slithery Four Hundreds in all your dancing dives in the United States. . . . There are lots of isolated islands throughout the United States where certain enterprising ones have rescued the country dances much as they would pluck a fine old handicraft out of near-oblivion, collect wooden implements our forefathers used, or do any one of a hundred things that would rate approval from the local Historical Society." Page authored *The Ralph Page Book of Contra Dances, Heritage Dances of Early America,* and a long series of articles on the history of square dancing that appeared each month during the years 1972, 1973, and 1974 in *Square Dancing* magazine.

In 1956 Page was sent to Japan by the U. S. Department of State Exchange of Persons branch. Concerning the latter, he noted, "We traveled to every city in that country teaching contra dances to people who had never seen one before and could not speak one word of English." In 1966 he went on a teaching tour of England under the sponsorship of the English Folk Song and Dance Society.

Square dance workshops and camps all over the United States and Canada have benefited from the fine leadership of this dedicated teacher. His popular square and folk dance camps were begun in New Hampshire in 1950. The New England Folk Festival, which was founded by Page, is now in its thirty-fourth year. The flavor of his camps is captured best in an article by Kirby Todd, a resident of Folk Valley, Illinois, that appeared in *Northern Junket* (edited and published ten times a year by Ralph Page). Together with Bob Howell, a resident of Cleveland, Todd attended Ralph Page's Year-End Camp at Keene State College, Keene, New Hampshire in 1977. Todd writes: "Winter Vermont was like driving through a book of Robert Frost's poetry: 'The woods are lovely, dark, and deep. . . .' And we had promises to keep with Ralph Page, the most knowledgeable man on contra dancing extant. I have known, admired and loved him for thirty years. The highest experience for me was just to see him again; meet his wife, Ada; his daughter, Laura, and two grandchildren, Seth and Erika. It was sweet nostalgia to be there. The first evening we had apple dumplings for dessert.

"Another high experience was dancing three times to live music: piano, banjo, tin whistle and hammered dulcimer made the sweetest dancing music under heaven, and it literally blew my mind; I didn't know where I was or what I was doing, but I knew that Contra is the wedding of music and dance.

"Folk Dancing under David Vinsky, Conny Taylor and Harry Brauser was spirited and delightful as Conny reintroduced some old-time favorites, but Charlie Baldwin was a heritage of American square dance in simple and traditional figures. Pure joy.

"Bob and I are agreed that neither of us have attended a camp with closer rapport between campers, staff and kitchen."

In October 1977 the state of Hew Hampshire honored Page with its prestigious Granite State Award—the first time any state has honored one of its citizens for doing work in traditional dance. He is currently president of the Historical Society of Cheshire County, the second largest historical society in New Hampshire, with two buildings open to the public during the spring, summer, and autumn: the Wyman Tavern, a period house; and the Colony Museum, housing a spectacular collection of New Hampshire glass and pottery as well as other objects of traditional interest to the area.

According to *Square Dancing* magazine, this son of an outstanding fiddler, grandson of a wonderful ballad singer, and dancer and nephew of a well-known prompter "has done extensive research on early American dances and is credited with digging up, preserving and making popular many an old contra, lancer and quadrille. He's also a mean folk dancer and can do a Hambo and Kolo with the best of them."

Grace Laura Ryan

by Carole Howard

The tiny rural town of Portland, Michigan, was chosen for the birthplace of Grace Laura Ryan, born August 23, 1894, predestined to become one of the pioneers in rediscovering and spreading country-wide the true joys of the American dance.

Her energetic pace led her into many varied experiences during her earlier years. As a child growing up in a small town in Michigan, Grace Ryan was naturally and quite easily brought into the joys of community recreation, which included the dances her parents and their friends enjoyed. "Our little town of Portland had a very unusual dance every so often in a hall with a fine floor. It was called the Blanchard Hall, and it was upstairs over the furniture store. All age groups came to waltz and two-step. Then we would sometimes have a change of partner dance. I never missed a dance, for I just loved the dancing. In fact, we used to do some rather unusual parties. Take New Year's, for instance. We all would go to a certain lodge hall, like the Masonic Hall, where we would have a beautiful dinner, perhaps a turkey dinner with all the extras, then after that about 4:00 or so, we'd all go back to the dance hall and dance until New Year's Eve came and after on into the morning. And that consisted of people of all ages. It was a delightful time. All of our crowd in the high school always went; we were like a big family."

In the early part of this century, rural schoolteachers were accepted without college or formal training, as long as they could pass comprehensive examinations in the grades they desired to teach.

After two years of teaching in a rural school outside Portland, Grace entered college in 1915, majoring in physical education. She chose Michigan Normal College at Ypsilanti, Michigan, later renamed Eastern Michigan University.

In 1917, after only two years of college preparation, as was common in the early part of the twentieth century, she left the college to take a job teaching physical education in Adrian, Michigan, for four years. In 1921 Grace Ryan was asked to return to Michigan Normal as a part-time instructor in the physical education department, where she finished her bachelor's degree. "I remember about 1921 or 1922 Elizabeth Burchenal, the very famous dance teacher, came to my college on a teaching tour. She was giving dance workshops in various colleges and universities throughout the United States. The interest was in European folk dance at that time. Well, she picked me out of the group to demonstrate how the polka was done, and that sure was good for my ego!"

She was graduated from Normal in 1923 and that same year accepted a position in the physical education faculty at Central Michigan Normal, Mt. Pleasant, Michigan, later named Central Michigan University. "I guess I can say I started the dance program at Central. I suppose there were others before me, but there certainly was nothing in the way of dance when I arrived there. I was teaching European folk dancing. I decided, however, that it was important to teach our own country dance. I remembered my parents dancing back in Portland, and I set out to find [out] more about our own dances, [especially] the square dance."

So, during the early 1920s, Grace Ryan started to collect the dances done by the early settlers of Michigan and the nearby communities around the Great Lakes. "I found they were all doing basically the same dances. The changes, the patterns, remained the same; they didn't initiate changes in those days. They stayed pretty much to the regular patterns. Later, when some teachers took out demonstration groups, they created new patterns for the dance. They didn't use the word "hoedown"; it was always called country dancing or square dancing.

"I remember talking to Pappy Shaw years later about [the] dances he had created. I told him that his new forms didn't resemble anything that looked like the old-time dances, but looked more like a gym-

nastics ensemble instead. I don't remember what he said, but I'm sure he didn't like it."

There was no music, nor were calls written down, so she would often take her friend, Dora Silver, along to the dances so she could transcribe the music for Grace. "When I went to watch the dancing, most times there would be only one musician playing, or whatever that village had in the way of talent. There was usually only one set dancing in the living room or kitchen, and one person called the sets. The older people were dancing; the younger ones hadn't yet caught on to that type of dance. The musicians of that time were mostly fiddlers, piano players, or an occasional accordionist or dulcimer player."

During her travels around the state, she noted similarities in dance posture, etiquette, and dance programs. "I noticed a very interesting thing as I was researching these dances; the women hardly ever smiled, and the men were likely to use a lot of fancy extra steps while they were doing the squares. There were very few longways dances: there were mostly squares and some waltzing and two-steps. I think very few people really knew how to waltz. They did a two-step to waltz-time.

"The foxtrot and polka came in later. I didn't see much of those two dances except in the 'thumb' area, where there were a lot of Germans and Poles. They loved to polka. They emphasized the polka with a hard step that didn't always come at the exact time with the music!"

Grace kept collecting dance material and writing down the old tunes with the express interest in writing a book for teachers to teach students their dance heritage.

"I had sent my manuscript to the publishers in New York, A. S. Barnes, and they rejected it, saying there was no demand for such a book. But when it appeared that the great Henry Ford of Dearborn, Michigan, was publishing his book *Good Morning,* which consisted of both European and early American dances, they wrote, asking me to return the manuscript. So my book, *Dances of Our Pioneers,* was published in 1926; it was accepted by the American Library Association immediately. And it was put in libraries and schools across the country."

Grace Ryan was able to attend one of the dances that Henry Ford sponsored at his spacious mansion, Fairlane, in Dearborn, Michigan. "Henry Ford's wife's sister, Mrs. Raymond, whose husband had the Ford automobile agency in Adrian, where I had taught, got an invitation for me to dance at Henry Ford's home. I was very thrilled to dance with this exacting, meticulous man. Everything had to be perfect at his dances, and they always were.

"He had hired a man from Boston to teach the

dances of Europe, but he taught the New England squares as well. They were very similar to what the older settlers in Michigan had been doing all those years."

Starting sometime in the 1930s, Miss Ryan took small groups of her dancers out to perform in public. This group, called the Country Dancers, has continued as a demonstration team up until the present time, under various leaders, but always demonstrating the degree of excellence and the joy of the dance that Grace Ryan initiated forty years ago.

She always used live music in her performance group, as well as in her daily teaching. The recording industry was barely beginning when she was collecting her dances and teaching at Central. It was her desire to collect and restore the old dances that kept many of them alive. Without her incessant drive to regain those old dances she had seen in her childhood, we may [n]ever have danced them again. "And I recall one time I was East and went to see the famous May Gadd and her Polish Country Dancers. They were doing my mother's favorite dance, the Fireman's Dance, but they were doing it wrong! So I got up my courage, and told the great Miss Gadd that they were dancing it incorrectly, and she asked me to teach it in the correct manner."

An article in the *Portland Review*, Portland, Michigan, in 1930 stated: "Still in quest of old dance music, Miss Grace Ryan, author of one book, may later publish a second volume. Physical educators make use of [the] first in classes. [The] talented lady goes to Columbia University this month for [a] master's degree."

She later earned her master's degree and did postgraduate study. Her innovative ideas at Central were always gaining notice in the Midwest as well as the nation. "I am sure I started the first coeducational dance programs way back in the '20s. Mr. Warriner, then the president of Central, used to ask me every spring if I would help plan the special program for the County Normal Teachers Meeting. So I remember planning a program named 'A Spring Day in the City Park,' and having activities that might happen in a playground in the park. Lyle Bennett dressed as the organ grinder man and he had a small boy posed as a monkey on his shoulder. I had nursemaids in the park, which were the college girls. Then I needed policemen in the park, so I asked the football players if they would be the policemen. Well, I had to have the nursemaids and the policemen dance, and that was the first time anyone had ever heard of such a thing! After that spring program I had football players and everyone else asking me if they could be in the spring program. And it became a very natural thing in my classes as well."

The folk dance camp concept was beginning in the 1930s, and she was sought out as a teacher. Grace attended many sessions of the Berea College Christmas Folk School, Berea, Kentucky, and was part of the staff in 1948. "I remember May Gadd was at Berea, too, and she didn't look very kindly at the early American dance. She rather looked down her nose at our kind of dance, thinking that the only proper dance to do was English Country Dance. I can still see her sitting on the balcony, just watching and never looking very enthusiastic."

Ryan was [a] member of the staff, Counselor Trainee program, Camp Sequoia, Asheville, North Carolina, for five years, from 1937 [to] 1941. Her experiences led her to believe that a similar camp located in Michigan would be beneficial to teaching teachers how to teach the American country dance. Her first dance camp was [held] in August, 1942, but [the plan to hold it annually] was interrupted by World War II, and [it] was continued for a few years after the war at Walloon Lake, Michigan. The early brochure read: "American Country Dance School. Central Michigan College of Education, August, 1942. The purpose: the one-week dance session is given for men and women who are interested in teaching the American square dances, contra dances, and couple dances; or for any who wish to learn them for their own recreation. A campus dormitory will be open to provide living accommodations for the guests of the dance session. Two persons in a room, single beds. Home cooking will be provided.

"Special features: lumberjack Orchestra, dancing on the green, a country barn dance, opportunities for golf, swimming, tennis, and riding. $25.00 will cover the total cost of room, board, local transportation and tuition."

With the advent of World War II, there came the need for trained recreation leaders, both for the American troops and the folks at home. Square dancing satisfied that need, and Grace Ryan was one of the natural leaders. "I was asked to go to many places to train recreation specialists. I can remember Minneapolis and the University of North Carolina right now. That was President Roosevelt's program, the WPA, or Works Project Association. It involved many citizens who were unemployed. Many of his programs involved recreation. I can remember sometimes I had all men in my classes and what good sports they were when they had to dance the girl's part in a dance. They would just tie on a scarf and that was it. They were wonderful."

Grace was not only involved with the university but with other interests as well. She was often asked to call square dances around the mid-Michigan area. Her tireless energy and devotion to teaching involved her on every level of state and national professional organizations, serving as president, Michigan Association of Health, Physical Education and Recreation in 1953–54. She also was active in her hometown activities such as the city recreation department, the Humane Society, National PTA Congress Board, Michigan Week Committee and Michigan Child Study Association.

A tragic accident happened on January 5, 1945, that altered Grace Ryan's life. On a very cold and windy day in January, Grace was hit by one of her horses. They rushed her to Ford Hospital in Detroit, where she underwent eight major surgeries, losing an eye in the process. "I stopped teaching soon after the accident. My interests started leaning toward health education, and that is where I remained until my retirement in 1958."

In the 1960s, after her retirement, Grace was asked to teach recreation leadership to Peace Corps students at Gainesville, Florida. Her job was to teach dance and play-party games to students who were going out to work in other countries such as the Bahamas or Honduras. They would, in turn, teach these simple activities to their students in whatever country they were assigned.

Besides writing a very important book, her curricular innovations gained her national recognition. Her daring coeducational programs were a first for the era in which [they were] introduced. Putting the dance of America into the public school curriculums was her greatest gift. She also pioneered the recreation program at Central. In 1937 she was responsible for the establishment of a minor in recreation, one of the four original universities and colleges in the nation [to offer this minor]. The other three were New York University, [the] University of Minnesota, and the University of North Carolina.

Grace Laura Ryan is not only a master teacher, she is a wonderful human being who has endowed her students and friends with a genuine respect and love for our country's heritage, and who, by the very example she has set for so many years, has made the word "teacher" shine with a different glow. *Dances of Our Pioneers* was created by the real pioneer, Grace Laura Ryan.

Lloyd and Dorothy Shaw

by Carole Howard

Lloyd Shaw and Dorothy Stott were wed September 3, 1913, after they were both graduated from Colorado College. Lloyd then taught biology and sophomore

Lloyd (Pappy) Shaw. Photo by Knutson Bowers

English at Colorado Springs High School and later became Superintendent of Cheyenne Mountain School.

Dorothy went to work as the librarian in Lloyd's school and together they created new programs for the students. Education included the out of doors and [involved] resource people from all over. They used the mountains for skiing and horseback riding, the roof of the schoolhouse for stargazing, and the campus for Indian encampments. For 34 years the Shaws brought exciting learning to the children of their school.

During Lloyd Shaw's college days, usually at the Sigma Chi fraternity dances, he didn't feel any special aptitude for dance. Dorothy says, "We tried to dance, and we two-stepped and waltzed. We did this ignoramous waltz, and I suppose that it started right there . . . his interest in the dance. Lloyd knew we weren't doing it right."

Pappy (the name by which Lloyd was lovingly called by thousands) saw that the dance could be another wonderful activity for his students at Cheyenne Mountain School. But first he had to learn it correctly. He pored over the books by Elizabeth Burchenal, the noted dance authority of the time. And he taught himself and his students European folk dance, including the waltz and two-step he could hardly master in college. Wednesday night folk dancing soon became one of the favorite activities of the school.

Dorothy tells us, "Yes, he learned how to dance out of a book. He used to say, 'You begin to dance just as soon as you are born . . . the minute those little legs start moving. Dance is a part of your being.' "

He heard of the dances held every weekend in the local Grange halls, and he and Dorothy made arrangements to be included. These people were just ordinary folk, mostly farmers, and mistrusted at the beginning "this school man" and his wife, but that soon gave way to mutual respect and friendship. The Grange sponsored square dance contests often, and Pappy entered his dancers and often won.

In the winter of 1933–34 Guy Parker, a caller who always competed in the El Paso County feed show, approached Lloyd Shaw asking if he could have a square of the Cheyenne students to train for his part in the callers' competition. He offered to come to the school and help with western squares for a couple of Wednesday evenings in return. "So he and Guy put together a set of students, met with them three times a week, and went to the feed show to compete. And, of course, they won the contest! They were perfectly lovely."

Lloyd Shaw continued with the Wednesday-night teaching and became intrigued with finding out as much as he could about our western American dance. His research was done in many places. If he had to go East to a convention, he would stop off at a place like Berea, Kentucky, and learn the unique dance figures they did there, such as the Kentucky running set. He and Dorothy spent countless hours tracking down dance patterns and music from the old timers in the mountains, just to bring them back to Cheyenne Mountain School.

The Shaws's daughter, Doli, said, "Nobody had any idea how much Mother knew about the dancing until Dad was gone. So much of her time had been as a spectator. I'm sure she danced a good deal more after he was gone than she had before. During the whole period of the reviving of this wonderful American dance form he had to be busy with teaching as well. Especially during the early days, there were always more women than men, and Mother always stepped back and didn't add to the imbalance. It was only a short time later that Dad, and not someone else, was almost always the caller."

In the early years at Cheyenne Mountain School, some changes were taking place that were unique for the times. "He was criticized at times for doing away with interscholastic athletics. He never really did entirely away with them; he just eradicated organized athletics. He included every child at Cheyenne, from the five-year-olds in kindergarten on up, in some kind of activity program. The dance was a very important part of physical activity for the whole school."

The Shaws bought a beautiful parcel of land in the mountains not far from the city and named it Coombie Corrie. Coombie Corrie was a very important, creative place where the Shaws could continue their research of the old dance patterns.

Doli recalled, "When I came home for the summer vacation he could hardly wait for a chance to put me in a square. In those days we always spent the whole summer at Coombie Corrie, and he would sometimes have a square of his seniors up for supper and the evening. He was so delighted in those early days with the directional quality of the western square, he wanted to try it out on me to prove it worked. I remember summer parties where some of the boys were eating popcorn and passing it from hand to hand during a right and left grand."

The dance expertise of the Cheyenne Mountain schoolchildren became well known in the area around Colorado Springs, and soon Pappy had formed a team from [among] his best dancers to go out on exhibitions. He wanted to show what American dance was all about.

Dorothy said, "I was the team mother. They sewed their own costumes, but I was in on all their decisions. Some had matching pantaloons for their long skirts and some didn't. No one ever wore hoops because they interfered with the movement of the dance. The boys wore western boots and the girls wore slippers."

Central City, Colorado, was one of the first places Pappy took his dancers, but because he wasn't sure it was a proper place for high school students, he took a team of alumni. But the alumni turned out to be a bit of a problem because they didn't feel they ought to be subject to the rules of conduct he expected of the high school students. Doli said, "The very first time he took a single square of alumni up for the weekend, we danced in the Teller House, an historic old hotel, and slept in an unused store down the road in Blackhawk. It was a wild and woolly weekend."

Because the weekend at Central City was such a success, Miss Ann Evans of that town arranged to have the dancers there for the full three weeks the next summer. They stayed in the Methodist parsonage. Doli said, "We ate over at the Teller House, but the living arrangements were something else again! The one bathroom had been converted from a sort of storage room when plumbing reached Central City. It has three doors, a closet, and a window. Poor Mother and Dad used to get up at six, use the bathroom, and go back to bed as the only way to avoid the rush. The second year we stayed in the Presbyterian parsonage, and the third in the Catholic priest's house. Finally, we ended up at the Lee House."

Dr. Shaw's research resulted in two valuable dance books, *The Round Dance Book* and *Cowboy Dances*, written during this time. Doli said, "The final work on *Cowboy Dances* took place at Coombie Corrie, and many was the time that Mother and I, along with an appropriate number of chairs, would be the guinea pigs while Dad checked to be sure his directions were valid." The Central City performances provided Pappy with the dancers needed in working out the old dances and some of the new patterns he was creating.

In 1940 the Cheyenne Mountain Dancers were asked to demonstrate the new western dances at the National Convention of the Association of Health, Physical Education, and Recreation in Chicago, Illinois. Their performance was amazing. Teachers flocked around Dr. Shaw, eager to learn the dances he had taught the exuberant students from Cheyenne Mountain School. It was a brand new, free kind of movement. He gave a workshop in Chicago, with the promise of more to come in Colorado.

Doli said, "He had his own ideas, his own principles. It seemed to me that during the early years of the revival of the American dance and the saving of these wonderful old patterns, there was an eagerness to share them with the rest of the world through his demonstration team. The fact that we exhibited was secondary. The fact that we were good enough to exhibit was first."

The demonstration team was asked to dance at Constitution Hall in Washington, D.C., in 1940, so Pappy drove the school bus East. Dorothy said, "We got to Constitution Hall early so we could practice, and it was brutally hot. We waited and waited for the speakers to stop talking. We had had no supper and had just driven straight from Colorado to do this show, and we were beginning to fade fast. Well, Lloyd finally went up to the head man and said, 'If we do not perform in the next ten minutes, we shall leave. We are exhausted from our drive to Washington, but if you do not have the courtesy to let us on that stage, we shall drive back to Colorado immediately!' We went on in the next few minutes and brought the city of Washington to their feet, wild with applause, as those Cheyenne Mountain kids brought a breath of fresh mountain air to Constitution Hall. We did many trips East after that and everyone loved us."

In order for a student to dance for the Shaws, he had to be not only a highly skilled dancer but a scholar as well, for they often stayed out of school a few days longer than the spring vacation permitted.

"Pappy said, 'Dance up to the stars.' And that's what we did every time we danced. People are not dancing for fun today or for the nourishment of their spirit. They just want to learn any old dance, just dance . . . rather than learn how to dance well."

The dance team continued to spread [its] joy of the dancing throughout the country for many years,

and [its] fame was worldwide. Pappy served as dance consultant for the very famous movie *Duel in the Sun,* starring Gregory Peck and Jennifer Jones. And he and Dorothy continued to sponsor all kinds of dance classes, making sure that the "reincarnated square dance" would never die again.

In 1948, Doli recalls, "he decided to terminate the Cheyenne Mountain Dancers. He felt they were doing it for the wrong reasons and they were not top quality anymore. That was the last team."

About this time Pappy believed that the dance he had researched and loved so well was falling into the wrong hands and being abused. He watched sadly what was happening on the dance floor after he had been calling squares for twenty years. The new callers were trying to race each other in making up new calls, with little flow or grace, in an attempt to outdo each other.

He renewed his fervor to pass on to teachers the necessity of learning our national dance, and he taught three classes each summer, limited to forty students each, in the old gym at Cheyenne Mountain School. Physical education teachers, recreation leaders, and professional callers flocked to that tiny gym to share his enthusiasm and ideas.

The long reign of Dr. Lloyd Shaw at Cheyenne Mountain School came to a close in 1954, when he realized that organized athletics and team sports had possessed the school. His set of ideals and high standards couldn't allow him to stay any longer. Dorothy tells how it happened. "Lloyd said, 'I can't help it. I cannot be superintendent of Cheyenne School while team sports is the most important thing in the school. I am too tired to fight anymore.' Lloyd could not have gone on any longer, anyway. He was exhausted from crippling arthritis that had settled in his hips, making every move painful."

After he left the school, he found he could no longer use the school facilities for his big dances nor his teaching sessions. He told Dorothy, "I can start all over again with forty people, so let's build a dance hall for forty." He called it La Semilla (the "seed" in Spanish). And it attracted the great callers and teachers of the United States. He continued his teacher workshops for the next three summers until his death from a stroke in 1958.

Remembering that sad period, Doli said: "The seed for the Lloyd Shaw Foundation was planted the afternoon of the day of his funeral service. It was amazing the number of dancers who got there. Bob Osgood and Kirby Todd were among the pallbearers. It turned out to be a most triumphant and joyous occasion. One of the questions Mother asked then was what should happen to the August dance class. We were in the period when he had three classes a summer, or just past that. Most of the old guard had settled into the August week, so when he gave up the big school gym on the summer classes, those who wanted to continue were already committed for the August sessions, so it was the natural one to continue. That particular summer the answer to her question was, 'We're continuing on, of course.' "

Dorothy Shaw proceeded with the plans for the pageant for the Denver convention of the National Square Dance Convention in 1959 even though Pappy was not there to continue the ideas he had conceived. She still continues, twenty years later, to lead the Lloyd Shaw Foundation, which was established in 1964, carrying on in the manner which Pappy would have admired. They still have their annual August meeting at La Semilla, and they still dance the dances the Shaws found up in those majestic mountains of Colorado. Through the foundation, teacher workshops are sponsored each summer, training teachers in the same fundamentals that were examined minutely at Coombie Corrie in the 1930s. The group has flourished under the little librarian's guidance, now even selling dance recordings and books. Under Dorothy's leadership and infinite wisdom, millions of people worldwide are enjoying the rhythms of early America.

People do not regard Dorothy Stott Shaw as the great dance teacher of the West. Instead, they view her place in history as one who picked up a banner and strode forward, making her own path. Her part in taking dance education to teachers and children of this land is monumental. Dorothy Stott Shaw has never stopped believing in dancing up to the stars.

(The preceding material was excerpted and is used with permission from a field study report made by Carole Howard for Central Michigan University.)

Many have paid tribute to Lloyd (Pappy) Shaw and the contribution he made to preserve America's dances. In his preface to *Cowboy Dances*, Thomas Hornsby Ferril wrote: "Lloyd Shaw is an American genius. We in Colorado are proud to share him with our sister states and neighboring countries, which have now caught up with what we have always known about him. The old square dances were never lost in America but, due to something temporarily lost in ourselves, got misplaced. Through Lloyd Shaw, more than any other man, we were able to restore our own dances to our own spirit. Now, in this new book, he is giving us renewed access to our old round dances. It is an adventure to move up with him, through something like a century of round dances, to where we are now.

"Over many years I've seen this thing happen— this thing Lloyd Shaw does in a lovely canyon under the shadow of Pike's Peak. I readily understand why his Cheyenne Mountain School (I say *his* although it's a public school) has become a shrine for people who want to know why the American dance is what it is and how to do it.

"They come from everywhere—New England, the Corn Belt, the Southern Mountains, Hollywood and the Northwest. Perhaps some of them think they are coming to learn dance steps, dance tunes and dance calls, just as some people think they can learn to write poetry by first learning how to make rhymes, meters and word patterns.

"Fortunately, these people get what they come for, but it happens the other way around. The steps, the calls, the tunes are taken in a sort of unconscious corollary to learning the dance itself. Lloyd Shaw, from the first moment, gives you the feeling of *being dancing,* which is quite different from being about to learn how to dance. Yet if the actual learning seems almost to come as an afterthought, there's no blundering on the way; he bears down with a radiant, booming discipline; your right hand knows what your left hand is doing and it doesn't forget."

When the American Academy of Physical Education made one of its rare citations, in 1949, "to the Lloyd Shaw Folk Dance Program, as a noteworthy contribution to physical education," the statement went on to say: "Dr. Shaw has pioneered in the field of folk dancing, and his institutes and other promotions have done much to popularize this area of dance, especially for young people. His books have contributed significantly to a better understanding of, and appreciation for, folk dancing and square dancing throughout the country."

III
SELECTED CAMPS AND ORGANIZATIONS

American Alliance for Health, Physical Education, Recreation and Dance

by Miriam Gray

(This article was written before the 94th Anniversary Convention was held in New Orleans in 1979, at which time the word *Dance* was added to the name of the Alliance, thereby changing the acronym to AAHPERD.)

The American Alliance for Health, Physical Education and Recreation, called AAHPER or the Alliance, is an umbrella organization encompassing seven associations: American Association for Leisure and Recreation (AALR), American School and Community Safety Association (ASCSA), Association for the Advancement of Health Education (AAHE), Association for Research, Administration, Professional Councils and Societies (ARAPCS), National Association for Girls and Women in Sports (NAGWS), National Association for Sport and Physical Education (NASPE), and National Dance Association (NDA).

AAHPER was organized in 1885 as the American Physical Education Association, and it has expanded, both in membership and variety of programs, undergoing several name changes and reorganizations along the way to becoming the Alliance in 1974. The Alliance emerged during a five-year reorganization of the long-term American Association for Health, Physical Education and Recreation (called AAHPER too) and its eight divisions, many of which became full-fledged associations with autonomy and greater visibility in the Alliance than under the previous structure.

The association with the greatest concern for dance is, of course, the National Dance Association. Several other associations and substructures of the Alliance do include dance in their ongoing work, in their publications, and in the National AAHPER Convention programs, either alone or in co-operation with the National Dance Association. Most frequently, those concerned with dance are AALR, NASPE, and the International Relations Council of ARAPCS, who present dance as part of their total scope in elementary and secondary school physical education and in leisure and recreation activities; and sometimes cosponsor convention programs with NDA. One cosponsoring project that some in NDA will never forget was in co-operation with the American Academy of Physical Education to bring the King Island Eskimos to the Seattle AAHPER Convention in 1970 for a demonstration of their dances, costumes, and culture. Program planners learned the hard way that Eskimo time is *different*—and unrelated to a tight convention schedule!

AAHPER, from its office in the nation's capital, protects its seven associations, including NDA, and provides them [with] many services: promotion and publicity, convention organization and housing, membership processing and publications.

Two AAHPER periodicals which all members receive, regardless of association affiliation, the *Journal of Physical Education and Recreation* (JOPER) and *Update,* both published nine times a year, carry dance in almost every issue. The *Journal* has a dance editor, appointed by NDA, and a section of the magazine reserved for dance articles and an occasional center feature of 16 pages, *Dance Dynamics,* which becomes available as a reprint. JOPER in 1978 contained 20 dance articles, 4 of them about folk and ethnic dance in whole or in part: "The Folk Dance Institute in Yugoslavia" by Marilyn Kocinski in April and, in the same issue, an advance listing of 11 "1978 Summer Dance Workshops," 4 of which were folk dance workshops in Michigan, Oregon, Utah, and Yugoslavia offering college credit if desired. The others were "The Spectacle of the Body as Exotic Dance" by Shirley Thomas in May and "Appalachian Clog Dance—Exciting and Challenging" by Jerry Duke in November-December.

Update, in newspaper format, includes a column or page five to six times a year on "Dance Information," bringing news of the increasing alignments of dance education with other arts education organizations and of federal aids to dance and grant programs, both public and private, available for dance projects.

The AAHPER National Convention held in Kansas City in April 1978 programmed two outstanding dance events sponsored by structures other than the National Dance Association, which planned sixteen programs of its own. One special feature was an All-Convention Square Dance sponsored by ARAPCS' Student Action

Council in co-operation with the Lloyd Shaw Foundation; Don Armstrong was the caller through the courtesy of the Lloyd Shaw Foundation. Another special all-convention event was the last General Session program—planned by the AAHPER president—presenting the Brigham Young University International Folk Dance and BYU Ballroom Dance teams titled "International Holiday Show." This marked the fifth time the BYU International Folk Dancers had appeared on General Session programs for AAHPER national conventions. Previously, they had danced at the 1975 Convention in Atlantic City, in Anaheim in 1974, Houston in 1972, and at an earlier date in Boston.

AAHPER supplies the headquarters office and an executive secretary for an affiliated organization, the International Council for Health, Physical Education and Recreation (ICHPER) which has published a book of some interest to folk dancers, *ICHPER Worldwide Book of Games and Dances* (1967) available from AAHPER Publications and Sales. Sixty-eight favorite children's games and thirty-nine dances from fifty-eight countries are useful in teaching international understanding in grades 1–6; the dances include diagrams and music.

A membership in AAHPER provides the opportunity to be a member of two of its associations for one membership fee; thus, one could join NDA as first choice, AALR as second choice, for example, and in addition be a member of AAHPER. The Board of Governors, in its fall 1978 meeting, voted to add [the word] *Dance* to the name of the Alliance, making it AAHPERD, subject to approval by the Alliance Assembly meeting at the 94th Anniversary Convention in New Orleans in March 1979.

Address inquiries to: American Association for Health, Physical Education Recreation and Dance, 1900 Association Drive, Reston, Va. 22091.

(MIRIAM GRAY, dance educator, Professor Emerita of Health, Physical Education, Recreation and Dance at Illinois State University, has taught dance and physical education on all levels from first grade through college in Missouri, Oklahoma, New York, and, during World War II, at the University of Texas. A bachelor's degree from the University of Missouri-Columbia was followed by graduate work leading up to a doctorate (Ed.D.) at Teachers College, Columbia University, New York.

During her twenty-six years at Illinois State University, she was in charge of the dance curriculum, developing a minor, a major, and a master's degree program in dance education. Her teaching-methods classes included folk, modern, round, social-ballroom, and square dance. With Dr. Gwen K. Smith, she was co-founder and codirector of a student recreational square

dance club, Shufflin' Shoes (1953), which continues to function today. For sixteen years Dr. Gray was director of the modern dance performing club Orchesis.

Miriam Gray has served in many capacities in recreational dance organizations. She was a charter member of the Illinois Square Dance Callers Association, serving four years on its board of directors—two years as chairperson. She edited *The Square Chute,* the newsletter of the Illinois Federation of Square Dance Clubs, for three years. She has contributed to *Viltis, American Squares,* and *Square Your Sets.*

Her most extensive and continuous contribution to dance organizations has been to the National Dance Association and its precursors. As a graduate student in 1932, Miriam Gray was present at the first official meeting in Philadelphia of the newly formed National Section on Dance (NSD) of the then American Physical Education Association (later renamed the American Alliance for Health, Physical Education and Recreation). Her leadership, beginning with the Illinois Dance Section chair in 1953, was followed by the Midwest District Dance Section chair, which first put her on the board of the National Section on Dance. She continued as NSD secretary, then held the NSD chair (equivalent to president) from 1958 to 1961. When NSD became the Dance Division of AAHPER, she was program chairperson of its first national conference on "Dance as a Discipline" in 1965. She served as editor of the Dance Division for four years, editing *Focus on Dance V: Composition* (1969). From 1970 to 1973 she chaired the Dance Division and was vice-president of AAHPER (1971–72). This put her in the driver's seat during an important phase of the long reorganization period during which AAHPER became an Alliance (1974) and the Dance Division became the National Dance Association (NDA).

Dr. Gray was honored at the national convention in Atlantic City in 1975 by being named the first Heritage Honoree under the new National Dance Association, the thirteenth recipient of the Heritage Award. She was selected as the second NDA Scholar, 1978–79. In 1977 she agreed to a taped interview as one of the dance education pioneers for the NDA Oral History Project. She chairs the NDA Honors Advisory Committee.

In 1978 Miriam Gray was named a special consultant for the NDA Projections Unit project, partially funded by the Alliance for Arts Education, to produce *Dance as Education* and the slide-tape "Dance Is . . . ." For the new book *Discover Dance* she served as one of several contributor-editors. Earlier, she had contributed articles to *Focus on Dance I, II, III, IV* and *VIII;* and to *Spotlight on Dance* and the *Journal of Physical Education and Recreation.*

Miriam Gray

At the national convention in Seattle in 1970 AAHPER made Miss Gray a recipient of its Honor Fellow Award. Among other awards were a Certificate of Recognition from the American Dance Guild and a Plaque of Appreciation from the Illinois Dance Association. Current biographical listings are included in *World Who's Who of Women, Dictionary of International Biography, Who's Who of American Women, Who's Who in the Midwest* and *Community Leaders and Noteworthy Americans.*

When Miriam Gray retired in 1972 after a teaching career spanning forty-five years, she moved back to the home where she was born and raised, the Wayside Farm, Route 1, Nevada, Missouri 64772. She continues to be active in dance committee work, editing, workshops, writing, and in local clubs and associations.)

Berea College Country Dancers

Berea College, Berea, Kentucky 40403
(See the essay on the Country Dance and Song Society in this section.)

Blue Star Folk Dance Camp

by Herman Popkin

It was the summer of 1947, before the State of Israel was established, that Fred Berk became known to me and my brothers. Our friendship began at Brandeis Camp Institute, in the Poconos, where he and his ex-wife, Katya Delakova, were on the faculty. It was my first experience with Jewish folk dancing. I took part in a modern interpretive dance entitled "Chiamisha (Hamisa)—The Story of the Five." It was an exciting opportunity and challenge, as well as an exhilarating experience. While at Brandeis I became a more knowledgeable and dedicated Zionist and expressed the hope to them then that one day, if and when I had my own camp, this creative, dedicated, and talented couple would find someone like themselves to teach for me at my camp. I did not have the courage to ask them, personally, to join my dream of a camp for Jewish youth in the Deep South.

Little did I know then that three years later, in the summer of 1950 (Blue Star's third season), Fred and Katya would join our staff and have such an impact and influence on our campers, as well as on the entire South, for the next seven years. Either both or one of the team would be a part of our key staff—teaching Israeli folk dancing, modern and interpretative dance, and even ballet. This revolutionized our thinking about dance and how it belonged to a good summer camp program with a positive Jewish approach.

In a section of the South (sometimes referred to, in more ways than one, as "The Negev") where the young took little or no interest in things Zionistic or even Jewish at camp, we had a great challenge to meet. Only through the skill, patience, dedication, and creativity of such a person as Fred Berk could we have had any success or made any progress. He was truly great. Katya only, remained a part of the team for three or four seasons, then Fred took over alone. He had all of us folk dancing—not only on Friday nights, as part of our Oneg Shabbat, but also as an optional choice activity and in performing groups.

He began at least three traditions at Blue Star that are still carried on today: (1) an Israeli performing group of older campers or staff that dances each summer before such places and groups as the Asheville Folk Dance and Music Festival; the B'nai B'rith Institute of Judaism, held at Wildacres in Little Switzerland, N.C.; the weekly Street Dances in Hendersonville, N.C.; and the Kanuga Episcopalian Conference, just a few miles from camp; (2) our own Dahlia Folk Dance Festival, which is modeled after the original one in Israel; everyone takes part before the overall Camp Oneg Shabbat program at the Dahlia Festival; it may not be equal to the real thing in Israel, but our six hundred campers and two hundred staff members think so; and (3) the Israeli Folk Dance Workshops, started in 1961 for one week with some fifteen participants. There was a three-year period (1958, 1959, and 1960) when Fred was not at Blue Star, but aside from this period and the first two summers of our existence, Fred Berk has been a vital, concerned, and beloved member of our Blue Star summer family. His contribution covers a three-decade period marked by many highlights and a dedication seldom seen in the world of dance.

It is fitting that this season's 18th Annual Folk Dance Workshops are dedicated to Fred. *Chai* means "life" in Hebrew. It also represents the number 18 and pays tribute to a great teacher, a master of creativity, and a kind, understanding human being who is loved by all who know him. It is said that he is like a Chasidic rabbi who has a dedicated following. The lives he has touched and influenced number in the thousands. Although the figures aren't exact, we feel that at Blue Star alone, either in the camps or in the workshops, Fred has brought his love for Israel, through dance, to some three thousand people, young and old.

There are other facets of Fred's great influence at national and regional festivals, workshops and seminars throughout the country, classes at the 92nd Street YMHA, the Jewish Theological Seminary, and tours to Israel for folk dance enthusiasts. We have not had the privilege of being a part of it all, but to us—deep in the South in the heart of the Blue Ridge Mountains, where the banjo and fiddle accompany the cloggers— we feel privileged to know such a professional artist, to be influenced by his kindly manners and his gentle personality, to become a part of his creative life and his legacy as a master dance teacher.

Fred Berk's name is on our outdoor pavilion overlooking the lake; the Folk Dance Workshops will forever carry his name. But in our hearts and minds, as though inscribed in letters of gold, there is a deep respect and love for one who has dedicated his life to an art form called folk dancing. Fred belongs to the people—to the folk who dance and sing, who create and enjoy, who are forever a part of the Jewish people in a way that never ceases, that comes from the deep roots of our very source of life. It is as though the earth cries out to honor one who loves his people and who, in turn, is beloved and blessed.

(Herman Popkin is founder and director, with his brother, Rodger, of Blue Star Camps.)

Address: Kanuga Road, P.O. Box 1029, Hendersonville, North Carolina 28739.

Buffalo Gap International Folk Dance Camp

by Mel Diamond

Buffalo Gap International Folk Dance Camp began Memorial Day 1969. The camp is held in Cold Stream, West Virginia, on Memorial and Labor Day weekends each year. Its directors are Mel and Phyllis Diamond, Larry Weiner, and Jean Bollinger.

The camp operates under the simple philosophy that if you give adult folk dancers a beautiful setting, outstanding dancing masters, a great dance floor, excellent meals, live music, and then just turn 'em loose and allow them to be themselves, without restrictions, they will have a simply marvelous time. It has never failed to meet our expectations.

We normally have between 200 and 250 persons attending and most weekends fill up very early. Waiting lists have at times had as many as 110 names on them.

Address: Buffalo Gap Camp, c/o Melvin H. Diamond, 2414 East Gate Drive, Silver Spring, Maryland 20906.

Country Dance and Song Society

by Genevieve Shimer

In 1959 the late May Gadd wrote a history of the then Country Dance Society (CDS). She wrote: "Towards the end of 1914, Cecil Sharp, pioneer collector of folk songs and dances and founder of the English Folk Dance and Song Society (EFDSS), came to the United States to work with Granville Barker on his production of 'A Midsummer Night's Dream.' Within a few months—in March 1915—the United States Branch of the English Society was formed, with centers in Boston, Chicago, New York, Pittsburgh, Cincinnati and St. Louis. The first four are still active. In 1915 Lily Roberts (later Mrs. Richard Conant) came from England to work with the United States Branch. She became the Society's national president, having succeeded Mrs. James Jackson Storrow in 1957. The English Folk Dance and Song Society of America

(EFDSSA) was adopted as the name of the national Society in 1937 and in 1940 it became the Country Dance Society of America.

During the first twenty-five years of its existence there was a growing recognition of the importance of the American aspect of the Society's program. The tremendous collection of Southern Appalachian songs and dances, made by Cecil Sharp between 1916 and 1918, led to further research which showed that a tradition of folk music and dance exists all over America, and that the English and American traditions are so closely interwoven that they cannot be separated without loss to both."

Now, almost twenty years later, it is time to bring that account up to date. The highlights in the life of the Society in the early sixties are certainly noteworthy. In 1961 Douglas Kennedy, president of the EFDSS at that time, came with his wife, Helen, to Pinewoods Camp, where he awarded the EFDSS Gold Badge to five members of the Country Dance Society; the award is given for "outstanding service to folk music through teaching and scholarship." The recipients were: Lily Roberts Conant, president; May Gadd, national director; Phil Merrill, music director; Louise Chapin, Boston Centre director; Evelyn K. Wells, scholar and authority on folk music and song. That same summer at Pinewoods also saw the addition of a fourth week to the CDS season—Chamber Music. The first year that recorder players began to hold a full week of instruction and playing was in 1958, when they shared the camp with folk musicians. By 1961 the number of devotees of both kinds of music had grown so much that they had to be divided—a welcome change for all. Since then the two music weeks have flourished and are consistently popular.

In 1962–63, the Society could feel very proud of its connection with the Berea College Country Dancers, a young performing group that was sponsored by the State Department for a tour of South America. After their highly successful tour, they were invited to dance at the White House in Washington, D.C., where they were presented to then President John F. Kennedy. Their director, Ethel Capps of Berea College, and CDS National Director May Gadd, as well as their outstanding musicians were with them on this occasion. In 1964 these Berea College Country Dancers joined the Society's group in the first of its performances at the New York World's Fair in the World's Fair Pavilion. Here a company of seventy dancers and musicians, directed by May Gadd and Phil Merrill, presented "An English Village Festival" in the series of Nationality Day programs directed by Walter Bacad. Dancers also came from Boston, New Jersey, and Pennsylvania to join the Headquarters Area group in an exciting and colorful program. The performance

was very professional; an incredible amount of volunteer effort went into making new costumes and props, rehearsals, publicity, and photographers, but everyone felt it was well worth the effort. The CDS repeated the same show (without Berea's young people but with a group of teen-agers from the Hindman Settlement School in Kentucky) on two subsequent occasions, at the United States Pavilion and at the Singer Bowl in 1965.

The Society celebrated its golden jubilee in 1965. In New York City, the opening birthday party was held in March at Metropolitan Duane Hall; the Golden Jubilee Festival was a great success at Hunter College. Many CDS centers also celebrated the fiftieth anniversary with gala events and special publicity in local newspapers; a fiftieth anniversary booklet was printed, with a press kit, and was widely distributed. (It is still available for anyone interested in receiving a copy.)

The year 1965 also saw an unprecedented event: the affiliation of the Pinewoods Morris Men [PWMM] with the Morris Ring in England—the first group outside of the United Kingdom to be so affiliated. The PWMM is also one of the Society's affiliated groups. That same year saw the birth of the Pinewoods Folk Music Club of CDS, founded by folk music enthusiasts who wanted to keep the spirit of Pinewoods Camp Folk Music Week going throughout the year. It operates through volunteers in the New York City area, publishes a monthly newsletter, sponsors concerts, and has a large membership, of which many are also National Society members.

Following up on some of the publicity generated by the golden jubilee, the CDS in the headquarters area participated in numerous public performances during the next few years on television, at museums, and in outdoor celebrations, as did many of the centers. These centers have for years been responsible for fine performances in their local areas, directed by members who have maintained contact with the Society and thus are carrying out its aims and keeping up its standards. In addition, of course, their most important contribution continued to be that of holding classes and parties and spreading the knowledge and enjoyment of our dances and music.

In 1967, by a vote of the membership, the CDS added the words "and song" to its name, changing the acronym to CDSS. This was evidence of the increasing interest in folk music and the growing number of members whose tastes leaned more towards the music than the dance. In 1968 the Society's magazine (published under the title *The Country Dancer*) changed its name to *Country Dance and Song*. About this same time, the Society began to print newsletters; these were more informal than the magazine, came out more frequently, with news of local activities, personalities, members' letters, and so forth; they convey the great variety of activities in which the centers and members are engaged, and are timely. Recently, they have been put out almost entirely with volunteer help.

From 1937 until 1970 the Society's national director, May Gadd, was responsible for the management of the headquarters office, which she was able to do with the help of a full-time secretary, occasional part-time workers, much invaluable volunteer help, and her unlimited devotion. In 1970 the executive committee decided that since the work load seemed to be increasing steadily, with volunteer help not as easy to obtain (more people working at full-time jobs than in the past), the Society should hire an assistant executive. In April 1970, therefore, Paul Skrobela became assistant director, a post he held until October, when he had to resign as a result of changes in his outside music teaching schedule. In November James E. Morrison was appointed assistant director. A recent graduate of Dartmouth College, where he majored in English, he had a keen interest as dancer and musician in both American and English folk traditions. Joining him as an assistant administrator in May 1971 was Robert Dalsemer, who held this post for several months until he moved to Baltimore. In July 1971 Jim Morrison was invited to England by the EFDSS to demonstrate the American clog in one of the EFDSS shows in London. He went as "co-dancer" and musician with Wayne Holland, of Brasstown, North Carolina, the CDSS granting him leave for the month and paying his fare. It was believed that his visit would further the contact between the EFDSS and the CDSS and give him some firsthand experience of the English people as well as English dance. It has proved a sound investment.

In 1972 May Gadd requested official retirement at the end of the year. The national council accepted her resignation with much regret, while fully understanding that at the age of eighty-two and after forty-five years of devoted labors at the helm of CDSS, she was entitled to lead a less strenuous life. She was released, therefore, with the title of Director Emeritus, and a successor was sought.

In January 1973 Genevieve Shimer was appointed national director by the national council. A member since 1940, she had been active in the Society's affairs as a longtime teacher at Pinewoods Camp and in New York City; as a member and chairman of the executive committee for several terms; and most recently as chairman of the New York Activities Committee. She agreed to assume the responsibility with the understanding that since this meant giving up her professional art work, it would be for a limited period—until, in fact, a new director could be found. She served as national director until September 1, 1975. During her tenure, Jim Morrison was the director of field work and special projects; he was appointed national director when Genevieve Shimer retired.

At the end of 1972, when May Gadd retired, the Society was showing signs of great vitality, and the next few years did indeed prove to be a period of considerable expansion; at a time when there was a nationwide growth of interest in folk music and dance, 1973 brought changes to the Society. It was saddened by the death of its honorary president, Lily Roberts Conant, a longtime friend. Those who had been privileged to dance in her classes will carry with them always the memory of a truly inspiring teacher; the Society owes her a tremendous debt, as owner of Pinewoods Camp, for her dedication to its summer programs. The national council was fortunate to find a successor in Norman Singer, CDSS member since the early forties and longtime friend and supporter of the society. He was at that time director of the New York City Center.

In 1973 the Society published a new dance book and a companion record (CDS #5) entitled *Okay, Let's Try a Contra,* by Dudley Laufman, a well-known New England caller who was on the staff at Pinewoods Camp for several years. This was the first book of American dances to be put out by CDSS; previously the Society had printed the two *English Country Dances of Today* books by May Gadd, and the popular records (CDS #s 1–4) of English dances, both traditional and of the seventeenth and eighteen centuries, under the direction of Phil Merrill.

Some reorganization of headquarter functions in New York City occurred in 1973. With the continuing growth of demands on staff time for truly national concerns, it was decided to shift the responsibility of organizing the dance classes and parties in the city to a committee composed entirely of volunteers. For many years, of course, the major time-consuming work had indeed been handled by volunteers (N.Y. Dancers' Council in the Fifties, followed by the New York Dance Activities Committee [NYDAC]). Now the need for more membership involvement was felt and NYDAC, a part of CDSS, was formed. Like the Pinewoods Folk Music Club, it is run by volunteers, but finances go through CDSS accounts. Festivals and weekends are still organized under CDSS auspices.

Several events of significance occurred in 1974, one of which was the first leaders' conference. An increase in both national membership and the number of centers was evidence of growing interest in the function of the Society itself; there was a need to improve communication between headquarters and the centers. This initial conference was held in New Jersey; thirty-six people attended the pilot project, the majority from the greater New York area, but others came from Baltimore, Boston, Bloomington, Chicago, New London, Philadelphia, Pittsburgh, Washington, D.C., and Woods Hole. The sessions were thought to be very productive; one of the themes discussed, a possible family week at Pinewoods Camp, was of great help and convinced us that we should take the plunge and initiate the week the following summer.

In 1974 Richard K. Conant announced that after discussions with family members he believed they could no longer operate Pinewoods Camp and would consider offering it for sale at a very reasonable price to a nonprofit organization. CDSS immediately asked for an expression of interest from its members and friends; the response was such that Mr. Conant decided he and his family were indeed willing to go ahead with a proposal. A committee—consisting of Carl Hiller, chairman of the executive committee; Norman Singer, president; George Fogg, vice-president; John Hodgkin, treasurer; May Gadd, Fred Bosworth, Mrs. Schuyler Chapin, Genevieve Shimer, and James Morrison—met and discussed the situation with Mr. Conant. After months of meetings and negotiations, the decision was finally reached that a nonprofit organization, to be known as Pinewoods Camp, Inc., should be formed, with a board on which the majority of members would represent CDSS but which would also include representatives of the other long-term users of the camp (CDS Boston Centre, Royal Scottis CDS), as well as the Conant family and Long Pond neighbors. A goal of raising $265,000 was set and the project was under way.

Another landmark in 1974 was the addition of four members to the select list of honorary life members of CDSS, in recognition of devotion and great contributions to the life of the Society. They were Richard K. Conant, Ethel Capps of Berea College, and Russell and Frances Houghton. The latter were dedicated supporters of CDSS programs in New York City for more than forty-six years, Frances also serving as CDSS assistant treasurer for a long time. (Other life members in 1974 were Louise Chapin, May Gadd, and Phil Merrill).

A major CDSS project was born in 1974. In 1973 the National Endowment for the Humanities had awarded James Morrison a grant in support of a study of American social dance in the eighteenth century that was renewed in 1974. As a result of this grant, Jim Morrison's research enabled the Society to organize the American Country Dance Ensemble [ACDE] a group of dancers and musicians from the headquarters area who were to participate in programs during the U.S. Bicentennial celebrations. The Ensemble itself put in many hours of rehearsals and performances, but a most rewarding aspect of the project was the

enthusiastic help and support of CDSS members, who donated a tremendous amount of time and energy to making costumes, wigs, props, and helping with transportation and publicity. Originally it was intended to have two groups, but the second one, which covered the early nineteenth century to the present, had to be disbanded in the face of the cost involved. A grant from the New York State Council on the Arts did eventually help to defray some of the production costs for the first group.

The ACDE gave a total of sixteen performances in the next two years, beginning with one in May 1975 at the historic Jumel Mansion in New York City. It was held outdoors with the temperature over ninety; it could truly be called a baptism of fire for the thirty performers in their beautifully designed authentic eighteenth-century-style costumes. (Even the underpinnings were as close to the genuine article as possible, since their structure influenced the way in which the dancers moved. The costumes were designed and many of them were made by Honey Hastings, aided by ladies and gentlemen in the cast who showed expertise at hand or machine sewing, as well as the volunteers mentioned in the previous paragraph. We considered ourselves quite expert in the fabrication of eighteenth-century corsets, for example.) In all, the Ensemble traveled from Newport News, Virginia, to Boonville in upper New York State, Connecticut, and Long Island, as well as numerous locations in the greater New York area. Jim Morrison directed the company, Phil Merrill and Marshall Barron arranged the music, and Edwin Durham was the manager.

During the Bicentennial celebrations, various CDSS centers developed their own performing groups. Boston CDS had one, as did the Larchmont Center, which gave several performances. Many centers concentrated on a few gala events; here mention should be made of the Williamsburg, Virginia, Center, which put on a truly splendid costume ball at the lodge in November 1976. It was the culmination of a two-year effort that involved holding classes and assemblies so that people would know the dances, and close co-operation with the Bicentennial Commission in Williamsburg. Two hundred and fifty dancers in costume attended the gala ball, which opened with a mass minuet adapted for present-day dancers who would not have liked the custom of having a single couple perform, as in 1776; the evening continued with a wonderful program of dances that only required a brief explanation since all the dancers had learned them. Gail and Leland Ticknor were the moving spirits behind this very successful event.

In 1975–76 the Society published two books of early American dances that proved extremely timely and useful to groups organizing Bicentennial shows, and which remain excellent sources for anyone needing material of the Revolutionary period. The first was *American Country Dances of the Revolutionary Era 1775–1795*, by Kate Van Winkle Keller and Ralph Sweet, with an introduction by Joy Van Cleef and edited by James E. Morrison. The second, *Twenty-four Early American Country Dances, Cotillions and Reels for the Year 1976*, published as the direct result of Jim Morrison's research (partially funded by the National Endowment for the Humanities), contains carefully selected dances by James E. Morrison, dancing master. In addition to the dances and tunes, it contains quotations from contemporary sources that add charm and distinction to the collection, as well as an excellent bibliography.

From September 1975 to June 1977 Jim Morrison was national director of CDSS. During this period, two more leaders' conferences were held in Washington, D.C., and New Harmony, Indiana. They are now firmly established on an annual basis, the fourth meeting to be held in Charlottesville, Virginia. One important topic discussed at the sessions was the relationship of the centers to CDSS headquarters; this, in turn, led to the decision to revise the constitution of the Society. A committee was established; after months of discussions and hard work, a revised constitution was submitted to the national membership and was finally accepted in February 1978.

While Jim Morrison was national director, he urged the inauguration of a sixth week at Pinewoods Camp featuring American dance and music. It was very well received in 1976 and promises to be a popular addition to the CDSS season at camp.

After a year in office, Jim Morrison announced that he could not continue as director if it meant living in New York City. The question of the location of CDSS headquarters had already been under consideration; a subcommittee had looked into alternatives but had finally recommended no change after studying them. A search committee was then set up by the national council with the task of writing a job description and seeking a successor. This committee was chaired by Norman Singer, president; it consisted of Genevieve Shimer, vice-president, Sue Salmons, chairman of the executive committee, and Christine Helwig and Jeff Warner, executive committee members. After long and exhaustive study, this committee submitted a proposal that eliminated the post of national director while creating the new positions of executive director (full-time) and associate director (part-time). The national council approved the redistribution of duties involved in the change; the search committee then recommended that Jim Morrison be retained as associate director, with a field office based in Charlottesville, Virginia. Much of the artistic direction would remain

in his hands, while the new executive director would assume administrative duties. Candidates were interviewed for the administrative post. Mrs. Nancy White Kurzman was eventually selected; the changeover took place in June 1977. Joan H. Carr, who had been serving on the headquarters staff, was retained as administrative assistant in the new regime.

In the opening months of 1978, the Society would seem to be thriving. More and more members and centers are realizing that they *are* the Society; workshops, weekends, and festivals are proliferating, both in music and dance. Membership is now over 1,300 after hovering around the 700–800 mark only a decade ago; there are more than 50 centers now, as against a consistent average of 15–20 for many years. Surely this healthy vitality supports the hope that, with ongoing support from its members and centers and dedicated staff, CDSS will continue to flourish and achieve its aim of spreading the knowledge of American and English dance and song across the country.

(Genevieve Shimer has served the Country Dance and Song Society in many capacities; one was as national director of the national council. An account of her other activities is included in this article.)

Address: Country Dance and Song Society of America, 55 Christopher Street, New York, N.Y. 10014.

Enumclaw Folk Dance Festival

1535 Myrtle Street, Enumclaw, Washington 98022

Feather River Family Dance Camp

Held annually near Quincy, California, in the Plumas National Forest of California.

Address: Oakland Parks and Recreation Department, 1520 Lakeside Drive, Oakland, California 94612

Folk Dance Federation of California

by Perle Bleadon

Organized folk dancing has been growing in California for well over thirty years. It has now (in 1977) reached a very high level, more so in California than in any other state.

There are at present about 400 folk dance clubs in California. These are not to be confused with square dance, round dance or ethnic dance groups, as we do dances from every country in the world that has a dance culture. The clubs usually meet weekly and an evening's program could consist of many dances from a large repertoire of hundreds of dances. In addition, in many clubs the first part of the evening could be devoted to the teaching of a new dance or reviving a dance that has been done previously by the group. The word "new" describes a dance that we have not done before—although that dance itself may be many, many years old and frequently is.

The Folk Dance Federation of California is a parent organization of these clubs. It has two basic units, one North and one South, each governing the clubs in its area. It is a nonprofit organization and is composed of officers and delegates from each club. Its activities cover a very wide range and contribute in important ways to the community.

Here are some of the activities in which we are involved: Institutes are held periodically (usually five or six each year). Here new dances are taught by experts in their given fields or by people who have visited other countries and have brought dances back to us. Frequently visiting teachers from other countries—such as Hungary, Scotland, Greece, Israel, the Philippines—teach at our institutes and at various clubs.

A tremendous interest has developed in the music, folklore, culture and especially in the costumes of the many countries whose dances we do. We have a costume committee that researches the costumes of each country and provides a wealth of material for those who are interested. Quite a few of our dancers make "authentic" copies of these costumes.

The Federation sponsors festivals that are held monthly. A given club will host such a festival to which dancers will come from all over the area. As a highlight of their program, several exhibition groups may be asked to present special dances in the costume of the country and of the particular dance they are doing. Some clubs have exhibition groups who perfect dances for special performances.

Teacher Training Seminars are held each year in both the North and the South. Many of these seminars are held in colleges or universities and college credit may be obtained for those who desire it.

Some of our most important activities are our summer seminars and workshops. Each one runs for a week or 10 days or longer. They are intensive training programs, each one with a faculty of 8 or 10 experts in their given fields. There is a full curriculum that runs all day long. In the evening, for relaxation, everyone dances the dances they have learned. Here, too, college credits are available and, as at our institutes, everyone brings the new dances back to their own clubs. Some of the summer camps are: San Diego State University Folk Dance Conference at San Diego; The Idyllwild [Folk Dance] Workshop at Isomata; University of Southern California at Idyllwild; University of the Pacific at Stockton, Mendocino and other places throughout California.

Our dancers and exhibition groups are constantly asked to perform for charitable organizations, churches, temples, and schools. But one of our most outstanding services involves our dancing for and with patients at various hospitals and particularly the outpatient section of mental departments of places like Gateways. This is a contribution to the community of inestimable value and seeing the immediate response and effect of involving these people is most rewarding.

The Federation sponsors beginner classes in many areas. Here, people who have never danced before are taught basic steps, beginner and intermediate dances. As soon as they feel they have sufficient background, they move on to a regular folk dance club.

For many years we have presented annually, over the Memorial Day Weekend, a Statewide Folk Dance Festival; one year it is held in the North and the following year in the South.

(This article originally appeared in *Viltis* magazine under the title "Folk Dancing in California—North and South" and is used here with permission.)

Address: Folk Dance Federation of California, Inc., 1275 "A" Street, Room 111, Hayward, California 94541.

Folk Dance Federation of California, Inc.

by Vi Dexheimer

Checking back into the early issues of *Let's Dance* revealed a most interesting history of folk dancing in California of which many of our new folk dancers are not aware.

According to notes compiled by Virgil Morton and an early article written by him in *Let's Dance,* Scandinavian folk dancing was introduced in the early 1930s by Valborg (Mama) Gravander in [the] San Francisco Pacific Heights district. Her house was always open to friends who were interested in her Swedish folklore and applied arts.

Among the visitors to Mama Gravander's home was (the late) Song Chang, a Chinese-American artist who became interested in folk dancing in 1931 while touring Europe. Feeling the warmth and the friendship surrounding him during these visits, he wondered why there weren't more organizations devoted to this form of recreation.

Folk dancing was extremely limited even among most ethnic groups. It was taught in some schools to a limited degree. Most of the classes or clubs were closed to the general public, preference being limited to persons of national origin. Outside of the William Tell Hotel, where folk dancing was open to the public, there were very few places where individuals could learn dances of other countries.

In 1938, with the aid of members of Mama Gravander's group, Song Chang developed a group open to everyone, where dances of all nations could be taught. He learned and taught Norwegian, Swedish, and German dances. The members of this group decided to give the club a name, and this club became Chang's Folk Dancers. The group performed [at] the first International Folk Dance Exhibition at the San Francisco World's Fair, on Treasure Island, in 1939–40. At that time the group met at 2226 Fillmore Street. In 1942 the club moved to 1630 Stockton Street in San Francisco, added the word "International" to its name, and established itself as the center of California folk dance activity, with an active membership of over 200. It attracted the best teaching talent to be found in the West.

Folk dancing by this time extended from one end of California to the other. Other folk dancers decided to form groups and by the middle of 1942 there were ten groups active in San Francisco.

The Folk Dance Federation of California [Inc.] Was Born. Leaders and dancers realized that with [a] concerted effort a unified folk dance program could be developed. At a meeting in Lodi on May 3, 1942, Henry (Buzz) Glass proposed the formation of the Federation, a thing he and others had been working on for a period of time. At that meeting Henry was appointed "temporary chairman of the committee" to solidify the proposed plan. Several meetings followed, but it was not until a meeting on June 14, 1942, that Henry was elected president and the Federation officially came into being. This meeting was held in Golden Gate Park, near the Conservatory. This was a part of a series of folk dance festivals which had been taking place at regular intervals for about a year prior to that time. These were sponsored by the many dance clubs then in existence.

In the early days of folk dancing, because of the handicap of wartime gasoline and tire rationing, the planning of festivals in various areas proceeded with difficulty. Nevertheless, interest in folk dancing continued to grow in California; festivals were planned in advance; the staff of officers and standing committees in the Federation increased.

Dance Descriptions Were Made Available. A group of members from Chang's International Folk Dancers wrote the first descriptions of the then popular folk dances to aid teachers of the other rapidly growing groups. These were far from the sophisticated style the Federation has since established, but the entire Volume I of *Dances from Near and Far* was later made from their original notes.

Originally organized as a short-term project to publish descriptions of the Federation dances, the Research Committee became, in 1946, a permanent appendage under the chairmanship of Lucile Czarnowski, followed by Mildred Buhler. Today, with Dorothy Tamburini as co-ordinator, it researches dances brought to Stockton Folk Dance Camp by teachers representing various countries, standardizes the descriptions so they may be interpreted by local teachers and dancers, and submits them to *Let's Dance,* the official publication of the Folk Dance Federation of California, Inc., for printing in easy-to-read form. Through the efforts of this committee, the Federation publishes these dances in volume form under the title of *Folk Dances from Near and Far, International Series.*

The first meeting of a Teachers' Institute was held on January 26, 1947, at the Mission Community Center in San Francisco. Since that first institute, hundreds of dances have been taught and reviewed at well-attended institutes planned by a committee that works closely with the research committee.

The Birth of Let's Dance *Magazine. Let's Dance*

originated as a two-page mimeographed paper in 1944, with Ed Kremers as its editor. It grew to a six-page bulletin, then a twelve-page brochure, and at the present time is a forty-page magazine circulated throughout the United States, Canada, Alaska, Hawaii, Mexico, Europe, and Japan. This official publication includes dance descriptions that will eventually be compiled into additional volumes. It also features invaluable costume information and sketches to enable folk dancers to make their own costumes to be worn at festivals.

The Southern Section of California Forms a Federation. (For more details, see Folk Dance Federation of California, South.) As early as 1941 groups in Pasadena were merging into co-operatives, and folk dancing was being taught in Los Angeles and Hollywood. The full strength of the statewide organization was realized when the southern section, later to become the Folk Dance Federation of California, South, was formed in April 1946, with Allen Pelton as its first president. By 1947 there were 65 groups actively engaged in folk and square dancing in addition to 17 ethnic groups. The bylaws of the North [section] were adopted after an explanation of their purpose by Walter Grothe. Although the North and South are two separate organizations, each with its own officers, it was the intention of the founders of the southern section that they act as two sections of one organization. Because of the distance from the northern part of California to the southern part, the creation of two working sections of the Folk Dance Federation of California made it easier to reach folk dancers throughout the state by a concentrated effort on the part of leaders in each area to promote the folk dance activity. The co-operation between the two has proved very successful and the two organizations act as one whenever a joint effort is needed.

Southern club membership extends from Santa Maria to San Diego and surrounding areas; northern club membership extends from Ukiah to Bakersfield. Once a year folk dancers gather together from all over California to meet old and new friends at a two- or three-day statewide festival—one year at a southern location and the next year at a northern city—where hundreds of folk dances, squares, and kolos are enjoyed by hundreds of folk dancers in their colorful costumes.

(This material first appeared in *Let's Dance* magazine and is here used with permission.)

Folk Dance Federation of California, South

by Perle Bleadon and Paul Pritchard

This is the story of the Westwood Co-operative Folk Dancers—how we began in the world and how we grew. It is a tale that soon became an account of the origin of the southern section of the Folk Dance Federation of California.

Katherine Jett, later known as Barnes, organized the group. Other attempts had been made at starting folk dancing in our area, but they just didn't catch on. Katherine did the job and it stuck. At first there was no telling what would happen. Most of the people didn't know what folk dancing was like—if it wasn't square dancing or the Virginia Reel—except that everyone danced with everyone else and there was a really friendly spirit. Some of us came back for more, and we brought our friends, and after several meetings it was pretty obvious that there was so much enthusiasm nothing could stop us.

The first meeting was held at the University Religious Conference Building in Los Angeles, May 26, 1945, and later meetings were at St. Alban's Church.

On September 5, 1945, Westwood Co-operative Folk Dancers officially came into being with Katherine Jett, president, Bob Satten, vice-president, and Esther Lipitz, treasurer. The purpose was recreation for campus and community.

Morry Gelman came in March, 1946—in fact, during the fall of 1946 Morry did most of the teaching. Mary Ann Herman was in Los Angeles during that time and she came and taught several Ukrainian dances. They were the first of a long list of dance specialists.

Then members began talking about festivals and participation with other groups in the area. With suggestions and encouragement from Walter Grothe and Madelynne Greene, an organizational meeting was held January 5, 1946, which eventually led to the formation of the very active southern section of the Federation.

[Paul Pritchard reported the following.] Under the lead[ership] of the Westwood Co-operative Folk Dancers, and supported by groups from Pasadena, Long Beach, Hollywood, Glendale, Whittier, Ojai and other nearby towns, the Folk Dance Federation of California, South, was formed in March 1946.

The first festival was promptly rained out, but by

May everything was under control and the first state-wide festival was held in Ojai, to which the northern groups were invited to participate. Several hundred dancers attended and there were numerous exhibitions of "new" dances, both by the ethnic and the folk dance groups. ("Ethnic" here means people belonging to a local ethnic cultural group, while "folk" means you and me and the people down the street.) By 1949 there were over 50 clubs in the organization and in addition there were associations of clubs devoted entirely to American square dancing and round dancing. Some Federation groups primarily interested in these latter aspects of dancing separated to join these kindred groups, and in mid-1951 the Federation was composed principally of clubs interested in general folk dancing as a whole rather than pertaining wholly to one type or national origin.

Folk Dance Scene, the official publication for the Folk Dance Federation of California, South, was begun in 1964 with Dick Oakes and Paul Pritchard as co-editors. It lists special events, items of interest, beginner classes, club teaching schedules, festival dates, and carries display and classified advertising. It is issued 11 times annually.

Frequent festivals are held to which all member groups are invited. Festivals are usually held indoors now, for the greensward, though pretty to view, is rough on the ankles, and dodging hidden rocks and "keep off the grass" signs while doing a Swedish hambo or a Ukrainian hopak can become somewhat of a hazard. All Federation clubs are nonprofit, and expenses for records to dance by, hall rental, refreshments, and an occasional out-of-town teacher come from donations or membership fees.

(Parts of this article originally appeared in *Let's Dance* magazine and are here used with permission.)

Folklore Village Farm

Route 3
Dodgeville, Wisconsin 53533
(For details, see the essay on Jane Farwell in Part II.)

Idyllwild Folk Dance Workshop

by Elma McFarland

The Idyllwild Folk Dance Workshop was established by the Folk Dance Federation of California, South, at the request of Dr. Max Krone, then dean of music at the University of Southern California and director of the Idyllwild Arts Foundation. In 1951 and 1952 we had only weekend folk dance programs, but in 1953 the one-week program was established. The one-week folk dance workshop programs proved very successful. From 1953 to 1977 the second week of July was the time set aside for the workshop.

At one time workshops were held for two weeks, included a children's program, and offered academic credit. In an article published in *Let's Dance* magazine, Nate Moore, then chairman, included the following descriptions of the 1963 program: "The Folk Dance Faculty . . . included such well-known leaders as Vyts Beliajus, widely traveled teacher and editor of *Viltis,* a national folk magazine; Madelynne Greene, famous for her interpretations of dancing and original research; Millie von Konsky, Oakland leader with an inexhaustible supply of material, especially known for her work with Bay Area teacher training programs and the Woodminster show; Grace Nicholes, who specialized in dances of the Latin Americas; Yovan Zwol, musician and Israeli specialist; and Gordon Engler, distinguished Southern California authority and teacher of Balkan lore and dance . . .

"Unique among all folk dance camps is the children's program offered at Idyllwild. Supervised by accredited teachers and assisted by specialists from the regular faculty in music, art, drama, and dance, a program for every age level is scheduled to coincide with the adult program so that dancing parents may relax and learn free of worry and enjoy a true family vacation in the mountains.

"Folk dancers who are also singers will have the opportunity to participate with and [get] to know such personalities as Sam Hinton, Pete Seeger, Bess Hawes, Marais and Miranda and many others, all of whom have earned a legendary fame for their recordings, concerts, and television work."

In 1969 Max Krone passed on and USC took over the Idyllwild Arts Foundation. It became the Summer Art and Music School of the University of California. The Idyllwild Folk Dance Workshop continued its folk dance programs at the Idyllwild campus of USC each summer until 1977.

The last five years we were not able to have housing on campus. It became increasingly more difficult to keep the unity that a folk dance program needs for real success. In 1977 we severed our connection with USC and moved to a private school, The Desert Sun School, in Idyllwild. There we have excellent meals and dormitory accommodations and a beautiful gymnasium, with hardwood floors for dancing. Now we are all together in one place. Our 1977 and 1978 workshops in the new location have proven a real help in re-establishing the unity of the group and everyone seems much happier.

Living accommodations increased from 40 in 1950 to 250 in 1963 on the USC campus. At the present site at Desert Sun School registration is limited to 80 for the week and is offered on a first come, first served basis for the weekend. The week-long package rate in 1978 was $165.00. It included tuition and room (furnish own bedding) and board on campus.

We now hold the workshop during the last week of June. The Idyllwild Folk Dance Workshop Committee, with Vivian Woll as chairman, includes Sam Schatz, Barbara Jones, Marguerite Clapp, Pat Coe, John Filcich, Bob Browne, Mark Gold, and me as executive secretary. We are looking forward to many more workshop programs at the Desert Sun School in Idyllwild.

Address: Elma McFarland, 144 S. Allen Avenue, Pasadena, California 91106, or Vivian Woll, 7908–70 Rancho Fanita Drive, Santee, California 92071.

Kentucky Dance Institute

by M. G. Karsner

The Kentucky Dance Institute [KDI] was begun in 1953. There have been many changes during the first twenty-five years. Only one thing has not changed—the philosophy that has dictated the type of program used from the very beginning. It was, and is, to develop more and better folk dance leaders.

Predating KDI, a New Jersey lawyer named Charley Thomas edited the first *American Squares* magazine and directed the first American Squares camps. This hobby gradually consumed more and more of Charley's time until, in April 1952, he found it necessary to pass the editorship of the magazine to Rickey Holden of San Antonio, Texas.

In 1953 Rickey and (the late) Frank Kaltman, at the time the folk dance and music director for Folkraft Records, arranged and conducted four dance camps to complement the last camp conducted by Charley Thomas at Lincoln Memorial University, Harrogate, Tennessee. One of the four, held at Branchville, New Jersey, was known as the Stokes Forest Summer Dance School. The faculty for these four camps included Rickey and Frank, with Olga Kulbitsky serving on three camps and Vyts Beliajus and Harold Harton joining the other three for the Stokes Forest Camp. One of the participants at Stokes Forest Camp was Shirley Durham.

By 1954 only the Stokes Forest Camp remained of the four held in 1953 and Charley Thomas failed to schedule any camps anywhere. To keep a camp in the South (and because of Shirley's influence), Frank Kaltman came to Kentucky to arrange for the first KDI, a joint venture sponsored by the University of Kentucky, Lee's Junior College, and Folkraft Records. It was held at Lee's Junior College as a ten-day camp, August 3–13, at a cost of seventy dollars per dancer.

The staff of this first KDI included Frank Kaltman (director), Vyts Beliajus, Shirley Durham, Harold Harton, Rickey Holden, M. G. Karsner, and Edna Ritchie. The program consisted of much that is included in present KDI offerings: squares, contras, rounds, international dances, calling techniques, teaching techniques, basics of folk dancing, recreation leadership, dancing for children, singing, folklore, and history. Although nonleaders were welcome, the purpose of the camp was to develop more and better leaders of folk dancing. Contrary to the belief of today's western square dancers, folk dance is not a minor part of their activity. Square dancing was an integral part of the folk dance scene. Western square dance was only on the drawing boards at this date.

Some outstanding remembrances: Everyone attended and participated in every scheduled session. There were no duplicate classes, so there were no crises over choice of material. Readiness to learn and to accept any phase of the program was manifested by all. No teaching or dancing in rat race style. Many wonderful new friendships were formed; some are still going strong, some were sadly terminated by death. Facilities for dancing were terrible in that there was no air conditioning, but it was a good wood floor. Food was adequate in quality and inadequate in quantity. Rosters of those attending were not distributed, but my memory seems to recall between thirty and thirty-five participants in addition to the teaching faculty.

In 1955 KDI consisted of two one-week sessions (August 22–7 and August 29–September 3) held at the Hazel Green Academy, Hazel Green, Kentucky.

The faculty was a repeat of 1954. The number of participants was greater than in 1954 but was still not sufficient to prevent the camp from operating in the red. The camp was subsidized for many years by Folkraft Records and the Dance Record Center, both then owned by Frank Kaltman.

In 1956 the length of the camp was reduced from two weeks to one week and was moved to Sue Bennett College, London, Kentucky. In 1957 KDI returned to Hazel Green Academy for the week of August 18–25, with a staff consisting of Kaltman, Beliajus, Durham, Kulbitsky, and Jerry Helt, who led the square dancing in the absence of Rickey Holden.

Rickey was absent due to the fact that he was in Europe researching traditional dances and collecting music for future record distribution by Folkraft Records. A list of sixty-three participants and staff members was made available for the first time.

Rickey had laid such a good groundwork in 1953 that Frank Kaltman, director of the first four KDIs, personally felt compelled to make further plans for producing and distributing traditional folk dance music and instructions on the Folkraft label. He went to Europe in 1953 for this purpose. Frank requested that this writer and Shirley run the 1958 KDI in his absence. The request was granted, with the stipulation that the change be made permanent. Thus began a second era of KDIs.

At this time the success of the institute seemed assured, but the continual change in facilities the first four years indicated a need for a permanent home. Because of the co-operation and backing of President Adron Doran of Morehead State College, Morehead, Kentucky, and the availability of necessary facilities at the desired time, Morehead was selected as the site of the 1958 KDI and the hoped-for permanent home for future institutes.

Over the next several years, the facilities moved from building to building and one end of the campus to the other, depending upon the need of certain buildings for college activities and the renovation of others. Everyone in the college community was not as co-operative as President Doran; more than once the president intervened on behalf of KDI.

The permanent teaching staff for the first four years consisted of Vyts Beliajus, Shirley Durham, and M. G. Karsner. In 1962 a fourth member, Stew Shacklette, was added. Other members of the teaching faculty were added over the years, depending upon individual needs; they included: Edna Ritchie Baker, Millie Chrisman, Nancy DeMarco, Harold Harton, and, from Antwerp, Belgium, Huig Hofman. Rickey Holden, Jack Hunter, Arden Johnson, Bob Johnson, David Johnson, Walter Koegler, George Lowrey, Margaret Pantalone, Pheane Ross, Al Schwinabart, and Paul-André Tétreault. Nonteaching staff members during this period included Lanadean Brown, Peggy Dunlap, Sue Lucke, Ed Moody, and Nancy Rhea.

Since the Dance Record Center, which prepared the syllabi for the first four years, was no longer involved, the university printed and collated the syllabi from 1958 to 1966. Group pictures were taken for the first time and distributed to each family or individual. In 1959 sixty-eight participants plus staff attended. For the first time that same year we had air-conditioned comfort—but at the expense of giving up a good wooden floor. Parties in the lobby and private rooms continued well into the wee hours. Approximately sixty-seven dancers attended. Paul-André Tétreault and his French Canadian dances were featured at the 1960 institute.

"Kolomania" was beginning to make headway with many dancers and leaders who were willing to sacrifice a well-rounded program, for reasons they deemed valid, in order to overemphasize the place of line dances in the program. Some of these dancers desired to have request dancing for the evening parties. The philosophy at KDI had always been to schedule dances for the night party that had been taught in the day classes and the requested change was therefore denied.

Many dancers requested additional dance sessions. Specialization and overcrowding were beginning to raise their ugly heads. Because of the increase in cost for bed and board, the tuition for 1960 had to be increased from sixty to sixty-six dollars. Seventy-five dancers attended in 1960 and seventy-one in 1962. In 1962 Stew Shacklette became a permanent member of the staff and Huig Hofman joined KDI for the first of three appearances. Many of the dances he taught have become standbys in any good program.

In 1963 Paul-André Tétreault returned and Frank Kaltman was able to attend KDI for the first time since 1957. Eighty-three dancers attended and the tuition was raised another dollar to sixty-seven dollars. The largest KDI, numbering 104 participants, opened the 1964 session. From an optimum number of 104 dancers the attendance abruptly dropped to 56 in 1965. At the same time tuition had to be raised again, this time to seventy-two dollars.

The first of three reunion weekends were held during the fall of 1967. The year 1968 was memorable for many reasons. For the first time the facilities were all located on the east side of the campus; Shirley first taught Likrat Shabit, now a KDI tradition; Ed Moody edited the first edition of the KDI *Daily Bulletin* and was instrumental in organizing the first scholarship auction. The first scholarship to KDI was awarded to Ellen Jump.

In 1969 Walter Koegler and George Lowrey joined the staff, and there were ninety dancers. The next year,

1970, was a year of confusion and inconvenience. Dancers were housed in Regent's Hall, on the east end of the campus, and had to go all the way to the other end of the campus to dance and eat. Jack Hunter joined the staff. Millie Chrisman brought her organ and talents to lead the singing in the lobby after the evening parties. The third edition of the KDI publication became the *Daily News*. Eighty-five dancers paid seventy-nine dollars to attend the seventeenth KDI.

In 1971 seventy-nine dancers paid eighty dollars to enjoy the last year of the second era in the history of KDI. The next year this writer found it necessary to leave the staff of KDI. The position of co-director of KDI was reluctantly transfered to the most able Stew Shacklette, and the third era of KDI was begun. Three new names were added to the staff: Shirley Durham Fort, Ya'akov Eden, and Mae Fraley.

This writer returned to the faculty for the 1973, 1974, and 1975 camps. What a pleasure it is to teach without shouldering the burden of administering the program. For those who have never been in the position of running a dance camp, the work and detail involved cannot be comprehended. And the anxiety caused by the concern for each dancer during the week weighs heavily. What a relief it is when Saturday morning arrives, with many congratulations, sad good-byes, and hopefully no maimed or sick dancers.

This writer hopes, and expects, that KDI will continue to improve and go on and on and on as it has during the first twenty-five years.

Address: Kentucky Dance Institute, 4516 Southern Parkway, Louisville, Kentucky 40214.

Lighted Lantern

by Paul Kermiet

The Lighted Lantern was born in the year 1944. It grew and came of age beautifully to mature into the enterprise that we know it to be today. In 1944 the pinch was very heavy on everything because our country was fighting a war. The acquisition of the old Flying Horse Inn property, later named the Lighted Lantern camp, was envisioned to be an enrich[ing] opportunity for the many activity groups which had their beginnings at Steele Community Center (in Denver). Represented were groups in dancing, art, drawing, music, crafts, specialized groups in play training and study, various athletic groups, the Sherwood folk dancers, [and] UNESCO activities. Only small groups were envisioned and were the norm in [the] early years, but

groups numbering a hundred and more soon became nearer the norm than the exception.

Literally thousands of people of varied ages and interests have known periods of great joy over the years because of the Lantern enterprise. Events and happenings have been far beyond the wildest dreams of its founders.

Five persons pooled money for an initial payment to secure title to a parcel of property at a purchase price that seems unbelievable in light of today's value. The group numbered five persons who were closely allied in [developing the] program . . . at Steele Center. They were: Lila Lynn Parke, drama and play production, a volunteer; Mary Seguin, group leader and university student, a volunteer; Kathleen Timmons, group leader and staff assistant; Frederick G. Enholm, staff administrator and program director; [and] Pauline R. Kermiet, group leader and staff assistant. (Paul Kermiet was on leave from the Center because of the war.) The Lantern buildings and operations are what they are today because of these five persons, their spouses, many helpers, and thousands who have frequented the Lantern to enrich program happenings over the years.

The Lantern enterprise benefited from no gifts of money outside the immediate Lantern group. The actual construction of the buildings (except for the original lodge and four cabins) was done by members of the group, with some paid help and volunteers. Volunteer help has been a factor in holding fees to a surprisingly low minimum. During twenty-three years of folk dance programs (twenty-eight for square dancing), the staff included some of the best known folk dance leaders.

The important reason that prompted this writing was to say something about the "why" of terminating the operation of the Lighted Lantern after the 1975 season unless some way developed for such programs to operate under leadership other than the Lighted Lantern group. The Lantern entertainment was established as a contribution [to] community social service for people and not for eventual sale to gain mone[tar]y profit for anyone.

The Kermiets have been the key people in operating the Lantern. The Kermiets and the Enholms are the two remaining active members of the initial group of five. The duty of the two remaining trustees was to keep faith and to carry forward the intention of the group. In 1958 an irrevocable trust was set up. The beneficiary selected was the American Friends Service Committee. The American Friends (Quakers) were very much in tune with the program activities at the Lantern and were in favor of helping the Lantern, as we knew it, to continue. But the question was "How?" Rather than waiting until the death of all the members of the trustee group, the Lantern property was turned over to them as of September 1975. After two years of inactivity at the site, Beryl Main, a leading square dance caller, purchased the property, took over operation of the Lantern, and continued with a folk and square dance program in 1978.

(Reprinted, with additions, by permission from *Viltis* magazine.)

Lloyd Shaw Foundation

by D. J. Obee

The Lloyd Shaw Foundation [LSF] is a chartered, nonprofit foundation with the stated objective "To recall, restore and teach the folk rhythms of the American people; in dance, music, song, and allied folk arts, as a tribute to the memory of Lloyd Shaw."

The Foundation encourages skills in teaching and leadership, especially among educated young people, building its teaching materials around the long view, both into the past and into the future. This puts them right to work, devising suitable curricula for various age groups and situations, and materials with which to present the curricula.

At first this looked like a sideline. Now it has developed into the main task. The program began by establishing week-long summer-session workshops at various universities, where they taught mostly young teachers how to present the American folk dance at two levels for elementary school children and for teenagers and adults.

There are three workshops each summer at three widely separated universities. The original master classes have met since 1965 at Colorado State University. The other two vary in location from year to year. Information about these will be furnished on request.

The curricula are subject to constant supervision, although, once stabilized, they remain remarkably static. At the present time (spring 1973) the secondary curriculum has been revised.

The organization was started from Lloyd Shaw Recordings, owned by Dorothy Shaw and Fred Bergin, who gave the inventories and other assets to LSF. The Foundation produces many of the records used in the curriculum kits, although it finds that there is virtue in a variety of labels. LSF has one of the finest dance libraries in the country. It is open for public use.

(D. J. Obee is president of the Lloyd Shaw Foundation.)

Address: The Lloyd Shaw Foundation, Inc., P.O. Box 203, Colorado Springs, Colorado 80901.

Maine Folk Dance Camp

Folk Dance House, P.O. Box 201, Flushing, New York, N.Y. 11352 (See the essay on Michael and Mary Ann Herman in Part II.)

Mendocino Folklore Camp

40 Glen Drive, Mill Valley, Ca. 94941 (See essay on Madelynne Greene, Part II.)

National Dance Association

by Miriam Gray

The National Dance Association [NDA] is the largest dance education association in the United States, with 3,033 members, 436 of whom are students, as of October 27, 1978. Dance educators and teachers at all levels, professional dancers, community leaders, students, and those professionally involved in any aspect of dance can become members. One goal of NDA is to increase membership to 5,000 by 1983. The only dance association with a nationwide network of officers and organizations at state, district, and national levels, NDA can reach every school, college, and recreational group in the nation; this includes Alaska, Hawaii, and several U.S. territories.

NDA is recognized nationally for its work with federal government agencies, state arts councils, foundations, and other educational associations, most notably the other three national arts education organizations in art, music, and theater. Through an executive director in the headquarters office in Washington, D.C., active liaison is maintained with more than 40 groups providing strong and able representation in legislative activities. Currently, NDA is generating funds of approximately $42,000 a year through grants and funding for travel.

As an Association of the American Alliance for Health, Physical Education and Recreation [AAHPER], NDA gains valuable assistance in promotion and public-information services, publications, and administration of conferences and conventions. (See the essay entitled "American Alliance for Health, Physical Education, Recreation and Dance" in this section.)

The stated purposes of NDA are to promote continuous development of sound philosophies and policies in all forms of dance and to provide leadership that will stimulate improvement in programs, materials, and methods in dance. NDA is as concerned with the folk forms of dance—folk, round, square, and social-ballroom—as it is with the theater forms—traditional, modern or contemporary and ballet, but increasingly including adaptations of folk forms for stage performance).

In 1931 what would later become NDA was conceived by five outstanding dance educators: Martha Hill, then at New York University; Dorothy La Salle, then with the East Orange, New Jersey, Public Schools; Ruth Murray, Detroit Teachers College (later named Wayne State University); and Mary P. O'Donnell and Mary Jo Shelley, both at Teachers College, Columbia University, at that time. Ruth Murray, noted for her book *Dance in Elementary Education,* served as temporary chairman. The Dance Section was born and was officially approved by the then American Physical Education Association at its 1932 National Convention in Philadelphia. Mary P. O'Donnell became its first elected chairman. For thirty-three years the National Section on Dance [NSD] matured and expanded, developing many standing and special committees to carry out its work and move its projects forward. During this time, the structure of state, district, and national dance sections was established. A considerable sprinkling of persons with a strong interest in the folk dance forms served in various leadership capacities; these included Lucile Czarnowski, who was chairman of NSD from 1939 to 1941; Don Begenau, Elizabeth Burchenal, Richard Kraus, Gertrude X. Mooney, Ralph A. Piper, Anne Pittman, Lloyd Shaw, Erma Weir, and Peter Wisher, who served on the board at various times.

In the midst of a major reorganization of the then AAHPER, which became official in 1965, NSD emerged as one of the eight divisions and was known as the Dance Division of AAHPER. The four substructures were sections named Dance Aesthetics, Dance Education, Dance Forms, and Dance Theatre. The Forms section was mainly concerned with the folk forms of international folk, round, social, and square dance. The ten persons who were elected chairmen of the Dance Forms section are mostly well known for their interest and work in folk dance: Don Begenau, Ralph Piper, Anne Pittman, Peter Wisher, Mary Bee Jensen, Alma Heaton, Miriam Lidster, Linda Hearn, R. Dwaine Goodwin, and Valerie Mof-

fett. Other folk-oriented educators who served the Dance Division as board members included E. Carmen Imel, Bob Oliphant, and Kirby Todd.

The changeover in the latest reorganization occurred in 1974. AAHPER changed from an association to an alliance but kept its same initials; and seven new associations were formed, NDA being one of them. The Dance Division had lasted nine years; and NDA will be five years old in March 1979, coincident with the 94th Anniversary Convention of the Alliance and its seven associations. Miriam Lidster, coauthor of *Folk Dance Progressions,* was one of NDA's presidents from 1976 to 1979.

The Board of Directors, consisting of nine voting members, represent the three main areas of responsibility within NDA: three presidents—elect, current, and past; three vice-presidents; and three directors, one for each of the three units. Throughout the ages, three has been a fortuitous sign! NDA is basically a three-pronged operation: the thinkers, the doers, and the districts. The *thinkers* are in the two divisions, headed by vice-presidents—Dance Curriculum and Dance Resources divisions and in the Projections Unit, which started as a Dream Committee. The *districts* are represented by the third vice-president. Among the *doers,* or workers, are the other two units: the Promotions and Publications units, headed by directors, and all of the standing and special committees. The three presidents are the administrators of the entire Association structure. An ex officio member of the board, the NDA executive director provides liaison with the Alliance.

The Dance Curriculum Division is subdivided into commissions: Children's Dance, Dance in Secondary Education, Dance in Higher Education, Graduate Education in Dance, and Dance Therapy. The Dance Resources Division has three commissions: Dance Culture, Movement Sciences and Techniques, and Theatre Dance. Folk dance is one of the concerns in all of these commissions. The vice-president of the districts seeks ideas from, and disseminates information to, the dance officers of the districts and states and co-ordinates the efforts of state, district, and national dance officer personnel.

The Projections Unit initiates ideas, concerns, directions, issues, and solutions to problems and suggests courses of action for NDA to take. The Promotions Unit promotes dance in general and in the schools, as well as NDA itself. The Publications Unit suggests needed publications, assigns authors and editors, and prepares for publication articles, books, a newsletter, pamphlets, periodicals, and other materials.

Of the fifteen or more books published by NDA that are still in print and available from AAHPER Publication and Sales, 25 per cent have a folk dance content. *Focus on Dance VI: Ethnic and Recreational*

Dance (1971) is entirely folk-based. *Focus on Dance VIII: Dance Heritage* (1977) contains seventeen articles, 40 per cent of which are folk-related: "Dancing as an Aspect of Early Mormon and Utah Culture," by Leona Holbrook; "Dance in Eskimo Society—An Historical Perspective," by Rick and Gail Luttman; "A History of Square Dance in America," by Ralph Page; "A Conversation with Ralph Page," by E. Carmen Imel; "Dance Heritage from the Bicentennial Perspective," by Lucile Czarnowski; "The Changing Scene in the Folk Dance Field," by Vyts F. Beliajus; and "Recreational Dance in the 1970s," by Dorothy Hughes.

The biennial *Focus on Dance* series was initiated in 1960 by the then National Section on Dance; to date eight volumes have been produced. Although now out of print, *Focus on Dance I,* with articles on a wide range of dance subjects, included six of folk dance interest: "Folk Dance in Education, 1925–1960," by Lucile Czarnowski; "A Square Dance Pioneer: Jimmy Clossin," [interview] by Miriam Gray; "Looking Ahead at Folk Dance," by Erma Weir; "Men in Dance Education," by Arden Johnson; and "Materials for Dance Teaching II: Folk Dances," compiled by Lucile Czarnowski, Fredericka Moore, and Ed Kremers.

A beautifully illustrated 1977 publication, *Dance as Education,* was prepared by the Projections Unit with a grant from the Alliance for Arts Education for the purpose of telling nondancers what dance is and why—*all* forms of dance, including folk dance. *Encores for Dance* (1978) contains a broad spectrum of eighty-six dance articles reprinted from the last ten years of the *Journal of Physical Education and Recreation* [JOPER], among them several concerning folk dance.

NDA publishes *Spotlight on Dance,* an eight-page newsletter, four times a year. *Dance Dynamics,* a JOPER insert, appears once or twice a year; it is written and edited by NDA personnel; the first two from the May 1977 and 1978 JOPERs have been reprinted in book form as *Dance Dynamics* (1978). Two articles may be of special interest to those with ethnic inclinations: "Dance of the Shakers" and "Dancers of the South Pacific."

Each year NDA members receive four issues of *Spotlight on Dance,* nine issues of the *Journal of Physical Education and Recreation,* and nine issues of the AAHPER newspaper *Update,* with its regular "Dance Information" column as well as other dance articles or profiles of dance personalities. A novel series of "Innovative Dance Games" was begun in the January 1979 JOPER by Jane Harris Ericson and others. In January Dance Bingo, a square dance game, and Team Dance Quiz to identify information about folk dance, were described; in February appeared Spoons, a folk dance game, and Tumbling Toes Social Dance Game.

With the able assistance of AAHPER through NDA's executive director, NDA sponsors frequent national and regional conferences focusing on a variety of dance issues and concerns scheduled at different times of the year and in a wide range of locations. The First Regional Dance Conference for Educators was held in Sacramento in the fall of 1977, with folk-ethnic dance excitingly developed from fourth grade through college by Bernardo Pedere (the Philippines); Iris Dragon (Polynesian); Susan Cashion (Mexico); Bruce and Denise Mitchell (international); and Millie von Konsky (simple and adapted dances for children). Square dance in three sessions, from elementary through advanced, was directed by Jack Murtha, a West Coast teacher and caller.

The highlight of the year is the national convention in conjunction with AAHPER, which supplies valuable aid in programing, scheduling, selecting a site, and providing facilities and housing. The convention runs from Friday to Tuesday; during that time, NDA presents approximately sixteen program sessions plus several special and social events. About 25 per cent of the April 1978 programing for the Kansas City Convention was devoted to folk dance forms, including "Jazz/Ethnic Dance," "Recreational Dance," "Black Dance," and a "Multidisciplinary Approach to Children's Dance," drawing raves and comments of delight and appreciation. Carol Cristocomo, of the University of Chicago, brought a group of Philippine-American children to perform on stage, with the dance, costumes, music, and total production done in an authentic style. The Philippine ambassador in attendance was introduced for brief remarks. Tentative scheduling for the March 1979 convention in New Orleans has a repeat appearance of Carol Cristocomo and her Philippine Dance Company of Chicago, whose members range in age from eleven to twenty; the session is titled "Dance in International Relations." Other planned programs feature "Middle Eastern Dance—Belly Dancing" and "Teaching Clogging and Kentucky Running Sets," with a performance and demonstration by the Dahlonega Cloggers of Georgia.

An eagerly awaited annual event at the national conventions is NDA's Heritage Luncheon, where the Heritage Award is presented to a dance pioneer who has contributed extensively to dance education; the Heritage honoree may be a dance educator, a professional dancer, or a person from a related area (criticism or accompaniment, for instance). The Heritage Award, initiated in 1963, has been bestowed upon two renowned folk dance personalities—Lucile Czarnowski in 1968 and Vyts Beliajus in 1972.

NDA and AAHPER co-operate with the U.S. Office

of Education, the Alliance for Arts Education, various dance organizations, and other arts and educational organizations on many projects that involve dance; they also serve as advisers on dance and arts education films prepared by other groups. A recent example is the thirty-minute color film *Something Special*, produced by the National Art Education Association under contract to the Alliance for Arts Education. In 1978 NDA prepared a twelve-minute color slide-tape presentation, developed as a companion to the book *Dance as Education*, which was partially funded by the Alliance for Arts Education. A series of eighty slides, with narration based on the text of the book, gives a visual panorama of dance in its many forms, cultures, and worldwide participation. A Carousel slide tray and cassette can be purchased from AAHPER Publications and Sales.

NDA and the Alliance are co-operating with the Association of American Dance Companies to spotlight dance during the second annual National Dance Week, April 23–9, 1979. The first National Dance Week coincided with the issue of the first-ever dance stamps by the U.S. Postal Service on April 26, 1978—a set of four brightly designed diagonal stamps depicting ballet, folk dance (a lively square dance couple in costume), modern dance, and theater dance.

Address: Dr. Margie R. Hanson, Executive Director, NDA, 1201 Sixteenth Street, NW, Washington, D.C. 20036.

Patricia Parmelee. Photo by Demetrio L. Guedes

National Folk Festival of America

The National Folk Festival of America is now called the National Council for the Traditional Arts, Inc.
Address: 1346 Connecticut Avenue, NW, Washington, D.C. 20036.
(See the essay on Sarah Gertrude Knott in Part II.)

New England Folk Festival

117 Washington Street, Keene, New Hampshire 03431
(See the essay on Ralph Page in Part II.)

New York Folk Festival Council

by Patricia Parmelee

It was never a club, never so called—always the New York Folk Festival Council, just and only that. It was the "brainchild" deliberately set up by one of our country's oldest and finest private-service organizations for the foreign born—The Foreign Language Information Service. It was affectionately called FLIS nationwide by [the] foreign-born whom it served. Headquarters were on lower Fourth Avenue in New York. It had ties with the entire foreign-language press throughout the United States. On its auxiliary staff were able foreign-born linguists who translated information of interest, and often of vital importance to the foreign born, for the press. Its central staff kept channels open to Washington and the Federal Government on laws and procedures, Federal, state and local, affecting the foreign born. The famous "Interpreter Releases" were based at FLIS headquarters. The service (still used, I believe) [is] used by individuals and agencies, public and private, nationally and internationally, as an authoritative up-to-the-minute clearinghouse for U.S. immigration laws.

Read Lewis was the executive director of FLIS and on its board were outstanding citizens devoted to the well-being of ethnic groups within the U.S. Exactly how and why the "Council idea" sparked and focused into action in the early thirties I do not know, but the board and staff must have wakened to the wealth of folk arts, latent and in active expression, to which it had access throughout the metropolitan area, and decided to do something about it. So, the Council was formed, open to anyone interested in the ethnic peoples and their folk arts.

To it gravitated such local leaders as Lola de Grille from the International Institute of the New York YWCA; Harvey Anderson, head of the International Dept. of the New York YMCA; Smith (can't recall his full name), head of The New School for Social Research; union leaders; Florence Cassidy from the National Institute of Immigrant Welfare, the national organization of the International Institutes, later named the American Federation of I.I.s and presently named the American Council for Nationalities Service, having amalgamated within fairly recent years with the Common Council for American Unity, a transitional name for FLIS in the forties.

Also attracted to the Council were individuals such as Stella Marek Cushing, Ella Sonkin and Mary Wood, lifelong, deep lover of "folk," who was living in New York at the time and residing at a fascinating professional women's residence-hotel started by Anne Morgan.

The first project dreamed up included two tremendous Sunday-night programs of music and dance at two of the larger theatres. Tom Cotton was added to the staff of FLIS to organize the events. Of course, the large group of translators on the auxiliary staff were open sesame to the ethnic communities. The programs were well publicized in the New York press and that's how I came into the picture. The publicity caught my eye, I attended and at once lost my heart, which had really always been "tuned it."

The already well-organized groups welcomed the centralized and broad exposure to each other which the Council activity offered and the leaders naturally gravitated to the meetings. Among those active were Tashimira and Desha Milcinovic from Yugoslavia (Croatian), Sture Lilja (Swedish), Aasmund and Sigmund Goytil (Norwegian), Hansen (Danish), the Aaltos (Finnish), Elba Farabegoli Gurzau (Italian), Michael Herman and Mary Ann Bodnar (Ukrainian), a wonderful folk-crafts woman from Romania, the Polish and Estonian leaders Matusz and Alice Zimmerman, Rosli and Hans Witschi (Swiss), May Gadd

(English), Stella Marek Cushing (Czechoslovakian), and others.

The Council was really never formally organized. It was always under the wing of FLIS, and meetings were sometimes held there and later at Mary Wood's residence-hotel, which was on the central west side of the city, and at the New School for Social Research on the edge of Greenwich Village. A fine little "Folk News" magazine was published (twice monthly, I think) at FLIS, ably edited by Arthur Leon Moore (another active member of the Council). One of the main functions was to plan interethnic get-togethers, some indoors, such as at International House on Riverside Drive, some outdoors, such as at Prospect Park in Brooklyn. At these events, the various ethnic groups would sing or dance and naturally drew in the rest of us to dance and sing with them, [with] any teaching done by the ethnic leader.

The activity of the Council was exclusively with the self-organized ethnic groups. True, they were encouraged to keep their heritage unspoiled, uncommercialized. Teaching was always done by their own leaders and members, recognizing that the most important and valued thing about "folk" is the subtle "style," "spirit," "nuance," "cadence," an inborn, instinctive quality which makes it unique to those peoples. (Some very few individuals, such as Vyts Beliajus, can feel and capture these intangibles.) The Council never trained leaders.

One of the most fascinating developments as the ethnic leaders and others mingled, and, to me, the most valuable, was the inspiration to open up one of their regular weekly rehearsal meetings to members of other groups and individuals. Soon, the Swedes were doing it on a monthly basis. There's where we really learned our hambos. Wow. Others would do it periodically, though not so often. This would take us into their "national" halls or churches all over greater New York, and was very enriching.

Another wonderful offshoot was a game we developed to discover new "pockets" of ethnic activity representing corners of the earth not yet out in the open. New York's resources were inexhaustible. Following clues, we would sometimes find ourselves right in the midst of an intimate circle of family and friends, singing and dancing. Or there were invitations to big banquets, such as Greek, where, when typical music struck up, you saw men in formal American attire suddenly burst into terrific squats and spirals as if back on their native heath.

The depression years of the thirties were, of course, perfect for the growth and spread of this wholesome grass-roots activity. Letters came into FLIS from all over the United States and Canada requesting help in starting something similar in their areas.

The most sustained and effective activity of the Council took place at the New School for Social Research on West 12th Street. Through Mr. Smith, mentioned above as an early member of the Council, we were offered the use of their dance studio for a weekly course added to their curriculum on Sunday evenings titled, "Folk Dances and Songs of Many Peoples." Every week, for several seasons, a different ethnic group, seldom repeating, would present their folk wealth and then invite us to join in. It drew a great variety of people. What a wonderful opportunity to see and feel the world in New York. The setting was perfect; there was a circular room with a slightly raised border around the lower central area where dances or songs were presented. If dances, it was then so easy and natural for those in the audience to just step down and be drawn in with them, or, if choruses, to sit around and join in. Words, music and instructions were reproduced at FLIS. This activity needed only a coordinator. First it was Mary Wood, later myself. You could enroll for the course or drop in for an evening. One never knew who might appear. Agnes de Mille, Doris Humphrey, Charles Weidman saw it as a valuable resource. Among the other cultures not mentioned before were American Indian, French, German, Bulgarian, Lithuanian, Irish, Philippine, Scottish, Dutch, Russian, Peruvian (Inca), Argentinian, Spanish, Albanian, Hungarian, Armenian and Portuguese.

The "bow out" of the Council was participation in the second and closing year of the New York World's Fair in 1940. It had been a dream of one of the Board members of FLIS, a distinguished architect who was "theme" vice president of the Fair, to provide a proper place for the ethnic groups in our great land to share their cultural gifts. But he met with no success. Then came the beginning of World War II in Europe. The Court of Peace at the Fair, with its impressive pavilions from many lands, was in jeopardy. The Soviet Pavilion, at the most strategic spot, right on the shores of a lagoon where lovely colored fountains played nightly to the music of a symphonic band, withdrew from the Fair. Here was the longed-for opportunity. Our ally stepped forward with his idea. And, that perfect location became the very popular American Common.

Picture an outdoor theatre seating about a thousand, with a large, well-lighted covered-shell stage and, at the other end next to the pedestrian paths, a large, open platform with the American flag aloft, just right for informal dancing. Setting the theme all around the border of the areas was a "Wall of Fame," a panel or panels devoted to every possible profession or type of productive work, with a listing of foreign-born Americans who had contributed significantly to that field of work. To produce that listing was a heroic

accomplishment in the short interval before the Fair reopened on May 1. But it was done.

The different ethnic groups could speak for a day, a weekend or a whole week, set up exhibits and, on the stage, present programs of the fine or folk arts. More than once the "Little Flower," Mayor La Guardia, was the coveted emcee and, one whole day, the President's Lady, Eleanor Roosevelt, was guest of honor and deeply pleased to be so. Professional stagehands never ceased to marvel at the good-natured, orderly discipline of all the folk performers, with nary a sign of temper nor temperament to which they were so accustomed.

The platform at the opposite end was the cherished place where many an innocent bystander or passerby had his or her first taste of dancing with an "original" foreigner.

For the record, the staff for the American Common was headed by Harvey Anderson, YMCA International chief, assisted by myself, Sture Lilja and a man from the rolls of WPA whose name I do not recall but to whom, I do remember, the value of the dollar had absolutely no meaning—and those were not inflationary days.

After the closing of the Fair, without a day between, I went to Boston on my first International Institute job and did not again live in New York. So far as I know, the Council gradually faded. Mary Wood had gone to California, Arthur Leon Moore was no longer with FLIS, and the war temporarily played havoc with the groups. But Michael Herman, whose leadership skills developed signally during the Council years, and who did a major job at the Fair, in the years immediately after, together with his gifted wife, Mary Ann, opened a Folk Arts Center in New York which grew and grew.

As I mentioned above, the Council made no effort to train leaders. However, consistent participation in its activities with the helpful exchange between groups just naturally developed the capacities of anyone desiring to learn.

The Council encouraged the use of native instruments wherever possible. I recall a dramatic incident that shows why.

The Bulgarians in New York, with their magic green thumbs, were often fine nurserymen in Westchester County. When a group presented a Bulgarian evening at the New School, with them was a worker who had recently arrived from the native mountains. In his black-braided brown wool typical garb, he looked like a little gnome. One of their dance melodies was played on the piano. He stood motionless. Then, suddenly came the sound of his native pipes. He was electrified, his feet and whole body joined in an ecstasy of motion. We were transported to his mountains.

Folk dancing is not just good exercise, nor a challenge of intricate steps and patterns. It is a subjective experience, if truly approached, very close to the roots of genuine brotherhood, all bars down.

(This article appeared in the May 1980 issue of *Viltis* magazine and is used here with permission. The author, Patricia (Pat) Parmelee, graduated from the University of Chicago in 1916, then took postgraduate training during the 1920s at the Noyes School of Rhythm in New York City and Connecticut under its founder-director, Florence Fleming Noyes. Parmelee subsequently qualified as a member of the professional Noyes Group and an authorized teacher of Noyes-Rhythm. From 1940 to 1970 she served as activities director of the International Institutes of Boston and Los Angeles in the field of leadership and administration.

Pat's lifelong love of people and the folk arts (especially dancing) took definite shape during the 1930s in New York City, where she worked as a leisure-time volunteer and became intensively involved with the Folk Festival Council described in the article. Her interest continued throughout her International Institute career and still glows in retirement.)

Oglebay Institute

by Mary E. Fish

Coming to Oglebay Institute in Wheeling, West Virginia, in the summer of 1940, Miss Jane Farwell brought with her a rural Wisconsin background combining Swiss, Irish, and Norwegian traditions, along with a talent for folk dance and enthusiasm for people. Beginning with contacts made at 4-H camps and the local YWCA, Miss Farwell spearheaded her interests into a growing and ever-widening circle of activities and events.

With assistance from the National Recreation Association, the Oglebay Folk Dancers, a group of about eighteen young people led by Jane Farwell, began to perform exhibitions and direct folk dance recreation for civic groups, schools, and churches. In the spring of 1942, the idea was born of getting together for seasonal festivals because, according to the camp program, "a handful of sentimental folk dance enthusiasts felt that a May Day, coming in the wake of a full moon, is an occasion to be celebrated." When it was over, everyone wanted to do it again and chose September, "for what could be a more proper time for peasants

to celebrate with merrymaking and dancing than the month of harvests." Since then, every Memorial and Labor Day weekend has been highlighted by an Oglebay Institute–sponsored folk dance camp, held at Camp Russel in Oglebay Park, Wheeling, West Virginia.

People are one of the primary reasons Oglebay camps have exerted a lasting influence on their participants. There is an opportunity to learn about other countries and their cultures, and to develop skills in associated fields such as crafts, music, and ethnic foods. Many recreation leaders come to these weekends in order to add valuable material to their repertories.

Camp instructors have included Yves Moreau, Jane Farwell, Al Schwinabart, Nelda Drury, George Lowrey, David Henry, Ken Spear, Conny Taylor, Ya'akov Eden, Walter Koegler, Eugenia Popescu Judetz, Glenn Bannerman, Jerry Joris, Ada Dziewanowska, Don Armstrong, Dick Oakes, and many others.

Address: Oglebay Institute, Oglebay Park, Wheeling, West Virginia 26003.

Pinewoods Camp

by Christine Helwig

Pinewoods Camp is located on Long Pond, a beautiful, clear lake situated between Plymouth and Buzzards Bay, a one-hour drive from Boston. Pinewoods has been a unique summer gathering place for dancers, singers, and musicians since its founding by Helen Storrow in the 1930s. For many years the camp was owned and operated by Lily and Dick Conant, under whose loving care the camp acquired a special atmosphere as a place where the natural beauty of the woods, ponds, trails, and the rustic setting of the buildings have added immeasurably to the joyful experience of sharing in the varied dance and music programs held there.

Pinewoods Camp, Inc., a nonprofit organization, was incorporated in 1975 for the express purpose of carrying on the traditions that have been established since the first invitational weekend for teachers of the English Folk Dance Society of America was held there in 1932. In 1933 the first summer dance camp of the Society—soon to become the Country Dance and Song Society of America [CDSS]—was scheduled and over the years Pinewoods has been a focus of the Society's activities, providing an opportunity for leaders and teachers to get together for instruction, practical experience, and inspiration, and to work with teachers of historic and traditional dance who were brought over from England to teach at the summer camps.

The first programs sponsored by CDSS were two dance weeks each summer featuring classes in traditional English country, ritual morris and sword and American contras and squares, including some folk music and recorder classes as well. In 1940 the Boston Centre of CDSS began to sponsor summer weekends, and in 1945, when the National Society did not organize a summer camp, Boston Centre conducted the two-week session. In 1950 a third week for folk music singers and teachers was offered; in 1958 Folk Music and Recorder Week became part of the summer program. By 1962 the CDSS program expanded to include the two dance weeks and a week each for chamber music and folk music. Family Week, combining the traditional elements of dance and music weeks with special activities and classes for children, was also added. In 1975 and 1977 a sixth week of American dance and song became part of the CDSS program.

In 1953 Mrs. Conant invited the Boston Branch of the Royal Scottish Country Dance Society [RSCDS] to hold their annual weekend at Pinewoods. The RSCDS has held its summer weekend there ever since; in 1972 it began sponsoring a full week in addition to its traditional weekend at camp.

The board of directors of Pinewoods Camp, Inc., is comprised of representatives from all three organizations that have used the camp for many years—the Country Dance and Song Society, the Boston Centre of the Society, and the Royal Scottish Country Dance Society—as well as members of the Conant family and neighbors. In 1975 the board initiated a capital fund drive to raise $265,000 for the purchase and improvement of the camp so that it could continue to serve as a center for the preservation and encouragement of traditional music, song, and dance. A major objective is to ensure that Pinewoods Camp will be self-supporting at the end of the capital fund drive in 1980.

Pinewoods comprises twenty-five acres of unspoiled woodlands, with waterfronts on two lovely ponds. Long Pond, the larger of the two, provides swimming and boating facilities for campers. The surrounding area has dirt roads for hiking and exploring bogs, brooks, and other ponds. For nature lovers there are many birds, wild flowers, and mushrooms visible in the woods. Although the camp has been primarily used by groups promoting traditional dance, music, and song, other groups interested in similar activities or in the preservation of the environment are eligible to use the facilities.

The camp accommodates up to 140 people in rustic cabins or cottages set unobtrusively amidst the trees. There are four open pavilions with excellent wooden floors for dancing, a kitchen–dining hall, a camp house for group activities, and an office for the use of sponsoring organizations. The camp season begins in June (weekends) and extends into September.

Pinewoods Camp has been extolled by those who have come from all over the world since 1932 to attend the programs. It has been described as "that increasingly rare thing on this planet, an earthly paradise . . . one of our few truly democratic societies where people of different ages, backgrounds and life philosophies mix, communicate, share and learn . . . [an] annual celebration of our common love of movement and music and the human values they affirm." Pinewoods Camp has provided the setting for programs that have inspired hundreds of people with a love for our heritage of dance, music, and song; it exists as a place in which these living traditions can flourish in the future.

Address: Pinewoods Camp, Inc., Box 245, Larchmont, New York 10538.

San Diego State University Folk Dance Conference

by Valerie Staigh

In January 1956 two Santa Barbara, California, folk dancers, Elizabeth Sanders and Frank Cole (both now deceased), suggested a site for a folk dance conference in Santa Barbara at the University of California. The job of organizing a folk dance conference was given to the Research and Standardization Committee of the Folk Dance Federation of California, South, by the president, Minnie Anstine. Valerie Staigh was appointed chairman, a post she has held for the entire history of the conference except for the two years she was president of the Folk Dance Federation. Through diligence and careful planning, the committee held the first conference in August 1956; there has been a conference held in August each year since that memorial year—for twenty-two years.

Santa Barbara was the home of the conference from 1956 until 1968. A teacher/leader workshop was added. Then, in 1969, the conference was moved to San Diego because of increasing costs and in order to gain three gyms with wooden floors for dancing.

The committee, no longer under the aegis of the

Research and Standardization Committee, works all year to plan a varied and well-structured program. Teachers of ethnic dance are invited from around the United States, Canada, and Europe. Attendees come from the United States, Canada, and Japan. The conference and the teacher/leader workshop have a great impact on folk dancing in California, Arizona, Colorado, and other states.

The staff for the 1978 Folk Dance Week included Andor Czompo, Ann Czompo, Ciga and Ivon Despotović, Bora Gajicki, Moshiko Halevy, Jerry Helt, Anthony Shay, and Vince Evanchuk. For the teacher/leader workshop the staff consisted of Ann Czompo, Moshiko Halevy, and Audrey Silva.

Registrations for the teacher/leader workshop and folk dance conference at San Diego State University are accepted after the start of each year. The conference is usually filled by the end of January, with a waiting list. The teacher/leader workshop can usually take reservations up to the date of the session. Attendance at the workshop ranges between fifty and ninety; the conference generally numbers over two hundred.

There are eight staff members. Classes start at 8:15 A.M. and end mid-afternoon; three classes are held consecutively during each class period, which lasts one hour and five minutes. After dinner there is usually a folklore hour, followed by an evening dance program that includes a review of the day's and week's teachings. Around 10:30 or 11:00 P.M. the evening program is over, but the dancers continue dancing at the all-request program after-party, which lasts as late as they wish.

The costs for the 1978 Folk Dance Week were: $148 (double occupancy), $170 (single occupancy), $75 (tuition only). The costs for the teacher/leader weekend workshop were: $61 (double occupancy), $68 (single occupancy), $35 (tuition only). One college credit may be earned. An $11 fee (1978) is included in the conference cost.

An Elizabeth Sanders Memorial Scholarship fund was established in 1959 to help teachers and potential leaders attend the conference. Usually six scholarships are awarded each year.

Address: SDSU Folk Dance Conference, 3918 Second Avenue, Los Angeles, California 90008.

Tennessee Octoberfest Folk Dance Camp

by Bernard Kaiman

The year 1978 marked the sixteenth year of the Tennessee Octoberfest Folk Dance Camp. It is always held on the Columbus day holiday weekend in early October and includes four or five teaching sessions, a party, and a review, with request dancing during free time. Usually some campers dance the whole night through, a sort of "twenty-four-hour nonstop dancing" or "till the last dancer drops." Campers are mostly fairly experienced dancers, with the same level of experience as at other folk dance camps. Large numbers of young people make up the bulk of our group. Campers come from Tennessee, Kentucky, Alabama, Florida, Georgia, North and South Carolina, Virginia, Ohio, Indiana, as well as other states. Most dance regularly at home with their own active folk dance groups, so our teachers usually can move along fairly rapidly and cover a fair amount of material—up to quite advanced and complicated dances. Thus, our camp dance program typically includes a fairly wide range of dances, including some easy fun dances and others that are quite demanding and challenging.

We usually have just one teacher at our camp to present the dance material. We started with Grace Wolff of Dayton, Ohio, and continued with Mary Ann Herman, Vyts Beliajus, Dick Crum, David Henry, Mel Diamond, Ken Spear, Bora Özkök, Larry Weiner, Steve Zalph, and David Vinski. Most of these individuals have national reputations as teachers of international folk dancing; all have proven themselves excellent teachers and have provided a lot of fun.

The camp location is quite comfortable and secluded, with spacious grounds and a pool. The dance floor is a good wooden floor and is easy to dance on. Since it's a little small, we've had to limit our dancers to sixty-five. The dormitory could hold over one hundred people, so with sixty-five, it's relatively uncrowded, with two or three to a room. We're very informal about meals; the campers do their own cooking in a well-equipped kitchen or run into town (just five minutes away) to any number of restaurants. One nice feature is our Saturday evening covered-dish supper. Everyone brings some favorite dish and the whole group shares in what turns out to be a festive, fabulous feast. And, of course, there's always the spontaneous late-night after-parties (for those who gave up on the dancing)!

Our philosophy has always been based on the concept that we think people do folk dancing for recreation and for fun. So, in organizing the camp we've tried to emphasize the fun aspect, taking things lightly. Informality is the rule. Folk dancing as we do it is for fun!

The camp location is just outside Crossville, Tennessee, in the heart of the beautiful Cumberland Plateau country. The sponsors are members of the East Tennessee State University Folk Dancers. This informal club has included both students and townspeople since its beginnings in 1961. We meet almost every Thursday except Thanksgiving, when we're too full of turkey to dance. The group does a wide variety of international folk dances and has also developed a performance repertoire that is presented at local functions. Along with the Octoberfest camp, the group tries to sponsor one or two other annual folk dance workshops.

(Dr. Bernard Kaiman is director of the Tennessee Octoberfest Folk Dance Camp. He teaches folk dance at East Tennessee State University, and is coauthor of the book *Folk Dancing for Students and Teachers,* 2nd ed., 1975.)

Address: Dr. Bernard Kaiman, 250 E. Main Street, Jonesboro, Tennessee 37659 or East Tennessee State University, Johnson City, Tennessee 37601.

Texas Folk Dance Camp

by Bobbi Gilotti

Texas Thanksgiving Folk Dance Camp. For so many of us it means a separate and very special world, a festival atmosphere filled with music and dancing, costumes, customs, and songs of countries and peoples far and near; friendships old and new; the delightfully exhausting tasks of creating and carrying on these wonderful traditions—just because it's fun and we love it!

The unique spirit of the Texas Folk Dance Camp [TFDC] was apparent from the beginning. The first camp, held January 27–30, 1949, in Dallas at the Kiwanis Club camp at Bachman Lake unexpectedly faced fifteen-degree weather and frozen water pipes. Wonderful Jane Farwell (then rural recreation leader in Wisconsin) was dance leader; her charm and personality soon warmed the feet and spirits of the freezing campers to such a degree that they decided there must be more folk dance camps! This was not a new reaction to Jane's contagious enthusiasm. The first folk dance

camp ever held in the United States was under Jane's leadership at Wheeling, West Virginia. It was at this camp that Margaret Clark Thompson got the inspiration for TFDC. Anne Pittman, Marlys Swenson, and Loyd Collier also worked hard and long in setting up the camp. Demonstrations by ethnic groups of the Czech Beseda and of some Greek dances highlighted one evening party, and the folksy traditions of ethnic meals and decorations—and dancing 'til all hours— were firmly established.

In November 1949 Jane and the ethnic groups returned. The 1950 and 1951 reports show that about twenty people attended. Attendance rose to fifty-seven in 1953 when Eleanor Boyer introduced New England contras. The 1954 staff included Jane Farwell, Bob Allison, Loyd Collier, Henry Lash, Alura Flores de Angeles, and Ralph Page (who brought to full flower the contra enthusiasm sparked by Eleanor Boyer).

In 1955 TFDC moved to Bastrop State Park. Chairmen Zibby and Roy McCutchan asked Alura Flores back and introduced Vyts Beliajus, who taught dances of various countries and performed some exotic dances. A Syrian meal and a Jewish Hanukkah ceremony were memorable events.

George and Mary Lowrey were avid supporters of TFDC during the early days. Before they moved to Illinois in 1966, George summed up TFDC activities to date in a report as follows: "Texas Camp has many meanings to different people. It is a place to learn 'new' old dances and review others, a workshop, so to speak. It is a place to awaken international understanding through exposure to customs, foods, costumes, songs, and dances of other peoples. It is most of all, however, a place to meet and greet old friends and make many new ones amongst that 'different breed'—the truly delightful and genuine personalities known as folk dancers."

TFDC is a place for the average folk dancer to meet and be inspired by some of the most outstanding leaders and teachers in the country. For a large majority of our campers, TFDC has "been" Bastrop and the leaders we have had there. In 1957 the old master, Vyts Beliajus, headed the staff, ably assisted by TFDC's own Alura Flores de Angeles and that winsome Polish lass from Chicago, Emily Mucha. In 1958 we had Mr. Personality, Dave Rosenberg, with his curled mustache and infectious enthusiasm. Assisting Dave were two other TFDC regulars, Miss Mary Tymkowich from Denver and Nelda Drury from San Antonio.

The year 1959 was almost too much, with Dave Rosenberg joined by the guiding light of TFDC, Jane Farwell Hinrichs. In 1960 we reached out to sunny California and chose Madelynne Greene. Mary Tymkowich returned to the staff along with two new beautiful and talented leaders, Altagracia Azios Garcia teaching Spanish dances and Ann Akiko Zavada teaching Japanese dances. In 1961 Jane Farwell was principal instructor, assisted by Eleanor Boyer (contra dancing) and Win Hirschman from Chicago. The year 1962 brought Michel Cartier from Canada, with Win Hirschman and Mary Tymkowich both returning.

With Jane Farwell returning for a workshop, 1963 was the first year for "Vic" the Viking, Mr. Gordon Tracie of Seattle. The year 1964 brought Hungarian Andor Czompo; 1965 was sparked by both Gordon and Andor. Jane was with us in 1964 and then returned this year to finish up at Bastrop. TFDC regulars have filled in at various times throughout the period, with Alura either being a staff member or camper. Nelda Drury helped during Dave's first year (1958) when we moved the camp temporarily from Bastrop to the Red Wagon Ranch School near San Antonio, and Roy McCutchan and I occasionally led Texas-style square dancing.

Dancing has improved somewhat over the years without losing the spirit and fun of camp. Music sessions—in spite of "us Texans being poor singers"—have improved to the point that the 1966 camp was the first in which we danced an entire evening to live music provided by the campers themselves. May it always continue as another tradition of TFDC.

The year 1966 was the end of another era. Bastrop will be no more. Some trouble had been brewing for a couple of years because of our insatiable desire to dance, sing, eat—or all three—until the wee hours (usually around breakfast time). This year tent and trailer campers were moved in much closer and on Wednesday (the first night), while the brass band was practicing, the great outdoorsmen and women became restless. The straw that broke the camel's back occurred when the band struck up "Stars and Stripes Forever" at 5:00 A.M. and apparently pulled out all the stops. (It even woke me up.) The next day brought complaints and curfew. Thursday night was strange indeed for TFDC: lights went out earlier than usual and all noise stopped; I think some of the dancers even went to bed! On Friday a pioneer spirit took over and prompted a mass exodus. At least nine cars—some say fifteen—loaded down with campers pulled out at curfew time, only to return just before breakfast. I don't yet know where all of them headed, but one seven-car caravan drove twelve miles to another state park and played music all night. Saturday night was "what-the-hell night" and we stayed up as usual, dancing with the music low and all windows closed. There were no music sessions! We cannot return to Bastrop!

In 1969 the twenty-second annual TFDC was held at a new campsite, where most of the Thanksgiving weekend meetings have been held ever since. Camp Hoblitzelle, owned by the Salvation Army and located near Midlothian, Texas, proved to be attractive and generally convenient, though the concrete dance floor "did in" the usual number of legs and feet. Dance leaders Atanas Kolarovski, Bev and Ginny Wilder, and Jean Forbes performed a variety of dances from many countries.

The 1972 silver anniversary of TFDCs was observed at Camp Soroptomist in Argyle, Texas, north of Dallas. A hearty group of dancers helped winterize an outdoor basketball court for dance sessions in cold weather. It was reminiscent of the first camp held in January 1949. Approximately 166 dancers attended. Colleen Moore was named executive secretary, a post she held for many years. Zibby McCutchan of San Antonio, who had attended each of the twenty-five folk dance camps, was crowned queen of the Saturday festivities.

Other teachers at TFDC have included C. Stewart Smith, John Skow, Germain and Louise Hebert, Marianne and Conny Taylor, John and Paula Pappas, Dick Crum, Ada and Jas Dziewanowski, and Yves Moreau. Texas Thanksgiving Folk Dance Camp continues meeting at Camp Hoblitzelle. For more information, write: Texas Folk Dance Camp, 5534-H Holly, Houston, Texas 77081.

(This article was excerpted from unpublished material provided by "Bobbi" Estella M. Gilotti and is here used with permission. Bobbi came from a family of square dancers and square dance musicians. She started international folk dancing in the fall of 1953 at the University of Texas at Austin. She was program director, taught dances, and held other offices in the Austin International Folk Dance group. She compiled the history of the Texas International Folk Dancers [TIFD], a state and area organization that sponsors the annual TFDC, for the 1969 camp syllabus, continued as the historian for the 1969, 1970, and 1971 camps, and was president of TIFD in 1971 and 1972.)

University of the Pacific Folk Dance Camp

by Walter Grothe

The idea for a camp started in 1948 after a folk dance festival held at the University of California at Berkeley. Lawton Harris, professor of religious education at the College of the Pacific (now the University of the Pacific at Stockton, California), and Walter Grothe, at that time president of the Folk Dance Federation of California, North, were standing on the cafeteria line waiting to be served and discussed the tremendous growth of folk dancing in California. Among other things, the idea of "why not try a folk dance camp in California" came up; the East had started a few very successfully. Lawton Harris then contacted the College of the Pacific and they showed an interest. The matter was presented to the Federation Council. After looking into other possible sites, such as Stanford University, an offer was made to the College of the Pacific and they accepted. Under the direction of Lawton Harris, a committee was formed to organize the camp. It was to be a part of the college's summer session and was to be jointly sponsored by the college and the camp committee. In the summer of 1948 the first camp was to take place on the beautiful campus of the College of the Pacific. Folders were sent out and the committee hoped that somebody would show up—and they did. The first year 135 people registered. The faculty then was small yet full of enthusiasm and classes lasted way into the night.

Since that first camp, many changes have been made every year based on past experience and comments from campers. The camp, now well established, is under the direction of Jack McKay, who took over after Lawton Harris's death. It consists of two identical one-week sessions, one held the last week in July and the other the first week in August. There were 233 participants registered for the July 1977 session. Almost every well-known teacher has, at one time or another, served on the faculty and many teachers from abroad have been invited to serve.

Almost every dance performed by folk dance groups in the United States has been taught at Stockton; many were originally introduced there. Weekly attendance now averages about 250 people drawn from all over the country and from abroad (e.g., Japan). All agree that, if you are interested in folk dancing, there is no better way of spending a one- or two-week vacation.

At the University of the Pacific's thirty-first annual Stockton folk dance camp held in 1978, dances from ten ethnic groups were presented by outstanding instructors; these groups included Serbia, Hungary, Switzerland, Armenia, the Philippines, Yugoslavia, Romania, Mexico, Holland, and the United States. Dancers were provided with a complete syllabus, international food, special classes in clogging, folk singing, and costume construction.

Each week offered six full days (and evenings) of study of folk dance, folklore, rhythms and motion, teaching techniques, dance practice, folk crafts, and other related activities. A one-semester credit unit per week was optional and partial scholarships were available. The cost per person for room, board, tuition, and fees was $190.

(Walter Grothe, an outstanding folk dance leader in California, was a cofounder of the UOP Camp and has been on the committee continuously for thirty-two years. He introduced Austrian and German dances at the camp. He is in his twenty-ninth year of weekly classes at the University of California International House, attended by some one hundred fifty dancers, mostly foreign students.)

Address: Jack McKay, Director, Stockton Folk Dance Camp, University of the Pacific, Stockton, California 95211.

IV
REPRESENTATIVE PERFORMING FOLK DANCE GROUPS

Aman Dancers

Introduction

Folk dance programs essentially performed to entertain an audience usually have a different format from those designed for group participation. Although based on original dances, for staging purposes the repetitive choreography of folk dances as performed in villages is sometimes changed to make it more visually appealing or more danceable for the group involved. A flourish is added here, an extra twirl there, or perhaps several dances are combined into a suite of dances.

There is an extremely wide variance in the types of folk dance programs and the groups performing them in the United States. They range from nostalgic renditions of a Polish polka or a Czechoslovakian csardas at an ethnic picnic to elaborately costumed professional extravaganzas involving dances from a dozen countries staged by trained performers. There are performances presented by Girl Scouts, city recreation departments, dance teachers, schools, folk dance clubs and enthusiasts, and professional dance troupes.

The following pages describe six formal performing groups, including their historical development and aims and an indication of their contributions to the folk dance scene. These were selected from among many others as representative examples of performing groups.

Aman Folk Ensemble

When the Aman Folk Ensemble [AFE] was founded in 1964 by Anthony Shay and Leona Wood, its first performances were little more than cabaret turns, with so few performers that the directors had to do frequent solos in order to provide time for the other dancers to make costume changes.

AFE began its fifteenth season in 1978. Since the company's formation at UCLA, it has grown into a professional and respected performing arts institution serving Greater Los Angeles with a variety of services and bringing its exciting performances to concertgoers throughout the West.

Under the artistic direction of Leona Wood and Anthony Shay, the eighty-five-member company of dancers, singers, and musicians has presented the music and dances of Eastern Europe, the Middle East, Africa, and America—all in authentic costumes and accompanied by the proper orchestra for each ethnographic region.

Anthony Shay, director and cofounder of AFE, studied dance ethnology in the Middle East for many years. Part of his university education included study in Iran, where he appeared as a vocalist on Iranian Radio with the National Orchestra. Upon his return to this country, he began staging Iranian folk dances and formed the Village Dancers at UCLA. In 1961 he expanded his choreography to include the musical folk art of Yugoslavia and Bulgaria, whose native dance forms he had performed as a dancer. Leona Wood, an internationally known painter and graphic arts designer, is recognized as one of the world's leading authorities on the dances, costumes, and music of the Middle Eastern and North African cultures.

AFE's major recognition has been achieved from performances at the Los Angeles Music Center. In 1971, after a sellout concert in the Dorothy Chandler Pavilion, Music Center Presentations offered to bring the company back for the first of its annual return engagements. The company has worked on a number of special projects as well, appearing in the Ahmanson Theater before two capacity audiences of ten-year-olds on the tenth anniversary of the Los Angeles Music Center, for the Bicentennial, the Grand People's concerts, and the rug concerts. Other southern California sponsors have engaged the company as part of their dance series, and special programs have been started to meet community needs for dance presentations of quality.

A special thirteen-member company was formed in 1974 to offer performances and lecture-demonstrations in the schools. Over two hundred were presented last year to southern California schoolchildren from kindergarten through high school. These are valuable experiences, introducing new audiences to the magic of the performing arts; school personnel find them an important addition to the regular academic work.

In 1975 AFE joined the National Endowment for the Arts Dance Touring Program, which enables companies to stay in a community for two-and-a-half days or longer, offering classes and workshops in addition to concerts.

AFE today stands as a museum of ethnic costuming. The collection, which includes hundreds of authentic costumes, has been assembled through direct purchases from Old World peasants, through the skill of village crafts people abroad, through gifts from foreign governments, and through purchases by travelers. When originals are not available, exact copies are made down to the smallest detail. Members of AFE have become expert at embroidery, leather craft, and dyeing fabrics.

The instruments also reflect years of collecting. While many are owned by the musicians, the company has a fine assortment of unusual folk instruments, ranging in size from small Serbian fipple-flutes, called frulas, to a large Romanian cimbalom. In a typical concert AFE uses over three hundred different costumes and up to seventy-five instruments, representing but a portion of the full collection.

AFE musicians have mastered such tongue-tangling musical instruments as the gadulka, the saz, the lijerica, the kemanjeh, the frula, the caval, and the zurna, as well as the better known Jew's harp, bagpipe, banjo, mandolin, fiddle, guitar, bass, and drums of every size and description. Almost as remarkable as AFE's versatility with exotic instruments is the ensemble's mastery of widely diverse folk singing styles, rhythms, and intonations in ten languages.

AFE's current membership includes a professional corps as well as many other talented and dedicated members whose devotion to the ethnic arts contributes to the quality of their performance in many ways. AFE's concert season, which runs from September through June, with occasional summer dates, includes performances for community concert associations, college arts series, museums, ethnic organizations, and private concert promoters.

The ensemble maintains a repertoire of over seven hours of music and dance and is constantly adding new material. Members travel abroad to research new material for the company and to arrange for the purchase and shipment of new costumes and instruments. AFE also works with visiting and local experts on music and dance and maintains a library containing films, records, and books to aid the directors in their work.

AFE has offered a number of special programs in co-operation with UCLA Extension. These include classes in dance especially designed for school teachers, a seminar called "Traditional Performing Arts in Selected Societies," and a ten-week course on the music, dance, costumes, and traditions of Yugoslavia.

AFE is organized as a nonprofit corporation, with a board of trustees and a support organization to help the ensemble continue to serve as a goodwill ambassador for Los Angeles and eventually to represent its home city in the major cultural centers of the world. The company wants to continue to reach out to the many communities that are developing a cultural awareness and wishes to bring programs of quality to their new audiences.

AFE rehearses in Los Angeles city schools in facilities such as basketball courts and gyms. Costumes are stored in the company members' homes. Long-range goals include a multipurpose center for rehearsals, housing a library, costume production and storage, and space for public workshops and classes.

Address: Aman Folk Ensemble, 15158 Morrison Street, Sherman Oaks, California 91403.

Brigham Young University Dancers

Brigham Young University International Folk Dancers

Mary Bee Jensen began instructing various folk dance forms at Brigham Young University [BYU] in 1956. When she was invited to provide "some Scandinavian dancers" for a local Provo, Utah, event, little did she realize that she was laying a foundation for a program that would end up with her students dancing in places like Lincoln Center in New York City; Disneyland in Los Angeles; Carnegie Institute Music and Lecture Hall in Pittsburgh; the famous Mercur Theater and

Tivoli Gardens in Copenhagen; the Trocadero in Paris; the Turku Konserttisali in Turku, Finland; the Circus Theater in Scheveningen and Doelen, Rotterdam; and a bullring in Abrantes, Portugal. Requests now flood into the university to have teams of dancers perform all over the world.

BYU has long realized the significance of all art forms and the importance of dance as an integral part of a broad education. Folk, ballroom, and modern dancing are taught regularly under the auspices of the College of Physical Education. Over twenty-five thousand students at the university are drawn from every state in the United States and from over seventy foreign countries; many become involved in folk dance programs. Over six hundred American Indians from a wide variety of tribes now attend the university; their dances are frequently included in the ever-increasing repertoire of the American Folk Dancers section. As the American Folk Dancers tour abroad, they exchange dance steps and ideas with dancers of other countries, thereby developing a common understanding as well as a deep appreciation for the dance styles of all peoples.

The program that started at BYU with seven couples under the leadership of Mary Bee Jensen now includes dances of other countries, thereby necessitating a changing in the name to International Folk Dance Club, comprised of two hundred members. It is of necessity a closed club, and now that it is well established, membership is highly competitive; during the fall of 1968, one thousand students tried out for one hundred openings. The group is under the sponsorship of two divisions, the College of Physical Education and University Relations. Students enroll in advanced folk dance classes that cover dance techniques, costuming, staging, as well as the history, geography, and culture of the countries in which the dances originated. Dances of all European countries are taught, as well as dances of the South Seas.

Invitations to perform in Europe have prompted extensive research into the history of our own American dances since the Europeans request that each group perform only those dances representative of its own culture at international folk dance festivals. Among the dances that have been thoroughly studied in preparation for European performances are those of the American Indians, New Englanders, Appalachian mountain people, Western pioneers, and fad dances from 1900 to 1940.

The dream of taking student performers on European tours became a reality in 1964 when the Danish Embassy extended an invitation to the BYU troupe to perform at Varde, Denmark, at their international folk dance festival. This started a program that has opened the doors and hearts of the people of Europe to these young American performers. And now, the history of America as illustrated through dance has been presented to people in every country of western Europe. European tours were completed in 1964, 1966, 1967, and 1968, with each tour lasting from ten to twelve weeks.

Friendships established over four summers have grown to such an extent that in many European villages the reception committee is larger than the arriving group. Tears of happiness greet the dancers, and homes are opened wide to welcome the students during their stay. What an experience it is to be taken into the homes of the European people and to partake of their food and generous nature. Immediately the fact is forgotten that the dancers are Americans and the hosts Dutch, Flemish, or Italian. All become one in friendship and in the exchange of ideas and experiences.

An example of such a priceless experience was the invitation to perform at the tenth annual folk dance festival in Schoten, Belgium, where the group had performed twice previously. This festival is one of the finest in Europe, providing many opportunities to meet and become better acquainted with the best European dance groups. For their tenth festival Schoten has invited the top five groups to participate for the past ten years. Invitations were extended to groups from Russia, Romania, Yugoslavia, Czechoslovakia, and the BYU International Folk Dancers. The BYU performers were the only group ever to have received three invitations to this outstanding festival, so a host of friends, including many performers from other countries, awaited the Americans' arrival. Previous friendships were renewed with performers from behind the iron curtain with whom our students had continued to correspond. They ignored the fact that they came from different parts of the world, with different cultural, social, and political backgrounds.

Folk dancing has opened the doors and hearts of the European people to a better understanding of America and the American people. It has opened the door of opportunity in practically every country of Europe for this American group to perform and to develop friendships. Plans are being made for the BYU group to return again and again in a continuing effort to improve understanding and appreciation among people of various countries and for Americans to become better informed about the people and living conditions in other lands.

In 1977 the BYU International Folk Dancers participated in one of the group's most extensive tours to date—a five-week European performing circuit that took them to such countries as Israel, Romania, and Great Britain.

Address: Brigham Young University, 115 Wilkinson Center, Provo, Utah 84602.

Duquesne University Tamburitzans

Duquesne University Tamburitzans

Forty years of music, song, and dance—that's how long the Duquesne University Tamburitzans have been around! When Dr. A. Lester Pierce first brought the musical group to Duquesne in 1937, there were only fourteen men who comprised the "Slavonic Tamburitza Orchestra." Matt L. Gouze was the director. Women orchestral members and dancers came later. The musical production adopted the format of a variety show, with dances and songs from everywhere between Mexico and Moscow.

The East European Performing Folk Ensemble, a section of the "Tammies," exists for the dual purpose of preserving and perpetuating the Eastern European cultural heritage in the United States and offering scholarship opportunities to deserving students. Hundreds have received more than two million dollars in financial aid since 1937.

The Tamburitzans take their name from the lutelike instrument called the tambura or, more properly, its diminutive, the tamburica. Originally the tambura was a twangy, rather loosely strung affair with a longish, narrow neck. Shepherds plucked out melodies on it

while singing songs as they tended their flocks. The modern tambura is a more refined instrument and comprises an entire family of picked musical instruments capable of producing a more technical and complex brand of music.

The tambura, however, is far from being the only musical instrument used in East European folk music. A wide range of pastoral flutes, single and multi-stringed bowed instruments, and various sizes and shapes of drums all combine to provide an exceedingly rich and intriguing set of musical sounds and rhythms.

Macedonian-Bulgarian folk music may feature the heavy, hypnotic beating of a large goatskin drum known as the tapan or tupan. Usually accompanying the tupan is a woodwind instrument called a zurla, which produces a strange sound generally considered harsh to Western ears. Also in evidence are the haunting sounds of the caval and the multistringed and bowed gadulka. The energetic dance, Lindjo, from Dalmatia, uses for its accompaniment a foot-stomping player of the three-stringed lijerica. The svirala, or pastoral flute, is an indispensable musical instrument in the Tamburitzans' repertoire. Whether it is a frula accompaniment to a Serbian dance or the twin-tubed dvoynice, the unusual sounds are captivating. Found throughout all of the Balkans is the ancient bagpipe, or gajde with its piercing, stringent tones, coupled with an ever-present drone, this instrument performs a wide variety of musical chores. Fascinating instruments such as the nai, or panpipes, from Romania and the taragot, a kind of soprano saxophone, provide still another dimension to the musical mosaic of the Tamburitzans' instrumental sound—like the Russian balalaika, the Greek buzuki, or the darabuka of the Near East.

In August 1947 the Tamburitzans (with an eye toward some degree of professionalism) started their annual training camp at Lake Nebagamon, Wisconsin, where they now spend six weeks every summer producing a new show. Dozens of dance choreographers and instructors are involved and rehearse the ensemble an average of fourteen hours each day.

Following camp training, the show is "put on the road" and tested before a great variety of different audiences. The show is criticized, corrected, changed, polished, re-evaluated, and reconstructed, with many weak spots taken out and replaced with better ones. The entire production is refined to such a degree that when the Tammies return to Duquesne after six weeks, the show is ready for the new season.

When the Tamburitzans perform the music of a specific ethnic group and dance their dances, they are always concerned with the proper portrayal of these cultures. From the gay little polkas and merry, lilting waltzes of the Slovenes to the fascinating and formerly seldom-heard Macedonian folk music, with its irregular rhythmic patterns, the Tamburitzans approach each ethnic group's music with great dignity.

Besides the old rituals and ceremonial songs and dances, the Tamburitzans also perform some of the new folk music of the postwar Eastern European countries. Proper instrumentation, whenever possible, is utilized. The Tamburitzans understand full well the great pride each national group displays for its own music and consequently approach these groups' musical traditions with loving care.

During the nine-month academic season, the Tammies perform about one hundred shows across the United States and Canada. In 1950 they initiated a long period of international travel, beginning with three separate tours to Yugoslavia and Italy. The 1950 tour came at a time when Europe was just recovering from the horrors of World War II. In 1952 it still wasn't much better, but in 1962 the Tammies witnessed a great change.

Walter W. Kolar took over the directorship of the Tammies in 1952. At about the same time, a nonprofit educational and cultural corporation called the Duquesne University Tamburitzans, Inc., was formed to provide financial and moral support to the musical organization. The dream of professionalism became a reality.

After the 1962 European tour, the expertise, popularity, and prestige of the Tamburitzans skyrocketed. The ensemble grew from fourteen performers in 1937 to forty performers today. New and authentic costumes, a wide variety of traditional and contemporary musical instruments, more rigid training and research programs—all of these changes made many people sit up and take notice of the Tamburitzans.

The U. S. State Department was impressed. It tapped the Tammies in 1968 to represent the United States as goodwill ambassadors on a ten-country Latin American tour. Known as Los Tamburas in South America, they made an extremely big hit! The following season, in 1969, the youthful Tammies increased their international acclaim by representing the United States on a goodwill tour to Romania, Poland, and the U.S.S.R. This time the Tammies included Americana in their musical productions.

In the normal course of operations and during a regular season of performance, the Tamburitzans' forte is in the East European field of folk music, song, and dance. Ever since 1952, when they adopted a policy of confining all major activities in one specific area, the emphasis was placed on the folk arts of Eastern Europe. Praise and prestige continued to grow and the Tamburitzans became recognized leaders in this field. To this day, this is still the area to which most of their efforts are diverted.

Some of the people represented through their folk concerts are the South Slavs (which include Croatians, Serbians, Slovenes, Macedonians, and Bulgarians), Hungarians, Romanians, Poles, Ukrainians, Czechs and Slovaks, Lithuanians, Russians, and many other national groups that make up present-day U.S.S.R. The Tamburitzans make every effort to portray these musical cultures with great dignity and on a high level.

The collection and acquisition of many original and authentic folk material has been going on for a quarter of a century. Thousands of pieces of music and books; hundreds of films, recordings, and audio tapes; forty years' worth of souvenirs, acclamations, proclamations, and just plain activity—all these, taken together, represent a substantial library, museum, and archive. This material serves to preserve the history of the Tamburitzans and is also valuable as research and resource material for serious students and teachers.

The Tamburitzans are still very actively engaged in the acquisition of material relevant to their area of interest. For example, they collect the old 78 rpm phonograph recordings, old photographs, musical instruments, embroidered fabrics, books, costumes—in fact, just about anything that sheds some light on the historical development of the immigrant cultures in the United States.

The collection of costumes down through the years has played an important role not only within the performing ensemble but within the total framework of the operation. Ever since the Tamburitzans received their very first original costume in Yugoslavia in 1950, there has been a constant, diligent effort to acquire appropriate outfits for practically everything portrayed by the Tamburitzans on stage. The veils that once shielded the faces of all Islamic women have all but disappeared in some areas, but their graceful memory lives on in the fluttering scarves of Tammie dancers.

Hundreds of original and authentic costumes and accessories found their way into the Tamburitzan organization. These will now become an entire section of the new Museum of the National Folk Arts Center. Besides this, the Tammies make patterns for these original costumes and offer them to many of the youthful enterprising folk dance groups around the country.

In the past seven or eight years, particularly when the Tamburitzans began touring around the world for the U. S. State Department, the emphasis (at the request of the State Department) has shifted to the field of folk and period cultures of the American people. An honest effort at researching this area revealed a great treasure of Americana, a culture that is every bit as rich as the East European heritage. The Tamburitzans dove into this field of Americana with great enthusiasm.

The Tammies created a full-scale production called

"An American Mosaic." This included a survey of Americana since the earliest days of the American Indian and his own culture—advancing chronologically through many periods of American history—and covered practically every region of the fifty states of the United States. Since it was not confined to the folk idiom, the production included some electronic musical instruments so popular in America today.

In a five-year period the Tamburitzans musical ensemble represented the United States during four of these years. The Tammies were first invited to take the Latin American tour and, immediately following this, were sent to the U.S.S.R. and then continued with a three-week stand at the Théâtre des Champs-Elysées in Paris. During this Paris concert engagement, the Tammies were asked to take their musical production into four additional countries the following summer.

This resulted in the European tour of 1972. The Tammies performed first in Czechoslovakia, followed by a festival in Marseilles, France, and then into Greece for a tour throughout the entire country. The summer was capped by a series of concerts in Bulgaria. Here, at the International Festival in Bourgas, on the Black Sea, they competed against some of the finest folk ensembles of Eastern Europe and won the gold metal for their efforts!

The Tamburitzans offer a unique and exciting opportunity to deserving young people in the form of educational opportunities and extensive travel throughout the United States and in foreign countries. Each year, individual scholarships in excess of sixteen thousand dollars are awarded to high school seniors who possess the necessary qualifications as singers, dancers, or instrumentalists. Of course, admission requirements to Duquesne University must also be met. Interested students may obtain application blanks from the Tamburitzans at Duquesne University. Upon receipt of the application, arrangements are then made for a formal audition, together with a possible interview. In return for their scholarship awards, the Tamburitzans students participate in the performing ensemble and travel throughout the world.

These young people come from all parts of America and are typical of American youth anywhere. They were generally leaders in their high schools, performed in a school orchestra or band, acted in plays, wrote and edited school newspapers, served as cheerleaders, or perhaps as athletes. Out of hundreds who apply annually only a select few are chosen. The applicants go through a strenuous audition and screening process before a final choice is made. They're generally very good in one specialized field and are adequate in several others.

These students receive a complete scholarship at Duquesne University for performing with the Tamburitzans and have an opportunity to study in the field of their choice within the academic programs of the university.

The Duquesne University Tamburitzans Institute of Folk Arts [DUTIFA] became a reality in 1973. DUTIFA is the formal name for an organization that had already existed. For the last twenty-five years, the Tamburitzans operation has included a community school program; a library, museum, and archive complex; publications; and all sorts of cultural and special activities that became part of the Tamburitzans Cultural Center complex. The one innovation is the recently established master's program in folk arts, a program unique in academic circles. In addition, DUTIFA has held major symposiums and has produced educational materials to be used in teaching ethnic heritages and world cultures.

Ever since the Tammies' first European trips in the early 1950s, there was an earnest effort to collect the necessary research materials such as books, journals, costumes, original musical instruments, films, recordings, etc., all pointed toward supporting the production of a better and more authentic musical performance.

All of this has found its way into a library, which today contains about ten thousand volumes, along with hundreds of recordings, films, graphics, and assorted research materials. There's a full-fledged wardrobe department containing hundreds of original and authentic items. The printed and recorded historical accounts of the Tamburitzans' operations have become a department of archives of Tamburitzans history and immigrant cultural information. Within DUTIFA, steady growth, creative development, and continuous research is a never-ending process.

Ever since 1937, the Tammies have been moving from house to house, storeroom to garage, all over Duquesne's campus, never really owning a place to live or rehearse in. By the early 1960s the situation was so critical that the Duquesne University Tamburitzans, Inc., established the Tamburitzan Cultural Center, which had ample room for the three staff members, rehearsal halls for an ensemble consisting of twenty-eight dancers and library and museum space for the one thousand or so books and costumes they had accumulated.

At that time the facility was adequate. Today the Tamburitzans again need room to accommodate the growing organization of eleven staff members, a forty-member ensemble, over ten thousand stage and museum costume pieces, historical archives, and operational inventories. The Tamburitzans Corporation, along with other supporting organizations such as the Ladies Auxiliary, General Membership, and the Alumni Association of the Tamburitzans, has undertaken the project of providing better facilities that will eventually become a national folk arts center.

One of the areas that has greatly expanded its operation and has served as a "farm system" for developing talent for the performing Tamburitzans since 1954 is the community school educational programs. Children learn about their own cultural heritage of music and dance. Youngsters begin the program when they are about seven or eight and continue until they graduate from high school. During their ten years or so in the community school educational program, children learn how to perform many of the same types of songs and dances that the parent Tamburitzans do at Duquesne. When they graduate from high school, many audition for the Tammies and are accepted. Today, the community school educational program encompasses a wide range of folk arts, including advanced tamburitza playing.

Address: Duquesne University Tamburitzans, Institute of Folk Arts, 1801 Boulevard of the Allies, Pittsburgh, Pennsylvania 15219.

Kopachka Dancers

Nancy and Dean Linscott started the Kopachka Dancers in September 1965, about a year after they moved to the Bay Area so that he could take a job teaching microbiology at the University of California Medical School in San Francisco. (He's now an associate professor there.) When they started the group, they (1) hoped to attract dancers from a wide range of nationalities who were equally interested in line dances and partner dances; (2) hoped to build a permanent, ongoing group rather than teaching a succession of classes; (3) wanted to be able to do a few performances for others from time to time, but not to the exclusion of learning and doing dances for the fun of dancing; and (4) hoped to instill in those who danced with them an interest in, and respect for, the proper style with which ethnic dances from different areas should be performed.

Now, twelve years later, they have an active group of about forty people and they feel very pleased with the way things have turned out. People come from as far away as fifty miles to dance with them; they have dancers of all ages and from all walks of life; and they dance regularly for four hours every Friday night. The seven musicians who constitute the Kopachka Band play for major parties and some of the performances.

Over the years the Kopachka Dancers have performed suites of dances from Poland, England, Greece, Yugoslavia, Norway, Finland, Estonia, Russia, Roma-

Kopachka Dance Director Dean Linscott

nia, and Hungary. In fact, they have made costumes for four different regions of Romania: Moldavia, Maramureş, Transylvania and, for men only, Caluşarii. Dean has taken about seven thousand feet of super-8 sound movies of dancing in Yugoslavia, Bulgaria, and Romania, from which they get some of their material. At their twelfth birthday party they invited over two hundred dancers from all over the San Francisco Bay Area.

In recent years some of the members have wanted to teach folk dancing and have started groups of their own in Mill Valley. At the present time, one such group and two classes are active in addition to the Kopachka Dancers. They have a beginner class, a low-intermediate class, and a high-intermediate group (the Dolina Dancers) affiliated in this way. They share largely similar dance repertoires to the extent that this is feasible, and have joint parties from time to time so the groups can get to know each other better. In fact, many people dance at least twice a week by attending two of these four groups. Total membership in all four groups is well over one hundred dancers.

Address: Kopachka Dancers, 40 Glen Drive, Mill Valley, California 94941.

Mazur Polish Dancers of Milwaukee. Photo by Milwaukee Journal

Mazur Polish Dancers of Milwaukee

The Mazur Polish Dancers of Milwaukee were organized in the fall of 1940 by Professor Alfred Sokolnicki, dean of the Marquette University College of Speech. The objective of the first group, which numbered 250 members, was preparation for the presentation of a simulated Polish wedding at the 1941 national convention of the American Legion. The "wedding," which was held on September 15, 1941, was heralded as "the largest group of Polish dancers ever to present any performance at one time on one stage in the United States" and "the largest folk group to present a single performance at one time on one stage in Milwaukee." Shortly after the performance, the group was reorganized to include only teen-agers. The enthusiasm and vigor the young people exhibit is evident in the dances and customs young people presented and perpetuated in Poland centuries ago.

Meticulous scholarship has woven these Polish dances and customs into "danscenes," just one of the many contributions the Mazur Polish Dancers have made to the folk dance world. While the danscene is similar to ballet and pageantry, it is unique in that it combines various dance routines, music, and temperaments with the spectacle of pantomime. This serves to give an authentic aura to the customs and dances being presented in their true folk flavor. Individual sets of costumes are used for numbers that represent distinctive regions of Poland: Łowicz, Cracow, Silesia, Pomerania, and the Polish mountains.

The Mazur Polish Dancers have earned tributes from several generations of audiences for their artistic endeavors. Utmost in their minds is the desire to present Polish dances and customs in their finest light. Contrasts of costume and dance moods have distinguished the Mazur Polish Dancers as America's leading Polish folk dancers.

The group has received much local and national publicity, including recognition in *National Geographic* and *Seventeen* magazines. The objectives of the Mazur Polish Dancers of Milwaukee are based on their rich American heritage of freedom, reflecting an appreciation of the varied cultural backgrounds of their fellow Americans. In interpreting the folk dances, legends, and customs of the Polish people, these young Americans learn to appreciate that culture more and, through it, the many allied cultures of the world.

The Mazur Polish Dancers have been regarded as both official and unofficial representatives of Polish culture at many festivals and programs, including the national folk festivals in Washington, D.C., Philadelphia, St. Louis, Nashville, and the United Nations Folk Festival in Barrington, Illinois.

The Mazur Polish Dancers of Milwaukee perform for nonpolitical organizations and sponsors.

Address: The Mazur Polish Dancers of Milwaukee, Inc., P.O. Box 1136, Milwaukee, Wisconsin 53201.

San Antonio College Folk Dancers

The San Antonio College Folk Dancers keep up a busy schedule of performances, workshops, and lecture demonstrations that, over the past eighteen years, have earned them recognition as one of the finest folk dance groups in the South.

The dancers, under the direction of Mrs. Nelda Drury, a professor of physical education, perform a variety of international dances from Poland, Germany, Italy, Hawaii, Yugoslavia, Mexico, South America, the Philippines, and other countries.

The majority of the forty students who comprise the group make most of their costumes, paying strict attention to detail, which has earned them a reputation for authenticity. Several former San Antonio College Folk Dancers are now touring with professional companies in different parts of the country and even outside the United States.

The San Antonio College Folk Dancers have given performances at the New York World's Fair, San Antonio's Hemisfair, the Texas Folklife Festival, and numerous other civic affairs. The students combine their performing skills with teaching skills when they are invited to attend a dance workshop. The dancers have taught and performed in Washington, D.C., Denver, Colorado, and Covington, Kentucky, at various national folk festivals. A highlight of the dance year occurs in April when the dancers host their annual folk dance festival.

Locally, the dancers have received special recognition from the Women's Department of the State Fair of Texas and the Texas Association of Health, Physical Education and Recreation.

The dance group was recognized in 1967 when it received the Burl Ives Award. Nelda Drury was chosen as San Antonio's Outstanding Artist for 1974. That year she also received the Kay Hart Award for her contribution to the Polish heritage in the area of dance. Earlier she was selected as one of a team to conduct a six-week series of European, American, and Mexican folk dancing in twenty-three cities throughout Japan for twenty-three thousand participants. The tour was sponsored by the Japanese State Department Ministry of Education, Asahi Press, Japan, and the National YMCA of Japan.

The San Antonio College Folk Dancers have two big projects during the year: a three-week Mexican dance workshop taught by Señora Alura Flores de Angeles, of the University of Mexico, and a program of the regional dances of Mexico, presented by Señora Angeles and her students, which culminates her classes.

The group sponsored their nineteenth annual folk dance festival in 1978. The festival features a variety of ethnic and folk dances and each year attracts such varied groups from across the state as the Austin International Folk Dancers, the University of Texas Dancers, the Scottish Dancers from Houston, and the University of Oklahoma Dancers.

The San Antonio College Folk Dancers receive numerous invitations each year. They have performed at the Jewish Purim Festival, the Polish Copernicus Ball, the German Wurstfest, the Danish Scandinavian Smorgasbord and, the Mexican Fiesta de Guadalupe. They have appeared in several national folk festivals; have held concerts in Madison, Wisconsin, Boston, Tucson, Arizona, the New York World's Fair, Toronto, and Oaxtepec, Mexico. In 1976 they toured Japan at the invitation of the Japanese Dance Federation. While in Japan, two of the dancers performed a Mexican dance for Prince Mikasa.

San Antonio College Dancers Director Nelda Drury and daughter Elizabeth

Director Nelda Drury has taught at workshops in Maine, West Virginia, Wisconsin, Colorado, New Hampshire, California, and New Mexico. In addition, she has taught at festivals in Canada, Japan, Mexico, Hawaii, and at the American University of Beirut, Lebanon.

Address: San Antonio College Folk Dancers, 1300 San Pedro Avenue, San Antonio, Texas 78212.

Silver Spurs

Spokane's dancing Silver Spurs completed a triumphant performing tour of several European countries during a five-week period in 1975. Director E. S. (Red) Henderson proudly proclaims that his twenty-seven high school goodwill ambassadors were welcomed with open arms by audiences in Scotland, England, France, Germany, Austria, Hungary, and Switzerland. Most performances closed with an enthusiastic audience complimenting the Silver Spurs with a standing ovation.

Silver Spurs programs abroad consisted of North American folk dances, including a variety of dances from Mexico, square dances, waltzes, contras and quadrilles, along with Philippine, Hawaiian, and South Sea dances. Authentic American Indian dances and show numbers such as the Cakewalk, Old Soft Shoe, Charleston, Varsity Drag, Jitterbug, and the Fox Trot were great favorites with European audiences.

The Silver Spurs, a nationally known high school western and folk exhibition dance group from the Spokane Public Schools and surrounding area, was started in 1947 when many of the students in physical education classes asked for a Saturday recreation hour in square, round, and folk dancing.

The exhibition group has made coast-to-coast tours, having appeared on NBC and CBS television shows, notably "Ted Mack and the Original Amateur Hour" and "Don McNeill's TV Club." Standard Oil of California produced a full-length color film of the young dancers. They have been featured in a textbook, pictured in *Life* magazine, and the story of the Silver Spurs has been sent to seventy-seven foreign countries by the United States Information Service.

The group was organized to bring parents and children together in order to participate in wholesome activities. The parents, through fund-raising affairs, promote the enlargement of these recreation interests for all youth.

The Silver Spurs are known throughout North America for their truly professional performances of authentic folk dances from almost every section of the globe. Their $40,000 wardrobe consists of bright, colorful costumes that add to the thrill and excitement of their shows.

Red Henderson organized the Silver Spurs and has directed the group since that time. These dancers have grown to fame through his constant efforts. Since 1951 the Silver Spurs has toured annually each summer, performing throughout the United States and Canada and visiting historical areas.

Beginning dancers from Spokane area schools start their training in the sixth grade; by the time they are ready to travel with the touring group, they can perform with proficiency over two hundred fifty dances.

So high is the morale of the Silver Spurs dancers that there is always a long line of students eager to be elected to fill the few vacancies left open by graduation. Those accepted for training must have talent and must maintain high grades in their studies. Most of the boys are among the best school athletes and the girls are usually recognized leaders in school activities. Smoking or drinking alcoholic beverages is frowned upon; dismissal from the group follows upon an infraction of this self-imposed rule.

Each spring the Silver Spurs dancers board a rented bus to start a trip that will take them into dozens of large and small cities. With them go complete sets of costumes, special lighting equipment, and other props used in their dance sets.

The annual tours are conducted primarily for the broader education and wholesome pleasure of the youngsters and secondarily to spread knowledge of, and interest in, this healthful and enjoyable form of recreation. All traveling is done by bus, with adult chaperones and supervisors in charge. The tour follows a prearranged schedule of sponsored engagements. The fees charged by the Silver Spurs dancers for their performances barely cover their costs.

In 1972 their twenty-first year of touring was marked by their first trip abroad, consisting of a six-week tour through eight European countries. This performing tour, arranged by the American Heritage Association as part of their cultural exchange program, gave the young people an opportunity to visit private homes.

The Silver Spurs Boosters is a completely nonprofit organization. No salaries are received. Show and tour bookings, costume design and construction, and all other tasks are a labor of love.

Red has given unselfishly of his time and devotion in order to make these young people into fine young men and women as well as fine performers.

The Silver Spurs group is sponsored by parents and alumni, the Spokane Public Schools, and the Parks and Recreation Department.

Address: Spokane Schools, Spokane, Washington 99210.

V

GUIDELINES FOR FOLK DANCE GROUPS

Format of a Folk Dance Group

by Betty Casey

The facades of international folk dance sessions—clubs, classes, camps, festivals—present a kaleidoscopic reflection of diversity.

Leaders range from trained professionals and enthusiastic volunteers who "just picked up a few steps" to second generation immigrants nostalgically sharing native customs. Dancers—adolescent or mature, novice or expert—gather in community halls, on campuses, at posh hotels, or at rustic campgrounds (complete with bedrolls) to share the joys of joining hands and stepping lightly to the music of live (if lucky) or, more commonly, recorded fife and fiddle.

Most groups meeting regularly are set up on an instructor-class-club basis. They start out by mastering basic steps and simple dance routines, organize into a club, and continue learning more steps and more complicated dances at club meetings. The progress and selection of dances is dependent on the interests of the group, the range of expertise of the teacher, and the music available.

With a little prompting from a knowledgeable teacher, many experienced international folk dancers can do several hundred dances from many countries. During a two- or three-hour session some forty different selections may be danced.

A basic procedure is for the teacher to choose one or two familiar dances at the beginning and to intersperse instructions for new dances during the session. Between dances, the dancers may list requests for favorite numbers on a paper or chalkboard provided for this purpose. This practice necessitates either very versatile musicians or access to a suitable sound system and a large selection of appropriate records. (See the essay on "Sound Systems for Folk Dancing" at the end of this section.)

At Mary Ann and Michael Herman's class-club, held in one of the many rooms at the magnificent Armenian Church in New York City, punch and cookies are served on a table side-by-side with two other large tables jammed with many record cases holding LPs, EPs, 45s, and 78s. "We have music for at least 1,100 dances," observes Michael. They take them along whenever they teach.

An extensive record collection is among an international folk dance teacher's most valuable assets, espe-

cially since many of the recordings are no longer being pressed. (See the essay "Records for Folk Dancers, Then and Now" in this section.) At Jane Farwell's Folklore Village Farm in Dodgeville, Wisconsin, she concentrates on providing live musicians and falls back on records when necessary. Ron Houston, a teacher in Austin, Texas, has an extensive library of tapes (many of which were made from records).

Sessions covering several days and offering instruction for new dances by more than one teacher—in addition to an opportunity to enjoy old favorites—have come to be called camps, whether held in formal modern settings or at an abandoned schoolhouse with no indoor plumbing. Jane Farwell, who began the custom of holding folk dance camps, has written: "We washed our faces in the May morning dew, midst the fairy rings on an Oglebay hillside in 1941 and began, without realizing it, a wondrous tradition that has no ending. It was the very first Folk Dance Camp—the beginning of so much for so many of us—the delving into folklore and customs of peoples all over the world." (*My Heart Sings* booklet.)

There are now dozens of folk dance camps held throughout the country. The largest is an annual folk dance camp held in two identical one-week sessions on the campus of the University of the Pacific in California. (For details, see the last essay in Part III.) Dancers may live in dormitories and can even receive academic credit for attending. Top instructors present a wide variety of exciting dances from many countries. Gala evening parties include reviews of the dances taught.

Yet it is the regularly held class-clubs that keep folk dancing vibrantly alive. It is the patient teacher and the eager dancer who, week after week, work together to progress from a stumbling simple step-hop to a confident, intricate hambo turn, that keep it moving and meaningful. It is the thrill of figuratively joining hands with folks from foreign lands.

Leslie Fernandez has aptly described the folk dance experience this way: "I am a folk dancer. At night, along with many friends, we crawl out of offices, schools, hospitals, factories, shops, on-the-go trucks, cars and airplanes, and land together in some tucked away place—a schoolroom, a college gym, a rec[reation] center, a coffeehouse—and we get wildly civilized together. We share the joys of the ancient life, living in a Middle Earth.

"We take on new forms as the evening progresses. We can have nine heads, eighteen feet; we whistle, stomp, jump, and run around to the craziest music you've ever heard if you're a modern day AM-radio-raised American. That's called a kolo line. Or we can be coupled up and move always in a counterclockwise direction around a dance floor until a ring forms, [making a] path of the average of all of our steps. We can be perspiring, drowning, but always grinning or working.

"Our teachers are our guides as we explore new countries, new dances, new music. Their world is people, the music, the dance. Their world is moving, circling new faces, opening up to a new style of life, always present in the here and now but with a balcony view of the past. We, the learners, need only pass by to see the images to be shared, glimpsed at like mirrors. Each dance we learn is like a gem with many facets. Some are more complex than others, taking time to learn and relearn the steps, the rhythm. But once learned, a folk dance can be transported with you—through you, like some great little message nature's given you to communicate itself with.

"It all began for me a year ago. I heard music that I felt at home with and met people who knew some-thing else about our time on this earth and the best way to spend it. I latched shoulders and tripped over some new feet that I learned were mine and moved differently than I thought they ever could. In that time and place, I traveled to a Russian village, a Yugoslavian mountain home where goats live, [and] to an Israeli kibbutz.

"We don't have Yugoslavian villages here or any rocky crags to climb, but our feet, in the forming of steps and styling of our movements, tell that story. We dance lightly and quickly over the desert sands in Yemenite dances because the Yemenite would burn his feet if he were to tread heavily on the sands.

"I rhymed with summer seasons in Israel, Greece and the modern/ancient places in that newest summer of my life. I spent it dancing, friends around, people's faces whirling . . . I traveled farther that summer than I'd ever have set out to if my trips had been planned.

"I've been glad to greet the dance with all my friends around. I think dances are glad not to be forgotten; they are grateful to have us translate their messages into our lives.

"Come join the magic of the folk dance! *Yassou* and *Shalom* and *Hopa!*"

(The foregoing remarks, excerpted from an article by Leslie Fernandez that originally appeared in *Folk Dance Scene* magazine, are used here with permission.)

How to Build a Folk Dance Group

by Dean Linscott

I. Three Main Types of Beginning Folk Dance Groups
  A. School class
    1. Captive audience
    2. All-girl class (frequently) or all boys
    3. Finite time
  B. Repeating-type group, starting over every 6–12 months
    1. Leave "graduates" to shift for themselves
    2. Feed "graduates" into a class on next higher level of instruction
  C. "One-shot" group intended to advance progressively to intermediate, advanced, and perhaps to exhibition level

II. Basic Requirements
  A. Good sound equipment
    1. Continuously variable-speed phonograph or tape recorder with variable speed
  B. Good hall
    1. Adequate ventilation, especially in summer
    2. Floor: smooth, not slick; concrete is undesirable; pillars in dance area are dangerous
    3. Adequate size but not too large; not long and narrow
    4. Water fountain
    5. Kitchen facilities desirable
    6. Storage facilities helpful
    7. Not too close to residences (noise at night)

8. Cost reasonable for number of people expected; sometimes can get help by being sponsored by recreation department

III. Recruitment

A. Local papers (use photo of dancers if possible)

B. Posters in stores, schools, recreation departments, churches, libraries, other dance groups

C. Announcements at festivals, dance exhibitions (especially informal ones); use sign-up list to get names and addresses

D. Assistance through local folk dance councils

E. Word-of-mouth through personal contact by other folk dancers very important

F. Very helpful to have a basic nucleus of people who know each other, especially if they have some dance experience

IV. Let's Dance

A. Start with dances that are simple, but *not dull,* and teach and dance with *enthusiasm!* If you are bored by what you're doing, you won't fool the others. Good music is a great help. Whoop and holler when you feel like it—it's contagious.

B. Use a number of nonpartner dances and some mixers. Remember, it is no accident that the greatest number of young and enthusiastic dancers are usually found in groups that stress Balkan and Israeli dances!

C. Make use of the great variety there is among folk dances.

D. Don't just teach steps, teach dances. When you teach a basic step or movement, always follow it with one or two dances incorporating that step.

E. First demonstrate the dance; then teach it while standing in front of a line of dancers, all facing the same way as you are, if this is possible. Later, when doing the dance in a circle, the teacher (and preferably someone else opposite him) should dance toward the center, where all can see.

F. When teaching without music, be very careful to maintain the correct rhythm, even when going very slowly. If possible, hum or sing the tune as you go along. Then, either gradually increase the tempo as the step is practiced, so that when the music is put on the dancers can keep up with it, or else start slowly with the record and gradually speed it up until the proper tempo is reached. (With a tricky step, this may take two or three sessions.)

G. Don't be afraid to play the same dance again later in the evening, especially during the first few months of the class.

H. Have a bulletin board on which you can write the name of each dance as it is taught, and on which you can put the dance program for the evening. This helps people to learn the names of the dances more readily.

V. Maintaining and Building Greater Interest and Enthusiasm

A. Always have a social time as well as a dance time so that people may get to know one another, and *you.* The best way is to have punch and cookies (provided each week by a different person or two) after dancing, before going home. Name cards are a help.

B. Learn to sing the songs that accompany some of the easier dances, such as Vranjanka, Ajde Jano, Oj Ti Pile, Šetnja.

C. Mimeograph prompt notes for such songs, and for dances with several patterns, if possible.

D. Always start dancing exactly at the appointed time. If you are on time right from the beginning, you'll avoid a big headache later on. If dancers know they may miss their favorite dance if they're ten minutes late, they won't often be late.

E. Encourage everyone to dance with several partners each evening. When a difficult step or figure is being taught, have people move up around the circle and try it with several different partners.

F. If a dance has a large number of patterns, don't teach them all [in] one night! Teach three or four or five, then next time review those and add one or two more. This helps make the step sequence easier to remember.

G. Arrange to do an occasional dance exhibition for others, be it only for a local service club or art festival. This will give your dancers incentive to learn certain dances extra well and to start thinking about a costume. It may also provide you with new recruits if you are interested.

H. Keep a checklist of all dances taught and mark it each time you do them. This way you won't forget to put certain dances on the program, and everyone will keep up with all the dances all the time.

I. Once in a while give people an opportunity to indicate which dances they like the most and which ones the least. Then you can do certain ones more often and perhaps consider dropping others.

J. When your dancers have learned the basic

essentials of a dance, then offer them some pointers on style. Some will be interested, others won't, but try to get them to dance with at least some of the proper style and feeling that are part of nearly every real folk dance. Your good example will be their best inspiration.

K. In the matter of styling, women dance teachers have to be particularly careful in teaching Balkan dances because very frequently there is a sharp difference between the masculine and feminine dance styles. Your male dancers should be encouraged to use the large leg movements that are proper, while the women should be feminine at all times. Of course, it is also important for men teachers to try to show the proper style for women, as well as for men, when they teach.

L. In this regard, it is often stimulating to bring in an outside teacher now and then; someone with particular competence in dances from a particular area. Have [this person] give an intensive workshop or, better yet, arrange for a whole weekend with such an individual [and] learn the songs that go with some of the dances.

M. Give a special dance party now and then and invite other dancers to come.

N. Subscribe to *Let's Dance, Viltis,* and other folk dance periodicals and encourage your people to check out and read the magazines and to attend festivals.

O. When you observe that people are forgetting a particular dance, schedule a short review stressing the troublesome step, or steps, and the proper style. If only a few people are having trouble, have them come early some night and review the dance with them alone, avoiding repetition for the whole group.

P. Allow time on the program for requests whenever possible, drawing from dances that have already been taught.

Q. Take particular care about your music. Always play records at a comfortable speed for dancing. Replace [scratched] or noisy records. If several records are available for the same dance, arrange to listen to them and buy the most appealing one. Sometimes the music can make or break a dance!

R. In general, don't teach a dance *you* don't like. Your lack of enthusiasm will help to kill it for the others.

VI. Maintaining Membership

A. Any group that fails to take in any new mem-

bers will sooner or later dwindle and die. At first, adding new members is no problem; if they come, you take them in and they learn along with the rest.

B. But after two or three years, a potential new member will be intimidated by the large number of seemingly difficult dances done by the group unless he is either one of those rare "natural-born dancers" that learns a dance the first time through or else has had considerable dance experience elsewhere. People of this calibre will probably be few and far between.

C. Thus, you may be faced with the problem of trying to start up a new beginning class to feed into the main group when they are ready. This works out best when the same teacher is teaching both groups, for several reasons, and when both groups meet in the same or nearly the same geographical area.

D. Expect to spend at least eight to ten months teaching a new class before [the dancers] will know enough dances to feel at home in the regular group. Teach them the basic steps, such as waltz, polka and schottische, and dances utilizing these steps, as well as the other dances done by the regular group.

E. Prepare them for switching over to the regular group very carefully; otherwise you may find that they want to continue as a separate group. Invite them to the regular group a few times, making sure they are not snowed under by seeing a lot of fast, difficult dances they don't know. Also, have some of the regular group come to the beginning group, when possible, so that they begin to get acquainted with one another. The main problem is a fear that the beginners (who are really no longer beginners, after eight to ten months of weekly meetings) will have that the regular group is so much better, that they will just be a handicap to the regular group.

F. In the same way, it is important for the regular group to realize it will have to make certain adjustments for the newcomers; and if they are not willing to make these adjustments, the beginner class should never have been started in the first place. These adjustments include a friendly willingness to dance with the less experienced dancers and to help them progress; a slowing of the pace at which new dances can be learned: more repetition of simpler dances that may be "old hat" to the older members of the group; and efforts on the part of everyone to make the newcomers feel that they are unqualified full-fledged members of the group.

(This article first appeared in *Let's Dance* magazine and is used here with permission. Dean Linscott, who has also written the essay "Dance Floor Manners" in this section, has been active as a folk dancer for over twenty years. Dr. Linscott has a Ph.D. in microbiology and is an associate professor at the prestigious University of California Medical Center in San Francisco. He and his wife, Nancy, are two of the five directors of the Mendocino Folklore Camp; they also originated, and continue to conduct, the North-South California Folk Dance Teachers' Seminar.

Besides teaching a full course load at the Medical Center, Dr. Linscott teaches a very lively folk dance group every Tuesday during lunch hour and again that evening in the Medical Center's gymnasium. He also teaches an advanced class in Mill Valley on Friday night and directs an exhibition group, the Kopachka Dancers.) [See essay on Kopachka Dancers in Part IV.]

From Words to Movement

by Fred Berk

Fundamentals of Folk Dancing

There are five basic elements which are necessary to know in order to be clear and specific about a dance: *Steps, Rhythm, Space, Dynamics,* and *Characteristics.* Following are the definitions:

Steps (See Lexicon of Folk Dance Definitions).

Rhythm is the organized division of time. To make the student more conscious of a rhythm, the teacher should clap it first and have the student repeat it. For example, if in a dance there are two slow steps and four fast ones, the student will have to clap slowly twice and fast four times. By so doing, it will be easier to transfer the rhythm to the feet.

Space includes Formation and Direction.

1. *Formation*—of couple dances, lines, squares, and circles. There are endless variations of space patterns which differ in almost every dance. Their differences should be made very clear to the students.

2. *Direction*—of forward, backward, sideward right, sideward left. A circle is a combination of the four basic directions. Diagonals are between the basic directions. There are two levels, high (jumps and leaps) and low (squatting or on the floor).

Every given instruction must include these three basic elements. For example:

Movement	Direction	Rhythm
1. step on right foot	2. forward	3. count 1

After the student learns the dance and knows it well, the last two elements should be introduced.

Dynamics is the strength or the accents in which a dance is performed. If such accents are not included, a dance will be dull and monotonous. Dynamics in dance relates to dynamics in music, in which various degrees of loudness and softness create the necessary expression.

Characteristics (style): Once a pupil masters all the above-mentioned points, the teacher will have to explain the characteristics of a dance. These characteristics determine its style and execution. There are love dances, gay and flirtatious ones. A dance might have a bouncy quality like the Arabic dances or be fluid and soft like the dances of the Yemenites. They can be vigorous and ecstatic like most horas. These differences will influence the movement quality and the style of a dance.

With added dynamics and characteristics, the pupils will become emotionally involved. They will not only do mechanical steps and movements but will also experience the essence of folk dancing.

Teaching Beginners

When a teacher meets a group for the first time, it is most important that he makes the pupils feel completely at ease. They must feel very comfortable about the steps they are about to learn and be given the feeling that they will be able to execute them without difficulty. When teaching beginners, the simplest dance should be selected. This way, no one in the group will have difficulty following the teacher's instruction. An atmosphere of enjoyment and unity is thus immediately created.

An important point to emphasize is that "anyone who can walk can folk dance." Folk dancing is actually "walking to music," and this is what they should attempt to do. Psychologically, this definition helps people a great deal; they usually tend to become very tense when thinking in terms of "dancing." When told to walk, however, they will feel much more comfortable and more relaxed.

Another important aspect in teaching folk dancing is that beginners should not be bothered with details about movements and steps. On the contrary, the teacher should simplify the steps if necessary and not trouble them with burdensome and complicated details. If beginners are forced to do steps they cannot execute, they will feel stiff and very awkward and unable to enjoy it. They will probably never try to folk dance anymore.

The main task in introducing the newcomers to folk dancing is to arouse the emotions of the participants and give them the feeling of accomplishment, of exhilaration, and of genuine fun.

Points for the Teacher

Be thoroughly prepared before facing a class. Know your material very well.

Tell the name of the dance. If possible, interpret the meaning. Then stress the formation. Which way to face—clockwise or counterclockwise. Always start with feet together, with equal distribution of weight on both feet. This way one can start with the right or left foot.

Do not teach a Yemenite step to beginners. It is difficult. If you have to, modify the step until your pupils are ready. Then teach it the proper way.

Teach every dance in sections. Repeat each section until the group remembers it well. Only then should you continue with the next part. To remember movements and steps is a new experience for beginners. Therefore, it is necessary to teach a dance in a gradual development.

If you feel a dance cannot be taught successfully in a circle, let the pupils form lines facing forward. You will have to stand with your back to your pupils in order to face the same way. After you are confident that your pupils have learned the steps, they can return to do the dance in the proper formation.

Use images to get movement qualities across. For example, a shuffling step can be taught by having your pupils pretend that they are walking on sand and creating a swishing sound. Or jumping in place can be accomplished much better if the students are told that the floor is burning hot and they cannot stop on the floor but must try to stop in the air.

Prompt steps in order to facilitate the learning process of a dance. Stop prompting only when you are sure that everyone remembers the sequence.

You have to be patient. You must never lose your temper.

You must make students understand that with practice the most difficult hurdle can be overcome.

You should give encouragement wherever you feel it is necessary.

You should be able to project to your students your enthusiasm about the material you are teaching.

Teachers have to have empathy. They should understand the problems a student has to go through while learning a dance. Then they will not just be teachers but very good ones.

(This essay was excerpted from *Ha-rikud, the Jewish Dance,* by Fred Berk, and is here used with permission.)

Costumes for Folk Dancing

by Betty Casey

There is no single international folk dance costume. Many dancers expend a great deal of time, money, and effort acquiring elaborate "authentic" costumes (or copies) with just the right braid or embroidered designs—often directly from the countries represented by particular dances. Others settle for casual modern clothing or a basic full skirt and peasant blouse for women and slacks, shirt, and colorful vest for men. (See the directions at the end of this essay on how to put together a basic folk dance costume.)

Though regional dress is still worn in many lands, modern clothes are slowly gaining the lead. It is increasingly difficult to find, or even emulate, elaborate foreign costumes because many provincial groups prefer new styles. Even the Eskimos are turning more and more to synthetic fabrics. When asked why she didn't wear wooden shoes, a young Dutch woman asked, "Why don't Americans wear high-top button shoes?"

As a rule, foreign costumes that appeared so quaint and appealing were not costumes at all; they were the everyday dress of the villagers or the ruling gentry in the country of origin. The dress of European peasants differed from that worn by those better off because of their work and the need for strong fibers in their clothing to withstand hard wear. Even if they were able to afford good cloth, they were prohibited from wearing it by sumptuary decrees that not only banned the use of fine fabrics but that of beautiful colors as well. The peasants were limited in their choice of dyes; they were thus compelled to use earth colors, which furnished the prevalent grays, browns, and dull greens. In addition, the coarse, homespun quality of their dress proclaimed their lowly status in society.

Sumptuary laws forbidding extravagant raiment date back to biblical times and were common in ancient Greece and Rome. They were so strictly enforced in the fourteenth and fifteenth centuries in Europe that penalties in the form of fines were imposed on those who disobeyed. This was the case even in the early years of the American colonies.

The discovery and settling of the new continents brought about an increase in commerce and wealth for the nobility and the upper classes. This gave rise to ostentatious displays in dress, which made use of handsome oriental fabrics: brocades, velvets, gold lace, feathers, and jewels.

Religious leaders who had long worn gorgeous robes

disapproved of the extravagance of the nobles but did not dare rebuke them. Denied these riches, the peasants decorated their plain homespuns with colorful hand stitchery and beautiful handmade lace. The general style of clothing remained somewhat constant but the embroidery became more and more elaborate. Cherished pieces were kept in handsome wooden chests and handed down as precious heirlooms from generation to generation.

Recognizable, unique designs developed in villages hemmed in by mountains and far from traveled roads. Many village fashions lasted a century or more and peasant dress did not become folk dress until around 1800, when it developed into festival dress for use in church, weddings, christenings, or funerals. For funerals a black armband was added and is still worn today in many places.

Elegant Spanish fashions influenced the mode of dress in European courts and became so familiar that the peasantry incorporated some of these fashion ideas into their own dress. These included the doublet, or short jacket, for men and the laced and corseted bodice for women, both of which are important features of folk dance outfits even today. Eastern, Oriental, and African dress consisted of beautifully woven lengths of cloth draped around the body in picturesque folds.

According to a bulletin reprinted from the Society for International Folk Dancing in England, in *Let's Dance* magazine, "A folk costume is not something which sprang up in the night; neither is it necessarily one particular style of clothing worn by any particular part of a community; nor is it a period costume. It is a collection of apparel put together over a number of years, often over centuries, and springs from the geographical, mental, historical, fashionable, and spiritual characteristics of a people.

"Many parts of a costume may be traced back to the Middle Ages and beyond. The short coats worn with so many costumes were worn all through the Middle Ages and were continually changing in detail up to the 18th and 19th centuries. The wide metal decorated belt dates from an even earlier age. Many pieces of clothing were added to the old costume, but often the old pieces were not discarded. Thus we are confronted with two hats or two jackets worn simultaneously. Elements from a particular style were adapted, presupposing the original fashionable style of high society. The lace bodices of women's dresses are adaptations from the corsets of the court lady, but the peasant, having no maid, had to have the lacing at the front instead of the back.

"Tight knee-breeches were in the fashionable world in the 17th century and were commonly worn by peasants in many countries by the 18th century, thus taking close to 100 years to infiltrate successfully the popular peasant taste. The military influence was great in Europe and traces may be found in almost every man's costume: the long coat, the frequent use of red and blue, the long boots, which were probably introduced into Europe by the Turkish invaders, and the headwear.

"Superstition takes a hand. Many parts of the costume were worn originally to ward off evil: edges decorated with fur on leather or with strips of red (a protective color); geometrical patterns in lace and embroidery (protective symbols); metal objects, rings, and buttons (the shining objects defeat the evil eye); embroidery patterns, left unfinished or with a deliberate inaccuracy in the design (so that the devil may not be imprisoned in the embroidery)—all were important to the credulous peasant.

"The strong trousers of the man, the useful skirt of the woman, the stout-heeled shoes, the footless socks (straw being considered cheaper, stronger, and more comfortable than socks), all combining with the ribbons, sequins, beads, laces, and embroideries to make one garment fit for both work and festive occasions. Folk costumes become reasonably static about 100 years ago, and any costume presenting style, color, or fabric introduced to the world after that period should be regarded with caution.

"From the above points you have a reasonable guide to authenticity; and when making a costume from a picture or postcard, bear these points in mind. As English [i.e., British] people we have no national right to a folk costume and our European friends have a natural reluctance to seeing us wear their costumes in a casual, sloppy, or inaccurate reproduction or manner. We would do well to remember the pride and affection they have for their national costume and watch ourselves to see that we do not offend through lack of knowledge or thoughtlessness."

A Basic Folk Dance Costume

A comfortable, basic costume can add enjoyment to practice sessions, evening dances, and folk dance weekend camps. Elaborate, delicate, or cumbersome authentic costumes are usually saved for special national programs.

Along with comfortable shoes—Balkan opankes, black pumps, boots, or slippers—there are three similar and basic components to costumes for both men and women from many countries. For women, they include a full skirt, a peasant blouse, and a weskit or bodice; for men, loose, dark pants, a long-sleeved shirt, and a vest.

The skirt, which may be a solid color or a print, can be gathered, ruffled, tiered, or full circle; the blouse can be long- or short-sleeved but should be loose enough not to bind. The bodice or weskit can be of contrasting color. The addition of appropriate embroidery, flowers, sashes, scarves, ribbons, a bonnet, or an apron (which can be made from a linen or cotton towel) will change the emphasis according to the nationality of the dance.

Men may tuck pant legs into boots, high stockings, or tie them at the knees as they switch from Russian to Scandinavian to Irish dances. They may add a sash and a sombrero if they wish to go Mexican; they can also add dash to the vest with gold or silver buttons.

The following books may be consulted for more detailed information on costuming: Emma Calderini, *Il Costume Populare in Italia* (Milan: Sperling e Kupfer, 1934); Varagnac, *French Costumes* (London: Hyperion Press); Joseph Leeming, *The Costume Book* (New York: Lippincott, 1938); Wasmuth, *Osteuropäische Volkstrachten* (Dr. Selle & Co.); Angela Bradshaw, *World Costumes* (New York: Macmillan, 1953); Kathleen Mann, *Peasant Costume in Europe,* 2 vols. (London: A & C Black Ltd, 1931–39); and Folk Dance Federation of California, Inc., *Costume Basics* (1275 "A" St., Rm. 111, Hayward, California 94541.

(Quoted material in this essay originally appeared in the form of a bulletin by the Society for International Folk Dancing in England, published in 1975 in *Let's Dance* magazine, and is here reprinted by permission.)

Dance Floor Manners

by Dean Linscott

Most of us dance for pleasure and would not intentionally diminish the pleasure of others on the floor by thoughtless behavior. But through lack of knowledge, overenthusiasm, or just plain carelessness, dancers sometimes offend others needlessly. Perhaps a word or two about dance floor manners would not be amiss.

In general, in couple dances that are not done in sets your main concern should be for your partner. Except in a learning situation (where most of the following would not apply), avoid asking a person to dance with you if you don't know the dance; and, conversely, don't drag someone out on the floor to do *your* favorite dance if that person doesn't know it unless it is very easy, you know it well, and you are sure that your partner can follow your lead. If you're not sure whether someone knows a dance, ask. Don't be one of those persons who hauls a poor, unsuspecting beginner through a ten-figure Russian dance, to the discomfort of others and the acute embarrassment of the beginner. And keep in mind that others besides your partner may be affected if either of you does not know the dance. If you go the wrong way and run into others, if you can't keep up and hold back those behind you or otherwise interfere with the progress of others on the floor, it won't be to your credit. In a fast-flowing dance such as the hambo, if for any reason you find you must stop, don't do it in the middle of the dance floor! People have been injured by running into someone who unexpectedly stopped in the middle of a fast-moving pattern. Get off the floor as quickly as you can, preferably by flowing with the traffic as much as you can. On the other hand, be patient with newer dancers and realize that only by practice can they become better. Just as in skiing or ice-skating, better dancers can make allowances for those less skilled without causing them unnecessary concern over their less-than-perfect performances. We were all in their shoes at one time or another!

In the matter of set dances, such as squares, contras, Scottish country dances and many others involving more than one couple in a co-ordinated unit, the dancer has a responsibility to others in addition to his partner. If you don't know the dance, you will spoil the pleasure of others in your set who do know it. Even if you realize your mistake at the last minute and withdraw, by that time the rest of the sets have frequently been formed, leaving the others in your set with no one with whom to finish it out. So before you get out on the floor, make *sure* that both you and your partner know the dance. And when you join a set, be sure you do so courteously, don't displace other couples from their positions if they got there before you did.

If a longways set is forming, *never* join at the head of the set (between the first couple and the stage, caller, or music); join at the opposite end. Even if there are only four couples forming up for a Scottish dance, such as the white heather jig, it is very discourteous to join except at the bottom end of the set; if two or three couples join at once, it may displace someone who was already there first. The last to arrive should be the first to leave if the set is overfilled. In a very long set it is the responsibility of the man in the head couple to go down the set and either number people off or divide them into groups, as required for the particular dance. And, lastly, we have all seen a case where a person or a couple who admittedly does not know the dance is asked to join in anyway to fill out the set. It is incumbent upon everyone else in that set to help this person or couple get through the dance; if they don't quite make it and foul things up, there is certainly no reason to blame them or get angry with them. Rather, they should be treated sympathetically and thanked for their effort.

In the matter of nonpartner or line dances, there are perhaps more misunderstandings about proper etiquette than with any other kind of dance. Although you don't have a partner to worry about, that does *not* mean that you are responsible only to yourself. You are responsible to those on either side of you in the line, to the extent that if you move the wrong way or do the step poorly it will directly interfere with the enjoyment of the dance by those next to you. You might even impede the progress of a whole line of dancers. If you do not know a line dance, the best place to learn it is *behind* the line, not in it. Most nonpartner dances are done in an open circle, or line, and consequently have a leader to whom others can look for proper steps, style, and clues as to changes in the routine.

Of the general mix of Israeli, Greek, Yugoslav, Bulgarian, Romanian, Turkish and other line dances done in the United States, I would estimate that about 95 per cent or more move predominantly to the right, and consequently have the leader on the right-hand end of the line. A small number of dances lead to the left and even fewer move equally in both directions; in the latter the leader is usually on the right. *Do not* join a line by displacing the leader! If you don't know which way it leads, wait until it starts. Conversely, do not take the lead position for a dance unless you know it *very well*. Others will look to you for help, and if you don't know what you are doing the whole thing will fall apart. Don't clown around or put Israeli styling in a Greek dance. Rather, put your best into it so that others will see how it is properly danced. If you are not up to that, don't lead.

In some dances the leader may from time to time do different variations. Only experience will tell you whether others in the line are expected to follow him by doing the new step or only watch and appreciate it. It is quite discourteous for someone other than the leader to try to initiate a new variation, except in those instances where any step may be done as long as it flows along with the general movement of the line. Since the leader may signal for everyone to change to a new step, it is important for everyone in the line to keep an eye on the leader and to be alert for such changes. On the other hand, the leader has a responsibility to do this at proper times in the musical phrase, and to avoid the temptation to show that he is better than everyone else by calling changes faster than the others can adapt to them. Don't forget that the dance is for the enjoyment of *all* the dancers, not just the leader.

A few words should be said about ethnic dance situations. If you are in a Greek nightclub (a real one, not a tourist trap) or at a Bulgarian picnic or a Serbian Church gathering, be a little modest and humble. Watch what is happening and be hesitant about barging in and showing everyone how well *you* can dance. You might even learn something by careful observation. And you might be thrown out the door, or worse, if you insist on grabbing hold of a few Greek buddies who have paid the band to play their favorite tsamiko so that they can dance together. If you are invited to participate, or if you see others joining in and are sure it is OK, and if you know the dance, then by all means get out there and do your best. Be open to learning; after all, chances are that some of those dancing have been doing so most of their lives, and their style and feel for the dance, though it might only be a simple pravo, are likely to be better than your thirteen-figure kopanica.

Dancing is fun. Enhance your own dancing pleasure, and that of those around you, by using good sense and common courtesy on the dance floor. You won't be sorry!

Records for Folk Dancers, Then and Now

by Ed Kremers

When the folk dance movement, as we now know it, was getting started in the last years of the 1930s, there were very few records being produced for this specialized field. Other than an odd one here and there, the only organized series was the RCA Victor "School" records, many of which were played by brass bands; they were mostly intended for the simpler dances such as Ace of Diamonds, Bleking, and Come Let Us Be Joyful. Because of the general availability of these records, they became the backbone of early collections. These dances were performed not only by children but also by adults, even at festivals.

The Henry Ford collection of Early American dance records—mostly covering such dances as the simple square, heel and toe polka, schottische, and the Virginia reel—was made available as a result of Mr. Ford's personal interest in old-time dancing. These pressings were discontinued after his death.

The record problem in those early days was generally solved in the following manner: A teacher would learn of a dance either in a discussion with elderly dancers about dances of their youth or by finding dance descriptions in old books or manuscripts; the teacher would first analyze the dance in terms of structure (measures, bars, counts, figures, repeats) and then look for a record that was fairly close to the dance in structure and in timing (polka, schottische, waltz, mazurka) and proceed to adapt the dance to the record. If the dance was, say, Russian, the teacher would attempt to find a Russian record—but if that was not possible, the dance would often be done to a record of another nationality—Scandinavian or whatever was available and fit the dance!

Since most of the records used had been produced by national orchestras for the general music trade, they were usually well played and the folk dancers thus got the benefit of good ethnic music. As the demand for folk dance records grew, a few companies began to produce records that could be sold both to the national and folk dance trade. Among the early companies were Kismet (mostly Russian at first; later expanded to include general folk dance and even squares), Scandinavia-Cordion (Scandinavian; many tunes played on an accordion, as the name indicates), and Sonart (Russian, other Slavic, and then general folk dance). All of these were New York firms.

Records in the "World of Fun" series (Methodist folk games records) were issued in groups of three, until they reached a total of twenty-one; then the entire series was reissued on seven LPs in a boxed set.

In California, Al Toft, a San Francisco folk dance teacher and orchestra leader, was hired by a new Los Angeles firm, Imperial Records, and recorded an initial series of eight "most-needed" dances on four records: Road to the Isles, Dashing White Sergeant, Black Hawk waltz, Laces and Graces, Wooden Shoes, Eide Ratas, Meitschi Putz Di, and Weggis dance. The recording session was supervised by Ed Kremers and other original members of the research committee of the Folk Dance Federation of California. For a time these were the most widely used records in folk dancing. As a result of success with these records, Imperial went on to produce about one hundred more records for folk, square, and round dancing.

After the folk dancers had popularized such Italian dances as Sicilian and Neapolitan tarantellas and the Italian quadrille, the major company records being used were no longer being pressed (as so often happens!). With the encouragement of the Federation (of which he had been an early president), Ed Kremers produced two records on the Oliver label containing the three dances previously cited plus an Italian danza. These are still available, as Festival 45 rpm records.

Michael and Mary Ann Herman, of the New York City Folk Dance House, started producing records on the Folk Dancer MH label. These were very successful; their catalog now contains several hundred titles. [Michael Herman's band was among the first to be recorded on RCA Victor folk dance records and the Methodist "World of Fun" series. His contribution to the beginnings of folk dance recorded music was among the most noteworthy.]

A few good dance records were produced in foreign countries, particularly England, under such labels as HMV, English DB and DX (Columbia), Parlophone, and Beltona. Later, Telefunken, Tanz, and Tanz der Volker came from Germany; some privately produced records were issued by folk dance organizations in Scandinavia; and U.S.S.R. (CCHP) records were received from Russia.

Frank Kaltman, an ex-Californian, moved to New Jersey, where he started the Folkraft Company with a few square dance records, moving into folk dance and building up a very useful catalog of several hundred records. Frank died, but the company is operating under his successor.

With the growth of the Balkan dance movement, records for the kolo dancers were furnished by Balkan Records of Chicago, Jugoton from Jugoslavia and, in California, Kolo Festival and Xopo (Horo). Several Philippine dance teachers have toured the United States, teaching dances mostly from the Mico (Manila) label, and some from the Villar label, also from the Philippines. Many of the early Israeli dances were performed to records furnished by the Israel Music Foundation in New York City—first as ten-inch LPs, then as twelve-inch LPs and also 45 rpm discs.

As the knowledge of how to go about having records made became more widespread, numerous teachers began to have records made for their own use; some of the first to try this included Madelynne Greene, Henry (Buzz) Glass, Virgil Morton, Grace Perryman Nicholes, and Grace West Newman. These were on the old ten-inch 78 rpm discs.

When the making of twelve-inch LP records became relatively easy, some of the professional dance teachers began to put their dances on that type of disc, preferring to use these rather than continuing to look for danceable music on records already produced by commercial record manufacturers. This trend has continued to this day (1981), with the result that most of the "new" folk dances are now available only on privately produced records; the old labels, such as RCA Victor, Columbia, and Decca, are seldom encountered in the folk dance business.

(As a country boy in rural northwest Oregon, Ed Kremers learned old-time dances, such as the three-step and Paul Jones, at Saturday night Grange dances performed to the music of a player piano. After earning three college degrees and putting in time as an office worker and a schoolteacher, he became an officer in the Navy Supply Corps during World War II. While stationed in the San Francisco area, Ed ran into folk and square dancing at a church party and was soon teaching and calling himself. He attended one of the first Lloyd Shaw summer camps in Colorado and was elected the second president of the Folk Dance Federation of California. At that time he founded and acted as first editor of *Let's Dance* magazine. After World War II, Ed opened the first shop anywhere to specialize in records and other supplies for folk, square, round, contra, and ballroom dancing; he also taught all of these dance forms professionally.

Ed has been on the staffs of many camps and workshops, including the camps at Stockton, Idyllwild, Santa Barbara, and San Diego. He has supervised the production of folk dance records and has written many articles on dancing. Besides serving as Federation president, he has been club president and president of the San Francisco Council of Folk Dance Groups. Currently he is a member of the committee that presents the annual San Francisco Kolo Festival each Thanksgiving week. He is a charter member of the Square Dance Callers Association of Northern California and has called at many national square dance conventions.)

Selected Record Sources

Compiled by Betty Casey

Aardvark Foreign Records
  Foreign and folk dance records and tapes
  259 E. Blake Avenue, Columbus, Ohio 43201
Alcazar Productions—Philo Records
  Producers of records for contra and square dancing
  8 Lindbergh Drive, Latham, N.Y. 12110
Aman Folk Ensemble
  LPs and 45s recorded by the Aman Orchestra
  1438 Gower Street, Rm. 371, Hollywood, Calif. 90028
Armadillo Folk Dance Records
  Small selection of IFD records
  P.O. Box 8575, Austin, Tex. 78712
Bay Records
  Small record company specializing in folk music recorded in this country—Balkan, Scottish, others
  1516 Oak Street, Suite 320, Alameda, Calif. 94501
Canada Ed. Media, Ltd. (Canadian F. D. Record Service)
  Folk dance and educational records; many labels
  185 Spadina, Toronto 2B, Ontario, Canada
Country Dance and Song Society of America
  Traditional American and English books and records
  505 Eighth Avenue, Rm. 2500, New York, N.Y. 10018

Country Dance in Connecticut, Inc.
  Country dance records
  Box 502, Bolton, Conn. 06040
Ed Kremer's Folk Showplace
  Folk and square dance needs
  161 Turk Street
  San Francisco, Calif. 94102
Festival Records
  Folk dance and foreign records
  2769 West Pico Boulevard, Los Angeles, Calif. 90006
Folk Arts Center of New England, Inc.
  Comprehensive record service
  62 Fottler Avenue, Lexington, Mass. 02173
Folk Dance Music International
  Domestic and imported folk dance, square dance, ballroom, and novelty dance records—45s, LPs; free catalog
  230 Seventh Avenue (bet. 23–24 Sts.), New York, N.Y. 10011
Folk Dancer Record Co.
  Comprehensive folk dance record service
  P.O. Box 201, Flushing, N.Y. 11352
Folk Dance Underground Records
  P.O. Box 2563, Culver City, Calif. 90230
Folklore Imports
  Scandinavian music for dancing and listening; catalog available
  800 Linden Avenue, Boulder, Colo. 80302
Folk Motif
  2752 E. Broadway, Long Beach, Calif. 90803
Folkraft Dance Record Center
  Free catalog
  10 Fenwick Street, Newark, N.J. 07114
Hebraica Record Distrib.
  Israeli and Jewish records
  402 Burns Street, Forest Hills, N.Y. 11375
June Appal Recordings
  Appalachian folk music
  Box 743A, Whitesburg, Ky. 41858
Kalox Record Co.
  316 Starr Street, Dallas, Tex. 75203
Kismet Record Co.
  Distribution of Russian and Ukrainian records
  227 E. 14th Street, New York, N.Y. 10003
Lloyd Shaw Foundation
  American and country dance records; educational records
  1890 Darlee Court, Lakewood, Colo. 80215
Merrbach Record Service
  Square and round dance records
  323 W. 14th Street, Houston, Tex. 75008
Minerva House of Greek Music
  2936 W. Broadway, Vancouver, B.C., Canada

Miro (Monitor) Music, Inc.
Many international records; free catalog
P.O. Box 342, Old Chelsea Station, New York, N.Y. 10011

Nama Records
Three LPs with dance descriptions by Dick Crum
2367 Glendon Avenue, Los Angeles, Calif. 90064

Phil Maron's Folk Shop
1531 Clay Street, Oakland, Calif. 94612

Request Records
Manufacturer of international ethnic music from 66 different countries, including folk and dance music; catalog
3800 S. Ocean Drive, Hollywood, Fla. 33019

Rhythms Production Records
Collection of folk dance standards and other records for school use
Box 34485, Los Angeles, Calif. 90034

Robertson Dance Supplies
Folk, school, square, and round dance records by mail; free brochure
3600 33rd Avenue, Sacramento, Calif. 95824

Steve Zalph's Folk Dance Record Service
Large selection of 45s and LPs
P.O. Box 174, New York, N.Y. 10016

Turkish Folk Dance Records
P.O. Box 9051, Berkeley, Calif. 94709

Worldtone Music, Inc.
Comprehensive folk dance record service
230 Seventh Avenue, New York, N.Y. 10011

Worldwide Records and Imports
Specializing in international folk dance music; send for free catalog
125 Lowry Avenue, NE, Minneapolis, Minn. 55110

Dance Descriptions

by Betty Casey

Throughout the history of the dance, various methods have been utilized for recording dance steps, movements, and routines in order to preserve them for future presentation. These have included crude stick figures scratched into walls by cave dwellers, written and oral descriptions, step patterns illustrated by footprints in books, and the very sophisticated abstract symbols used in a method called Labanotation. The method is named for its creator, Rudolph Laban.

Outside of actual filming, Labanotation is the most accurate method for showing all facets of dance routines—footwork, arm and hand movements, and precise torso and head movements. The method has been used for several years in Europe to record ballets and is being used increasingly in the United States by dance specialists. For use with their Selectric typewriter, International Business Machines Corporation (IBM) has designed a Labanotation element that makes it possible to type an entire dance. "Isn't it marvelous," said Fred Berk, an Israeli dance authority, "that now the beautiful dance forms, complete with details, can be preserved accurately for posterity. A dance can be written, like a music score, and the dance reproduced at will."

However, using Labanotation isn't quite that simple. It is a complicated new language requiring training for use and interpretation. Although some folk dances have been Labanotated, it has not yet become generally used in writing folk dance directions.

The dance descriptions presented in this book are basically similar but differ slightly since they were written by various instructors. Interpretation requires the understanding of abbreviations, terms, movements, formations, step descriptions, and rudimentary musical terms that are defined and described in the Lexicon of Folk Dance Definitions. The usual format followed in the latter includes an introduction giving the name of the dance, the source, a label and number for a suitable recording, the appropriate formation and steps, and the musical meter. The pattern description is presented in chart form, with the measures numbered in a left-hand column and corresponding instructions for precise steps and counts described in the right-hand column.

Publications for Folk Dancers

by Vytautas Beliajus

The very first folk dance magazine to appear on the scene was *Lore* (1936–38), for which I was editor. It was published by the Chicago Park District with WPA money. *Lore* resembled the current *Viltis;* in a way, it was a forerunner of *Viltis.* When WPA was eliminated, so was *Lore. Viltis* still has at least four subscribers I am aware of who also received *Lore:* Pat Parmelee, Gretel Dunsing, Jerry Joris Lindsay, and Charlotte Chen.

Then two good little magazines appeared on the scene: *The Folk Dancer,* by Mary Ann and Michael

Herman, and *Rosin the Bow,* by Rod LaFarge. Both had good material, but they were short-lived. During the early 1940s, in two widely separated areas, two seeds that proved to be of lasting importance were planted. *Viltis* began in Fairhope, Alabama, first as a mimeographed "strictly service" newsletter to friends in the armed forces and later in printed form (as of September 1944), with a gradual incorporation of folkloric and folk dance material. In San Francisco and the Bay Area, the Folk Dance Federation of California (presently with North and South divisions), started *Let's Dance* magazine (1275 "A" Street, Rm. 111, Hayward, Calif. 94541) as a Federation organ. Both of these magazines have served their subscribers' needs well. *Viltis* specializes in background material and ethnic news. Many articles that first appeared in *Viltis* have been reprinted in many magazines in the United States, Canada, England, and also by various institutions. It has a worldwide reputation.

As with folk dance teachers, there has been a proliferation of folk dance magazines that has been phenomenal. Many were short-lived—the spirit was willing but the flesh (i.e., money) failed to rise to the occasion, most often while these magazines were still in their infancy. Others survived early obstacles and are serving their readers well. There are many "strictly club" magazines that stick with the news and activities of their member clubs; examples are *Latest Steps* (Sacramento) and *Scandia News Notes* (Seattle).

A number of federational (regional) publications that include additional folkloristic "goodies"—background material, dance descriptions, songs, recipes— such as those found in *Northwest Folkdancer* or *Ontario Folk-Dancer.* Two publications in particular stand out: *Folk Dance Scene* (Los Angeles) and *Folk Dance Scene* (Baton Rouge). Both are published in mimeographed form.

The Los Angeles *Folk Dance Scene* (Paul Pritchard, 13250 Ida Avenue, Los Angeles, Calif. 90066) serves its region (southern California) exceptionally well. Nearly every folk dance club and activity is listed and described; it is a real guidebook to Los Angeles and the South (and elsewhere, to a lesser degree).

Of course, the folk dance "scene" in Baton Rouge can hardly compare with what is taking place in Los Angeles. However, what is lacking in directory-type information is replaced with good background articles; Louisiana is rich in diverse ethnic lore. *Folk Dance Scene's* editor and publisher, Vonnie Brown (4431 Blecker Drive, Baton Rouge, La. 70809), follows a *Viltis*-type "personalized editorship."

Another publication, now defunct, appeared in New York City under the title *Mixed Pickles* (Ray LaBarbera, P.O. Box 500, Midwood Station, Brooklyn, N.Y. 11230). It was basically a calendar of events such as that which appeared in Ray's *Folk Dance Directory.*

Northern Junket (Ralph Page, 117 Washington Street, Keene, N.H. 03431) has been around for many years even if it does appear irregularly. It is produced in mimeographed form and is published by contra dance authority Ralph Page, a delightful gentleman whose New England sense of humor is reflected in his publication. The pages of *Northern Junket* are filled with nostalgia, folklore, and contra and square dance background material.

Tradition, published by the National Council for the Traditional Arts in tabloid-newspaper form, is now in its seventh year (although not in the same format). Basically, it is the organ of the National Folk Festival Association [NFFA], which was organized by Sarah Gertrude Knott way back in 1934. It mainly discusses the NFFA and participating groups and individuals; it also provides some background information and lists events (*Tradition,* 1346 Connecticut Avenue, NW, Washington, D.C. 20036).

Le Troubadour (8440 Boulevard St. Laurent, #205, Montreal, Quebec, Canada H2P 2M5) is the very latest publication to appear on the scene. It is unique because it is bilingual (French and English). Its editor, Yves Moreau, is well known in the folk dance world. Published by the Canadian Folk Arts Council (Le Conseil Canadien des Arts Populaires) *Le Troubadour* is a slick magazine containing many photographs. Some of the articles are only in one language while others are in both languages. On the whole, this is a very handsome magazine.

Karikazo (Judith Magyar, 257 Chestnut Avenue, Bogota, N.J. 07603), is a Hungarian-oriented folk dance publication published in English. It carries news about Hungarian folk dance clubs, related problems, and background information.

Hora (Editor, American Zionist Youth Foundation, 515 Park Avenue, New York, N.Y. 10022) is published three times per year. Its six pages cover folk dance news from Israel as well as Israeli dance personalities and events.

The *Baltimore Ethnic Identity* (Kalevi Olkio, Editor, 28 S. Gay Street, Baltimore, Md. 21202) is a four-page bimonthly that publicizes ethnic activities taking place in that city.

There are also single-sheet publications serving club memberships. One with a unique name, published in Sacramento, is B.B.K.M. (Benevolent Brotherhood of Kolo Maniacs), founded by Bill and Barbara Pompei and continued by Bruce Mitchell. It comes out monthly. (B.B.K.M. is no longer published.)

A new directory-type annual publication, the *People's Folk Dance Directory* (P.O. Box 8575, Austin, Tex. 78712), was launched in 1977. It lists many folk dance groups and their meeting places by state, plus contacts, camps, shops, and other information of interest to folk dancers.

There are many more publications that would be of interest to folk dance readers. However, not having seen copies, I am unable to comment on them.

Besides the many types of folk dance publications and newsletters, the square dancers also have numerous publications. Their efforts would require a separate chapter. However, I do want to mention the most influential publications for square dancers. They are *Square Dancing* (Bob Osgood, Editor, 462 No. Robertson Blvd., Los Angeles, Calif. 90048) and *American Square Dance* magazine (Stan and Cathie Burdick, Co-editors, Box 788, Sandusky, Ohio 44870).

(This article originally appeared in *Viltis* magazine (June–Sept. 1977) under the title "Media for Folk Dancers." It has been updated and is used here with permission.)

Sound Systems for Folk Dancing

by John Casey

The sound system used can determine whether a folk dance session is a satisfying experience or a disappointing, frustrating one. Having the right type of system and using it properly is every bit as essential for the teacher or leader as knowing how to teach and do the dances. It is a necessary tool that makes it possible for each dancer to hear the music and instructions.

There are many sound systems on the market especially designed for this purpose. There is a difference between them and hi-fi sets. For folk dancing, the turntable (record player) should have three speeds (33⅓, 45, and 78 rpm) to accommodate different size records. It should have a variable speed or tempo control for varying each of the three speeds as much as 20 per cent faster or slower. This makes it possible to adjust the speed of music recorded at the wrong tempo for dancing and slow it down while learning. The turntable should be equipped with a durable pickup cartridge of high quality (commonly ceramic) and with a diamond stylus (needle). The diamond is more expensive than the sapphire but will last many times longer and will not wear out the record as fast.

The amplifier should have enough power to reach your entire group without overloading or distorting the music or voice. It should be as lightweight and compact as possible. In modern equipment, the amplifier is either transistorized or is of the solid-state type. It is built into the turntable base, with controls on the front or in the turntable carrying case. There should be separate volume and tone controls on the turntable for the music and the microphone. This will permit adjustments to achieve proper volume and tone balance between the music and voice. An auxiliary input jack on the amplifier will permit the use of a tape recorder in place of a record. This jack is usually wired into the circuit so that when the cable from the tape player is plugged in, the pickup is disconnected and the controls for the pickup can be used for the tape player.

The cost of a microphone is seldom included in the price of the sound system. It is the most personal component of the sound system; a microphone that is just right for one person may not be suited for another. The buyer should arrange to try one out before buying, to check it together with the equipment, and to determine whether it carries his or her particular voice well. The microphone should be especially designed to operate with low feedback, low room noise pickup, and the capability of close-to-the-lips use without distortion. Microphones made for radio, television, and recording studio use are not suitable for use with a sound system. The sound system microphone is especially engineered with directional characteristics to minimize feedback (an annoying squeal or high-pitched hum when the microphone picks up the output from a speaker). It is designed to be used close to the lips, without annoying plops and hisses caused by the speaker's breath. A convenient on/off switch is desirable. A ten-foot cable allows the operator plenty of freedom while moving around the equipment. The most popular and commonly used microphones for public address use are made by the Electrovoice Company. Two good models are the EV 660 and EV 635, from $65 on up. (All prices quoted are approximate, based on 1978 listings.)

Many sound systems are especially designed for instructional purposes. They are usually of rugged construction and are designed to produce a high quality of music and speech under adverse conditions usually found in gymnasiums and recreation halls. Prices range from around $400 to over $2,000. A good sound system, if properly cared for, should last for several years; therefore, a true evaluation of immediate and future needs should be made before purchasing a system. Here are some important points to consider (1) the size of group you will be working with; (2) whether you will be working in one central location or setting up and removing the equipment for each session; and (3) whether the equipment will be transported by automobile.

Some systems in the lower price range have the amplifier and turntable housed in one case, with one open-back speaker mounted in a housing that attaches itself to the amplifier case to form a single carrying unit. One of these systems is the Newcomb model T-40-S, selling for $420 (excluding the microphone). It weighs only 36 pounds, is an extremely portable single unit, and would be adequate to cover small groups or small halls. Other systems are available with two open-backed speakers that snap together to form one carrying case; the amplifier has its own detachable cover. The two speakers permit more flexibility in dealing with poor acoustics; in most instances they provide better coverage and double the power capabilities of a single-speaker system. The output power of the amplifier is divided between the two speakers. It is recommended that the two-speaker system be chosen over the single-speaker system in most instances when open-back speakers are to be used. Two systems of this type, with approximate costs, are: Newcomb, model T-40, 36½ lbs, $475 (excluding microphone); and Califone, model 1875K (weight unknown), $400. There are other similar systems available.

Single amplifier-turntable units that do not include speakers are available in the $500 to $600 range. Some of these, with approximate costs, are: Clinton P-200, 160 watts, 18 lbs, $516; Hilton Micro-75, 11 lbs, 33⅓–45 rpm, $550; Newcomb, model T-40 #100, 85 watts, 27 lbs, $500. Each of these units is capable of covering large halls or groups of people when used with adequate speakers.

Some traveling square dance callers use lightweight units with a single column-type high-power speaker and have no problem covering up to 250 people. Higher-power units for huge crowds have between 225 and 460 watts.

The speakers must be capable of handling the output of the amplifier without overloading and distorting the sound. With open-back speaker enclosures there is little choice since the speakers are included as a part of the system. With proper understanding and use, the open-back speaker can give a very satisfactory performance; when the need arises, auxiliary speakers can be added to increase coverage.

There are many types of speakers and enclosures on the market. Here, as with amplifiers and microphones, speakers are especially designed for public-address-system use. A speaker that is engineered for hi-fi use is not necessarily the best for folk dance purposes.

The column speaker consists of a tall, narrow cabinet with from two to six small high-quality speakers mounted in it. The speakers are wired in a series-parallel arrangement to produce the correct impedance (usually 8 ohms) to match the amplifier output. The power capability will equal the total rating of the speakers used (six 10-watt speakers would equal a total of 60 watts). The column speaker is becoming more popular all the time.

Other types consist of a heavy cabinet with a high-quality, high-power speaker mounted in it. Most speaker equipment is produced by sound equipment manufacturers. The sound equipment distributors can usually make a qualified recommendation as to the speakers best suited for your particular needs.

The user should know how to set up and operate the equipment for maximum performance quality. The proper location for the amplifier/turntable, as well as the speakers, will vary with the size, shape, and acoustics of the hall and the number of people involved.

A combination social hall/gymnasium in a church, school, or recreation facility, with a stage at one end and a large expanse of floor space, usually has poor acoustics. This is caused by the sound reflecting off such flat and reflective surfaces as the floor, walls, and ceiling. The sound reaches the ears of the listener from all reflective surfaces as well as from the speakers, creating a sort of whirlpool of garbled sound and making the words difficult to understand.

There is nothing the sound operator can do about acoustical conditions, but there are a few things that can be done to improve the situation. The more people there are in a hall the less sound reflection there will be. Placing the speakers about shoulder level (or higher, but never on the floor) and tilted slightly downward and toward the center of the group will help in some instances. Varying the height of the speakers may help. Speakers should not face toward each other or toward the microphone. This is a common cause of feedback (squeal). In a large room two (or more) speakers are better than one. At a reduced volume they spread the sound so everyone can hear and no one is blasted. For even coverage, speakers should be spaced apart so that they cover the area without overlapping the sound.

Buying sound equipment for folk dancing purposes is a major investment. The system should be selected with care and used properly for best results.

(John Casey, husband of the author, is a radio engineer. His experience includes several years as chief engineer of domestic radio stations in the United States and twenty years on the foreign service staff of the Voice of America. He and his wife have taught and conducted folk and square dance classes and programs in some twenty countries. Acting as sound engineer on these occasions, he has met the challenge of providing suitable sound in such places as recreation halls, airplane hangars, castles, embassy ballrooms, and on open concrete slabs.)

VI
OVERVIEW

The Changing Scene in the Folk Dance Field

by Vytautas Beliajus

During the more than 40 years since I have been teaching folk dancing, great changes have taken place. For one, the popularity of folk dance since the early thirties has increased a thousandfold. Ethnic demonstration groups existed during this time and in ethnic neighborhoods the simple ballroom type of folk dances was used at social functions. But international folk dancing among nonethnics as a hobby and as recreation was still unknown.

Some folk dancing was utilized in certain schools as a regimented physical education activity, done mostly by a few girls in bloomers. But now—gone are the bloomers! Many schools and universities are featuring folk dancing and many students of both sexes find it a favorite subject and pastime. In some universities, registration in folk dance classes is in the hundreds. Brigham Young University, in Provo, Utah, is a good example. In lesser numbers, folk dancing is favored at Ricks College, in Rexburg, Idaho; Illinois State University, Normal; Ball State University, Muncie, Indiana; UCLA at Los Angeles; State University of New York, Cortland; University of Arizona in Tucson, and many other places.

[The] popularity of folk dance often depends upon the teacher's knowledge and ability to convey the element of fun while teaching. In "olden" days many leaders tried to maintain authenticity while doing and enjoying the dances. Some went overboard, while others viewed authenticity as a minor factor. The joy of dancing and the companionship it afforded was deemed uppermost for the hobbyist and recreational dancer; fortunately this idea prevails.

Originally, the most favorite dances were those done in couple and quadrille formations. These were dances from Scandinavia, Britain, and Central, Eastern and Western Europe. I introduced dances from the Balkans around 1937. The dances of Yugoslavia were readily accepted, but those from Greece were more difficult to make popular. It was not the dances which kept people away, but the music and tempo, which seemed strange and like something from another world. Nowadays the Balkan dances, which include those from Greece, Yugoslavia, Romania, Bulgaria, Turkey, and Armenia, have a large following, especially among the

upper teen- and college-age students. They certainly have come a long way since I organized the first kolo group in Chicago in 1938–39. [A kolo is a Serbo-Croatian circle dance.]

Line dances have great merit in that partners are not required. In situations where there are more women than men (often the case), the line dance (actually [this] is [a] misnomer since these dances are usually done in circles or broken circles) is a problem solver because no one has to sit out. Unlike set dances, when one error-making participant can wreck the entire set of 4, 8, 16 or more dancers, in a line dance the antics of one individual do not hurt the line unless it happens to be a demonstration group.

Because of these two factors—no requirement for partners and teamwork—the line dances have gained favor to such a point that often a club is overbalanced and topheavy with these dances at the expense of other types of folk dances. Line dancers are often impatient and intolerant of other dance forms. This can be noted at request programs where these so-called "kolomaniacs" will take over. One individual will often write down about 10 or more dances from the Balkans and Israel, with the rest of them following suit. They will sit out when a couple dance is played and refuse to participate even when only one couple or person is needed to fill the set, thus preventing 6 or 7 other people from participating. I have encountered this type of rude behavior on many occasions.

For many years—from about 1937, when I first started traveling, until well into the sixties—I was about the only teacher of folk dance who traveled widely. Michael and Mary Ann Herman, from New York, did a certain amount in later years. I've been in every state except Hawaii and have also taught in Canada and Mexico. Thus dance forms from many countries were first introduced by me. Now there are large numbers of teachers of every kind teaching specialized dances. International folk teachers are on the wane, while line dance teachers in particular, and some specializing in a particular nationality, have increased tremendously. This trend fills the demand for new materials. Meanwhile, traditional favorites are being pushed out by these new works, some of which are not of general use and can be performed only by the most agile enthusiasts. Institutes are constantly held for the teaching of new dances to groups, which can hardly absorb all the material thrown at them. All traveling teachers, despite their great numbers, are regularly engaged, a condition testifying to the fact that people have a great thirst for learning folk dancing and a lively interest to see what each teacher has to offer.

The states with the greatest number of folk dancers are California, first and foremost, New York, Washington, Illinois, Oregon, Texas, New Jersey, Ohio, Michigan, Indiana, Florida, Utah, New Mexico, Arizona, Massachusetts, Connecticut, Louisiana, Colorado, and a few others. They are practically nonexistent in the Dakotas, South Carolina, and Arkansas. These last-named states do have square dancing. This form of folk dance, which outnumbers the international folk dance forms, is found in every nook and cranny of our country.

The growth of folk dancing is especially not[iceable] among college students. A university town folk dance group will sometimes have an 80 per cent constituency of college students, as in Chapel Hill, North Carolina; Boulder, Colorado; Tucson, Mesa, and Phoenix, Arizona; Albuquerque, New Mexico; Ann Arbor, Michigan, and others. In fact, some of the finest exhibition groups are often found within universities; for example, Brigham Young University, Ball State University, Ricks College, and Illinois State University. An excellent group of high school students exists in Paw Paw, Michigan.

(This article first appeared in *Focus on Dance, VIII: Dance Heritage*, and is here used with the permission of the National Dance Association of the American Alliance for Health, Physical Education and Recreation.)

Authenticity of Dances

by Betty Casey

Responsible dance teachers and leaders are concerned about whether their material is authentic. Dancers want to be reassured that they are learning the original steps and style as practiced at festivities in the Gasthäuser of Germany or in outdoor pavilions in Greece.

Some researchers and collectors have learned dances through representatives from various countries travel-

ing in the United States; others shared the dances brought by immigrants who settled here. A few research their dances firsthand at folk festivals held in faraway places.

Yet even these fortunate folk dance enthusiasts sometimes bring back differing choreography or music—from the same country. Also, the same dance taught by one teacher may be presented differently by another. How can this happen? Who is right? Perhaps everyone is right.

Dick Crum, noted researcher and choreographer, told of researching dances in a Balkan village where two brothers in the same dance line were doing different steps. How could he write up an instruction sheet? Include both sets of steps and let the dancers choose? Make a selection himself and note that there were also other authentic steps?

Anthony Shay, who studied dance ethnology in the Middle East, explains some basic concepts regarding the conception of dances in their native setting by claiming that "improvisation is an extremely widespread phenomenon." He explains that dancers draw from an inventory of movements particular to their society and that this selection is cued by the type of dance event, the music, and each dancer's emotional and psychological state and physical condition. Improvisation by especially fine dancers is encouraged in some societies. "Improvisation permeates most dance traditions beyond the imagination of most American folk dancers."

Vyts Beliajus, folk dance authority and editor of *Viltis,* says, "Crying for *authenticity* in this age is like trying to climb a greased pole—you'll get nowhere." He says that versions abound and cannot be eliminated. During his travels from coast to coast, he has noted a great number of variants to popular and "standardized" dances. (Standardized dances are those about which a research committee or group of Americans have reached a consensus concerning style and choreography.) He reports that he's "seen at least six ways of doing the Karagouna or Pentazali, four ways thus far of the Greek Gaida Gidas, and a great number of versions of the Bulgarian girls' dance Dobrudjanska Reka (or Ruka) including different versions for men."

Vyts cites a report written by Miriam Lidster, a member and devotee of the California Federation Research Committee, after her visit to Macedonia, in which she noted, "The dance is changed by the area, the tempo, and given style of the village. No wonder a research committee could have such difficulty."

Concerning Greek line dances, where the leader has the discretion of determining the choreography almost at will, Rickey Holden and Mary Vouras have noted in their book *Greek Folk Dances*, "It's pretty hard to select one 'pure' form of most Greek dances because often the same dance varies from village to village." They added another explanation that could easily be applicable to instructions for dances from many lands. "We have leaned heavily on routines . . . because we are *writing it in English for non-Greeks* and it's difficult for foreigners to ad lib properly—*authentically*—in a strange culture."

Mountain villagers in the Philippines perform a much more complicated version of an igorot war dance than the version danced by a University of the Philippines dance troupe. "These steps are too difficult for them to teach," explained the village mayor, who was one of the dancers.

Some dances that are discovered and resurrected but prove unusable because the instructions are incomplete, or because appropriate music is not available, must be rechoreographed if they are to be preserved and enjoyed. In a deliberate effort to redirect national values in the 1930s, clubs and organizations in Germany did just that. They came up with the popular dances Kreuz König and Das Fenster.

The Czechoslovakian dance Tancuj was presented by Madelynne Greene at the Teacher's Institute (California) held in conjunction with the 1954 Statewide Festival. The steps were taken from a longer dance of the same name which was taught to the Festival Workshop by Mr. J. Slavik of Czechoslovakia and fitted to recorded music.

In his book *The Teaching of Ethnic Dance* Anatol Joukowsky says, "Folk dance, as we use this term, describes a dance which initially was an ethnic dance which has undergone some change through the years. It has gone from dancer to dancer, teacher to dancers, from book to dancers and teachers and has been altered in the process of evolution."

In The Folk Dance Federation of California's *Folk Dances from Far and Near* we read: "Since folk dancing is a living human activity, changes and variations in the spirit and pattern of the dances occur as they are performed by ethnic groups far from the homelands from which they originated."

Dances considered to be truly traditional in this country have been conditioned by the same processes. In *The Round Dance Book* Lloyd Shaw confesses, "I must frankly admit that when I . . . found an old dance in various forms, and all of them seemed somehow wrong, I have submitted the matter to my legs and let them work it out. I have asked the rhythm in my blood what was the matter. I have asked my memory and my heart about the likeliest form of the thing."

Shaw also relates the following anecdote: "I remember once at the National Folk Festival in Washington, D.C., the leader of a southern mountain group, who evidently felt some pity and scorn for the brash new-ness of our western land, where newcomers brought dances from every part of the country and dumped them into a common melting pot, said to me, 'The difference between your dances and mine is that every step my young people do is authentic. Every single step has been done in exactly the same way in the same valley of our mountains for generations and generations.' And I winced a little, for where there is no growth there is no life; the tree is dead . . . However, his boys did have a dandy do-si-do . . . Then I asked them what they knew about it, and just how long it had been danced in that valley, and they laughed at me.

" 'Why, Bill here made it up last winter. Ain't it a slick one? We kids kept working on it, till we got it down smooth.'

"I protested, 'Your leader tells me that every step you dance is authentic, and has been danced just that way for generations in your valley.'

" 'Baloney,' the boy answered. 'Sure he talks that way and he likes to think it's so. But just the same he's always glad when we slip in something new, especially if it's showy.' And I felt better. The dance is still alive in their valley."

Anthony Shay says that "when dances are standardized they become cultural fossils or relics because the possibility of change is curtailed and the form becomes dead and unchanging. This is the reason that dances so often change after they have been introduced in the United States, and why we find dances that have been introduced by one teacher done differently all over the country. This is only natural and happens in quite the same way in a native setting, where a dance may be performed differently by neighboring communities, or even individual dancers in the same community. Change is a natural process, however much one may not like it."

The purists decry these changes and label them heresy. The real dispute occurs when a choreographer borrows indiscriminately from various national sources and creates a "patchwork" job, or when a teacher deliberately or carelessly makes major changes in a dance. Such contrivances or distortions do folk dancing a disservice.

Lucile Czarnowski notes that putting the dances into written form and teaching them from an authorized description has contributed to a stabilization of the form of dances. She provided a usable pattern for recording and presenting dance instructions that has been almost universally accepted among folk dancers.

In an article published in *Let's Dance* magazine, this venerable folk dance authority admonishes would-be teachers and leaders that "the traditional folk dances are like rare tapestries woven through with many cultural threads of the past and representing a unified creation. Cutting any one into pieces and rearranging the parts destroys the continuity and beauty of the whole. Likewise, cutting out a segment and supplying in its place some material foreign to its texture, quality and age results in a patched, unsatisfying result. Yet this is exactly what happens when dance figures are omitted or rearranged, or when the wrong music is used, or embellishments in the nature of turns, claps, and spins are put in at will. We, as teachers and leaders of folk dance groups, should feel a responsibility toward our priceless heritage in folk materials, and the use we make of them, and be mindful of the trust put in us by the groups taught."

Fortunately, responsible folk dance teachers and choreographers carefully select and combine figures, steps, and movements that are most typical and fitting—and are culturally valued in the native environment. From a practical standpoint, they match them with the available music within the time limit of the phonograph record. Thus, we compromise but are rewarded with a usable piece of choreography available for the enjoyment of all.

Hopefully, this admittedly diluted product retains enough of the authentic flavor and styling of its cultural origin to promote a bond of common enjoyment between the native who danced it on a Serbian hillside or a sun-drenched Greek island and the American international folk dancer at the local Y or community hall.

VII
SELECTED FOLK DANCES FROM MANY LANDS

Dances representing many more countries, provinces, and categories than those listed here are popular with international folk dance groups. Some dances are popular in one place and not in another. Due to space limitations, all of the areas, including representative dances from each, could not be included here. The specific selection of countries, categories, and dances from various areas was made from among those frequently programmed at folk dance camps, seminars, and workshops throughout the United States.

Under the heading "Children," dances suitable for children were selected from several countries. These dances may also be enjoyed by beginning adult dancers. The other dances described are grouped according to the individual countries or areas they represent. An introductory essay, providing an overview of the origin and general characteristics pertinent to the dances of each geographical area, precedes the individual dance descriptions. The overviews and selection of dances included were provided by outstanding specialists, either in specific ethnic categories or in the broader scope of international folk dancing. These specialists have used different formats in presenting their dance descriptions. Therefore, although there is a great deal of similarity in the way these dances are described, there is also some degree of difference (see the essay "Dance Descriptions" in Part V).

Here, then, is a description of 191 selected international folk dances, representing some 28 countries and areas of the world, as they are currently performed in the United States.

CHILDREN

Folk Dancing for Children

by Mildred (Millie) von Konsky

A good teaching plan combining folk dancing and rhythmic activities will refresh the body and the mind of the young participant. It will offer variety, action, and color. It will teach the young the folkways of different countries and will establish a systematic program for the development of skills and acceptable social behavior.

However, these objectives can only be accomplished through the knowledge, skill, and aspirations of a qualified teacher. General considerations include knowing the group that you will work with, including their needs and desires as these relate to their age level and interests.

The group objectives to be determined include whether they are to increase learning and skills, occupy leisure time (recreation), develop acceptable patterns of social behavior, study folkways of various cultures, or develop an appreciation for cultural values and intercultural relationships.

Consideration should be given to learning (attention) span, physical activity, and social participation. Other factors to be considered include the time allowed for a lesson or meeting, the size of the activity area, safety factors (obstructions on floor), health factors (ventilation, dress, footwear), and equipment (phonograph, piano, drum).

The teacher should tell the participants the what, when, and how of a folk dance activity. He or she should explain the fundamentals of locomotion, or basic skills, which are natural expressions of a fundamental instinct. The even rhythm movements include:

Photo by Walt Metcalf

Oakland Junior Dancers International

A folk dance is a related series of basic skills and traditional folk dance steps danced to a melodic pattern and performed with a single national style. Types of folk dances are determined on the basis of: making, renewing, or retaining friendships on a social level; traditional customs and ceremonies in the events of daily living; imitation of work activities in occupations and trades; and the agility and skill of the performer in competitive and individual skills.

The teacher should relate the rhythmic pattern and step pattern by explaining the elements of music. Rhythmic structure means the number of beats per measure and the rhythmic patterns of varying note values superimposed upon these beats. Music suitable for walking, running, jumping, hopping, and leaping has an even structure, or *even rhythm*. As an example, 4/4 meter or four evenly divided beats to the measure can produce four walks, jumps, hops, or leaps. Music suitable for skipping, galloping, and sliding has an uneven structure containing an uneven divided beat, or *uneven rhythm*.

It is helpful for students to know the following definitions:

Accent	rhythmic stress or emphasis
Beat	rhythmic pulse
Measure	beats grouped by an accent
Meter	a division into measures of a uniform number of beats, or a pattern of strong and weak beats in a measure
Phrase	two or more measures forming a sequence
Tempo	rate of speed at which the music is played (quick, moderate, slow)

walk—an even change of weight from one foot to the other as steps are taken; run—fast springing steps causing both feet to leave the ground for an instant as steps are taken; hop—leave the ground from one foot and land on the same foot; leap—leave the ground from one foot and land on the other foot; and jump—leave the ground with both feet and land on both feet. Uneven rhythms include: slide—step sideways and close the other foot; gallop—a step followed by a leap to the other foot; skip—a hop followed by a step on the same foot; and cut—a quick displacement of one foot by the other. Among the principles that guide movement (meter), tempo, and national styles are: time—measured movement (meter-tempo, fast-slow); force—qualities of movement (vigor, effectiveness), and space—direction, level, and range of movement (size-pattern).

Children easily learn traditional folk dance step patterns, which are combinations of the basic skills. These patterns include:

Making a lesson plan is helpful. If the lesson is offered for increasing learning and skills, a standard should be established and maintained. Evaluate each lesson in terms of achievement and objectives. Make brief notes of the results for the following lesson.

Teach the basic skills over a series of lessons, including appropriate dances when needed. Teach traditional dance steps over a series of lessons, including some appropriate dances in a progression. Teach dances that can be related to social behavior. Allow time for reviewing material covered in each lesson. Plan a rest and discussion period, offering information that will evoke, dramatize, and sustain interest in the activity

Schottische	step, step, step, hop	4/4	even
Two-step	step-close-step	2/4–4/4	uneven
Polka	hop, step-close-step	6/8–2/4–4/4	uneven
Waltz	step, step, close	3/4	even
Mazurka	glide, cut, hop	3/4	even
Pas de basque	leap, step, step	3/4–6/8–2/4–4/4	uneven

by showing costume plates and maps, discussing the use of authentic material and the folklore and folkways of a given area. Planning a special demonstration of skills learned and a special group participation event also sustain interest among children. Conclude each lesson with a fun dance or request. Expect various reactions in attitudes and abilities and consider the welfare of all concerned, thus offering a maximum amount of participation.

(This material, covering the elements of instructing a folk dance activity for children, is taken from an outline made by Millie von Konsky for the Teacher Training Program co-sponsored by the Folk Dance Federation of California, Inc., California State University (Hayward), Laney College (Oakland), and the Alameda County School Department. The material is used with permission.)

(Mildred von Konsky has wide experience as a leader and teacher in adult folk dance activities, as well as those for children. She has served as president and concert director of the Folk Dance Federation of California, as editor of *Let's Dance* magazine, and as an instructor at International House, Berkeley, California. She served as co-ordinator and was one of several instructors for a seven-college teacher-training program sponsored by the Folk Dance Federation of California.

She has conducted and assisted many folk dance workshops as dance specialist and instructor; these workshops were held at Brigham Young University as well as seven California universities and colleges.

Millie and Vernon von Konsky

This talented folk dance leader is currently dance specialist and consultant for the Oakland Recreation Department and instructor-director of the Oakland Junior Dancers International performing group. She is director for the annual citywide Children's Folk Dance Festival, in which from eight hundred to one thousand children participate.

For ten years she has, together with her husband, Vernon, been program leader and instructor for the Oakland-sponsored Feather River Family Folk Dance Camp, which specializes in folk and ethnic dance. For twenty-seven years she has instructed folk dance activities at St. Bernard elementary school and many other places.

Millie was the recipient of both the 1971 Service Award from the California Parks and Recreation Society for her distinguished contribution to the field of public recreation and the mayor of Oakland's Service Award.)

FOLK DANCES SUITABLE FOR CHILDREN

Although children are capable of mastering most folk dance steps, the following dances, described elsewhere in this book, have proven suitable and enjoyable for children.

Alunelul	Romania
Apat Apat	Philippines
Cotton-eyed Joe	United States
Doudlebska Polka	Czechoslovakia
Fjäskern	Sweden
Highland Quadrille	Scotland
Hora	Israel
Klumpakojis	Lithuania
Mayim, Mayim	Israel
Mexican Mixer	Mexico
Oklahoma Mixer for Three	United States
Šetnja	Yugoslavia
Square Dance	United States
Teton Mountain Stomp	United States

Duquesne University Tamburitzans

ARMENIA

Armenian Folk Dancing

by Tom Bozigian

In the United States there are approximately four hundred thousand Armenians scattered across the country. There are fifty to sixty thousand Armenians in Los Angeles, where there is a large community of Russian Armenians who moved there prior to 1915. Fresno has a large Turkish-Armenian community that also moved there in 1915. Life in Armenia was highly agricultural; that was one of the reasons these immigrants decided on Fresno.

When I was a youngster, I danced where there was still much of the old tradition. But freedom of expression in the United States rubbed off on the Armenians. As the second and third generations were born, they continued to do the dances, but the dances began to change. The current style became less dramatic and the original style was lost.

The original immigrants brought their dances with them. When they attempted to teach these to their children, many didn't take an interest. But right now there has been a rebirth, a rediscovery of the national identity. Many Armenian dances have been created recently. Ten years ago, there were ten to fifteen dances that all Armenians performed all over the country. So, in order to have more dances, they started creating them. They used to have contests, and the best dance creation would win a trophy. I teach some of these dances. I still remember the 1956 contest; about ten dances originated there. I teach the dances that are being danced.

But Armenian dances are quite different in Turkey and in the Caucasus; Turkish Armenians have a dance style that has more of a Middle Eastern influence. Armenian history and geographic location have influenced the types and styles of dances. Occupying a landlocked area just south of the great mountain range of the Caucasus, between the Caspian and Black seas, and fronting on the northwestern extremity of Asia is the Armenian Soviet Socialist Republic [S.S.R.], popularly known as Armenia. It is the smallest of the fifteen republics making up the Soviet Union. To the north and east, Armenia is bounded by the Georgian and Azerbaijan Soviet Socialist republics, while its neighbors to the west and southeast are, respectively, Turkey and Iran.

Modern Armenia is part of ancient Armenia, one of the world's oldest centers of civilization, whose peoples have long inhabited the highlands of the area.

Once a backward Russian colonial province, Armenia has been transformed, in a remarkably short period, into an industrial country with an advanced form of agriculture.

Armenians were continually subjugated by the people around them, which kept them from becoming a strong, independent nation. They were successively ruled by the Iranians, Romans, Greeks, Byzantines, and Arabs. Ghengis Khan assumed control about 600 A.D., followed by the Seljuk Turks about 1200 A.D., who moved west until they took Constantinople in 1453 A.D. Armenians were considered a separate entity in that they were tradesmen who traded with the other minorities. All the people were subjugated under the Turks.

Later Armenia joined the Transcaucasian republics located between the Caspian and the Black seas. The folklore in this area is very rich. Whenever you have a strip of land between two seas, a lot of people are going to pass through. Yet who can say who influenced whom? The Turks had dominated much of the Balkans, North Africa, and the Arab countries. Who's to say they didn't pick up dances from these countries and bring them back to Turkey? And who's to say the Armenians weren't dancing some old dances when the Turks conquered them?

For ten years I had longed to study in Armenia. Finally, through the Committee for Cultural Relations with Armenians Abroad, I was accepted to study Armenian folk dance and choreography in Yerevan, capital of the Armenian S.S.R. Only a handful of students of Armenian descent from outside Armenia have taken the course. It requires four years of study for Soviet

Duquesne University Tamburitzans

Duquesne University Tamburitzans

vast amount of Armenian dance material drawn from several Armenian communities throughout the United States and Canada. He also conducted research during the fifteen months he spent in Armenia while studying at the Sayat Nova Choreographic School, working with both state ensembles, performing with an amateur stage ensemble and, finally, traveling with the Ethnographic Institute of the University of Yerevan to several selected regions in the interior to research, film, and record native dances.

Tom Bozigian began dancing as a young teen-ager in Fresno, California—at that time containing the largest Armenian community in the United States—where immigrants from all the folk regions of both Caucasian and Anatolian Armenia were well represented. He excelled in various sports throughout his school years: All-Conference football player at Roosevelt High School; member of the Fresno Olympic Club Valley Soccer Champions; and 1967 All-American and Player of the Year with the Fresno Power Volleyball Association. Tom has a master's degree in education, a bachelor's in Russian, and has taught in both the Fresno and Los Angeles school systems.

Moving to Los Angeles in 1968, Tom Bozigian had the privilege of working with the renowned dancer-choreographer Jora Makarian, which proved to be an extremely valuable experience in preparing Tom for his study terms in Armenia. He has presented his workshops throughout the United States and Canada, as well as parts of Europe and the U.S.S.R. Having taught in many folk dance conferences in the western United States, he produced the first University of California–Santa Barbara International Folk Dance Symposium in September 1975, which proved very successful.)

citizens wishing to earn a diploma in dance choreography and the certificate of Professional Dancer of the Soviet Union. Generally, for the noncitizen one to two years is suggested. In addition to Armenian folk dance, students study classical ballet plus character and international dance forms. Various types of examinations are given periodically during the four-year period; the final examination consists of a large concert at the philharmonic hall in Yerevan.

There are three state dance ensembles, two in Yerevan and one in Kirovakan, located in upper Armenia. Many schools and factories throughout the Republic sponsor dance organizations; the majority are quite good. Folk dancing in the villages throughout these regions is still very much a part of the daily routine. Most of the new incoming dancers for the state ensembles are selected and auditioned from the list of graduates of the Sayat Nova school. However, some exceptionally talented outsiders and even village locals have made the grade.

Armenian folk dances are divided into two types: the Eastern, or "Kavkaz," Armenian, and the Western, or Anatolian, style. These, in turn, are also subdivided. The Eastern Armenian dance style covers three regions (Leninakan, Lori, and Karabakh-Zangezoor), while the Western style is divided among four areas (Sassoun-Taron, Vaspoorakan, Shatakh, and Kareen).

(Tom Bozigian is an Armenian researcher-choreographer of song and dance and a 1975 graduate of the Soviet Armenian State Choreographic School of Yerevan. In past years he has collected and compiled a

Tom Bozigian

ARMENIAN FOLK DANCES

Styling and Important Arm Positions

Male arm positions

1st pos: Arms extended together straight fwd, palms away.

2nd pos: Arms extended straight out to each side, parallel to floor, palms away.

3rd pos: Arms curved to overhead pos, fingers touching and palms up.

4th pos: Combination of 2 and 3 with either arm. (One arm curved overhead, other arm out to side.)

Female arm positions

1st pos: Arms extended fwd and rounded (parallel to floor) at chest level, palms away, wrists wider apart than elbows, and fingers in "Y" form. ("Y" signifies yeghneek, an Armenian mountain deer which the formation of fingers symbolizes—middle finger and thumb rounded to point toward each other while other fingers are extended and curved above.) (Wrists bent up and palms facing same dir as forearm.)

2nd pos: Arms extended to sides—fingers in "Y" pos.

3rd pos: One arm in front of chest, elbow bent slightly lower than wrist (from elbows to wrist parallel to floor) and other arm extended to side—fingers in "Y".

4th pos: One hand near side of face, elbow bent, pointing down (head slightly turned in opp direction) and other arm raised above head on same side as first hand—fingers in "Y".

Note: There are many other arm positions plus movements built around the above. All arms extended to side are parallel to floor.

AGHCHEEKNEROO PAR

Source: This dance was learned by Tom Bozigian at the Sayat Nova State Choreographic School in Yerevan under Director Teresa Grekoryan, merited artist of the Soviet Union, and Norig Khachaturyan, ballet maestro. The music was written recently by composer Khachatur Avetisyan, now director of the Armenian State Song and Dance Ensemble. This dance was presented by Tom Bozigian to the third-level class of the Sayat Nova Choreographic School, which presented the dance at the final school recital in May 1974 at the Yerevan Philharmonic.

Record: Music for Dances GT 2001-A, band 3

Formation: Women in closed circle

Meter 6/4   Pattern

Meas Intro—2 meas

Figure I

R arm extended above head, hand in "Y" pos, L hand very slightly in back of R waist of neighbor, body facing diag LOD.

1	R to R (cts 1, 2, 3) L over R (cts 4, 5, 6).
2	R to R in plié (ct 1–2) straight back on L, L heel raised (cts 3) step R beside L, heel raised (cts 4–6).
3–4	Repeat meas 1–2 with opp ftwk, except on meas 2, ct 6 step R to R, heel raised.

Figure II

1	Step L across R in plié as eyes follow hand (cts 1–2) R to R, heel raised (ct 3) repeat cts 1–2 (cts 4–5). Repeat ct 3 (ct 6). *Note:* R hand makes 2 inward circles in "Y" pos.
2	Repeat cts 1–5, pivot on L to face RLOD, R arm ends twd RLOD (ct 6).

Figure III

1	Backing in LOD, take 5 small steps on ½ toe beginning with R (cts 1–5) step on whole L ft (ct 6).
2	Rock bwd on R (cts 1–3) rock fwd on L (cts 4–6).

Figure IV

1	Moving to outside of circle to make one small individual CCW circle, step R fwd, as hands are lowered to R, shlder ht (ct 1) hold (ct 2) continue in circle, step L as arms move to L (ct 3) step R as arms move to R (ct 4) plié on L in place as hands in "Y" pos, do inward turn (ct 5) hold (ct 6).

Do fig IV—4 times in all, ending to face ctr of circle.

Figure V

1	Step bwd on R to face LOD as L arm is raised along body straight overhead, palm in, hand in "Y" pos, and at the same time, R arm moves straight down in back. Head facing twd ctr of circle (cts 1–2), step L, R, L, turning ½ turn in place CCW, L palm ends facing out (cts 3–5) plié R in place, as R arm raises to chest ht, palm in, and L hand is lowered to waist ht, palm out (ct 6).
2	Repeat cts 1–6 with opp ftwk and direction and arm movement.
3–4	Repeat meas 1–2, but on 6th ct of meas 4, arms return to pos as in beginning of dance, and L steps across R on ct 6 with no plié, body facing LOD. Repeat figs I thru V one more time.

Transition VI

1 Facing ctr with plié on L, swing R over L & to floor as arms open to side, then legs straightening heels up to execute 360° CCW turn, L ft ending in front of R ft & arms doing inward "Y" turn to end R across L chest level.

2 Deep plié, R knee to floor, L ft in front, hands to L in "Y" pos, chest ht (cts 1–6) (R instep is on floor).

Figure VII

There is only arm action in fig VII. Hands in "Y" pos throughout.

1 Arms swing to R as hands wave once (cts 1–3) arms swing to L as hands wave once (cts 4–6).

2 Arms swing to R and make 1 CCW circle in front of body—hands wave twice (cts 1–6).

3–4 Repeat meas 1–2 in opp direction.

5 Arms do 3 revolutions around each other with an inward motion (from down to up) in front of chest (hands in "Y" pos & waving with each turn) ending R arm up, bent at elbow, L fingers touching R elbow (cts 1–6).

6 Repeat meas 5 with opp movements.

7 Repeat meas 5.

8 Repeat meas 6.

Figure VIII

Hands in "Y" pos throughout. Facing diag RLOD, rise to standing pos with wt on L, R behind, arms remain straight—R arm raises above head level, wrist bends down, at same time L is lowered below waist level, wrist bends up (cts 1–3); repeat cts 1–3 with opp hand motions (cts 4–6).

Repeat cts 1–3 in one ct (ct 1); repeat cts 4–6 in 2 cts (cts 2–3).

Repeat fig VIII one more time.

Figure IX

1 Step R to R on ½ toe as hands are raised up from L to R above head, hands in "Y" pos (cts 1–3) cross L over R in plié as arms move down and up to L in a CCW circular motion (windmill) (cts 4–6).

2–4 Repeat first meas 3 more times but R remaining up on last CCW arm circular motion & L extends to orig beg pos in fig I.

Repeat figs I through V one more time, except in fig V, meas 4, L hand is placed on front neighbor's L waist, as R ft moves on floor in an arc to LOD and body turns to face LOD, R arm and head turning to outside of circle.

GUNEEGA

Source: Armenian Youth Organizations of Los Angeles

Record: Express X-106-B (G-H), side 2, band 1

Formation: Open, mixed cir with little finger hold at shldr ht

Meter 2/4   Pattern

Meas

1 Facing diag, R and moving LOD, step L over R with slight plié as arms are lowered ½ from elbow (ct 1); step R to R as arms are raised to orig pos (ct 2).

2–3 Repeat meas 1, cts 1, 2, two more times (cts 3–6).

4 Extend and touch L heel on floor across R (ct 7); touch L to RLOD (ct 8).

5 Repeat ct 7 (ct 9); step L beside R (ct 10).

6 Extend and touch R heel on floor, ahead of L (ct 11); step R beside L (ct 12).

7 Repeat ct 7 (ct 13); repeat ct 8 (ct 14).

KAFAN WEDDING DANCE

Source: Learned by Tom Bozigian from Kafan (Ghapan) Village Dance Collective in southern Armenia, just west of Soviet Azerbaijan border

Record: Music for Dances GT 2002-A, band 1

Formation: Mixed line—little finger hold at shldr ht

Steps: *Kafan-Armenian three plus one-step*—Facing slightly diag LOD, step R, leap slightly L beside R, step R (cts 1–3); swing L across R (ct 4); step L to L (ct 5); swing R across L (ct 6). Arms swing, beg with & before ct 1, bwd, and thereafter, fwd, bwd, fwd, bwd, fwd, bwd (cts 1–6).

(Dvel) Western Armenian two-step: Facing diag & moving LOD with slightly less than full wt, step R to R (ct 1); L ft is placed more quickly beside R than in conventional two-step (ct and); slight leap R to R as L lifts behind (ct 2).

Armenian Kertsee: Leap on both, L arm swings slightly across front of body and R arm across back (ct 1); leap on R, L heel lifts behind arms remain as in ct 1 (ct &); repeat (ct and) with opp ftwk & arms (cts 2).

Meter 2/4   Pattern

Dance described in counts—each meas has 2 cts. No intro

Figure I

Do Armenian 3 plus 1 step—three times (18 cts); on 18th ct, body turns to RLOD hopping on L as R lifts behind and arms raise above head; do one Armenian 2-step to L beg with R ft (cts 19–20); stamp L beside R with wt (ct 21); pivot to face diag LOD (ct 22).

Figure II
Moving LOD, do 15 Armenian 2-steps beg with R ft (30 cts); stamp L beside R, with wt (ct 31); arms come down, hold (ct 32).

Figure III
Do one Armenian 3 plus 1 step (6 cts) but on ct 6 turn slightly RLOD, hop on L in place, raising R knee in front as arms raise overhead; touch R over L (ct 7); arms come down, hold (ct 8). Repeat fig III once again.

Figure IV
Releasing little finger hold, hands raised even farther up—do 5 Armenian Dvel steps beg with R as arms move slightly to side of each lead ft (10 cts); clapping hands in front of body, leap on L (ct 11); leap on R turning to LOD, lowering hands as L lifts behind (ct and); leap L to LOD as R heel lifts behind (ct 12).

Figure V
Facing LOD, starting hands down to side, do 9 Armenian Kertsee steps (18 cts); stamp R beside L without wt (ct 19); hands come down and hold (ct 20). Dance entire dance three times in all.

KAROON (Springtime)
Source: Armenian Youth Organizations of Los Angeles
Record: Songs and Dances of the Armenian People, GT 3001-LP, side 1, band 1: Garoon
Formation: Open, mixed cir with little finger hold at shldr ht

Meter 2/4   Pattern

Meas
1–2   *Step 1.*
      Facing slightly & moving LOD, 2 two-steps to R starting with R (arms bend R from elbow on 1st two-step and L on 2nd) (cts 1–4).
3   Step R to R (ct 1); raise L in front of R (ct 2).
4   Step L in pl (ct 1); raise R in front of L (ct 2).
5   Releasing finger hold, walk 2 steps to LOD (R-L) as hands clap twice on ea ct at chest level (cts 1–2).
6   Cross R over L turning to face ctr and holding fingers again (ct 1); hop bk on R as L lifts behind (ct 2).
7   Continuing bkwd, step on L as R toe pivots outward and arms bend L (ct 1); repeat ct 1 with opp hand-ftwk (ct 2).

8   Repeat meas 7, ct 1 (ct 1); stamp R beside L (ct 2).
1   *Step 2.*
      Facing slightly and moving LOD, step on R as arms go down (ct 1); hop on R as L lifts behind (ct 2).
2   Step L-R-L as arms raise again (cts 3 and 4).
3–4   Repeat *Step 2* meas 1–2 (cts 1–4).
5–6   Releasing finger hold, make complete revolution to R with R-L-R touching L to R on 4th ct as hands clap (cts 1–4).
7–8   *Repeat Step 2,* meas 5–6 with opp ftwk & direction (cts 1–4).
      Note: Step 1 done to chorus "Karoun Karoun" and step 2 done to verses.

OEE NAZE (girl's name)
Source: Learned by Tom Bozigian at the Institute of Ethnology of the University of Yerevan from Zhenya Khachturyan, researcher, in June 1975. A Kurdish Armenian dance.
Record: "Songs and Dances of the Armenian People," GT 3001-LP
Formation: Mixed, open line with hand hold

Meter 2/4   Pattern

Each meas described in 2 cts
Meas   Instrumental intro: 10 meas
1–2   Facing ctr, with hands joined at side, do 4 side steps to R starting on R (R-L-R-L) as arms swing with each step bk, fwd, bk, fwd (cts 1–4).
3   Step R to R as arms swing bk (ct 5); step L behind R as hands are raised to shldr ht (ct 6).
4   Step R to R (ct 7); touch L beside R (ct 8).
5   Turning to face R, dip on L as L arm is drawn to small of bk & R arm extends to front neighbor's bk (ct 9); bounce twice on L (ct 10, and).
6   Turning ¼ to R, step fwd, on R as hands are released (ct 11); step L-R in place turning R to face LOD as hands clap in front at chest level when stepping on L (ct 12, and).
7   Step L to L as hands are again grasped swinging bk (ct 13); touch R beside L as arms are raised to shldr ht (ct 14).
8   Step R across L as arms from elbows up bend to R (ct 15); step L to L as arms bend to L (ct 16).
       Note: Dance is done 7 times in all.

SEV ACHEROV AGHCHEEK (Girl with the Black Eyes)

Source: Learned by Tom Bozigian at the Youth Palace in Yerevan, capital of Soviet Armenia, in May 1975.

Record: "Songs and Dances of the Armenian People," GT 3001-LP. Used with the permission of the Armenian State Estrada Ensembles.

Formation: Mixed line dance with little fingers grasped

Meter 2/4   Pattern

Each meas described in 2 cts

Meas   Instrumental intro: 10 meas

Figure I

1   With leader at L of line and little fingers held at shldr ht (dancers facing diag L) step L to L (ct 1); touch R toe beside L (ct 2).

2   Repeat above with opp ftwk (cts 3–4).

3   Step L to L (ct 5); step R in pl as body turns to R (ct and); step L across R (ct 6).

4   Facing ctr, step on ball of R pivoting both heels slightly R as body turns slightly L (ct 7); pivot heels slightly L as body turns slightly R (ct and); repeat opp action of above ct and (ct 8).

Figure II (in 3 parts)

1–2 Facing and moving ctr, walk 4 steps starting L as arms are lowered gradually to side (cts 1–4); arms swing slightly fwd (ct and).

3   Turning to face R, dip on L to L as L arm is drawn to small of bk and R extends fwd (fingers remain grasped) (ct 5); bounce twice on R (cts 6, and).

4   Dip again on L (ct 7); bounce once on R (ct 8).

5   Facing and moving R, step on L as hands clap in front at chest level (ct 9); step on R as L hand is placed on front neighbor's L shoulder and R hand is extended straight out to R, palm facing out (ct 10).

6   Do 2-step (L-R-L) (ct 11 and, 12).

7–8 As hands remain in same position, repeat meas 5–6, cts 9–12 (13–16).

9   Pivoting on R to face diag R (line now facing outside of ctr) as hands (little fingers grasped) are lowered to side, step L across R with plié (ct 17); step R to R (ct 18).

10   Touch L beside R (ct 19); step L across R as body turns slightly R (ct 20); step R to R as body turns slightly L (ct and).

11   Repeat ct 17 (ct 21); touch R heel to R (ct 22).

12   Do 2-step starting R (R-L-R) (cts 23–24).
     Notes: Dance fig I and II three times in all.
     In first transition from fig II to start fig I again

execute approx 360° CW turn with 4 walking steps in pl starting with L, hands remaining down (4 cts). In second transition, execute turn with only 2 walking steps. For ending when on fig II, third time, repeat cts 17–20 but this time holding with no weight on L, and execute turn again with 4 walking steps (4 cts) stamping L in pl (ct and).

SIRDES (Armenian misirlou)

Source: Armenian Youth Organizations of Los Angeles

Record: Express A101-B(S), side 1

Formation: Open, mixed cir with little finger hold at shldr ht

Meter 4/4   Pattern

Meas

1   Facing ctr, touch L across R (ct 1); touch L to L (ct 2).

2   Repeat meas 1, cts 1–2 (cts 3–4).

3   Step L over R (ct 5); cross R over L (ct 6).

4   Cross L over R (ct 7); step R to R (ct and); step L behind R (ct 8); step R to R (ct and).
     Note: Dance begins where musical phrase begins.

BULGARIA

Bulgarian Folk Dancing

by Yves Moreau

The great variety of movements and steps as well as the intricate rhythmic structures found in Bulgarian folk dances indicate the various developments undergone throughout hundreds of years.

In the 7th century A.D., the Bulgars, under their leader, Asparoukh, settled in the Balkan Peninsula. They eventually mixed with the Slav tribes which were already there. Both of these cultures integrated, thus forming a new and rich cultural heritage which has evolved until today and which still occasionally carries traits of Thracian, Hellenic and Roman times.

Very little is known as to the precise types of dances which were done during the early years of the new Bulgarian state; however, old books contain information related to chain-type dances and point out that these songs and dances were quite popular among the

Amateur Ensemble, Bulgaria

people. Furthermore, many of those manuscripts, which were written by religious writers, suggest that dancing was very much frowned upon by the Church Elders, [who] attributed the devil as the main Instigator.

Old paintings and frescoes which depict various forms of folk dances and which throw some light on their nature during the Middle Ages have been found in monasteries and churches. Some good examples may be found in the Rila Monastery in southwest Bulgaria as well as in several churches throughout the country.

Slav peoples (Ukrainians, Serbs, Macedonians) utilize many common dance forms in their folklore which have developed differently through the centuries according to each nation's characteristic features (e.g., chain dances).

The only information as to the folk dance traditions in Bulgaria during the Ottoman rule (1396–1878) is found in diaries and travel accounts of foreigners who would be passing through the country on their way to Constantinople (Tsarigrad). Their actual descriptions of the dances were very vague, however. One

of the best reports was written by a French scientist, Ami Boué, in the early 19th century. He clearly made mention of the *horo*, danced in open circles with belt hold, as well as the couple dance *râčenica*, with the dancers holding a handkerchief in their hands.

It is most important to state that the long Turkish rule did not destroy the old song and dance traditions of the Bulgarians. In fact, because of their oppression, the people became more conscious of their cultural heritage. The monasteries became underground "houses of culture" where books were secretly published and where education was offered. This movement produced such key figures as Otec Pajissi, Rakovski, and Botev, whose names were synonymous with Bulgaria's cultural and political liberation.

The first serious scientific collections of Bulgarian songs and dances were written in the 19th century by such scholars as the Midodinov brothers (1891), Vassil Čolakov (1872), and Ivan Šismanov (1889). These books gave a detailed picture of the many types of dances in each region as well as the existing songs, rituals and musical instruments.

Another serious scientific account on the dance folklore of the 19th century was by a Czech music teacher, Karal Mahan, and was entitled "Choreography from Vidin and Lom Counties." Mahan's research, however, was concentrated on that particular region of northwest Bulgaria.

[Even] today, folk dances in Bulgaria undergo transformations as they are passed down from the old to the new generation. Many dances known to have been danced in the 19th century are still done today. This is easily proven by the accounts of the old folk, who remember those dances from their parents. Therefore, in a given village dance repertory one usually finds a mixture of old and new dances.

Tunes and rhythms go through a renewal process. Among the most common sources of change are Gypsy musicians who continuously experiment with new musical ornamentations and, more recently, radio broadcasts where many musicians hear new tunes from other parts of Bulgaria and the Balkans.

The horo, or chain dance (derived from the Greek xopós) holds a central place in the socio-cultural activities of rural Bulgaria. The horo is mostly a community dance which, until recently, could be observed every Sunday in the village square. Today, due to the greater choice of free-time activities and the lack of interest on the part of the younger generation, folk dancing has been confined to a few specific occasions.

Most weddings, whether held in small villages or big cities, will include much horo dancing with exciting music provided by good local Gypsy bands, generally using brass instruments. There are regional fairs and festivals held annually or at specific intervals which

Shope Dancers. Photo by Sofia Press

will include spontaneous folk singing and dancing. Among the most famous are the Rožen fair, held in August near Smoljan, in the Rhodope mountains; the Pirin festival at Predel, near Blagoevgrad; the National Folk Festival in Koprivŝtica ([held] every five years); the Rose festivities in Kazanlŭk and Karlovo in May; and the Haskovo Thracian Festival in June.

Most towns and villages organize festivities including folk dancing at some specific time in the year, but, due to poor scheduling and lack of communication within the country, it is quite hard to find out exactly when and where these manifestations take place.

Every village has its local repertoire of horos and other dances which reflect the local character of the people. It is important to note, however, that there are four basic horos characterized by their rhythm and steps and danced throughout the country. They are:

1. the Pravo, or straight dance, in 2/4 meter
2. the Pajduško, or limping dance, in 5/16 meter
3. the povârnato, or turning dance (sometimes known as Šareni Čorapi or Svornoto), in 9/8 meter
4. the Râčenica (literally meaning small handkerchief) in 7/16 meter

The Râčenica is probably the most widespread dance in Bulgaria, for it can be performed in many ways: solo, couples, trios, segregated and even in a horo form (this type is usually referred to as horo-râčenica or hvanati-râčenica [hooked râčenica]).

The râčenica is considered by many as the liveliest of all Bulgarian dances, for in it dancers can show their greatest skills.

Other dances which are widespread throughout most regions of Bulgaria include Eleno Mome (Elenino Horo), Dajčovo Horo (especially popular in the West and North) and Gankino (also known as Kopanica or Krivo), which is found in most regions except East Thrace and the Rhodopes.

The horo can be danced in a closed or open circle formation, or in a straight or "crooked" line. The best dancers are usually located at each end of the line (na dva tanca). Both of them guide the group through exciting patterns while waving a kûrpa (handkerchief) in the free hand. The leader is called horovedec, vodač, glava or čelo.

There are many hand positions and formations used in Bulgarian horo dancing. Hands can be joined down at sides or up at shoulder height; or crossed in front or back in a basket fashion; or the arms may rest on the neighbors' shoulders. Perhaps the most characteristic of all positions is the na pojas, where the dancers hold each other by their belts or waistbands. When a group of dancers uses this particular hold and dances

in a straight line, this formation is known as na lesa (on a stave). Other formations include crooked or twisted lines, open or closed circles with mixed or segregated groups of dancers.

The names of some dances and tunes often refer to the town or village from which they come: Radomirsko, Kulsko, Jambolsko, for example. Other dance names originate from a person's name: Gankino (Ganka's), Denjovo (Denjo's), Dajčovo (Dajčo's). Often, dances are related to the milieu in which they are danced or may indicate a craft or trade guild: Grânčarsko (potter), Kasapsko (butcher), Kalajdžisko (tinsmith).

The exact character of the dance can also be defined precisely in its name: Čukanoto (stamped), Kucano (limping), sitno (small). The character of the dance may sometimes be described by using names of animals: Zaješkato (rabbit), Konskato (horse), Ovcata (sheep). Many names of horos also show a foreign origin: Čerkeska (Circassian), Šumadijsko (from Šumadija, Serbia), Vlaško (Vlach). In a reverse manner, some dances of other Balkan countries show a definite Bulgarian origin. Pajduško and Râčenica dances are done in Romania and Greece and there is a Turkish dance known as Bulgaristan Usulu (in the Bulgarian way).

[Even] today, many weddings are accompanied by special songs and dances. A honey loaf is baked on Friday before the wedding and a horo is danced around it. The dance is led by the brother-in-law holding the oruglica, the wedding banner decorated with flowers and ribbons (this is sometimes replaced with a flag). While the bridegroom is having a shave, his mother circles around him three times with a small kettle of water in her hand dancing the râčenica. On leaving her father's house, the bride dances a slow râčenica, with deep bows, next to the godfather, who is the leader. Brothers- and sisters-in-law dance the râčenica with small steps before the wedding procession. The mother-in-law, or her son, with candles held in their hands or stuck in a bowl full of flour, meets the young couple. Then the bride gives presents to the guests and all who have received such gifts dance a special darovno (gift) horo led by the brother-in-law holding the oruglica (banner).

Kukeri or carnival dances can still be observed today throughout Bulgaria. Most carnival celebrations take place during the week preceding Lent, but some other manifestations occur throughout the year as well. Carnival dancers generally wear fantastic masks and tie copper cowbells around their waists. Each region has its typical costumes and masks. In the past, carnival dancers performed each dance to the sound of musical instruments, usually a gajda (goatskin bagpipe). Now they content themselves with the noise of the brass and copper bells which hang around their waists. The carnival dances are of a free-style nature, including leaps, hops, jumps and turns, and are usually performed individually.

The 2/4 is the most common measure found in Bulgarian folk dance music. However, the most characteristic rhythms are the ones which are the foundation of many unequal beats (5/16, 7/16, 9/16, 11/16) or even intricate combinations such as 7/16 + 11/16.

Such rhythms are typically Balkan and are best thought of as combinations of quicks and slows rather than using Western time signatures. A Bulgarian village musician can rarely identify the time signature of a dance tune. Just like the drummer, he will relate to the melody in terms of quick or slow stresses.

Bulgarian dancing is done mostly with the feet. There are, however, certain dance stylings which are characteristic of specific regions of Bulgaria. I use the term regional styling here to make a clear distinction from the term "style," that misconceived word which has to do with each individual dancer's degree of emotional involvement with a dance which makes him move in a certain way. "Stylings" can be taught, style can't be. Dances of the Šop area (named after the Šopi, an ethnic group found in western Bulgaria and eastern parts of Serbia and Macedonia) are usually quite fast, with tricky movements and wild tunes, while dances of Thrace are more solemn and generally slower. The dances from the western part of Thrace, west of Plovdiv and around Panagjurište and Ihtiman, are livelier and are sometimes confused with the Šop ones.

Dances of the Pirin region (named after the mountains of the same name) use larger steps and tricky movements as well. The dances of the Pirin region, which is in fact the eastern portion of Macedonia, are very much related to the types found slightly to the west of Yugoslav-Macedonia in such towns as Kriva Palanka, Strumica, Delčevo, and so forth. Many of these Pirin (Macedonian) dances begin slowly, using an improvised pattern which develops later into a more regular form at a faster tempo.

North Bulgarian dances are in general quite energetic and exuberant. Dances of the northwest have a similar character but have [a] more marked influence from nearby Serbia as well as a strong Romanian flavor radiated by the imposing number of Vlachs in that area. The dances of Dobrudža are probably the most exciting to watch. Dobrudžan dances are done generally at moderate tempo, using slightly bent knees, with the dancers' backs arched backward. Shoulder and arm movements play an important role in their dances. It is quite probable that some of these stylings were influenced by the Turks, as similar forms are found along the Black Sea coast in Turkey.

Not too many dances have been collected in the Rhodopes (named after the mountain range). The types of dances observed there very much resemble those in eastern Thrace. Dances in the western part of the Rhodopes have much in common with those in the Pirin. In the eastern section, there are many Turkish settlements which have kept up specific traditional dances. The entire region, however, is perhaps the richest treasure-house of folk songs in Bulgaria. The Strandza area is also a subdivision of eastern Thrace, where singing tradition is predominant. The area used to be famous for the Nestinarsko (fire-dance) ritual. The râčenica po trojki (for three) is widespread in that part of the country.

One must not forget the various minority groups throughout Bulgaria who have kept up specific dances and traditions. Among them are the Vlachs in northern Bulgaria (mostly northwest); the Kapanci, descendants of the first Bulgar settlers of the 6th century A.D., who live around Razgrad in northeast Bulgaria; the Turks in the northeast and southeast parts of the country; and the Gypsies, as well as the Armenians, Serbs and Greeks.

The Folk Dance Department of the State Choreography School offers a three-year course for young boys and girls who would like to work with a performing folk ensemble. The course gives basic information on ethnography, ethnomusicology, basic steps, regional styles, choreography and staging. Upon graduating from this school, the boy or girl is usually assigned to one of the thousands of groups in Bulgaria or is asked to form a new one.

Bulgarian Folk Dancing in America

What sparked interest in Bulgarian folk dancing and folklore in America? Why is it still quite popular? To answer these questions, one has to go back to the beginning of the folk dance movement in the United States. Before Americans started flying to Europe every summer to bring back new dances, the main source of material was from the various ethnic communities living here. This is where such pioneers as Michael and Mary Ann Herman and Vyts Beliajus taught many of the dances.

The Bulgarian community in America is not a very large one compared to the Italian, Greek or Ukrainian. The main migration from the Balkans started in the early 20th century and continued through World War II. Most of the Bulgarians settled in such industrial areas as Pittsburgh, Toledo, Chicago and Detroit. The biggest communities today are found in Canada, in the greater Toronto area, as well as Hamilton and Windsor.

Photo by Jacques Bourassa

Some of the first basic Bulgarian dances appeared on the folk dancing circuit in the early fifties, filtering out from Bulgarian parties (večerinka) or social picnics. The Detroit Bulgarians, for example, did such favorites as: Eleno Mome, Šana Horo, Ciganskoto, Pajduško and Zmirna Horo. Anatal Joukowsky and John Filcich in California popularized many Bulgarian dances on the original XOPO 78 rpm disks such as Gankino, Narodno and Trakijsko.

The first North American to travel to Bulgaria for the sole purpose of researching folk dancing and spreading it over here was Michel Cartier from Montreal. Michel was then director of a famous amateur folk dance group in Montreal, Les Feux Follets, and co-ordinator of folk dancing activities for the city of Montreal. As a member of the jury at the Moscow Youth Festival in 1956, he became fascinated with the Bulgarian groups there. He quickly made friends with members of the Bulgarian delegation and a year later had an official invitation to visit Bulgaria. In Sofia, he had special classes with such specialists as Haralampiev, Dženev and dancers from various other ensembles. He learned many steps . . . from all regions of Bulgaria. Up to that moment, very little had been known here about such ethnographic zones as Dobrudža and Strandža. After this work in Bulgaria, Michel toured the United States and Canada several times and presented many of these new dances. Most important, he brought back some excellent recordings (Folk Dancer label) and many are considered the best: Dajčovo (Zizaj Nane), Trite Pâti, Ekizlijsko.

From that moment, Bulgarian folk dancing was "in." Dick Crum, then choreographer of the Duquesne University Tamburitzans, researched some material for the Tammies and the Tammies always had a Bulgarian suite in their show. Kolo festivals and parties always included horos and râčenicas.

The first appearance of the Filip Kutev Ensemble in 1963 across America did much to stimulate further interest. This great ensemble presented a fascinating concert with colorful costumes, emotional songs and intricate yet down-to-earth dancing. Several groups of folk dancers got the opportunity to learn some dances and styling points from the Kutev group during their tour.

The next person to do additional research in Bulgaria was Dennis Boxell. Dennis brought back mostly original village dances unchanged and used village folk music, relased on the Folkraft label.

Finally, dozens of excited folk dancers have been combing Bulgaria in the last ten years learning material and adding it to the ever-growing Bulgarian repertoires. Martin Koenig from New York and Yves Moreau from Montreal spent many months in Bulgaria and brought back many village and ensemble dances. In that same period of time, Dick Crum introduced new material, as did Ronnie Wixman, Steve Glaser and members of the Aman group from Los Angeles.

What will happen in the next ten years? In the last five, folk dancers have developed a taste for simpler dances with primitive music. This trend is continuing.

More people have traveled to the Balkans and have "seen the real thing." Some of those traveling folk dancers have even stopped dancing completely in folk dance halls and clubs because they couldn't take the hassle of fighting their way for a place in the line to dance a 56-figure Kopanica to a scratchy Boris Karlov record. Their minds were still at that village wedding in the Rhodopes where they had danced a Pravo for three hours to the sound of three gajdas.

I believe that the Bulgarian Folk Dance Machine should take a rest. Already [there are] over 150 dances . . . in the repertoire. Most of them have been forgotten or badly butchered and still people ask for MORE . . . MORE. . . . People tire fast of the old dances; they seek new steps, new tunes and new rhythms. The teachers and researchers easily become caterers feeding the masses. Local teachers who can't afford time or money to go to the Balkans want MORE for their group and people attending the 683rd Balkan Festival want MORE for their money.

Bulgaria deserves a break. The trend right now seems to be moving East to the more exotic stuff: Turkey, Arab countries, North Africa. But WAIT . . . WAIT! We can't go too far East. We forgot one tiny spot in the Balkans: Albania. Folk dancers, teachers, researchers, musicians, record companies: on your mark, get set, GO!

(The preceding article was excerpted, with permission, from material provided by Yves Moreau.) (Yves Moreau started folk dancing as a Canadian Boy Scout. He danced with several recreational folk dance groups in the Montreal area, where he developed a particular interest in Balkan folklore and culture and became active within the Serbian community as a leader of the performing group as well as a member of the Serbian Choir. In 1966 Yves traveled to Bulgaria for the first time, then spent a year codirecting the Koleda Ensemble in Seattle. He was a guest teacher for the 1967 San Francisco Kolo Festival, taught in several West Coast cities, including the Aman Folk Ensemble in Los Angeles. In 1968, at the Kolo Festival in San Francisco, he introduced the famous Dobrudjanska Reka. Yves calls this dance ill-fated since it has been taught and retaught in so many different ways ever since.

In 1969 Yves spent a year in Bulgaria learning the varied regional stylings of dances and making tapes and films as a special guest of the Bulgarian Committee for Friendship and Cultural Relations with Foreign Countries. While in Bulgaria, he supervised the production of a special LP with twelve new Bulgarian dances pressed by Balkanton, the state firm. On this record were such popular dances as Dospatsko, Denjovo, Kulsko, and Bičak. The years 1970–71 marked a long tour across the United States and Canada in-

Yves Moreau. Photo by Barry Korn

volving teaching at many camps. In 1971 he choreographed a special suite of Dobrudjan dances for the Duquesne University Tamburitzans. This suite was presented by the Tammies in their North American tours and their appearance in France.

Since 1972 Yves has been very active in folk dance activities in Montreal and elsewhere in Canada. He has served as co-ordinator of folk dance activities for the City of Montreal Parks & Recreation Department and workshop co-ordinator for the Quebec Folk Dance Federation. He was guest speaker at the Dance Canada Conference in Edmondton and the Canadian Association for Health, Physical Education and Recreation Conference in Saskatoon. He has produced several radio broadcasts on international folk music for the Canadian Broadcasting Corporation (CBC) French network and produced more recordings of Bulgarian dances with Worldtone Records in New York. With a grant from the Canada Council he researched the Bulgarian-Macedonian communities in Canada. He returned to Bulgaria and the Balkans for more collecting in 1973, 1974, 1975, and 1976, and has conducted workshops in Mexico, England, Switzerland, the Netherlands, and twice in Japan.

In 1976 Yves was technical co-ordinator for all folklore performances organized by the Olympic Committee's Arts & Culture Programme at the Montreal Summer Games. He is currently on the staff of the Canadian Folk Arts Council at the Montreal office, where he edits that excellent Canadian folk arts magazine *Le Troubador*. Since 1972 he has been director of Les Gens de Mon Pays, a Montreal-based performing group of twenty-four dancers and five musicians specializing in Bulgarian and French-Canadian dances. The group toured Bulgaria in 1975 and France in 1976.)

BULGARIAN FOLK DANCES

BREGOVSKO HORO

Source: Bregovsko Horo (BREH-gohf-skoh hoh-ROH) was learned by Yves Moreau in the fall of 1969 at a local festival in Novo Selo, Vidin District, Northwest Bulgaria. It is widespread in the vicinity of Bregovo near the border with Serbia and Yugoslavia. It is of the "Čačak" type, with a ten-measure pattern. Bregovsko is danced by Bulgarians and Vlachs living in the area.

Record: Worldtone BG-1001, side A, band 1

Formation: Short mixed lines of M and W; belt hold, L over R; face center; wt on L

Style: Small steps, sharp movements, knees slightly bent, arms relaxed. Often the dancers at both ends of the line make the line bend and twist sharply ("na dva tanca").

Meter 2/4　　Pattern

Meas　Dance may begin at beginning of any musical phrase.

1　Facing ctr, step R to R (ct 1); step on L behind R (ct 2).

2　Repeat action of meas 1.

3　Step on R to R (ct 1); small hop on R bringing L slightly across in front of R (ct 2).

4　Step on L across in front of R (ct 1); small hop on L, bringing R ft slightly fwd and across L (ct 2).

5　Step R across L bending fwd, and face L of ctr (ct 1); small hop on R (ct 2).

6　Step L to L of ctr (ct 1); step on R in front of L (ct 2).

7　Facing ctr, step onto L (ct 1); small hop on L in place (ct 2).

8　Small step on R twd ctr (ct 1); small hop on R (ct 2).

9　Facing slightly L of ctr, small step on L to L (ct 1); step on R across L (ct 2).

10　Facing ctr, small step on L to L, bending upper part of body slightly (ct 1); small, sharp stamp with R next to L, no wt (ct 2).

DENJOVO HORO

Source: Denjovo Horo (DEHN-yoh-voh hoh-ROH) was learned by Yves Moreau in the winter of 1970 from Stefan Stojkov, from the village of Lovnidol, near Gabrovo, northern Bulgaria. The dance is very popular throughout most villages in Gabrovo District. It is often referred to as the North Bulgarian Četvorno.

Record: Balkanton BHA 734, side 1, band 6. 7/16 meter: 1-2-3, 1-2, 1-2. Counted here as *1*, 2, 3. Slow down record slightly.

Formation: Mixed lines of M and W, hands joined down at sides, face slightly R of ctr, wt on L ft

Steps: Pas de Basque: to L—Step L to L (ct 1). Step R in front of L (ct 2). Step back on L in place (ct 3).

　　to R—Reverse ftwk.

Style: Moves quickly, with very light, sharp, small steps. Leader starts at the beg of any 8-meas musical phrase. He may change to next pattern at his discretion and should signal change by raising his R hand.

Meter 7/16　　Pattern

Meas

Figure I: Basic

1　Moving in LOD, step R (ct *1*). Lift on R (ct 2). Step in LOD with L (ct 3).

2　Facing ctr, step R to R (ct *1*). Close L to R, bouncing twice on both ft (cts 2, 3).

3　Repeat action of meas 2, Fig I, reversing ftwk and dir.

4　Repeat action of meas 2, Fig I, exactly.

5–8　Repeat action of meas 1–4, Fig I, reversing ftwk and dir.

Figure II: Pas de Basque

1　Facing and moving LOD, repeat action of meas 1, Fig I.

2　Facing ctr, Pas de Basque R.

3　Facing ctr, Pas de Basque L.

4　Facing ctr, Pas de Basque R.

5–8　Repeat action of meas 1–4, Fig II, reversing dir and ftwk.

Figure III: Jump

1–2　Repeat action of meas 1–2, Fig II.

3　Facing ctr, wide jump onto both ft in stride pos, R ft remaining on spot, L ft to L side (ct *1*). Hold (cts 2,3).

4　Pas de Basque R, but take small leap to R on ct *1*.

5–8　Repeat action of meas 1–4, Fig III, reversing ftwk and dir.

Figure IV: Heel Bounce

1　Facing ctr, small hop on L ft (ct "uh"—upbeat ahead of *1*), take a large reaching step to R

with R ft, dragging L ft twd R (ct *1*). Jump
to R side, ft together, knees bent (ct 2). Hold
(ct 3).

2   Small leap onto R, throwing L lower leg back
and to L side (ct *1*). Extend L heel fwd close
to R ft, bounce twice on R ft, at same time
touch L heel twice on floor (cts 2, 3).

3   Repeat action of meas 2, Fig IV, reversing ftwk
and dir.

4   Repeat action of meas 2, Fig IV, exactly.

5–8   Repeat action of meas 1–4, Fig IV, reversing
ftwk and dir.

DOBRUDŽANSKA REKA

Source: Dobrudžanska Reka (doh-bruh-ZHAHN-
skah RUH-kah) was learned by Camille Brochu,
of Montreal, from "Ansamble Sredec" in Sofia, Bulgaria, during the summer of 1968. It was first presented by Yves Moreau at the 1968 Kolo Festival
in San Francisco. The dance, as learned by Camille,
was choreographed for and performed only by
women, but Dobrudžan men also dance rekas (a
generic term referring to dances which involve hand
movements; reka means "hands").

Record: XOPO (45 rpm) X-318, Nama 2 (LP) 1002;
2/4 meter; must be slowed down

Formation: *W only* in short lines of 6 to 8 dancers.
Hands joined at shldr level, "W" pos. Hands back
near shldrs, not pushed fwd. Face slightly R of ctr,
wt on L ft.

Steps and Styling: *Basic Step* (1 meas to complete):
With a preparatory lift on ball of L ft, step on ball
of R ft (ct 1); come down on full R ft as L full ft
stamps beside R, both knees bent (ct &). Repeat
with opp ftwk, including preparatory lift (cts 2 &).
Throughout dance the Basic Step always begins by
stepping onto R ft for ct 1 of meas involved. There
is more emphasis on lift of body from ball of supporting ft than in covering distance. Body bends
from waist twd side of stamping ft—the head and
shldrs tip from side to side as a result of bending
at the waist; the hands remain in orig pos—do not
pump up and down. The emphasis of the steps is
more vertical than horizontal; the ball of the ft contacts the floor first. However, the stamps are firm
and done with full ft.
The W of Dobrudža dance with simplicity and calm-
ness and, at the same time, exhibit strength and
firmness. There is contrast throughout the dance
between soft lyricism and sharp, quick, strong movements. The W occasionally shout in a high-pitched
voice "lju, lju, lju, lju, lju, lju, lju" (pronounced
lyoo), stressing the seventh shout.

Meter 2/4   Pattern

Meas

4   Intro—no action

Figure I: Entrance
This fig is never repeated.

1–16   With 16 Basic Steps move in LOD.

Figure II: Solo
Release hands, put fists on hips (do not break
wrists), face ctr, use Basic Step throughout.
The area of movement is confined within a radius of a normal-sized step to the R, to the
L, fwd, and bk to place in a continuous, smooth,
flowing manner.

1   During the preparatory lift begin to turn ¼
CW and finish facing in LOD (ct 1); move twd
ctr, L shldr leading (ct 2).

2   Retrace steps.

3   Turn ¼ CCW and move twd ctr, R shldr leading (ct 1); turn ¼ CW to face ctr and move
to L (ct 2).

4   Retrace steps, but continue to face RLOD on
ct 2.

5–16   Repeat action of meas 1–4, fig II, 3 more times
(4 in all). On each repeat of meas 1, ct 1 involves
a ½ turn CW to face LOD.

Figure III: Moving Sideward
Join hands down at sides, elbows locked. Face
ctr exactly, but move LOD.

1   Step R sdwd R, arms thrust bkwd (ct 1); step
on L across in front of R, arms brought fwd
but not high (ct &); repeat action for cts
2, &.

2   Step R sdwd R, arms thrust bkwd (ct 1); stamp
L beside R, no wt, arms fwd (ct &). Step L
sdwd L, arms thrust bkwd (ct 2); stamp R beside L, no wt, arms fwd (ct &).

3–16   Repeat action of meas 1–2, fig III, 7 more times
(8 in all). The arm swings are short, tense, and
strong; elbows remain locked.

Figure IV: Moving Forward

1–2   Face ctr and move fwd with 2 Basic Steps.
Arms swing fwd on ct 1, bkwd on ct 2, and
the arms are much more relaxed than in fig
III. Elbows are straight, but not rigid. Arm
movement is softer because it is half as fast
as in fig III. Head tips from side to side (same
side as stepping ft), but this action must be
natural and not forced and is achieved only
after great familiarity with ftwk, arm motions,
and mood of dance.

3   Hop on L, simultaneously raising hands up at
about a 45° angle from shldr (ct 1); stamp R

beside L, no wt (ct &); leap onto R in place (ct 2); stamp L beside R, no wt (ct &).

4   Leap onto L in place (ct 1); stamp R beside L, no wt (ct &); stamp R again, no wt, bring hands down sharply to "W" pos (ct 2).

5–16 Repeat action of meas 1–4, fig IV, 3 more times (4 in all). Always move fwd twd ctr on first two meas of the fig.

Figure V. Basic and Stamps

1–2 With hands raised high, elbows fairly straight, face R of ctr, move in LOD with one Basic Step. Turn to face L of ctr, move bkwd in LOD with one Basic Step. Bring hands sharply to "W" pos on & before ct 2.

3   Turn to face R of ctr and move in LOD with one Basic Step. Push hands up, fwd, swing down and bkwd on cts 1, &, 2; swing fwd (not high) (ct &).

4   Stamp R beside L, no wt, arms thrust bkwd (ct 1); arms fwd (ct &). Repeat actions for cts 2, &. Arm motions are again sharp and tense as in fig III.

5–16 Repeat action of meas 1–4, fig V, 3 more times (4 in all).

Figure VI. Finale

1   Face ctr and move fwd with one Basic Step. Arms swing fwd on ct 1, bkwd on ct 2 with soft motion as in fig IV.

2   Step bkwd on R (ct 1); close L to R (ct &); step fwd on R (ct 2); scuff L heel fwd, rising on ball of R ft (ct &). Arms swing rhythmically as in meas 1—fwd on ct 1, bkwd on ct 2. On "scuff" arms begin to come up fwd.

3   Turning to face slightly L of ctr, step on L to L, hands high (ct 1); stamp R beside L, no wt, bring hands sharply to "W" pos (ct &); *facing ctr,* step bkwd onto ball of R ft, knee straight (L ft stays in place and may turn in slightly as body turns to face ctr); extend arms fwd at shldr level, elbows almost straight (ct 2); hold (ct &). There is no exaggerated movement of arms or head. Total wt is on ball of R ft on cts 2, &.

4   Take wt on L ft in place, hands start to come back to "W" pos (ct 1); stamp R beside L, no wt, hands in "W" pos (ct &); hands go up a little (ct ah); stamp R beside L again, no wt, hands come back to "W" pos (ct 2); hold (ct &). The hand motions are short and sharp.

5–16 Repeat action of meas 1–4, fig VI, 3 more times (4 in all). *Dance repeats from fig II.*

DOSPATSKO HORO

Source: Dospatsko Horo (dose-PAHT-skoh hoh-ROH) was learned by Yves Moreau in December 1969 from Nasko Dimitrov in Smoljan, Bulgaria. The dance comes from the small town of Dospot, in the Smoljan District. It is done by the Bulgarian-Mohammedans in the western part of the Rhodopes.

Record: Balkanton BHA 734, side 1, band 3. 7/8 meter: 1-2-3, 1-2, 1-2. Counted here as *1, 2, 3.*

Formation: Segregated lines; M use shldr hold, W use "W" pos; face ctr; wt on L ft.

Style: Smooth, quiet, controlled—somewhat heavy in feeling. Has a Macedonian flavor. W arms move up and down with the rhythm, and their movements are not as large as those of the M.

Meter 7/8   Pattern

Meas

     No intro

     Figure I: In Place

1–2 In place, step R, L, R (cts *1, 2, 3*). Repeat for meas 2, begin L.

3   Step R to R (ct *1*). Lift on R, bringing L around behind R (ct 2). Step L behind R (ct 3).

4   Step R to R (ct *1*). Step L across in front of R (ct 2). Step back in place on R (ct 3).

5–8 Repeat action of meas 1–4, reversing ftwk and dir.

     Figure II: Grapevine

1   Step R to R (ct *1*). Step L across in front of R (cts 2, 3).

2   Step R to R (ct *1*). Step L across in back of R (cts 2, 3).

3–4 Repeat action of meas 3–4, Fig I.

5–8 Repeat action of meas 1–4, Fig II reversing ftwk and dir.

9–16 Repeat Fig II, meas 1–8, exactly.

     Figure III: Rocking

1   Step bkwd on R, leaving L in place (ct *1*). Rock fwd onto L (ct 2). Rock bkwd onto R (ct 3).

2   Large, smooth walking step fwd on L (ct *1*). Step fwd R, bending knee, simultaneously bring L ft up behind R leg, L knee turned out (cts 2, 3)

3–4 Moving bkwd, step L, R, L (cts *1, 2, 3*). Repeat for meas 4, begin R.

5–8 Repeat action of meas 1–4, Fig III, with opposite ftwk.

9–16 Repeat Fig III, meas 1–8, exactly.

     Figures IV, V, VI
     Repeat Figs I, II, and III exactly.

     Figure VII: Traveling

1–2 Facing slightly R and moving LOD, step R,

L, R (cts *1*, 2, 3). Continue for meas 2, begin L.

3　　Face ctr, step R to R (ct *1*). Lift on R, bringing L around behind R (ct 2). Step L behind R (ct 3).

4　　Facing slightly R and moving LOD, step R (ct *1*). Step L (cts 2, 3).

5–16　Repeat Fig VII, meas 1–4, 3 more times (4 in all)

Figures VIII, IX, X

Repeat Figs I, II, and III. On final meas, close R to L (ct 2). Hold (ct 3).

SANDANSKO HORO

Source: Sandansko Horo (sahn-DAHN-skoh ho-ROH) was learned by Yves Moreau in October 1969 from members of a folk ensemble from the town of Sandanski, Blagoevgrad District, Bulgaria. This dance is quite popular in the villages of Liljakovo and Ogražden, located in the Pirin (eastern Macedonia) area in the southwestern part of Bulgaria. It has an interesting rhythmic structure of $^{22}/_{16}$, a combination of a $^{9}/_{16} + ^{13}/_{16}$. The most popular instrument of this region is the tambura. Many of the players are Gypsies and have adopted some musical ornaments and styles from nearby Greece.

Record: Worldtone WT-YM-004, side A, band 1 (45 rpm)

Formation: Mixed lines of M and W, hands joined down at sides; face slightly R of ctr; wt on L ft.

Style: Slight knee bend, with upper part of body erect; Steps small and light (balls of feet); arms relaxed.

Meter $^{9}/_{16} + ^{13}/_{16}$　　Pattern

Count as follows: 1-2, 1-2, 1-2, 1-2-3 + 1-2, 1-2, 1-2, 1-2-3, 1-2, 1-2. Counted here as 1, 2, 3, *4* + 1, 2, 3, *4*, 5, 6.

Meas

1　　Small hop on L ft in place simultaneously raising R ft a little from ground and pointing it R (ct 1) step on R to R (ct 2) small low leap onto L ft directly behind R (3) step on R to R (ct 4).

2　　Repeat pattern of meas 1 reversing ftwk (cts 1–4). Small leap onto R ft to R (ct 5). Small step on L to R (ct 6).

3　　Small hop on L ft, simultaneously lifting R leg and pointing it to R (ct 1). Hop again on L; R leg now points to ctr (2). Hop again on L; R leg now points to L (ct 3). Facing L, step on R ft (ct 4).

4　　Facing and moving in reverse LOD, small leap fwd onto L (ct 1), small step on R ft (2) small

leap fwd onto L (ct 3) small step on R (ct 4). Small hop on R ft, simultaneously turning to face ctr (ct 5) small leap on L ft turning to face LOD (ct 6).

SILISTRENSKA TROPANKA

Source: Silistrenska Tropanka (SIH-lihs-trehn-skah TROH-pahn-kah) is a type of dance that is widespread throughout Dobrudža, in northeast Bulgaria. This particular version is especially popular in and around the small town of Silistra, situated on the Danube.

Record: Request SRLP 8142, side 1, band 5

Formation: Mixed or segregated lines of M and W, hands joined at shldr ht ("W" pos); face slightly R of ctr; wt on L ft.

Style: Rather heavy; definite knee bend; movements proud and strong; arm movements are rather strong, as well as stamps.

Meter 2/4　　Pattern

Meas　No intro. Dance may begin at beginning of any musical phrase.

Figure I: Basic Step

1　　Step on R (ct 1). Low, heavy brushlike stamp with L ft, no wt (ct 2).

2　　Same pattern as meas 1 but with opp ftwk.

3　　Turn to face ctr, small step back onto R ft (ct 1), small step back on L ft (ct 2).

4　　Small step fwd onto R ft (ct 1). Small stamp with L ft next to R, no wt (ct 2).

5　　Step in place onto L ft (ct 1). Stamp sharply and heavily with R next to L, no wt (ct 2).

6　　Stamp again sharply with R ft next to L, no wt (ct 1). Hold (ct 2).

Arm Movements

1　　Arms extend up and fwd straight elbows and then down.

2　　Arms swing bkwd straight elbows.

3　　Arms swing fwd straight elbows.

4　　Arms swing bkwd straight elbows.

5　　Arms swing fwd and come back up to "W" pos (ct 1). Pull hands strongly dnwd in "W" pos on first stamp (ct 2).

6　　Pull hands again in same fashion on second stamp.

Figure II: Variation

1–5　Repeat pattern of meas 1–5, fig I (ft and arms).

6　　Take fairly large and heavy step bkwd and slightly to R onto R ft (ct 1). Hold (ct 2). L ft remains on ground, knee slightly bent.

7　　Repeat pattern of meas 5, fig I.

8　　Repeat pattern of meas 6, fig II.

9–10 Repeat pattern of meas 5–6, fig I.
Arm Movements
1–5 Same as in meas 1–5, fig I.
6 Extend arms smoothly up and fwd to a parallel position with floor.
7 Hands come back to "W" position.
8 Same as meas 6, fig II.
9–10 Same as meas 5–6, fig I.

Duquesne University Tamburitzans

CZECHOSLOVAKIA

Czechoslovakian Folk Dancing

by Anatol Joukowsky

Czechoslovakia is divided into three parts. In the north is Bohemia, in the middle Moravia and in the southeastern part is Slovakia. When the author was the Vienna Opera House choreographer, he had many opportunities to visit Slovakia. It was the first place where he had a chance to study ethnic dance in intact form. The southwestern slopes of the Carpathian mountains and the Danube River lead to Bratislava, the capital city of Slovakia. North and northwest from Bratislava

in the neighboring villages one can find very nice traditional dances. The mountain people preserve the treasures of dance.

In Slovakian folklore the important dance form is the *Couples Dance*. The Szardash (Czardas), an Hungarian dance, was adopted by the Slovaks but changed considerably. The music they use is typically Slavic and the steps are more vigorous and free than in the Hungarian version. Each village has its own interpretation . . . Every tune has its special approach by the dancers. In the mountain region of Visoke Tatri there are Slovak mountaineers who dance in a kind of moccasin. They do not wear typical boots.

In the region of Chichmani the dancers wear a costume called Chichmani Kroj which is unique in all of Europe. It is a brightly colored, beautifully embroidered costume. Going down into the valleys like Horehronsko or Dolnehronsko by the Hron River, one can see another form of Czardas Z Kozickyh Hamrov. The Nitrianski Tanz presented here is still another Czardas. The third one, Zahraite Me, means "Gypsy Play For Me." All are different in their patterns yet each is Slavic and represents this very particular temperament. This set of Slovak dances was learned before changes were made in them, and are presented for the first time in the United States in published form [in *The Teaching of Ethnic Dance*]. . . .

In the search for new material one day in the Opera House of Brno in Moravia, the author became reacquainted with the choreographer, a ballet master named Vania Psota. He was a long-time solo dancer in the original Ballet Russe. Many years before we had worked together. He is now gone, but he provided a great impetus to building ethnic dance for the stage. He researched primarily in ethnic dance in Czechoslovakia, and he has left much fine material for those of us who have followed him.

The music for Slovakian dances, except in the high mountain regions, is very close to symphonic music. It is not as good as it would be if it were really ethnic. Up toward the northern part of Czechoslovakia the music is even more of a disaster. In each Bohemian village there is a little band made up of not quite enough instrumentalists to give a true symphonic sound. But—because all Czechs, Slovaks, and Moravs are good musicians, the music is good. Think what it would be like if the musicians were not talented! In Slovakian Tatri the rustic flute, the shepherd's clarinet and other native instruments provide the clear accompaniment that is truly ethnic. The cimbalo is an Hungarian instrument adopted in Slovakia. This is a fine instrument for use in ethnic dance. Then the Gypsies with their violins producing soft, lyric music take the dancer's heart and he becomes a blind follower of the tune of the violin.

The Slovak State Ensemble today presents the folk-lore of Slovakia. These people are trying to preserve for posterity what is left of the old culture of the mountainous Slovaks.

(Anatol Joukowsky is established as a world-renowned expert in ethnic dance. The people who have attended his workshops, particularly on the West Coast, know of his high standards, his personal and professional integrity, his ability to analyze, his first-hand knowledge of the countries and the native dances, his ability to touch each whom he teaches with a bit of his own humor, his own *joie de vivre*.

As Eleanor Wakefield said in an article in *Impulse* (1956), Anatol Joukowsky and his talented wife, the great Yugoslavian ballerina Yania Wassilieva, emigrated to the United States in 1951. They arrived in New York direct from France after having had fascinating lives centered not only in artistic circles but political ones as well.

Professor Joukowsky was born in the Ukraine. His father was a colonel in the cavalry of Emperor Nicholas II. After World War I his family settled in Salonika, Greece. His parents wanted him to have a Slavic education, so he attended school in Yugoslavia. It was in Belgrade that the ballet master of the state theatre suggested that Anatol should have dance lessons. At the age of 14, he began a two-year term of ballet study. His interest grew and when Pavlova visited a school performance she singled him out for special commendation. This aided materially in his decision to make

dance a career. Subsequently, however, he studied engineering at the University of Belgrade, but never gave up studying ballet. Concurrently he attended the Yugoslavian State Theatre Ballet School and graduated in 1926. In 1935 Professor Joukowsky was named choreographer and director of the ballet for the State Theatre of Belgrade.

During 1936, Professor Joukowsky organized a small professional group to specialize in ethnic dance. This group performed at a Sokol festival in Prague in 1938. His performers won the first prize in the competition. He was not only permitted but encouraged by the director of the State Theatre to repeat the performance under its auspices. In March 1941, his first exhibition of ethnic dances at the State Theatre of Belgrade was presented. It was entitled The Book of Yugoslavia and provided the entr'acte for two ballets choreographed by Joukowsky. Mr. Joukowsky's works were enormously well received in Belgrade.

During this period, Yania Wassilieva, whom Anatol Joukowsky had married in 1932, was an active participant in many of the performances, and in the scientific hunts which took them into the native hills and countrysides to find authentic dances, notate music and photograph the natives in costume. During the interim between the two world wars, Professor Joukowsky was the only professional choreographer who was doing this research, and this was the last era when some of these dances could be found alive in these particular countries. At the end of World War II, Yania performed with him in programs staged by the Special Services Division of the French Army to which Anatol Joukowsky was attached. Later, they both joined de Basil's Ballet Russe Company and toured with them for two years. Anatol Joukowsky was dancer and choreographer. . . .

Mr. Joukowsky has danced in every country in Europe and the Middle East. In addition to his many accomplishments, he has been awarded the Cavalier Cross of Bulgaria from King Boris III in 1938; the Order of St. Vladislav of Czechoslovakia from President Benes in 1938; and the Order of St. Sava from Prince Paul of Yugoslavia in 1941. . . .)

(This introduction, written by Ann Paterson, professor of Physical Education at San Francisco State University, appears in Anatol Joukowsky's book *The Teaching of Ethnic Dance,* published by J. Lowell Pratt and Company. The preceding article and three of the following dances from the book are used with permission, courtesy College Division, Charles E. Merrill Publishing Co.)

CZECHOSLOVAKIAN FOLK DANCES

A JA TZO SARITSA

(Ah Yah Tso Sah reet sah) I Am Like A Queen

Source: A Ja Tzo Saritsa is a Moravian couple dance that takes its name from the first words of the song that is sung.

Record: Folk Art, FALP-I, side 2, band 2. A Ja Tzo Saritsa, National (45 rpm) 4561

Formation: Lines of 5 or 6 cpls, ptrs facing, M back to music. M join hands in line, W same. Free hands of end M just behind hip, palms out. End W hands on hips, fingers fwd. Lines about 6 ft apart.

Steps: *Couple Turn:* Take modified shoulder waist pos (W L and M R hands joined, palm to palm, and held on W L hip. W R hand on M L shoulder. M L hand on W R forearm). Step fwd on R and bend knee slightly (ct 1). Bring L ft to R heel, taking wt on ball of L (ct &). Repeat action for cts 2, &. Usually takes 1 meas to make 1 full turn CW.

Meter 2/4, 3/4   Pattern

Meas

¾   No intro

Figure I: Passive Pattern (Both Lines)

1   Turning to face R, walk R, L, R. (All walking steps in Passive Pattern take 1 ct).

2   Making ½ turn to L, walk L, R, L.

3   Making ¼ turn R to face ptr, walk fwd R, L, R. On last step on R, bend knee.

4   Walk bkwd to place, L, R, L.

5–12   Repeat action of meas 1–4 (Fig I) twice (3 in all).

Figure II: Woman's Active Pattern (Vocal)

1   Woman: Walking diag fwd R twd M line, step R (ct 1), L (ct 2), R (ct 3), stamp L next to R (no wt) (ct &). As L is brought fwd to be stepped on (ct 2), bend R knee a little. Hands on hips, fingers fwd.

2   Walking diag fwd L twd M line, repeat action of meas 1 (Fig II) but start with L.

3   Moving slightly fwd twd M line, step R (ct 1), L (ct &), R (ct 2). Stamp L next to R (no wt) (ct 3). As L is stamped, strike bottom of R fist against top of L fist as if to say, "I want my way."

4   Make ½ turn to R, stepping L, R, L (cts 1 & 2). Hands are returned to hips and W back is to M. No action rest of meas.

5–8   Starting with back to M, repeat action of meas 1–4 (Fig II). W will move away from M line. After ½ turn R on meas 8, W will again face M.

9–12 Repeat action of meas 1–4 (Fig II). W end with back to M.

Man: During 12 meas of W Active Pattern, continue Passive Pattern (Fig I), dancing it 3 more times.

Figure III: Man's Active Pattern

1   Man: With hands just behind hips, walk diag fwd R twd W line, stepping R (ct 1), L (ct 2), R (ct 3). Slap outside of L heel with L hand (ct &). On the slap the L ft is brought up behind to knee level.

2   Walking diag fwd L twd W line, repeat action of meas 1 (Fig III) but start with L. Slap R heel with R.

3   Moving slightly fwd twd W line, step R (ct 1). Close L to R, bending knees in preparation for a jump (ct 2). Jump into air, spreading legs apart sdwd (ct &). Land ft together (ct 3).

4   Make ½ turn R, stepping L, R, L (cts 1, & 2). On each step clap back of R hand against palm of L as if to say, "Why must that be so?" Hands are returned to pos and M back is to W. No action for rest of meas.

5–8   Starting with back to W, repeat action of meas 1–4 (Fig III). M will move away from W line. After ½ turn R on meas 8, M will again face W.

9–12 Repeat action of meas 1–4 (Fig III). M ends with back to W.

Woman: On meas 1–2, walk 6 steps (starting R with back to M) to beginning pos. Hands are on hips. On meas 3–4 turn R to face M line and join hands. On meas 5–12 dance Passive Pattern (Fig I, meas 1–4) two times.

Figure IV: Woman's Active Pattern (Vocal)

1–12 Woman: Repeat action of Fig II.

Man: On meas 1–2 walk 6 steps (starting R with back to W) to beginning pos. Hands just behind hips. On meas 3–4 turn R to face W line and rejoin hands. On meas 5–12 dance Passive Pattern (Fig I, meas 1–4) two times.

Figure V: Man's Active Pattern

1–10 M and W repeat action of Fig III, meas 1–10 as given for each.

11–12 M make R turn and walk (2 steps to a ct) to ptr. Join hands with ptr. Cpls at both ends of line curve around so as to form a double circle, ptrs facing, M back to ctr. All cpls adjust a little to help form circle.

Meter 2/4 *Figure VI: Couple Turn and Progress*

1–2   Take modified shoulder waist pos as described and make 2 CW turns with ptr.

3   Using joined hands (M R, W L) for lead, M turn W ½ turn R. Both step R, L, R (cts 1, &, 2). Hold ct &. Do not drop joined hands. Ptrs end side by side, W to R of M. Free hands on hips or at sides.

4   Both stepping L, R, L (cts 1, &, 2) M turn W one full turn L to again end side by side, W to R of M. Joined hands now encircle W waist. Hold ct &. Do not catch W R arm at her side.

5   Repeat action of meas 3 (Fig VI) but W makes one full turn R. During meas 3–5 M dances almost in place.

6   Both stepping L, R, L (cts 1, &, 2) M moves to W on his L. W moves to M on her R (M moves up one place (CCW) in circle.

7–42 Repeat action of meas 1–6 (Fig VI) six more times (7 in all). On meas 42 do not progress to new ptr. Instead repeat action of meas 4 (Fig VI).

CZARDAS Z KOSICKYCH HAMROV
(Czardas from Ko zich'ke Ham'rehv)

Source: The Slovakians have borrowed the Hungarian Czardas and given it a flavor of their own. This particular Czardas has been danced by the Slovak Company in Bratislava.

Record: National (45 rpm) V-7801

Formation: Double circle, M on inside, facing LOD (CCW). M R arm around W, holding W RH at her waist. M LH on hip. W L on M R shoulder.

Steps: *Czardas:* Step to R with R (ct 1). Close L to R, bending knees (ct 2). Step to R with R (ct 3). Close L to R, wt still on R (ct 4). Next step would start to L with L. Close ft together; this usually results in a heel click if the shoes and the mood of the dancer permit. The M particularly like to click their heels.

Description is same for M and W unless otherwise noted.

Meter 4/4   Pattern

Meas

No intro.

Figure I

1   Step diag fwd R with R (ct 1). Close L to R, bending knees (ct 2). Repeat for cts 3–4.

2   Walk in LOD 4 steps starting R.

3–4   Repeat action of meas 1–2.

5–6   Czardas step to R and L.

7   Step to R with R (ct 1). Close L to R, bending knees (no wt) (ct 2). Step to L with L (ct 3). Close R to L, bending knees (no wt) (ct 4).

8   M: Step to R with R (ct 1). Close L to R (ct 2). Step R in place (ct 3). Hold (ct 4).
W: With 3 steps (R L R) turn out to R, go behind M and end on L side of him. Close L to R (no wt) (ct 4). M puts L arm around W, holding W LH at her waist. M RH on hip. W R on M L shoulder.

9–11   Beginning L instead of R, repeat action of meas 5–7.

12   M: With 2 steps (L R) make ½ turn R to face RLOD. Close ft together (ct 3). Hold (ct 4). Release W Hs.
W: With 3 steps (L R L) turn out to L and end facing M. Close R to L (no wt) (ct 4). Cpls are in single circle, M facing RLOD, W LOD. H on hips.

Figure II (Vocal)

1   Czardas to R.

2   Bokazo: With little hop on R, cross L in front of R (ct 1). Touch L out to L side (ct 2). Close ft together (ct 3). Hold (ct 4).

3–4   Repeat action of meas 1–2 to L. Bokazo done with hop on L and crossing R.

5   Join RH, shoulder level (elbow also shoulder level). L still on hips. Step R, taking a ¼ turn to L so M R side is to R LOD and W R side is to LOD (ct 1). Close L to R (ct 2). Step to R with R (ct 3). Touch L behind R, bending knees (ct 4). After ¼ turn on ct 1, M has bk to ctr of circle, W faces ctr. Ptrs are facing.

6   Release RH. Make ½ turn R on 2 steps thusly: Step bkwd on L twd original pos (ct 1). Step R, completing ½ turn R (ct 2). Close ft together and place LH on ptr L forearm, RH on hip (ct 3). Hold (ct 4).
Note: Original pos refers to place where dancer stood at end of meas 4.

7   Change places on meas 7–8. Moving fwd to ptrs place, step L (ct 1). Close R to L, bending knees (ct 2). Step fwd L (ct 3). Close R to L, bending knees (ct 4).

8   Walk L R (ct 1–2) into ptrs place. Close ft together (ct 3). Hold (ct 4). End single circle, W facing ctrs, M bk to ctr. RH on hips. L on ptrs L forearm.

9   Step to L on L (ct 1). Close R to L (ct 2). Step to L on L (ct 3). Touch R behind L, with bend of knees (ct 4). Elbows bend to enable ptrs to face each other after ct 1. This pattern is similar to meas 5.

10   Release LH. Make ½ turn L on 2 steps thusly: Step bkwd on R twd original pos (ct 1). Step L, completing ½ turn L (ct 2). Close ft together and place RH on ptrs R forearm, LH on hip (ct 3). Hold (ct 4). Cpls now in single circle, M facing ctr, W with bk to ctr.
Note: Original pos refers to place where dancer stood at end of meas 8.

11–12   Changing places, repeat action of meas 7–8 but starting with R. End single circle, ptrs facing, M looking RLOD. Hs on hips.

13–24   Repeat action of meas 1–12. On meas 24, W makes ½ turn R to face RLOD. Cpls in single circle facing RLOD, M behind W. W Hs on hips, M Hs on W shoulders.

Figure III

1   Step fwd R (ct 1). Hop R (ct 2). L ft is crossed behind R about mid-calf on hop. Step fwd L (ct 3). Hop L (ct 4). R ft crosses behind L leg.

2   4 light runs in RLOD (R L R L).

3–4   Repeat action of meas 1–2.

5   Step to R side with R (ct 1). Close L to R, bending knees (ct 2). Step to R with R (ct 3). Touch L behind R, bending knees (ct 4).

6   M: Step L R (cts 1–2). Close ft together (ct 3). Hold (ct 4). M starts W into her turn and then removes Hs from her shoulders.
W: Make 1 turn R in front of M. Step L R (cts 1–2). Close ft together (ct 3). Hold (ct 4). M puts Hs bk on W shoulders at end of turn.

7–8   Repeat action of meas 5–6 but moving to L with L. W turns L.

9–10   Repeat action of meas 5–6 exactly except that W makes only ½ turn and ends facing ptr. Both place Hs on ptr's shoulders.

11   Step to M L with L (W R) (ct 1). M close R to L (no wt), bending knees (ct 2). W close L to R. Repeat to M R (W L) (cts 3–4).

12   M shifts Hs to W waist. Prepare to lift W (ct 1). Lift W (ct 2). Put W dn (cts 3–4). End Hs on hips, single circle, ptrs facing (M facing RLOD).

Figure IV (Vocal)

1–5   Repeat action of Fig II, meas 1–5.

6   M turns W to L 1½ times under joined RHs. Both step L R L (cts 1, 2, 3). Hold (ct 4). M dances in place. W ends at M R side. M holds W RH at her waist with his RH. LH on hips. Cpls facing RLOD.

7   Czardas step to L.

8   Click heels 3 times. Hold (ct 4).

9   Step to L with L (ct 1). Close R to L, bending knees (ct 2). Step L with L (ct 3). Touch R behind L, bending knees (ct 4).

10   With joined RH M turns W to R. W make 1 turn. Both step R L (cts 1–2). Close ft together (ct 3). Hold (ct 4). W stops at MR but a little behind M. Hold joined RH at shoulder height with M R arm outstretched in front of W. W R arm bent, elbow shoulder height. W L on M R shoulder. M L on hip.

11   Moving RLOD, step R (ct 1). Close L to R, bending knees (ct 2). Repeat (cts 3–4).

12   M makes ½ turn R to face W. W dances in place. Both step R L (cts 1–2). Close ft together (ct 3). Hold (ct 4). End single circle, M facing LOD. W facing M. Hs on hips.

13–23   Repeat action of meas 1–11 exactly. After meas 17 ptrs will be facing LOD.
In meas 22 movement is LOD.

24   Repeat meas 12 exactly but W also makes ½ turn R to end with bk to M. Cpls in single circle facing RLOD. M H on W shoulders, W Hs on hips.

Figure III (repeated)

1–12   Repeat action of Fig III. Dance ends with M lifting W.

DOUDLEBSKA POLKA

Source: This polka mixer was learned in Czechoslovakia by Jeannet Novak.

Record: "Doudlebska Polka," Folk Dancer MH-3016-B

Formation: Couples in closed position any place on the floor

Steps: Polka, walk

Meter 2/4   Pattern

Meas

4   Intro

Figure I: Polka

1–16   Take 16 polka steps turning CW and progressing any place on the floor.

Figure II: Walk and Star

17–32   In open position, W free hand on hip, walk CCW into one big cir. (When group is large, smaller cir of any number of couples may be formed.) M form star with L arms outstretched, hands on L shoulder of M in front. All sing "Tra-la-la" throughout this fig.

Figure III: M Clap, W Circle

33–48   M face ctr and clap hands throughout fig as follows: Clap own hands (ct 1), clap own hands (ct &), clap hands of M on sides, shldr high (ct 2). W turn ½ CW and take 16 polka steps CW around M cir. (If there is more than one cir, W may change freely from one M cir to another.) W hands on hips. At end of meas 48, M turn around and begin dance with new ptr.

Note: Extra M may join dance during Fig II, joining star without ptr. Extra W may join dance during Fig III.

HOREHRONSKY CZARDAS

Source: Horehronsky (hoh-reh-HROHN-skee) Czardas is a women's dance from the Upper Hron Valley in Slovakia. It shows a Hungarian influence, but it is still basically Slovakian. It was introduced by Anatol Joukowsky.

Record: Apon 45-2126

Formation: Cir of W facing ctr, hands at sides. During intro join hands to make a closed cir.

Steps and Styling: *Box Pattern:* 4 meas for 1 pattern. Knees straighten on the beat and relax on the off-beat. Not too staccato.

Meas 1: Step L to L side (ct 1); close R to L (ct 2).

2: Step L fwd twd ctr (ct 1); close R to L (ct 2).

3: Repeat action of meas 1.

4: Walk 4 small steps bkwd, beg L, to bring the cir back to orig size (cts 1, & 2, &).

Diagonal Pattern: 4 meas for 1 pattern. Knee action is not visible as it is in the Box Pattern.

Meas 1: Moving diag L twd ctr, step L (ct 1); close R to L (ct &); step L diag L (ct 2); close R to L, bending knees, no wt (ct &).

2: Repeat action of meas 1, but use opp ftwk and move diag R twd ctr.

3: Moving diag L, step L (ct 1); close R to L, no wt (ct &); low leap fwd onto R (ct 2); close to L to R, bending knees, no wt (ct &).

4: Beginning L, walk 4 steps bkwd to bring cir to orig size.

Side Steps: 1 to a meas. Knees straighten and relax the same as in Box Pattern. Step L to L side, leading with the heel and turning the body in a little to the R (ct 1); close R to L, turning body to face ctr again (ct 2).

Open Rida Steps: 2 to a meas. Step to L on ball of L ft (ct 1); step on full R ft across and in front of L ft (ct &). Repeat action for cts 2, &.

Meter 4/4, 2/4   Pattern

Meas
4/4
4 meas Intro. Join hands in a cir.

Figure I: Walk

1   Turning to face a little L of LOD, walk R, L in LOD (cts 1, 2). Turning to face ctr, step R to R side (ct 3); close L to R (ct 4).

2   Repeat action of meas 1.

3   Moving twd ctr, step diag fwd R to R, turning body a little to L (ct 1); close L to R, no wt (ct 2). Very low small leap fwd diag L on L, turning body a little to R (ct 3); close R to L bending knees (ct &); hold pos (ct 4). Joined hands will rise naturally.

4   Walk bkwd out of ctr 3 steps R, L, R (ct 1, 2, 3); close L to R (ct 4).

5–24 Repeat action of meas 1–4 five more times (6 in all). On meas 24 walk bkwd R, L (cts 1, 2); close R to L (ct 3); hold pos (ct 4).

2/4

Figure II: Box, Diagonal

1–8   Dance 2 Box Patterns
9–12 Dance 1 Diag Pattern
13–16 Dance 1 Box Pattern
17–20 Dance 1 Diag Pattern
21–24 Dance 1 Box Pattern
25–48 Repeat action of meas 1–24 (fig II).

Figure III. Side Steps, Diagonal

1–8   Dance 8 Side Steps moving to L side.
9–12 Dance 1 Diag Pattern
13–16 Dance 4 Side Steps
17–20 Dance 1 Diag Pattern
21–24 Dance 4 Side Steps
2/4

Figure IV. Rida, Diagonal

1–3   Moving to L, dance 6 Open Rida Steps.
4   Turning to face a little R of RLOD, run 4 steps beg L (ct 1, &, 2, &).
5–8   Repeat action of meas 1–4 (fig IV).
9–12 Dance 1 Diag Pattern.
13–16 Repeat action of meas 1–4 (fig IV).
17–20 Dance 1 Diag Pattern.

21–23 Moving to L, dance 6 Open Rida Steps.
24   Step L to L side (ct 1); close R to L (ct &); rise onto balls of ft and raise joined hands high (ct 2); hold pos (ct &).

VRTIELKA

(Vrr-tiel-kah) Turning Dance

Source: This Slovak Czardas, from Nove Zamki, was presented by Anatol Joukowsky, who learned it while on tour in Slovakia, 1935–36.

Record: Kolo Festival KF 803-B.

Formation: Couples, spaced freely about the floor; ptrs facing, in ballroom pos (M L—W R well extended) with M R at W waist. M face LOD.

Steps: Czardas, Bokazo, Pivot. *Note:* Throughout dance, bend knees on each closing step of Czardas and on Bokazo.

Meter 2/4, 4/8   Pattern

Meas

2/4   *Figure I: Sideward Czardas and Bokazo*
1   *M:* Step R to R (ct 1), close L to R, bending knees (ct &) step R to R (ct 2), close L to R, bending knees and keeping wt on R (ct &).

2   Step L to L (ct 1), close R to L, bending knees (ct &), step L to L (ct 2), close R to L, bending knees and taking wt on R (ct &).

3   Bending both knees, turn L heel diagonally outward and close (ct 1), turn R heel diagonally outward and close (ct &), turn both heels out and quickly close (ct 2), hold (ct &). *W:* Dance counterpart throughout action of meas 1–3.

4–6   Repeat action of meas 1–3.

Figure II: Czardas and Woman Pivot

Ballroom pos, as described above. M dance directly fwd and bwd in this fig.

1   M step R fwd (ct 1), close L instep to R heel (ct &), step R fwd (ct 2), close L instep to R heel (ct &). W step bwd L (ct 1), close R heel to L instep (ct &), step bwd L (ct 2), close R heel to L instep keeping wt on L (ct &).

2   M step in place L, R, L (cts 1 & 2), hold (ct &); W pivot on R CW (one complete turn) under their joined hands (ML-WR) (ct 1), step L in place (ct &), close R to L (ct 2), hold (ct &).

3–4   Repeat action of Fig II, meas 1–2, M starting bwd L, W fwd R. (W end meas 3 with wt on L to prepare for pivot.)

5–7   Repeat action of Fig I, meas 1–3.

Figure III: Diamond With Turn
Hands on hips, ptrs facing.

1   Both step fwd diagonally R, R shoulder leading (passing ptr face to face) (ct 1), close L to R (ct &), step diagonally R (ct 2), close L to R (ct &).

2   Pivoting ¼ turn R (CW), both step L to L, continuing the diagonal pattern with L shoulder leading (back twd ptr) (ct 1), close R to L (ct &), step L to L (ct 2), close R to L, keeping wt on L (ct &).

3   Both turn CW in place to face ptr (½ turn) stepping R L R (cts 1 & 2), hold (ct &).
       Note: Action of Fig II, meas 1–3 completes half of the diamond fig, ptrs having changed places.

4–6   Repeat action of Fig III, meas 1–3, to finish in original place. M end with wt on L.

Figure IV: Czardas and Woman Pivot
1–7   Repeat action of Fig II, meas 1–7.

Figure V: Diamond With Turn
1–6   Repeat action of Fig III, meas 1–6.

Figure VI: Czardas and Woman Pivot
1–7   Repeat action of Fig II, meas 1–7. On meas 7, W steps L R L making ¼ turn CW to end at ptr's R side, both facing same direction. Assume open pos. FAST PART.

4/8   *Figure VII: Open Czardas and Woman Cross-Over*

1   Open pos, outside hands on hips. Both step L to L (ct 1), close R to L (ct 2), step L to L (ct 3), close R to L (ct 4).

2   Both starting R and moving R, repeat action of Fig VII, meas 1.

3   M step in place L R L (cts 1, 2, 3), hold (ct 4), while W turns CCW (L) in front of M, stepping L R L (cts 1, 2, 3) to end at M L side, (R arm on his L shoulder in open pos) hold (ct 4). M should assist W in cross-over.

4–6   Starting R and moving to R, repeat action of Fig VII, meas 1–3. W end on M R side on open pos for next fig.

Figure VIII: Crosshold With Couple Turn

1   M take W L hand from his shoulder with his L, her R with his R (L over R, chest high) as both step fwd R (ct 1), close L to R (ct 2), step fwd R (ct 3), close L to R (ct 4). W keep wt on R.

2   M step in place R L R, making ½ turn R (CW) while he turns W 1½ turns CCW under their raised joined hands (cts 1, 2, 3), hold (ct 4). W pivot CCW stepping L R, close L, keeping wt on R (cts 1, 2, 3), hold (ct 4).
       Note: At end of meas 2, W is on M L, hands joined R over L, ptrs with backs to original direction of Fig VIII.

3   Both step L fwd (ct 1), close R to L (ct 2), step L fwd (ct 3), close R to L (ct 4). W keep wt on L.

4   M step in place L R L, making ½ turn CCW while he turns W 1½ turns CW under their raised joined hands (cts 1, 2, 3), hold (ct 4), W pivots CW, stepping R L; close R, keeping wt on L (cts 1, 2, 3) hold (ct 4). End in open pos, facing original direction of Fig VIII.

5–7   In open pos, both starting R, repeat action as described for M in Fig I, meas 1–3.

26 meas Repeat action of following figures in sequence: Fig VII, VIII, VII, VIII.

Turn and Pose
R hands joined, M turn W L (CCW), completing 1 turn under his R arm. As second turn is started, joined R are lowered to end at W R waist as M draws her to him in pose.

ENGLAND

English Folk Dancing

by May Gadd and the Country Dance and Song Society of America

GADD: Country dances originated many centuries ago in the form of ceremonial circles and processionals but have long since evolved into dances for men and women to be used on any social occasion. The steps are simple and natural yet the patterns can be complex. Innumerable combinations of the basic patterns of intercrossing lines, stars, circles, and right and left weavings have been developed for sets composed of two, three, four, or any number of couples in square, circle, or line formation. Many have been adopted by city dancers from the villages where they have been danced for many generations; others are taken from seventeenth- and eighteenth-century dance collections, when the dance was at the height of its popularity in fashionable ballrooms as well as on the village green.

CDSS: In the seventeenth and eighteenth centuries England was renowned as a dancing nation. A wealth

Country Dance and Song Society Dancers. Photo by Suzanne Szasz

of printed and manuscript information dating from this period has been interpreted and reintroduced by twentieth-century dance historians and scholars, beginning with Cecil Sharp. The finest sources are the books published by one John Playford; indeed, historic country dances are sometimes referred to as "Playford Dances."

These early dances were composed by dancing masters and were danced in the ballroom, but they also included elements of the dances that country folk did at the time. The style in which they are danced today is influenced by contemporary and traditional country dances. The earliest recorded country dances, those of the seventeenth century, are in many forms; in the eighteenth century the progressive longways dance dominated; in the nineteenth century dances in square formation reappeared, and the influence of the waltz and polka was felt in the longways dances.

The music of these early dances is exceptionally beautiful and sophisticated, matching precisely the figures of the dance. These figures are often intricate and always graceful, whether the dance is lively and quick or slow and stately.

GADD: Morris dances were originally performed by the young men of a village at the time of the spring celebrations. The dance has been interpreted by anthropologists as a kind of dynamo, furnishing an output of energy designed to quicken all growing things.

Today it is danced by teams of six men who enjoy the vitality and exhilaration of the various dances. Tapping sticks, waving handkerchiefs, and jingling bells all add to the vital character of the dance. Based

Kopachka Dancers

on a rhythmical jigging, the steps sometimes develop into leaps and turns, thus offering a considerable challenge. The patterns are basic and simple. There are a few solo Morris jigs.

CDSS: . . . The traditional Morris costume is white, with bright ribbons and vests or baldricks, and bells strapped to the legs.

GADD: Sword dances were originally part of a midwinter folk drama in which a victim, or scapegoat, died symbolically in order to rid the community of the evil of the past year. The five, six, or eight dancers are linked in a circle by their swords and weave patterns culminating in the display of the sword woven into a star—the "lock" or symbol of sacrifice. The rhythmical teamwork of the dance, the changing patterns, and the unity of feeling and movement have great appeal for present-day dancers—especially men. The Society uses both the long sword dances of Yorkshire and the flexible short swords and "stepping" of Northumberland and Durham.

CDSS: Sword dances come from the north of England and are of two types: the long sword and the short sword. In both types the swords serve as links between the hands of five or six dancers; they are not placed on the ground, as in Scottish sword dancing. The dancers and their swords go through a series of intertwining figures, ending with the lacing of the swords into a star shape. The long sword dances—which are very old and are related to mummer plays, with their symbolic death and resurrection—are slow, open, and hypnotic. The rapier dances, which developed in the nineteenth century, use shorter, more flexible swords

and are thus tighter in formation. The tempo is fast and the excitement is increased by the rapid stepping done by the dancers.

GADD: Morris and sword dancing had nearly died out during the Industrial Revolution, but a few traditional teams survived in rural parts of England. The work of collectors in the early part of this century has sparked a renewal of interest and the appearance of hundreds of revival teams. In the last five years there has been a surge of interest in the United States; the number of teams in this country is growing rapidly. Though traditional ritual dance is the province of men, both men and women dance in revival teams.

CDSS: Traditional dances are those that are being danced in the villages and small towns of England by people who learned them in the community. The dances are descended from those danced by previous generations of Britons, but they have changed gradually as they were handed down orally, and have incorporated influences from the ballrooms of the cities. Only in the last seventy-five years have these rural dances been collected and written down. The style of dancing varies from country to country, but some form of fancy footwork is common. There are many polka dances, and others include steps borrowed from the Scots or from clog dancing. Floor patterns tend to be simple, and figures, such as "swing and change," and reels reappear often.

(For background information on May Gadd and The Country Dance and Song Society of America, see appropriate headings in Parts II and III, respectively.)

ENGLISH FOLK DANCES

CIRCASSIAN CIRCLE

One version of this dance is performed by a single circle of dancers, the other by a double circle.

Single Circle
Record: "Irish Washerwoman," Victor 45-6178; or any reel or hornpipe tune
Formation: Single circle of partners (W at M's right side) with hands joined
Step: Walk

Meter 6/8   PATTERN

Meas	A	PROMPTS
		All join hands
1–4	All walk to ctr (4 steps), and back up (4 steps).	Everybody IN
		Everybody OUT
5–8	Repeat	Everybody IN
		Everybody OUT
9–12	M stand in place. W walk to center (4 steps) and clap on the 4th step, then back up to place (4 steps).	Ladies IN
		Ladies OUT
13–16	L stand in place. M walk to center (4 steps), turn left around and walk to L who was originally left side in the cir (4 steps) (new ptr).	Gents IN
		TURN and
		go OUT

Country Dance and Song Society Dancers. Photo by Stan Levy

B

1–8	Swing new ptr (square dance swing pos, elbow hook or two hand swing).	SWING new partner
9–16	Promenade.	Promenade
	Repeat dance until music stops.	

Double Circle, Progressive
Record: "Irish Washerwoman," Victor 45-6178; or any reel or hornpipe tune
Formation: Sets of two facing cpls (one facing LOD, one facing RLOD) in a cir (W at M's right side)
Step: Walk

Meter 6/8   PATTERN

Meas	A	PROMPTS
1–4	Couples make a R-hand star and turn the star (8 steps).	R-hand star
5–8	Make a L-hand star and turn it (8 steps).	L hand
9–12	Ptrs face and do 4 balance steps (or 2 set steps).	Balance partners
13–16	Partners swing.	Swing your partners

B

1–4	Two ladies chain across.	Two ladies chain
5–8	Two ladies chain back.	Ladies chain back
9–12	Cpls walk 4 steps twd each other, then 4 steps bkwd.	Forward and back
13–14	Couples pass through to a new couple.	Pass through
15–16	All do-sa-do the new person faced.	Do-sa-do
	Repeat entire dance.	

CUMBERLAND SQUARE

Source: Cumberland is a county situated in the Northwest of England along the Scottish border.

Record: "My Love She's But a Lassie Yet," Methodist
109A; Folkraft 1143

Formation: Square formation, cpls in closed pos, M
with L shldr and W with R shldr to ctr of square.

Steps: Slide, walk, buzz step, polka, sm repp step

Meter 4/4   Pattern

Meas

A

Figure I: Slide Across and Back

1–4   Head cpls take 8 sliding steps across to opp
place, M passing back to back.

5–8   Keeping same position, return to own place
with 8 sliding steps, W passing bk to bk.

1–8   Side cpls cross and return as described for head
cpls in meas A 1–8.

B

Figure II: Star

1–4   Head cpls join R hands in ctr, forming a R-
hand star, walk fwd 8 steps in CW dir.

5–8   Changing to L-hand star, walk 8 steps in CCW
dir, returning to place.

1–8   Side cpls repeat same action as directed for
head (repeat) cpls in meas B 1–8.

A

Figure III: Basket

Head cpls form basket in this manner: All step
to ctr. W hook arms thru arms of M on either
side and join hands across with opp W. M join
hands behind W back. All this is done simultaneously.

1–8   In basket formation circle to L with 16 buzz
steps, R ft crossed in front of L.

1–8   Side cpls form basket and cir L with 16 buzz
steps.

B

Figure IV: Circle and Promenade

1–8   All join hands and move to L with 16 skip
or 8 polka steps.

1–8   Arm in arm with ptr, promenade CCW (repeat)
to place with 16 walking steps.

OSLO WALTZ

Source: A waltz mixer danced in both England and
Scotland.

Record: Folk Dancer MH 3016 A

Formation: Cpls with hands joined in a single cir;
W at M's R

Steps: Waltz balance, waltz, step-draw; opp ftwk

Meter 3/4   PATTERN

Meas

8   Intro

A

Figure I: Balance and W Progress

1   Waltz balance fwd, ML, WR (ct 1, 2, 3).

2   Waltz balance bwd, MR, WL (ct 1, 2, 3).

3–4   M balances L, R in place and leads W at his
L across in front to his R side while W makes
one complete turn CW and two waltz steps
(ct 1, 2, 3; 1, 2, 3).

5–16   All rejoin hands and repeat action of meas 1–
4 three more times. On meas 16 M faces new
ptr on his R.

B

Figure II: Turn and Waltz

1   Join both hands and waltz balance sdwd twd
ctr, ML, WR (ct 1, 2, 3).

2   Waltz balance away from ctr, MR, WL (ct 1,
2, 3).

3–4   Turn individually once around, M CCW, W
CW (with one waltz step) (ct 1, 2, 3), plus
two more steps moving slightly twd ctr (ct 1,
2) and hold (ct 3).

5–8   Repeat B, beginning away from ctr, MR, WL,
and this time M turns CW, W CCW, both moving slightly away from ctr.

9–10   Join both hands, both step twd ctr (ct 1, 2),
draw (ct 3); step-draw; step-draw.

11–12   Both step-draw twice away from ctr. On last
step-draw M end bk to ctr, W facing M.

13–16   In closed pos take 4 CW turning waltz steps
while progressing CCW.
All join hands and repeat entire dance.

SQUARE TANGO

Record: "Square Tango," English Columbia DX 1322;
Decca 27511

Formation: Cpls in closed ballroom pos; standing anywhere around room. M facing LOD with W facing
him.

Steps: Box, draw, slow walk, dip, and cross steps.

Meter 2/4   Pattern

Meas

Figure I: Box, Draw Step

W does the counterpart of all the steps.

1–2 *a.* M beg on L ft step dir fwd (ct 1), hold (ct &), step directly to the R with R ft (ct 2), close L ft to R and change weight to L ft (ct &). Step directly bwd on R (ct 1), hold (ct &), step to the L with L ft (ct 2), close R ft to L and change wt to R ft (ct &), completing one square "box" pattern.

3   *b.* M steps directly to the L with L ft (ct 1 &), draws R ft to L with an accent (ct 2), hold (&).

4   Repeat action of meas 3, stepping to the R with R ft and draw L to R.

5–8 Repeat action of meas 1–4.

Figure II: Slow Walk, Dip

1–3 *a.* M beg on L ft take six slow, gliding steps fwd (ct 1 & 2 &, 1 & 2 &, 1 & 2 &).
     Note: Step only on count, pause on &.

4   *b.* M steps directly fwd on L, bending L knee, and he takes all his wt onto L ft, keeping R leg outstretched bkwd with R toe touching floor but with no wt on R ft (ct 1), hold (ct &). M steps directly bwd on R ft, straightening L knee (ct 2). M keeps wt on R ft, bringing L ft to R in preparation for next step (ct &).

Figure III: Cross Step

5–7 Moving in LOD in open ballroom position, M steps fwd L (ct 1 &), fwd R (ct 2 &), fwd L (ct 1), step R beside L (ct &), without dropping hands turn inward twd ptr to face CW and step L across R (ct 2 &); step fwd in CW direction on R (ct 1), step L beside R (ct &), turn inward toward partner and step R across L (ct 2 &).

8   Turning slightly L to face LOD and assuming closed ballroom position, M steps fwd on L (ct 1), steps directly R on R (ct &). Close L ft to R (ct 2), hold (ct &). This last step (cts 1 & 2) are done in a quick, sharp fashion.
     Note: The W on (ct 1), meas 8, takes a large step with her R foot to place herself directly in front of her ptr in closed ballroom pos.

A

To ctr and out, chasse, waltz.

1–4   M beg L, W R, take 4 slow steps (1 to each measure) toward ctr of cir, M bwd, W fwd).

5–8   With W moving bwd, M fwd, take 4 slow steps twd outside of cir.

9–10 Beginning M L (W R) moving CCW around the room, take 1 chasse (step sdwd, cts 1, 2, close, ct 3. Step sdwd, ct 1, hold, cts 2, 3 with M R and W L foot pointed CW, raising joined hands above shldr ht and looking in the CW dir.

11–12 Repeat action of A, meas 9–10, in opp dir.

13–16 Take 4 waltz steps, turning CW and progressing CCW around cir.

B

Dip and balance, chasse, waltz.

1–2   Face CCW in open ballroom pos. Step fwd on outside ft (M L, W R) (cts 1, 2, 3). Step fwd on inside ft, turning toes slightly twd ptr and bending knee in slight dip (cts 1, 2, 3).

3–4   Balance fwd on outside ft, bringing instep of closing ft to heel of supporting ft without changing wt (cts 1, 2, 3).
      Balance bwd on inside ft, bringing toe of closing ft to instep of supporting ft without changing wt (cts 1, 2, 3).

5–8   Repeat action of B, meas 1–4.

9–12 Repeat action of A, meas 9–12.

13–16 Repeat action of A, meas 13–16.

To dance as a mixer, during meas 1–4 of second and subsequent sequences back away from first ptr. During meas 5–8 advance diag L to new ptr.

FRANCE

French Folk Dancing

by Louise and Germain Hébert

TANGO WALTZ

Record: "Tango Waltz," Columbia DX 1218

Formation: Couples in ballroom pos in double cir with M back to ctr.

Steps: Waltz, chasse (step, close, step), dip, waltz balance.

Meter 3/4   Pattern

Meas

A few years ago, we knew nothing—or, like many folk dancers, almost nothing—about French dances. Historically, our ancestors were French; we spoke the same language, but our contacts with the mother country were lost many generations ago. We were hoping, like many French-Canadians, to visit France one day, but these intentions were more or less dreams. A succession of events occurred in 1963 that changed the entire situation.

During autumn 1963 the French Government sponsored an industrial fair in Montreal. The emphasis was on industrial products rather than wines, silks, or perfumes, which are usually the hallmarks of France. At the same time they felt that cultural aspects were not to be neglected, so they also sent theatrical companies and two folk dance groups, one from Basque and one from Berry. Besides exhibitions in Montreal, these groups offered their services for a tour of important cities. They wrote to our local Folk Dance Federation and were referred to us for a local exhibition. This was the first time we saw them.

The contrast between the two groups was striking; Basque dances were so close to ballet and Berry dances so rustic. We must confess that on the stage Basque dances were very well received by audiences; Berry dances, with their strange music and peasant style, were politely applauded.

We had an opportunity to meet these people behind the scenes. The Basque people were a little distant; the Berry folks appeared friendlier to us. The Berry folks even spoke our dialect (French-Canadian is still very rich in old expressions that Parisian French lost many years ago). Pierre Panis, their leader and a national instructor in folk dancing and the foremost authority in Berry dances, had spoken to the president of our Federation about a possible exchange of instructors between our two countries. Our names were mentioned as possible candidates. We accepted this offer with the feeling that it was much too good to be true.

At the beginning of March 1964 we received the official invitation. Our Federation helped us to get a grant from the provincial government, and from July 25 to September 1 we lived in Berry, taught our repertory, and learned bourrées.

It would be presumptuous to pretend that the boundaries of Berry can be identified on a map by a simple pencil mark. The inhabitants themselves tend to confuse slightly the limits of their province with those of the counties of Cher and Indre.

Geographically situated exactly in the center of France (not to be confused with the Massif Central, more to the South), centuries ago Berry found itself politically divided by the river Le Cher; to the West, the Bas-Berry (Lower Berry); to the East, Haut-Berry (Upper Berry). This division still exists today on the geographical plan, and the departments of Indre and Cher represent it. In fact, there is only one Berry. Folk dancers tend to maintain a psychological division, as is indicated by the differences in the style of the dances, especially the bourrées.

Musical Instruments

The instruments used to accompany these dances are the vielle, which is built with a wheel acting as a continuous bow turning under ten strings, and the cornemuse or musette (bagpipe). These old instruments were preserved best and are still much in use today in Berry. An important society, which has its office in Nohant, was founded in 1888 by Jean Beffier, a famous sculptor. The group today includes more than sixty maîtres sonneurs (players of the vielle or cornemuse), old and young—and this is only for the department of Indre.

Many beliefs and superstitions are attached to these musicians and their rustic instruments, who were very dear to the writer George Sand. Speaking of these players, she wrote: "They are fierce, jealous and envious of the success of their neighbors; they often have a bad reputation. Some say they are related to the evil spirits, and it is even believed they have concluded a solemn pact with the devil. . . ."

At the present time no one believes in evil spirits or in the devil. Error! No one will admit it, but the superstitions and the beliefs are still there, and everyone is more or less influenced by them. The significance of these beliefs may have been lost, but the practice has stayed just the same, almost untouched.

Twenty-five years ago not a single player from Bas-Berry would have been allowed inside a church with his vielle or his cornemuse. On wedding days they always waited for the groom and the bride outside the church. Meanwhile, it was the custom to offer them a drink in one glass only, which was promptly broken immediately thereafter "lest anyone who might drink after them would encounter bad luck."

Dances

In spite of the great numbers of players, the dances were often done only to the sound of people singing. The folklore is largely dominated by the bourrée, which already forms a very important repertory. The bourrée was, and still is, the most popular form of dancing in the central part of France. The branles are more ancient than the bourrées even if the latter predominates. Many dances from Berry formerly were connected in some way with a trade or custom, while others that were very attractive and pleasant to practice were performed purely for entertainment. Throughout Berry these dances remain very much alive, and any kind of holiday or celebration is a pretext to leave work aside and get together to dance. In a tiny village we even saw the people of the place take over the stage after a foreign group had just finished its performance and dance without stopping for most of the afternoon. Much more remains to be said about these friendly Berrichons and their province than is possible in this brief essay.

(Germain and Louise Hébert, from Quebec, Canada, are regarded as the finest French dance authorities in North America. Largely through their efforts American and Canadian folk dancers have been introduced to the unusual and fascinating music and dances of France. Perhaps the Héberts' most noteworthy contribution to the folk dance repertory has been the introduction of the French bourrées.

The Héberts' first intensive study of French dances began in 1964, when they were invited to France to teach international folk and ethnic dances as well as to study French dances. With a grant from the provincial government they departed for Berry, in central France, where for several months they studied the dances of that region. The Héberts returned to France again in 1967 and 1972 to do further research and to study with such notable French dance authorities as Pierre Panis, Paul Bouard, Geneviève His, Michel Piot, and Nicole Andrioli.

In 1966 the Héberts were invited to teach at the University of the Pacific Folk Dance Camp in Stockton, California, which was their first major teaching assignment in the United States. A warm reception followed and they were invited back to this camp in 1968, 1969, 1972, and 1975. They also taught at the San Diego State University Folk Dance Conference.

Since their introduction at Stockton ten years ago, the Héberts have taught at workshops, festivals, and camps throughout the United States and Canada. They are skillful and knowledgeable teachers who take a serious interest and a special delight in teaching the dances of France.)

FRENCH FOLK DANCES

Basic Steps for Bourrées
Note: Bourrées are the "real" French dances. Their origin is unknown, though they are widely dispersed throughout France, especially in the central region, the Massif Central, Auvergne, Rouergue, Limousin, and, of course, Berry. In Berry bourrées are danced in a very sober style—no gesturing with the hands (as in Auvergne). M convey most of the typical style with their knee action, which is strictly forbidden for W, who dance in a very delicate way.

Louise and Germain Hébert. Photo by A. C. Smith

Figure I: Pas de bourrée (bourrée step)—3/8 or 2/4 meter
Starting on L ft, step fwd with the full wt of the body touching the ground and bend both knees (ct 1); step-close on ball of R ft, straightening the knees slightly (ct 2); step on ball of L ft, straightening the knees slightly (ct 3). Repeat, starting with R ft.
Note: All steps should be kept well under the body and close to the ground.

Figure II: Avant-deux (fwd and bk)
1: *Avant-deux droit* (straight move for 2 dancers) Two dancers face each other (4 ft apart).
1st meas: Both starting with L ft, dance one bourrée step fwd and meet your opp on R shldr. (*Note:* The first step is a large one.)
2nd meas: Dancing on the spot, do one bourrée step if you are a W. M bend both knees on the 1st ct of the meas.
3rd meas: Move bkwd with one bourrée step, starting with L ft.

4th meas: Do one bourrée step in place.

2: *Avant-deux épaulé* (épaulé—shldr)

This figure takes 4 meas, like the straight avant-deux. It is frequently used in "bourrée croisée." Two dancers face each other.

1st meas: Starting with L ft, take one big step twd each other, turning ½ turn to L (ct 1).

Step on R ft close to L ft (ct 2). Step on L ft in place (ct 3). This brings ptr's R shldr to R shldr.

2nd meas: Step on R ft and at same time throw L ft sdwd L (ct 1). Step on L ft (ct 2). Step on R ft, close to L ft (ct 3).

3rd meas: Step on L ft in place, beg a ¼ turn to R (ct 1). Step on R ft in place (ct 2). Step on L ft, close to R ft (ct 3). This brings ptrs face to face.

4th meas: Step on R ft diag R bkwd (ct 1), beg ¼ turn to R. Step on L ft across R ft (ct 2). Step on R ft in place (ct 3). This brings ptrs pointing L shldrs twd each other.

Note: For teaching purposes, avant-deux épaulé can be started with L shldr pointing to opp dancer. When the steps are mastered, dancers should remember that all types of avant-deux start *facing* opp dancer.

3: *Épingle à cheveux* (hairpin or U-turn)

This is a variation of the avant-deux épaulé and takes 4 meas.

1st and 2nd meas: Repeat meas 1 and 2 of avant-deux épaulé.

3rd meas: Take a fast ¾ turn on L ft (ct 1). Step on R ft near L ft (ct 2). Step in place on L ft (ct 3).

4th meas: Repeat meas 4 of avant-deux épaulé.

4: *Avant-deux du Haut-Berry* (Avant-deux from Upper Berry)

1st meas: Starting with L ft, large step fwd (1). Scuff R heel fwd (2). Hop on L ft (3).

2nd meas: Cross R ft over L ft (1). Step on L ft a little bit bkwd to free R ft (2). Step on R ft close to L ft (3).

3rd meas: Move bkwd with one bourrée step, starting with L ft.

4th meas: Do one bourrée step in place. There is a great emphasis on the first step.

Figure III: Croisements (crossing over)—4 meas

1: *Croisement du Bas-Berry* (Crossing over from Lower Berry)

1st meas: Repeat meas 1 of avant-deux épaulé.

2nd meas: Step sdwd R on R ft, changing place with your ptr (ct 1). Step L ft close to R ft (ct 2). Step on R ft in place (ct 3).

3rd meas: Take ¾ turn on L ft (ct 1). Step on R ft close to L ft (ct 2). Step on L ft in place (ct 3).

4th meas: Repeat meas 4 of avant-deux épaulé.

2: *Croisement du Haut-Berry* (Crossing over from Upper Berry)

1st meas: Starting with L ft pivot ½ turn CCW "around" the opposite dancer (1). Step on R ft in place (2). Step on L ft in place (3).

2nd meas: Step on R ft in place, throwing L ft swd L (1). Step on L ft close to R ft (2). Step on R ft in place (3).

3rd and 4th meas: See meas 3 and 4 of avant-deux from Upper Berry.

Figure IV: Bransiller

These steps are done on the spot and are used as a transition between avant-deux and crossing over. Basically, they are pas de basque or bourrée steps done on the spot.

1: *Lower Berry Style*

Steps for M are done very neatly, crossing on the 2nd ct. Step on L ft swd L (1). Cross R over L (2). Step on L ft in place (3). Reverse. W *do not* cross on 2nd ct. They do it on each side.

2: *Upper Berry Style*

M and W do not cross on 2nd ct.

Note: These steps need 2 or 4 meas, depending on the dance. The last step becomes a preparatory move for crossing over. This anticipation characterizes the whole style.

BAL DE JUGON

Source: This is a dance from upper Brittany, but it is also very popular in other areas of France.

Record: Uni-Disc Ex 33-147, side B, band 4; Vogue EPL 7 711; Worldtone WT 10014

Formation: Cir of cpls in Varsouvienne pos, facing LOD

Meter 2/4   Pattern

Meas

A

3   Intro

Figure I: Heel and Toe

1   Both start L, do a heel and toe in front of the supporting ft (R).

2   With 3 steps (L, R, L) each ptr makes ½ turn to R (CW) to face RLOD. Do not release hands. M now to R of ptr.

3–4   Repeat action of meas 1–2, with opp ftwk. Turn to L (CCW).

5–8   Repeat action of meas 1–4.

1–8   Repeat action of meas 1–8.

Repeat A

B

Figure II: Promenade

1–14 Dance 14 two-steps moving in RLOD, begin L.

Repeat dance from beginning.

Note: The above description fits the Uni-Disc record. On the Vogue record there is no introduction and there is a pause after Fig II, during which we can stamp twice (L & R).

LA BOURRÉE DROITE DU PAYS FORT

Source: This bourrée, which was learned from Pierre Panis and Paul Bouard, means "straight bourrée from the strong country." It comes from the region of Sancerre in Upper Berry, which is called the "strong country" because of its energetic dances.

Record: "La Bourrée Droite du Pays Fort," Rhythm 4001, side A; "Bourrée Croisée de Sologne," Barclay 820138, side 2, band 4 (substitute)

Formation: Cpls in longways formation. Line of M with L shldr twd head of hall, facing line of W, with ptrs 4 ft apart. Ptrs should be able to touch each other's hands when arms are straightened. This dance is *never* danced in cir. Hands free at sides, or W may hold skirt or edge of apron where hands fall naturally. Do not swish skirt.

Steps and Styling: In Berry, bourrées are danced in a sober manner, with the M conveying most of the typical styling in their knee action. In the long step fwd, M lead with heel, then put full body wt on whole ft. M knees are kept apart (turned out) and never fully straightened throughout dance. W are strictly forbidden to copy M styling; they dance in a very delicate way. Ftwk identical for both M and W.

Pas de Bourrée (Pah deh boor-RAY)—Bourrée step (1 meas). Step fwd on L, bending knees outward (ct 1); step on R near L, beg to straighten knees slightly (ct 2); step in place on ball of L ft (ct 3). Next bourrée step would beg with R. The step can be done moving fwd or bkwd, to R or L, or turning.

Avant-deux du Haut Berry—from Upper Berry (4 meas): 2 dancers face each other 4 ft apart.

1st meas: Beginning L, take 1 long step fwd (ct 1); scuff R heel fwd (ct 2); hop L in place (ct 3).

2nd meas: Step on R across L (ct 1); step slightly bkwd on L (ct 2); step R close to L (ct 3).

3rd meas: Beginning L, dance 1 bourrée step moving bkwd to original place.

4th meas: Beginning R, dance 1 bourrée step in place.

Note: There is great emphasis on first step.

Bransiller. This is basically a pas de basque or bourrée danced in place; used as a transition step between avant-deux and croisement. In true Upper Berry style, there is no cross step on ct 2. The last bransiller step before crossing becomes a preparatory move. This is accomplished by quickly turning so that the L shldr is twd ptr to initiate the crossing step. This quick change of dir momentarily before crossing is vital, traditional, and *always done*. This anticipation characterizes the whole style of Berry dances.

Croisement du Haut Berry from Upper Berry—Crossing over (4 meas)

1st meas: Beginning L, take 1 long step twd ptr, at same time pivoting L, CCW around each other to finish in ptr's original line and facing each other. Step R beside L (ct 2); step L in place (ct 3).

2nd meas: Step R in place, throwing L ft sdwd L (ct 1); step L beside R (ct 2); step R in place (ct 3).

3rd meas: Beg L, dance 1 bourrée step, moving bkwd to opp place.

4th meas: Beg R, dance 1 bourrée step in place.

Épingle à cheveux—hairpin or U-turn (4 meas). Two dancers in a single line facing head of hall, M behind W.

1st meas: Beg L, take 1 long step, each to own L, at the same time pivoting ½ turn L, CCW. (Dancers are now facing foot of hall, W behind M.) Step R beside L (ct 2); step L in place (ct 3). Do not dip shldr.

2nd meas: Beg R, dance 1 bourrée step in place.

3rd meas: Repeat action of meas 1 of épingle à cheveux. (Dancers now are again facing head of hall, M behind W.)

4th meas: Beg R, dance 1 bourrée step in place.

Meter 3/8   Pattern

Meas	A
4	Intro

Figure I: Avant-Deux

1–2 M move fwd twd W, with meas 1–2 of Avant-deux du Haut Berry. W remain in place; no action.

3–4 M move bkwd to orig place with meas 3–4 of Avant-deux du Haut Berry. W dance action of meas 1–2, as described for M.

5–16 M repeat avant-deux steps (fwd and bkwd) 3 more times (4 in all). W continue steps as described for M.

Note: W steps will carry over into next phrase of music.

B

Figure II: Croisements and Bransiller

As fig II beg, M are in orig pos. W, who started 2 meas later, are in the middle of formation.

1–6   M dance 6 bransiller steps in place. W complete last 2 meas of avant-deux and then dance 4 bransiller steps in place.

7–10   All dance Croisement du Haut Berry (4 meas). Dancers are now in ptr's orig place.

11–14 All dance four bransiller steps in place.

15–16 Beg L, take 1 long step twd each other, at same time turning L, CCW, but *do not cross over*. M turns ¾ CCW, and W turns ¼ CCW to finish facing head of hall, M behind W. Dancers are now in single file in ctr of formation.

A

Figure III: Épingle à Cheveux

1–16   All dance steps of épingle à cheveux 4 times.

B

Figure IV: Croisements and Bransiller

1–2   All dance 2 bransiller steps, backing up into orig pos. M make ¼ turn CW, W turn ¼ CCW to face M.

3–6   All dance 4 bransiller steps in place.

7–8   All dance Croisement du Haut Berry (4 meas).

9–14   All dance 6 bransiller steps in place.

15–16 M pivot full turn in place, turning CCW on L, then dance 1 bourrée step in place. W dance 2 more bransiller steps in place. Ptrs have now exchanged places. From ptr's place, repeat dance from beg. This time, at end of fig II, dancers will have backs to head of hall. At end of dance, custom decrees that M kiss ptr first on her L cheek, then on her R cheek.

       Note: Rhythm record—4 meas intro; allows for performance of entire dance 2½ times; has no additional music for kiss. Barclay record—8 meas intro; allows for performance of entire dance 1½ times; has additional music for kiss.

LA BOURRÉE PASTOURELLE

Source: La Bourrée Pastourelle (lah boo-RAY pahs-too-REL) is a circle bourrée from the region of Pouligny-Notre-Dame in Lower Berry. Without any doubt, this is the most popular dance in Berry. Groups usually performed it for exhibition purposes. It was learned from Pierre Panis and Paul Bouard at Pont-Chrétien in 1964 and 1967.

Record: "Bourrée Croisée de Sancerre," Barclay 820138, side 2, band 10; Rythme 4002 (45 rpm)

Formation: A cir of 6 to 10 cpls. W at M R, all facing ctr, free hands at sides for M; W hold skirt.

Meter 3/8   Pattern

Meas
8   Intro:
4   (on the Rythme record)

A

Figure I: Avant-deux

1–4   All M move fwd with steps of Avant-deux droit. W do the same starting 2 meas later.

5–8   Repeat meas 1–4.

1–8   Repeat meas 1–8.

Figure II: Chaîne

As fig II starts, W are on inside cir. They will not complete their avant-deux but will do ½ turn CCW to face their ptr.

B

1–2   Join R hands with ptr and move and change places with ptr, using the 2 first meas of Avant-deux droit.

3–8   Keep moving diag out and in, like in a grand R and L.

1–8   Repeat meas 1–8, fig II.

Figure III: Avant-deux

At the end of fig II, M finish on outside cir.

A

1–4   All move twd next ptr, meeting with R shldr using Avant-deux droit steps (W face out, M face in).

5–8   Repeat meas 1–4, fig III, meeting same ptr at L shldr.

1–8   Repeat meas 1–8, fig III.

Figure IV: Souricière (Mousetrap)

During this figure W dance on the spot with bransiller steps (Lower Berry style). M circle 3 W, turning the 3rd W ½ CCW at end of fig.

B

1–2   Starting with L ft, M, using same steps as in fig II, turn around ptr. After 2 meas, M are behind W.

3–4   Completing their turn, M are in front of W.

5–6   M move to the next W.

7–8   Repeat meas 1–2, fig IV.

1–2   Repeat meas 3–4, fig IV.

3–4   Repeat meas 5–6, fig IV.

5–6   Repeat meas 1–2, fig IV. M takes W R hand with his L hand and they begin to turn ½ CCW as a cpl.

7–8   Cpls complete turn, finishing facing ctr.

A

Figure V: Avant-deux

1–8   All starting with L, W and M move fwd with Avant-deux droit steps.

1–6   Repeat meas 1–6, fig V.

7   M join inside hand with W on their R, drop the other, M turn ½ CW to face out of ctr.

8   W turn full turn CCW under joined hands.
M dance on the spot with a bransiller step as W move on outside cir to next M (moving CW).

B

Figure VI: Pastourelle

1–2   M and W join R hds. Balancing the hands sdwd to M R, then L, 2 bransiller steps (L, R).

3–4   W turn CCW under joined hands and move CW to next M. All is done with bransiller steps.

5–8   Repeat meas 1–4, fig VI with new ptr.

1–8   Repeat meas 1–8, fig VI. On last 2 meas M do ½ turn CW, moving out to W cir to finish with 4th W at L.

Dance repeats one more time, plus fig I and fig II with the Rythme record.

GERMANY AND AUSTRIA

German and Austrian Folk Dancing

by Paul Dunsing and Morry Gelman

German folk dances have been, are now, and will be in the future, expressions of the communal life of the people. Communities change, the people change, and of course the dances change. Life itself means change. And yet, it appears sometimes as though time had stood still.

In the year 1951 the traveler runs into a ducal wedding party in a small southern German town and he sees—and, if he wishes, participates in—the life of the Middle Ages. Of course this is magic pageantry. Only hours later he might arrive in a small village or in a big, pulsing city—it really does not matter— and he finds himself dancing with the home folks a tango, a rumba, a foxtrot, or even a jitterbug. And then he arrives back home on these shores and the first thing into which he happens to run might be a folk dance party where hundreds dance the *Windmueller* or the *Rheinlaender zu Dreien*. It depends on his background, his personality development, and his philosophy of life [as to] how he reacts to all that.

There seems to be a fundamental urge of the human being to express his feelings in movement first, then in music of some sort, then in speech, and then in a multiple of other ways. At the primitive level there is stamping of feet, clapping of hands, turning or twirling; then chanting or singing is added, perhaps also drum beats and pipes; then a story is told through a combination of movement, speech, and chanting; then music of various kinds takes over for speech and chanting while movement remains; and again singing, chanting, and speech are reintroduced to supplement movement.

Along with this basic development goes an increasing consciousness and a refinement of order in pattern of movement, in music, and in form and style generally. It would be possible to name examples of German dances for each of these developmental stages. Furthermore, it would be possible to detect traces of these stages in most of the old German dances. The folk dancer of today is little concerned with the early development of his *Tanzgut* (dance material) but he does stand reverently and in wonderment when he watches still existent folk customs, such as dance processions in the Rheinland or the *Perchtenlaufen*, a bit of mummery to ban evil spirits in the Alps.

But the older German folk dancer of today might have been taken in more by another sort of experience. In his youth and as a member of the *Jugendbewegung* or the *Wandervogel*, which history is beginning to recognize not only as a youth movement but also as a cultural epoch, he had thrilling experiences at solstice festivals. On the hilltop and around a huge fire, *Jungfrau'n kommet zu den Reihen*, a solstice dance, was imbued with meaning which speech or any other form of communication has never been able to convey. True,

Photo by Henry L. Bloom

this is a nice dance and fine music. It is so good, in fact, that audiences in Washington [D.C.]'s Constitution Hall during National Folk Festivals also were thrilled by it. Some still talk about it after 12 years. Certainly the thousands in that hall had a worthwhile experience. But in the eyes of this old folk dancer it fades away behind that hilltop experience 25 years ago. There, humanity wound a tight circle around that fire as a symbol of its own essential unity and recognizing that beyond that circle there was something bigger, better, and even more important than any of its links. Perhaps this means coming as close to the original intention of the dance as one will ever get.

Not only have German folk dances been "performed" in Germany at festive occasions in such places where thousands and thousands could congregate to watch, but they have been performed in this way here in the United States. Brief reference already has been made here to the National Folk Festivals. Let us look only at one more incident.

At the Inn of the Crown, as it [i.e., this dance] is known to a lot of folk dancers all over the United States—to singers and choral groups it is known as Catherine's Wedding or, if they are German, *Beim Kronenwirt*—this dance had its real start at a pageant in Chicago in 1936 sponsored by the German Day Association and named *Ein Deutsches Leben* (a Ger-

man life). There were 2,000 participants in the pageant and probably 12,000 people in the stands on Soldiers Field. There was portrayed an elaborate wedding party to which the guests came in the typical costumes of their provinces. This in itself was a nice picture. When they had all assembled—hundreds and hundreds of them—they danced At the Inn of the Crown to the accompaniment of the German United Choruses—again numbering almost a thousand—and a 50-piece orchestra.

Let us look at the *Foehringer Kontra*. German folklorists say nothing else about its origin than that it is an old, traditional Frisian dance. It is at home on the little island of Foehr in the North Sea. There is little doubt that this dance has been saved from obscurity by the work of German Youth Movement groups and their leaders before the First World War. In the same way other dances from other localities were brought back to life. But everyone knows today that these young people were not folklorists; they were wanderers, explorers, reformers, and radicals. They had pledged that they would not only live their own lives according to what they felt was right and decent and human, but that they would also change society in keeping with their ideals. At its peak after the Second World War this movement counted perhaps several hundred thousand of the best German youth among its members. Society did change considerably. Now, knowing even that much, one can draw a first and very important conclusion as to the fate of the German dances.

While being a rather healthful link with the past, these German dances became a sturdy and altogether appropriate expression of this stormy age. German folk dances today are likely to vary according to the experiences of the people and their leaders and according to the published materials used.

Paul Dunsing

(This material was excerpted and used with the permission of Gretel Dunsing. See the essay on Paul and Gretel Dunsing in Part II for a discussion of the important contribution they have made to folk dance activity in the United States.)

In recent years there has been a strong revival of folk dancing in Upper and Lower Bavaria, and the adjoining Austrian regions of Salzburg, Upper Austria, and the Tirol. Except for the highly organized Schuhplattler clubs, in the early 1950s one could hardly find a folk dance group in Bavaria that danced *Laendler* (waltz), *Boarischer* (schottische), or *Dreher* (pivoting) dance forms. Now Munich and other cities and towns abound in folk dance opportunities and there's hardly a village in Bavaria that doesn't have a Friday or Saturday night dance with young and old alike doing patterned couple folk dances such as are described below.

Following World War II, folk activity was at a low ebb since recovery from the devastation of war was underway. Surprisingly, the Schuhplattler clubs were vital and active. In 1951 a directory of Schuhplattler federations (sixteen in all) in southern Germany listed over three hundred active Trachten Vereine (folk costume clubs specializing in the schuhplattler) with about eighty-five in the Munich region alone.

Any regional revival of folk activity usually can be attributed to the lifelong efforts of natives who have earned the respect and love of the local populace by their devotion to researching and preserving the customs, music, songs, and dances of the region. Such a man was the late folklorist Kiem Pauli, of Upper Bavaria, who in the war-torn forties and recovery period fifties brought the folk music of Bavaria to the fore with his research, books, radio programs, and seminars. His protégé and successor, Wastl Fanderl, carries on the folk music traditions in Upper Bavaria today.

The work of Kiem Pauli sparked a general interest in dance. In the latter fifties the late Erna Schutzenberger, of Passau, Bavaria, collaborated with Hermann Derschmidt, of Wels, Upper Austria, to produce *Spinnradl Unser Tanz*, five volumes of folk dances from the broad regions of Upper and Lower Bavaria and Upper Austria. *Spinnradl Unser Tanz* has become the handbook of folk dance throughout these regions.

In the adjoining Austrian provinces of Salzburg and Tirol, two outstanding folklorists must be mentioned. They are Tobi Reiser and Dr. Karl Horak. The late Tobi Reiser, of Salzburg, researched and helped preserve the rich musical and dance traditions of his native Salzburg with his orchestra, trio, quartet, and sextet. He notated and recorded music and songs that had never been written down before and inspired a whole generation to think "folk" in Salzburg and neighboring Upper Bavaria. Dr. Horak also spent a lifetime researching and putting in book form the music and dances of the magnificently mountainous land of the Tirol, where each valley has its own unique dress, music, songs, and dances. Many folk dance-minded Americans are familiar with the Zillertaler Laendler. This dance was found by Dr. Horak in the Ziller Valley, where he recorded it in its mountain valley environment.

Due to the efforts of these leaders, as well as many others who contributed to the postwar revival, it is now possible to dance most every night of the week in and around Munich. On Friday and Saturday nights many a village hall and Gasthof resounds with the music of a Zwiefacher, Spinnradl, Waldjaeger, Boarischer, and Laendler.

Mention must be made of the famous Schuhplattler dance, which is indigenous to Upper Bavaria and the Tirol. These rather small regions of Germany and Austria joyously share the north *Kette* (chain) of the German-Austrian Alps, with a common border of only 150 miles. Although separated by a geographic line on the map, the people of these regions are quite similar, sharing a common language, food, dress, music, songs and dances. The Schuhplattler dance they share has found its way into other areas of Germany and Austria, but its heart and soul remain in Upper Bavaria and the Tirol, where it is enjoying vigorous activity today. A widespread movement also exists in the United States and Canada, with about fifty Bavarian and Austrian folk dance clubs actively preserving the dance form and co-ordinating their efforts through an International Federation of Clubs.

The Schuhplattler dance form has not made any headway in the recreational folk dance arena in America because of the difficulty of teaching the dance and the physical difficulty in learning the dance. A form of the Schuhplattler did enjoy some success on the West Coast in the fifties and sixties, but its resemblance to Bavarian or Tirolean Schuhplattler was only incidental.

Morry Gelman

(Morry Gelman started square and folk dancing in

high school and continued while in college in Connecticut and New York. This activity accelerated to become a full-time avocation as folk dance teacher and
dancer after he moved to California. A move to Minneapolis brought him into contact with many European
ethnic folk dancers.

He taught many groups. Together with Ralph Piper
he founded the Minnesota Folk Dance Federation,
with himself as president. He expanded his knowledge
under such leaders as Vyts Beliajus, Michael and Mary
Ann Herman, and Dr. Lloyd (Pappy) Shaw.

Several years in Germany as an aircraft engineer
with the United States Air Force provided him with
an opportunity to become an active member of Gebirgs
Trachten Vereine (Mountain Folk Costume clubs) and
to dance extensively in Germany and Austria.

He later taught at California workshops and the
Stockton Folk Dance Camp. He organized the Oberlaender (a Schuhplattler club) there and another
Trachten Verein in Maryland. In the seventies he made
several return trips to Bavaria and Austria to dance
(once in Munich with two thousand dancers), and to
do extensive dance research.)

Morry and Nancy Gelman

GERMAN AND AUSTRIAN FOLK DANCES

ALTE KATH (Zwiefacher)

Source: The Zwiefacher is a very popular and unique
form of folk dance found in Bavaria. This is one
of many, each with different mathematical changes.
The music alternates between 3/4 to 2/4 tempo and
the dancer adjusts steps accordingly between waltz
and pivot steps. This particular dance is the easiest
of the Zwiefachers.

Record: Folkraft (45 rpm) 1506; Folk Dancer (45 rpm)
MH-2017; Tanz (EP) 56-908

Steps: Take social dance position and alternate by doing 2 waltz steps and 2 pivots (dreher) throughout
the record (WWDD). Note that pivots are slow
steps, not double time.

W = waltz, D = dreher (pivot).

DREISTEYRER

Source: Introduced by the Austrian Student Goodwill
Tour, 1951. This dance for one M and two W comes
from Styria, one of the Austrian *Bundesstaaten*
(provinces).

Record: Folk Dancer (45 rpm) MH 2018; Express
(45 rpm)

Formation: Sets of three, one M and two W; M in
center, usually in triple cir. Except in beg and end,
hands are joined and must not be broken. In beg
and end free hands of W on hip.

Step: A Laendler step on whole foot. The step developed from a fast walking step and consists of one
large (1) and two small (2 and 3) steps. Step, step,
close. Large, small, small. Must be executed in an
even-flowing manner without swaying, bouncing, or
stamping, like the even flow of water. The step is
executed all through the dance, even in place where
needed. Posture firm and erect. A great deal of flirtation and play between the M and his two partners
all through the dance.

Meter 3/4   Pattern

Meas   Figures
1–8   1. Entrance. With their backs to the wall,
                the threesome enters, M in center, two W
                at his side. M holds inside R hand with R
                W shoulder high, extends left arm across his
                chest and L W holds his L hand in back of
                M at his R side. All 3 facing LOD and move
                in above pos twd center, starting on L foot.

9–16   2. M unwinds under his own R arm and both W turn inward under M raised hands at his side, all now moving in line of dir.

17–20   3. M raises R hand, L W moves under the arch back to her side. M turns with her (R hand up, L hand under). Free hands of W on hip. Inactive W steps in place.

21–24   Same with R W going under L hand arch.

25–32   4. All join hands and cir CW. Cir well extended; hands remain joined until last fig, without breaking hold.

33–40   5. Single Window. M swings both arms fwd under W arms, W turn out and form window. M has his arms straight in front of him with elbows bent up at about 90°. W face M. R W right arm and L W left arm rest on M arm, the other arms high to form window. M flirts through windows with both W. All turn CCW in this position. R W moves backward.

41–48   6. Unwind and all circle CW.

49–56   7. Form single window, as in fig 5, but turn CW.

57–64   8. Unwind and all turn CW.

65–72   9. All circle CW.

73–80   10. Single Knot. M bends over at about 90° angle from waist, places both hands under his R armpit, turns CCW one complete turn, then rises, pulls the R W thru and then the L W, arms well extended.

81–88   11. All circle CW.

89–104   12. Double Knot. M bends over as in single knot, turns, 2 complete turns CCW, while W continue circling with him. Then M rises and pulls both W thru twice, first R W, then L W, then R again, then L again. Finish circling CW.

105–112 All cir CW.

113–120 13. Double Window. M raises L arm, turns R, steps through under joined hands of W, all lower hands and cir CW in crossed-hand pos.

121–128 14. W turn out to form double window, same as in single window pos (fig 5); all turn CW.

129–137 15. Unwind and cir CW.

138–153 16. M raises both hands over and behind W heads; W likewise raise joined hands over and behind M head; all rest arms on each other's shldrs. In this pos cir CW for 8 meas, then reverse and cir CCW for 6 meas and unwind on 2 meas.

154–161 17. R W raises L arm, turns R so that her back is towards the joined hands of L W and M. M and L W kneel down on outside knees (M R, W L). R W steps over joined hands

bkwds, the other two rise, unwind and cir CW.

162–169 18. Same with L W stepping thru.

170–177 19. Same with M stepping thru.

178–185 20. M raises L arm, turns R, then breaks hold with both W, places arms on W outside shldrs. W take firm inside hand wrist hold (outside hands on hips). M sits on joined inside hands of W, supports himself strongly on outside shldrs. W carry M off in this position.

JAEGERMARSCH (March)

Record: Folk Dancer (45 rpm) MH 2013

There are many different versions of the Jaegermarsch. This is the German version of the American Paul Jones.

Note: You do not have to use all the figs given here; use all or as many as needed.

Figure 1: Cpls march side by side CCW around the ring, W to R of M inside hands joined, W has hand on hip. M has his L thumb thrust into his real or imaginary suspenders. 32 steps.

Figure 2: M continue going the same way, but W turn around and march the other way, with both clapping hands, the W clap on the "oom" and the M on the "pah." 32 steps.

Figure 3: Take new partner and waltz 32 cts around room.

Figure 4: March with new partner as in Figure 1.

Figure 5: This time W continue going in a CCW dir and M turn back the other way, and all march in opp dir 32 cts. Clap as above.

Figure 6: Take new ptr and waltz 32 cts around room.

Figure 7: March with new ptr around circle 32 counts.

Figure 8: M face center, join hands raised high to make arches. W drop hands and moving to R go in and out arches, weaving around ring.

Figure 9: Take new ptr and waltz around ring.

Figure 10: March new ptr around ring.

Figure 11: W face center and make arches, as M weave in and out arches, leading to R.

Figure 12: Waltz new ptr around ring.

Note: Any extra W or M can join during parts of dance where dancers are moving in opp dir or not waltzing.

There will undoubtedly be people without ptrs at end of each sequence, so leaders should instruct dancers to go to "lost and found" department, which is in center of ring.

KREUZ KOENIG

Source: This German dance has long been a favorite among American folk dancers. It has been done in many different ways. The choreographer of this dance was Ludwig Burkhardt. It was presented by Paul and Gretel Dunsing.

Record: Folk Dancer MH 1022

Formation: Two cpls joining hands in a cir.

Steps and Styling: Grapevine step; running step; mazurka step. The dance should basically be danced with measured reticence. The transitions of the different dance patterns must be well harmonized. Parts A, C, and D are to be danced calmly and with controlled strength (not boisterously). Running steps change with mazurka steps and give swing to the Kreuz koenig. Part B, the Straight Chain, has faster music but allows ample time for execution of the figure with hop-steps. The "flying figure" (meas 1–8 repetition) has never been intended to be used widely.

Meter 3/4   Pattern

A

Meas

1–4   Starting on left ft, do one grapevine (facing center) that is step L sideways, step R behind L, left sdwd and R in front of L and follow with 8 running steps CW, facing slightly into CW dir.

5–8   Repeat meas 1–4 at the end. Quickly take open hip-shldr pos with ptr, M join L arms with an elbow hook. In this pos take small running steps fwd.

Drop hold, W take a small step sdwd to the R and turn to face M.

B

Straight Chain (straight hey) done with hop-step (hop-waltz)

9–10   M change places by giving L hand to each other, passing by L shldrs; W hop in place adjusting to meet M with R hands (2 hop-waltz steps).

11–12 M join hands with other W, pass R shldr (in a wide circular movement) with 2 hop-steps (hop-waltz), bringing the W to the inside.

13–14 W join L hands in center, pass each other by L shldrs with 2 hop-waltz steps while M hop in place adjusting pos to meet W.

15–16 Join R hands with own ptr and change places; *M are again on the inside,* ready to do the repetition.

Note: There is much time to execute this straight chain and care should be taken to have a wide circular movement when exchanging places, especially when rounding the end of the line.

9–16   Repeat per above, but with meas 15–16 M pulls his ptr (R hands joined, arms stretched) to his R side, takes a small step to the L, lets go of her R hand and immediately takes her L hand. All four then join hands in a cir four. W does ½ turn L as she swings to M side.

C

Circle Four and Circle Two

17–20 Starting on L do 4 mazurka steps CW, release hold with corner.

21–22 Join both hands fwd with ptr, 2 mazurka steps CW.

23–24 Do 6 running steps. *Then join hands in a circle four.*

17–22 Repeat per above; smooth transition from cir to cir important.

23–24 Do running steps as above, but use last 3 steps to change from cir in two-hand position to R hands joined (straight arms) and lead W to center in such a way that they will be standing side by side, R shldrs adjacent facing ptr. M join L hands with other W.

D

Running CW with Exchanging Places

25–28 Both M, leaning back a little with loosely stretched arms, run 12 steps CW while W turn almost in place. M should dance as tall as possible "as if they were trying to look at each other above the W's heads."

29–32 Drop L hands, M lead W to outside—exchanging places with 6 running steps. Both W join L hand with other M's L hand and keep on running CW.

25–32 Repeat. Keep running CW and exchanging places.

Note: The exchanging comes on the first few running steps of every 12 steps. Then finish this part as follows:

29–32 As above, but on meas 32 M make a R about-face jump, landing to the R of their own ptrs; all join hands and start dance again with cir four with the other W as new ptr.

SAUERLAENDER QUADRILLE NO. 5

Source: This quadrille is a very old traditional dance from Neheim-Hüsten, Westphalia. It was learned in Germany by Gretel and Paul Dunsing.

Record: Folk Dancer MH 1129

Formation: Four cpls in square formation: cpl 1 facing music; cpl 2 opp them; cpl 3 to R of cpl 1; cpl 4 to L of cpl 1

Steps and Styling: Neheimer Schritt (Neheimer step, meaning step from the village of Neheim) is used throughout dance. Each Neheimer Step (N.S.) takes 2 meas or 8 cts.

Bodies are carried tall and straight. Hands are down at sides. Face ctr of set at all times except when actually dancing. On first hop (ct 1), and not before, take pos necessary to carry out step. As each dancer completes his portion of a dance fig, the last movement of closing ft together (ct 7) done facing ctr. Action of this dance is very subtle.

Neheimer Step: (described for L ft)

meas 1 (done in place) Hop lightly on R ft; at same time touch L toe to floor beside R ft, with heel turned out to side, knee turned in (ct 1). Hop lightly on R ft; at same time touch L toe to floor beside R ft, with heel turnd in twd R, knee turned out (ct &). Hop lightly on R ft; at same time touch L heel to floor beside R instep with ft parallel (ct 2). Hop lightly on R ft; at same time touch L toe to floor beside R toe, with ft parallel (ct &). Also to be done on R ft by hopping on L ft, touching R toe, and so forth.

2 (moving) *(a)* Moving sdwd to L: step to L on L ft (ct 1), step R behind L (ct &), close L to R with wt evenly divided between both ft (ct 2), rest (ct &). (Reverse ft and dir when moving fwd on R.)

(b) Moving fwd: step fwd on L ft (ct 1), step fwd on R (ct &), close L to R, with wt evenly divided between both ft (ct &). (Also to be done starting fwd on R.)

Note: The second half of N.S. is danced in same style as first—the "bounce," as in the hop, is always present. Moreover, the "rest" is a rest only when a step ends. If the movement is not finished, or if it leads immediately into next, the "rest" becomes a preparatory "bounce" for next step.

Meter 2/4   Pattern

Meas
1–4   Intro
        Honor your own (meas 3). Honor your corner (meas 4).

Figure I. Peek-a-Boo
1–4   M 1 and W 2 dance 1 N.S. sdwd, M to L, W to R, playing a sort of "peek-a-boo" around cpl 4 and back to their places with 1 N.S. sdwd, M to R, W to L.

5–8   M 2 and W 1 repeat action of meas 1–4, peeking around cpl 3.

9–12   M 3 and W 4 repeat action of meas 1–4, peeking around cpl 1.

13–16   M 4 and W 3 repeat action of meas 1–4, peeking around cpl 2.

Figure II. Couples to Right and Back
9–10   M and W of cpl 1 face each other and do 1 N.S. to R

11–12   and 1 N.S. to L, ending in orig pos facing ctr.

13–16   Cpl 2 do N.S. to R and L as in meas 9–12 (fig II).

17–20   Cpl 3 do N.S. to R and L as in meas 9–12 (fig II).

21–24   Cpl 4 do N.S. to R and L as in meas 9–12 (fig II).

Figure III. Couples Cross Over
1–2   Cpls 1 and 2 dance twd each other with 1 N.S., starting R ft. (Cpls are momentarily in line of four in ctr of set, M on outside, W with L shldrs adjacent.)

3–4   With 1 N.S. starting L ft cpls 1 and 2 continue fwd to opp place, turning in twd ptr on last movement (ct 7) to face ctr again.

5–8   Cpls 3 and 4 repeat action of meas 1–4 (fig III).

9–16   Repeat action of meas 1–8 (fig III), with cpls ending in orig places (W on outside, M with L shldrs adjacent.) Pass opp person by R shldr throughout this fig.

Figure IV. Handtour Right
9–10   Cpl 1 face ptr, join R and do 1 N.S. starting L, to ptr's place.

11–12   Continue CW to orig place with 1 N.S. starting R.

13–16   Cpl 2 repeat action of meas 9–12 (fig IV).

17–20   Cpl 3 repeat action of meas 9–12 (fig IV).

21–24   Cpl 4 repeat action of meas 9–12 (fig IV.)

Figure V. Grand Slam (all 4 cpls working)
1–4   (a) Cpls 1 and 2 cross over as described in fig III, meas 1–4, while cpls 3 and 4 dance sdwd to corners and back as described in fig I, meas 1–4.

5–8   Repeat action of fig V, meas 1–4, with cpls 3 and 4 crossing over as cpls 1 and 2 dance to corners and back.

9–16   Repeat action of fig V, meas 1–4, with cpls returning to original places on the crossover.

17–20   (b) All 4 cpls repeat action of fig II, meas 9–12 (to R and back).

21–24   All 4 cpls repeat action of fig IV, meas 9–12 (handtour R).

25–32   All 4 cpls repeat action of fig V(b), meas 9–16 (to R and back and handtour R).

SPINNRADL (Spinning Wheel)

Source: There are many versions of this dance form.
This one is taught in the eastern United States. It
is from the Muehlviertel region of Upper Austria.

Record: Tanz (EP) 58129

Formation: Cpls in Varsouvienne pos on line of cir.

Meter 2/4   Pattern

Meas

1–4   With 4 step-step-close steps fwd in LOD, beg
on outside ft. W moving to inside of cir on
meas 1 and 2, then moving to outside of cir
(M R side) on meas 3 and 4.

5–8   With 4 step-step-close steps as above but with
W staying on M side, cpls move LOD.

9–12   With hands still joined, W moves once around
M, making a full CW turn as she passes in
front of and behind him, ending outside of cir,
facing each other with joined hands crossed
(R on top).

13–20   Joined hands are raised, cpl turns under joined
hands alternately, W turns CW on the outside
of the cir, M CCW on inside of cir. Cpl moves
fwd slightly in LOD while turning. W has 3½
turns, M 3 turns, so that with meas 16 they
are facing each other. Turns must run smoothly
one into the other without a stop.

21–24   Couples move LOD with joined hands in front
with 4 step-step-close steps. Take Varsouvienne
pos to start dance again.

ZILLERTALER LAENDLER

Source: This dance was introduced in the United States
by the Austrian Student Goodwill Tour in 1951.
It had its origin in the Ziller Valley in the Tirol
and, as researched by Dr. Karl Horak, does not
have the large window figures, numbers 10 and 11;
these large windows were added by the Goodwill
Tour members. Unfortunately, the original music
was not available on a record in the United States
in 1951, so the dance was done to Bavarian Laendler
music on a 78 rpm Victor record entitled "Schwan-
taler Hoher." The music has now become associated
with the dance in this country; while it is a lovely
piece of music, it is almost twice as fast as the original music as played for the dance in Austria. Slowing
the record down helps restore some of the character
and charm to this lovely Laendler.

Record: National (45 rpm) 4561; Victor (78 rpm) 25-
4147

Formation: Cpls, inside hands joined to start, facing
LOD.

Steps and Styling: Laendler waltz throughout, 6 steps
to 6 cts of music, to be executed as smoothly and

quietly as possible, to be danced on whole ft (not
toes) as much as possible. No dipping or flexing
knees; no shldr dropping; keep body erect when
fig allows it.

Meter 3/4   Pattern

Meas

1–2   1. Partners side-by-side facing CCW (LOD),
inside hands held, free hands on hips. Both
starting outside ft, M L, W R, waltz fwd, swinging straight arms fwd and back.

6–8   M keeps moving fwd, turns W in front of him
under her own arm, inside hands still held.
W keeps waltz, turning in front of M under
her own arm, turning CW, progressing CCW.

9–16   2. M facing CCW (LOD), W C (RLOD), join
both hands, W R in M L and W L in M R.
Move CCW (LOD) swinging straight arms into
ctr and out. (W backing up here.)

17–24   3. With both hands still joined, M raises R
arm, turns W to her L until her L arm is extended in front of M chest, then cir in place
CCW (takes 4 meas to get into pos and 4 to
cir).

25–32   4. Reverse procedure, unwind, and then, raising M L arm, W turns under, cpl turn CW.

33–40   5. Change hands so that hands are crossed
with R on top. W goes down on her R knee.
M steps over joined L hands in a crouched
position, R first, then places both joined hands
under his R armpit and turns in bent-over pos
twice CCW while W rises. With hands still
joined, unwind. (Hands at end of figure are
still crossed above W head.)

41–48   6. M dancing in place, facing CCW, leads W
with R hand (both hands are still joined) high
CCW around him so that she ends behind him
facing CCW. Both hands remain joined L on
M L hip. R arms in a rounded pos fwd. Both
turning in this pos W behind M R arm in place
CCW. W leads M.

49–56   7. Reverse procedure. W stepping slightly to
L behind M, joined R hand on M R hip, L
arms fwd, turning CW, W behind M L arm.

57–64   8. Both hands still joined, M backs out and
under, turning W twice in front of him into
R little window position and turn. (In this position M may call through window "cuckoo.")

65–72   9. Reverse window to L little window pos,
turning W 3 times and turn CCW. (W may
call "cuckoo.") In both windows W elbow must
rest adjacent to M shoulder.

73–80   10. Unwind window and keep turning W with
L hand high until big-window pos is reached,
L high overhead, R low and R shldrs adjoining.

Keep turning CW (use 4 meas to get into pos and 4 to turn). (In this pos M may give kiss to W through big window.)

81–88 11. Reverse procedure, turn W 3 times CCW R hand high. (W not wanting to accept anything without giving in return may give kiss to M through window.)

89–96 12. Drop hands, take Laendler pos, supporting each other on shldr blades, arms high and round, W arms resting on M, dance Laendler waltz turning CW, progressing CCW (LOD), to be danced smoothly on whole ft.

97–192 Repeat entire dance, ending up with lifting W with shoulder-waist lift.

GREECE

Greek Folk Dancing

by Athan Karras

The forceful way in which Greeks defend their cultural identity makes us realize the important role dance plays in their lives. It is no accident that their dance traditions can be traced back to their ancient heritage. From the earliest times in the development of their civilization, great significance and emphasis was placed on the arts. Their attention to the expression of movement was inspiring and unique, resulting in very specific forms of dance—initially in religious ceremonies and later in secular activities. Dancing was one of the leading forces of expression. It remained strong in the hearts and feelings of the Greek people as a kind of assurance of their existing identity and reflected the eminence of their declining leadership as a world power. The ensuing invaders plowed through their landscape and subjected them to domination, but they managed to preserve their dances. This nonverbal means of communication was emphasized even more as a way of holding on to one's identity in the midst of an invasion by an invader who, along with political, social, and economic subjugation, attempted to impose foreign cultural influences. A question that has confused laymen and scholars for years is: Who truly had a greater influence on whom, the conquered or the conqueror? The answer becomes simple when we draw significant parallels with other forms of expression.

Their language remained the same, with only the natural evolution and development, and their religion was still relevant. Thus, there is reason to believe that customs, traditions, music, songs, folk tales and folk-lore remained constant. The dance can also be considered to have been consistent throughout their history. Furthermore—and it may be one of the strongest clues we have about Greece as well as the Balkan countries—perhaps because of their dominant position during the great European Renaissance, cultural influences were being disseminated at a rapid pace and great changes and innovations were taking place.

The latter gave rise to the great Industrial Revolution, while the Middle Eastern or Balkan peninsula nations remained divided from what became known as Western Europe. This is one reason why the tip of Eastern Europe is enjoying a belated renaissance and why the folk arts have been kept alive and vibrant in these countries. Culturally speaking, these nations are just now beginning to catch up with Western Europe.

In every society dance plays an important role in depicting the temperament and environment of its people. For instance, after the rage of the ballroom era and dancing cheek to cheek, youth, always in the forefront of new trends, broke loose and championed the twist. Rock 'n' roll followed. Then the sheer abandonment of movement gave way to a solo type of dancing. Now our so-called solo dancers are slowly beginning to reach for one another on the dance floor—again touching, so to speak, relating to our times by moving away from "doing your own thing" to getting to know one another.

In Greece today, local traditions have been abandoned almost inadvertently. Even in the villages, holding on to these ideas is considered old-fashioned; most people are concerned with keeping apace with the latest trends and fashions.

The growing importance of tourism in Greece and the advent of such films as *Never on Sunday,* and *Zorba the Greek* had a definite impact, particularly outside Greece. The films created an interest in contemporary Greek culture and traditions; in some cases a certain notoriety resulted. But the outside world viewed these cinematic excursions as two rather vibrant and strong affirmations of life and considered them tremendous forces. Not only were they cinematic experiences, but they began to influence aspects of general culture.

Buzuki music emerged from its "dens of iniquity" to share the spotlight with other major forms of music as entertainment. The celebrated Athenian—who was becoming a kind of European snob, subject to British and French influences, seeking entertainment in the music halls, theaters, and nightclubs—began to turn to the buzuki tavernas. Having to deal with the koutsa-vakia or manghes (an elite group considered an underworld subculture), the Greek dance gained in popularity among the upper and middle classes. The syrtaki dances and the hassapiko were exploited as an affectation rather than as a visible form of expression. Nevertheless, most Greeks continued to keep their eyes on the Western World and to follow their trends.

However, outside Greece an awareness was growing of Greek music and dancing as offering a feeling of abandonment. This form of line dancing, which had been restricted to the Greeks in the past, was accepted as a form of expression where people related to each other in a direct and meaningful manner. It gave them a feeling of belonging and being part of a cultural heritage that had deep roots in history.

Greek immigrants in various parts of the world attempted to hold on to their Hellenism, as well as their religion, language, and traditions. In the United States, in many instances, a ghetto existence satisfied the emotional needs of these people and gave them a sense of security in the new world. But, like all people, those who had been here for a couple of generations were losing touch with the past. Organizations, institutions, churches, festivals, and social events were established to maintain those traditions. Dances performed near the local church steps and in the recreation rooms resulted in magazine articles, short stories, novels, and films. The Greek immigrant living in the United States had emerged and demanded a place beside other cultures.

In his new home, the Greek immigrant strived to uphold his identity by passing on to his children the language, religion, customs, folklore, and the various dances of his native land. He was proud to see his children in his native country's national dress, recapturing a moment of past glory. Although he did not possess a coat of arms and could not boast of being a descendant of a founding father, he, too, could show that he came from a substantial background. Thus, he would endure and live side by side with his neighbor in the city or suburb.

(Athan Karras has taught Greek folk dances throughout the United States and Canada, and has lectured and written articles for several magazines. His services are sought not only among the many amateur dance ensembles but even among top professionals in Las Vegas and big show palaces, in movies, television, and concerts.

Athan has worked in Greece with various folk ensembles and periodically visits his native Greece to update his research and record new ideas in dance, music, and costumes. Karras was lead dancer with the National Dance of Greece Ensemble under the direction of Dora Stratou. He has produced several outstanding Greek folk dance albums that have won many initiates to Greek dancing, and has extended the musical range to include the regional sounds of the mountains and the islands.

Athan Karras

Athan was cofounder of the Intersection Folk Dance Center in Los Angeles in 1965. It has become the inspiration of Greek dancing nationally and has brought a vitality into folk dancing as something for all to enjoy in an atmosphere that breaks down barriers even among the most uninterested parties. The Intersection Folk Dance Center successfully and enthusiastically makes folk dancing the vital experience it has always been. Athan has extended his services by opening up a center in Greece and working with individuals in other countries and cities all over the United States.)

GREEK FOLK DANCES

HASSAPOSÉRVIKO

Source: The hassápika dances became popular in Greece within the last thirty years. Prior to that there were several different variations of the hassápiko dance, with characteristic styles and tempos reflecting the area or province. The hassápika dances of Thrace differ from the hassápika dances of Macedonia and the islands. The hassápiko was originally danced by butchers in Constantinople, thus explaining how it received the name Butcher's Dance. Greek seamen roaming the Aegean did much to disseminate this dance. They created a style and mood of their own at the seaside tavernas they frequented, and developed a tradition which, following the advent of the rebetika music and the mood of the buzuki, was reflected in the dance known as Sailor's Dance (also called hassápiko). The sense of freedom and abandon that was inherent in this dance form was almost immediately accepted by all Greeks; they could easily identify with the vitality of this particular dance form. The hassaposérviko is another style that evolved from the hassápiko dance, utilizing the steps of the Butcher's Dance and the Sailor's Dance in a kind of tempo that falls between slow and fast.

Record: Soul Dances of the Greeks, Peters International, Piltis-33; Hit Parade Trio Bel Canto, Grecophon GRS-310

Formation: Arms stretched out shldr hold

Meter 2/4   Pattern

Meas *Figure A*

1   Step with R ft to R (ct 1); step L to R, crossing behind R (ct 2).

2   Step R to R (ct 1); bring L to R, no wt (ct 2).

3   Step L to L (ct 1); step R to L, no wt (ct 2).
    Repeat four times.

Figure B

1–2   Repeat meas 1 and 2 of fig A, except in meas 2 raise L up to ankle.

3   Step fwd to ctr with L (ct 1); swing R in air fwd and into the air (ct 2).

4   Bring R behind L and step (ct 1); bring L behind R and step (ct 2).

5   Step R to R (ct 1); bring L to R (ct 2).

6   Repeat fig A: Step L to L (ct 1); step R to R, no wt (ct 2).
    Repeat four times.

Figure C

1–4   Repeat fig B, meas 1–4.

5   Syncopated steps (pas de basque), step R to R, cross L in front and step on it, changing wt to R (cts 1 & 2).

6   As above, step L to L, cross R in front and change wt to L (cts 1–2).
    Repeat four times or continue with crossing R ft behind and continue sequence of meas 5 and 6.

Figure D

1–2   Repeat fig A, meas 1–2.

3   Drop arms and slap hands (ct 1); slap back of R heel with R hand (ct 2).

4   Swing R ft fwd and bring directly front of L (ct 1); hold (ct 2).

5   With wt on L, pivot all the way around, on ball of ft, shift wt to R, ft crossed (cts 1–2).

6   Step L with L, bring R to L with wt (cts 1–2).
    Repeat twice.

Figure E

1–3   Repeat fig B, meas 1–3.

4   Bring R in front of L, lift L off floor (ct 1); in place, shift wt onto L, leaving R in place (ct 2).

5   Cross R behind (ct 1); cross L behind (ct 2).

6   Step R to R (ct 10); bring L to R (ct 2).

7   Step L with L, bring R to L (cts 1–2).
    Note: From the above steps many other combinations can be selected and combined so that the lead dancer is improvising within the form.

MÍSIRLOU

Source: The mísirlou, a Greek-American dance meaning "beloved," is based on the Krítikos Syrtós from Crete.

Record: Kolo Festival 45-4804; Festival F-3001, side 2, band 1; Festival Records FLP-1505; T-131-A(78); RCA Victor 45 EPA 4129A1; Folkraft 1060x45A; Festival F-3505(45 rpm); Balkan S-7000A(78 rpm); Mercury 70145(78 rpm); Columbia 7217F. Meter may vary with recording.

Formation: Dancers in a broken cir with leader at R end. All join hands at shldr ht, hands near shldrs.

Steps and Styling: Walk, grapevine (cue: S = slow, Q = quick). The dance is characterized by a graceful and flowing movement, with easy turning of the hips. When knee is lifted, keep inner side of ft near supporting leg. The leader at the R end may lead the dancers in any direction, serpentining.

Meter 2/4, 4/4, 7/8   Pattern

Meas

Intro
(Measures of intro may vary with recordings). Dancers wait in place.

	I. Point, Grapevine, and Walk	Cue
1	Moving LOD, step sdwd R (ct 1); hold (ct 2).	S
2	Point L toe in front of R (ct 1) and describe an arc with L in preparation for next step (ct 2).	S
3	Step L behind R (ct 1); step R to R (ct 2).	QQ
4	Step L in front of R (ct 1) and pivot ¼ turn on L to face RLOD (CW), raising R knee (ct 2).	

The hips turn easily with each step.   S

5–6   Take 3 steps fwd in RLOD, R L R
(cts 1, 2, 1); hold (ct 2). On last step
rise on R toe, lifting L knee.   QQ S

7–8   Still facing RLOD, take 3 steps bkwd
in LOD, L R L (cts 1, 2, 1); hold
(ct 2), pivoting ¼ turn to face ctr
on last step.   QQ S

Repeat dance from the beginning.

PENTOZÁLI

Source: This dance comes from the island of Crete.
It is believed to be derived from the ancient Minoan
dance of Kouretes. *Pento* is five and *záli* means
dizzy; thus, a five dizzy step in Cretan dialect provides the name for this dance. As the music gets
livelier, the dancers leap higher and improvise many
variations.

Record: Panhellenion KT1001
Formation: Arms at shoulders

Meter 2/4   Pattern

Meas

Figure I

1   Jump onto L ft directly fwd, bending R leg,
on (ct 2) hop on L ft.

2   Jump bwd on R ft, bringing L ft in front of
R; on (ct 2) jump on L ft to the L, crossing
R ft in front, stepping L R L.

3   Jump on R ft to R, crossing L ft in front, stepping R L R.

4   Raise L ft off floor and hop on R ft (ready
to start phrase all over again).

Figure II

Repeat meas 1 and 2.

3   Jumping onto R, do three little quick brush
steps R L R.

4   Same as in fig I.

Figure III

Repeat meas 1 and 2, same as in fig I, three
brush steps on R L R, and repeat three little
brush steps on L R L.

4   Same as above.

Figure IV

Repeat meas 1 and 2, jumping with ft apart,
hop onto R ft, bringing L ft behind, hop onto
R ft, bringing L ft in front.

4   Same as above.

Figure V

Repeat meas 1 and 2 same as above.

3   Jump on R ft to R, cross and bring L leg high
in front of R, brushing and touching L toe.

Same as above.

Note: Other variations may be developed from
these in various combinations.

SYRTÁKI

Source: Syrtáki (Seer-tah-ki) is the name given to the
combination of various hassápika dances, both in
style and variation of tempo. Syrtáki, meaning "little
syrtó," was applied after the popularization of the
dance performed in the motion picture *Zorba the
Greek.* The hassápika dances of northern Greece,
known as the Butcher's Dances, became very popular because of the ritualistic elements contained
within the dance, and the idea of a kind of personal
dialogue among dancers through movement. The
seaports of the Aegean captured this type of expression. In time several forms of this hassápiko evolved,
each retaining the name hassápiko, which dates back
to the days of Byzantium and the slaughtering of
swine in Constantinople. Today this version is of
particular interest to people from all walks of life,
and perhaps is still inspiring the same ritualistic
feelings in each person.

Record: Soul Dances of the Greeks, Peters International, Piltis-33; Hit Parade Trio Bel Canto, Grecophon GRS-310
Formation: Lines with shldr hold

Meter 2/4   Pattern

Meas

Figure I: Basic Slow Hassápiko Step

1–2   Side steps to R with R, slowly bring L to R.

3–4   Repeat with opp ftwk.

1–2   Feet together, drop on to ctr with L, leaning
body fwd (ct 1); slowly bring R ft fwd as if
to brush, swing it fwd as body recovers and
straightens (ct 2), swing R leg, making a semi-
circle in air and crossing directly behind L (1
& 2).

3   Raise L and quickly cross it behind R, and
hold (cts 1–2).

4   Step R to R (big step), cross L in front of R
(very close together) raise R and step in place,
lifting L and only touching heel on floor, in
front of R (cts 1 & 2 &).

Repeat first pattern three times.

Figure II

1   As L is in front of R, continue with L 3 little
steps RLOD (step LR, LR, LR).

2   Do same as above, only bring R in front of
L and move LOD (LR, LR, LR).

Figure III

1–2   Repeat fig II, except take only 2 steps to R
and 2 to L.

Figure IV

1–2 Cross over 4 single steps, starting with R and ending together.

Figure V

1–2 (Four counts) open toes, open heels, close toes, close heels.

BASIC HASSAPOSÉRVIKO STEP (tempo changes)

Figure A

1 Step R to R (ct 1); step L to R, crossing behind (ct 2).

2 Step R to R (ct 1); bring L to R, no wt (ct 2).

3 Step L to L (ct 1); step R to L, no wt (ct 2).

Figure B

1 Repeat fig A, meas 1.

2 Repeat fig A, meas 2, except raise L ft up to ankle ht.

3 Step fwd to ctr with L leg (ct 1); swing R leg fwd into air (2).

4 Bring R ft crossing behind L and step on it (ct 1); bring L behind R crossing and step on it (ct 2).

5 Step to side to R with R (ct 1); step L together R (ct 2).

6 Repeat fig A, meas 3, ct 2.

Figure C

1–4 Repeat fig B, meas 1–4.

5 Do 3 syncopated steps twd ctr, L R L; swing R leg through.

6 Repeat above, meas 5.

Repeat fig A of hassaposérviko.

BASIC FAST HASSAPIKO (tempo changes)

1 Step R to R (ct 1); step L to R, cross in front (ct 2).

2 Step R to R (ct 1); swing L in front of R (ct 2).

3 Step L with L (ct 1); swing R leg in front of L (ct 2).

Repeat five times.

BASIC SLOW HASSAPIKO STEP (Repeat as fig I, 3 times)

Figure B: Grapevine or "Zorba" step

1 As L is free, step L across R, step R to R.

2 Step L behind R, step R to R.

3 Step L in front of R and hold.

1–3 Repeat meas 1–3 in opp dir and opp ftwk.

1–3 Repeat meas 1–3 with L to begin.

1–2 Cross 4 little steps R, L, R and L together.

1–2 Open R toe, open L heel, close R toe, close L heel.

HASSAPOSÉRVIKO

Repeat fig A of Hassaposérviko twice.

Repeat fig B of Hassaposérviko twice.

Repeat basic step of fast hassápiko 8 times; then fast hassápiko step 10 times, except that at the start instead of stepping to R, cross R, then pas de bas to L, and finish the syrtáki dance.

TRÁTA (Trah-Tah)

Source: The tráta is believed to be an ancient dance. A description has been found on a tomb in Apoulia, an ancient Greek colony active about 400 B.C. This fresco depicts women dressed alike, holding hands crossed over with the left foot pointing and the body bending away. The dance represents fishermen dragging the nets of the fishing fleet (Tráta). The dancers are like little boats of the fleet led by the master boat, simulating the fishermen heaving in their nets when they return to shore. It is danced on the island of Salamis, where the women ritualistically do this dance while the men are preparing to ship out to the sea. It is also danced in Megara during Lent and at the big Easter Sunday festival. The leaning away steps and the imitative pull are imitative of the heaving of nets.

Formation: For women only, in a line with arms extended open and crossing with the next person in line of R arm over L.

Record: Aegean Echos LP66—Panegyris Folk Ensemble

Meter 2/4   Pattern

Meas

Figure A

1 Step R ft to R, step with L ft crossing front of R ft with a dip (bend) and slightly leaning body opp.

2 Step with R ft to R, point L ft (toe) and lean fwd to R.

3 Close L ft to R ft, point R ft (toe) to R and lean away twd L.

Repeat above 6 times.

Figure B

Tráta is also a Nesiotiko syrtó: The following description presents a version of the Nesiotiko step. It is similar to the regular syrtó step, only with smaller steps and without the return step.

1   Step R ft to R. Step L ft behind R ft. Step R ft to R side.
2   Same as above, only with opp ftwk counts 1 & 2. Close L ft to R ft.
     Repeat meas 1 and 2 to complete phrase. For musical sequence complete twice the full fig B.

Figure C
1   Step R ft to R. Step L ft behind R ft.
2   Step R ft behind L ft. Step L ft behind R ft.
3   Step R ft to R. Step with L ft crossing front of R ft and bending (dip), leaning body in opp dir.
     Fig A and fig C can be connected by 2 phrases of 2 plain syrtó steps (12 counts each).

HUNGARY

Hungarian Folk Dancing

by Kálmán Magyar

In the 1950s the Hungarian Academy of Sciences established a special group of professionals to collect and categorize the Hungarian national dance heritage. Dr. George (György) Martin was one of the folklorists who undertook the enormous task of organizing the material at hand and initiating additional field collections. (*Hungarian Folk Dances*, G. Martin [translated by Rudolf Fischer] Budapest: Corvina Press, 1974.)

In 1978 Dr. Martin reported that there are 426,504 feet (130,300 meters) of movies and approximately 12,000 dance variations from over 800 locations in the possession of [the] Musicological Institute (Zenetudomanyi Intezset) in Budapest. The next phase will be comparative studies in order to trace the evolution [of] dance.

In a somewhat different form, there have been 200–300 folk dances introduced to the American recreational dance community in the last 20 years. Some of them may be criticized because they do not express ancient traditions. Yet most could easily be classified into the same categorical system that was developed by Dr. Martin.

Dublin Folk Dances

Hungarian folk dance is categorized by *styles* and/or *dialects*.

STYLES

This systematic grouping observes the importance of chronological development in the dance culture of Hungarians in Europe. Following are examples of old-style dances.

KÁRIKAZÓ (The Maidens' Round Dance)

Chain round dances accompanied by singing, the dominating form of the Middle Ages in Europe, were soon superseded by the fashion of modern couple dances. The girls' circle dances resemble those earlier dance forms and often they combine childrens' games. This latter characteristic is not found in the more highly developed and, as a rule, instrumentally accomplished chain dances of the Balkans.

Today the Kárikazó is usually done on festive occasions, when the musicians are resting, or on a Sunday afternoon on the village square, for the young girls' self-amusement.

Although this old-style dance type may be found in many geographical areas, it is most popular in the southern and northern regions of Hungary.

The most popular examples of recreational dances of this type introduced in America are: Somogyi Karikázó (A. Czompo), Lassú Sergé (Cs. Ṕalfi), Paloc Karikázó (J. Magyar) and Sárkö zi Karikázó (A. Czompo, J. Magyar).

HERDSMEN'S DANCES (Pásztortánc, Botoló)

Weapon dances, or war-like dances, may be found in almost every ethnic culture. The Hajdútánc (or Hayducken Dance) of 16th–17th-century Europe may be considered as a root to this dance type. It was used to display virtuosity at victory feasts and wakes, and at jollifications at court. But hájdu dances amidst the battlements in the heat of battle are also recorded. They may be characterized by fast twirlings of weapons (daggers, swords) as well as acrobatic crouching and leaping figures that sometimes lay flat on the ground.

The musical accompaniment to the herdsmen's dances were bagpipes, shawms, fiddles and drums.

Although mostly men cultivated [the] hájdu dance, stories tell about some women's participation as well.

The Botoló (Stick Dance) dances of the north-eastern part of the Great Plains (mostly Szatmár region) and the Kanásztánc (Swineherdsmen's Dance) of Transdanubia (mostly Somogy region) and the Kanásztánc (Swineherdsmen's Dance) of Transdanubia (mostly Somogy region) are living proof of the wild hájdu dances of old times.

To my knowledge none of the recreational folk dances are done with a stick, but the following examples will illustrate dances that might be grouped under this heading: Somogyi Kanústánc (K. Magyar), Kanásztánc (A. Czompó).

LEGÉNYES AND UGRÓS (Lad's and Leaping Dances)

This dance form is closely related to the above-discussed herdsmen's dances; however, unlike the former type, they are still one of the most popular dances of the Hungarian ethnicon and they may be found in almost all geographic areas.

They may be characterized as jumping, running, heel-clicking dances and their musical accompaniment is instrumental, ranging from bagpipe and zither to full Gypsy bands.

The following sub-groups were designated by Dr. Martin:

I. Southern, western and northwestern areas of Transdanubia. We find the Kanásztánc (danced without a stick or any utensil): Ugrós, Háromugros, Cinege, Pajtástánc, Szakáctánc. Several recreational dances were introduced that may be classified here: Cinege (A. Czompó), Szakácsnetánc (J. Magyar), Csillagatánc (Cs. Pálfi), Sárközi Ugros (K. and J. Magyar).

II. Marching dances (Menettancok—are popular in the Lower Danube region, Kalocsa, South Great Plains (Alföld). These dances are mostly processional and are used to march down the street, or around the house or yards, to the music of a band. Examples are: Kalocsai Mars, Cs. Pálfi (K. and J. Magyar).

III. Dus, Ugrós, Oláhos dances are known from northern Transdanubia and the Great Plains region in Hungary. They are solo and also couple dance, with somewhat more complicated movements, performed mostly as exhibition dances on festive occasions. The best example may be the popular Oláhos (A. Czompó). Other examples: Rábaközi Dus (K. Magyar), Ugrós (A. Czompó).

IV. Bukovina leaping dances, Silladri and Fel-Olahos, are two rare dance forms found only among the Csángós and the Zsékely people (Secklers) in Transylvania. The format of these dances are similar to the Ugrós dances of Transdanubia, but they are not as well developed. To my knowledge, this type of recreational folk dance has not been introduced to date in America.

V. Erdélyi Legényes (Transylvanian Lad's Dance) is the most developed and unequivocal in virtuosity among all the East European dances. It is exclusively danced by men of Kalotaszeg, Mezőséd, Central Maros River area as a performance, solo, improvisational dance and it forms an important bridge between the Ugrós (leaping dance) and the Verbunk (discussed below) dance styles.

Several well-known dances belong to this group, under various synonyms: Pontozó, Csúrdöngölő, Sűrű Tempó, Sűrű Magyar. Unfortunately, due to the extremely complex figures and styles, this dance does not suit the requirements of the average recreational folk dancer. Nevertheless, attempts have been made by the following instructors to teach some of these intricate dances: Andor Czompó, Károly Falvay, Sandor Tímár, K. Magyar.

VI. Lassú Legényes ("Ritka" tempo, or slow Lad's Dance), is mostly found in the Mezoseg region of Transylvania and it is the slower version of the dance described above. However, only the music is slower; the steps are executed in double tempo, making the dance even more difficult and demanding than the Erdélyi Legényes (above).

This type of dance was introduced to America by Károly Falvay [and] Sandor Tímár and was taught to recreational folk dancers by A. Czompó and K. Magyar. The Gypsy dances found in Hungary also belong to this Ugrós category.

Old Couple Dances are old-style Hungarian dances. They are unique, since the very popular, later-developed csárdás did not assimilate them. These dances are surviving remnants of the late Medieval and Renaissance Western European couple dances.

The Lassú, Lassú Magyaros are found today among the Csángó Székelys in Gyimes and among the Hungarians of the Mezőség. As the music increases in tempo, other dances become evident. Almost all the Transylvanian couple dances belong to this general

type, and the following are danced also in America: Marosszéki Forgatós (A. Czompó, K. and J. Magyar), Osszerázós (K. Falvay), Szeki Csárdás (S. Timar [and] also A. Czompó).

It is important to note that this group represents a transition from the old style (ugrós). However, the movements sometimes resemble the steps of the csárdás, as noted below.

New Style Hungarian dances include the verbunk and the csárdás.

VERBUNK (Recruiting Dance)

When the Habsburg, Austro-Hungarian armies were established, starting with the second half of the 18th century, musical entertainments and jollifications were generally used for recruiting.

Professional dancers neatly dressed and well trained in the art of recruiting went around the countryside to sell poor peasants on the advantages of army life. During the entertaining, dancing and drinking, the potential soldier's virtuosity awakened and he joined the military—for a lifetime. This method seemed to be effective in obtaining volunteers.

The dance itself is improvised and specific variants are found in different geographic locations. The verbunk is always the first dance in a dance cycle (táncciklus, táncrend) of the area and it is usually followed by the couple dance, the csárdás. It is either danced in a circle (Körverbunk—circle verbunk) or as a solo performance.

The verbunk dances are well known by recreational folk dancers in this country. The best examples are Kapuvári Verbunk (A. Czompó), Danátúli Verbunk (Cs. Pálfi) from the western region of Hungary, Magyar Verbunk (K. Magyar), Szatmári Verbunk (A. Czompó) from eastern Hungary, Vasvári Verbunk (K. Magyar) from [the] northern Palóc region and Kun Verbunk (A. Czompó, Cs. Pálfi, K. Magyar) from the southern part of the country.

The most important differentiation between the verbunk and the Ugrós-Ingényes (Leaping Lad's Dance) is the musical accompaniment. The verbunk rhythm is always characteristic [of] the even rhythms (every measure of the 4/4 beat is accented) as opposed to the faster tempo "esztam" (oom-pah) beat, which is used in the old-style dances (e.g., Ugrós-Legényes).

CSÁRDÁS

The development of the csárdás may be traced back to the Renaissance; however, the present form of the dance appeared in the first half of the 19th century. The dance became popular throughout the country because it was hoped [that it would] be established as the national dance of Hungarians.

The csárdás music is closely related to the verbunk. The slow csárdás has the even rhythmic pattern explained above and the quick csárdás is played with an esztam (oom-pah) beat.

There are numerous variations to this dance. Each one is characteristic [of] the locality it is found in. Always danced with a partner, improvised, first slowly, then in an increasingly faster tempo, climaxing the táncciklus (dance cycle).

There are many recreational forms of this dance known in America today. A few popular examples are: Kevi Csárdás (A. Czompó), Békési Páros (A. Czompó), Friss Magyar Csárdás (Cs. Pálfi), Nagyecsedi Csárdás (K. and J. Magyar).

There are two additional forms of csárdás styles. They are Hármas Csárdás (threesome csardas) such as Borozdánfutó (A. Czompó) and Körcsárdás (circle csárdás) (J. Magyar).

The above-discussed six groups could be used to categorize and identify every existing Hungarian recreational folk dance in America. Therefore, we may conclude that a respectable and knowledgeable expert of Hungarian dance cannot create choreographies only for the sake of dancing and dancers. He must present material which is honest and representative of Hungary's folklore and which bears all the markings of hundreds of years of heritage.

DIALECTS

The other method Dr. Martin uses to define Hungarian folk dances is by dialectical differences. The reason for the regional variations is the uneven development of each dance style discussed above, due to various geographic and cultural factors.

Three major dialects for Hungarian folk dance are noted as follows:

1. Western or Danube region—including Transdanubia, the western half of the Highlands (Felföld), the western part of the Danube-Tisza mid-region (Duna-Tisza Koze).

Rábadöz, Somogy, Kalócsa [and] Sárköz are well-known areas of origin for many recreational dances.

2. Middle of Tisza region, includes the Great Plains (Alföld), and the eastern half of the Highlands (Felvidék).

Alföld Szatmár, Nagykunsag [and] Borsod are best recognized for the dances of this area.

3. Eastern Transylvanian dance dialects. In discovering the past of Hungarian dancing and the story of its development, Transylvania must be considered the most important field of research.

Several dances from the land of the Székelys (Székelyföld) and the Mezoseg region are popular in America among recreational folk dancers. Examples are: Forgatos (A. Czompó, K. and J. Magyar) and Székley Friss (A. Czompó).

Hungarian folk dance research is not complete; additional studies are being conducted and new revelations will be forthcoming. However, it is certain that Dr. Martin's system of categorizing types and dialects will be the basis for future publications.

(This article originally appeared in the January–February 1979 issue of *Viltis* magazine and is used here with permission.

Kálmán Magyar and his wife, Judith, both natives of Hungary, came to the United States in the early sixties. He was born in Kiskunhalas in 1945; she was born in Budapest in 1947. Kalman started his dance training at an early age. At age ten, he was accepted into the Hungarian Ballet Institute. Judith's early artistic environment revolved around the literature, music, and history of her native country. Both have had an excellent background in the arts and crafts relative to the music and dances of Hungary.

Soon after his arrival in America, Kálmán joined the Hungária Dance Ensemble in New York and soon became its dance director. From that point on, his interest in Hungarian folklore and dance intensified. He has utilized his ability in numerous choreographed works for Hungaria and other folk dance ensembles in the United States and Canada. After Judith arrived

in this country, she continued her study of the arts, received a degree in interior decorating, and worked for some years in this field. She joined Hungária in 1964. This was the start of a strong involvement in Hungarian folk dance and folklore. She served as costume director for them and the now inactive Nomad group. She also is a choreographer and, like Kálmán, has taught at numerous camps. Regarding the education of children of Hungarian ethnic communities as important, she teaches folk dance and folklore in Passaic, New Jersey. Both are experts on the zither. Judith produces and edits, *Karikazó,* a Hungarian folklore publication. Kálmán is the organizer and director of Pontozó, an annual Hungarian folk dance festival. They are a driving force in the folk cultural scene of the New York–New Jersey–East Coast Hungarian communities.)

LŐRINCRÉVI CSÁRDÁS

Source: A dance from Lőrincréve, Transylvania. Presented by Kálmán and Judith Magyar.

Record: Hungarian Folk Dances of Transylvania, Folkraft LP-41, side, A, band 3

Formation: Couples in shoulder-waist pos M facing LOD

Steps and Styling: Step 1. Két Lépéses Csárdás (Two-step or double csárdás)

a) Step on L ft to L (ct 1); close R ft next to L ft, taking wt (ct 2); step on L ft to L (ct 3); close R ft to L ft, wt shared momentarily by both ft (ct 4).

b) Same action as Step la, but with opp ftwk and direction.

Step 2. Forgó (Turn)

a) (Forgó step L) Turning CW in place with ptr and facing L, step on L fwd (ct 1); continuing turn, step on R ft (ct 2). This step takes only ½ meas.

b) (Forgó step R) Same as Step 2a, but with opp ftwk and direction of turn.

c) (W turnout step) W turns out CW (R turn) under M L arm with three steps, beg R ft (cts 1, 2, 3); close ft together (ct 4). Make 1 turn or 2.

Step 3. Kopogós (Heel stamp)

Facing slightly L, step on R ft diag bwd to R (ct 1); stamp L heel next to R ft without taking wt (ct &); step on L slightly bwd (ct 2); stamp R heel next to L ft without taking wt (ct &). This step takes only ½ meas.

Meter 4/4   Pattern

Meas No Introduction

I. Csárdás

1   M: Dance one double csárdás step L (Step 1a), moving diag fwd L.

W: Dance one double csárdás step R (Step 1b), moving diag bkwd R.

2   M: Dance one double csárdás step R (Step 1b), moving diag fwd R.

W: Dance one double csárdás step L (Step 1a), moving diag bkwd L.

3–4   Repeat action of meas 1–2 (Fig. I).

II. Forgó
Ptrs change to the following turning pos: Ptrs facing but turned slightly L, R hands on ptr waist, L hand on ptr R elbow.

1–5   Do the forgó (turn) step L (step 2a) 10 times, turning CW in place with ptr. On last 2 cts (cts 3, 4 of meas 5), W turns slightly to R, opening up the pos a bit, M L hand taking W R hand (M R hand and W L hand are still in shoulder-waist pos). On the very last ct (ct 4, meas 5), close ft together in preparation for next step (movement is for both M and W).

III. Kopogó and Forgó

1   M: Still facing slightly L and starting to turn CCW as a cpl, dance the kopogós (heel stamp) motif (step 3) twice. During last 2 cts turn slightly R in preparation for next step.

W: Facing slightly R and starting to turn CCW as a cpl, do the forgó (turn) motif to the R (step 2b) twice.

At the end, ptrs assume the following turning pos: Ptrs facing but turned slightly R, L hands on ptr waist, R hands at ptr L elbow.

2–4   Turning CCW as a cpl, do the forgó (turn) motif to the R (step 2b) 6 times.

5   M: Do the forgó motif to the R once more, while turning W under L arm, then click R ft to L ft (ct 3), hold (ct 4).

W: Dance the turnout step (step 2c) once. On last ct close ft together.

Repeat dance from beg.

MAGYAR VERBUNK

Source: Men's recruiting dance from the Szatmár region. Presented by Kálmán and Judith Magyar.

Record: Folk Dances and Folk Music of Hungary, Folkraft LP-40, side B, band 5, Nagyecsedi Magyar Verbunk.

Formation: M individually in a circle or line. Arms free, or place either or both fists at waist.

Meter: 4/4   Pattern

Meas No Introduction

A1   *I. Hajlongó (Sway), Cifra and Záró (Close)*
1   Turning slightly to R, fall on R slightly

fwd diag R, knees together and bent, L ft remaining on floor (ct 1); in this pos, and keeping R on floor, tap R heel 3 times (cts, 2, 3, 4) as R chugs slightly fwd and body twists a bit more to R with each ct.

2   Continuing slightly fwd, repeat meas 1 with opp ftwk and direction.

M usually hold R hand fwd somewhat above head level during meas 1–2.

3   Fall on R fwd, turning knees and body to R, keeping knees together and bent, L ft remaining on floor (ct 1); continuing fwd, repeat ct 1 with opp ftwk and direction (ct 2); repeat cts 1, 2 (cts 3, 4).

4   Repeat meas 3.

M usually have both fists on waist during meas 3–4.

5   Step on R heel across in front of L, knee bent slightly (ct 1); step on L in place (ct &); step on R across in front of L, knee bent slightly. While raising L lower leg in back, knee bent (ct 2); repeat cts 1, &, 2 with opp ftwk (cts 3, & 4).

6   Bring R ft around (prior to ct) and jump on both heels in place, ft together and parallel (ct 1); jump on both ft apart but knees together (ct 2); click ft together (ct 3); hold (ct 4).

7–8   Repeat meas 5–6.

Note: It is important to keep knees together in this fig.

A2   *II. Bokázó (Click), Cifra, and Tapsos (Clap)*

1   Raise L ft slightly, with knee bent, and slap L thigh with L hand (ct 1); click L to R ft as you hop on R sdwd to L to meet the L ft, wt on both ft (ct &); repeat cts 1, & (cts 2, &); step on R heel sdwd to R (ct 3); step L behind R (ct &); step on R sdwd to R (ct 4). The steps on cts 3, &, 4 are small.

Note: The slaps may be omitted.

2–3   Repeat meas 1 twice (3 times in all).

4   Click L to R and clap hands in front of body (ct 1); clap in back (ct 2); clap in front again (ct 3); hold (ct 4).

Note: You may add a click R to L ft on ct 2 and a click L to R ft on ct 3.

5–8   Repeat meas 1–4.

Fig II may also be done with opp ftwk, handwork, and dir.

B1   *III. Hátrafonó (Weave back or reel step), Harang (Bell), and Csapó (slap)*

Note: On meas 8, ct 4, fig II, you may add a fall onto L in place to initiate this next fig.

1   Hop on L in place, swinging R lower leg bkwd

in a slight arc (ct 1); step on R behind L while kicking L fwd (ct 2); repeat cts 1, 2 with opp ftwk (cts 3, 4).

2   Repeat meas 1.

3   Beg with wt on L and with R slightly out to the side, step on R in place next to L, almost like a cut step except the L is not displaced (ct 1); step L in place (ct &); step on R in place, while swinging L leg out to the side, knee straight (ct 2); repeat cts 1, &, 2 with opp ftwk and dir (cts 3, &, 4).

4   Leap onto R in place, swinging L lower leg to L and slightly back and slapping L outer boot with L hand (ct 1); repeat ct 1 with opp ftwk and handwork (ct 2); click R to L; end with wt on both (ct 3); hold (ct 4).

Note: Again, on ct 4 you may add a fall onto L in place to repeat the reel step.

M usually place R hand on head, holding the hat, especially during meas 1–2, fig III.

5–8   Repeat meas 1–4. On ct 4, meas 8, stamp R fwd with wt and raise R hand across in front of body to prepare for the slapping fig that follows.

B2   *IV. Csapó (slap) and Tapsos (Clap)*

1   Do a small hop in R in place, while swinging L fwd, knee straight, slapping L boot top with R hand (ct 1); slap L thigh with L hand (ct &); step on L in place while slapping R thigh with R hand (ct 2); slap L thigh with L hand (ct &); do a small hop on L in place while swinging R fwd, knee straight, slapping R boot top with R hand (ct 3); slap L thigh with L hand (ct &); step on R in place while slapping R thigh with R hand (ct 4); slap L thigh with L hand (ct &).

2–3   Repeat meas 1 twice (3 times in all).

4   Repeat meas 4, fig II. On ct 4 stamp R fwd with wt and raise R hand across in front of body to prepare for the slapping.

5–8   Repeat meas 1–4. On ct 4, meas 8, hold.

Repeat dance from beg for a total of 4 times.

RÁBAKÖZI CSÁRDÁS

Source: A couple dance from the Rábaköz region. This is the basic form of a freestyle dance with many variations. Figures I and II may be interchanged with figures III and IV, and vice-versa, at any time. Presented by Kálmán and Judith Magyar.

Record: Folk Dances and Folk Music of Hungary, Folkraft LP-40, Side A, band 3, Rábaközi Friss Csárdás.

Formation: Cpls facing each other in shldr-waist pos.

Steps: Double Csárdás (2 meas): Step on L to L (ct 1); step on R next to L (ct 2). Step on L to L (ct 1); close R to L (ct 2). Bend knee slightly with each step (on each ct) and straighten knee between cts, thus making this csárdás step rather bouncy. This step is also done beg with R ft.

Double Csárdás, M Variation (with cpl turn) (4 meas): Beg with wt on R, L ft slightly raised behind, step on L, crossing behind R ft, bending knee and pulling ptr into a CCW turn as a cpl (ct 1); step on R sdwd to R, completing ½ turn (ct 2). Step on L sdwd to L, bending knee slightly (ct 1); close R to L, straightening knees (ct 2). With bouncy steps (as described above for the basic double Csárdás) take a small step on R to R (ct 1); step on L next to R (ct 2). Take a small step on R to R (ct 1); do a slight lift on R, while raising L ft behind, knee bent, preparing to repeat this step from the beg (ct 2). This step is done turning ½ CCW each time, so that if it is repeated a full CCW turn as a cpl would be made.

Szökkenös (Step-hops) (W only) (2 meas): Step on R with a slight accent, very slightly sdwd to R, bending knee (ct 1); hop on R in place, bringing L ft to R ankle (ct 2). Repeat with opp ftwk and direction (cts 1, 2).

Sarkazó (Step-hops with heel-touches) (M only) (2 meas): Step on L slightly sdwd to L, with accent, bending knee (ct 1); hop on L, straightening both knees and touching R heel to floor in front (ct 2). Repeat with opp ftwk and direction, touching L heel fwd (cts 1, 2).

Meter: 2/4   Pattern

Meas   No Introduction

A1   *I. 2 Pépéses Csárdás (Two-step csárdás or double csárdás)*

1–4   M dance one Double Csárdás step to L and one Double Csárdás step to R, while W do likewise but with opp ftwk (W start to their R).

5–16   Repeat meas 1–4 three times (4 in all). On ct 2, meas 16, M do a slight lift on R, while raising L ft behind, knee bent, in preparation for fig II.

A2   *II. 2 Lépéses Csárdás Forduloval (Double csárdás with half turns)*

1–4   M dance one Double Csárdás, M Variation step, turning with ptr 1/2 CCW as a cpl.
W repeat meas 1–4, fig I. Take larger steps on the Double Csárdás to R and smaller steps on the Double Csárdás to L.

5–16   Repeat meas 1–4, fig II, completing 2 full CCW turns. On ct 2, meas 16, M omit the raising of the L ft behind.

Note: M tilts upper body slightly to the L as he leads W into each 1/2 turn. Cpls turn approximately on the spot without much traveling.
Repeat figs I and II two more times (3 times in all). This corresponds to music A 3–6.

A7   *III. Kiforgás (Individual turns)*

1–8   M dance the Sarkazó step 4 times, while W dance the Szökkenös step 4 times.

9–16   Release hold. Repeat meas 1–8, turning individually CW more or less in place. W ordinarily make 2 turns, M 1 turn, but the number of turns is optional. W usually place free hands at waist, while M usually hold hands up or clap.
Resume shldr-waist pos at end.

A8   *IV. Nő-Forgatás (M turns W)*

1–8   Repeat meas 1–8, fig III. On meas 8 M L hand takes W R hand from his shldr and prepares to turn her.

9–10   M dance one Sarkazó step in place while turning W once CW under his L arm. Make sure to bring joined hands all the way down at the end. W place free hand on waist (forming a handle) and turn once CW with one Szökkenős step.

11–12   Repeat meas 9–10 but reverse the direction of the W turn.

13–16   While doing 2 Sarkazó steps, M grasps W L arm slightly above the elbow with his R hand and, using that as a handle, leads her into a CW spin, releasing both hands as she starts her turn and then making 1 CW turn himself. W, with 2 Szökkenős steps, make 2 CW turns individually. W usually place free hands at waist, while M usually hold hands up or clap. End facing ptr, ready to resume shldr-waist pos. Repeat figs III and IV three more times (4 times in all). This corresponds to music A 9–14.

SOMOGYI KANÁSZTÁNC

Source: A Shepherd's dance from Somogy. Presented by Kálmán and Judith Magyar.

Record: Folkraft LP-40, side A, band 5.

Formation: Individually in a circle, M with fists on waist, W with hands on waist. May also be done in circles with low handhold or in couples holding R or L hands or in shoulder hold.

Steps and Styling:

Step 1:   Bokázó (Clicks)
Click R ft to L ft (this movement is accompanied by a slight CCW pivot on the ball of the L ft

so that the L heel moves slightly to R to meet the R heel) (ct 1); repeat the preceding movement with opp ftwk (ct 2).

Step 2: Dobogós Cifra (Stamping cifra)
Meas 1: Facing slightly to R, stamp R ft to R, taking wt (ct 1); stamp L ft next to R ft, taking wt (ct &); stamp R in place, taking wt (ct 2).
Meas 2: Repeat action of meas 1, step 2, with opp ftwk and direction.

Step 3: Kopogós (Heel stamp)
Facing slightly R and moving R, stamp onto R ft, bending knee (ct 1); stamp L heel in front of R ft, taking wt on L (ct &). This stamp takes only 1/2 meas.

Step 4: Cifra
Facing slightly R, stamp fwd on R (ct 1), stamp on L, moving in same direction (ct &), stamp on R (ct 2).

Step 5: Előre Dobogós (Stamp forward)
Meas 1: Stamp fwd on R ft, taking wt, bending knees, and turning slightly to R (ct 1); repeat action of the preceding ct with opp ftwk and direction (ct 2).
Meas 2: Repeat action of meas 1, step 2.
Meas 3–4: Repeat action of meas 1–2, step 5, with opp ftwk.

Step 6: Légbokázó (Click in Air)
Meas 1: Jump on both ft in place (ct 1); click heels together in air (ct &); repeat action of cts 1, & of this meas (cts 2, &). The jumps are with feet apart but parallel.
Meas 2: Land on R ft (ct 1); step on L ft, crossing behind R ft (ct &); stepping into straddle pos, stamp R ft to R (ct 2).
Meas 3–4: Repeat action of meas 1–2, step 6, with opp ftwk and direction.

Meter: 1/4   Pattern

Meas   No Introduction

1–8   *I. Bokázó*
Dance the bokázó motif (step 1) 8 times.

II. Dobogós
1–8   Dance the dobogós cifra (stamping cifra) motif (step 2) 4 times.

III. Kopogós
1–7   Dance the kopogós (heel stamp) motif (step 3) 14 times.
8   Do the cifra step (step 4) once more.
9–16   Repeat action of meas 1–8, Fig III, with opp ftwk and direction (move to L).

IV. Előre Dobogós
1–8   Dance the előre dobogós (stamp fwd) motif (step 5) twice.

V. Légbokázó
1–8   Dance the légbokázó (clicks in air) motif (step 6) twice.

SZANYI KÖRVERBUNK

The Szanyi Körverbunk is a men's circle verbunk (recruiting) dance from the village of Szany, in the western part of Rábaköz and of Hungary.

The changes of figures are called by the *hej-legeny*, who shouts *"hej!"* before a new step is to be done. The sequence is predetermined, but not the number of times a given step is done. (For the purpose of learning the dance, however, each step is described below as having a fixed number of repetitions.)

The set structure does not mean that the dance is the same in all the villages of the region. It is practiced in small groups, village by village, and also by groups of lads. Each group strives for individuality in the figures and sequences. Learning the verbunk played an important role in the dance life of Rábaköz. Practice during the months preceding the yearly patronal festival of a certain village is taken seriously. The performance of the verbunk takes place at the fair, during the festival, for the enjoyment and judgment of the crowd. Any dancer making a mistake has to pay a penalty. Presented by Kálmán and Judith Magyar.

Record: Folk Dances and Folk Music of Hungary, Folkraft LP-40, side A, band 1.

Formation: M individually in a circle (or line), facing ctr. Stand a little closer than normal (dancers will start dance by backing away into proper places).

Steps: Bemérés (Measuring-in) (2 meas): Start with ft together, knees bent. Straighten knees and extend arms straight fwd, palms more or less facing, R hand slightly higher (ct 1); bend knees and elbows, bringing hands closer to body but still around chest level (ct 2); straighten knees and clap hands in front (ct 3); bend knees again (ct 4). Straighten knees and clap hands in front (ct 1); bend knees and clap hands in front (ct 2); straighten knees and clap in front (ct 3); bend knees (ct 4). Every fig of the dance will be introduced by this measuring-in step.

Meter: 4/4   Pattern

Meas

1–3   Introduction
After some words of greeting, a 3-meas musical introduction is heard. Stand in place for the first two meas. On meas 3 run bkwd 3 steps R, L, R to form a larger circle (cts 1, 2, 3); click L to R (ct 4); with ft together, bend knees (ct &).

I. Bokazo-Fordulassal (Click with turn)
1–2   Do one measuring-in step.

3   L fist on waist, R hand above head level. In place, turn 1/4 CW with 2 steps L, R (cts 1, 2); close L to R with a small heel click (ct 3); hold (ct 4). End facing 1/4 to the R.

4   Repeat meas 3 with opp ftwk and direction (but hands remain in same pos as before). End facing ctr.

5–8   Repeat meas 3–4 twice (3 times in all).

9–16 Repeat meas 1–8 with opp ftwk, handwork and dir.

II. Berugós (Kick in)

1–2   Do one measuring-in step. On ct 4, meas 2, step heavily onto L ft in place, raising R lower leg diag bkwd R.

3   Hop on L in place, kicking R leg fwd across in front of L, straightening knee (ct 1); leap onto R sdwd to R, kicking L lower leg to L, L knees bent and turned in (ct 2); click L to R (ct 3); bend knees (ct 4).

4–9   Repeat meas 1–3 twice.

10–18 Repeat meas 1–9 with opp ftwk and dir.

III. Csapós (Slap)

1–2   Do one measuring-in step.

3   Hop on L in place while slapping inner side of R boot top with R hand, in front (ct 1); leap onto R sdwd to R, kicking L lower leg to L, knee bent and turned in (ct 2); click L to R (ct 3); bend knees (ct 4).

4–9   Repeat meas 1–3 twice.

10–18 Repeat meas 1–9 with opp ftwk, handwork, and dir.

IV. Hosszú Futó (Long running)

1–2   Do one measuring-in step.

3   Straighten knees while extending R arm straight up and snapping fingers (ct 1); bend knees and bring arm down (ct 2); straighten knees while extending L arm straight up and snapping fingers (ct 3); bend knees again (ct 4).

4   Do a small hop on R, raising L leg in front, knee bent, and slapping inner side of L boot top with L hand (ct 1); step on L in place, with accent (ct 2); do a small hop on L, raising R leg in front, knee bent, and slapping inner side of R boot top with R hand (ct 3); turning to face diag R, run fwd on R in LOD (ct 4).

5   Continuing in LOD, run fwd on L (ct 1); step on R in LOD, turning to face ctr and swinging L leg out to side (ct 2); click L to R (ct 3); with ft together and parallel, bend knees (ct 4).

6–20 Repeat meas 1–5 three more times (4 in all). Repeat dance from beg, without the introduction.

Note: The dance figs do not follow the musical phrase. If this sequence is followed, the claps and shouts of *"hej"* will not correspond to those heard on the record. For this version of the dance, the call *"hej"* will come on the first ct of the measuring-in step of a new fig or new direction, except during the fig with the 1/4 turns (fig I). Here a call is needed to signal the end of the 1/4 turns, so the call is made on ct 1 of the last 1/4 turn; since this signals the start of a new fig or direction as well, it is not necessary to make the call again on the following measuring-in step. Also, during the introduction the call is made on ct 4, meas 2, to start the dance.

SZATMÁRI CSÁRDÁS

A couple dance from Szatmár. Presented by Kálmán and Judith Magyar.

Record: Folk Dances and Folk Music of Hungary, Folkraft LP-40, side B, band 6: Nagyecsedi Csárdás.

Formation: Cpls in open pos, W on M L side, inside hands joined and held low, ptrs turned slightly twd each other.

Meter: 4/4   Pattern

Meas No Introduction

A1   *I. Előre-Hátra (Forward and back)*
     Steps are described for M; W use opp ftwk. Move fwd with 3 steps beg with R (cts 1, 2, 3); close L to R, or bring L near R, touching (or without touching) the floor, while marking time on the supporting leg with a slight bounce or knee flex (ct 4).
     Variation for ct 4: Do a small hop on R in place while kicking L fwd, slightly off the floor.

2   Repeat meas 1 but move bkwd with opp ftwk. In the variation, swing and raise R lower leg behind L, R knee bent.

3–8   Repeat meas 1–2 three more times (4 in all). Variation for M: On any ct 4 of meas 1–8 above, M may lift the free leg higher than described above and slap the upper part of the boot with the free R hand.

A2   *II. Harang (Bell) and Dobogó (Stamp)*
     Steps are described for M; W use opp ftwk. Face ptr.

1   Beg with wt on L and with R slightly out to the side, step on R in place next to L almost like in a cut step, except the L is not displaced (ct 1); step on L in place (ct &); step on R in place while swinging L leg out to the side, knee straight (ct 2); repeat cts 1, &, 2 with opp ftwk and direction (cts 3, &, 4).

2–3   Repeat meas 1 twice more (3 times in all).

4   Do 3 stamps in place R, L, R (cts 1, 2, 3); hold (ct 4).

5–8   Repeat meas 1–4.

A3   *III. Sergő (Turn) and Dobalós (Switch sides)*
M and W use same ftwk. Assume shldr-waist pos as first step is taken.

1   Turning CW in place with ptr and facing slightly to L, step on L diag fwd L, rolling slightly from heel to toe (ct 1); continuing the turn, step fwd on R, L, R (cts 2, 3, 4).

2   Continuing the turn, step fwd on L, R (cts 1, 2); M stamp L fwd with wt, stopping the turn, leaning body fwd and in the direction of the turn, and opening into a semiopen pos, W on his R side, her L hand on his shldr, his R hand on her back, above the waist, while W pivot CW on R (prior to the ct) and jump onto both ft, arriving at M R side as described above, leaning slightly fwd, ready to go in opp direction (ct 3); hold (ct 4). Ptrs are turned inward slightly twd each other.

3–4   Assuming shldr-waist pos again, repeat meas 1–2 with opp ftwk, handwork, and direction of turn. (W first step will be fwd, while M first step will be more like a side step.)

5   Beg in open shldr-waist pos (semiopen pos) with W on M L side, ptrs turned slightly twd each other. Ptrs switch sides, M without much of a turn, W making almost a full CW turn, thus: M face slightly L and step on L diag fwd L (ct 1), leading W into her turn with his L hand; step on R fwd across in front of L (ct 2); turning slightly CW, stamp L with wt sdwd and slightly fwd, leaning body the same way and holding W at her back with his R hand (ct 3); hold (ct 4).
W step fwd L, R (cts 1, 2) going across in front of M and starting to turn CW; pivot on R (prior to the ct) and jump into pos on both ft (ct 3), completing the turn and arriving at M R side in open shldr-waist pos, turned slightly twd ptr and leaning slightly fwd, ready to go in opp direction; hold (ct 4).

6   Repeat meas 5 with opp ftwk, handwork, and direction.

7–8   Repeat meas 5–6. M do not put full wt on last stamp.
Variation for M: In meas 2, 4, 5, 6, and 7, after the stamp on ct 3, M may add 2 more weighted stamps (cts &, 4) in place.
Repeat dance from beg, then repeat fig III once more.
Variation for fig II: This fig may also be done individually with or without clapping.

Overleaf:
Kálmán and Judith Magyar.
Photo by Aida Loussararian

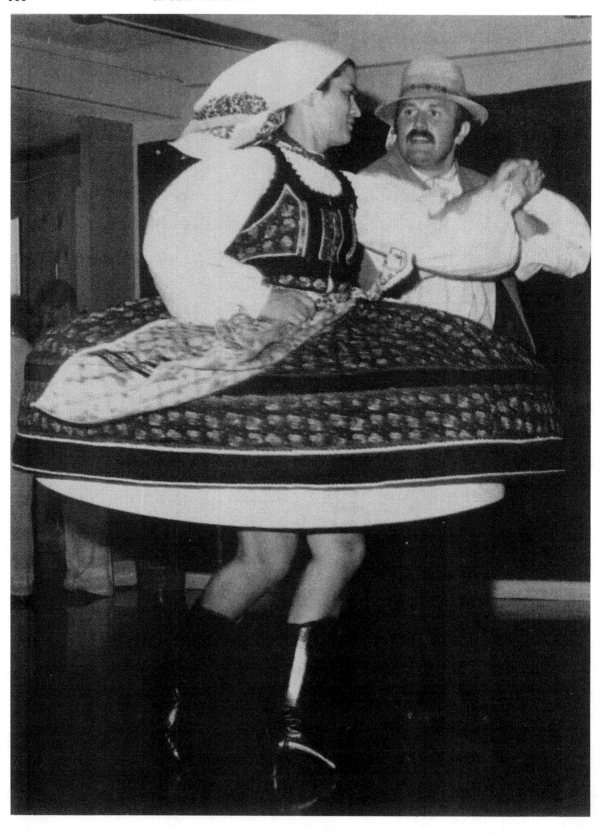

IRELAND

Irish Folk Dancing

by Margie Lenihan Tiritelli

The Gaelic word "feis" (pronounced "fesh") denoted a custom or form of thanksgiving coming after a plentiful harvest, where the nobility of Ireland, with their ladies, harpers, and bards, would gather at the castle of an Irish king to celebrate and compete in music and dancing. At this particular time, the popular dance was Rinnce Fadha (pronounced reenka faudha) which was originally an old Irish peasant dance.

Since this dance was a favorite of the reigning King Leoghaire (pronounce it "Leery" "Leary"), who was the ruler when St. Patrick came, it was frequently performed at court. It was also known as the "long dance," meaning of unusual length. The Rinnce Mor, or Great Dance, is a later version. The Sir Roger de Coverley is a dance that was derived from this long dance, and which eventually became known in America as the Virginia Reel.

Religion has played a role in the surviving dances of Ireland. It is said that in the 4th century A.D., when the Celtic settlers converted to Christianity, the new priests allowed these Celts to retain some of their pagan elements in tunes and dances by transforming their gods into saints. St. Patrick was one such example.

Because history records these priests as of two distinct types—aesthetic and worldly—conflict soon arose over two forms of Catholicism which later caused further confusion when Protestant reformers extended English sovereignty over Ireland in the 16th century. This is why Irish dancing varies. On the one hand, you'll see a light, leaping, gay spontaneity or [on the other hand] perhaps only a very rigid stance where the only movement is that of the feet. Therefore, ancient ritualistic dancing is almost completely lacking in Ireland as a result of this dissension.

With the Danish invasion of the 9th century came a polishing of some dances that were later to catch the eye of the 16th century English invaders. Dancing instructors were engaged to refine these dances so that they would be acceptable at the court of Queen Elizabeth I. Hence, it is said that their efforts were largely responsible for the lack of expression worn by Irish dancers.

The traditional dances of Ireland are the reel, jig, hornpipe and, of course, set dances. But it is in the first three mentioned that the difficulty of foot steps is encountered. The reel, of Scottish origin, is a classic dance that is performed smoothly and rapidly, but without any noise. The jig and hornpipe are similar in that both use clogging and shuffling. At some parts in the dance, the feet tap the floor 75 times in a quarter of a minute. This uniqueness is what sets Irish dancing apart from other ethnic groups, as concentration is primarily centered only on the movement of the legs and the erectness of the body. However, there is a jig that is danced to "Tune of the Occupation" that does involve the use of the hand in a clenched fist.

The set dances are performed by couples and are somewhat simpler in motion and music. They consist of hop jigs, slip jigs, single and triple jigs, and are executed in 9/8 meter. The single jig and slip jig evolved from the double jig, which is the commonest of all Irish dances. There is little doubt that the double jig is the oldest.

The period 1300–1350 A.D. [contains] the oldest recording of Irish dancing [which] has been set down in English dialect peculiar to that age. William Butler Yeats is said to have based his poem "I Am of Ireland" on this, but it wasn't until the latter part of the 16th century that the beginning of modern Irish set down the words for dance—"Rinnce" and "Damhsa." It is probable that these words stem from the English "rink" and the French "danse."

In the 17th century we become aware of the withy dance, Rinnce an Ghadaraigh; the sword dance, Rinnce an Chlaidhimn; the warlike dance, Rinnce Treasach; and the long dance. It is not known for sure if the Irish dance conformed to the sword dances as did Scotland and North England (Northumbria). Little is known of the withy and warlike dances, but it is presumed that the rinnce fadha was the best known. This latter dance, as we mentioned earlier, was performed on festive occasions like the May Day ceremonies, held out of doors, where the dancers decked themselves with flowers. This dance is said to have entertained the Duke of Ormonde in 1662 and again when James II landed at Kinsale in 1689.

The tunes played for many of these dances have been mixed so thoroughly between the Irish and Scots that it is difficult to determine their origins. Both of these countries have even incorporated certain English regimental characteristics during times of war into their tunes.

The most common costume worn by the colleen dancers, subject to modification, is generally a green dress having an embroidered ancient Celtic design, black stockings, a fichu, and cuffs. A cloak or cape-like effect is attached at the shoulder, ending on the opposite side near the waist, held in place by the ancient-designed Tara Brooch.

The written word, no matter how descriptive, can in no way convey the vibrancy of color, execution of gracefulness, or splendiferous pageantry of an Irish feis half as well as the pipers and dancers will at an "old time Irish faire and Hibernian games."

(This article appeared previously in the *Hibernian Independent* and *Folk Dance Scene* and is used here with permission. Despite her Italian last name [she married into it] Margie Tiritilli is as Irish as the Lakes of Killarney or the sands of Galway Bay—or, at least, as much so as any Irish-American is. She is not a professional dancer or dance teacher, although her article might suggest this due to its thoroughness. She is a journalist for the *Hibernian Independent*. Assigned to write an article on Irish dance, inspired by her roots, and fascinated by what she saw and remembered, she did a thorough research job and came up with this result.)

IRISH FOLK DANCES

BAINT AN FHEIR

Source: Baint an Fheir (bwint-un-air), or Haymaker's Jig, is best done with 5 couples. This Irish jig was taught by Una and Sean O'Farrell.

Record: "Come To The Ceili," Top Rank Records of America, "Jigs," side 2, band 5. Also "My Ireland," Capital T 10028, side 2, band 1, or any good jig.

Formation: Longways formations of 5 cpls. M stand in one line, with hands joined, facing their ptrs, who are in a similar line. M L shldr is twd music.

Steps and Styling:

Basic Threes (Promenade) for jig: hop L (ct 1), step on R (cts 2, 3), step on L (ct 4), step on R (cts 5, 6). Next step would start with hop on R and use opp ft. This step may be done in place, moving in any dir or turning either R or L.

Jig Step: hop L, at the same time touching R toe on floor slightly in front of L (cts 1, 2, 3); hop on L again, raising R in front of L leg (ct 4, 5); hop on L again, bringing R back (ct 6) to step R, L, R, L (cts 1, 2, 3, 4, hold 5, 6).

Buzz Step: M and W are on same ft throughout dance. Keep bodies erect and steps light. Free hands hang at sides.

Meter 6/8	Pattern

Meas

    Intro

1–8   *Note:* Always wait for 8 meas before starting any Irish dance.

I. Advance and Retire

1–2   M line and W line move twd each other with 2 promenade steps, starting with hop on L ft (ct 6 of previous meas).

3–4   Lines move back to place with 2 promenade steps.

5–8   Repeat action on fig I, meas 1–4. Drop hands.

9–10   All do 1 jig step beginning with hop on L ft.

11–12   Repeat action of meas 9–10.

13–16   Repeat action of meas 1–4.

II. Ends Meet

1–4   With 4 promenade steps (start with hop on L), head W and last M move to ctr of set, join R H, make 1 turn CW, and return to place.

5–8   Head M and last W repeat action of meas 1–4 (fig II).

9–16   Repeat action of meas 1–8 (fig II), but joining L and turning CCW.

17–24   Head W and last M go to ctr and join R as before; then each grasps the R elbow of the other with his L, as they turn CW with buzz steps.

25–32   Head M and last W repeat action of meas 17–24 (fig II).

33–36   Head cpl take R arm hold and make 1½ turns CW with 4 promenade steps. End with M facing 2nd W, W facing 2nd M.

III. Reel

1–20   Head W joins L with 2nd M, head M joins L with 2nd W, and they turn 1 time CCW with 2 promenade steps. Continue reeling down the set with cpl 3, 4, 5, in turn, at the side of the set, and with each other in the ctr.

21–28   Head cpl joins both hands at foot of set (R in R, L in L), and they swing (turning CW) with promenade steps back to the top of the set.

29–44   Heads cast off (M turns L and all M follow him; W turns R and all W follow her). Head cpl promenades to the foot of the set where they face each other and join hands to form an arch. The others pass through the arch. Cpl 2 is now at the top of the set and becomes the new head cpl. Repeat the dance from the beginning with each cpl getting a turn as head cpl.

CADHP AN CUIL AIRD

Source: Cadhp an Cuil Aird (kipe-un-cool-oyard), or High Cauled Cap, is an Irish reel for four cpls in a square formation. It was presented by Una Kennedy O'Farrell of Dublin, Ireland.

Record: Any good reel or selection of reels. For example, "Rakes of Mallow," Capitol 79-40203; tin whistle music in Decca album (No. 12098) good, and others.

Formation: Four cpls in square formation: cpl 1 with back to the music, cpl 2 to L of cpl 1, cpl 3 opp cpl 1, cpl 4 to R of cpl 1.

Steps: Sidestep, promenade, and swing. Promenade step used throughout unless otherwise stated.

Meter 2/4   Pattern

Meas

I. Lead Around (Intro)

1–16   Cpls face CCW, join inside hands at shldr ht (M R, W L) and progress fwd CCW with 8 promenade steps. Drop hands, turn inwardly to face CW dir. Join inside hands (M L, W R) and return to place with 8 promenade steps.

II. The Body (Chorus)
a. Sides

1–4   Cpls join hands in promenade pos. 1st and 3rd cpls sidestep to R to pos of 4th and 2nd cpls; at the same time 2nd and 4th cpls sidestep L to pos of 3rd and 1st cpls, respectively. (1st and 3rd cpls pass in front of 2nd and 4th cpls.)

5–8   All sidestep again, same dir as before, to next pos. (2nd and 4th cpls pass in front of 1st and 3rd.) All cpls are now opp their orig pos.

9–12   All sidestep again in the same dir to next pos. (1st and 3rd pass in front of 2nd and 4th.)

13–16 All sidestep in same dir to orig pos in square. (2nd and 4th pass in front of 1st and 3rd.)
       Note: A change of wt must be made to continue to sidestep in same dir.

b. Double Quarter Chain

1–16   Cpls join R hands, make one turn CW to orig pos. (Allemande R with ptrs.) M join L hand with W on L, make one turn CCW. (Allemande L with corner.) Cpls again join R hands and turn CW 1½ times. (Allemande R with partner; go 1½ times around.) M now joins L hand with W on his R (not his ptr), turn once CCW. (Allemande L with R-hand lady.) Cpls again join R hands, turn CW 1½ times. (Allemande R with ptr, go 1½ times around.)
       Note: From the turn W move into next fig, i.e., "Ladies Off," without actually going back to their orig pos.

c. Ladies Off (Figure-eight)

1–8   Use promenade step throughout fig. All W face L, pass in front of ptr, then behind and around in front of M on L; continue fwd, passing behind own ptr to orig pos.

9–16   All W form R-hand star in center and turn CW (¾ turn), drop R hand and give L hand to M on R of orig pos (corner); turn once CCW; join R hand with ptr and turn once CW to orig pos.

d. Gents Off (Figure-eight)

1–8   M repeat action of W, but move to R in front of ptr, behind and around W on R, behind his own ptr and back to orig pos.

9–16   M form R-hand star in center and move CW (¾ turn), drop R hand and give L hand to W on R of his orig ptr; turn once CCW; join R hand with ptr and turn CW (½ turn) to orig pos.

e. Clap and Tramp

1–2   Standing in pos, clap hands together: Clap (ct 1), clap (ct 2), clap (ct 1), clap (ct &), clap (ct 2). Stamp lightly with R ft in same rhythm as claps. (Stamp on meas 3 & 4.)

5–8   Ptrs change pos with one sidestep; W passes in front of M.

9–12   Repeat clap and tramp; action of meas 1–4 (d).

13–16 Sidestep back to place; M passing in front of W.

III. First Figure

1–8   1st cpl face each other and join R hands; sidestep twd 3rd cpl and back to own place.

9–16 Keeping R hands joined, turn ptr once in place. 1st M takes L hand of W on L (corner), makes one turn CCW while 1st W takes L hand of M on R (corner) and makes one turn CCW. Then 1st cpl joins R hands and makes one turn CW in place. Use promenade step on turns.

17–32 3rd cpl repeat action of 1st cpl; fig III, meas 1–16.

33–48 2nd cpl repeat action of 1st cpl; fig III, meas 1–16.

49–64 4th cpl repeat action of 1st cpl; fig III, meas 1–16. Repeat the action of fig II (the body of the dance).

IV. Second Figure

Cpls join inside hands at shldr ht.

1–4 1st cpl advances to opp cpl (3rd cpl); 3rd couple separates slightly and 1st cpl passes between 3rd cpl. As 1st cpl passes through 3rd cpl they join outside hands with 3rd cpl (W R to M R and M L to W L), and turn opp person into a R-hand star.

5–8 All four make a R-hand star (use a cluster handhold, elbows bent), and turn CW.

9–12 Release hands in star formation and join R hand with ptr. 3rd cpl makes one turn CW in place; 1st couple at the same time makes one turn CW while moving back twds orig pos.

13–16 1st and 3rd M move across the set, R shldr leading slightly, give L hand to opp W and make one turn CCW. M again move across the set, L shldr leading slightly, give R hand to ptr and make ¾ turn CW to place.

17–24 1st and 3rd cpls take "swing position": M and W join L hands under joined R and beg M R (W L), dance around each other with 8 promenade steps.
Cpls rotate CW while moving around the other cpl CCW.

25–48 3rd cpl repeat action of 1st cpl; fig IV, meas 1–24.

49–72 2nd cpl repeat action of 1st cpl; fig IV, meas 1–24.

73–96 4th cpl repeat action of 1st cpl; fig IV, meas 1–24.
Repeat action of fig II (the body of the dance).

V. Third Figure (Ladies' Chain)

1–8 1st and 3rd W move to center, join R hands, continue across to opp M, give L hand and make one turn CCW; W return to own ptr (passing R shldrs), without rejoining hands; join R hand with ptr and make one turn CW in place.

9–16 1st and 3rd cpls repeat action of fig IV, meas 17–24.

17–32 2nd and 4th cpls repeat action of 1st and 3rd cpls, fig V, meas 1–16.
Repeat action of fig II (the body of the dance). This repeat is left to the discretion of the dancers.

VI. The finish

1–4 All join hands in cir. Move toward center with 2 promenade steps. Return to place with 2 promenade steps.

5–8 Repeat action of fig VI, meas 1–4.

9–16 Sidestep to R; sidestep to L.

17–24 Repeat action of fig VI, meas 1–8.

25–32 Repeat action of fig VI, meas 9–16.

VII. Lead Around

Repeat action of fig I, meas 1–16.

COR CHIARRAIGHE

Source: Cor Chiarraighe (curr KEE-rree), or Kerry Reel, was presented by Madelynne Greene, who learned it from Maureen Hall, a noted authority on Irish dancing from Cork, Ireland.

Record: "My Ireland"—Capitol T10028, side 2, band 3; "Snow on the Mountains" or any Irish reel. Since there is extra music on the recommended record, lift the needle at end of dance or repeat dance until music ends.

Formation: Trios facing audience, M between 2 W, inside hands joined at shldr level, elbows almost touching. Free hands are held at sides, arms relaxed, inside edge of wrist close to body, palm facing bkwd.

Steps and Styling:

Threes: These are danced like small pas de basque steps, keeping toes turned out, and they may be done either traveling or in place.

Traveling: Leap fwd R (ct 1), step on ball of L across in front of R (ct &), closing step R to L (ct 2). Next steps start L.

In Place: Leap R close beside L (ct 1), step on ball of L across in front of R (ct &), step R in place (ct 2). Next step starts L.

Sevens (2 meas): To move sdwd L begin with wt on L and swing R behind L (ct & of preceding meas), step R behind L, bending both knees slightly (ct 1), step on ball of L to L (ct &). Repeat action of cts 1, & two more times (cts 2, &; meas 2, cts 1, &). Step R behind L (meas 2, ct 2), hold (meas 2, ct &). . . . To move sdwd R reverse ftwk and dir. Knees are bent on accenting cts so that the feeling is "down"; on unaccented cts step on ball of ft.

A tall, straight, good posture is important throughout the dance. Unless otherwise specified, Threes are danced throughout—even when waiting in place. All steps start R also unless otherwise specified.

Meter 2/4   Pattern

Meas

8   Intro. Trios stand in place with R toe pointed fwd on floor.

I. Lead Out

1–4   All dance fwd with 4 threes.

5–6   All dance in place, while W make one complete turn inward under joined hands with M (R W turn CCW, L W CW).

7–8   R W go under arch formed by M and L W, M follow R W under arch as L W moves fwd CW around them. Trio finish with backs to audience.

9–16   Repeat action of meas 1–8, with L W going under arch while R W go around them. Finish facing audience.

II. Sevens in a Line

1–2   Release hands and all dance sevens sdwd L.

3–4   Dance sevens sdwd R back to place and do ¼ turn CW individually on last ct &.

5–8   All dance sevens again sdwd L twd audience and then back sdwd R, making ¼ turn CW on last ct &.

9–12   Again dance sevens L and R, with ¼ turn CW on last ct &.

13–16   Dance sevens once more sdwd L away from audience and back sdwd R, with ¼ turn CW on last ct &, to finish in orig place.

III. M Turns W

1–4   M and R W join R hands with handshake hold about shldr level, with an easy tension in the arms, and turn once CW; L W in place.

5–8   M and L W join L hands with handshake hold and turn once CCW. M return to front of R W on meas 8 to finish R hands joined with hers, R shldrs adjacent, the set forming a small triangle.

IV. Arches in a Triangle

1–2   L W dance under arch formed by M and R W joined R hands.

3–4   L W turn ½ CW in place as M and R W change places by drawing elbows close together on first "Three" and then turning ½ CW and backing into opp place.

5–8   Repeat action of meas 1–4 (fig IV), L W returning to place.

9–16   Repeat action of meas 1–8 (fig IV), with R W going under arch formed by M and L W.

Finish with M and L W still with joined R hands.

V. Star

1–4   All join R hands in a 3-hand star and turn once CW.

5–8   M release R hand and dance in place facing W, while W continue in a 2-hand star turning once CW.

9–16   Repeat action of meas 1–8 (fig V) forming a L-hand star and turning CCW. Finish with W L shldr and M R shldr twd audience.

VI. M Splits the Line

1–4   All dance Sevens sdwd L (not traveling too far), and 2 Threes in place as dancers turn to face ctr of set and all join hands to form ring.

5–8   With one "Seven" sdwd R circle ½ CCW and then dance 2 Threes in place. W are now in opp places. Finish with W L shldr and M R shldr twd audience.

VII. Forward and Back

1–2   All dance fwd as M moves away from audience, W twd audience.

3–4   All turn ½ CW in place.

5–8   Repeat action of meas 1–4 (fig VII) to return to place. Finish with M back to audience, W facing audience.

VIII. M Fig 8

1–8   W dance in place facing audience, as M dance fig 8 around W, going fwd and CCW around L W and then over to circle R W once CW to finish between W in orig pos.

XI. Lead Out

1–16   Repeat action of fig I, meas 1–16.
Lift needle or continue dance to end of music.

FALLAI LIMNIGHE

Source: Fallai Limnighe (FAH-lee LIM-nee), or Walls of Limerick, is an Irish reel that was taught by Una Kennedy O'Farrell, of Dublin, Ireland.

Record: "Walls of Limerick," Rex 15008A (Pipes); "Siege of Ennis," Columbia 3321-F—or any reel.

Formation: Sets of 2 cpls facing each other in a cir, one facing CW, the other CCW. Inside hands joined at shldr ht, W on R of M. Outside hands hang at sides.

Steps: Promenade, Sidestep

Meter 2/4   Pattern

Meas

I. Advance and Retire

1–2   Take two promenade steps fwd—R, L.

3–4 Take two promenade steps bwd—R, L.

5–8 Repeat action of meas 1–4. Drop hands.

II. Sidestep to Change Places

1–4 Both W turn L shldrs twd each other and, passing face-to-face, exchange places with one "seven." They make ¼ turn to the R to face partner as they do the two "threes" in place.

5–8 M turn R shldrs twd each other and exchange places, passing face-to-face on a "seven," then make ¼ turn L to face opp W on the two "threes."

III. Sidestep to Change Places

1–4 Both M join R hands with opp W and take one Sidestep to M L. (Cpls separate, one moving into cir, the other moving away from center of cir.)

5–8 All take one Sidestep to return to place.

IV. Swing

1 Original ptrs now join L hands under R and beg M R (W L), take one Promenade step in place.

2–8 Continue with seven more Promenade steps turning CW, while traveling CCW 1½ times around opp cpl to finish back to back with orig cpl and facing a new cpl from next group. Repeat dance from beg.

Note: On swing, ptrs are close, elbows bent, forearms upright. Variation on hold for swing: M rolls joined R hand twd him and under their joined L hands to finish with R hands near W, L hands near M, W arms resting on M arms with elbows held out horizontally.

SIAMSA BEIRTE

Source: Siamsa Beirte (SHEEM-suh BER-tah), or Two-Hand Frolic, is an Irish couple dance in slow hornpipe time. This dance was introduced by Sean and Una O'Farrell.

Record: "Bluebell Polka," Parlophone MIP 306; Folkraft 1422, or any good hornpipe.

Formation: Ptrs face with R hands joined at shldr ht, elbows bent and down, M with back to ctr. Free hands hang naturally.

Steps and Styling: Threes, Rock, Promenade

All steps are danced up on ball of ft, in a relaxed, easy style. The steps are described for M; W does counterpart.

Note: The step pattern for Siamsa Beirte begins on 4th ct and each meas description includes 4th ct of preceding meas.

Meas	Pattern
1–8	Intro

I. Threes and Rock

a. Moving to M L (LOD) hop on R in place (ct 4).

1 Step to L on L (ct 1), step on R behind L (ct 2), step to L on L (ct 3).

2 Repeat action of meas 1, beg with hop on M L and moving RLOD.

b. The following step is done in place and is very quick and subtle. Do not move away from ptr. One ft replaces the other after the hop. On the rock the wt is transferred from ball of one ft to other ft.

3–4 Hop on R ft in place, bringing L around behind R (ct 4), step L across behind R (ct 1), hop on L, bringing R around behind L (ct 2), step R across behind L (ct 3); hop on R, bringing L across behind R (ct 4) and rock L R L (cts 1, 2, 3). The rock is a swd movement from ball of one ft to other.

5–8 Repeat action of meas 1–4, beg with hop on M L (W R) and moving RLOD.

II. Change Places, Promenade

9–10 a. Repeat action of meas 1. Then M and W change places, both using 1 three: hop, step, step, step (cts 4, 1, 2, 3). M makes ½ turn CW while W moves CCW into M place, turning under R hands which are still joined.

11–12 Repeat action of meas 9–10, moving RLOD and changing places so M is again on inside of cir.

13–16 b. Join both hands with ptr—R joined over, L joined under. Dance promenade steps (hop, step, step, step—cts 4, 1, 2, 3) continuously turning CW and moving in LOD.

Note: On the Promenade (swing), ptrs are close, elbows bent, forearms upright. Variation on handhold for promenade (swing): M roll joined R hands twd himself and under their joined L hands to finish with R hands near W, L hands near M, W arms resting on M arms with elbows held out horizontally.

SOLAISAI NA BEALTAINE

Source: Solaisai na Bealtaine (so-law-SHEE nuh BYOWL-thuh-nuh), or Sweets of May, means the pleasure or joys of May and should have a feeling of spring. It comes from the North of Ireland and was presented by Sean and Una O'Farrell.

Record: "Come to the Ceili," Rank Records of America, #RM310, side 2, band 2.

Formation: 4 cpls in square formation, cpl 1 with backs to music.

Steps: A seven in jig time (2 meas): When moving to the L, hop L (ct 6 of preceding meas), step R back of L (ct 1), step L to L (ct 3), step R behind L (ct 4), step L to L (ct 6), step R back of L (meas 2, ct 1), step L to L (meas 2, ct 3), step R behind L (meas 2, ct 4). The seven may also be done to the R, reversing ftwk and dir. A three in jig time: Hop L (ct 6 of preceding meas), step R (ct 1) step L (ct 3), step R (ct 4). Next step starts hopping R and stepping L R L. A three may be danced in place or moving in any dir.

A Sidestep consists of one seven and two threes. If the sidestep is danced to the L, the first three starts hopping R and stepping in place L behind R, R in front of L, L behind R and the second three starts hopping L, etc.

All Irish dance steps are done up on the ball of the ft in a relaxed, easy style.

Meter 6/8   Pattern

Meas
1–8   Intro. All join hands at shldr ht.

I. Sidestep in Circle
1–4   All cir L with sidestep to L.
5–8   Cir back to place with sidestep to R. On last three take an extra step R (meas 8, ct 6) to adjust wt for next step.
9–12   Continue to cir R with sidestep to R. (rptd)
13–16   Cir back to place with sidestep to L.

II. Chorus
a. *Promenade Across*
1–2   Ptrs join inside hands at shldr ht, outside hands free. Cpls 1 and 3 exchange places through the ctr of set with two threes, M passing L shldr. Cpls 2 and 4 dance two threes in place.
3–4   All dancing two threes, cpls 2 and 4 exchange places while cpls 1 and 3 release hands, turn individually, M ½ CW, W ½ CCW, and join new inside hands at shldr ht.
5–6   With two threes cpls 1 and 3 return to orig places through ctr of set, W passing L shldrs, while cpls 2 and 4 turn individually.
7–8   With two threes cpls 2 and 4 return, while cpls 1 and 3 turn individually, M ½ CCW, W ½ CW.
b. *Forward and Back*
1–2   With two threes, cpls 1 and 3 move fwd twd each other, while cpls 2 and 4 repeat action of cpls 1 and 3 in fig IIa, meas 15–16.
3–4   With two threes cpls 2 and 4 move fwd twd

each other, while cpls 1 and 3 move bwd into place.
5–6   With two threes cpls 1 and 3 move fwd again, while cpls 2 and 4 move bwd.
7–8   Cpls 2 and 4 do two threes in place, while cpls 1 and 3 move bwd into place.
c. *Clap and Change*
1   All face ctr of set and clap thighs twice (ct 1, 4).
2   Clap own hands together twice (cts 1, 4).
3–4   Repeat action of fig IIc, meas 17–18.
5–8   Exchange places with ptr with one sidestep, M to R and W to L, W passing in front.
9–16   Repeat action of fig IIc, meas 17–24, returning to orig places, M moving to L and W to R, M passing in front.

III. Lead Around
1–8   Ptrs with inside hands joined at shldr ht face CCW around set and lead around (promenade) with eight threes. Release hands and turn individually, M ½ CW, W ½ CCW on last 2 meas.
9–16   Join new inside hands and promenade back to orig places.

IV. Chorus
1–32   Repeat entire action of fig II.

V. Arches
1–2   Ptrs join inside hands. Cpls 1 and 2 face each other. Cpls 3 and 4 face each other. Cpls 1 and 3 raise joined inside hands, forming an arch, and all move fwd with two threes, cpls 2 and 4 going under arches made by cpls 1 and 3.
3–4   All release hands and turn individually, M ½ CW, W ½ CCW, with two threes. Join new inside hands.
5–6   Cpls 2 and 4 make arches while cpls 1 and 3 go under and back to orig places.
7–8   Ptrs join both hands and turn ½ CW with two threes, finishing so that cpls 1 and 4 face each other and cpls 2 and 3 face each other, W on M R.
9–14   Repeat action of fig V, meas 1–6, facing new cpl.
15–16   All release hands and turn individually to face ctr of set, M ½ CCW, W ½ CW.

VI. Chorus
1–32   Repeat entire action of fig II. All join hands in a cir on last 2 meas.

VII. Thread the Needle
1–8   #1M and #4W release hands. Cpl 1 raises joined hands to form arch. #4W dances under arch, leading others behind her. She passes behind #1W and moves CCW back to orig place

in cir with eight threes in all. #1W turns once CCW under her L hand joined with ptr R to re-form circle.

9–16 Repeat action of fig VII, meas 25–32, with cpl 4 forming arch while #1M leads others through and around CW. #4M turns CW under his hand joined with ptr.

VIII. Sidestep in Circle

1–8 All join hands in single cir and repeat entire action of fig I.

9–16 Repeat action of fig VIII, meas 1–8.

STAICIN EORNAN

Source: Staicin Eornan (STACK-een OR-num), or Stack of Barley, is a couple hornpipe that was brought to the United States by Una Kennedy O'Farrell of Dublin, Ireland.

Record: "Stack of Barley," Imperial 1039A; "Stack of Barley," Celtic CI-1002

Formation: Cpls in cir, ptrs facing with R hands joined at shldr ht, elbows bent, M with back to center and M L shldr twd LOD. When not held, hands hang at side.

Steps: Sevens, Threes, Tramp, Promenade

Meter 4/4   Pattern

Meas

I. Four Sevens

M hops on R, lifting L, W hops on L, lifting R (upbeat, ct 4).

1–2 Take 1st seven, moving to M L (CCW). On hop to begin 2nd seven, couple makes ½ turn R (CW) exchanging places. (M is now on outside of cir.)

3–4 Complete 2nd seven, moving CCW (to M R). On hop for 3rd seven, couple again makes ½ turn R. (M is now on inside of cir with L shldr to LOD.)

5–6 3rd seven—repeat action of meas 1–2.

7–8 Complete 4th seven moving CCW, as in meas 3–4, but do not make ½ turn on hop. (M now remains on outside of cir, W with back to center.)

II. Threes and Tramp

9 M and W now join L hands under joined R and move to center with one three, M begins by stepping fwd on L; W begins by stepping back on R. Finish with hop (M L, W R).

10 Tramp in place (3 little steps) (M R, L, R), (W L, R, L). Finish with hop (M R, W L).

11 Move out from center with one three (M back on L, W fwd on R). Finish with hop (M L, W R).

12 Repeat action of fig II, meas 10, but make ¼ turn R so M faces LOD.

III. Swing

13–16 M beginning L (W R), hands still joined, cpl travels CCW with 4 promenade steps, making ½ turn R (CW) on each meas. Finish in orig pos, M with back to center.

Note: On swing, ptrs are close, elbows bent, forearms upright. Variation on handhold for swing: M rolls joined R hand twd him and under their joined L hands to finish with R hands near W, L hands near M, W arms resting on M arms with elbows held out horizontally.

ISRAEL

Israeli Folk Dancing

by Fred Berk

There is, sadly, relatively little accessible material for studying the history of Jewish dance. While we know from the Bible that dance was a vital and integral aspect of Jewish religious life in the pre-Diaspora period, its form and style have been lost over the centuries. The Jewish people were forbidden to make or carve graven images; therefore, there are no original pictures or sculptures of dances, costumes, or instruments. In order to understand the revival of Jewish dance, we will have to go back to its beginning.

ISRAEL

At the turn of the century, *chalutzim* (pioneers) came to Palestine and brought with them the songs and dances of their respective countries, mainly European. One dance from Romania, the Hora, became transposed into the national dance of Israel.

In 1944 a group of teachers decided to organize a meeting at Kibbutz Dalia both to show and learn folk dances. It resulted in three hundred dancers performing to an audience of three thousand spectators. This became known as the first folk dance festival at Kibbutz Dalia. The dances presented were mostly European. The gathering was most impressive. The organizational committee decided to continue its work and to stimulate the creation of new folk dances that were specifically Jewish and linked to Israel.

One of the most dynamic organizers of the group was Gurit Kadman. As a result of her foresight and drive—she continually shaped, inspired, and developed new ideas and new Israeli folk dance projects—she is considered today "the mother of Israeli folk dance." Kadman spearheaded the creation of new dances in our own lifetime through a conscious effort that was contrary to the time-honored way other cultures slowly evolved their arts and dances over the centuries.

Jewish dance, as we know it from descriptions in the Bible, was lost as the Jews wandered the face of the earth during the last two thousand years. The newly created dances were inspired by the Bible, by the new life in Israel, and also by folk motifs and dance steps of different ethnic groups residing in the country. These included Arabs, Druz, Yemenite Jews, Hasidim, and others.

Among the creators of Israeli folk dance was Rivka Sturman. Her first dances succeeded in capturing the real flavor of the new country and the spirit of the people. Some of her dances are known all over the world and are seen wherever folk dancing takes place: Hine Ma Tov, Harmonica, Zemer Atik, and Kuma Echa. Other creators of Israeli folk dances during this period were Yardena Cohen, Leah Bergstein, and Sara Levy Tanai.

In 1945 another impetus was given to the development of Israeli folk dance through the formation of a folk dance department sponsored by the Cultural Department of the Histadrut (Labor Union). In 1952 Tirza Hodes became the director of this organization, whose many functions include training folk dance leaders and teachers, organizing performance groups, stimulating the creation of new dances, and publishing folk dance material. In 1947, at the second Dalia Festival, only newly created Israeli folk dances were performed. This enormous accomplishment was achieved in only three short years.

More folk dance choreographers emerged, among them Shalom Hermon and Jonathan Karmon. Hermon intended to create not folk dances but mainly choreography for pageants. Some of these dances were so well liked by the dancers and the audiences that they were danced again and again, becoming true folk dances. He also started the first Independence Day folk dance parade in Haifa, which subsequently became a very popular annual event. Hermon is still an active member of the Histadrut folk dance committee. Karmon created popular folk dances too, but he mainly concentrated on the performing and staging of folk dances with his own groups. At many international folk dance festivals his groups represented Israel. Later, with his "Music Hall of Israel," he traveled all over the world.

Over the years, additional festivals were held at Kibbutz Dalia. The biggest and last festival was held in

San Antonio College Dancers

1968. Sponsored by the Histadrut and the Ministry of Education, three thousand dancers performed for some sixty thousand spectators. Today, Kibbutz Dalia is considered the cradle of Israeli folk dance.

The younger folk dance teachers and creators developed Israeli dance activities in many cities rather than in kibbutzim. In Tel Aviv, Yoav Ashriel and his wife, Mira, teach practically every night of the week. In Haifa, Yonathan Gabai and Yaacov Levi teach and lead performing groups. In Jerusalem, the most active dance leader is Ayalah Goren. Folk dancing also takes place in some kibbutzim, in the army, and in public schools and universities. In fact, Israeli folk dance is established all over the country.

New Israeli dances are constantly being created and introduced to the public. These new dances are hits for a year or two and are later discarded to make room for yet newer creations. A completely new element was recently introduced—disco dances. The choreographers use popular hit songs and fit them to jazz movements and folk dance motifs. The accepted folk dance formations of circles, lines, couples, and squares are changed, so that the participants all face the same direction, performing the steps separately but in unison. The disco flavor is very popular because of its pseudo-American dance accent. Today, an evening of folk dancing in Israel usually includes a lot of disco dancing, with a few international dances thrown in for good measure. Some teachers create so-called folk dances just to satisfy the demands of their students to continually teach something new. This reflects the low quality of dances presented today.

To preserve the authentic dance material still found among the different ethnic groups, a new organization was formed by Gurit Kadman in 1974. The Israel

Ethnic Dance Project has begun collecting exciting anthropological field experiences in their research on the dances of the Jewish Yemenites, Kurds, and Druz in Israel. This organization is sponsored by the Histadrut and the Ministry of Education in connection with the Folklore Department of the Hebrew University in Jerusalem.

AMERICA

When I arrived in the United States in 1941, I found much Jewish dance activity amidst modern dance. Modern dancers would interpret Jewish themes and present these dances at concerts at Jewish community centers, at Y's, and at fund-raising affairs mostly for Jewish audiences. After the establishment of Israel in 1948, interest in these dance performances disappeared. These dancers were replaced by dance groups from Israel.

There was Jewish folk dancing going on as well. Most of the dances, done to Hasidic melodies, were choreographed in America. European dances, so popular in Palestine, were also being danced by Zionist youth movements in America at the same time. In these organizations, folk dance games were created to the tunes of Hebrew songs and were very enthusiastically performed at every occasion.

Folk dance records did not exist and a good accordionist was rarely available, so the musical accompaniment consisted of singing while dancing. The American-Jewish dances, as they were called, incorporated the zest and swing of American square dancing. Among the dances that had their origins in America were the Double Hora, Dundai, and Ari Ara.

In 1946, for the first time, I saw a dance that came from Palestine, the very popular Mayim Mayim. It was introduced by a cultural emissary (Shaliach) on a Hashomer Hatzair Zionist Youth Organization farm. It was exciting to see a dance that had its origin in the new country! Over the years, more and more dances were introduced in America—all new creations coming from Israel. These dances replaced the American-Jewish dances, which are almost totally forgotten today.

San Antonio College Dancers

In 1951 I started a weekly Israeli folk dance session at the 92nd Street YM-YWHA in New York City. It was the first time such sessions were attempted in an organized way. Of course, in the beginning they were poorly attended, but eventually more and more people came and sometimes there was not even enough room for all the dancers. In the same year I was also asked by the American Zionist Youth Foundation to organize an Israel folk dance festival in New York City, which has become an annual event. We just celebrated the twenty-sixth festival with performances at Lincoln Center.

Dvora Lapson, another folk dance pioneer in America, brought Israeli folk dances to Hebrew schools. Today she still organizes an annual children's Israeli folk dance festival, supervises teachers, and publishes dance articles. Her activities are sponsored by the Jewish Education Committee of America in New York City. Visiting Israeli dance leaders have come to many U.S. cities to teach the newest dances throughout the years, spreading enthusiasm as well as knowledge.

In 1968 the Zionist Youth Foundation established a department of Israeli folk dance under my direction. Its purpose is very similar to the Histadrut folk dance department in Israel. Leadership training sessions are offered and a summer program for Israeli folk dance enthusiasts in Israel is an annual project. *Hora,* a publication appearing three times a year, reports on Israeli folk dance activities. Through this department a book and record service is also available.

Over the years, Israeli folk dances were included in the international folk dance repertory. A large audience of non-Jews was thereby reached. In this way, Israeli folk dance became tremendously popular. Today its popularity is exceeded only by Yugoslavian and Greek folk dances.

In most big cities one can participate in Israeli folk dance activities practically every evening. Hillel organizations on college campuses offer Israeli folk dancing and many even have performing groups. In most Jewish and Zionist summer camps Israeli folk dancing constitutes a very important part of the programming. A concluding dance festival, Rikudia, often ends the season with every youngster participating. At many colleges there are credit courses on Israeli folk dancing. Israeli folk dance festivals are annual events in many American cities.

On the West Coast, in San Francisco and Los Angeles, there are very charming international folk dance cafes. These are places where friends may meet, eat, and dance. Each evening usually features a different national dance, with Israeli dancing at least once a week.

Because there is such an interest all over the country, almost every Israeli folk dance has been recorded on LP records, the latter usually accompanied by an instruction booklet. By now, hundreds of dances have been recorded and new ones are constantly being added.

While traveling all over the United States to teach, I am always amazed by the fantastic interest in Israeli folk dance. Workshops are now very common and serve several purposes: to acquaint the community with an Israeli folk dance specialist; to teach new dances; and to inject excitement and new interest into a community of folk dancers.

Finally, I would like to mention an American Israeli folk dance phenomenon—the emergence of the professional Israeli folk dance choreographer. A few Israelis living in America fit this description. These choreographers create Israeli folk dances in America, teach them at their workshops, and sell records of the music. Every year, newly created dances, along with their records, swamp the market. Unfortunately, the whole process has become a business venture and an unhealthy, competitive spirit has developed, defeating the philosophy of folk dance.

As one who has visited Israel many times and, since 1968, spends part of every year in Israel, I am able to observe the Israeli folk dance situation very closely in both countries. Wherever and whenever I asked American-Jewish students why they joined Israeli folk dance activities, the unanimous answer was: to establish ties with Israel, to create a link with their Jewish heritage and tradition. Therefore, one may come to the conclusion that the popularity of Israeli folk dancing is based on the fact that American-Jewish youth identify with Israel through folk dance.

In the repertory of Israeli folk dances, the name of the choreographer and composer of every dance is known. Therefore, some international folk dance circles do not consider Israeli folk dances as real examples of folk dance. These groups rightly claim that folk dances have to evolve over the years, without knowing who created the dance or who composed the music. But Israeli folk dance is well established in Israel, America, and wherever people perform folk dances.

(Fred Berk was well known throughout the country as one of America's outstanding authorities on Jewish and Israeli folk dance. He was the founder and director of the 92nd Street YM-YWHA Jewish Dance Division. He was cofounder of the Merry-Go-Rounders dance company. For five years he headed Stage for Dancers, producing modern dance concerts at the Brooklyn Museum in New York City. Since 1951 he directed the annual Israeli Folk Dance Festival at Lincoln Center, conducted leadership training sessions, and directed the Israeli Folk Dance Department under the auspices of the American Youth Foundation. Many Israeli folk

Fred Berk

dance records were issued under his supervision. He also published three books: (ed.) *Ha-Rikud: The Jewish Dance, Chasidic Dance Book,* and *Mechol Ha'am: Dance of the Jewish People.* Since 1968 he conducted summer folk dance seminars in Israel with American students. Fred Berk died on February 26, 1980.)

ISRAELI FOLK DANCES

DODI LI
Dance: Rivka Sturman
Music: Chen
Record: Tikva LP 138
Formation: Cpls face each other, boy with back to ctr, girl faces ctr, boy's R hand joins girl's L, ptrs start with opp ft. Boy's steps are described.

Meter 4/4   Pattern

Chorus

Meas
1–3	Yem L.
4	Pivot on L, ¼ turn to L side, face CCW.
5	R fwd.
6	Hold.
7–10	Tcherkessia L. On first step bend both arms fwd and bend left knee. On third step arms down. On fourth step pivot on R. Face each other again.
11	L in place.
12	Hold.
13–16	Yem R.
17–32	Repeat 1–16.

Part One
1–5	Repeat 1–5 Chorus.
6	Pivot R, ½ turn to R side. Release hands. Both face CW.
7–10	Join inside hands. 4 steps bwd, L R L R. On last step pivot on R. End up facing each other again.
11–16	Join orig hands and repeat 11–16 Chorus.
17–32	Repeat 1–16.
	Repeat Chorus.

Part Two
1–6	Repeat 1–6 of Part One but do not change hands.
7–8	2 steps bwd, L R. On second step pivot on R, ½ turn to L side. Face CCW.
9–10	2 steps fwd L R. On last step pivot on R, ¼ turn to R side. Ptrs face each other again.
11–16	Repeat 11–16 Chorus.
17–32	Repeat 1–16.
	Repeat Chorus.

Part Three
1–5	Repeat 1–5 Chorus.
6	Pivot on R, end up facing each other.
7–10	Mayim step L (move CW).
11	L crosses in front of R.
12	Hold.
13–16	Yem R.
17–32	Repeat 1–16.
	Repeat Chorus.

EREV BA
Dance: Yoav Ashriel
Music: Lavanon
Record: Tikva 98
Formation: Cir, face ctr, join hands

Pattern

Part One
1	R to R side.
2	L crosses in front of R.
3	R bwd.
4	L to L side.
5–7	Face CW. 3 steps fwd, R L R.
8	Pause.
9	L bwd.
10	Face ctr. R swd.
11–14	Mayim step L.
15	L crosses in front of R.
16	Pause.
17–32	Repeat 1–16.

Part Two

1–2	Release hands. Travel to R side with 2 steps, R L, while completing a R turn once around.
3	R to R side.
4	L crosses in front of R.
5	R bwd.
6–8	Reverse 3–5, start L to L side.
9–16	Repeat 1–8.

Part Three

1	Face CW. R to R side, arms open.
2	L crosses in front of R, cross arms, and snap fingers.
3–6	Repeat 1–2 two more times.
7	R to R side.
8	L to L side.
9	R crosses in front of L, cross arms, and snap fingers.
10	L to L side, open arms.
11–14	Repeat 9–10 two more times. On last step face ctr.
15–16	Repeat 1–2 of Part Two.

HARMONICA
Dance: Rivka Sturman
Music: Alconi
Record: Tikva 138
Formation: Cir, join hands, face ctr of cir

Pattern

Part One

1–4	Mayim step L.
5–6	Face CCW. Step-hop L fwd.
7–8	Step-hop R fwd.
9–32	Repeat 1–8 three more times.

Part Two

1–4	Face ctr. Harmonica step L. Clap on first ct, arms up high. On next 3 cts arms down.
5–8	Harmonica step R.
9–12	Repeat 1–4.
13–14	Face CW. Step-hop R fwd, arms crossed behind back.
15–16	Step-hop L fwd.
17–32	Reverse 1–16.

Part Three

1–2	Face center, arms on each other's shoulders. Step-hop L to L side.
3–4	Step-hop R to R side.
5–8	Face CW. 4 running steps fwd L R L R.
9–32	Repeat 1–8 three more times.

HAROA HAKTANA
Dance: Jonathan Karmon
Music: Willensky
Record: Tikva 69
Formation: Cir, face ctr, arms down close to body

Pattern

Part One

1–2	Step-hop on R to R side and ½ turn to R.
3–4	Step-hop on L to L side and ½ turn to L.
5–6	Step-hop on R to R side and ½ turn to L.
7–8	Step-hop on L to L side and ½ turn to R.
9–10	Step-hop on R to R side and ½ turn to R.
11–12	Step-hop on L to L side and ½ turn to R (face center).
13–14	Balance R, raise hands, and snap fingers.
15–16	Balance L and snap fingers.
17–32	Repeat 1–16.

Part Two

1–2	Step-hop on R in place and ¼ turn to R (face CCW).
3–4	Step-hop on L to L side.
5–6	Step-hop on R to R side and ½ turn to L (face CW).
7–8	Step-hop on L to L side and ¼ turn to R (face ctr).
9–12	Repeat cts 13–16 of Part One.
13–24	Repeat 1–12.
25–26	Step-hop on R in place. Kick L fwd, arms fwd, palms up.
27–28	2 running steps in place L R, arms down.
29–32	Reverse 25–28.

HINE MA TOV
Dance: Rivka Sturman
Music: Jacobson
Record: Tikva 138
Formation: Line, join hands, face CCW

Pattern

Chorus

1–2	Step-bend R fwd.
3–8	3 more step-bend fwd, L R L.
9–16	8 running steps fwd, start R.
17–32	Repeat 1–16.

Part One

1	Face center. R to R side.
2	Hold.
3	L bwd, arms bwd.
4	Close R to L.
5	L fwd, arms up high.
6	Hold.
7	Close R to L.

8   Hold.
9–12   Yem R.
13–16 Yem L.
17–32 Repeat 1–16.
      Repeat Chorus.

Part Two
1–8   Face center. 8 running steps fwd, start R, lift arms up high gradually.
9–12   Yem R.
13–16 Yem L.
17–24 8 running steps bwd, start R, arms down gradually.
25–32 Repeat 9–16.

HORA

Music: Folk
Record: Tikva 106 or any recorded Hora fits the dance.
Formation: Cir, all join hands or hold on to each other's shldrs. Face ctr.

Pattern

1   R to R side.
2   L crosses behind R.
3–4   Step-hop on R to R side.
5–6   Step-hop on L to L side.

MA NAVU

Dance: Raya Spivak
Music: Spivak
Record: Tikva 100
Formation: Cir, face ctr, join hands

Pattern

Part One
1–2   Point R fwd.
3–4   Point R swd.
5–8   Yem R bwd.
9   L bwd.
10   Hold.
11   R fwd.
12   Hold.
13   L bwd.
14   R fwd.
15   Close L to R.
16   Hold.
17–32 Reverse 1–16, start L fwd.

Part Two
1–3   Yem R.
4   ¼ turn on R to R side.
5–7   3 steps fwd L R L.
8   ¼ turn on L to L side, face ctr.
9–32   Repeat 1–8 three more times.

MAYIM MAYIM

Dance: Folk
Music: Amiran
Record: Tikva 106
Formation: Cir, all face ctr, all join hands, move CW

Pattern

1–16   4 Mayim steps, start R.
17–20 4 steps fwd, start R. Raise arms.
21–24 4 steps bwd, start R. Lower arms.
25–32 Repeat 17–24.
33–36 Face CW, run 4 steps fwd, start R.
37–44 Face ctr. Hop 8 times on R. On uneven cts point L fwd toward ctr. On even cts point L to L side.
45–52 Release hands and reverse 37–44. Raise arms and clap on uneven cts 4 times.

TZADIK KATAMAR

Dance: Jonathan Gabai
Music: Neeman
Record: Tikva 147
Formation: Cir, face CCW, all join hands, arms shldr level

Pattern

Part One
1–4   4 steps fwd, R L R L.
5–8   Face ctr. 4 steps in place from side to side, R L R L.
9–16 Repeat 1–8.

Part Two
1–2   Face CCW. R L fwd. ½ turn to L side on L, face CW.
3–4   R L bwd. ¼ turn to R side on L, face ctr.
5–6   Release hands. 2 steps, R L, at the same time one complete turn to R side. Face ctr.
7   R to R side.
8   L crosses in front of R.
9   R bwd.
10–12 Reverse 7–9.
13–16 Face ctr. Join hands at shldr level. 4 steps in place, from side to side, R L R L.
17–32 Repeat 1–16.

VE'DAVID YEFE EYNAIM

Dance: Rivka Sturman
Music: Shelem
Record: Tikva 138
Formation: Cpls in cir facing CCW, boys inside, girls outside; join inside hands.

Pattern

Part One

1–4 4 steps fwd, start R.

5–8 4 steps, start R. Boys walk bwd, girl in place. All end up in one big cir and join hands.

9–12 4 steps fwd, start R, raise arms.

13–16 4 steps bwd, start R, arms down. Release hands.

17–24 Girls 4 steps fwd and 4 steps bwd, start R, while boy stands in place and claps each ct.

25–28 Boys 4 steps fwd, start R. On last step make ½ turn to R side. Girls clap 4 times in place.

29–32 Boys 4 steps fwd, start R. Do not return to own ptr. Move to L side, change ptrs. Girls stand still.

33–40 R arm around each other's waist, L arms up. Pivot on inside foot (8 steps).

ZEMER ATIK

Dance: Rivka Sturman

Music: Neeman

Record: Tikva 100

Formation: Cpls in cir, face CCW. Girl in front of boy. L arm bent and touching own shoulder. R arm extended fwd. All join hands. Both same ft.

Pattern

Part One

1–4 Four steps fwd, R L R L.

5–6 Step-bend R fwd, lift arms and clap on ct 6.

7–8 Reverse 5–6, start L fwd.

9–32 Repeat 1–8 three more times.

Part Two

1–2 Face ctr. Step-bend R fwd, snap fingers on ct 2 (arms shldr level).

3–4 Step-bend L fwd, snap fingers on ct 2.

5–8 4 steps bwd, R L R L, arms gradually down.

9–32 Repeat 1–8 three more times. On last 4 cts ptrs end up side by side. Boy inside of cir, girl outside facing CCW. Join inside hands.

Part Three

1–4 Four steps fwd, R L R L.

5–6 R fwd and face each other.

7–8 Close L to R and bow.

9–32 Repeat 1–8 three more times.

Part Four

1–2 Face CCW. Step-bend R fwd.

3–4 Step-bend L fwd.

5–8 Lift inside hands (still joined), walk 4 steps in place, R L R L. Girl at same time takes ½ turn to L side, she faces CW. R shldrs next to each other. Boy brings his R arm down, girl's L behind her head. Her R arm extends behind ptr's back.

9–12 Move CW. 2 step-bend fwd, R L.

13–16 4 steps, R L R L, at same time returning to CCW pos. Ptrs end up side by side.

17–32 Repeat 1–16. On last 4 cts girl ends up in front of ptr, as in the beg.

ITALY

Italian Folk Dancing

by Elba Farabegoli Gurzau

Italy is today a modern country where for years interest has been directed toward the fine arts, an area in which the country has excelled. The folk arts, and folk dancing in particular, are little known or appreciated by the people. However, if enough time and funds were available to go and do research in the remote parts of the country, perhaps there would still be material that could be collected. This ought to be done very soon, for dances in particular are disappearing uncomfortably fast.

In northern Italy some of the names one would look for are *la furlana, la monfrina, il trescone*—all generic terms which have different versions—plus some fun dances, such as the dance of the chair, the mirror, the candlestick, and the washerwoman. These would add much to the spirit of joy in our folk dance evenings if we knew them.

In central Italy the name that comprises many dances is the saltarello, meaning "to jump." In southern Italy most of the dances fall under the heading tarantella. The short essay which follows provides details of background and variations.

The quadrille (quadriglia) or cotillion (codiglione) seems to have been danced in many parts of Italy; some believe it originated in Tuscany. It can be done in a square of eight, sixteen, or in a circle.

A few other names to look for are: La Galletta from Emilia, a dance for one man and two girls; La Gogliarda from Lazio; La Danza dei Ladroni from Calabria; and Pizzica Pizzica from Puglie, a gay dance from the heel of Italy.

The sword and stick dances have attracted some attention since the publication of the book *La Danza della Spada* in 1942 by Bianca Maria Galante. This comes as a surprise for those of us who hitherto have associated sword dances mainly with England.

Much research must be done by dedicated people, but perhaps we in the United States can help awaken an interest in the folk arts among Italians in Italy.

A conference and festival is being planned by the Nationalities Service Center of Philadelphia on Italian folk arts. One can speculate on what long-range developments may ensue.

Long before Betty Casey honored me with the request to write the Italian section of this book, I was conducting research to find out which dances were being done by folk dancers and Italian-American groups in the United States, with the purpose of preparing the second edition of my book, *Folk Dances, Costumes and Customs of Italy.* I found that because of the current emphasis on ethnicity and the widespread interest in folk dancing of many lands in the United States in the last few decades, many people of Italian background and others have been searching for Italian folk dances.

In response to two notices in the folklore magazine *Viltis,* letters have come to me from all over the country from people and groups wanting Italian dances both to dance for personal enjoyment and to perform before an audience. They all told the frustrating story of trying to find someone who knows Italian dances, and of the greater disappointment when they met new arrivals from Italy and discovered that they knew nothing about such dances and that they, the Italians, were surprised at our interest.

It was exactly for this reason that I went to Italy a few years ago with the sole purpose of finding dances and subsequently published the above-mentioned book. But my book contains only eight dances and there is much more that should be done.

Now, looking at the overall picture, I find that the only name of a dance that everyone identifies as Italian in this country is the tarantella, known only in southern Italy. But that is not surprising since the majority of the Italians who came to the United States were from southern Italy (the northern Italians tended to go to South America) and also because the tarantella is a gay, colorful dance, rich in flirtation and emotions certainly worth preserving.

There are a number of tarantella arrangements done in different parts of the United States. Some folk dance leaders and researchers, in need of Italian dances, have found Italians who remembered a few figures. Special arrangements were made, sometimes built around a good record available at that time. I am grateful to Rod LaFarge—one of whose dances I present here—for having provided the source of his information.

In some countries of Europe committees have been appointed to study their dances, standardize them, and keep them alive. We hope that will happen in Italy too, especially now that they have an active Federazione Italiana delle Tradizioni Popolari.

In the United States progress has also been made. Under the auspices of a United Way agency, Nationalities Service Center, and the efforts of Elba F. Gurzau, a weekend conference and festival was held in September 1978. The purpose was to bring together the various Italian folk groups in the Mid-Atlantic states and others to exchange information and make plans for study and the preservation of Italian folk music, dance and folk arts.

A nationwide organization resulted, The Italian Folk Art Federation of America (IFAFA), which was incorporated in 1979 as a cultural, nonprofit organization. The organization's newsletter, *Tradizioni,* begun in 1980, is distributed widely in the United States, Canada, and Australia. The mailing address is: IFAFA (NSC), 1300 Spruce Street, Philadelphia, Penn. 19107.

Italian Folk Dance Group, Nationalities Service Center of Philadelphia

(On June 2, 1975, Elba Farabegoli Gurzau, who contributed all of the material for the Italian section of this book, was awarded the title of Cavaliere by the Italian Government because of her long service to new arrivals to the United States and because of the publication of her book *Folk Dances, Costumes and Customs of Italy* as part of her effort to keep alive the folk arts of Italy.

Elba was born in New York City. At the age of twelve she was taken to Italy, where she studied in Florence and Bologna, graduating from L'Istituto Magistrale, which accounts for her being bilingual.

Returning to the United States, she attented New York University and graduated with a bachelor of science degree in education. Later, in Philadelphia, she became activities director of the International Institute, now the Nationalities Service Center, a United Way agency.

In 1975 Temple University awarded her a master's degree in TESOL (Teaching English to Speakers of Other Languages), a study which she pursued in connection with her work at NSC as co-ordinator of their English program.

Dancing has been Mrs. Gurzau's lifelong avocation. She has taught classes in folk dances of many lands and started several groups. Especially dear to her are the dances of Italy, the country from which her ancestors came.

In 1977 Mrs. Gurzau was assigned by NSC to a special project to stimulate and keep alive the folk arts and culture of Italy among Italian-Americans and others in the Philadelphia area and vicinity and integrate them into the ever-evolving fabric of American culture.

The following dances appear in her book *Folk Dances, Costumes and Customs of Italy*, unless otherwise noted, and are presented here with permission.)

ITALIAN FOLK DANCES

BALLO SARDO (or BALLO TONDO)
Ballo Sardo (Bahl-lo Sahr-do), or Ballo Tondo (Bahl-lo ton-do), is a dance from Sardinia. Although there are few Sardinians living in the United States, Mrs. Gurzau was able to locate Mrs. Julia Nuscis and her family, from Pittsburgh, from whom she learned this dance.

Sardinia is the only region of Italy that still has a line dance similar to the ones of the Balkan countries and the Near East. It is called Ballo Sardo, Sardinian dance, or Ballo Tondo, round dance. We know it was danced in pre-Christian times because Homer, the Greek poet, mentions it and has Ulysses marvel at the agility of the dancers of the island.

It is often danced by couples standing side by side in open circle formation, but also in an open circle or spiral with no partners. In old[en] times a man and a woman who were not married were not allowed to hold or touch hands. In some parts of the island it is danced rather sedately, often to the singing of three or more people standing in the middle of a circle. In other parts of Sardinia it is very lively and [is] danced to the music of the launeddas, the goatskin bagpipe or, more recently, the accordion; and in the absence of all of these to the ringing of church bells.

The launeddas is a primitive instrument, made of

canes of varying lengths, separate one from the other, which the player interchanges, depending on the sound desired . . . I am told that because some of the pipes are quite long, when there is much excitement the musicians stand in a corner facing away from the dancers in order to avoid the possibility of accidents.

There is no bouncing or springing in the Ballo Sardo; it is always done close to the ground, almost giving the effect of skating; however, when the music becomes lively, the men will kick higher and add a little fancy footwork. The women continue to dance smoothly in a very dignified manner, as becomes their regal-looking costumes. A few notes of the music of his favorite dance is all a Sardinian needs to get up and dance.

The figures follow each other according to the music and to the whim of the leading couple. However, from observing the Sardinian people dance, a pattern similar to the one described below seemed to emerge.

Record: Folkraft No. 1407 B
Formation: Open circle composed of couples or individuals facing center. A couple may be composed of 2 women or 2 men. *Leading couple is at left.*
Position: Partners stand side by side, very erect and serious, shoulder touching shoulder, arms straight down holding nearest hand. Occasionally all hold

San Antonio College Dancers. Photo by James F. Bartlett

hands in the open circle, but more often just partners hold hands.

Pattern

Introductory Figure

Dancers move rhythmically in place to the music for 12 counts (4 to a meas). The movement comes from a springing motion in the legs. At the 9th count, the leading couple raises the arm and hand, holding partner straight forward; all others do the same; then on the 11th count all arms are lowered rapidly to indicate the beginning of the dance.

Figure 1

Music A *Throughout the dance the group inches gradually to the left, clockwise.*

Step on R foot (count 1), point with L foot in front of R (count 2), step on L foot (count 3), point with R in front of L (count 4). Repeat 5 more times (meas 2 to 6, counting 24).

Figure 2

Music B Step on R foot (count 1), point with L in front of R (2), then, moving to the left with L foot, step-together-step (count 3 & 4), feet hardly leaving the ground. Repeat 5 more times (meas 7 to 18, counting 24). Music accelerates.

Figure 3

Music C *All moving toward the center of the circle* & Repeat *and back.* Walk forward on R foot (count 1), L (2), R (3), point with L in front of R (4); step to the left on L foot (5), swing R foot across the L (6); back, away from center with R foot (7), L (8), R (9), point with L foot in front of R (10) step on L (11), swing R foot to the left (12), (meas 13 to 18 & Repeat). *Repeat this figure 3 more times.*

Note: Each time this figure is started again, the R foot, which has just swung toward the left, makes a little circular motion in the air while the shoulders and upper part of the body help by moving forward momentarily.

Figure 4

Same as figure 2 except usually faster.

Music D When the music accelerates, the men enliven their dancing by lifting their leg higher and tilting foot instead of just pointing or swinging leg. Girls continue to dance close to the ground, smoothly.

Repeat as many times as desired.

To join the circle or change position, couples often take several small slides in one direction or another in time with the music.

IL CODIGLIONE

A quadrille is generally a dance with 4 couples and sometimes 12 or 16 couples. It often has a series of figures which the dancers memorize and there is no need for a caller. The cotillion, on the other hand, needs a caller, or *caposala*. He is free to arrange the figures in whatever order he wishes and to adapt them to the ability and liking of the group.

It seems that quadrilles and codigliones have been danced all over Italy for many centuries—some say as far back as the time of the Romans—by both the peasants and the upper classes. It is recorded that at the time of the golden era of the Medici family in Florence, during the 15th and 16th centuries, there was much reason for rejoicing and that there was much dancing among all classes of people. When Catherine de Medici married King Henry II of France, she and her entourage brought the quadrille to France, where it was introduced at court. It met with great favor and it promptly was given French calls. It later came back to Italy with a new foreign flavor. (Studies were made by Anton Giulio Bragaglia and presented at the International Folk Music Conference in Venice in 1949.)

The codiglione, with any number of couples in a large circle, lends itself well to our folk dance parties because, having a caller, it can be adapted readily to the ability of the group. It can be made very simple for new dancers and elaborate for more experienced dancers. The speed also can be adjusted, young people will use a light running step, or even a skip, while older people prefer a walking step. There is no particular order that one must follow.

ITALIAN QUADRILLE

The following dance can be done to the same music as the codiglione, but it is a quadrille (a square) done with four couples. It is from Vyts Beliajus' book *Dance and Be Merry*, volume II, from which most of the Italian quadrilles done by folk dance groups around the country seem to have come. The dance has many more figures than those given here, but the more interesting ones have been selected.

The phrases of the music are all eight measures in length; no particular phrase goes with any particular figure. A lively walking step, in time with [the] music, is used throughout the dance.

Record: Harmonica H 2051, or any Italian quadrille record.

Position: A square of four couples with the girl to boy's right. Free hands at side. The couple with backs to music is couple No. 1; pair to the right is couple No. 2; couple opposite No. 1 is couple No. 3, and to the left is couple No. 4.

Pattern
Meas

Figure I: Circle

1–8   Join hands in a circle. Walk sixteen steps to L.

1–8   (rptd). Sixteen steps to R.

Figure II: Salutation

1–2   In couples with inside hands joined. Couples 1 and 3 with three steps walk to the center of square and bow to each other.

3–4   Walk back to place.

5–6   Same couples walk three steps forward again, release joined hands, and join inside hands with opposite partner (boy 1 with girl 3, boy 3 with girl 1).

7–8   Boys return to own place with new partner as follows: As he returns home he makes a complete turn L about, leading new partners round in front of him toward his L.

1–8   (rptd). Couples 2 and 4, same as in meas 1–8 of this figure.

1–16   (and rpt). Repeat meas 1–8 (and repeat), bringing back original partners.

Figure III: Cross

1–4   All boys join L hands in the center to form a cross. Girls are still to their partners' R and inside hands joined. All walk forward six steps. Boys release own partners' hands and with two longer steps join inside hands with the girl ahead (girls keep on walking—eight steps in all).

5–8   Repeat same three times more finishing beside own partner.

Figure IV: Lines

1–8   Couple 1 leads into two straight lines, end about six feet apart; boys in one line, girls in the other facing partners. Pause until the end of the phrase of music.

Figure V: Salutation in Lines

1–2   Boys walk toward partners three steps, bow.

3–4   Boys walk back to place.

5–8   Girls repeat meas 1–4.

1–8   (rptd) Same as above, boys saluting first, then girls.

Figure VI: The Reel

Couple No. 1 join R hands, walk one and a half times around each other until boy faces girl's line and girl boy's line. Boy joins L hands with girl next in line while his partner joins L hands with boy next in line. Turn once completely around each other and face own partner, join R hands with partner, turn once around each other and join L hands with the next in line. Continue doing this until reaching foot of set, where boy remains last in boys' line and girl last in girls' line (just like in a Virginia Reel). As soon as couple No. 1 reaches 3rd couple, the new head couple begins reeling as described for couple 1. Likewise each couple starts until each couple has had a turn to reel and all are in original places again.

Figure VII: Grand Right and Left

Both lines turn to face opposite directions so that their R shoulders are toward their partners. Girls' line walks in place. Boy No. 1 leads boys' line forward and around to the L of boys' line, reaching foot of set to face last girl. Boy No. 1 and last girl join R hands, pass R shoulder to join L hands with next person in line (boy with next girl, girl with next boy). Pass L shoulders and join R hands with next person in line. Continue doing this (Grand Right and Left) until own partners are met for the second time. The girls' line begins moving forward when head boy meets foot girl with R hand. At the end of the Grand Right and Left couples are again in a circle.

Figure VIII: Promenade

All face forward, with boys on the inside of the circle and the girls to their R. Girl raises her hands, shoulder high. Boy standing somewhat behind and to the L of the girl, joins his L hand with her L hand and his R hand with her R. His R arm is over her shoulders, her L arm across his chest.

1–2   All walk forward four steps.

3–4   With four walking steps each boy passes his partner around behind him as follows: With hands still joined as in meas 1–2, boy raises R arm to form an arch and passes his R arm forward and across in front of him, at the same time turning the girl to the L and under the arch. Without pausing he continues leading girl around to his L and behind him by passing under the arch formed by his R arm himself. All hands remain joined until girl is behind, then release hands and join hands with the new girl in front.

5–8 Repeat meas 1–4 with new girl.

1–8 (rptd) Repeat meas 1–4 with each of the two remaining girls, finishing with own partner in original position.

Figure IX: The Knot

All join hands and circle to R for eight steps. Then, only boy No. 1 and girl No. 4 release hands, all others keep hands joined. Boy No. 1 stands still. Girl No. 4 leads the line around the boy until all are wound around him. Then boy No. 1 leads line out underneath the joined hands of the dancers around him toward and under the arch formed by the joined hands of couple No. 4. He may lead back into a circle and finish with a bow or lead the dancers off the stage.

TARANTELLA

The tarantella (Tah-rahn-tel'la) comes from southern Italy. Anyone who has ever heard anything of Italian dances has heard of the tarantella. The name is known because of many descriptions which have appeared in books, and because its music has been used by so many composers. Still, our information on how to dance the tarantella is very limited, particularly since it does not have a set pattern, but is composed of a number of figures in any order dictated by the mood of the dancers. Many people have stylized tarantellas, putting several of the basic steps together; all are created dances and not traditional. One can see the real tarantella in this country only if a group of old Italian people get together and dance it. They will take little steps, clap, turn, and become quite exhilarated by the gay and fast music; it is simple but real and one gets the feeling of wanting to join them.

In pursuing the study of the tarantella, one is discouraged at the lack of information on the actual steps of the dance, but one is fascinated by its long history. Movements of the tarantella are depicted on old Greek vases, drawings of the dance are on the walls of the ruins of Pompeii, and reference to it was made by dance masters of many different periods in history.

A popular legend has it that the tarantella comes from the jumping that doctors once ordered for those bitten by the tarantula spider. There was considerable discussion on this topic at the Venice Congress and Folk Festival in September 1949, but the consensus of opinion seemed to be that the dance had no relation to the bite of the spider and that the confusion might have come from the similarity of names.

There is another charming legend regarding the tarantella of Sorrento—the Sorrentina. It tells that the mermaids, half women and half fish, were humiliated and piqued because the famous Ulysses did not respond to their songs [having lashed himself to the mast of his ship and put wax in the ears of his sailors to remove temptation]. They asked the Graces to teach them something very effective that could help them conquer the King of Ithaca through his eyesight. The Graces, it is said, perhaps for the fun of it, created the Sorrentina, which of course the mermaids could not dance, not having legs. It was thus that the girls of Sorrento and Capri learned the gay and graceful dance.

It is not really known where the name tarantella came from, except that it might be from Taranto, a city in Le Puglie where dancing was always a favorite pastime even at the time the ancient Greeks settled there. The tarantella appears with its present name only in the last four or five centuries; earlier it was referred to as Lucia, Sfessania, Villanella, and by other names.

It seems that the tarantella underwent some changes and acquired the use of castanets when it was fused with the fandango, which appeared in Italy with the domination of southern Italy by the Spaniards in the fifteenth century.

There is an interesting reference to the tarantella in an almanac of the year 1891, which is reported by Anton Giulio Bragaglia in his article in the December 1949 issue of *Ricreazione*. It says: "Let us take ourselves to Italy, to this cradle of choreography and of all the arts. To the sound of castanets and of tambourines and to the music of mandolins the vivacious tarantella jumps and designs voluptuous movements in Taranto and in Calabria, and also in Le Puglie and in Naples. Its steps and its evolutions, the pauses of the two dancers dramatize flirtation, jealousy, disdain, pleasure, regret, all the expressions of that great poem of the heart which is called love!"

Although its origin is lost in the past and clothed in legend, the tarantella became a favorite pastime in every part of southern Italy, acquiring through the centuries special characteristics in different regions. Following are some of the differences as pointed out in several publications on [the] folk arts of Italy by the Opera Nazionale Dopolavoro of Rome.

The Tarantella in Puglia

The distinguishing characteristic in Puglia is the shyness of the woman, who dances mostly with her head bent and eyes to the ground; and even in the liveliest part of the dance she is always dignified and reserved. The instruments used are the accordion, castanets, and tambourine.

Ballet Basques de Biarritz, Oldara

The man invites the girl to dance by dancing around her while playing his castanets and singing to her. She is slow to accept but finally starts by keeping time with the music. She holds her hands on her hips or holds the ends of her apron; then she starts dancing, moving around very little and carefully avoiding the advances of the man.

He later unfolds his handkerchief and waves it while dancing. The most stirring moment comes when she takes the other end of the handkerchief, thus giving her approval to his suit, much to the delight of friends who surround them shouting words of encouragement and clapping their hands in time with the music.

In Puglia and in other localities, the tarantella is often danced by one couple while the others form a circle around them. When the woman is tired she will fall back in the circle and the man will invite another partner, or some other man may start dancing inside the circle, indicating to the other that his turn is over.

The Tarantella in Calabria

Here again the dance does not have a definite pattern; it is the actions and movements of the body that give it its character. The motions are both elastic and robust, typical of the people of that mountainous region. The man bends toward the girl with hands at shoulder level, snapping his fingers; his knees are slightly bent and his attitude has an air both of respect and boastfulness.

The woman faces him. She is always graceful and does not move around much, but imitates his steps as he takes long strides, making wide circles around her. She lifts her skirt a modest bit in front. She also may take the two ends of the kerchief which she wears on her head or around her neck and pull it from side to side in time with the music. Occasionally they will touch shoulders and turn with faces looking in opposite directions.

The Tarantella in Sicily

For the Sicilian people, who love gaiety and mimicry, every festivity, public or private, was and often still is a pretext to get a group of friends together, rapidly improvise an orchestra, and dance the tarantella. They dance at home or in the public squares, just a few couples or many, adapting the figures to the number of dancers.

The Sicilian tarantella is full of movement and abandon, expressing the joy of being alive. Yet its actions and movements are never immodest, for that would not be tolerated by the chaste habits of La Conca d'Oro, the golden basin, so-called because of the many orange groves which abound in the region.

At weddings the tarantella is part of the ceremony, for when the bride is taken to the groom's home, together with her many gifts and her trousseau, the guests immediately dance the tarantella in honor of the newlyweds.

The dance starts with each man holding his partner by the hand and moving forward; this is followed by many figures to which the popular sentiment attributes such meanings as: greetings to the lady, discord, flight, reconciliation, and the kiss of peacemaking. The Sicilians do not generally use castanets or tambourines while dancing, their sole accompaniment being the rhythmic beating of the hands.

The Tarantella in Campania (Naples and Sorrento)

The difference which is most remarkable about the tarantella as it is danced in Naples and Sorrento is the attitude of the woman. Here she is more free, more sure of herself; she dances with her head up, proud of her appearance, flashing her sparkling eyes and abandoning herself to the joy of the dance.

Old records show that in this area oftentimes girls danced the tarantella together, at times three girls, one playing the tambourine while the others danced, changing places as one got tired. Occasionally the girls used a long ribbon or sash which was held loosely by the ends to make graceful patterns.

Then again, as in other regions of southern Italy, the tarantella is danced by couples who do the steps as they please and as the mood moves them. But for the purpose of performances in Naples and in Sorrento, many tarantella figures have been arranged in stylized patterns, particularly for the benefit of tourists.

In Sorrento, where the tarantella is a bit different from the one in Naples, a certain Gioacchino Napoletano (who came from Nola, east of Naples, in the 19th century and domiciled himself in Sorrento) arranged and regulated the Sorrentina (tarantella of Sorrento). He then formed the first group of tarantella dancers; and recently his son Edoardo, a barber, still directed the group, which is composed of workers from the countryside. They use every available instrument—mandolin, guitar, tambourine, whistle, castanets—making a very lively ensemble which always reaps long and loud applause at performances.

Most tarantellas are written in lively 6/8 meter—*tempo vivace*. The beating of tambourines, clapping of hands, snapping of fingers or playing of large castanets is in time with the main beat of the music, once or twice to the measure.

The instruments used, as mentioned before, are the goatskin bagpipes, especially in the mountains, the ac-

cordion, which is extensively used even though it is of recent introduction. The tambourines are sometimes very large, particularly in Sicily, where they are used by the musicians, not by the dancers. In Naples, where the dancers use them, they are often decorated with multicolored ribbons about three quarters of a yard long to create a festive mood.

The dance is composed of a series of figures, each in turn composed of many different types of little jumping steps. Each measure of the music is for two steps. Since the dance has a continuous jumping motion, it is quite strenuous and often older people and the less energetic ones just accent the beat rather than perform the actual jump.

Following are some of the favorite steps and figures which can be varied and used in any order desired:

Steps

1. Hop twice on left foot, with right foot pointing forward and touching the ground (one beat), repeat on right foot, then on left and right again several times, generally until the end of the musical phrase.
2. Hop on left foot and with right pointing to the left (in front of left foot), then on second hop point to the right with right foot. This can be done for half the musical phrase, then repeat, hopping on right foot pointing with left.
3. Hop on left foot, lifting right foot in front of left knee and extend to right; repeat several times, then on other foot. This figure is done only by men.
4. The following step is also done only by men. Alternating feet, hop on one foot and kick forward with the other leg high enough to clap hands under bent knee. The man does this figure while moving around the girl. His agility is judged by the height he can lift his legs.
5. The men of Calabria favor this step. Move around in any direction by jumping on the ball of the left foot and keeping the right foot forward with the heel touching the ground, just enough to keep in equilibrium. The person's weight is always on the foot behind; position of feet may alternate. The hands are held at uneven heights while snapping fingers. Body bent slightly forward.

Figures

1. The man moves around the girl while she claps or beats the tambourine and vice-versa.
2. Partners touch shoulder to shoulder, leaning a little on each other with body turned in opposite directions; they turn with running steps, moving either backward or forward in a little circle of their own. Sometimes their faces are turned away from each other; sometimes they look at each other while turn-

ing. Their hands are on their hips or held high with fingers snapping.

3. Holding right arm around each other's waist, right hips touching, free arm bent up and hand about head level—turn forward with small running steps to the end of the musical phrase, then reverse the position of the arms and run in opposite direction.

4. La Morra is a game favored by men on the farms. It consists of two or more men extending the right hand forward and down with a certain number of fingers extended while another guesses the total number. This motion is used as a dance figure. The partners stand about four feet apart, lunging forward with the right knee bent; they flick their tambourines smartly, imitating the motion of La Morra. In the meantime they come closer and closer, leading with the right foot and pushing with the left.

5. The girl pirouettes by herself, holding skirt or apron while the boy dances around her, often with step number four, described above.

SICILIAN TARANTELLA

Dance description as modified by Elba F. Gurzau

Record: RCA 442-0208

Formation: Two couples, partners facing each other diag. Several sets can form a double line, M on one side, W on other. W hold tambourines in R hands.

Steps and Styling: Run, skip, buzz (wt on R ft, push with L). The dance is done with a light walking or skipping step, moving fast, with much noise from tambourines and lots of flirtation.

Pattern

Introduction

16 cts Each dancer facing person in front, men snap fingers at shldr level; women shake tambourines.

Step kick

16 cts Both men and women step on R ft and small kick with L ft; then step on L and kick with R (8 kicks).

Forward and Back—4 times

32 cts Each person walks fwd twd person in front, keeping a little to the L until R shldrs are near. Hit tambourine (men clap) (4 cts). Back (4 cts). Fwd and back again, keeping a bit to the R until L shldrs are near, clap. Repeat both R and L shldr.

Elbow turn with partner

32 cts M 1 and W 1 hook R elbows, turn CW back to place. M 2 and W 2 do same. Couple 1

Elba Farabegoli Gurzau. Photo by Pacita T. Cruz

repeat with L elbow, Couple 2 repeat with L elbow.

Shoulder turn

32 cts Couple 1 go fwd, put R shldrs adjacent and turn CW 4 cts and back to place. Couple 2 repeat. Couple 1 do same with L shldrs adjacent. Couple 2 repeat.

All 4 elbow turn

16 cts All 4 dancers dance fwd, put L elbows tog, hand on hip or held shldr level and walk 7 steps CCW, hit tambourine and reverse dir (tn CCW), walk 8 more steps CW with R elbows to center.

All 4 hold L hands together high

16 cts All four walk CCW holding L hands tog up high, 7 steps, hit tambourine, and turn on 8th ct. Reverse, walk 8 steps CW back to orig pos.

MUSIC STARTS OVER AT THIS POINT

Girls pivot

16 cts W pivot CW with a buzz step; M bend low, snap fingers and pretend to turn W by brushing edge of skirt.

REPEAT ENTIRE DANCE

On third repeat, girls twirl, step-kick and end with dancers facing each other. Put R arm around waists, turn 16 counts, reverse, L arm around waists, other arm held high, shake tambourine. End in open pos with W at R side of M, shout "ah" on last beat. (Optional: solo double turns on counts 14, 15, 16 before reversing.)

TARANTELLA MONTEVERGINE

This description of the Tarantella Montevergine (Mon-teh-VER-gee-neh) [1] is by Rod LaFarge. I collected the steps for this dance by attending an endless procession of fiestas held by various Montevergine societies in New York, New Jersey, Pennsylvania, and Connecticut. I would like to extend special thanks to members of these societies, who were so helpful in persuading old time fiesta dancers to demonstrate their favorite steps and figures, and who helped me through the difficulties of the dialect.

Music: The fiesta celebrants dance many steps and figures to almost any tarantella music, but the recording we recommend fits the following set routine: Very fast—"Cinderella Tarantella," RCA No. 25-0127; Special—"Montevergine Tarantella" (flip side, "Graziella Mazurka")

Position: Two couples facing, lady on the right of the man (own partner).

Steps: A light running step on the ball of the foot except where otherwise specified. [2]

Pattern

Figure 1: Join hands, shoulder level, and circle to the right with a shuffle step (16 counts). Repeat going left.

Chorus: Face own partner and perform 4 (leaping) pas de basque steps starting with a leap on the left foot swinging right over left [3] and snapping fingers with upraised arms swaying from side to side. (Castanets are often used instead of the finger snapping.) Now, without actually touching partners enclose each other with outstretched, encircling arms; in this position they turn together (clockwise) with four fast walking steps. [4] This "don't touch them" embrace is called "sorellina" (little sister). Turn singly (clockwise) out of each other's embrace, raising arms overhead. Repeat all with opposite partner. Total 32 counts.

Figure 2: Right-hand moulinet. 16 counts. Repeat left-handed.

Chorus

Figure 3: Link right elbow with own partner, turn once around together clockwise. Reach behind the other man's back and, linking left elbow with opposite partner, turn counterclockwise. Repeat all. Now turn own partner with right elbow once more, then all turn singly clockwise. Total 32 counts.

Chorus

Figure 4: Facing *opposite* partners, the men back the ladies until the men can pass back to back (as in dos à dos). The ladies then walk forward, the men backwards, the couples thus exchanging places. 8 counts. Face own partner and repeat manoeuvre. Repeat all. Total 32 counts. The polka step is used in this figure and the arms are raised overhead, swaying from side to side with much finger snapping.

Chorus

Figure 5: Join inside hands with partner. Couple 2 (the couple facing the music) raise joined hands to form an arch, both couples walk forward, exchanging places, couple one passing under the arch. Retaining handholds, turn around, man walks backwards, lady forward, facing other couple again. 8 counts. Repeat with couple 1 raising the arch. Repeat all. Total 32 counts.

Chorus

Figure 6: The two men, who are in a diagonal position, join right hands and exchange places, with three steps and pull on count 4, then without releasing hands exchange places three more times, 16 counts, ending with right hands joined. The ladies join right hand under the arch, exchange places twice without releasing hands. Still with right hands joined, the ladies reach over the men's right hands and join left hands with partner and the whole formation revolves clockwise with four chassé steps. Release hands and turn singly.

Chorus

Figures at a glance

Fig 1	All four circle R (16) and L (16)
	Chorus
Fig 2	Moulinet moving CW 16, then CCW 16
	Chorus
Fig 3	Elbow Swing R and L
	Chorus
Fig 4	Shuttle dos à dos starting with opposite partner
	Chorus
Fig 5	Couples arches
	Chorus
Fig 6	Exchange places and chassé
	Chorus

[1] Montevergine, which means Mount of the Virgin, is a tiny village with a breathtaking view which can be reached by the famous Amalfi Drive going Southeast from Naples. It has a sanctuary built in the year 1119.

[2] LaFarge describes a grapevine step, but I think a light running step more Italian.

[3] It is more of a leap; on one description it was called "Calcio di cavallo," which means horse's kick.

[4] A bouncing chassé step is often used, says Rod LaFarge.

Photo by Edward Mankus

LITHUANIA

Lithuanian Folk Dancing

by Vytautas Beliajus

The Lithuanians are people of the land in the fullest sense of the word, for not only are they farm folk but they have a love of the soil they work so tenderly. They love the arable land as well as the prairie, the forest as well as the pasture lea, the tree as well as the reed. Flower and weed, bird and insect, lakes, streams, bogs, and fens are beloved. And as the Lithuanian comtemplates them tenderly, he creates legends, songs, and folk dances about them. The Lithuanian finds a reason for the existence of each thing, and he gives a mythical reason why certain trees, animals, insects, flowers are the way they are: why the aspen trembles, why the swallow has a forked tail, why the mosquito bites humans, and so on. Everything animate and inanimate has a legend and a folk song. Certain objects receive greater notice from the folk singer than others: among birds, the cuckoo ranks first; among animals, the steed; and among flowers, the rue (ruta). The rue is also the prime object of the body of Lithuanian folklore. Even when singing of obnoxious weeds, the terms are used diminutively and tenderly, without scorn. They don't say *pikta dilgė* (that obnoxious nettle), but *pikta dilgelėle* (that obnoxious, dear, cute little nettle).

Lithuanian folk dance is based almost exclusively on agriculture and nature subjects. Most of them concern birds, flowers, animals, grain, and weeds. Dances involving other subjects can be counted on the fingers of one hand. Some dances are allegorical, some are based on legends or fables, while others are based on festive agricultural rituals.

The Lithuanians are a singing people. Of course, the Italians also bear this title, but while the Italians are an operatic people, a people of brilliant voices, the Lithuanian will sing regardless of his voice.

In olden days there were many dances: liturgic or festive in character; dances with candles held in the hands; dances in which the *laumės* (fairies) were invited; virile, rough dances performed by men, with hatchet-throwing contests to win the hand of the maiden. Some of these dances are mentioned only by name in various old documents; many survived in remote villages located deep in the forest and are still danced by the old timers, who are never too old to dance.

Prior to 1940, the Lithuanian Government, taking great interest in the survival and revival of this phase of national culture, sponsored research on the subject. Hundreds of thousands of songs and dances were thus recorded. With the aid of a government subsidy, they were introduced into schools, recreation centers, and physical education departments; the dances were seen in the ballrooms on all festive occasions.

Marija Baronas, of Kūno Kultūros Rūmai (physical education department) was a pioneer in the revival of these dances. Under her direction, Lithuanian folk dances achieved recognition and won awards whenever they were performed at European dance competitions.

For the past fifty years, Lithuania's neighbors have strongly influenced and overshadowed the Lithuanian folk dance. For a while, only the non-Lithuanian forms were known and were danced either under their foreign names or Lithuanianized titles. Such dances still appear; one, the Klumpakojis, considered a Lithuanian dance, is really an adaptation; it is also found among the Czechs, Germans, Dutch, and Swedes. Other adaptations are the various forms of Vengierka, which are of Hungarian origin, the Greiž, which is the Teutonic Kreuz (Cross) polka, the Kokietka, Krakowiak, and Padespan, which are of Polish and Russian origin.

(For a detailed study of Vyts Beliajus; including his background and the important role he has played in the history of folk dancing, see the essay devoted to him in Part II.)

LITHUANIAN FOLK DANCES

JAUNIMĖLIS
Jaunimėlis (yow-nee-MEY-lis), which means "the youth," is a mixer dance. It is a dance of leave taking and gratitude for a lovely party.
Record: Folkraft LP-34, side A, band 4
Formation: Single circle of couples facing center, woman on partner's right.
Position: All hands joined.

Meter 2/4   Pattern

Meas
1–8   Circle right with sixteen *walking steps.*
9–10   Pause, releasing hands (counts 1–2), *clap* own hands twice (counts 3–4).
11–12 Pause (counts 1–2), two *stamps* in place (counts 3–4).
13–20 Starting with partner as number 1, *grand right and left* to eighth person, who becomes new partner.
       Repeat entire dance, starting *with new partner.*

JONKELIS
Jonkelis (YOHN-kya-lis), which means "little Jack," is a quadrille from Žemaitija. It is often performed at weddings to suggest that the bride's future life will be full of weaving and spinning.
Record: Folkraft LP-35, side A, band 1
Formation: Quadrille: four couples form a square set, each woman on partner's right. Couple 1 has back to music and couples are numbered counterclockwise 1-2-3-4.
Note: All movements throughout this dance are with *walking steps,* two (right, left) per measure.

Turn (in this dance): Pivot clockwise in place with walking steps in Lithuanian position.
Lithuanian position: Partners facing opposite directions with right sides adjacent, man's right arm in front of woman and hand holding her left waist, man's left hand holding woman's left upper arm, woman's right hand on man's left shoulder and her left hand on man's right shoulder (or holding her skirt.)

Meter 2/4   Pattern

Meas   Intro
1–2   Pause (counts 1–4).
3–4   *Stamp* right foot three times without taking weight (counts 1–3), pause (count 4).

Figure I: Weave Across

1–4   Woman 1 and 2, leading with right shoulders, move forward, passing back to back in the center (measure 1–2), then turn slightly so as to lead with left shoulders and move forward to opposite place while men 1 and 2, leading with left shoulders, move forward, passing back to back with opposite woman (measure 3); women 1 and 3 make ½ turn to left to face oncoming partner, while men 1 and 3 turn slightly so as to lead with right shoulders and move forward, passing back to back in the center (measure 4).
5–8   Men 1 and 3 each *turn* partner in opposite place; couples 2 and 4 *repeat* the weaving of measure 1–4.
9–12   Men 2 and 4 each *turn* partner in opposite place; couples 1 and 3 *repeat* the weaving of measures 1–4, returning to place.
13–16   Men 1 and 3 each *turn* partner in original place, couples 2 and 4 *repeat* the weaving of measures 1–4, returning to place.

Figure II: Turn Opposites

1–2   Men 2 and 4 *turn* partner in original place; men 1 and 3 move forward to opposite place, passing right shoulders in center.
3–4   Men 1 and 3 each *turn* opposite woman at her place; men 2 and 4 *repeat* the crossover of measures 1–2.
5–8   *Repeat* measures 1–4. Men 2 and 4 *turn* opposite, then cross over to original place; men 1 and 3 cross over to place, then *turn* partner.
9–16   Couples 1 and 3 continue turning and *all* couples *turn* in place.

Figure III: Turn Corners

1–8   Each man moves in front of own partner, *inside* the square, to woman on his right (measures 1–2) and *turns* this woman (measures 3–4); then each man returns *outside* the square to own partner (measures 5–6) and *turns* own partner (measures 7–8).
9–16   *Repeat* measures 1–8 except each man moves *outside* the square to woman on his left, then returns *inside* the square to own partner.

Figure IV: Men 1 and 4, etc.

1–2   Men 1 and 4 move forward toward each other with four steps and on the fourth step, with right shoulders adjacent and looking at each other, *clap* own hands; men 2 and 3 do the same.
3–4   Each man makes ½ turn to right and returns to place.
5–8   Each *turns* own partner in place.
9–10   Men 1 and 4 move forward and change places, passing right shoulders; men 2 and 3 do the same.
11–12   Each man *turns* new partner.
13–16   *Repeat* measures 9–12. Each man returns to place and *turns* own partner.
17–32   *Repeat* measures 1–16, except men 1 and 2 work together, as do men 3 and 4.

Figure V: Trios

1–4   Partners right *elbow swing* with eight steps, except that couple 1 stops after six steps and woman 1 remains in place while man 1 moves to couple 2.
5–8   Man 1 with couple 2 *circle* left as a trio for six steps, then man 1 ducks under arch formed by joined inside hands of couple 2 and moves to couple 3; meanwhile couples 3 and 4 continue to right *elbow swing*.
9–12   *Repeat* measures 5–8, man 1 with couple 3, then moving to couple 4; meanwhile couples 2 and 4 continue to right *elbow swing*, except that couple 2 steps after six steps and woman 2 remains in place while man 2 moves to couple 3.
13–16   *Repeat* measures 5–8, man 1 with couple 4, then returning to partner, man 2 with couple 3, then moving to couple 4.
17–20   *Repeat*, man 2 with couple 4 while others *elbow swing*.
21–24   *Repeat*, men 2 and 3 with couples 1 and 4, respectively.
25–28   *Repeat*, man 3 with couple 1 while others *elbow swing*.
29–32   *Repeat*, men 3 and 4 with couples 2 and 1, respectively.
33–36   *Repeat*, man 4 with couple 2 while others *elbow swing*.
37–40   *Repeat*, man 4 with couple 3 while others *elbow swing*.

Figure VI: Circle

1–8   All four couples *circle* left once around in "W" position (elbows bent, hands joined at shoulder level, resembling the letter W).

Figure VII: Ending

1–16   As in Figure I (weave across and back).
17–24   All *turn* partners in original place.
25–32   All promenade with inside hands joined and

outside arms raised freely, hands waving in tune with steps. (This may be used to *exit* for demonstrations.)

KALVELIS

No dance of Lithuanian origin has won greater favor among American folk dancers than has Kalvelis (kahl-VYA-lis), which is now known in almost every part of the country. Among the Lithuanians, too, it is the first dance they learn in their repertoire. Because of its popularity, it is no wonder that many folk dance groups in the United States created new versions or elaborated on its simple playfulness. In some regions, the version is a far cry from the original, which I first introduced to American folk dance audiences in the late 1930s. However, the version that follows is authentic and is set down in a Lithuanian governmental publication. This dance may be considered an occupational dance, though the only thing that discloses the smithy's occupation is the hand clapping in the refrain, which represents the striking of the hammer on the anvil.

Record: Folkraft 1418

Formation: Any number of cpls. All join H in a cir, W on M R.

Meter 2/4   Pattern

Meas

Part I

1–7   Polka in cir to R, 7 polka steps.

8   Stamp 3 times.

9–16   All polka to left, ending with 3 stamps, facing ptrs.

Refrain

1   Clap own H twice (R over L) (1), L over R (2), to imitate hammer hitting anvil.

2   Same as meas 1. Refrain.

3–4   Hook R arms with ptr and turn once in place with 4 skips.

5–6   Clap as in meas 1–2. Refrain.

7–8   Hook L arms and turn in place.

9–16   Repeat meas 1–8. Refrain.

Part II

1–3   All face ctr of cir. W dance twd ctr with 3 polka steps.

4   3 stamps and turn to face ptr.

5–8   Back to place with 3 polka steps, finish with 3 stamps, and turn to face ctr.

9–16   M polka into cir and out, as in meas 1–8 of this part. However, their steps are more vigorous, stamping on the first beat of each meas.

Refrain

Part III

1–16   Face ptrs and do a grand R & L. If the group

Brigham Young University Dancers

is small, continue grand R & L until ptrs meet a second time. If ptrs meet before end of music, hook R arms and turn in place with polka steps. If group is very large, repeat music as long as necessary.

Refrain

Part IV (Optional)

1–16   Polka around in cir CCW with own ptr.

Refrain

The dance either begins again or, if desired, dancers exit from floor during polka of part IV before reaching refrain.

KLUMPAKOJIS

Klumpakojis (kloom-pah-KOH-yis), which means "the wooden shoe," is a favorite of the Lithuanian ballroom dance. It resembles many other dances of the Dutch, Germans, Swedes, Czechs, and other nationalities.

Record: Folkraft 1419

Formation: Cpls anywhere in a dance pos

Meter 2/4   Pattern

Meas

1–8	Polka in a CCW dir, cpl behind cpl.
9	Release hold and walk to R 2 steps.
10	Stamp 3 times.
11	Walk 2 steps to L.
12	Clap 3 times.
13	Shake R index finger 3 times.
14	Shake L index finger 3 times.
15	Slap twd ptr R H, make one complete turn CCW, and face ptr.
16	Stamp in front of ptr.
	Repeat to end of music.

KOJA, KOJA

Koja, koja (KOH-yah KOH-yah), a ballroom type of folk dance, seems to be another variation of the Russian Oyda or, as the Lithuanians call it, Anelkute, Kaire Koja (Little Anna, Your Left Foot). This version is found among the Lithuanians of Baltimore. The tune was shared with Vyts Beliajus by Kazys Stupuras, who danced it in Tryskiai, in the district of Siauliai, and brought the dance to this country.

Record: "Hip Hip Polka," Folkraft 1418X45

Formation: Cpls anywhere on the floor, both H joined, facing ptr

Meter 4/4   Pattern

Meas

Part I

1	Step R, L, R, turning slightly to R until L shldrs are adjacent and joined H are stretched across each other's chest.
2	Stamp in place twice with L ft.
3	Step L, R, L, turning slightly to L until R shldrs are adjacent and joined H are stretched across each other's chest.
4	Stamp R ft twice.

Part II

1	Same as meas 1, part I.
2	Hit L hips against each other twice.
3	Same as meas 3, part I.
4	Hit R hips against each other twice.
5–8	Polka in dance pos anywhere on floor. Repeat to end of music.

KŪBILAS

Kūbilas (KOO-bill-lahs), which means "the tub," is a merry autumnal dance performed within the house, around the huge vat in the center of the floor, after all the vegetables have been gathered.

Record: Folkraft LP-35, side B, band 3

Brigham Young University Dancers

Formation: Single circle of couples, each woman on partner's right

Starting Position: Back chain position. Right foot free.

Meter 2/4   Pattern

Meas

Figure I

1–7	Fourteen *gallop steps* sideward to right (counts 1–14).
8	*Jump* on both feet in place (count 1), pause (count 2).
9–11	The circle breaks up into couples in open position and each couple turns clockwise in place (man moves forward, woman backward) with six *gallop steps* (counts 1–6).
12	Release partners and *jump* on both feet in place, man turning clockwise in the air before landing (count 1), pause, and all men form a circle in "T" position (arms extended sidewards, hands on neighbors' shoulders).

Figure II

1–8	*Men* circle left in "T" position with fourteen *gallop steps* sideward, then *jump-pause* as in fig I, while *women*, with left hand raised and right hand holding skirt, face center and move sideward to right with fourteen *gallop steps*, then *jump-pause* as in fig I.
9–11	Continue with six more *gallop steps* in the same direction, timing it to finish near partner.
12	Men release shoulder holds and all *jump* on both feet in place, men making ½ turn to right to finish facing partner (count 1), pause (count 2).

Figure III

1–8	Partners join both hands, right shoulders adjacent, left elbow bent and right arm across partner's chest, leaning away from each other, and

turn clockwise in place with fourteen *gallop steps* (counts 1–14), *jump* on both feet, pulling backward away from each other (count 15), pause (count 16).

9–12 Repeat measures 5–8 (six more *gallop steps* then *jump-pause*).

Figure IV

1–8 Partners facing, with man's right hand holding woman's left waist, woman's left hand on man's right shoulder, man's free arm curved above head and woman's free hand holding her skirt. Fourteen *gallop steps* sidewards in line-of-dance (counterclockwise) to man's left (counts 1–14), then *jump-pause* as in fig I (counts 15–16).

9–12 Release partner and *men clap* hands eight times while *women* raise arms curved above head and *walk* eight steps clockwise 1½ times around partner to finish in center in a circle in "T" position (counts 1–8).

Figure V

1–8 *Women* circle right in "T" position with fourteen *gallop steps* sidewards, then *jump-pause* as in fig I, while *men* join hands outside in a circle stretched as wide as possible and circle left in similar fashion.

9–11 Six more *gallop steps* in the same direction, timing it to finish near partner.

12 Women release shoulder holds and all *jump* on both feet in place, women making ½ turn to right (count 1), pause, each woman returning to partner (count 2).

Figure VI

As in fig I, except circle left and, after first jump, break circle at central point to straighten out line, ending with a jump and a bow.

MALŪNAS

Malūnas (mah-LOO-nahs) means "the mill."

Music: Folkraft LP-34

Formation: Cir of 8 cpls, M on inside facing out, W facing ptr, both hands joined. During dance, whenever hands are not joined with ptr, M place free hand on hips; W hold skirts.

Step: Light running step

Meter 2/4 Pattern

Meas *Entrance* (optional)—Cart with horses bringing grain for grinding.

1–32 Four groups of four with number 1 (leading) cpl acting as the "horses" and number 2 (behind) acting as the "cart." Cpl 1 join inside hands and stretch inside arms straight fwd like a pole between a team of horses, outside hands

resting on outside shldrs, which hands are held by outside hands of couple 2; couple 2 join inside hands, arms downward. Group follow group in this formation, enter, and form a double cir. Finish facing ptr, M's back to center, both hands joined.

Intro. 3 chords

I. Winnowing

1–8 Standing in place, swing joined hands, first to M's R, then to L (meas 1). Repeat action 7 more times.

9–16 Release hands. M circle once CW, W, CCW with 16 running steps, finishing in own home pos.

II. Individual Weaving

M progress CW; W CCW.

1–2 Beg L ft, ptrs exchange places, R shldr leading and passing R shldrs, with 4 running steps. (M move out of cir, W move in).

3–4 ½ turn R in place with leap L, R ft raised (ct 1); run in place R, L, R (cts 2, 1, 2).

5–6 Beg L ft, exchange places with new person, L shldr leading and passing L shldrs, with 4 running steps. (M move twd ctr of cir, W move out.)

7–8 ½ turn L in place with leap L, R ft raised (ct 1); run in place R, L, R (cts 2, 1, 2).

9–32 Continue weaving, repeating action of fig II, meas 1–8, until ptrs meet.

III. Couple Weave

Join both hands with ptr. Cpls 1, 3, 5, 7 progress CW—in for 2 meas and out for 2 meas. Cpls 2, 4, 6, 8 progress CCW—out for 2 meas and in for 2 meas.

1–2 Cpls 1, 3, 5, 7 move twd ctr of cir, M moving bwd; while cpls 2, 4, 6, 8 move away from ctr of cir, M moving fwd—all using 4 running steps.

3–4 Turning just so as to move diag CW, cpls 1, 3, 5, 7 move out of cir, M moving fwd, passing next cpl moving in; while cpls 2, 4, 6, 8, turning just so as to move diag CCW, move twd ctr of cir, M moving fwd, passing next cpl moving out—all using 4 running steps.

5–16 Continue weaving, cpls 1, 3, 5, 7 progressing CW and cpls 2, 4, 6, 8 CCW, passing a new cpl to M's R during each 2 meas until home pos is reached. (Pass neighboring cpl once; remain in pos when meeting second time.)

1–8 Winnowing: Repeat action of fig I, meas 1–8.

IV. Spokes of Wheel ("Wings")

Everybody facing LOD so as to move CCW,

form a large mill wheel with 2 cpls to each spoke. (An odd # cpl with the nearest fwd even # cpl form a spoke. Even # cpls in ctr.) Even #M form hub with L hand on next M's L wrist, R arm about ptr's waist. Even #W place L hand on ptr's R shldr, her R hand on L shldr of odd #M forming her spoke. The odd #M places his L arm about waist of W on his L, R arm around ptr's waist. Odd #W place L hand on ptr's R shldr, free R hand holds skirt.

1–8   With 16 running steps, turn the mill wheel CCW.

V. Spokes ("Wings")
Release handhold. M turn R about to face CW; W remain facing LOD.

1–2   All run fwd 2 steps (outer dancers take long strides, inner take smaller strides) and fit into a new spoke, stamping 3 times in place.

3–8   Continue repeating action of fig V, meas 1–2, until meeting own ptr for second time.

VI. Spokes ("Wings")
Form a large mill wheel exactly as in fig IV, all facing LOD.

1–2   All run fwd 4 steps, turning wheel in LOD.

3–4   While rest of wheel moves fwd slightly, odd #M (on outer part of spoke) release hold on W and leap turn to own R, then with 3 more steps fit into spoke (or "wing") behind, taking hold of new W.

5–16   Repeat action of fig IV, meas 1–4, until M #1, 3, 5, 7 are back in their original spokes.

VII. Grindstone
Release hold on W. M only form solid spokes, inner hub remaining intact, as in fig VI. M in each spoke join near hands to form arches, outside M's free hand on hip. Odd #W step fwd of own spoke; even #W step behind own spoke, then all W join hands to form a cir under arches formed by M.

1–8   W run fwd to R (CCW) under arches as M move bwd (CW).

9–16   Reverse dir: W run fwd to L (CW) as M run fwd (CCW). At end of this fig, W move to R of own ptr.

VIII. Circles and Little Mills

1–8   Cpls in each spoke ("wing") form cir(s) of 4 persons; turn cir(s) to R, CCW, with running steps.

9–16   Cir(s) form into little mills of 4 persons, R hands joined and raised high; turn mill CW with running steps.

IX. Gear (music increases tempo).
All M step in to form one large cir. W step to R of own ptr and place their L hands over the clasped hands of the M, thus forming a cir of M with "teeth" made by W.

1–16   Cir CCW with running steps.

1–16   Exit. M place R hand around ptr's waist, W places her R hand over ptr's hand at her waist; L hands joined in front of M. Run off or same as entrance, with carts leaving with flour.

NAŠLYS

Našlys (nah-SHLEES), which means "the widower," is a mixer.

Record: Folkraft LP-35, side B, band 9

Formation: Column of cpls facing same dir, each woman on ptr's R, with one M (the widower) alone at head of column.

Starting pos: Inside hands joined. *Swing* for this dance means: pivot CW in place with walking steps in Lithuanian pos. All movements in this dance are with *walking steps.*

Meter 4/4   Pattern

Meas

Part I (Music A—slow)

1–12   Widower lead column anywhere around floor.
       Part II (Music B—fast)

13–28 Widower swings W 1 just a few times, then releases her and *swings* W 2 while M 1 swings W 1, then both release these W and widower *swings* W 3 while M 1 swings W 2 and M 2 swings W 1, then continue with widower moving down the line of W and each M following in turn until music stops, at which point M without ptr becomes new widower.

NORIU MIEGO

Noriu Miego (NOH-ryoo MYEH-goh), which means "I Want to Sleep," is a dance for four people. This is one of the oldest Lithuanian dances. The song tells about a young man who wants to sleep but is kept awake by the sweet voice of a maiden in the flower garden. Lithuanian orchestras often change the dance tempo suddenly at almost any point.

Record: Folkraft LP-35, side B, band 8

Formation: Groups of 4 people, no ptrs, scattered anywhere

Starting pos: Hands on own hips, R ft free

Meter 2/4   Pattern

Meas

1   A small *leap* onto R ft in place and touch L heel fwd (ct 1), pause (ct 2).

2   A small *leap* onto L ft in place and touch R heel fwd (ct 1), pause (ct 2).

3–4   *Repeat* meas 1–2 four times (i.e., twice as fast, no pause).

5   *Clap* hands twice (meas 1–2).

6   Stamp 3 times in place (cts 1-and-2).

7–8   R-hand *star* with 4 *skips*.

9–12   *Repeat* meas 5–8 except with L-hand *star*.

SUKTINIS

Suktinis (sook-TIN-nix) is a couple dance that means "the turner."

Record: Folkraft LP-34, side B, band 5

Formation: Couples facing line-of-dance (counterclockwise), woman on partner's right.

Position: Man's right arm around woman's waist, his left hand holding her left hand in front of his chest, man's left elbow shoulder high, woman's right hand holding her skirt.

Meter 2/4   Pattern

Meas

1–7   Seven *Suktinis polka steps* forward: with weight on left foot, hop on left foot and kick right foot slightly forward (count -ah before count 1), step forward on right foot (count 1), step forward on left foot (count -and), step forward on right foot (count 2); and *repeat* six more times (seven times in all), alternating footwork.

8   Three stamps (left, right, left) in place (counts 1-and-2).

9–11   Six *skips* turning counterclockwise in place (woman moves forward, man backward).

12   Two *skips*, changing places: with left hands still joined, woman passes sideward under man's left arm to finish with his left arm across her chest and her right arm around his waist, man's right hand on hip.

13–15 Six *skips* turning counterclockwise in place (man moves forward, woman backward).

16   Change places, as in meas 12, man passing under woman's left arm to finish in original starting position.

VOVERAITĒ

Voveraitē (voh-vyah-RYE-teh) which means "Miss Squirrel," is a dance for four couples. It tells of a rabbit who met a squirrel in the lane. The rabbit took off his hat with a flourish, greeting the squirrel with a "labs ryts" (equivalent to our "Good mornin' "), and proposed to her. But other animals with more sense advised the squirrel to wait awhile, for, who knows, something better may turn up.

Record: Folkraft LP-35, side B, band 4

Formation: Longways or contra: four couples in a line or set, men in one line and women in another line, each woman opposite and facing partner about six feet apart. Head end of the set is near the music; the other end is the foot. Men wear straw hats.

Meter 2/4   Pattern

Meas

Figure I

1–4   Four *polka steps* in place.

5–8   Partners change places with four *polka steps*, passing right shoulders.

9–10   Two *polka steps* forward toward partner.

11–12 Each man takes off his hat and *bows* deeply to partner; she bows too.

13–14 Partners hook right elbows and change places with two *polka steps*.

15–16 Each man takes off his hat and *bows* deeply to partner; she bows too.

Figure II

1–2   Partners join right hands and balance toward and then away from each other with one *polka step* each way.

3–4   With right hands still joined, change places with two *polka steps*.

5–8   *Repeat* meas 1–4.

9–10   Release hands and all face the "head": all *step-close step-touch* sideward (men to the left, women to the right).

11–12 *Repeat* meas 9–10 to place (women move left, men right).

13–16 *Repeat* meas 9–12.

Figure III

1–8   All with *polka steps*, man 1 turns left and woman 1 turns right, each leading own line toward foot of set, where they form a line in single file, each woman in front of own partner, then start to form a circle moving clockwise.

9–10   Continue to move in a clockwise circle with *polka steps*, each woman in front of partner.

11–16 Stop, each woman makes ½ turn to face partner, and *repeat* the bow and elbow hook of fig I, meas 11–16.

Figure IV

1–8   As in fig II.

9–16   Grand right and left with polka steps.

Figure V

1–3   All join hands in the circle and move forward to center with three *polka steps*.

4   Three *stamps* in place (counts 1-and-2).

5–8   Move backward to place, three *polka steps* then

three *stamps*, and finish with partner in Ballroom position, each couple standing on one side of a square "set."

9–12   Couples 1 and 3 turn clockwise in Ballroom position with *polka steps* and exchange positions in the square, while couples 2 and 4 *repeat* fig II, meas 1–4.

13–16   *Repeat* meas 9–12 reversing roles: couples 2 and 4 now exchange positions with *polka steps* while couples 1 and 3 *repeat* fig II, meas 1–4.

Figure VI: Ending

1–8   Release hands and women, only, *repeat* fig V, meas 1–8.

9–12   All face audience and *polka* backward until they are in one straight line, each woman on partner's right, in Back Chain position.

13–16   All move forward with three *polka steps*, then *bow* (to audience).

ŽIOGELIS

Žiogelis (zhyoh-GYAH-lis), which means "little grasshopper," is a dance for two trios. This dance depicts the presumed movements of a grasshopper cavorting in a rye field.

Record: Folkraft LP-35, side B, band 2

Formation: Trio (normally one man between two women) facing trio about eight feet apart.

Position: Men's arms around women's waists, women's inside hands joined behind men's backs, free hands holding skirts, right foot free.

Meter 2/4   Pattern

Meas   *Chorus*

1–4   One *polka step* forward, starting with hop on left foot (counts -ah-1-and-2). Two *walking steps* (left, right) forward (counts 3-and), *stamp* on left foot, taking weight, and simultaneously bend body forward and extend right leg backward (count 4), and repeat, moving backward (lean backward and extend right leg forward at the end) (counts 5–8).

5–8   Repeat meas 1–4.

Figure I (music BB)

9–12   The two right-hand women, leading with right shoulder and passing back to back, exchange places with eight *gallop steps* sideward to right (counts 1–8); meanwhile the others (men's hands on hips, women's hands holding skirts) balance flirtatiously, turning toward each other (count 1), away from each other (count 2), and so forth.

13–16   The two left-hand women, leading with left shoulder and passing back to back, exchange

places with eight *gallop steps* sideward to left while others balance similarly.

Figure II

1–8   *Repeat chorus.*

9–12   With four *polka steps* the two right-hand women right *elbow swing*, then return to place; man and left-hand woman do the same. (Right-hand women *clap* own hands on count 1 before hooking.)

13–16   The two left-hand women left *elbow swing* similarly; man and right-hand woman do the same.

Figure III

1–8   *Repeat chorus.*

9–12   *Men:* Four *gallop steps* sideward to right, moving in front of partner and counterclockwise ¼ turn around the set (counts 1–4); facing each other, four *bleking steps* (hop on left foot and touch right heel forward, same reversing footwork, and repeat) (counts 5–8).
Women: Each pair join inside hands and exchange places with four *polka steps*, one pair going under arch formed by other pair.

13–16   *Women:* Release hands, turn individually, and return to place with four *polka steps*, the other pair now going under arch.
Men: Four more *bleking steps* (counts 1–4), then return to original positions with four *gallop steps* sideward to left (counts 5–8).

Figure IV

1–8   *Repeat chorus.*

9–12   Men join inside hands with both partners and, with four *polka steps*, women move forward, changing places with right-hand woman going under arch formed by man with his left-hand woman, to finish facing out with backs toward other trio.

13–16   *Repeat* meas 9–12, except left-hand woman goes under arch. Trios finish facing.

Figure V: Circle Three

1–8   *Repeat chorus.*

9–12   Each trio forms a circle-of-three and all circle right with four *polka steps*.

13–16   Circle left.

Figure VI: Circle Six

1–8   *Repeat chorus.*

9–12   Trios form a circle-of-six and all circle right with four *polka steps*.

13–16   Circle left. Finish in original formation (two trios facing) and bow.

MEXICO

Mexican Folk Dancing

by Alura Flores de Angeles with Ron Houston

I started teaching foreigners the Jarabe Tapatío in 1932 and have never taught it exactly the same way twice. I teach part of a living folk process which, like the butterfly, changes to become more beautiful.

Indigenous influence. There remains none! Anyone claiming to know an Aztec dance is in error. Spain subjugated the native population for four hundred years by killing the better-educated musicians, priests, and dancers, and selling the rest into slavery.

Spanish influence. There are two types of dances in Mexico: bailes and danzas. Bailes are couple dances derived from Spanish couple dances. Danzas were taught by missionaries and conquistadors to acculturate the natives. In Spain this form represented the conflict between Christian and Moor and evolved into Mexico's danzas, which are group dances incorporating an argument or story.

Chilean influence. La Cueca, the national dance of Chile, spread along the Pacific Coast as La Chilena, the Chilean dance. In Mexico, Las Chilenas is a family of beautiful couple dances performed to such tunes as "Las Amarillas" and "La Sanmarqueña."

European influence. In 1864 Mexican traitors asked Napoleon III to set his cousin, Maximilian, on the throne of Mexico. European influence then penetrated all aspects of Mexican life. The schottische, waltz, polka, varsouvianna, redova, and quadrille became the dances of Mexico.

Natural influence. Like many rural populations, the Mexicans love nature and imitate natural objects, particularly animals (how do you imitate a cactus?), and especially that most noble of animals, the horse. The *vaquero* of the north and the *charro* of Jalisco created cultures in which the horse was a central figure. Their dances reflect the mannerisms and gaits of both horse and rider.

Folclórico influence. After World War II, folk ballets developed in Europe and the Americas. Amalia Hernández formed the *Ballet Folclórico de México* and changed the world's perception of Mexican folk dance. While the folk ballet is based on traditional patterns, it is entirely different from the dances of the people and should never be confused with folk dance.

Common errors. A large *sombrero* and multicolored, sleeveless *cotorina* do NOT represent Mexico. Mexico is almost two thousand miles in length; every five miles the costumes, food, language, and traditions change completely. Please do not underestimate our culture.

I am sad that, of the many dances done at folk dance gatherings, few are termed Mexican. Of those that are, few really are Mexican. Mexico has no couple-mixer type dances. The Mexican Mixer is an American folk dance performed to Mexican music. The Mexican waltz is an American dance done to the Mexican tune "Las Chiapanecas." Please do not call it a Mexican dance. "Over the Waves" was composed by a Mexican, Juventino Rosas, in the 1800s. It is properly titled "Sobre las Olas."

A *corrido* is a Mexican epic poem or ballad. There are thousands extant and others are being written constantly. The folk dance known as Corrido is actually a pasodoble dance choreographed by my student, Avis Landis, an American. It should be referred to as an American dance with Mexican influence and called Eso Si, Como No. "Tehuantepec" was composed by Pepe Guizar. The folk dance to this tune was choreographed by an American and should always be referred to as an American dance with Mexican influence.

A personal note. I would like to take this opportunity to thank the Americans, particularly those at the Texas International Folk Dance Camp, for inviting me to teach in the United States for the last twenty-five years. I would also like to thank all those who have come to Mexico to study with me at the University of Mexico (Universidad Nacional Autónoma de México) for the last forty-five years, particularly those who have shared with us the Festival Folclórico Folk Dance Camp December.

(Alura Flores de Angeles was born in Cuernavaca, Mexico, of an American mother and a Mexican father. Her world has always been filled with music. Her mother was a concert pianist and singer, her father a singer, and she was given the gift of dance. The Universidad Nacional Autónoma de México graduated Alura in physical education, and she has been researching, dancing, teaching, and choreographing Mexican dances since the late twenties. In 1928 she started collecting unrecorded dances by going into remote villages as a member of a government-sponsored cultural mission.

For more than twenty years Alura has taught for three weeks each year at the University of Mexico's

*Alura Flores
de Angeles*

affiliate campus in San Antonio, as well as at San Antonio College. She has also been a visiting professor of dance at various schools and folk dance camps in the United States, including the camp at Stockton, California. Some of the most outstanding folk dancers and teachers have been students of Alura or were affiliated with her, including Nelda Drury, Buzz Glass, and several other California Folk Dance Federation presidents.

Señora de Angeles coached women's basketball and volleyball teams for twenty-five years. Representing Mexico City, her volleyball team won six national championships; three of her players were on the Mexico team in the 1968 Olympics. Her government asked her to act as a cultural representative at the Olympic Games in Rome (1960), Tokyo (1964), Mexico (1968), and Munich (1972). As busy as she was in athletics, however, she always had time for dancing.

Alura is head of the Department of Dance of the Temporary Courses Division of the Universidad Nacional Autónoma de México in Mexico City. She is also director of the Festivales Folklóricos Internacionales, a folk dance camp held twice yearly in the Centro Vacacional of Oaxtepec, Morelos.

Alura is also choreographer for, and director of, an exhibition group called Yolo Xochitl, which is made up of students from the university. According to legend, Yolo Xochitl was a boy born into an Indian village who was very dear to his mother. She watched over and protected him carefully, and as he grew to be a man he became very wise and wealthy and his village prospered. Yolo Xochitl, meaning "the flower of the heart," came to represent the spirit of prosperity. Alura used the name as an inspiration to both herself and the group. They have performed at statewide folk dance gatherings in California.

In 1977 Señora de Angeles was commissioned by the Mexican National Federation of Charros to accept an invitation to present a program of Mexican dances before the King and Queen of Spain. In 1978 she traveled again to Europe, where she taught the dances of Mexico in Stuttgart, Hamburg, Berlin, Zurich, and Vienna.

Alura Flores de Angeles has contributed much to the world of folk dancing, and she has presented and choreographed many dances that are done today.)

MEXICAN FOLK DANCES

Two of the following dances—El Jarabe Tapatio and Jesusita en Chihuahua—are used with permission from the forthcoming book *The Mexican Dances of Alura Flores de Angeles,* compiled by Ron Houston (see Bibliography).

CABALLITO BLANCO
A dance from Mexico

Record: Festival (45 rpm) F-3603; Standard T 124 A, "Fado Blanquito," Staff F D 1A; Decca 2164 B, "World of Folk Dances," EPA-4136.

Formation: Couples in a line, W in front of M (with her back to him). W arms are folded at shoulder height, L over R. M holds her L hand with his R hand and her R hand with his L.

Note: Throughout dance, unless otherwise stipulated, M keeps hands clasped low behind him. W holds skirt lightly in front with both hands.

Steps: Fado Step, Jump-hop, Walk (stroll), Buzz-Step, Dos-à-Dos.

Meter 4/4   Pattern

Meas Intro
1–3   M gives W slight impetus by slightly pulling her L hand with his R, starting her off clockwise. W takes 6 step-hops moving directly fwd, starting with R foot, revolving clockwise and stopping 6 or 8 feet from partner. W holds skirts with both hands. M in place, with hands clasped loosely behind back, sways very slightly in time to music.

4   Partners facing, stamp lightly R, L, R (cts 1, 2, 3), hold (ct 4).

5–8   Both beginning L, M and W stroll across to change places, passing R shoulders. (Step pattern: slow, slow, quick, quick, slow.) Repeat beginning R. When in opposite position both turn to face each other.

Vamp

1   M slaps thighs R, L, R, L (cts 1 and 2) and claps hands together twice (cts 3, 4). W, holding skirts, steps R (ct 1), points L toe across in front of R (ct 2), steps L (ct 3), points R toe across in front of L (ct 4).

2   Repeat action of meas 1.

I. (a) Long Fado Step and Buzz-Step Turn

1   Step diagonally to R on R (ct 1), hop R (ct 2); step L in front of R (ct 3), hop L (ct 4).

2   Step R behind L (ct 1), hop R (ct 2), step diagonally to L on L (ct 3), hop L (ct 4).

3   Step R in front of L (ct 1), hop R (ct 2), step L behind R (ct 3), hop L (ct 4).

Note: When L ft is in front, L shoulder is toward partner and the R foot is raised back. When the R foot is in front the R shoulder is toward partner and L foot is raised. M keeps hands clasped in back. W holds skirts and both look back over own shoulder toward partner.

4–9   Repeat action of meas 1–3 twice.

10 Repeat action of meas 1.

11–13 Beginning R, buzz-step turn clockwise (6 slow buzz-steps), making 3 complete turns to finish facing partner.

14 Stamp R, L, R (cts 1, 2, 3), hold (ct 4).

(b) Jump-hop Step

1 Jump to easy stride position, with knees bent slightly, toes turned out (ct 1), hop on L ft, straightening L leg and turning R knee to R and pointing R toe down in front of L calf (ct 2), jump to stride position (ct 3), hop on R foot, bending L leg in front of R with L knee pointing to L and L toe down in front of R calf (ct 4).

2 Jump to stride position (ct 1), hop on L ft, bending R leg (ct 2), hop L (ct 3), hop L (ct 4). (Make one complete turn clockwise on the 3 hops on the L foot.)

3–4 Repeat action of meas 1–2, hopping first on R foot and turning counterclockwise.

5–8 Beginning L, M and W stroll across to change places as in the Intro, passing R shoulders. (Now in original positions.)

9–12 Repeat action of meas 1–4.

13–16 Repeat action of meas 5–8, but instead of changing places partners do a dos-à-dos (pass R shoulders, move to R around each other and back into place). As the dos-à-dos is completed, M makes ¼ turn L, and W makes ¼ turn R to finish on M's R. Both face in same direction and at R angles to original position.

(c) Short Fado Step

San Antonio College Dancers

1–3 In skating position (R hands joined on top of the joined L hands), partners do one fado step (6 step-hops), starting on R.

4 Stamp R, L, R (cts 1, 2, 3), hold (ct 4), weight on L.

5 Repeat action of meas 1–4.

(d) Vamp

1–2 Partners face each other and back away to position 6 or 8 feet apart while they repeat action of Vamp as described above in Intro.

II. Long Fado Step

1–14 Repeat action of I(a).

Jump-hop Step

1–16 Repeat action as in I(b), except that instead of a dos-à-dos at the close, M and W again stroll across to change places.

Short Fado Step

1–8 Repeat action as in I(c) above, but in double line formation, partners facing each other (M clasping hands loosely behind back, W holding skirt) as in the long fado.

Jump-hop Step

1–16 Repeat action as in I(b) with the dos-à-dos. Since partners have now changed places, couples will face in opposite direction to that originally taken in B.

Short Fado Step

1–8 Repeat action of I(c) as before. On final stamps, without releasing hands, lean away from partner to pose.

CORRIDO (Eso Si, Como No)

The Mexican corrido is a true folk ballad. Historically, this form is descended from the Spanish romance, which flourished most brilliantly during the fourteenth and fifteenth centuries in Spain. The earliest Mexican example that bears a date was issued in Mexico City on August 19, 1684.

The music for secular folk dances is in the form of songs. This dance, corrido, has developed from the ballad form. Three characteristic steps are noted in this dance: soldado, a soldierly style of dancing dating back to revolutionary days; a dipping step, commonly called the grapevine; and a typical sideward step-close. Avis Landis introduced this dance.

Record: Star (45 rpm) B412, Mexican Columbia 1613-C, Imperial 1137

Formation: A double circle of couples in closed dance position, M with back to center and W facing center

Steps: Step-close, soldado; grapevine (Mexican dipping step)

Meter 4/4   Pattern

Meas   *I. Step-close*

1–5   In closed position, couples move swd CW with

10 step-close steps. The hips sway easily in typical Mexican fashion.

II. Grapevine (Mexican Dipping Step)

1–7 Beginning with M's R and W's L, execute 7 grapevine steps moving CCW. Grapevine step (described for M; W begins with opposite ft): Step R ft across in front of L (ct 1), step swd L with L (ct 2), step R ft across in back of L (ct 3), step swd L with L (ct 4). In this step partners watch feet and keep close to each other.

8 Step R ft across L (ct 1), stamp L ft in place (ct 2), stamp R ft in place (ct 3), hold (ct 4). (W do same with opposite ft.)

III. Step-close and Soldado

9–10 In closed pos, repeat swd step-close step 4 times in CW direction.

11 Soldado: In closed pos and starting with M's R ft and W's L ft, couples move to the center of the circle, M moving bwd, W fwd. The step is a relaxed shuffle step in typical Mexican manner, keeping ft on floor. 4 steps moving twd center.

12 Reverse direction, moving away from center of the circle and slightly to M's L, with 4 steps (M: R, L, R, L; W: L, R, L, R).

13–17 Repeat soldado 5 more times, continuing to move toward and away from center of circle, at same time progressing fwd in LOD.

18 Moving away from center of circle, M steps fwd on R (ct 1), M stamps on L ft (ct 2), M stamps R (ct 3), hold (ct 4).
W stamps with opposite ft. Both change weight for grapevine.

IV. Grapevine

1–8 Repeat 7 grapevine steps, progressing CCW with same ending as in fig II.

REPETITION WITH VARIATIONS

I. Step-close

1–5 Action same as in fig I.

II. Cross Step with One Turn

Partners facing, M hands clasped behind back, R hand holding L wrist, W holds skirt at sides. Moving to M's L, W's R, take the following step (described for M; W begin with opposite ft).

1 Step R across in front of L with an accent, lifting L off the floor in back (ct 1); step L in place (ct 2); step R beside L (ct 3); step L, across R with accent; lifting R ft off floor in back (ct 4). During this action shoulders point alternately toward partner.

2 M takes a 4-step turn to his L away from partner, starting with R ft in back of L. W does same with opposite ft.

3–6 Repeat action of meas 1–2 twice.

7 Repeat action of meas 1.

8 Facing partner, M steps with R behind L (ct 1); stamp fwd L (ct 2); stamp R beside L (ct 3); hold (ct 4). W does same with opposite ft.

III. Step-close and Soldado

9–18 Repeat action of meas 9–18 in first section.

IV. Grapevine with Two Turns

1–8 Partners face each other, holding R hands shoulder height, M's L hand held in back, W's L hand holds skirt. Progressing CCW, M takes grapevine step throughout as in meas 1–8, figure IV, first section. While M dances this plain grapevine step, W dances as follows:
Meas 1: Grapevine step
   2: Two turns to R in 4 cts
  3–4: Repeat action of meas 1–2
  5–6: Repeat action of meas 1–2
   7: Grapevine step
   8: Pivot turn, stepping on L (ct 1); facing partner, stamp R (ct 2); stamp L (ct 3); hold (ct 4).

SECOND REPETITION

This is performed exactly as in first section, with a slight variation in part IV as follows: Couples hold inside hands for grapevine step; W holds skirt with outside hand, M has outside hand in back; W accentuates movement of skirt with R hand and the dance ends with sharp stamps.

EL JARABE TAPATÍO (Dance of the Tapatíos)

Independence fighters from all parts of Mexico formed a dance known as *Jarabe Largo Ranchero,* set to the *sones* of Jalisco. In the early 1920's, the

Mexican National Board of Education synthesized the much shorter (2 min. 30 sec.) *Jarabe Tapatío* from this overly long (6 min.) original. By proclamation of the Federal Government, it became the national dance of Mexico, signifying the integration of the Republic. Los Tapatíos are the people living on the outskirts of Guadalajara, capital of Jalisco. As the people of Jalisco have a strong horse culture, bowed legs for the men are entirely appropriate for this dance. As in many Mexican *Jarabes,* courtship of the *china* by her *charro* is the central theme. During the dance, the *charro* throws his sombrero on the ground for the *china* to dance on. She has accepted him when she dances on the brim and puts the hat on her own head. The dance ends with *La Diana,* a military tune signifying triumph and expressing congratulations to the *charro* for winning his *china*. The dance presented here by Alura F. de Angeles, is sometimes called *The Mexican Hat Dance.*

Costume: *Rancheros* may be used but the right costumes are the *Charro* and *China Poblana.*

Record: RCA Victor MKS-1448, *Bailes Regionales;* A-1, *Jarabe Tapatío;* others

Formation: Cpls in a line, facing top of set. W on M R, near hands joined with ptr.

Meter 6/8, 3/4, 2/4, 2/8   Pattern

Meas	Action
	Introduction

You may preface the dance with a CCW turn in place for the W under the M R arm; followed by both backing away from each other, 6 to 8 feet.

(6/8) *1. Zapateado triple.* This mimics the galloping of a horse as the *charro* rides to see his *china.*

1	Small step fwd with R ft (ct 1), close L ft to R ft (ct 2), step in place with R ft (ct 3), repeat cts 1–3, using opp ftwk (cts 4–6).
2–7	Repeat bar 1, advancing to meet ptr with R shldrs adjacent.
8	Stamp R ft in place (ct 1).
9–16	Repeat bars 1–8, advancing to ptr's place and turning CW to face ptr.

2. Knocking step. This mimics the *charro*'s knocking on the *china*'s front door.

1. Step fwd onto R heel with R toe raised (ct 6 of preceding bar). Turning R ft slightly to R and leav[ing] R heel on the floor, stamp slightly fwd onto L ft (ct 1), step onto ball of R ft by L ft (ct 3), turning R heel slightly outward, stamp slightly fwd onto L ft (ct 4), start step again with R heel (ct 6).

2–7	Repeat floor pattern of step 1, bars 2–7, using ftwk of step 2.
8	Stamp R ft in place (ct 1).
9–16	Repeat bars 1–8, advancing to original pos and turning CW to face ptr.

3. Zapateado triple. The *charro* takes his horse to the stable. Using step of step 1, advance to ptr's place and turn CW to face ptr.

(3/4) *4. Coqueteo (flirting).* The *china* does not want to say yes.

1. Run 3 steps twd ptr: R ft, L ft, R ft (cts 1, 2, 3).

2. Pivot CW on R ft by swinging L toe across R ft and pushing with it. Shift wt onto L ft (ct 3), having made 1 full turn. The turn starts and ends with R shoulders adjacent.

3–4	Repeat bars 1–2, moving to ptr's place and turning CW to face ptr. End with wt on R ft.
5	Turn CCW once with 3 steps, starting L ft.
6	Stamp R ft in place.
7–8	Repeat bars 5–6, using opp ftwk and direction.
9–12	Repeat bars 5–8.
13–24	Repeat bars 1–12.

Note: These turns may be done using push steps instead of the 3-step turns. M places sombrero on ground.

5. Atole (corn mash) or Borrachito (drunkard) step. Facing rejection, the *charro* seeks solace in his tequila bottle.

1	Fall fwd onto R ft (ct 1), step onto L ft behind R ft (ct 2), step to R onto R ft (ct 3).
2	Repeat bar 1 to L, starting with L ft.
3–6	Repeat bars 1–2 for a total of 3 times, advancing to ptr's place.
7–8	Rock fwd onto R ft (ct 1), rock back onto L ft behind R ft (ct 2), repeat cts 1–2 for a total of 6 rocking steps, turning CW to end facing ptr.
9–15	Repeat bars 1–7, returning to own place.
16	Stamp R ft (ct 1).

(6/8) *6. Hojas de té (leaves of tea) step.* The *china* serves the *charro* hot tea to sober him up.

1	Stamp slightly fwd onto R ft (ct 1), stamp slightly fwd onto L ft (ct 2), stamp slightly fwd onto R ft (ct 3), stamp slightly fwd onto L ft (ct 4), pause (ct 5), hop in place on L ft.
2	Repeat action of bar 1. Step does not alternate feet.
3–16	Execute floor pattern of step 1, using *hojas de té* step.

(2/4) *7. El Palomo (the dove).* Flirting resumes.

1–2	Run fwd 4 steps, R ft, L ft, R ft, L ft (cts 1, 2, 1, 2).
3	Step to R onto outside of R ft (ct 1), step across R ft with L ft (ct 2), turning CW once.
4	Facing ptr, stamp in place with R ft (ct 1).
5–6	Turn CCW, moving back to place thus: step to L onto L ft (ct 1), close R ft to L ft (ct &), step to L onto L ft (ct 2), close R ft to L

ft (ct &), step to L onto L ft (ct 1). M places sombrero on ground.

7–12   Repeat bars 1–6, remaining in ctr of set and near to ptr. Or:

1–3   Repeat step 4, bars 1–2, cts 1–6.

4–6   Circling CW, back-to-back around ptr, return to place with 6 push-steps as described in bar 5 of version 1 of step 7. M places sombrero on ground.

7–12   Repeat bars 1–6, remaining in ctr to circle ptr CCW.

8. Mecedora (rocking)

1–8   Circle sombrero CW with 16 push-steps.

9–16   Rock back onto L ft behind R ft (ct 2 of previous bar), rock fwd onto R ft in front of L (ct 1), continue rocking from ft to ft until end of bar 16. Continue circling CW. Or you may do the following alternate step for bars 9–16:

9–16   With R ft always behind L ft, W leaps into hat brim with L ft, touching R toe to brim behind L ft (ct 1), small leap bkwd onto R ft, touching L toe to brim in front of R ft (ct 2). W travels around brim CW with 2 rocking steps per bar; leaving hat on ct 2 of bar 16. M continues push-step.

17–19   W drops to R knee, picks up sombrero, places it on her own head (signifying acceptance of the *charro*), and stands up. M swings R leg over kneeling W's head, crosses R toe over L ft, and pivots CCW in place.

(2/8) *9. La Diana*

1–2   With inside (M R, W L) hands joined, both move fwd with 4 step-hops, starting R ft.

3–4   Repeat 1–2, moving bkwd.

5–8   Repeat 1–4.

9–10   Hop 3 times on L ft (cts 1, 2, 1), touching R heel diagonally fwd (ct 1), R toe across in front of L ft (ct 2), and R heel diagonally fwd (ct 1). Hop, landing with both feet together (ct 2).

11–12   Repeat 9–10, using opposite ftwk.

13–16   Repeat 9–12.

17–23   Repeat 1–7.

24   M turns W CCW under his R arm and drops to his L knee. W places L toe on M R knee to end dance in a pose. Or: Both hide behind hat and kiss, as they are now engaged.

EL SHOTIS VIEJO

El Shotis Viejo (Old-Style Schottische) is a type of Mexican dance that was popular in Mexico from 1815 to 1910. The schottische was introduced into Mexico about 1830, along with the polka and mazurka, and in the cities the people immediately adopted it. As the dance increased in popularity in the rural areas,

its style became more rustic. This shotis is in the classical style and is typical of the last half of the nineteenth century, when people imitated European culture more than their native culture. The music used for the dance was written by a young mariachi player, Miguel Martinez, one of the most popular composers of music of this type.

El Shotis Viejo was learned from an elderly gentleman of Oaxaca, who taught the dance to native schoolteachers and young people during a research trip made by Al Pill into the rural areas of Mexico. The teacher remembers dancing many figures in his youth, of which only a few representative examples have been included in this version.

Record: Express (45 rpm) 233

Formation: Ptrs in a circle, facing each other, M back to ctr, R hands joined. W hold skirt with free hand; M place L arm across small of back and hold L hand almost over R hip. Throughout the dance M R hand hangs naturally at side whenever it is free.

Steps and Styling: *Viejo Two-Step:* Step fwd L (ct 1), step R to rear of L (ct 2), step fwd L (cts 3–4). Do not pass R ft by L on closing step (ct 2), but allow it to close behind L heel. Step has smooth "lifting" motion. Repeat step, beginning R.

Viejo Shotis Step: Beginning L, walk 3 steps (cts 1–3), lift slightly on R toe while raising L ft with knee turned out to L (ct 4). Step may also begin with opp ft. This is a light, dignified step without an exaggerated hop.

Balance in Place: Step fwd on L, lifting R ft off the floor (cts 1–2), shift wt to R in place (cts 3–4), lifting L just off the floor.

Promenade Pos, Heel-Toe, Walk: Description is written for M; W does counterpart unless otherwise instructed.

Meter 4/4   Pattern
Meas

Intro: 3 pick-up notes, no action

I. Heel Toe and Cross Over

A 1–2   Bend bodies fwd from waist, extend L heel to L side (cts 1–2), touch L toe to floor with L heel across instep of R ft (cts 3–4). Beginning L, walk 3 steps fwd in LOD (CCW), gradually straightening bodies (cts 1–2), lift slightly on L (ct 4).

3–4   Repeat action of meas 1–2. Begin R and move RLOD (CW).

5   Face ptr. With bodies bent slightly fwd from waist, extend L heel fwd (cts 1–2), touch L toe to floor with L heel parallel to R ft (cts 3–4).

6   Hands remain joined. With 3 walking steps (gradually straightening bodies as in meas

2) exchange places with ptr (cts 1–3), hold (ct 4). Ptrs make ½ turn CW on last crossing step. Release hands.

7 Dance 1 Viejo Shotis step moving LOD (CCW).

8 Dance 1 Viejo Shotis step in RLOD (CW).

9–16 Rejoin R hands to repeat action of meas 1–8. Begin M R, W L, M on outside of circle, W on inside.

II. Two Step, Balance, Woman Pivots

B 1–2 Ptrs take promenade pos, facing LOD. With 2 Viejo two-steps, move fwd LOD.

3 Balance in place (cts 1–4).

4 Release L hands. M repeat action of fig II, meas 3. W take short step fwd on R, bend knees, lean fwd from waist and pivot one complete turn CW under joined R hands (cts 1–2), step L in place (cts 3–4).
Note: M must hold joined hands high and his hand flexible to assist W in turn.

9–16 Repeat action of fig II, meas 1–4, three times.

III. Heel Toe and Cross Over

A 1–15 Repeat action of fig I, meas 1–15.

16 With 2 steps (R L) M move twd RLOD; on 2 steps (R L) turn CCW in front of ptr to face ctr (cts 1–2, 3–4) and stand at W L side as W move fwd to ctr with 1 Viejo Shotis step. M put L hand just above elbow of W L forearm, W hold skirt out to the side with L hand. Ptrs join R hands high above W head. As they face ctr, M is slightly behind W.

IV. Shotis, Balance, Woman Pivot

B 1 With 1 Viejo Shotis step, both beginning R, ptrs move to the R but turn slightly twd L.

2 Repeat action of fig IV, meas 1, but move slightly to L and turn to R to finish facing ctr.

3–4 Repeat action of fig II, meas 3–4 (Balance, Woman Pivot).

5–12 Repeat action of fig IV, meas 1–4, two times (Shotis in LOD, RLOD and Balance and Pivot).

13–14 Repeat action of fig IV, meas 1–2 (Shotis LOD and RLOD).

15 Repeat action of fig II, meas 3 (balance fwd and bwd).

16 W repeat pivot, but turn to own R twd outside of circle. With 2 walking steps (R L) M turn ½ CW to face ptr, back to ctr. Release joined hands.

V. Solo Shotis, Woman Pivot

B 1 With 1 Viejo Shotis step, move to own R (M-RLOD, W-LOD).

2 With 1 Viejo Shotis step, move to own L (M-LOD, W-RLOD).

3 Join R hands. M Balance fwd and bwd in place. W Pivot Turn under joined hands (cts 1–2). Step L in place (cts 3–4).

4 M keep ft in place, bow from waist. W place R ft behind L and curtsy (cts 1–4), holding skirt to side with L hand.

5–16 Repeat action of fig V, meas 1–4, three times.

VI. Heel Toe and Cross Over

1–5 Repeat action of fig I, meas 1–15.

16 With three walking steps (M-R L R, W-L R L) ptrs move RLOD. Ptrs look at each other as dance ends.

EVANGELINA

Evangelina (ay-vahn-hay-LEE-nah) is a polka from northern Mexico. The description was provided by Nelda Drury.

Record: Peerless (45 rpm) 5811, ECO (LP) 207

Formation: Cpls scattered anywhere on floor, facing LOD. W is to R of M, inside hands (M R-W L) joined. M free hand at waist, thumb stuck in belt. W holds skirt in R hand.

Steps and Styling: Slide; Polka; Taconazo or Northern Zapateado: Leap onto R (ct 1); step on L heel beside R (ct &); step on R in place (ct 2); strike L heel beside R without taking wt (ct &); wt stays predominantly over R leg with R knee bent. Repeat of step would beg leap onto L, etc. This dance has lots of "up and down" motion in it, especially in polka step. Dancers yell, whistle, and shout freely, especially in "push" step.

Directions given for M; W use opp ftwk throughout.

Meter 2/4   Pattern

Meas Intro: 1 pick-up note.

I. Taconazo (Northern Zapateado)

1–16 Beg M L-W R, dance 16 Taconazo steps mov-

Brigham Young University Dancers

ing fwd (LOD). When on L turn face-to-face, when on R turn back-to-back. End in open ballroom pos facing ctr (M L-W R shldr twd ctr).

II. Brush and Slide

1–2   Brush L toe bkwd on R side of R (ct 1); brush L fwd (ct &); brush L bwd on L side of R (ct 2); tap L toe in back (L side of R) (ct &).

3–4   Move twd ctr with 4 Sliding steps.

5–8   Still retaining open ballroom pos (M L-W R shldr twd ctr) ptrs turn to face out of circle and repeat action of fig II, meas 1–4, with opp direction and ftwk.

9–16 Repeat action of fig II, meas 1–8. On last slide M turn to L and end facing LOD.

III. Polka

1–2   In closed ballroom pos cpl moves fwd LOD with 2 polkas; at same time turn once CW.

3–4   With 2 polkas M follows W as she turns once CW under joined hands (M L-W R), W holds skirt with L hand on turn.

5–16 Repeat action of fig III, meas 1–4, three more times (four in all). End in closed ballroom pos, M facing LOD.

IV. Forward, Back and Turn

1–2   M step fwd on L (ct 1); step in place on R (ct 2); step bkwd on L (ct 1); step in place on R (ct 2).

3–4   Beg L cpls turn once CW with 4 steps (cts 1, 2, 1, 2).

5–16 Repeat action of fig IV, meas 1–4, three more times (four in all). End M back to ctr.
      Note: M L hand may hold W R on his L hip or hands may be joined, and arms move freely fwd and back with the step. Ptrs should be very close together.

V. Push

A 1–4 Ptrs join hands with arms extended sdwd. Beg M L, cpls dance 4 Taconazo steps away from ctr (M fwd, W bkwd) as though M were pushing W. Body bends and arms move freely with the step.

5–8   Cpls move twd ctr (as though W is pushing M) with 4 Taconazo steps.

9–16 Repeat action of fig V, meas 1–8.
      Repeat dance from fig II (omit fig I).
      Repeat fig I, doing only 15 Taconazo steps.
      End dance with 2 stamps.

JESUSITA (or CHUCHITA) EN CHIHUAHUA

This tune, not to be confused with *La Jesusita,* was composed by Quirino Mendoza y Cortéz during the 1912 revolution against Porfirio Diaz. The composer, who was Alura's pianist, also wrote the very popular

Cielito Lindo. Chuchita is a nickname for Jesusita, which is a diminutive form of the name Jesus. The tune is also known as the *Jessie Polka. Jesusita en Chihuahua* was choreographed by Alura in the 1930's as a teaching device for Mexican dance steps. It was well received and continues to be a popular dance.

Costume: *Traje de polka,* or the special Adelita costume

Record: Peerless 45-3248-B—*Jesusita en Chihuahua*

Formation: Cpls in varsouvianne position; all facing CCW in a circle, M on inside.

Meter 2/4   Pattern

Action
Introduction

1–4   No action.

1. Polka CCW and CW

1–15 Starting with R ft, dance 15 polka steps CCW around circle, 1 polka step per bar.

16   Turn to face CW with 1 polka step, M remaining on inside of circle.

17–32 Repeat bars 1–16, moving CW.

2. Walk and turn

1–2   Walk fwd 4 steps: R ft, L ft, R ft, L ft (cts 1, 2, 1, 2).

3–4   M walks fwd 4 more steps while W turns once CW under M L arm with 4 walking steps.

5–16 Repeat bars 1–4 for a total of 4 times.

3. Polka CCW

1–16 Starting with R ft, dance 16 polka steps CCW around circle, 1 polka step per bar.

4. Slow turns. Change handhold to "courtesy turn" position.

1   Stamp R ft fwd (ct 1), close L ft to R ft (ct 2).

2   Stamp R ft back in original position (ct 1), close L ft to R ft (ct 2). Turn 90° CW with each 2-bar step.

3–32 Repeat bars 1–2 for a total of 16 steps and 4 turns.

5. Heel-toe step

1   Hopping on L ft, touch R heel diagonally fwd to R (ct 1), hopping on L ft, touch R toe across L ft (ct 2).

2   Repeat bar 1.

3   Moving away from ctr of circle, step to R with R ft (ct 1), close L ft to R ft (ct &), step to R with R ft (ct 2), close L ft to R ft (ct &).

4   Step to R with R ft (ct 1), close L ft to R ft (ct &), hop on both feet (ct 2).

5–8   Repeat bars 1–4, using opp ftwk and direction.

9–16 Repeat bars 1–8.

6. Slow turns

1–16 Repeat action of step 4, bars 1–16.

7. Polka CCW

1–16   Repeat action of step 3.

    8. Walk and turn

1–16   Repeat action of step 2.

    9. Taquachito—assume ballroom position

1   Step to M L with M L ft, W R with W R ft (ct 1), close free ft to wt-bearing ft (ct 2).

2–16   Repeat bar 1 for a total of 16 repetitions.

    Note: This step has a slight lean twd the wt-bearing ft, similar to the Merengue step. You may turn CW as a cpl during this step.

LAS CHIAPANECAS

This dance (Chee-AH-pah-NAY-kahs) was arranged by Señor Mariano Tapia, of the Palace of Fine Arts, Mexico City.

Record: Falcon FEP-29, Mariachi Nacional de Arcadio Elias

Formation: Dancers in 2 lines about 8 ft apart, M in one line with L shoulders twd music, W in opp line facing ptr. M clasp hands behind back, and W hold skirt high at both sides throughout dance. Keep rounded arms extended swd with elbows out unless otherwise directed. Skirt work is described with each fig of dance.

Steps and Styling: *Riding Step (2 meas):* Step fwd with L ft, toe turned out (ct 1), hop on L (ct 2), step fwd R (ct 3); step L slightly fwd (ct 1), hop on L (ct 2), step bwd R, toe out (ct 3). This step may also begin with R ft. When moving fwd, most of the traveling is done on ct 1 of meas 1.

Meas

1   *Riding Step Variation with Stamp (4 meas):* Stamp L across behind R (ct 1), hop on L, raising R over L instep, knee turned out (ct 2), step R slightly to R in front (ct 3).

2   Repeat action of meas 1, continuing to move twd R.

3–4   Step L (ct 1), hold (ct 2), stamp R L (cts 3, 1), hold (cts 2, 3). M only clap while stamping. This step may also be used turning R (CW). Beginning with stamp R across behind L, this step pattern may be used moving to L or turning L (CCW).

    Riding Step with Grapevine (4 meas): Moving to L, beginning with step-hop on R, dance one Riding Step pattern in place.

3–4   Step R across in front of L (ct 1), step swd L with L (ct 2), step R across in back (ct 3); step L to L (ct 1), step R across in front (ct 2), hold (ct 3). When moving to R, begin Riding Step with step-hop on L.

    Hook Waltz and Turn (2 meas): Moving fwd, step R L R (cts 1, 2, 3); small leap fwd onto L (ct 1); bending knees, hook R ft across behind L and make a full turn R (CW), shifting wt

from R to L ft during pivot. Next pattern repeats exactly. To face opp direction turn 1½ times.

Riding Step with Twist (2 meas): Step L (ct 1); hop L, turning R knee and toe twd R, R heel over L instep (ct 2); step R beside L (ct 3). Step L (ct 1); hop L, turning R knee in, R heel out with knee bent and toe raised from floor (ct 2); step R beside L (ct 3). This step pattern may also begin with step-hop on R. It may be used turning or moving fwd.

Balance, Leap, and Turn (4 meas): Small leap to L with L (ct 1), step R beside L (ct 2), step L in place (ct 3). Small leap to R with R (ct 1), step L beside R (ct 2), step R in place (ct 3). Step L to L (ct 1); leap and turn L (full turn CCW), completing turn with step on R (cts 2, 3); step L beside R (ct 1), hold (cts 2, 3). (M clap twice at end of pattern [cts 3, 1], hold [cts 2, 3].) This section is done on the balls of the ft. When pattern begins R to R, turn is to the R (CW).

Stamp and Shake Step (4 meas): Stamp L slightly behind R (ct 1), raise R ft fwd with a quick shake (modified mazurka) while hopping on L (ct 2), step R ft in front of L (ct 3).

2–3   Repeat action of meas 1 two more times.

4   Step L (ct 1), leap R to R (ct 2), step L in front of R (ct 3). Next pattern begins with stamp R behind L.

    Stamp Ending (2 meas): Stamp (ct 1), hold (ct 2), stamp R L (cts 3, 1); hold (cts 2, 3).

    Running Waltz: Three light running steps per meas (cts 1, 2, 3) with slight accent on ct 1 of each meas.

Hop, Leap

Throughout the dance, ftwk is identical for M and W except in figs III and VI.

Meter 3/4   Pattern

Meas

    Intro: 2 upbeats, no action

1–4   Both beginning R, stroll twd ptr with 4 steps (one step per meas) and make ½ turn R (CW) on last meas.

5–8   Return to own place with 2 steps (R L) and step R, turning R to face ptr (ct 1), hold (ct 2), stamp L R (cts 3, 1), hold (cts 2, 3). (Skirt: Both hands move skirt twd active ft.)

    I. Riding Step

1–6   Both beginning L, dance 3 Riding Steps to exchange places with ptr. Pass R shoulders.

7–8   Turn ½ CW with 4 quick steps, L R L R (cts 1, 2, 3, 1); hold (cts 2, 3). No wt on last step.

9–16 Beginning R, repeat action of fig I, meas 1–8, returning to own place.

17–32 Repeat action of fig I, meas 1–16, except that on meas 31–32 dancers finish with Stamp Ending as they turn to face ptr. (Skirt: When step is fwd hands move fwd; when step is bwd, hands return to place.)

II. Riding Step Variation with Stamp and Turn

1–4 Beginning with stamp L behind R and moving to own R, dance one pattern of Riding Step Variation with Stamp.

5–8 Beginning with stamp R behind L and moving to own L, dance one Riding Step Variation with Stamp.

9–12 Repeat action of fig II, meas 1–4, turning once CW in place.

13–16 Repeat action of fig II, meas 5–8, turning once CCW in place. (Skirt: On ct 1 move skirt to L; on ct 3 to R. Begin away from direction of travel.)

III. Riding Step with Grapevine

This pattern is performed changing places with ptr, beginning with M L shoulder near W R shoulder, both with backs twd music.

1–4 Both move swd to exchange places with ptr with one Riding Step with Grapevine pattern; M begin step-hop with R, W with L ft. W cross in front of M.

5–8 Beginning step-hop with M L, W R, repeat action of fig III, meas 1–4, returning to own place, with M crossing in front.

9–16 Repeat action of fig III, meas 1–8, except that on last meas M turn ½ R stamping L R (cts 1, 2), no wt on R; hold (ct 3), to finish with R shoulder twd ptr. (Skirt: On Riding Step use skirt as in fig I; on Grapevine hold skirt with no movement.)

IV. Hook-Waltz and Turn

1–4 Face ptr and both beginning R, change places with 2 Hook-Waltz and Turn patterns, passing R shoulders. Finish facing ptr.

5–8 Repeat action of fig IV, meas 1–4, returning to own place.

9–16 Repeat action of fig IV, meas 1–8, except that on meas 15–16 ptrs dance Stamp Ending R L R. (Skirt: Out to sides on fwd waltz; both hands in to chest on Hook Turn.)

V. Riding Step with Twist and Turn

1–6 Both beginning L, dance 3 Riding Step with Twist patterns to exchange places with ptr, passing R shoulders.

7–8 Turn in place to own R (CW) with 4 stamps, L R L R (cts 1, 2, 3, 1) hold, no wt on last stamp (cts 2, 3).

9–16 Repeat action of fig V, meas 1–8, again passing R shoulders and turning R to face ptr.

17–24 Repeat action of fig V, meas 1–8, turning once to own R (CW).

25–32 Repeat action of fig V, meas 17–24, beginning R behind L and turning to own L (CCW). Both finish with back twd music. (Skirt: Keep skirt still.)

VI. Balance, Leap, Turn, and Stamp

1–2 Beginning M L-W R, balance swd twd ptr and away from ptr.

3–4 With Leap and Turn pattern, ptrs exchange places, W crossing in front.

5–8 Beginning M R-W L, repeat action of fig VI, meas 1–4, returning to place. M cross in front.

9–16 Repeat action of fig VI, meas 1–8. (Skirt: Move skirt in direction of balance; keep still on turn.)

VII. Stamp and Shake Step

1–8 Face ptr and exchange places with 2 Stamp and Shake Step patterns, passing R shoulders. Finish turning R to face ptr on last leap.

9–16 Repeat action of fig VII, meas 1–8, returning to own place. Pass R shoulders. Finish with stamps R L. (Skirt: When R ft leads, hold R skirt fwd, L bwd. Change skirt pos on leap.)

VIII. Waltz, Turn, and Pose

1–4 Beginning R, change places with 2 Hook-Waltz and Turn patterns, passing R shoulders. Finish facing own place.

5–8 Repeat action of fig VIII, meas 1–4, returning to own place. Finish facing ptr.

9–12 Ptrs exchange places with 4 Running Waltz steps. Begin R and pass R shoulders. Finish facing ptr on last waltz (turn R).

13–14 Return to own side with 2 Running Waltz steps.

15–16 Stamp R (ct 1); hook L over R ft, turning R to finish beside ptr with back to music (M make ¾ turn, W ¼ turn), M L arm around W waist (ct 2); stamp L R (cts 3, 1), hold in pose (cts 2, 3). (Skirt: In meas 1–8, same as in fig IV; on Running Waltz, skirt follows leading ft.)

MEXICAN MIXER

A Tex-Mex dance presented by Nelda Drury, to be danced in a strutting northern Mexican style.

Record: Any good Mexican polka. Las Perlitas AFLP 1898 Viva Mexico; Atotonico Columbia EX 5110 Mariachi! The Sound of Mexico; RCA LP 1619.

Formation: Couples in a double circle in promenade crossed hand position (R to R, L to L) facing LOD, W to R of M. Step directions are for M; W does counterpart throughout dance.

Part I

M starts on L ft, W does counterpart beg R.

Take 4 steps in LOD (ct 1, &, 2, &). Turn to face ptr, continue LOD, M step to side with L ft (ct 1), step R in back of L (ct &), step L to L (ct 2), touch R beside L (ct &). Repeat Part I in opp dir, M beg on R ft, W on L. Finish by dropping L hands, M facing out, W facing in, R hands joined.

Part II

Form a single circle by joining L hands with person in adjacent couple. All balance fwd, M step R (ct 1), tch L (ct &); and bwd, M step L (ct 2), tch R (ct &), (M away from center, W twd center). Release L hands, turn half CW with ptr (ct 1, &, 2, &), rejoin hands in a single circle, M facing center, W facing out. Balance fwd and back (release R hands, turn CCW with joined L hands until W faces LOD, M continues turn until facing LOD (same ct as before for balance and turn). Take promenade crossed hands pos with new ptr. Repeat entire dance as many times as desired.

SANTA RITA

Santa Rita (SAHN-tah REE-tah) is a couple dance from northern Mexico. The dance description was provided by Nelda Drury.

Record: "Santa Rita," Express (45 rpm) 411B; C.B.S. EPC 393 (Columbia—45 rpm)

Formation: Cpls in open pos facing LOD with free hands joined and pointing twd LOD. Steps are described for M. W use opp ftwk unless otherwise noted.

Steps and Styling: Santa Rita should be danced gaily and with exuberance. Polka, Stamp, Push

Bounce: With wt on both ft, raise heels (upbeat). Lower heels (downbeat).

Taconazo: Step on R (ct 1), strike L heel on floor (pick it up immediately) (ct &); lift R heel, leaving ball of ft on floor, and snap R heel on floor (ct 2); strike L heel on floor, picking it up immediately (ct &). Repeat of step begins with step on L.

Quebrado or "Broken Ankle" (without wt)—as done in fig VI: Step on one ft, turning ankle of free ft out, no wt. (Be sure to transfer wt supporting ft before turning ankle of free ft.) Ft alternate on these steps, which are danced in even rhythm.

Quebrado or "Broken Ankle" (with wt): See end of fig II.

Meter 2/4   Pattern
Meas

Intro: No musical intro. Dance begins after the words "Santa Rita" and 2 pick-up notes.

I. Fwd Polka and Stamps

1-4   Begin L, dance 4 polka steps fwd in LOD bend-ing the body fwd on meas 1 and 3 and holding the body upright on meas 2 and 4.

5   Facing ptr, step on L in front and slightly to R of R (ct 1), step on R in front and slightly to L of L (ct 2).

6   Facing LOD, bend body from waist and point joined hands twd floor as you stamp L (ct 1), stamp R (ct &), stamp L (ct 2), hold (ct &).

7   Moving in RLOD but facing ptr, step sdwd on R (ct 1), close L to R (ct &), step sdwd on R (ct 2), hold (ct &).

8   Bending body from waist and pointing joined hands twd stamping ft, stamp L (ct 1), stamp L (ct 2).

9-16   Repeat action of fig I, meas 1-8.

II. Sdwd Two-Step and "Broken Ankle"

1   Facing ptr, step sdwd L on L (ct 1), close R to L (ct &), step sdwd L on L (ct 2), hold (ct &).

2   Step on R in front and slightly to L of L ("Broken Ankle") (ct 1), step on L in front and slightly to R of R (ct 2).

3-4   Repeat action of fig II, meas 1-2, in opp direction with opp ftwk.

5-16   Repeat action of fig II, meas 1-4, three more times.

"Broken Ankle" (with wt) is optional. Place the outer side of R ft on floor far enough to side to prevent foot and leg from making a sharp bend. The ankle must bear wt for a moment. Be careful! It can be dangerous.

III. Polka

1-16   In closed ballroom pos dance 16 turning polka steps traveling in LOD and turning CW. This polka is like a bouncy two-step with no hop. Arms go down and up with the movement of the body.

IV. Balance and Wrap

1-2   Facing ptr with both hands joined straight across, M facing LOD, both beg R; balance fwd (twd ptr) with one polka step (R shldrs adjacent); balance bkwd (away from ptr) with one polka step.

3-4   Dance 2 polka steps into "wrap" pos: With M R-W L joined hands at waist level and M L-W R joined hands held high, W turn L (CCW) under raised joined hands to finish at M R side. M drop M L-W R joined hands over the W to waist level.

5-6   In "wrap" pos balance fwd and back with 2 polka steps.

7-8   M dance 2 polka steps in place as you help W turn back to place. Dancing 2 polka steps, W turn R (CW) under M L-W R raised joined hands.

9-10   Repeat action of fig IV, meas 1-2, but this time L shldrs adjacent.

11–12 Repeat action of fig IV, meas 3–4, but W turn R under M R-W L raised joined hands to finish at M L side.

13–14 Repeat action of fig IV, meas 5–6.

15–16 Still in "wrap" pos, again balance fwd and back with 2 polka steps. (*Do not* unwrap!)

V. Taconazo and Push

1–4 Facing LOD and still in "wrap" pos, dance 4 Taconazo steps in place: R, L, R, L.

5–8 Beg R, dance 7 push steps to the R, finishing with a bounce on both ft.

9–16 Repeat action of fig V, meas 1–8, beg L and moving L.

Interlude

1–2 Dropping M R-W L hands, M step R, L, R, hold in place while W dance a three-step turn to the L (L, R, L, hold).

3–4 Both turn with 4 steps to finish in closed ballroom pos, M facing LOD: M make one full turn L (CCW) stepping L, R, L, R; W turn 1½ to R (CW), stepping R, L, R, L.

VI. "Apache" Step and "Broken Ankle"

This whole figure is danced "cheek-to-cheek" and bent fwd at waist so that the derrière protrudes.

1–2 Moving in LOD, step fwd on L, pushing joined hands fwd twd W hip (ct 1), step in place on R (ct &), step bkwd on L, pulling joined hands back twd M hip (ct 2), step in place on R (ct &). Repeat action of meas 1.

3–4 With joined hands at M hip and beg L, M walk fwd 8 steps, turning heel of trailing ft out with each step (keep front of ft in contact with floor—hips do not turn or twist). W walk bkwd with "Broken Ankle" (no wt) on trailing or fwd ft.

5–16 Repeat action of fig VI, meas 1–4, three more times.

VII. Bouncy Heel and Toe (to ctr and out)

1 Standing upright in closed ballroom pos with M facing LOD, hop on R placing L heel out to L (ct 1), hop on R placing L toe across in front of R (ct 2).

2 Moving twd ctr, step sdwd L on L (ct 1), close R to L (ct &), step sdwd L on L (ct 2), hold (ct &).

3 Step on R in front and slightly to L of L "Broken Ankle" (ct 1), step on L in front and slightly to R of R (ct 2).

4 Step on R beside L (ct 1), bounce on both ft (ct 2).

5–8 Repeat action of fig VII, meas 1–4, with opp ftwk and moving in opp direction.

9–16 Repeat action of fig VII, meas 1–8.

VIII. Fwd Polka and Stamps

1–16 Repeat action of fig I, meas 1–16.

IX. Sdwd Two-Step and "Broken Ankle"

1–16 Repeat action of fig II, meas 1–16.

X. Fwd Polka and Stamps

1–15 Repeat action of fig I, meas 1–15.

16 Still facing LOD, stamp L with body bent from waist and joined hands pointed twd stamping ft (ct 1), stamp L with joined hands extended overhead and body upright (ct 2).

THE ORIENT

Oriental (Belly) Dancing

by Ibrahim Farrah

In the early 1970s what many people referred to as a craze was actually a resurgence of interest in dance. A further resurgence took place in what dance specialists call "oriental dancing" and lay people "belly dancing." The movement that began at this time surprised many skeptics. Long-time professionals viewed it as one of those momentary periods where people became curious about this form of dance. Others viewed it as a very commercial craze, one where serious practitioners of the art became skeptical because they felt that a misunderstood art form was being further misunderstood because of resulting commercial developments. This commercialism produced unqualified professionals to teach and merchants who sold a lot of junk. But the movement has survived this commercialism and people have begun to understand the course this form of dance has taken and to view it in a different perspective.

In the course of the 1970s, much has been written about the expanding dance audience in America. This growth serves to strengthen our credibility and enables us to find a place in the dance scene. Furthermore, more and more is being written about the physical and emotional benefits to be derived from dance. This, of course, aids the movement in general. A lot of this interest is actually rooted in the early 1960s, when the Kennedy era put a great deal of emphasis on physical fitness in our country. As a result, we saw the growth of health clubs throughout the United States. Many people eventually became bored with machines and straight exercise classes. Today these clubs offer "dancersize" as well as classes in various forms of dance to impress upon its members the fact that movement can be fun. Amazingly, what has come about is a resurgence of interest in ethnic dance, customs, and music. What is amazing about this phenomenon

Süheyla Dancers. Photo by Milwaukee Journal

is the intensity with which people are seeking to discover their roots.

America has in the past been referred to as a melting pot; at the present time it is once again living up to this image. Though many people began by studying oriental dancing, this served as a stepping stone, whetting their appetites for greater exposure to the folkloric dances of the Middle East as well as exotic oriental dances. Americans are not the only ones to benefit from this renewed interest; all folk dancers will benefit as well. People are again dancing the traditional dance forms of their ancestors. Even more unique is the fact that interest of this nature often leads people to become interested in other ethnic dance forms. Thus, ethnic dancing is currently being offered in dance schools, recreational centers, Y's, adult education centers, health clubs, and social centers. People several generations removed from their immigrant ancestors have begun to study these dances as part of their heritage. Once they start to study, they become aware of the real fun involved in this sort of exploration. At weddings, when the participants have an ethnic background, the music and festivities that follow the ceremony have begun to embrace the American as well as the ethnic backgrounds of the families. People from all walks of life and all races seem to be participating in this new mood. In a typical class one finds a diversity of backgrounds and reasons for attending.

The student may be a nurse, a college student, a secretary, or an artist. Once again dance is proving to be a universal language.

(Ibrahim Farrah is involved in this field as a performer, a director and chief choreographer of his own troupe (the Near East Dance Group), a noted teacher and lecturer in classes and seminars given across the

Ibrahim Farrah Near East Dance Group. Photo by Lee Marshall

Ibrahim Farrah. Photo by Richard Sutor

country and, since 1975, as editor and publisher of *Arabesque,* a journal dedicated to Middle Eastern dance and culture. He has made several trips to the Middle East, undertaking intensive research on the dance and music traditions of that part of the world. His dance troupe has been in existence since 1975.)

Danse Orientale (Belly Dancing)

by Süheyla (Kate McGowan)

"The dancing was so ancient, so unchanging, that I found it soothing and refreshing. For how many thousands of years had the village women danced so . . ." Joyce Roper, *The Women of Nar* (London: Putnam, 1975).

Dance in the Near and Middle East, like other areas of ancient culture, falls into two main categories. One is folk dance, or dances with no specific creator, which grows out of communal expression. The other is traditional dance, which, along the way, has achieved a near-classical form, being a more formal distillation of all dance forms that preceded it, both ritualistic and folk, and performed by a smaller group selected

for its skill. Here we will briefly describe the evolution of the latter category—a dance form derived from ritual and folk elements, both aristocratic and peasant, and performed down through the ages by professional musicians and dancers, from temple priestesses and court-trained artists to street dancers.

A traditional form still observed by professional dancers—having specific sequences of mood, rhythm, and tempo changes—may have been shaped during the ninth and tenth centuries A.D., when Baghdad was the cultural center of Islam and Arabic music was being cultivated and annotated. Yet the most essential characteristics of this dance—a rhythmical and repetitive rocking and swaying of the body, an undulation of the torso—have their source in ancient societies, particularly those in which a female deity reigned over the life cycles.

Some vivid examples of societies in which this dance is rooted range from the settlement at Catal Hüyük (Chatal Hooyook) in Asia Minor, dating from about 7000 B.C., where female statuettes depict the fruit of the womb emerging from the navel, to the temples of Isis in Egypt and the cults surrounding the goddess Astarte, first in Syria and later in Carthage in North Africa.

From the beginning, rhythmical movement and sound were the instruments through which man sought to create a balance and harmony between himself and a mysterious universe. To achieve this harmony, the vibrations of voice and instrument were completely integrated with body movement. True *danse orientale,* still related to its original concept, exists only in connection with the music. Terms used to describe the mood or style of the dance are often musical terms and, conversely, rhythms trace their descent from dance movement, further confirming their inseparability.

Drawing on this concept of the "music of the spheres" and the music of the ancient world, extending from India to Syria, Egypt, and North Africa, scholars like Avicenna and al-Farabi codified Arabic music, which in turn delineated the shape of *danse orientale.* This was but one moment in history that helps to define the nature of this dance.

Given the profusion of religious and cultural differences in the Near and Middle East, it is impossible to trace a single chronological skein in the evolution of music and dance, just as it is impossible to draw definite lines between the sacred and secular (i.e., ritual and folk) motivations that influenced *danse orientale.* A few other moments in history illustrate the exposure of formerly sacred dance rites, to the general populace: the fluid, serpentine movement of Asian dancers sent as tribute to the Pharaonic courts of the Middle Kingdoms, which had been more familiar with strong, angular movement and acrobatic feats; the dispersement of the dancers into the North African countryside to make their own way after the destruction of the temples of Astarte at Carthage; the appearance in the Mogul (Moslem) court of *devadassis,* who until then had danced only for their Hindu gods in the temples of southern India.

Over the centuries, myriad ethnic groups have added their influence, including the peoples of the Caucasus and Central Asia, Turks, Slavs, Berbers and other nomadic groups, and Africans.

In each region, from North Africa through the eastern Arab world to Afghanistan, some distinct style of *danse orientale* is known. It is referred to either by a musical mode or rhythm, such as chiftitelli, karshilama, taqsim; by a regional style, such as the beledi of the village or rakasi, the undulating style of movement of women in the Levant; or by the name of a caste or tribe of professionals who perform publicly.

The specific technique of *danse orientale* corresponds completely to the manner of dance popular among the people of the Near and Middle East. There is an emphasis on: isolated movements of the torso; strong emotion conveyed through arm and hand gestures and facial expression; pride of carriage and balance; small and precise steps right under the body, where footwork is involved; and a sense of community among dancer, musicians, and audience. But the dictates of society, particularly under Islam, forbade dancing in public except by those who were often trained since childhood to perform that role, and who were members of guilds and tribes and made their way through life as entertainers.

In Morocco belly dancing is done by women called Shikhat; the Almeé of Egypt were highly skilled performers who were welcomed into the *sarays* of the wealthy and powerful; while the Ghawazi were street dancers who often performed in *beledi* or village style. The dance called rakasi in the Levant is called the Arab dance in Persia, and chiftitelli in Anatolia and the Balkans means the lively dance of the Gypsies, without whom no wedding, circumcision celebration, or festival can properly proceed. Even the Nautch dancers of northern India, whose movements—both elegant and ribald—describe the adventures of the god Krishna in human form, share some of the elementary movements of *danse orientale.*

Styles differ greatly from one region to another, but the term *traditional* nevertheless best describes the dance known to the Western world by the French *danse du ventre,* or the North American belly dance. Both terms fall short of describing the real dance, and no Arab terms refer to the belly as such, although the primary focus of the dance, in its many variations, is on the abdomen as the physical center and as the source of all movement. Unfortunately, twentieth-century dance historians usually refer to belly dancing as though it were a tangential—and always decadent—phenomenon in the Near East, neglecting to explore or analyze its intrinsic role in the culture.

The *danse orientale,* which has captured the imagination of so many people in the Western world and has motivated thousands of women to participate in dance classes, was born in the 1920s in the cabarets of the Near East. Until then, as we now realize, the movements, steps, melodies, and rhythms that make up *danse orientale* were not a single entity. Skilled professional dancers who later became fine artists, like Badia Messabni, Tahia Carioca, Samia Gamal, and Hoda Shems Edin, presented general audiences with artful interpretations of dances previously known only in their natural context, the latter ranging from sophisticated salons to village festivals and tribal rituals.

Consciously or unconsciously, today's artist draws on these following diverse sources: the elemental undulating, serpentine, and cyclical movements that celebrate the source of life; the lyrical beauty of facial expression and hand gestures originating in the Far East; the rhythmical energy of pelvic thrusts, dips, snaps, and swings typical of North African dance; and the trembling, whirling, and trancelike states of the shaman and the dervish. She practices the age-old custom of rhythmical self-accompaniment with finger cymbals, and the mysterious illusions created by veiling to enhance expression of mood. These are the elements necessary to present a complete *danse orientale.*

Like an arabesque motif in a mosaic pattern, the *danse orientale* is mysterious and intricate. What appeal, then, does it have for those who learn the basics of this dance in private classes, YM-YWCAs, and adult education and community college facilities across the nation? Two threads link these ancient practices to our own lives. First, of all traditional dance techniques, *danse orientale* is the most direct descendent of ancient rhythmical motion. Second, it provides a direct and natural communication between the body, mind, and spirit that often answers the need in our lives for heightened personal awareness.

(After spending two years at the Martha Graham dance studio in New York City in the mid-fifties, Süheyla (Kate McGowan) became involved with folk dance, primarily of the Balkans and the Middle East. Since then she has studied and performed with amateur groups in Belgrade, Yugoslavia; with the Turk Folker Kurumu Association in Istanbul, which included tours to festivals in Bulgaria and Spain; and with the international dance ensemble Westwind in San Francisco.

Süheyla. Photo by Lannie Robbins

Under her direction, the Art Worlds dance troupe Ta' ammulät fi Buhayrit al-Zaman [Reflections in the Pool of Time] offers performances of Middle Eastern dance. Süheyla is the author of *The Ancient and Enduring Art . . . Danse Orientale* (Ann Arbor, Mich.: Edwards Brothers, 1977), and has written articles for *Arabesque* and *Viltis* magazines.)

Danse Orientale Technique

by Süheyla

Records: Music for an Orientale Dance, Vols. 1 and 2, label: Voice of Lebanon, Peters Intl., dist." Kanoon and Flute, Phillips; How to Make Your Husband a Sultan (Özel Türkbas), Elay.

No matter what the individual style of a performer, or which the ethnic or ritual tracings in a single *danse orientale* interpretation, there are throughout the Middle East several related elements to concept and technique of movement that define it as a *Middle Eastern* dance and distinguishes it from the other dance forms.

The lower spine and the sets of muscles which form the pelvic girdle become the physical center for a dancer. The elements which distinguish *danse orientale* from other forms are also related to the physical center,

and how movement is created around it. The flow of movement in *danse orientale* is from the center outward through hips, chest, arms and hands, and even facial expression, with a sense of giving and reaching out that, once expended, cycles back to its own center for renewal of energy. The whole has a quality of continuous cycles—gestures that move from center are completed with a return to center—drawing the focus to the movements of the torso itself.

The most basic movements that compose all variations of *danse orientale* are undulation, thrust, rotation, shaking and pulsing of the whole body, but especially of the torso. Artful refinement of these basic movements results in alternating fluid, serpentine torso movements to quick, controlled thrusting or shaking of separate parts of the body in isolation.

The physical technique used to create such dance movements is a highly developed sense of inverted pyramidal balance, with knees and feet always closely parallel, knees never locked to allow a free yet weighty and earthbound quality about the hips and, in contrast, a proud yet easy, high carriage of the chest, head and arms. Success hinges on the skill to control and move each part of the body in isolation, and then, through various combinations, to create beautiful patterns of movement in a small space. Much of the beauty lies in subtle movement when it is done simply and wholeheartedly—the lift of a shoulder, the snap of a hip, or a glance.

The intent is to express emotions ranging from joy to mourning, from playfulness to worship in a manner in keeping with a continuing, though evolving, way of life that is centuries old. The effect within a whole dance moves from compelling excitement and hypnotic reiteration to soothing sensuousness then back again to joyful resolution.

Terms: plié—to bend or flex both knees deeply; relevé—to lift the body by raising up to the balls of the feet, i.e., onto half-toe; [if] properly done, the muscles on the inside of the legs to up under the buttocks tighten; pivot—to turn the body around itself as though whirling around an axis, i.e., the spinal column; forward/back/diagonal, usually abbreviated as fwd./bk./diag., refers to pelvic or rib cage movement in relation to one's own center, and not to a traveling movement unless specifically stated as such.

The first position for *danse orientale* is a basic centered stance from which all step variations begin and end; rib cage lifted out of the waist so little hollows appear just under the lower ribs, and chest open so one feels wide between the shoulders, shoulders relaxed . . . arms out away from the body, slightly rounded at the elbow and the hands a natural extension of the arms, fingers open . . . knees and feet close together and parallel, with enough flex in the knees so they do not lock—ever—and toes slightly turned out for balance . . . the pelvis held correctly by the small contraction necessary to straighten out the lower spine and to smooth out the crease where the lower abdominal muscles run into the thighs.

A second basic position in this technique is to place one foot forward, only so far that the fwd. foot-heel is even with the bk. foot-big toe. This changes the alignment of balance: weight on the bk. foot and the corresponding arm held more fwd. of the body . . . arm corresponding to fwd. foot held out to side . . . the head and gaze also turn in the direction of diag. pointed by the fwd. foot. All else remains the same. This position directs the focus of the dance gesture to the side of the body which has the foot forward.

Shoulder isolations very quickly become part of the *danse orientale* vocabulary. One movement is to circle the shoulders, holding arms curved out from body, hands at hip level . . . alternate from right to left, and concentrate on moving only the ball of the shoulder: right fwd./lift/pull back/relax. Left: repeat to four counts, always starting the fwd. move on count 1: a moderate to slow *masmudi saghir* or *rhumba* is fine music for this.

For another, holding arms out wide at chest level, start slowly: shrug the ball of the right shoulder in a tiny move fwd. and relax immediately . . . alternating with the left . . . count 1–2, 1–2. When this [movement] is done . . . quickly (never very fast) so that alternate shoulder moves fwd. on each count 1 as the opposite relaxes, it [represents] the basic movement for a shoulder or bust shimmy.

The general points to remember about basic placement of arms and hands are: (1) they are carried out and slightly forward of the body so elbows are visible from the corners of the eyes, rounded at the elbow with the hands a simple extension of the arm, fingers open and the thumb held in opposition to the middle finger; (2) each arm has its own territory—from center front to center back, from hip level to high over head, and does not generally cross the center line of the body; (3) the arms work in opposition, the lower, outreaching gesture corresponding to the dancing hip while the other is drawn into the side bearing the weight.

For snake arms—or rippling arms—the nature changes somehow with the size of the movement: hold arms wide and slightly rounded; then, starting from the center of the back, lift and roll the ball of the shoulder so the back of the elbow and then the wrist lift toward the ceiling . . . to lower it, drop the shoulder first, then the elbow, and the hand last. Counting to four beats to the measure, the alternate shoulder starts the lift on each count 1, and the focus is on the lifting arm.

For Egyptian (or Pharaonic) arms: the technique is the same—shoulder, elbow, hand last, but the arms are held forward of the body.

The dance is structured around the natural and possible movements that the torso can make. These fall into a few large family groups that are related by their essential similarity in execution and effect; rotation, thrust, undulation and trembling or shaking, i.e., shimmy. Once the basic technique becomes natural, along with some of the essentials of music and traditional sources, using one's imagination will keep *danse orientale* alive and fresh.

Conscious of the dancer's physical center, with half the body above it and half below, try to sense in the space around you the four sides of a square: front, back, right and left sides; and the diagonals through the body from the four corners; and, of course, the circles.

A simple illustration of how we use geometrically defined space is to imagine that with four thrusts of the right hip, you will turn once around yourself. Each time the thrust starts, control or place the initial lift of the hip toward each of four sides of the square: fwd./left side/back/right side.

Rotation refers to the slow, full circling of *one* hip repeatedly, while the figure 8 refers to the alternate circling of both hips. There are four possible basic patterns. All share several points in technique for graceful execution: (a) beginning and finishing in one of the two basic positions; and (b) since the pattern is circular, the move extends around four touch points: starting center—back-1/side-2/fwd.-3/return center-4, for example.

Forward to back rotation: the hip twists fwd. to accent count 1 . . . presses out to side . . . back . . . finishes circle center. The plane of rotation is parallel to the floor, so keep both knees flexed and the weight on the heels. To glide smoothly into alternate hip rotation, or figure 8, do not pause in center on count 4 but glide on through to accent the next count 1. This is true for all figure 8 patterns.

Side to side rotations are on a *vertical* plane to the floor, so the circle is shaped by a much deeper plié in the knees as the hip slides down and extends out to the side on count 1 . . . begin to straighten both knees, but press the ball of the extended hip toward the floor and lift the heel, raising that hip on count 2 . . . draw into alignment on count 3 . . . center on count 4.

Back to forward rotation, also called *hip-roll;* on count 1 press the hip up toward the back by straightening the knee . . . circle side to forward by turning the knee inward and twisting the heel outward. This rotation has a more snaky quality because the exaggerated lift in the rib cage, needed to counterbalance the hip pressed back, results in an abdominal undulation, giving the movement a strong, fluid quality that is especially beautiful.

The fourth rotation differs from the others because the muscles of the torso, not the legs, do most of the engineering. Contract the muscles of the torso on the side as though pulling up under the rib cage, lifting the hip upward so the toe nearly leaves the floor . . . extend hip out to side and lower it, flexing the knees to allow the drop . . . draw hip in and up to center to complete movement. The particular isolation in this rotation has an unusual, disjointed effect rather than [a] flowing [one], and may be from North African dance.

Hip thrust is best defined as an energetic lift/sit-to-center of one hip, with the hip pressed up on an *and* count, then dropping to center on the accent beat of the music. This step represents the earthbound character of *danse orientale,* in which the tossing hips must drop as though weighted by loads of sashes and jewelry.

Forward hip thrust: assume second basic position so right toe is forward, weight on left foot, holding upper torso centered, twist the pelvis so that hip bone is pressed fwd./up by straightening both knees a little, but turning the right heel outward . . . relax the knees, the hip drops back to center position.

Side hip thrust differs only in that the hip is lifted to the side, so the feet must be placed side by side. To move *to* the side in either direction with hip thrust—to the right, for example: step right, press hip up at the same time, counting *and* . . . release hip while closing left foot to right and centering, counting the beat. Thus, four hip thrusts to side are counted: and 1, and 2, and 3, and 4. Done very quickly it becomes a hip bounce. An interesting movement would be to move in the same way with a fwd. thrust, in a fwd. diagonal line, but usually to travel fwd. and back, alternating fwd. hip thrusts are used. This is called:

Egyptian walk, which has a very grand and deliberate air to it. The pattern is: right hip lift/sit —and 1 . . . step to right foot —2 . . . left hip lift/sit —and 3 . . . step to left foot —4.

Hip movement variations include the hip lift, the hip dip, and hip swings. The hip snap is a short and quick hip move that comes to a sudden stop by deep contraction in the thigh and buttock muscles.

To pivot slowly turn around oneself in one spot with a fwd. hip thrust, or a back/fwd. hip rotation.

Undulation (abdominal rolls), or the rippling, fluid tightening and relaxing of the abdominal muscles, is probably the most elemental and earthy movement in *danse orientale.*

The basic fwd./back undulation is a body wave that starts each time with a lift of the rib cage and finishes in a pelvic contraction so the lower spine is straight and the buttocks tucked down and under. Standing with one foot fwd., weight on back foot, knees relaxed, the back of the hands resting on hip back—and remembering the little clockwise sequence: stretch rib cage fwd./up —1 . . . relax abdominal muscles from diaphragm, to waist, to lower abdomen—and ah 2 . . . swing pelvis down and forward into flexing knees —3 . . . contract, pulling in deeply at the waist and continuing contraction down spine so buttocks tuck under and small of back is flat —and 4. To repeat from this contracted position, release the rib cage first to lift into the initial forward stretch.

Remembering the sequence by this image still works—a large drop of jasmine-scented, jade-green oil has fallen into the hollow of your throat: pretend, as it starts to slither down your body, that you will slow its course, first by lifting the bosom, then relaxing forward the stomach, the waist, the belly, then, as a last movement, you tilt the navel upward and catch the drop of jasmine oil, to hold it there like a jewel.

The basic shimmy is essentially [composed of] very short, quick up/down or back/forth alternations of the hips. If it is possible, basic posture and isolation are even more important to successful shimmies, so that the upper torso and arms do not shake along with the hips. The technique is the same: flex the knees and keep them close together, keep the heels stationary—either flat on floor or on half-toe, move hips by pressing knees back and tightening thigh muscles alternately.

Traveling steps and walks are infinite in their variations but share the single rule of keeping all steps small and right under the body. The *Persian* walk is to step/close/step, keeping the shoulders parallel forward, so that any hip movement is isolated. Usually one glides along because the feet hardly leave the floor, and the flexed knees absorb any jarring or jerking.

The *Beledi* walk does not continue forward but moves from and to the center, like the spokes of a wheel, in four steps, so each repeated sequence starts on the same foot. Step forward right —1 and left —2 . . . step back right —3 and left —4.

The tradition of dancing in and with great swaths of diaphanous fabric has very early origins and has been enriched by custom over the centuries. As we dance we use our veils to reflect images of these many origins and [to] express [our] feeling about them in our time.

Some of the general points to remember about handling the veil: as you tuck the veil drape to start, hold the veil by the upper long—three yard—edge, so that you know approximately where the center edge and the corners are. Hold the veil firmly between thumb and the index and ring fingers. The arms, when moving the veil around the body, must have especially full reach, still slightly rounded at elbow. When holding one veil section overhead, place the hand high and back of the head; otherwise the line of the flowing fabric is broken. When placing the veil over the nose or under the chin to frame the face, hold edge with hands about 30 inches apart, place the edge as you wish first, then, as you raise your hands to meet back of the head to hold veil in place, spread your elbows wide, and out to the side, under the fabric. This drapes beautifully, frames the face, keeps arms covered, and the veil where you put it.

Dancers have been keepers of their own rhythm by means of some hand-held device since ancient times. Finger cymbals serve this purpose traditionally. *Zill* is the Turkish word for a cymbal, *ziller* is plural; in Arabic they are called *sagât*. Usually they are played to accent certain sequences and high points of the dance.

THE PHILIPPINES

Philippine Folk Dancing

by Francisca Reyes Aquino

Because of the scattered positions of [its more than seven thousand] islands, a great variety of dances are found in the Philippines. As a people, the Filipinos love singing, dancing, and feasting. For centuries, singing, playing musical instruments, and dancing have been the recreational activities of the people. They have dances and songs for all occasions.

Philippine folk dances of today have the peculiar combination of Spanish and oriental movements. The majority of the dances found in the Philippines are of Spanish origin, and a few bear French, English, American, and Malayan influences. They have become traditionally Filipino. Some examples of dances showing marked foreign influences are: (1) La Jota, Areuana, Pandango—with Spanish influence; (2) Ba-Ingles—with English influence; (3) Alcamfor, Pasakat—with French influence; (4) Birginia, Lanceros—with American influence; [and] (5) Kandingan, Sua-Sua, Kapiil sa Munsala—with Malayan influence.

Some 25 years ago, Philippine folk dances were in danger of extinction and replacement by foreign dances. No books or music on folk dances were available, for none had been written. They were simply

handed down from generation to generation, undergoing changes from time to time as they were performed.

Interest in Philippine folk dances was revived in 1927 when Dr. Jorge Bocobo, then Acting President of the University of the Philippines, decided to send th[is] writer, then instructor of physical education at the State University, to some provinces of Luzon, the Visayas, and Mindanao to do research on such dances. There the old people were the living source of materials and information.

In 1934, Dr. Bocobo created an Advisory Committee on Folk Dances and Songs in the State University. From 1934 to 1938, the Committee made an intensive study of folk music, songs, and dances. Not only were songs and dances collected, but also authentic costumes and musical instruments. As a result of this research a book entitled *Philippine National Dances* was published. People became more enthusiastic about learning folk dances, witnessing folk dance demonstrations and attending lectures on folk dances.

In 1937, the University of the Philippines Folk Song and Dance Club was organized. In 1940, the Bureau of Education Folk Dance Club was organized under the auspices of the Department of Physical Education,

Betty Casey

Instruction Division, of that bureau. This club was composed of public school teachers and high school students. In 1949, the Philippine Folk Dance Society was organized, with members from all walks of life. The interest of the people in folk dancing has become permanent.

Philippine dances include national and local or regional dances. There are occupational dances, religious and ceremonial dances, courtship and wedding dances. There are dances performed in connection with a celebration, a feast, a barrio fiesta, good harvest, good fortune or favors granted, and other social gatherings. The majority of folk dances belong to this group. War dances show imaginary combat. There are comic dances and game dances. Philippine dances, like many other dances, are affected by climatic conditions. The warm climate is not conducive to vigorous or strenuous movements. Hence, energetic and fast movements are seldom found in them.

Philippine dances may have special distinguishing features. There are dances with songs and with the use of objects or implements. Among the implements used are coconut shells, wooden sticks, fans and hand-

kerchiefs, glasses of wine, lighted oil lamps *(tinghoy)*, bamboo poles or pestles struck together by the helpers, hats, anklets or bells *(singuel)*, bamboo or wooden castanets, *anahaw* leaves (a kind of palm) and war implements such as bolos, spears, shields, *kris*.

As a rule the dances begin and end with a *saludo* (salute) to partner, to audience, or to honored guests. A *saludo* is a three-step turn in place and a bow. Partners dance about six or eight feet apart from each other. There is little, if any, bodily contact.

There are about 50 fundamental steps used in Philippine dances. Some of them are of foreign origin, like the polka series, step-swing series, waltz series, close, mazurka, change, *paso español*, touch, gallop, slide, *habenera*, and bleking steps. The traditional steps indigenous to the country are the *papuri, haplik, chotis, kuradang, contradansa, itik-itik, panadyak, piangpiang*, sway balance series, *engaño* series, *espunti, bacui*, pivot turn with *sarok* and point.

The arm positions used are: lateral position, fourth position, one hand on waist and the other holding the skirt, both hands on waist, arms in lateral position with forearm turns, fifth position to fifth amplified, fifth position moving sideward right and left, both hands holding skirt, arms bent forward, arms in *hayon-hayon* (one forearm bent in front and the other bent behind the body, both forearms at waist level), one hand encircled overhead and the other bent forward at shoulder level. Generally, there is a *kumintang* (turning of wrist clockwise or counterclockwise) at the close of a movement.

(The above material, condensed from an article that appeared in the December 1952 issue of the *Journal of the American Association for Health and Physical Education* [vol 23, no. 10, p. 10] is used here with permission.

In 1924 the late Francisca Reyes Aquino began to collect folk dances, songs, and games. A portion of the material gathered from 1924 to 1926 was used in her master's thesis, which was later revised and published in book form as *Philippine Folk Dances and Games.* For several years further research was officially conducted by Lt. Antonino Beunaventura, the late Ramon P. Tolentino, Jr., and the author under the auspices of the President's Committee on Folk Dances and Songs, University of the Philippines. Costumes, music, and musical instruments were collected, as well as songs and dances. A later book, *Philippine National Dances,* was coauthored by Reyes-Tolentino (Aquino). The manuscript for the book, representing years of research by Francisca R. Tolentino (Aquino), was sent to the United States just prior to the Japanese invasion of the Philippines. Publication was delayed for five years until the end of hostilities. The beloved Mrs. Aquino is known as the mother of Philippine folk dance. She devoted her adult life to teaching and sharing dances she loved with her own people and the world. She taught at many folk dance sessions in the United States.)

Visayan Dances of the Philippines

by Libertad V. Fajardo

The Philippines are divided into three regions, namely, Luzon, Visayas, and Mindanao. Located South and Southwest of Luzon are the Visayan islands. Visayan folk songs and dances have been handed down as survivals of early culture and heritage.

While barrio life retains some real native dances and music, Filipino town life in the eighteenth and nineteenth centuries drew the great majority of its music, dancing, social graces, and even its games and amusements from Mexico and Central American sources. The older native dances were decidedly mimetic in type and were always rather serious, joyousness or pleasure being seldom if ever expressed. The Spanish influence brought in a quite different psychology, in which active rhythmic movement and open expression of pleasure or emotion were characteristic. The *fandango, curacha, balitao, cariñosa,* and *surtido* are all certainly derived from Spanish or Spanish-American prototypes.

Teodoro A. Agoncillo has said, "The Visayan is a happy-go-lucky man and is more interested in the here and now than in the past or in the future. He exceeds the Tagalogs in his love for the finer things of life . . . but like his northern Ilocano brother, he is adventurous and afflicted with wanderlust. The Visayan . . . is a lover like the Tagalog, but he expresses his love in music . . ."

In an effort to preserve the hidden wealth of Visayan folk dances, I started to seriously research and collect Visayan folk dance materials in 1960. By 1961 the first volume of *Visayan Folk Dances* had been published, followed by a second volume in 1964 and a third in 1975. My source persons were farm workers and old people from several towns in the Visayan regions. Except for the pioneering works of Mrs. Francisca Aquino, Philippine folk dance literature is definitely meager. I am proud to say that my contribution, in the form of the above-mentioned three volumes, is the second such effort to be recorded and published on the topic of Philippine folk dances.

(Libertad V. Fajardo studied Philippine folk dancing under Mrs. Aquino. She was a dance director and instructor for several organizations, including the University of the Philippines, Philippine Women's University, and the Bayanihan Philippine Dance Company. She has accompanied the Bayanihan Company on tours of Europe, the Middle East, the United States, Canada, and Australia. Ms. Fajardo is the author of *Visayan Folk Dances (vols. I, II, III)* and *See the World in Dances.*)

PHILIPPINE FOLK DANCES

Three of the following dances—Liki, Cariñosa, and Chotis de Negros—are used here with permission from *Visayan Folk Dances,* by Libertad V. Fajardo. The remainder, from *Philippine National Dances* and notes by (the late) Francisca Aquino, are used here with the permission of her daughter, Celia Martinez.

APAT APAT

Apat Apat (AH-paht AH-paht), a Philippine folk dance mixer, was introduced in the United States by Francisca Aquino.

Record: Folk Dancer MH-2031, Mico MX 626-B

Formation: Cpls in a circle facing LOD, Girl to Boy's R with inside hands joined at shoulder height, elbows bent. When hands are free, they hang naturally at sides.

Steps: Smooth walking step

Meter 4/4   Pattern

Meas

8   Introduction (Last music has castanets in it.)

I. Walk with Partner, Away and Together
Begin with vocal.

1-2   Both beginning R, walk 4 steps in LOD.

3-4   Release hands, both turn ½ R, join inside hands (boys L, girls R) and walk 4 steps in RLOD.

5-6   Release hands, turn to face ptr and walk 4 steps bwd (boys twd ctr, girls away from ctr).

7-8   Walk 4 steps fwd twd ptr.

II. Opposite Circles, Star and Progress

1-2   Both turn ¼ R (L shoulder twd ptr) and walk fwd 4 steps (boys RLOD, girls LOD).

3-4   Both walk bwd 4 steps (B LOD, G RLOD).

5-6   Ptrs join R hands, shoulder height with elbows bent, and walk 4 steps CW once around.

7-8   Release hands and B walk 4 steps in LOD to next G, while ptr turns ½ CW with 4 steps to face LOD.
             Repeat dance with new ptr.

CARIÑOSA

This is an old and most popular courtship dance of the Visayan Islands. This version comes from San Joaquin, Iloilo.

Record: Mico MX 570A. Music has two parts, A & B.

Formation: Partners face each other about six feet apart, W at R of M when facing audience.

Costume: The W wears *patadyong* and *camisa* or kimono with a soft *pañuelo;* M wears *barong tagalog* or *camisa de chino* and any color of trousers.

Equipment: Comb, powder puff, handkerchief.

Meter 3/4   Pattern

Meas

          Introduction: Partners face audience.

1-2   Three-step turn in place (cts 1, 2, 3) and pause

(cts 1, 2, 3), R hand in reverse "T" pos, L hand on waist.

I. Music A. Partners face each other

1-6   (a) Three sway balance steps with a close (R, L, R), arms in 4th pos, R and L arm alternately high.

7-8   (b) Three-step turn left in place, arms down at sides (ct 1, 2, 3). Bow to each other, hands in front, parallel to each other at waist level, elbows close to waist, palms up (cts 1, 2, 3).

9-16   (c) Repeat all (a–b), starting with L ft, reverse pos of arms.

II. Music B: Cross Hands. Partners face each other.

17-18   (a) Starting with R ft, take three steps fwd to meet at center (cts 1, 2, 3) step L close to R (cts 1, 2, 3), hands down at sides.

19   (b) Join R hands, take one waltz step sdwd R (cts 1, 2, 3).

20   (c) Release R hands and join L hands, repeat (b) to left.

21-22   (d) Drop L hands. Repeat (b) and (c).

23-24   (e) Start with R ft, take three steps fwd to ptnr place, passing each other by R shoulders (cts 1, 2, 3). Turn L about and step L close to R ft. Finish facing each other (cts 1, 2, 3).

25-32   (f) Repeat all (a–e), finishing in original places.

III. Music A: Palms Touching. Partners face each other.

1-2   (a) Repeat fig II(a).

3-6   (b) Four touch steps in front, R and L alternately. Hands in front parallel to each other at waist level, elbows close to waist. With palms touching each other, M hands down, W hands on top (cts 1, 2, 3), reverse pos of H every meas.

7-8   (c) Repeat fig II(e).

9-16   (d) Repeat all (a–c), finishing in original pos.

IV. Music B: Combing. Partners face each other.

17-18   (a) Repeat fig II(a).

19-22   (b) Four waltz steps sdwd, R and L alternately. M takes comb from pocket and makes motion with his R hand combing W hair, L and R sides alternately.

23-24   (c) Repeat fig II(e).

25-32   (d) Repeat all (a–c). W gets comb from ptnr, combs M hair.

V. Music A: Powdering. Partners face each other.

1-2   (a) Repeat fig II(a).

3   (b) M takes puff from his pocket. Waltz sdwd R, gently powdering W L cheek (cts 1, 2, 3),

while W takes one waltz step R in place, hands flaring skirt.

4–6 (c) Repeat (b) three more times, powdering R, L, R cheek alternately and both waltzing L, R, L.

7–8 (d) Repeat fig II.

9–16 (e) Repeat all (a–d), this time the W does the powdering motion.

VI. Music B: Hide-and-Seek with Handkerchief. Partners face each other.

17–18 (a) Repeat fig II(a). M takes handkerchief from pocket. Ptnrs hold handkerchief at corners in perpendicular pos between their faces, with the W hands on top at face level.

19–22 (b) Partners take four touch steps in front, R and L alternately. Invert the handkerchief at every measure with M hands on top first, then the W hands. When hands are up, look at other's face from below handkerchief; when down, peek from below.

23–24 (c) Girl releases handkerchief. Partners exchange places as in fig II(e).

25–32 (d) Repeat all (a–c), finishing in original places.

VII. Music A: Kneeling. Partners face each other.

1–2 (a) Start with R ft, take three steps fwd to center (ct 1, 2, 3). M kneels on L while W passes around on his R side to stand behind him, facing same direction. Both place hands on waists (ct 1, 2, 3).

3–6 (b) W, with hands held at side, takes four waltz steps sdwd, R and L alternately. At the same time M gently turns his head while they look at each other alternately over his R and L shoulders. M hands at his waist.

7–8 (c) W turns R about and exchanges places with ptnr as in fig II(e). Finish facing each other.

9–16 (d) Repeat all (a–c). This time W kneels in (a). Finish in beginning place.

VIII. Music B: Ballroom Waltz. Partners face each other.

17–18 (a) Repeat fig II(a). Finish with partners in closed ballroom pos.

19–30 (b) Waltz in any direction.

31–32 (c) Join inside hands, W turns inward (1 M.), and both bow to audience, free hands in 2nd pos (1 M.).

CHOTIS DE NEGROS

The Chotis or Shotis was one of the ballroom dances learned by Filipinos from early European settlers. In the old days no social gathering was complete without

this dance. This version comes from Negros Occidental.

Record: Mico MX 735 A

Formation: Couples scattered, inside hands joined.

Step, Styling: Chotis. Walk three steps, starting L or R, (ct 1, 2, 3), step and hop slightly, swing free ft fwd (ct 4).

Meter 4/4   Pattern

Meas

I. Music A: Partners face audience, inside hands joined, W free hand flaring skirt, M on waist.

1 (a) Starting R ft, take one chotis step diag fwd R (ct 1, 2, 3, 4).

2 (b) Repeat (a) beginning L ft, retracing steps bkwd.

3–6 (c) Repeat (a) and (b) twice more, moving straight fwd and bk the second time and diag L the third time.

7 (d) Release hands. Partners face away from each other, W flaring skirt, M hands on waist.

8 (e) Repeat (b), ending facing, inside hands joined.

9–16 (f) Repeat all (a–e), moving in any desired direction.

II. Music B: Partners face each other about two feet apart

17 (a) Three step-close slides to R (ct 1 and, 2 and, 3 and), pause (ct 4 and), W flare skirt, M hands on waist.

18 (b) Repeat (a) to L. Take ballroom dance pos.

19 (c) Begin M R and W L ft, turn in place (M fwd, W bkwd) in four steps (ct 1, 2, 3, 4).

20 (d) Repeat (c) turning L (M bkwd, W fwd).

21–24 (e) Repeat (a–d).

25–32 (f) Repeat (a–e).

Note: Repeat as many times as desired.

LIKI

Liki is a dance of a coquette. It is characterized by a graceful swaying of hips and lifting of skirt. The dance should be done in a flirtatious manner, always looking at and flirting with partner. This simple dance comes from Bago, Negros Occidental.

Record: Mico MX 685 A. Music has A and B parts

Formation: Partners stand about six feet apart. One to any number of pairs may take part in this dance.

Meter 3/4   Pattern

Meas

Music Introduction.

1–3 Three-step turn right in place (1 M.), bow to audience or partner (1 M.), pause (1 M.). Girl holds skirt, Boy's hands on waist.

I. Music A: Partners face each other.

1   (a) Brush R foot forward and step on it immediately forward (ct 1), step L foot backward (ct 2), step R foot sideward right (ct 3). Girl holds skirt, swaying it in time with the music, Boy's hands on waist.

2   (b) Point L foot in front (cts 1, 2, 3), hands as in (a).

3–4   (c) Repeat (a) and (b), starting with L foot.

5–6   (d) Starting with R foot, take two close steps forward to partner's place, passing by R shoulders. Hands as in (a).

7–8   (e) Three-step turn right about, hands as in (a). Finish facing partner.

9–16   (f) Repeat all (a–e), finishing in proper places.

II. Music B: Partners face each other.

17   (a) Step R foot forward (ct 1), step L foot close to R foot (ct 2), step R foot backward (ct 3), hands as in figure I(a).

18   (b) Point L foot in front (cts 1, 2, 3). Arms in 4th position, R arm high.

19–20   (c) Repeat (a) and (b) starting with L foot. Reverse the position of hands in (b).

21–22   (d) Two waltz steps forward (R, L) to partner's place, passing by R shoulders. Arms in lateral position moving sideward right and left.

23–24   (e) Waltz turn right about, arms in forward-bend position with a forearm turn R and L. Finish facing each other.

25–32   (f) Repeat all (a–e). Finish in proper places.

III. Music A: Partners face away from each other.

1–4   (a) Repeat figure I(a–c).

5–6   (b) Take two close steps backward (R, L) going to partner's place, passing by R shoulders. Girl holds skirt, swaying it in time with the music, Boy's hands on waist.

7–8   (c) Three-step turn right about hands as in (b), finish facing away from each other.

9–16   (d) Repeat (a–c), finish facing audience.

IV. Music B: Partners face the audience.

17–20   (a) Repeat figure II (a–c), moving little by little forward. Partners face each other.

21–24   (b) Repeat figure II (d) and (e). Finish in partner's place.

25–32   (c) Repeat all (a–b), finishing in proper places. Execute the last turn slowly, bow to partner or audience.

PALAY DANCE

Palay literally means either the plant or the grain from which rice is obtained. Husked rice is the staple food of the Oriental people. This dance has an interesting story. The first figure depicts the graceful swaying of the palay plants in the breeze. Other lovely figures portray the cutting, harvesting, and threshing of palay. It can be danced on any occasion but is most appropriate as an after-harvest celebration.

This dance was arranged for the Agricultural Pageant which the University of the Philippines presented in 1929 at the Philippine Carnival Auditorium.

Costume: Dancers were dressed in peasant work costumes. They are barefoot and carry stalks of palay in both hands.

Formation: Partners stand opposite each other about eight feet apart, W at their partners' right when facing the audience.

Record: Mico MX 567 B. Music has three parts: A, B, and C.

Meter 3/4   Pattern

Meas

I. Music A: Dancers face the audience.

1–16   Execute sixteen waltz steps sideward R and L. Hold arms in fifth position, swaying sideward R and L.

II. Music B: Partners face each other.

17–18   (a) Take two close steps sideward right (cts 1–6). Hands in fifth position swaying sideward right (cts 1–2), sway to sideward left (ct 3). Sway arms sideward right (cts 1, 2, 3).

19–20   (b) Take two close steps sideward left. Arm movements as in above, starting from sideward left.

21–24   (c) Four waltz steps forward R and backward L. Arms swinging forward-upward (cts 1, 2, 3) and downward-backward (cts 1, 2, 3).

25–32   (d) Repeat all (a, b, and c).

III. Music A

1–16   Eight sway-balance steps with a point, R and L. R arm in fifth position and L hand on waist when going to the right, reversing the hand positions when going to the left.

IV. Music C: Partners face the audience.

17–20   (a) "Sarok" (1 M.) and pivot turn with point to the right (3 M.). Cross the hands down in front in "sarok" and have the R arm up and L hand on waist in the pivot turn with point. Turn the wrist of the R hand at every measure.

21–22   (b) Repeat (a) to the left. Reverse the hand positions.

23–32   (c) Repeat (a and b).

V. Music A (slower): Partners face the audience.

1   (a) Starting with the inside foot, take three steps sideward to partner's place (cts 1, 2, 3).

W pass in front of their partners. W sway arms parallel sideward right, M sideward left (cts 1, 2, 3).

2 (b) Point sideward with inside foot. Sway arms to opposite side (W sideward left and M sideward right) (cts 1, 2, 3).

3–4 (c) W move the arms in a double-arm-circle counterclockwise, M move the arms clockwise (cts 1–6). The inside foot remains pointing for six counts.

5–6 (d) Repeat (a and b) going back to places. W pass in front of their partners. Arms in opposite direction.

7–8 (e) Repeat (c), reversing the directions of the arms.

9–16 (f) Repeat all (a, b, c, d, and e).

VI. Music D: Partners face each other.

17–20 (a) M take four (small) waltz steps backward, starting with the R foot. Arms in lateral position moving sideward R and L. W take four (big) waltz steps forward, starting with the R foot. They follow their partners, arms as in above. Finish with partners standing near each other.

21 (b) M hands down shaking "palay" stalks three times (cts 1, 2), pause (ct 3). W shake "palay" stalks overhead in the same manner.

22–24 (c) Repeat (b) three times more, reversing hand positions every measure.

25–26 (d) W turn right about. Partners execute mincing steps sideward right, R foot in front (cts 1–5). Point L in front (ct 6). Hands on waists.

27–28 (e) Repeat (d) going sideward left, L foot in front.

29 (f) Three quick stamps in place (R, L, R) (cts 1, 2), pause (ct 3). Hands on waist.

30 (g) Repeat (f) (L, R, L).

31–32 (h) Take four steps forward going to proper places, starting with the R foot (cts 1, 2, 3, 4). Hands on waists. The W, upon reaching their proper places, turn right about. Partners bow to each other. Arms in second position (cts 5–6).

(i) Repeat all (a, b, c, d, e, f, g, h). This time M move forward and W backward. Reverse the arm positions in (b) and (c). M face right about in (d). M turn right about in (h) in place.

VII. Music A: Partners face the audience and join inside hands.

1–8 (a) Take eight step-swing steps forward, R and L alternately. Place free hands on waists.

9–16 (b) Turn inward to face about and repeat (a).

17–18 Saludo: Three step turn right in place and bow either to partner or to audience.

PANDANGO SA ILAW

Pandango Sa Ilaw (Dance with Oil Lamps), a version from Mindoro, is the most difficult of all the pandangos. It is quite unusual and colorful. The female dancer gracefully and skillfully balances three lighted *tinghoy,* or oil lamps—one on her head and one on the back of each hand.

A few boys and girls may take part as townsfolk or onlookers. They clap their hands in time to the music, adding life and gaiety to the dance.

Costume: The girl is dressed in *balintawak,* the boy in long red trousers and *barong tagalog.*

Record: Mico MX 420 B. The music is divided into three parts: A, B, C.

Formation: Partners stand about six feet apart facing the audience. The three lighted oil lamps are placed on the floor between them. The girl stands at partner's right. The oil lamps are of two sizes, the one to be placed on the head (no. 2) being larger than the two for the hands.

Meter 3/4 Pattern

Meas

Music Introduction

1 (a) Standing on the L foot, tap R in front (cts 1, 2), tap once more (ct 3). Place left hand on waist, R hand hanging loosely at the side.

2 (b) Repeat (a).

3–5 (c) Three-step turn right in place and bow to the audience. Place both hands on waist.

I. Music A: Partners face right.

1–4 (a) Take two waltz steps forward (R, L—2 M.), one waltz turn right (2 M.). Arms in lateral position moving sideward R and L with forearm turns.

5–16 (b) Repeat (a) three times more, moving clockwise around the oil lamps.

17–32 (c) Turn right about and repeat all (a and b) moving counterclockwise. The W finishes with the lamps in front of her.

II. Music B: W Part:

1–24 (a) Cross R foot in front of L and bend knee slightly (this position is held for 32 measures), arms bent forward at shoulder level. Move right (1 M.) and left elbows (1 M.) upward twice on cts 1, 2 of each measure. The wrists are relaxed so that the hands dangle at every movement.

25–32 (b) Place a lamp on the back of the right hand.

M Part:

24 (a) Repeat the movement of fig I, going clockwise around the W. Take the same arm movement of the W in figure II(a).

25–32 (b) Take lamp no. 1 and help the W place it on the back of her right hand.

III. Music C

1–16 *Cross-waltz step:* With a spring, step R (L) forward across L (R) in front, raising the L (R) in rear at the same time (ct 1), step L (R) in rear of R (L) (ct 2), step R (L) in the same place (in front) (ct 3).

1–16 (a) Starting with the R foot, take sixteen cross-waltz steps around the lamps clockwise. M hands on waist, W free hand holding the skirt.

16–32 (b) Turn right about and repeat (a) moving counterclockwise. Finish in proper places facing the audience.

IV. Music A

1–8 (a) Starting with the R foot, execute waltz steps (tiny steps) backward. The W bends left arm upward and flutters the fingers in time to the music. M hands are placed on the waist.

9–16 (b) Repeat (a) moving forward to original places.

17–24 (c) M gets lamp no. 2. Partners repeat (a). Free hand of M on the waist.

25–32 (d) M puts the lamp on the head of the W who stands still.

V. Music B

1–2 (a) Take one waltz step sideward R and L (2 M.), waltz-turn right (2 M.). Arms of M and L arm of W in lateral position at shoulder level, moving sideward R and L alternately, or L hand of W holding the skirt.

3–16 (b) Repeat (a) seven times more, moving around the lamp clockwise.

17–24 (c) The M gets the third lamp and places it on the back of the left hand of the W. The W stands still while the M is placing the lamp on her hand.

   W Part:

25–26 (1) Step R across L in front and bend right knee slightly. Raise L foot in rear at the same time (cts 1, 2) step L in rear of R foot (ct 3). Step R foot sideward (cts 1, 2, 3). Hold lamps in front or obliquely forward at shoulder level.

27–32 (2) Repeat (1) three times more (L, R, L).

   M Part:

(1) Continue waltzing around the W counterclockwise (8 M.).

VI. Music C

   W Part:

Stand with feet in third position, R foot in front, knees relaxed. Do the following hand movements, hands first at shoulder level in front:

1–2 (a) Raise R hand and lower L hand slowly (cts 1–6).

3–4 (b) Reverse the movements of the hands.

5–6 (c) Cross the hands in front, R over the L hand.

7–8 (d) Back to the starting position.

9–12 (e) Repeat (a) and (b).

13–14 (f) Lower both hands and bend the knees slightly.

15–16 (g) Raise both hands and straighten the knees.

   M Part:

17–32 (a) Repeat fig I, going clockwise around the W.

VII. Music C

1–16 (a) Partners execute eight sway-balance steps with a point, R and L, moving counterclockwise little by little, arms in third position, R and L high alternately.

VIII. Music C

The M takes the two lamps from the hands of the W (one in each hand), leaving one on her head.

1–14 (a) Partners repeat the steps of fig I, going in any direction with the M following the W.

15–16 (b) Three-step turn right in place and bow to the audience.

   M Arm Movements:

17–24 (a) The M moves the lamps, one up and the other down (2 M.), crosses the hands in front, R over L (2 M.), L over R (2 M.), circling R hand clockwise and L counterclockwise (2 M.).

25–30 (b) Repeats (a) up to 6 Meas.

31–32 (c) Hands at the sides while bowing.

   W Arm Movements:

(a) Repeat the arm movements of fig I for 14 measures.

(b) Takes the glass from her head with the R hand and opens the hands sideward while bowing (2 M.).

RIGODON (Rigaudon)

This dance was first introduced in the court of Louis XIII by a dancing master from Marseille named Rigaud. Introduced in the Philippines, the rigodon has become the most popular of the quadrilles. It is usually performed at the beginning of formal dances, with government officials and people of high social standing in the community participating. The music is lively. There are many versions of the rigodon. The one described below is the most common and the simplest to perform.

Costume: Evening dress should be worn if the rigodon opens a formal dance, but any kind of Filipino costume may be used on other occasions.

Record: Mico MX 843 AB

Formation: Partners stand side by side with the ladies always on the right side unless otherwise indicated. The dancers are arranged in a square formation. From four to any number of even pairs may take part. Couples 1 and 2 are head pairs or *cabeceras*, 3 and 4 are side pairs or *costados*.

Meter 2/4, 4/4   Pattern

Note: The definite number of steps to be taken will depend upon available space. Consequently the repetitions of the music cannot be stated. After a figure is finished the musicians are signaled by clapping or stamping. The steps may be started with R or L foot, one step for each count.

I. Ladies Meet
Music A

Head Pairs:

(a) Pairs 1 and 2 cross-over (going to opposite places).

(b) Cross-over again (going to proper places).

(c) Ladies 1 and 2 meet at center (followed at four paces by their partners), join right hands and swing around half-way. Drop right hands. Lady 1 joins left hand with left hand of Gentleman 2, and Lady 2 does the same with Gentleman 1. Swing half-way around.

(d) Gentlemen take own partners to opposite places. This means that Pair 1 will be in the place of Pair 2 and vice-versa.

(e) Cross-over (going to proper places).

Side Pairs:
Pairs 3 and 4 repeat all.

II. Zeta (Letter Z)
Music B

Head Pairs:

Lady 1 and Gentleman 2 dance first.

(a) Face right. Starting with the R foot, take three steps forward (R, L, R) and close L to R.

(b) Starting with the L foot, take three steps backward (L, R, L) and close R to L.

(c) Face each other and advance forward to opposite place, passing by right sides.

(d) Face right and repeat (a) and (b).

(e) Face each other and go to proper places, passing by left shoulders. About three-fourths of the way they stop, turn and bow to each other, then walk backward to proper places.

(f) Lady 2 and Gentleman 1 repeat all.

Side Pairs:

(a) Lady 3 and Gentleman 4 repeat all.

(b) Lady 4 and Gentleman 3 repeat all.

III. Casamiento (Wedding)
Music C

Head Pairs:

(a) Lady 1 and Gentleman 2 meet to the center, join R hands and swing a full turn around clockwise. Finish standing sideways still with R hands joined. Lady 2 and Gentleman 1 advance forward and join left hands with own partners.

Ladies stand in one line side by side facing the Gentlemen, who are also in one line side by side facing them.

(b) Swing the joined hands three times from side to side.

(c) Drop hands. Partners go to opposite place with inside hands joined.

(d) Cross-over, going to proper places.

Lady 2 and Gentleman 1 repeat all.

Side Pairs:

(a) Lady 3 and Gentleman 4 repeat all.

(b) Lady 4 and Gentleman 3 repeat all.

IV. "Hatid" or "Visita" (Visit)
Music D

Head Pairs:

(a) Pair 1 join inside hands. Advance forward and stop in front of Pair 2. Pairs 1 and 2 bow to each other.

(b) Pair 1 drop hands. Gentleman 1 crosses hands in front, palms up. He receives the left hand of his partner with his left and the right hand of Lady 2 with his right. Then he walks backward towards his proper place, leading the two ladies who walk forward with him. Gentleman 2 walks behind the two ladies following them.

(c) About three-fourths of the way they release hands and the gentlemen take their own partners to opposite places.

(d) Cross-over, going to proper places.

(e) Pair 2 starts first and repeats all.

Side Pairs:

(a) Pair 3 starts first and repeats all.

(b) Pair 4 starts first and repeats all.

Note: Sometimes the "hatid" or "visita" is done in this manner. Gentleman of Pair 1, upon reaching Pair 2's place, gives his partner to Gentleman 2. Gentleman 2 crosses his hands and walks forward with the two ladies.

V. Cadenilla (Small Chain)
Music E

Pairs 1 and 2:

(a) Each couple join R hands, walk forward to the center or one pair may approach the other pair. Partners swing once clockwise.

(b) Couples drop hands and join left hands with the left of the opposites, that is, Lady 1 joins left hand with left of Gentleman 2 and Lady 2 with Gentleman 1. Swing once counterclockwise with the new partner.

(c) Finish facing in.

(d) Gentleman 1 crosses hands in front and receives his partner's right hand with his right and the left hand of the opposite lady with his left. Both ladies are facing him. He walks backward to his proper place with the two ladies walking forward. Gentleman 2 follows them.

(e) Upon reaching Pair 1's place, Gentleman 1 releases the hands of the ladies. Gentleman 2 then crosses his hands in front and receives the ladies in the same manner, his right hand with the right hand of his partner and his left with the left hand of the opposite lady. Gentleman 2 walks backward to his proper place with the two ladies. Gentleman 1 remains in his place.

(f) Lady 1 goes back to her proper place. Gentleman 1 and Lady 2 execute the do-si-do movement. They bow to each other before returning to their proper places.

(g) Repeat all with Gentleman 2 taking the ladies first to his place. Do-si-do is done by Gentleman 2 and Lady 1 this time.

Side Pairs:

(h) Repeat all with Gentleman 3 taking the ladies first to his place. Do-si-do by Gentleman 3 and Lady 4.

(i) Repeat all with Gentleman 4 taking the ladies first to his place. Do-si-do by Gentleman 4 and Lady 3.

VI. Cambio Pareja (Change Partners)
Music F

Head Pairs:

(a) Pairs 1 and 2 meet at the center and exchange partners. Gentlemen receive opposite ladies' left hands with their left.

(b) Gentlemen walk backward to proper places with the new partners who walk forward with them. Place the new partner at the left side.

Side Pairs:

(c) Pairs 3 and 4 do the same.

All:

(d) All gentlemen step in front of the new partner and bow to each other.

(e) Gentlemen then go to the lady at their left. Join both hands with the new partner and swing once clockwise. Gentlemen place their partners at their right side after the turn.

(f) Repeat all (a, b, c, d, e). The head pairs always

changing partners first, then the side pairs. These movements are repeated as many times as necessary until the partners meet at their proper places.

Note: If many pairs are taking part, this figure may be omitted.

VII. Cadena (Grand Chain)
Music F

Execute the "Grand Chain" movement as described in the foregoing explanations.

VIII. Saludo (Bow)
Music F

Ladies take the right arm of their partners ("Abrasete").

Head Pairs meet to center and bow to their opposites. Walk backward to places.

Side pairs do the same.

Note: Sometimes at the end of the Rigodon an old-time waltz is danced to open the ballroom dancing.

TINIKLING

This dance is a favorite in the Visayan Islands, especially in the province of Leyte.

The Tikling is a bird with long legs and a long neck. The Tinikling dance, therefore, imitates the movements of the Tikling birds as they walk between grass stems or run over tree branches. This spectacular dance is usually accompanied by a song.

The performers dance along the sides and between two bamboo poles, about nine feet long, which are placed horizontally on the ground. The poles are struck together in time to the music. Skill is demonstrated in dancing between the bamboos, and in keeping the feet from being caught when the poles are struck together. There is much fun, however, when the bamboo players catch the feet of the dancers.

Two bamboo players sit opposite each other on the ground holding the ends of the bamboo poles (sometimes long pestles). Two pieces of board or bamboo, about thirty inches long and two inches thick, are placed under the poles, about one foot from the ends.

Costume: Girls wear *balintawak* or *patadiong*. Boys wear *barong tagalog* and long red trousers with one leg rolled up. They dance barefoot.

Formation: Dancers stand at the left side of the bamboo poles, girl in front, facing the audience.

Record: Mico MX 342 B; RCA Victor EPA 4126

Bamboo Rhythms (abbreviation is B. R.):

B. R. I. Strike bamboo poles together once by sliding them against the boards or lifting them an inch or so (ct 1), open the bamboos about a foot apart and strike them twice against the boards (cts 2, 3). This is repeated as many times as necessary in regular rhythm:

M. 3/4 RHYTHM

	LIFT,	STRIKE,	STRIKE,	
	1	2	3	

B. R. I. Strike bamboos once as above (ct 1), open bamboos a foot apart and strike them three times against the boards (cts 2, 3) with R, L, R hands of bamboo player number 1 and with L, R, L hands of number 2. The whole measure is played like this:

M. 3/4 RHYTHM

		No. 1-R L	R	
		No. 2-L R	L	
	LIFT,	STRIKE-STRIKE,	STRIKE,	
	1	2	3	

Tinikling Steps:

Tinikling Step Right—Hop on L foot outside (at the left side) the bamboos (ct 1), hop on R between the bamboo poles (ct 2), then hop on the L foot on the same spot (ct 3) and raise R. (That is, when the bamboos are struck together on count *one,* the hop is done outside and when they are far apart the two hops are done between or inside on counts *two, three.*)

Bend R arm upward about head level and "kumintang" the hand counterclockwise, girl's L hand holding the skirt and boy's on waist.

Tinikling Step Left—Hop on R foot outside (at the right side) the bamboo poles (ct 1), hop on L between the poles (ct 2) and hop on R on the same spot (ct 3). Reverse hand positions.

Meter 3/4   Pattern

Meas   Music Introduction
1-4   (a) Starting with the R foot, dancers take four waltz steps forward going to proper places, the girl holding the skirt, the boy's hands on the waist.
Bamboo Rhythm—silent for (1 M.).
Strike bamboo poles together once at every first beat of the second, third and fourth measures (2-4 M.).

5-8   (b) Dancers stand at the left side of the poles on the L foot. Tap with R foot twice between the poles on counts two and three of measure 5 (c). Repeat (b) three times more (6-8 M.). B. R. I. Play four times (4 M.).

I. Music A (B. R. I.). *Tinikling Step*
1-7   (a) Take seven tinikling steps R and L alternately. Hand positions as described above. The

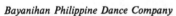

Bayanihan Philippine Dance Company

first hop on count one of measure one may be omitted.

8 (b) Step R foot outside pole No. 2 (ct 1), hop twice on the L foot between, turning right about (cts 2, 3). Girl holds skirt, boy's hands on waist.

9–15 (c) Take seven tinikling steps L and R alternately. Hands as above.

16 (d) *Girl* hops on L foot outside pole No. 2 (ct 1), hops on R twice between the poles, going backward near bamboo player No. 1 (cts 2, 3). Hands as above in 8 M.
Boy hops on L foot outside pole No. 1 (ct 1), turns right about by hopping twice on the R foot between the poles going near bamboo player No. 2 (cts 2, 3). Hands as in 8 M.
They finish facing each other.

II. Music A (B. R. I). *Clockwise and Counterclockwise*

17–18 (a) Girl stands at the left side of pole No. 2 and boy at the left side of pole No. 1. Starting with the L foot, take four steps forward outside the poles (cts 1, 2, 3, 4); turn right about and hop on L (ct 5) and R foot (ct 6) between the poles. Girl holds skirt, boy's hands on waist.

19–24 (b) Repeat (a) three times more, going clockwise. On the eighth measure hop on L twice between the poles (cts 5, 6).

25–31 (c) Repeat all (a, b, c), starting with the R foot on the other side of the poles (boy at right side of pole No. 2, and girl of pole No. 1). Reverse direction.
Note: This time the figure is started by hopping on the R (ct 1) and L foot (ct 2) between the poles.

32 (d) *Girl* takes three steps forward about two feet away from pole No. 2. *Boy* takes three steps forward about two feet away from pole No. 1. Finish facing each other.

III. Music B (B. R. II). *Kuradang Step*

1–16 (a) Take eight kuradang steps R and L alternately. Arms in fourth position, R and L high alternately. At the last measure the boy jumps over to the left side of his partner, facing the same direction.

IV. Music B (B. R. I). *Tinikling Steps Sideways*
Open the poles wider to accommodate the feet of the dancers. Partners join inside hands. Free hand of the girl holding the skirt, and boy's free hand on his waist.

1 (a) Hop on L foot outside the poles (ct 1), hop on R (ct 2) and on L between the poles (ct 3).

2 (b) Hop forward on R foot outside across pole No. 1 (ct 1), hop on L (ct 2), and R foot between the poles (ct 3).

3–7 (c) Repeat (a) and (b) five times alternately.

8 (d) Hop on R twice, outside pole No. 1, turning right about. Release the hold of inside hands (cts 1, 2). Hop on L close R foot in place (ct 3).

9–15 (e) Join inside hands. Repeat (a, b, and c).

16 (f) Hop on R foot outside pole No. 2. Release the hold of inside hands (ct 1), pause (ct 2).

V. Music A (B. R. I). *Feet Apart*

1 (a) Girl turns right and boy left (facing each other), jump with both feet apart outside the poles (No. 1 and No. 2), join both hands and swing them sideways (ct 1), jump twice with feet together between the poles, swing hands down in front between them (cts 2, 3).

2–3 (b) Repeat (a) twice more.

4 (c) Jump with feet apart outside the poles (ct 1), release hands and jump twice between the poles turning right about (cts 2, 3). Partners are in back-to-back position.

5–8 (d) Repeat (a), (b) and (c) except hand movements. Girl holding skirt, boy's hands on waist.

9–16 (e) Repeat all (a, b, c, and d) except on the sixteenth measure, the girl does not turn. The boy turns right about facing the audience.

VI. Music A (B. R. I). *Cross-Step*

1 (a) Hop on L foot across pole No. 2 and raise R foot in rear (ct 1), hop on R twice between the poles (cts 2, 3). Girl's right hand on waist and L holding skirt, boy's hands on waist.

2 (b) Hop on L outside pole No. 1 and raise R foot in front (ct 1), hop on R twice between the poles (cts 2, 3). Hands as above.

3–8 (c) Repeat (a) and (b) three times more. On the last two counts of the eighth measure hop on R foot twice turning right about.

9–15 (d) Repeat seven times (a) and (b) alternately.

16 (e) *Girl* hops on L outside pole No. 2 (ct 1), hops on R twice between poles moving backward near bamboo player No. 1 (cts 2, 3). *Boy* hops on L outside pole No. 1 (ct 1), hops on R foot between poles moving forward near bamboo player No. 2 (ct 2), hop on R again and face right about (ct 3).

VII. Music B (B. R. I). *Diagonal*

1 (a) Hop on L foot outside the poles (girl outside pole No. 2, boy pole No. 1) (ct 1), hop on R diagonally forward to the center of the poles (ct 2). Hop on L on the same spot (ct 3). Join R hands on counts 2, 3.

2   (b) Hop on R foot diagonally backward across the other pole (girl across pole No. 1, boy No. 2). Release the hold of R hands (ct 1), hop on L (ct 2) and R (ct 3) between the poles as above. Join R hands on counts 2, 3.

3–7   (c) Repeat five times (a) and (b) alternately.

8   (d) Leap to exchange places.

9–15   (e) Repeat (a), (b) and (c).

16   (f) Boy leaps to the left side of pole No. 1 and girl at the right side of pole No. 2 near bamboo player No. 2.

VIII. Music B (B. R. II)—8 M. *Waltz Steps*

1–4   (a) Starting with the R foot, take four waltz steps forward. Arms in lateral position moving sideward R and L alternately or inside hands joined.

5–8   (b) Repeat (a) moving backward.
(B. R. I)—8 M.
Girl dances in front of her partner.

9   (c) Hop on the outside foot once outside the poles (girl outside pole No. 2, boy pole No. 1) (ct 1), hop on the inside foot twice between the poles (cts 2, 3). Girl holds her skirt, boy's hands on waist.

10–14   (d) Repeat (c) five times more, moving forward little by little.

15–16   (e) Boy jumps over to the left side of the girl and they join R hands. Girl makes a three-step turn left in place passing under the arch of arms (1 M.), and both bow to the audience (1 M.).

POLAND

Polish Folk Dancing

by Alfred Sokolnicki

Polish dances are as old as the traditions and customs of Poland. They began with the Slavic tribes in the sixth century. The dances were religious and recreational.

Primitive Polish tribes—the Polanians, Masovians, Lechites, Pomeranians, and Sarmatians—worshiped idols through dances, songs, and sacrifices. They also worshiped the forces of nature—wind, sun, and thunder—and regarded fire as a sacred symbol of the gods.

Shrines were built in groves and forests for the various gods and it was there that the ceremonials took place. Together with sacrificial offerings of animals,

Alfred J. Sokolnicki

honey, fruits, and shrubs, dances were offered to the gods to ensure abundant crops, rainfall, blessings in the coming seasons and at the beginning of a new undertaking. They also performed rites corresponding with the various changes of the moon.

When Christianity was introduced into Poland in 965, during the reign of Mieczyslaw (Mieceslaus) I, some dances continued to be performed as part of the religious ceremonies. Religious processions held at various church feasts consisted of walking dances similar to the polonaise.

Lyrics of some of the Polish Christmas carols sung during church ceremonies were set to the dance tunes of the time. The carol "W Zlobie Lezy" (He Lies in a Manger) is a stately polonaise. Another carol, "Bog Sie Rodzi" (God is Born) was set to the music of the coronation polonaise written for King Ladislaus IV in 1648.

Some dances formerly used for religious purposes were later commonly used for recreation and enjoyment. Simple and mixed couple dances became prevalent. The dances of the time consisted of exaggerated beating out of time in a song, and the music consisted of repetitions of shouts and, later, of words.

The most popular music was played on bugles, drums, kornety (animal horns), and various types of whistles. Young people liked to play the dromla (Jew's harp—little metal spring instrument played with the lips). Others delighted in playing piskliwe gajdaki (small violin-type instruments).

Dances were filled with mimicry and pantomime, representing such various trades as fishing, hunting, and harvesting. Some dances were used in war ceremonies. There were also vigorous dances such as the zbojnicki, the dance of the Polish mountain brigands. They danced around fires, waved their mountain climbing sticks, or *ciupagi*, and jumped over the fires in imitation of their legendary leader, Janosik, the most daring of brigands.

Dances were an index to people's temperaments. Polish people danced before and after attempting a new venture, during their spare time, and during feasts and holidays. Harvest festivals, weddings, and other traditional customs were preserved and elaborated through dances. The same was true of festivities among the poor and gala parties among the wealthy. Folk songs were dramatized and improvised during the dances.

Dances were an integral part of the pre-Lenten traveling carnival, the "Kulig." Shrove Tuesday festivals, Eastertime, St. John's Eve (midsummer eve), harvests, weddings, local village festivals honoring patron saints, shepherds returning with their flocks, or fishermen returning safely with their catch were occasions for dancing.

In time, the polonaise was recognized as a national dance and was performed at the opening and closing of important events. Dances that are identified as indigenous to specific areas or regions include: mazur (Masovia), krakowiak (Kracow), kujawiak (Kujawy) and cashubian (Pomoria).

Polish dances are renowned for their many formations and variations. The variety of movements and motifs depends on the ingenuity of the dance leader— usually the man in the lead couple, *wodzirej*. He inspires the flow of the dances as bridges, wheels, windmills, chains, and various changes of partner constitute the particular dance. Sometimes the dances are unusually long, this being due to the leader's enthusiasm, strength, and determination.

In the sixteenth century, the Polish dance was known all over Europe as *chorea polonica, polonisch dantz*, and awakened the admiration of the aristocratic dancers and nobility by its inimitable national characteristics, beautiful melody, and stately rhythm. The Poles called this dance the chodzony (walking dance). It later became the polonaise. This dance is said to have been invented by King Henry Valois (Henryk Walezy) when he ruled Poland in 1573.

(Alfred J. Sokolnicki's introduction to Polish cultural activity occurred at South Division High School, where he wrote and directed skits and plays for the Polish Club. This activity then extended to the neighborhood social center at the Forest Home Avenue School, conducted by the Milwaukee Public Schools Recreation Department, where he was active in the Marshal Pilsudski Club. This teen-age group presented weekly improvisations for a large audience. The group eventually was invited to present a serialized radio program in Polish dealing with "our youth." The commedy series, for which he wrote the scripts in Polish, was broadcast on Sunday afternoons from December 1939 to March 1940 on station WEMP.

Folk dancing began as an extension of the group's activity. Several dance teachers were invited to teach the better-known Polish dances to the teen-agers in the group. The group was one of several invited to participate in a Polish folk dance presentation in Milwaukee's Midsummer Festival, 1936–41, at the city's beautiful lakefront. Sokolnicki was appointed dance director.

This led to an invitation requesting Sokolnicki and the Polish-American youth of Milwaukee to present a folk dance number in the 1941 national convention of the American Legion in Milwaukee. For this presentation Sokolnicki created the cultural form of "danscene" (dance scene) of a Polish wedding. Over 250 young people, accompanied by a symphony orchestra, presented this number. Several days before the presentation, the lead dancer became ill and Sokolnicki had to dance the part of the groom.

The dancers wanted to stay together since they enjoyed the idea of presenting national customs in the form of dance. Thus, the Mazur Polish Dancers of Milwaukee (see essay in Part IV) were formed, with Sokolnicki as dance director and choreographer. His interest in research and in the dance were combined as he began to import manuals and materials from Poland (before World War II) and from various parts of Europe in order to create "danscenes" of customs, regional dances, potpourri, and occasional festivals.

Milwaukee soon became a leading center of folk dances of the Polish people and the Mazur dancers' large collection of dance materials was constantly consulted.

Sokolnicki has frequently lectured on Polish dances and customs at universities, seminars, and various programs. He has served as director of community festivals, has hosted television programs on Polish dances and customs, as well as other programs. Most of the danscenes in the repertoire of the Mazur Polish Dancers of Milwaukee are the result of his painstaking research.

Alfred Sokolnicki is currently dean of the College of Speech at Marquette University and is the founder and former supervisor of the University's Hearing Laboratory School of Speech.

In 1973 he was awarded the Polonia Restituta by the Polish Government in Exile in London. His many publications on cultural subjects include articles on Polish customs and dances for the *Polish-American Encyclopedia.*)

POLISH FOLK DANCES

KRAKOWIAK

The krakowiak (krah-KOHV-yahk), one of Poland's most popular dances, traditionally does not follow a set pattern, the figures being called by a leader. When danced by American folk dancers, they are usually arranged to fit a particular record. This krakowiak has been arranged by Anatol Joukowsky, who has danced the krakowiak in Krakow, Poland, but may be rearranged to fit any particular krakowiak music.

Record: National (45 rpm)-4524; RCA (45 rpm) EPA-4127

Formation: Double circle, cpls facing CCW (LOD), W to R of M. Inside hands joined at shoulder level. M L hand a little behind hip, palm out. W takes skirt in R hand about 6 inches below waist and holds it on R hip (palm out, fingers bwd).

Steps:

Basic Step: Leap onto L (cts 1, &). Step R (ct 2). Close L to R (ct &). Next step would start with leap onto R. Knees are flexible.

Click Step: Starting with wt on L, hop and land on L. While both ft are off floor, click heels a little to R side. Takes 1 ct. May be done hopping on R and clicking heels a little to L side.

Meter 2/4   Pattern

Meas

Duquesne University Tamburitzans

I. Back-to-Back and Face-to-Face

1–16 Starting outside ft (M L, W R) do 16 basic steps traveling in LOD. On first leap (meas 1) swing joined hands fwd and assume a slightly back-to-back pos. Second step (ct 2) is in LOD. On leap in meas 2, turn to face ptr, swinging hands back to starting pos. Second step is still in LOD. Finish facing ptr, M back to ctr. Hands still joined. End wt on M R, W L.

II. Click and Turn

1 Description is for M; W does counterpart. Hop twice on R and click heels each time. Move in LOD. M raises L arm out to L side, about shoulder height, palm up. W R on hip.

2 Stamp L (ct 1), R (ct &). Hold (cts 2, &).

3 Stepping on L, brush R across in front of L to start pivot turn to L (ct 1). M only clap on ct 1. Step R, completing pivot turn (ct 2).

4 W brush L across in front of R, pivoting R. Facing ptr, stamp L (ct 1), R (ct &), L (ct 2). Hold (ct &). Hands on hips.

5–8 Repeat action of meas 1–4 (fig II), but starting with hop on L and reversing hand pos. Move to RLOD.

9–16 Repeat action of meas 1–8 (fig II).

III. Couple Turn

1–8 Assume modified shoulder-waist pos. M R hand on W L hip, L arm extended out to side, palm down. W L hand on M R wrist, R hand on M L shoulder. Starting M L, W R, turn CW, progressing in LOD. Use 8 basic steps to make 4 turns. M accents leap on L of each odd-numbered meas by bending knee. L hand moves down twd floor on each odd meas and back to place on each even meas.

IV. Men into Center

Man:

1 Hands on hips, walk into ctr, R (ct 1), L (ct 2). Join hands in circle.

2–3 Hop 4 times on L and click heels each time. Move to R.

4 Stamp R (ct 1), L (ct &), R (ct 2). Hold (ct &).

5–7   Hop 6 times on R and click heels each time. Move to L.

8   Stamp L (ct 1), R (ct &), L (ct 2). Hold (ct &).

9–12   Repeat action of meas 5–8 (fig IV), but hop on L and move to R. On first ct hands are placed on upper arms of neighbors.

13–16   Repeat action of meas 5–8 (fig IV), hopping on R and moving to L.

Woman:

1   Hands on hips. In LOD, walk R (ct 1), L (ct 2).

2   Continue, walk R (ct 1). Facing ctr, stamp L (no wt) (ct 2).

3–4   Repeat action of meas 1–2 (fig IV), but start L and move RLOD.

5–8   Repeat action of meas 1–4 (fig IV).

9   Facing ctr, step R to R side (ct 1). Stamp L next to R (no wt) (ct 2).

10   Step L to L side (ct 1). Stamp R next to L (no wt) (ct 2).

11   Into ctr walk R (ct 1), L (ct 2).

12   Moving back out of ctr, walk R (ct 1), L (ct 2).

13–16   Starting R, walk 7 steps into ctr under ptr R arm and close L to R (no wt). On last 3 steps turn L to face ptr. W L ft free, M R.

V. Couple Turn with Man's Arms Outstretched

1–16   W places hands on M shoulders. M arms are outstretched to side, palms up, a little above shoulder level. Starting M R, W L, turn with 16 basic steps CW and moving in LOD. Make 7½ turns so M ends on inside of circle. As turn is done, widen circle back to original size.

VI. Click and Turn

1–16   Repeat action of fig II.

VII. Couple Turn, Lifting Woman

1–8   Starting M L, W R, dance 8 basic steps, turning CW and moving in LOD. Make 4 turns. M R hand on W L hip, L hand on own hip. W L hand on M R wrist, R hand on M L shoulder. On ct 1 of each even meas, W leap high and onto L as M lifts with R hand. On last meas W remove hand from M R shoulder and cpls finish in single circle, facing ctr, W to R of M.

VIII. Women into Center

Man:

1   Facing ctr, move to R. From stride pos jump into air and click heels. Land with L crossed behind R, wt on L (ct 1). Step R to R side (ct 2).

2   Step L in front of and to R side of R (ct 1).

Step R next to L (ct 2).

3   Repeat action of meas 1 (fig VIII).

4   Stamp L next to R (ct 1). Stamp R (ct &). Stamp L (ct 2).

5–8   Repeat action of meas 1–4 (fig VIII), but after click land with R behind L and move to L.

9–16   Repeat action of meas 1–8 (fig VIII). On last stamp R, do not take wt.

Woman:

1   Moving diag R and twd ctr, walk R (ct 1), L (ct 2). Hands on hips.

2   Facing ctr, hop twice on L and click heels each time.

3   Walk R (ct 1), L (ct 2) in LOD.

4   Facing ctr, hop on L and click heels (ct 1). Stamp R (ct 2).

5–8   Repeat action of meas 1–4, but start with L and move RLOD.

9–15   Repeat action of meas 1–7.

16   Step L (ct 1) making ½ turn R (CW) to face M. Step R (ct 2). End M R, W L ft free.

IX. Couple Turn with Woman's Hands Behind Head

1–16   M holds W as in shoulder-waist pos, but hands are a few inches above her waist. W clasp hands behind head. Starting M R, W L, use 16 basic steps to make 8 CW turns in LOD. On last meas M release W and all join hands in a single circle, W to R of M.

X. Click and Turn the Woman

1   Hop on R twice and click heels each time. Move to L.

2   Stamp L (ct 1). Stamp R (ct &). Hold (cts 2, &).

3   M stamp L (ct 1) and pull ptr across to L side. Stamp R (ct 2). W, with lead from M, turn twice CCW (L) and move to ptr L side. Use 4 steps starting L. Rejoin hands.

4   All stamp L (ct 1), R (ct &), L (no wt) (ct 2). Hold (ct &).

5–8   Repeat action of meas 1–4 (fig X). M pulls new R-hand W to his L side. On last stamp L take wt.

9–14   Repeat action of meas 1–6 (fig X), but hop on L and move to R. This time M will pull L-hand W over to his R side.

15   Action same for M as in meas 7 (fig X). W moves to R side of M but stays in twd ctr. W make only 1 turn.

16   On stamps (R, L, R) W join hands in circle. M grasps W L wrist with R. M L arm out to L, a little above shoulder level, palm up.

XI. Star Circle

1	All look a little L of ctr of circle. Move to RLOD. Step L in RLOD (ct 1, &). Close R to L (ct 2). Hop on R and click heels (ct &).
2–6	Repeat action of meas 1 (fig XI) five times.
7–8	M pull W out of circle to his L side. Pose facing ctr with inside arms around ptr's waist and outside hands high.

KUJAWIAK

Kujawiak (koo-YAH-vee-ahk) is a Polish couple dance that originated in the Kujawy region, the agricultural lowland located northwest of Warsaw. It became popular all over Poland as a ballroom dance and is, therefore, one of Poland's five national dances, suggestive of the grain blowing gently in the fields. Kujawiak has many steps and figures, and only a few have been chosen for this arrangement, which was introduced by Ada Dziewanowska and has consequently been called Ada's Kujawiak No. 1. The figures may be rearranged to fit other Kujawiak music.

Record: "Pozegnanie Ojczyzny" (Farewell to My Country), side A, band 3; "Na wierzbowym listku" (On a Willow Leaf), LP Muza XL 0203

Formation: Cpls around the room, M and W face each other, M back to ctr of circle, fists or knuckles on own hips slightly fwd, elbows also fwd.

Steps and Styling: An erect posture with slightly bent knees. From time to time the M performs more elaborate steps than the W.

Basic Step: Keep knees slightly bent throughout this step. Step on L (R) (ct 1); slightly smaller step on ball of R (L) (ct 2); small step on ball of L (R) near other ft (ct 3). Repeat same pattern with opp ftwk. This is a type of waltz step, with the first step longer than the other two.

Heel-Step-Step: Step fwd on L heel, knee almost straight (ct 1); step fwd on R (ct 2); step fwd on L (ct 3). The first step is longer than the other two. Repeat same pattern in the next meas with opp ftwk.

M Slap-Turn Pattern: Step fwd on R (ct 1); pivot CW on R ft during remainder of meas (cts &, 2, &, 3). Meanwhile raise L knee (ct &) and with a wide movement slap the top (*not* side) of L thigh twice with L hand (cts 2, 3).

Flat Step (3 per meas): Flat walking steps in even rhythm done with bent knees.

Meter 3/4   Pattern

Meas

Intro

1–4	M invite W to dance; ptrs face each other and join inside hands with free hands held out to sides.

I. Away and Together, Move LOD, Cpl Turn

1–3	Starting with outside ft, move fwd in LOD with 3 basic steps turning to open away from ptr (meas 1), face ptr (meas 2), open away (meas 3). The extended outside arms do not do any special movements, but move naturally as the body turns.
4	With 1 basic step, M lead W from his R side across in front of him to finish in shldr-shldr blade pos facing ptr, M facing LOD.
5–7	Move in LOD with 3 basic steps (M fwd, W bkwd). On last ct & rise slightly on balls of ft in preparation for dip in meas 8.
8	Both do a slow dip, bending knees and pointing them to L (ct 1); then recover by straightening knees (cts 2, 3).
9–11	Still in shldr-shldr blade pos, both beg L ft, turn CW around each other with 3 heel-step-step patterns.
12	Stamp twice, R L (cts 1, 2), hold, as ptrs turn L hips adjacent (ct 3).
13–15	Repeat action of meas 9–11, reversing ftwk and direction.
16	Stamp twice as ptrs resume starting pos of fig I.
17–32	Repeat action of meas 1–16. On last meas finish facing ptr in open pos with outside fist on own hip, M back to ctr of circle.

II. Away and Together with Slap-Turn Pattern

1–3	With M R arm around W waist, W L hand on M R shldr, and free hands in fists on own hips, repeat action of fig I, meas 1–3.
4	Moving across in front of ptr, M dance 1 slap-turn pattern, as W moves bkwd with 3 small flat steps.
5–7	Cpl turn CW (M fwd, W bkwd) with 3 flat step patterns (9 steps in all).
8	M stamp R L, W stamp L R (cts 1, 2) to finish M back to ctr, facing ptr; hold, adjusting wt to M R, W L (ct 3).
9–16	Repeat action of meas 1–8 (fig II).
	Interlude
1–4	Ptrs join both hands straight across. Balance bkwd away from ptr, arms extended fwd (meas 1); balance fwd twd ptr, arms extended sdwd (meas 2). Repeat balance bkwd and fwd (meas 3–4).

Note: This is the same musical phrase as the intro.

MAZUR

The figures used in this dance were done by a Polish group at the World's Fair at San Francisco's Treasure

Island. They were taught to Madelynne Greene, who arranged them to fit this record. These figures are to be used as an exhibition dance for sets of four couples. There are many Mazur figures.

Record: National (45 rpm) 4001

Formation: Circle of 8 or 12 couples, all facing CCW, W to R of M, inside arms extended slightly fwd, chest high, elbows bent. W forearm resting lightly on M, fingers clasped in his hand. Outside fist on hips.

Steps and Styling: This dance should be done vigorously and accurately, but not so stylized that it loses a feeling of vitality.

Mazur Step: An accented running step to 3/4 meter. Accent the first beat of each measure by bending the supporting knee slightly and touching the opposite heel beside the supporting foot, i.e., step fwd on L, bending L knee slightly (ct 1), the foot is flat (not just the ball of the foot), step on R heel beside L or slightly in front of it (ct and), roll weight from heel to ball of foot (ct 2), step fwd on L (ct 3). The feet are parallel and close to the floor. The dip and rise are from the bending of the knees. Repeat starting R.

Note: According to Madelynne Greene, this step is more authentic than the next one. When the dance was first taught, the following step was used.

Mazur Step: An accented running step to 3/4 meter. Accent the first beat with a heavy step, bringing the opposite foot up sharply in back with a knee bend. On cts 2 and 3 the steps are small and unaccented.

Mazur Turn: Partners face each other, right hips adjacent, R arm around partner's waist, L hands high; 2 Mazur steps turning CW, starting M L, W R. Reverse, placing L arm at partner's waist, R arm high, turn CCW with 2 Mazur steps. Stepclose with heel clicks; starting M L, W R, step to side (ct 1), close opposite foot to leading foot (ct 2), jump on supporting foot, clicking heels together in air (ct 3).

Mazurka, Pas de Basque.

Meter 3/4   Pattern

Meas

1–2   Intro: Stand in formation.

I. Balance and Click Steps and Mazur Turn

1–4   Progressing fwd in LOD with 4 Mazur steps (starting M L, W R), balance away from each other, pushing joined hands fwd and turning slightly back to back. Balance toward each other, bending elbows again. Arms are kept chest high throughout step. Repeat balance away and together.

5–8   Face partners, release inside hands and sweep them down between partners and up, finishing with M R, W L, hands curved over head, outside fists remain on hips. At the same time take 4 step-close with heel click steps in LOD.

9–12   Mazur turn.

13–24   Repeat fig I, meas 1–12.

II. Circle Right and Left (Mazur Turns)

1–4   All join hands in single circle, facing R. Circle CCW with 4 Mazur steps, starting M L, W R.

5–8   W turn toward partners, Mazur turn.

9–12   Repeat meas 1–4, facing L and progressing CW.

13–16   M turn toward partners, Mazur turn.

III. Double Circle

1–4   All face center, with 4 Mazur steps W move forward, forming small circle by linking arms at the elbows, fist on hips. If each W puts her R arm through the L elbow of the adjacent W, this will avoid confusion. At the same time the M move in with 4 Mazur steps to join hands, arms extended to form outer circle.

5–8   M Circle L, W circle R with 3 Mazur steps, accent last meas with 2 stamps.

9–12   Repeat meas 5–8, reversing direction, M circle R, W circle L.

1–2   "Weaving the Basket" Position
On *two chorded measures* partners should take places, W to R of M. W slide hands down, joining them to form a circle, M lift joined hands over W heads, forming a basket.

IV. The Basket

1–8   Circle CW 7 Mazur steps, all starting with L ft. Accent 8th meas with 2 stamps.

9–16   Circle CCW 7 Mazur steps starting with R, 2 stamps on 16th meas.

V. Forming Lines

The next two figures are done with M in one line, W in another line facing partners, in groups of 4 couples. Couples are numbered 1, 2, 3, 4 CW around circle. For festival dancing, the two couples with backs nearest the music break the circle and swing back into line, all facing the music. For an exhibition, the couples with backs to the audience break the circle and all move into a line facing the audience.

1–8   W of couple 1 and M of last couple release hands and join them with own partners so that all dancers are in a chain. The end couples move backward and the center couples slightly forward with 8 Mazur steps to form a straight line.

San Antonio College Dancers

9–12 Release hands. M dance forward with 4 Mazur steps, turning to face partners on the last meas. Arms are crossed on chest. W turn CW in place, L hand on hip, R hand high. The lines should be 6 or 8 feet apart with a space between each group of 4 couples.

VI. Solos

Each couple does a solo while the other couples in the lines keep time with small Mazur steps in place, clapping their hands. M clap on the first beat, W on 2 and 3. This is supposed to be an impromptu step to show the skill of the dancers; however, four figures are suggested:

1–4 Couple 1 in each group dance down the center of the set with 4 Mazurka steps, facing each other, M L, W R, hands high, other fist on hip.

5–8 2 Mazur steps backing even with lines, both fists on hips, elbows slightly forward. Dance 2 Mazur steps toward each other.

9–12 Mazur turn at foot of group of four.

13–16 Couple 1 returns to place with 4 Mazur steps, M going up outside of M line, W outside W line. While couple 1 returns to place, couple 4 dances up the center of the lines; with inside hands joined, balance away, together; the W turns R under joined hands to face partner.

17–20 Mazur turn at head of sets.

21–24 Couple 4 returns to own place with 4 Mazur steps, each going down outside of respective lines. While couple 4 returns to place, couple 2 dances down the center of the set with 4 step-close heel clicks.

25–28 Couple 2 does Mazur turn at foot of set.

29–32 Couple 2 returns to place with 4 Mazur steps, dancing up the outside of respective lines. While couple 2 returns to place, couple 3 dances up the center of the set with inside hands joined, free hands on hips, balance away, together, away, together, with 4 Mazur steps.

33–36 Couple 3 does Mazur turn at head of set.

37–40 Couple 3 returns to place with 4 Mazur steps, outside respective lines.

OBEREK

This Oberek (oh-BAIR-ek) was introduced by Anatol Joukowsky.

Record: "Oberek," Harmonica 1015 A, or any Oberek music.

Formation: Circle of cpls, facing CCW, inside hands joined at waist level, M L hand in fist on his L hip. W takes skirt 8 or 10 inches below the waist (in R) and holds it up (waist level) on front of R hip (palm out, fingers bwd). This is the skirt hold whenever R is free.

Steps: Steps are indicated for M; W steps are counterpart unless otherwise indicated.

Pas de basque, Walking step, Waltz Balance

Mazur Step: An accented running step to 3/4 meter. Accent the first beat, bringing the opposite ft up sharply in back with a knee bend. On ct 2 the step is small and unaccented and a heavy accent on ct 3.

Step-Close with Heel Clicks: Step to own R on R (ct 1), close L to R (ct 2), jump on L ft, clicking heels together in air (ct 3).

Dish-Rag Turn: Ptrs facing, both hands joined straight across; retaining both handholds, M turns L under his L arm while W turns R under her R arm, to end facing ptr in original position. Variation: W only turns once completely to R (or L), while M assists her in her turn as he dances in place.

Meter 3/4   Pattern

Meas

1–4 Intro: Face ptr and bow.

I. Pas de Basque, Step-Stamp, Dish-Rag Turn

1–8 Starting outside ft (M L, W R), cpl progresses fwd in LOD with 8 pas de basque steps (in a reaching manner), turning out on outside ft, and in twd ptr on inside ft, swinging joined hands fwd and bwd (1 pas de basque step to each meas).

9 Cpl facing (M back to center of circle), join both hands straight across. M step L (ct 1), bring R to L with small stamp (ct 2), hold (ct 3).

10   Repeat meas 9, starting M R.

11–12 Cpl does dish-rag turn moving CCW with scuff steps as follows: Step twd LOD (M L, W R), scuff heel (M R, W L) twd LOD and complete turn pivoting on M L, W R. Momentum of the scuff carries you through on the pivot.

13–16 Repeat action of meas 9–12, moving CW (starting M R, W L).

1–8   Repeat action of meas 1–8.
       (rpt)

II. Pivot-Turn (Oberek Step)

1   Cpl in semiopen pos, except M L hand is extended outward at shoulder level, and W R hand holds her skirt. M steps L with heavily accented dip, pivoting to R, turning CW (cts 1, 2, 3); W takes 3 small steps R, L, R while turning to her R.

2   M takes 3 small steps R, L, R to recover from dip of meas 1, while W pivots R on heavy dip on L ft (cts 1, 2, 3).

3–16   Repeat meas 1–2 seven more times (8 in all). End facing CCW. Change pos on last meas to starting pos, inside hands joined.
       Note: During the M dip on his L ft, he may insert heel-clicks, if he prefers, as follows: Dip on L (ct 1), click R heel against L twice (cts 2, 3) in air. This variation is done only by M.

1–8   Repeat action of fig I, meas 1–8.
       (rpt)

III. Walk with Dish-Rag Turn

1–4   Cpl facing CCW, inside shoulders together, W L arm in back of M joined in his L hand over, or slightly above, his L shoulder; M R arm extended across in front of W, chest high, holding W R hand. Cpl moves fwd with 3 reaching pas de basque steps, both starting R and reverses direction with 4th pas de basque. Reversal of direction is performed by turning in twd ptr without breaking handhold. Cpl now faces CW, M L hand in back of W, joined with her L hand over her shoulder.

5–8   Moving bwd, cpl repeats meas 1–4, turning inward on 8th meas to face CCW once more. During meas 8, both take 2 steps only, L R (cts 1, 2) holding ct 3, leaving L ft free to start next fig. M places R hand behind W at her waist, W holds skirt with R.

9–16   Cpl makes 2 turns almost in place CCW (both moving in very small circle) with following step: M step L (ct 1), tap R heel beside L (ct 2), step R (ct 3). W step L (ct 1), brush ball of R ft slightly fwd beside L (ct 2), step R (ct 3). Repeat step 7 times, making 8 in all.

During meas 16 both take 3 steps (L, R, L), ending with wt on L ft.

1–8   Repeat action of fig III, meas 1–8, both completing 8 pas de basque steps.

IV. Circle Turn (Butterfly)

1–7   Cpl in open pos, bend deeply at waist (heads of ptrs adjacent, nearly touching). Outside arms are extended sdwd at shoulder level. Both starting R ft, cpl turns twice in small circle CW, M moving fwd, W bwd, using 7 small pas de basque steps.

8   M changes W to his L side by taking 2 quick steps (L R), moving slightly to his R. W makes a complete L turn in 2 steps (L R), changing to M L side.

9–16   In new pos, cpl makes 2 turns CCW (M again moving fwd) with 8 small pas de basque steps, starting L ft.
       Interlude

1–4   W spins to her L away from ptr, to join hands in center and form a circle with all other W, facing out; M form circle facing in, fists on hips.

1–3   Both circles move to R using step-close with heel click steps. Repeat step 2 more times (3 in all).

4   Take 3 stamps in place (R, L, R).

5–7   Repeat meas 1–3 moving to L, starting L ft.

8   M takes 2 stamps (cts 1, 2) hold ct 3, wt on R ft. W takes 3 stamps, L, R, L (cts 1, 2, 3), wt on L ft.

9–11   Facing ptr, hands joined in cross-hold pos, take 3 Mazur steps (beginning M L, W R) moving out of center (M bwd, W fwd).

12   W turn to R once without breaking handhold (dish-rag) using 1 Mazur step (L, R, L) while M does 1 Mazur step in place (R, L, R).

13–16 Repeat meas 9–12, returning to center (W bwd, M fwd), with W turning L on 16th meas while M takes 2 stamps (R, L) cts 1, 2, holding ct 3, wt on L.

1–8   Repeat action of fig V, meas 1–8.
       (rpt)

9–12   Repeat action of fig V, meas 9–11. On meas 12 change to back hold pos (no dish-rag turn for W).

13–20 Cpl turns CW (twice) in own circle with 8 Mazur steps, M starting L, W R. End in cross-hold pos.

21–24 Beginning M L, W R (M fwd, W bwd), return to center with 4 Mazur steps. W does not dish-rag turn; M takes 2 stamps (R, L) ending with wt on L.

Duquesne University Tamburitzans

7–8   With both hands joined straight across, cpl does a dish-rag turn to M L (LOD), using scuff step. Cpl bends low and close to each other on the turn.

9–32   Repeat action of fig VII, meas 1–8, three more times (4 in all).

VIII. Pas de Basque and Pose

1–6   Repeat action of fig I, meas 1–6.

7–8   Ending pose: M turns W under their joined hands (CW) (meas 7) and drops to R knee, with L knee up and fwd in LOD (meas 8) W sits on M L knee, L hand in lap, R hand holding skirt at side, facing out of center. M R arm extended out from shoulder, L arm at W back.

1–8   Repeat action of fig V, meas 1–8, both starting R and moving R.
(rpt)

9–16   Moving out of center in cross-hold pos, repeat action of fig V, meas 9–12, two times (8 Mazur steps), omitting the dish-rag turns for W.
Note: On last 3 meas M maneuvers W (CW) to outside of circle. On meas 16 assume position for Oberek step.

VI. Pivot-Turn (Oberek)

1–16   Repeat action of fig II, meas 1–16, only. Join inside hands on meas 16.

VII. Mazur, Heel-Click, and Turn

1–2   Cpl facing, inside hands joined, free hand in fist on hip. Beginning M L, W R, dance 2 Mazur steps (slightly back to back and face to face).

3–4   Moving in LOD, M starts L and does 2 heel-click steps, with L fist on his hip and his R arm swinging down and up in a circle, flicking W skirts (as W turns alone). W with fists on hips, takes 2 turns to her R with scuff steps (same step as in fig I, meas 11–12).

5–6   Cpl facing, inside hands joined, dance 1 Mazur step to M L (LOD) and 1 Mazur step to M R (RLOD).

POLKA

This arrangement of typical Polish polka steps and figures was made by Eugene Ciejka.

Record: any Polish polka music

Formation: Cpls in a circle, both facing LOD. M on inside, W outside. M holding W L hand with his R. Free hand on hip. Thumb behind, fingers front and curled under.

Steps and Styling: Keep the steps small and low except where specified. Work off the balls of the feet and the ankles, keeping the knees slightly bent at all times. The accented spots where the heels must hit the floor are noted.

Polka (Polish "hop"): Hop on R foot (ct uh). Touch L toe to floor (ct 1). Hop on R ft while bringing L ft up sharply with bend at knee so sole of L ft shows (ct &). Leap onto L ft while bringing R ft up sharply with bend at knee so sole of R ft shows (ct 2), hold (ct &). Repeat action, with opp ftwk, for next meas. Steps are described for M; W dances with opp ftwk.

Meter 2/4   Pattern

Meas

Figure 1: Walk in LOD

1–7   Seven basic polka steps in LOD. No side-to-side movement. On ct 1 when touching ft to floor, touch in front, advancing with each step.

8   Stamp 4 times, taking wt on each (cts 1, &, 2, &).

Figure 2: Circle Around Each Other Facing LOD

1   Still facing LOD, and placing both hands on hips, M take one basic polka moving forward

slightly, as W take one basic polka moving backward slightly.

2–3   M, making CW circle around spot partner was in while facing LOD, returns to original spot to L of W. W does same as M, but moves CW behind M and then to front to return to same spot.

4   Face partner and stamp 4 times, taking wt on each ct with hands on hips and slight bend at waist (cts 1, &, 2, &).

5–8   Repeat meas 1–4.

Figure 3: Balance Out and In

1–2   M, using basic polka, balance out and in. W, using basic polka, balance out and in.

3–7   Repeat meas 1 and 2 2½ more times, finishing on balance out. M R hand holding W L hand, with free hand on hip.

8   Turn to face partner. Retaining handhold, stamp 4 times, taking wt on each ct.

Figure 4: Basic Polka with CW Turn.
Basic Step: Same as noted except where touch of ft is indicated. M: On each even meas places R ft behind and beyond L ft. The M odd meas have no cross over and are considered as recovery steps. All this is done in closed position while turning CW. W: Does same step but her even meas are recovery steps and odd meas are cross over steps.

1–7   Seven basic polka steps turning CW ½ turn per meas, finishing with M on inside (turn a little more on last meas).

8   Stamp 4 times, taking wt on each ct (cts 1, &, 2, &).

Figure 5: Basic Polka with CCW Turn
Same as above but now W even meas are recovery steps and M odd meas are recovery steps. In short, M now does W steps and W does M steps of meas 1–8.

9–15 7 basic polka steps turning CCW, finishing with M inside circle (turn a little more on last meas).

16   Stamp 4 times, taking wt on each ct (cts 1, &, 2, &).

Figure 6: Move to New Partner

1–3   Both hands on hips and on inside of circle moving RLOD. M takes 3 basic walking polka steps to W behind him. W takes 3 basic polka steps to M ahead of her.

4   Both make ¼ turn CCW while stamping 4 times, taking wt on each ct (cts 1, &, 2, &) to face new dancer, bending slightly at waist.

5   With basic polka M makes ¼ turn CW to face RLOD. W takes one basic polka to make ¼ turn CW to face LOD and moving slightly forward.

6–7   M moving RLOD, W LOD, progress towards next dancer with two basic polka steps.

8   M and W turn CCW to face partner while stamping 4 times, taking wt on each ct (cts 1, &, 2, &).

9–16 Repeat meas 1–8. Except on meas 16, M makes ½ turn CCW to face LOD. W does not turn at all but remains facing LOD.
      Repeat entire dance.

POLONAISE

The polonaise (poh-LOH-nez) is Poland's "Grand March" and is danced to open the festivities on such ceremonial occasions as weddings and community gatherings. The Polish name for the dance is "Polonez," but it is popularly known by the French name Polonaise. The dance dates back to the fifteenth century and has many variations. The following variation comes from the region of Warsaw and was taught in the United States by Anatol Joukowsky.

Record: Bruno BR 50071, side B, band 8, or any other Polish polonaise music

Formation: Cpls in double circle facing LOD (CCW), M to L and slightly behind W, ptrs L joined and extended fwd about shoulder height. W hold skirt with R; M R at small of back, palm out, or extended at shoulder level in a protective arc behind W but not touching her. Ptrs should not be too close to each other.

Steps and Styling: Basic Step: Step fwd R (ct 1), step fwd L (ct 2), step fwd R, bending knee and almost at the same time lightly brush L fwd (ct 3). Next step starts fwd with L. Description same for M and W unless otherwise noted.

Meter 3/4   Pattern

Meas

I. Promenade

1–3   Both beginning R, dance 3 basic steps fwd in LOD.

4   Both beginning L, W dance 1 basic step almost in place while M dances 1 basic step bwd twd ctr. Finish M facing almost RLOD, W LOD, L hands still joined.

II. Cross over and Return
Change places by moving fwd in an arc, L hands still joined.

5   Beginning R, dance 1 basic step twd ptr's place.

6   Continuing fwd movement, step L (ct 1), step

R (ct 2), point L toe and shoulder twd ptr (ct 3). W is now on inside of circle facing RLOD; M on outside facing LOD.

7–8 Cross over to take starting pos of meas 1 (Promenade). M move straight across and W turn R, backing under raised joined L hands with one basic step (meas 7). Continuing movement, step R (meas 8, ct 1); step L (ct 2); stamp R beside L, no wt (ct 3). Cpls are now in pos to start the dance again.

ROMANIA

Romanian Folk Dancing

by Eugenia Popescu-Judetz

Romania, situated in southeastern Europe, is located in the Carpatho-Danubian space, in the area between the Carpathian Mountains and the Danube River. The country is bordered by the Soviet Union, Hungary, Yugoslavia, and Bulgaria, and has an eastern coast washed by the Black Sea.

Romanians are the descendants of the Geto-Dacians, a branch of the Thracians, and the Romans, who conquered Dacia in the year 107 A.D. and turned Dacia into a Roman province.

Duquesne University Tamburitzans

The folk traditions of Romania are linked with the origin of her people and are related to the neighboring peoples of the Balkan region. The historic regions of Romania include: Muntenia, Oltenia, Moldavia, Dobrudga, Banat, and Transylvania. Muntenia was known in the past as Walachia. These divisions represent traditional styles in folk productions. They, in turn, are subdivided into smaller areas, identified with the administrative districts of the country, which are further subdivided into particular zones of folk styles.

Romanian folk dances constitute a vast repertoire of categories and variants displayed in a wide spectrum of distinct examples. The variants combine the basic national elements of dancing, which are common to all the regions of the country, into particular units and variations. The contents of the dance variations from the different regions emphasize both unity of style and variety of particular features.

The repertoire of each village and locale is rich in dances, ranging from at least twelve or fifteen dances to as many as forty to sixty specific dances known and practiced in a single village. The titles of the dances suggest folk imagery and symbolism. The subject qualifier may reflect the name of a place, district, or region; nationality or ethnic community; age and status; class qualification; occupation; girls' or boys' names; plants and flowers; domestic and wild animals; birds and fish; household objects; dance characteristics like direction and style; psychological distinction of individuals; and ancestral cult symbols.

The repertoire of dances is not differentiated in terms of age. The same dances are performed by all generations. Children practice the village dances. They learn by watching the teen-agers while they engage in dancing, and they practice the new dances for a while before attempting to perform them in front of the community. This usually happens when the children reach the right age to enter the community dance gathering. Children do have their own games. Dance is only a small part of their games' structure, one of the constituent elements along with rhymes, singing, pantomime, and acting.

Romanian folk dances are either performed by both men and women, by men alone, or only by women. There are a great number of dances for men, whereas dances for women are very scarce.

The dance gathering of the village is called a *hora* or *joc*, both terms meaning dance in a general sense. The dancing session is held after lunch on Sunday afternoons and on holidays, generally till sunset. The gathering is held in the village main square or in the outskirts of the village. In winter the dancing moves to a room in the clubhouse, at the village pub, or even in a barn or a cabin.

In present-day Romania every village and hamlet

has its own cultural home, with a room and a stage platform where the dance gatherings and folk shows are presented.

Traditionally, the individual performer is ready to enter the group of village dancers at the age of fourteen or fifteen. This is the time when the individual girl or boy is welcomed into the community as a new member of the teen-age group, with the full status of an adult looking ahead to the exercise of his or her working duties, getting married, and raising a family.

The candidate comes to the gathering thoroughly prepared for the event. A girl will be dressed in a new outfit made especially for this event, with rich embroidery and bright colors. A lad also wears a new costume sewed by his sisters or cousins.

The male candidate has to prove, before the community, his dancing ability and his strength in athletic movements, both considered by the community as precious values of his malehood and the capacity for work he is expected to pursue. The girl who is accepted in the hora feels like a debutante; her graceful appearance reflects the promise of a kind future bride and housewife.

The hora event is the highlight of the community's social life. The performers, consisting only of teen-agers and nonmarried individuals, are surrounded by a large audience of parents, relatives, friends, and the whole community. The emphasis in the hora event is on the social function of the gathering. After enter-ing the hora, the young performers will get engaged and will later marry.

The community watches the performers, standing about in silence and not interfering in their performance. However, their attitude is rather critical, reserved, and contemplative. They do not applaud or praise the dancers. Sometimes the bystanders express their criticism of the dance style of the performers and their interpretations of traditional steps.

Married couples continue to dance only at family parties, ceremonies, during holiday festivities, and at smaller gatherings of friends and relatives. The old people still dance on special occasions, at weddings, and at celebrations—after warming up with some drinking.

Romania's traditional life-style has undergone many changes. Folk dancing is mostly an organized activity. Every village has a dancing group that participates regularly in folk competitions and performs at folk festivals in its own area and elsewhere. The amateur groups and clubs have a busy agenda, traveling constantly to perform at shows. However, the Sunday hora is a tradition still very much a part of the social scene of the village community.

Besides the hora event, balls and celebrations are held around the year, bringing together the young as well as the old people of the community. At these occasions, there is no restriction preventing married people from dancing side by side with the teen-agers.

Romanian folk dances fall into many categories, including: ensemble dances, performed on all occasions by everyone; group dances, performed by a select group of virtuosos possessing a great deal of skill and training, or by specialty dancers; couple dances; solo dances; dances with one soloist or several soloists, performed by an ensemble with solo parts during the performance; command dances, with movements executed in response to the particular command shouted by the leader or by all the dancers; song-dances, involving dancing and singing at the same time; ceremonial and ritual dances; mask dances; entertainment dances; and dances involving objects.

The following classification defines dance types by grouping dances with identical structure patterns in terms of rhythm, steps, design, and form. There are three major types, representing the basic dance forms:

Hora, the national and standard dance, with variants grouped into three forms: walking, leaping, and stamping horas.

Brîul is the second major type. Mostly intended for men, it is characterized by syncopated and intricate step patterns. The main categories are brîul pe opt (with a musical phrase of 4 bars 2/4), brîul pe şase (with a musical phrase of 3 bars 2/4), brîul of Banat, brîul from Oltenia, corăgheasca from Moldavia.

Sîrba, another major type, is very entertaining and popular.

Other minor types contain many variants, including denominations such as geamparalele, schioapa, rustemul, fecioreasca, calabreaza, hategana, invîrtita, dealungul, and bota. All these types have further subtypes, with specific denominations and structures.

Căluşul is a unique dance, being both a type and a particular dance at the same time. Intended to be performed only by men, it is a ritual of spring. A model for agricultural rites, it includes dance virtuosity, drama, and pantomime.

The majority of Romanian dances have a binary rhythm. There are also dances with an *aksak* and ternary rhythm. The spectrum of dance rhythm is dominated by syncopation, recurring in short formulas and also involving long, intricate combinations of accents and values.

The dynamics are very distinctive. The dances are mainly energetic, lively, and set to a vivid tempo. The mood is lyrical, but the coloring is cheerful, bright, outspoken, and intense. The dances are for the most part fast. However, there are also examples in moderate tempo and a few in slow tempo.

Research into Romanian dances has not been completed at present. The results of these findings, in the form of collections, studies and surveys, indicate an exceptional wealth of variants, with many thousands of specific dances evenly distributed all over the country. The great variety of examples underscores the vital creative spirit and ingenuity of the Romanian people.

Romanian dances were first introduced to the United States by Romanian immigrants who came to America in the late nineteenth century. Those immigrants, mostly peasants from Transylvania, Banat, and Bukovina (north of Moldavia), brought to the new country their own folk songs and dances from the regions where they originated.

In the period before World War I, there were many folk dance groups in the Romanian communities of Michigan, Indiana, Ohio, and Illinois. But when the old-timers retired from this activity, the groups faded and the second generation concentrated on other forms of ethnic entertainment. A revival of interest in folk dancing occurred after World War II, particularly in the fifties and sixties, when instructors (such as Larisa Lucaci) started to teach Romanian dances in Romanian communities and American dance groups and clubs. Interest in Romanian dances has increased in recent years. New instructors, including both American teachers (such as Martin Koenig and Sunni Bloland) and native Romanian teachers (such as Jacob Lascu and Mihai and Alexandru David) have worked to develop a knowledge of Romanian dances by holding workshops and organizing performing groups.

Following are several types of Romanian dances that have become popular in the United States.

Alunelul is a well-known Romanian dance in the United States, having reached this country with the first Romanian immigrants from Oltenia. Originally a regional dance, the simple alunelul was first introduced in Romanian grammar schools and soon became popular all over the country. It is a rare example of a children's dance, having a charming melody and

Duquesne University Tamburitzans

children's rhymes. Oltenia is the homeland of alunelul dances. The alunelul is performed in a straight line, in basket or shoulder position, and contains many crossing and stamping steps.

Hora, the national Romanian dance, is performed all over the country and on any occasion. The symbol of unity and national solidarity, a hora opens all official ceremonies and closes celebrations. The main hora or simple hora is performed with basic walking steps, with a continuing movement of the circle in counter-clockwise direction. Hora also means the main circle dance, since the characteristic formation of this dance type is a circle. The hora has many variations of steps, ranging from simple walking steps, through grapevine steps, to stamping steps with syncopation. The meter is basically 2/4, with other variants having 3/8, 3/4, or 6/8 meter.

Sîrba is currently a very popular dance all over the land, ranking above the other specific dances. Its rhythm is binary, very fast, and alluring. The main formation is an open circle, in shoulder position. The basic pattern is a movement in a counterclockwise direction with three steps and in a clockwise direction with one step. The steps performed are mostly hopping steps with much leg swinging. Other steps common to sîrba-type dances are crossing steps, grapevine steps, and hopping steps with fluttering movements. The sîrba-type dance has many variants.

Ciuleandra, a sîrba-type dance with a beautiful, flowing melody, is based on running steps. The main trait of the dance is the circular movement around the space, the dancers flowing and floating and never coming to rest. The dancers assume the shoulder position and move in very small circles or in ever-widening circles. The dance ends with these circles spinning rapidly.

Rustemul is similar to the Bulgarian pajduško. An entertaining dance with many variants, rustemul comes from the region of Oltenia and parts of Muntenia. It is performed either in a straight line or in a circle, with various arm positions. Its meter is basically 5/16. However, Romanian variants frequently contain other meters, such as 6/8, 3/8, and even 2/4.

Invîrtita, a dance which originated in Transylvania, is a model of syncopation. It is an elegant couple and group whirling dance. Performed in small circles of from four to eight individuals, it moves in two directions, with almost continuous spinning. The binary melody is sensuous and attractive.

Ardeleana is popular in Banat and some parts of Transylvania. This couple dance has varied positions for the partners; they switch direction and arm position. The dance ends with a swinging and spinning section.

Eugenia and Gheorghe Popescu-Judetz

(Eugenia Popescu-Judetz was born in Romania and was educated as a choreographer and ethnomusicologist. She studied at the University of Bucharest and the Institute of Balkan Studies. Her husband was the late Gheorghe Popescu-Judetz, artist emeritus, outstanding folk dance researcher and choreographer, author of ten volumes containing descriptions of approximately one thousand Romanian folk dances [including explanations and notations], with information on many more, and creator of an efficient dance notation method for use by folk dance researchers known as the Judetz folk dance notation. Together with her husband, Eugenia Popescu-Judetz carried out research in the field and collected thousands of dances of Romania. They have also performed together in dance concerts.

Her experience includes nine years as ballet soloist with the Romanian Theatre and Opera of Bucharest and sixteen years as choreographer and ballet master of Perinița, a Bucharest-based professional folk ensemble. She was also a ballet and character dance teacher at the School of Choreography in Bucharest, has choreographed TV shows, and was artistic supervisor of the National Opera of Baalbek in 1968. This talented folk dance authority has conducted teaching tours in folk dancing in India, Yugoslavia, the United States, Finland, Belgium, and England from 1969 to 1972.

Since 1973, she has been a professor at the Duquesne University Tamburitzans Institute of Folk Arts.

Eugenia Popescu-Judetz is the author of various books and articles on Romanian folk dances and Turkish music and arts. She has won many awards, including: first prize at the International Dance Competition in Prague in 1950 [with her husband]; Cultural Merit Order, Labor Order, and Labor medal of Romania; first prize at the international dance festivals of Vienna, and Tunis, and Agrigento, from 1959 to 1964, for her choreography with Perinița.)

ROMANIAN FOLK DANCES

ALUNELUL

Alunelul (ah-loo-NEH-lool), which means "Little Hazelnut," is a Romanian circle dance that was first introduced by Larisa Lucaci.

Record: Folk Dance (45 rpm) MH-1120; Folkraft (LP) F-LP-31; Elektra (LP) EKS-7206

Formation: No ptrs necessary; closed circle, all facing ctr; bodies held erect, arms straight out to sides, hands on nearest shoulders of adjacent dancers. Small circles of 8–10 persons are suggested. Dancers face ctr of circle during entire dance.

Steps: Sideward Run, Stamp

Meter 2/4   Pattern

Meas

4   Intro

I. Five Steps and Stamps

1   Move sdwd to R with 4 light running steps, beginning R and stepping L, behind R; R (ct 1); L (ct &); R (ct 2); L (ct &).

2   Step R sdwd to R again (ct 1); lightly stamp L heel beside R, no wt (ct &); lightly stamp L heel beside R again, no wt (ct 2); hold (ct &).

3–4   Beginning L and moving sdwd to L, repeat action of meas 1–2.

1–4

5–8   Repeat action of fig I, meas 1–4.

II. Three Steps and Stamp

1   Step to R on R (ct 1); step L behind R (ct &); step to R on R (ct 2); lightly stamp L heel beside R, no wt (ct &).

2   Beginning L and moving to L (CW), repeat action of fig II, meas 5.

3–4   Repeat action of fig II, meas 5–6.

III. One-Step and Stamp
(Music repeats meas 5–8)

1   Dance in place. Step R (ct 1); stamp L heel

beside R, no wt (ct &); step L (ct 2); stamp R heel beside L, no wt (ct &).

2   Step R (ct 1); stamp L heel beside R, no wt (ct &); stamp L heel again, no wt (ct 2); hold (ct &).

2–4   Beginning L, repeat action of fig III, meas 1–2.

Repeat dance from beginning. It is done 5 times to the record.

ARDELEANA CU FIGURI

Ardeleana Cu Figuri (ahr-dehl-YAH-nah coo fee-GOOR), which translates literally as "Dance from Transylvania with Figures," was introduced by Dick Crum, who learned it from natives in several villages surrounding the town of Varset, in Banat, Romania.

In its native setting, the Ardeleana is frequently improvised, variations being performed according to the whim of the dancer.

Record: National (45 rpm) N-4513; Cristea CR-507

Formation: Cpls anywhere on the floor

Steps and Styling:

Basic Ardeleana Step (2 meas): Ptrs face each other, turning slightly to own L. W hands on M shoulders, M R hand at W L shoulder blade, his L hand grasps her R arm just below elbow. M and W use identical ftwk. *Meas 1:* Step diag fwd L with L (ct 1 &), step fwd with R passing L (ct 2), step diag fwd L with L (ct &). *Meas 2:* Hold (ct 1), step diag fwd L with R, passing L (ct &), step diag fwd L with L, passing R (ct 2 &). During these 2 meas cpls revolve CW as far as possible comfortably. To reverse, each dancer turns slightly to own R; W keep hands on M shoulders, M reverses hold so that his L hand is at W R shoulder blade, his R hand grasping her L arm just below elbow. Reverse ftwk by stepping diag fwd R with R and revolve CCW.

Continuation Step (2 meas): This step is added to the Basic Ardeleana Step to form the "Short Turn," the "Long Turn," and is the step used in the "Arches." When done to the L: *Meas 1:* Step diag fwd L with R (ct 1 &), hop on R (really a smooth lift) (ct 2), step diag fwd L with L, passing R (ct &). *Meas 2:* Hold (ct 1), step diag fwd L with R, passing L (ct &), step diag fwd L with L, passing R (ct 2 &). During these 2 meas cpls revolve CW. When done to the R, cpls revolve CCW. Begin stepping diag fwd R with L.

Men's Show-off Steps: These steps are actually personal improvisations done by the M. Ptrs face each other, M R and W L hands joined. W R (back of hand) on hip. M may place his L hand behind head, elbow out to side, or it may be on his hip or held low out to side. While M does Show-off Steps, W takes small walking steps as she follows him from side to side, or does Basic Ardeleana Step.

Show-off Step #1 (2 meas): *Meas 1* (moving to R): Hop R, kicking L out quickly (ct 1), step L (ct &), hop L, kicking R out quickly (ct 2), step R (ct &). *Meas 2:* Dip slightly on R leg, swinging L ft down and across in front of R with inner edge of ft up (ct 1 &), hop R (ct 2), step L in place, turning to face L (ct &). Moving to L: Repeat above 2 meas with opp ftwk.

Show-off Step #2 (1 meas): Hop on R, swinging L fwd slightly (ct 1), step L to R of R so that outer edges are touching and roll so that outer edge of R is on floor (ct &); keeping ft in same pos, shift wt onto full R so outer edge of L is on floor (ct 2), in same pos shift wt onto full L so outer edge of R is on floor (ct &). Repeat action of above meas with opp ftwk.

Note: During steps in Basic Ardeleana pos, the farther the cpls can revolve the better. Basic Ardeleana and Continuation steps are done rather flat-footed, although as the cpls revolve faster, the steps become a walking heel-toe motion.

Meter 2/4   Pattern

Meas

2   Intro

   I. Basic Ardeleana Step

1–8   Beginning L, dance 4 Basic Ardeleana Steps.

   II. Short Turn

1–4   Beginning L, dance 1 Basic Ardeleana Step followed immediately with 1 Continuation Step to L (beginning with R).

5–8   Beginning R, repeat action of meas 1–4, Short Turn.

   III. Arches
   Beginning L, dance a series of 8 Continuation Steps.

1–2   M touches W L hand (fingers up, palm out) with R hand (at R angle to floor, thumb up, palm out) as he moves diag fwd L, raising his R arm under which W makes ½ turn CCW as he turns ½ CW. Both begin L and dance 1 Continuation Step. Finish facing ptr, releasing hands.

3–4   With 1 Continuation Step moving twd each other, M touches W R hand with his L and they pass, W makes ½ turn CW, M makes ½ turn CCW under the joined hands.

5–8   Repeat action of meas 1–2 (fig III).

9–10   With 1 Continuation Step dancers move twd each other, M takes W L hand in his R (thumb down) and turns her one full turn CCW under the joined hands as he dances in place.

11–12 M takes W L hand in his L (thumb down) and turns her again one full turn CCW as each does 1 Continuation Step. As W finishes turn, M brings her L hand to the small of his back and places it in his R hand there; simultaneously she places her R at the small of her back and he passes his L hand under her L arm and takes her R hand where she placed it. L shoulders are now adjacent, hands grasped at each other's backs.

13–14 In above pos dance 1 Continuation Step moving CCW, as a cpl.

15–16 M releases W R hand and withdraws his L. M dances 1 Continuation Step in place, turning slightly to his R and pulling W around CCW to face him as she does 1 Continuation Step.

   IV. Long Turn

1–8   Dance 1 basic Ardeleana Step to L, followed by 3 consecutive Continuation Steps to L, turning CW.

9–16   Repeat action of meas 1–8 (fig IV), beginning R and turning CCW.

   V. Men's Show-Off Steps

1–8   Do M Show-off Step #1 four times, starting with hop on R.

9–16   Do M Show-off #2 eight times, starting with hop on R.
   Repeat dance from beginning.

   VI. Finale—Short Turn

1–4   Dance 1 basic Ardeleana Step to L, followed by 1 Continuation Step to L (beginning with R).

5–8   Repeat action of meas 1–4 (fig VI) with opp ftwk.
   Dance may end with stamp. The natives do not bow at the end in Ardeleana.

CIULEANDRA

Ciuleandra (choo-LAN-druh) was first presented by Mihai David. He learned the dance while performing with the Romanian State Folk Dance Ensemble during the years 1963–65. The dance comes from the region of Oltenia, in southern Romania.

Record: "The Lark," FLDR-A, 10″ LP; "Gypsy Camp" (LP) GC 5201.

Formation: Mixed lines of 10 to 12 dancers, leader at R end. Arms extended sdwd at shoulder level, hands on nearest shoulder of adjacent dancer (T position). Free hand of end dancers may be extended sdwd at shoulder level or be placed on hip, fingers fwd.

Styling: Posture is erect. Ftwk is precise and controlled. The steps in fig I diminish in size as the tempo increases. In fig II the movement is swift and the steps are done lightly.

Meter 4/4   Pattern

Meas

8   Intro: no action

I. Sway, Forward, Grapevine

1   With plié (bend of knee), step onto R ft and sway body wt completely over R, leave L in place (ct 1); raise on ball of R ft, straightening L knee (ct &); lower R heel and bend knee slightly (ct 2); raise on ball of R ft (ct &). Repeat action of cts 1, &, 2, &, reversing ftwk and direction (cts 3, &, 4, &).

2   Repeat action of meas 1 (fig I). During meas 1–2 face ctr; do not look from side to side.

3   Step fwd on a slight R diag twd ctr on R heel (ct 1); closing L to R (no wt) and bending both knees slightly, take wt on full R ft (ct 2). Repeat action of cts 1, 2, but reverse ftwk (step diag fwd L) (cts 3, 4).

4   Small step R sdwd R (ct 1); raise L leg fwd, knee bent, ankle relaxed (ct 2); step L to L (ct 3); stamp R beside L, no wt (ct 4).
Note: Dancers often join vocalist during meas 4, singing (phonetically) "HOPE shah SHAH shah SHAH."

5   Grapevine: Step R across in front of L (ct 1); step L to L (ct 2); step R across in back of L (ct 3); step L to L (ct 4).

6–7   Repeat action of meas 5 (fig I) two more times.

8   Step R across in front of L (ct 1); step L to L (ct 2); close R to L (ct 3); hold (ct 4).

9–56   Repeat action of meas 1–8 (fig I) six more times. As the tempo increases, the action of the first 2 meas of the 8-meas phrase becomes: R, bounce, L, bounce.

II. Travel (No vocal at beginning of phrase)

1–2   Step R to R (ct 1); step L across in back of R (ct 2); repeat action of cts 1, 2 three more times, except on ct 4 of meas 2 do not cross in back but stamp L beside R (no wt). The 7 steps are small and evenly stressed.

3–4   Repeat action of meas 1–2 (fig II), reversing ftwk and direction. Continue to cross in back.

5–8   Repeat action of meas 1–4 (fig II).

9   Small step R to R (ct 1); stamp L beside R, no wt (ct 2); small step L to L (ct 3); stamp R beside L, no wt (ct 4).

10   Small step R to R (ct 1); step L behind R (ct 2); step R to R (ct 3); stamp L beside R, no wt (ct 4).

11–12   Repeat action of meas 9–10 (fig II), reversing ftwk and direction.

13–16   Repeat action of meas 9–12 (fig II).

17–32   Repeat action of meas 1–16, (fig II).

33–40   Repeat action of meas 1–8, (fig II).

DE-A LUNGUL

De-A Lungul, a couple dance from central Transylvania, translates as "Along the Line." De-A Lungul falls into the category of couple dances, although its name suggests that it is a line or group dance. It has the function of opening a suite of dances (and thereby, the Sunday Hora) due probably to its slow, stately, formal character. Sunni Bloland learned this variant from Puiu Vasilescu.

Record: Roemeense Volksdansen Nevo LP 12153
Formation: Couples in a circle facing LOD
Steps and Styling: Walk, Leg Swing. The dance is stately and the body is held erect.

Meter 3/4   Pattern

Meas

No intro

I. W Circles M CCW (both hands joined)
Woman:

1   Step fwd on L (ct 1); step R in place (ct 2); close L to R (no wt) (ct 3).

2   Step fwd L, R, L (ct 1, 2, 3).

3–4   Raising hands, W circles CCW around M, passing in front of and behind M with 4 walking steps (R, L, R, L), (ct 1, 2, 3, 4). On ct 5 W steps onto R, pivoting CCW (making a full turn) into Varsouvienne pos. Close L to R (no wt) (ct 6).
Man:

1–2   Does the same action as W, meas 1–2.

3–4   Step sdwd on R (ct 1); step L across in front of R (ct 2); step fwd on R (ct 3); step sdwd on L (ct 4); step R across in front of L (ct 5); close L to R (no wt) (ct 6).

5–8   Repeat action of meas 1–4.

II. W Circles M CCW (L hands joined)

1–8   Repeat action of meas 1–8, fig I, except that R hands are not joined.

III. W Circles M CW (R hands joined)
Woman:

1–2   Repeat action of meas 1–2, fig I.

3–4   Drop L hands. Turn outward (CW) to circle M, passing CW behind M, returning to orig pos with 5 walking steps (R, L, R, L, R) (cts 1, 2, 3, 4, 5). Pivot CW on L heel as R ft

takes wt (ct 6). This turn places the W in Varsouvienne pos.

Note: The turn may be a ¾ turn or a 1¾ turn.

Man:

1–4   Repeat action of meas 1–4, fig I (M).

5–8   Repeat action of meas 1–4.

IV. W Inside Cir, M Leg Slap (L hands joined)
Woman:

1   Step fwd on L (ct 1); step R in place (ct 2);
       step L beside R (ct 3).

2   Drop R hands. Begin R. With 3 walking steps,
       pass in front of M to stand at his L side facing
       fwd (ct 1, 2, 3).

3   Hold (ct 1, 2, 3), giving firm support to M
       with L hand.

4   Small leap sdwd R (ct &); step in front of M
       on R (ct 1); step on L, pivoting CW (ct 2);
       close L to R, returning to Varsouvienne pos
       (ct 3).

Man:

1   Step fwd on L (ct 1); step R in place (ct 2);
       step L beside R (ct 3).

2   Having dropped R hands, step sdwd R on R
       (ct 1); step L across in front of R (ct 2); close
       R to L (no wt) (ct 3).

3   Bend knees (ct 1); hop on L, swinging R leg
       fwd with straight knee and slapping R thigh
       or front of lower leg with R palm (ct 2); hold
       with leg raised in front (ct 3).

4   Small leap sdwd on R (ct &); step sdwd L
       on L (ct 1); step R across in front of L (ct
       2); close L to R without wt (ct 3).

5–8   Repeat action of meas 1–4.

1–32   Repeat entire dance from beginning (do each
       fig twice).

1–16   Repeat entire dance from beginning, except
       that this time dance each fig only once.

       There are other possible fig variations; several
       have been added to the preceding figures by
       Ms. Bloland in recent years.

FLORICICA OLTENEASCA

Floricica Olteneasca (floh-rih-CHEE-kah ohl-tehn-
yah-skah) is from the region of Oltenia. It was learned
by Mihai David while dancing with the Romanian
State Folk Dance Ensemble. The instrument played
is the well-known Jew's harp.

Record: "The Lark" (10″ LP), FLDR; "Gypsy Camp"
  (LP), GC 5201

Formation: Open cir of mixed M and W with hands
  holding shoulders of neighbors in "T" pos.

Meter 4/4   Pattern

Part One

Meas   Intro

1   Facing slightly to R in LOD, walk R, L, R
       (cts 1–3), close L to R facing ctr (ct 4).

2   Reverse action of meas 1 in opp dir (RLOD)
       with opp ftwk.

3–4   Repeat action of meas 1–2.

I. Step-Hop and Swd

1   Facing ctr, step slightly R on R (ct 1), hop
       R, raising L knee slightly in front (ct &), step
       slightly L on L (ct 2), hop L, raising R knee
       slightly in front (ct &), step R swd to R (ct
       3), step L behind R (ct &), step R swd to R
       (ct 4), hop R, raising L knee slightly in front
       (ct &).

2   Reverse action of meas 1 in opp dir with opp
       ftwk.

3–4   Repeat action of meas 1–2.

II. Step-Hop, Step-Stamp

1   Step slightly R on R (ct 1), hop R, raising L
       knee slightly (ct &), step slightly L on L (ct
       2), stamp R beside L, no wt (ct &). Repeat
       action of cts 1 & 2 & (cts 3 & 4 &).

2   Repeat action of meas 1.

III. To Ctr, Back

1   Walk to ctr R, L, R, L (cts 1–4), stamp R,
       no wt (ct &),

2   walk bwd out of cir R L R (cts 1 & 2), stamp
       L, no wt (ct &), walk bwd out of cir L R L
       (cts 3 & 4), stamp R, no wt (ct &).

IV. Travel in LOD

1   Facing to R, step R (ct 1), hop R (ct &), step
       L (ct 2), hop L (ct &), step R (ct 3), close L
       to R, taking wt (ct &), step R (ct 4), hop R
       (ct &).

2   Reverse action of meas 1, continuing in LOD.

3–4   Repeat action of meas 1–2.

       Repeat action of fig I through fig IV.

       Repeat action of fig I through fig III.

Part Two

Intro

1–4   Repeat action of meas 1–4 of Intro to Part
       One.

I. Travel in LOD

1–4   Repeat action of meas 1–4 of fig IV, Part One.

II. In Place

1   Jump in place, spread ft apart (ct 1), click an-
       kles together in air (ct &), land on L (ct 2),
       step on ball of R across in back of L, thrusting
       L fwd in air (ct &), hop R (ct 3), slap L in
       front of R (ct &), hop R (ct 4), slap L diag
       to L (ct &).

2 Step L in place (ct 1), quickly step R in front of L (ct uh), quickly step L in place (ct &), step R in place (ct 2), quickly step L in front of R (ct uh), quickly step R in place (ct &), jump in place, ft spread apart (ct 3), click ankles together in air (ct &), land on L, thrusting R fwd in air (ct 4), slap R in front of L (ct &).

III. To Ctr and in Place

1 Moving twd ctr: Hop L, touching R in front of L (ct 1), hop L, touching R diag to R (ct &), hop L, touching R in front of L (ct 2), leap fwd R (ct &), hop R, touching L in front of R (ct 3), hop R, touching L diag to L (ct &), hop R, touching L in front of R (ct 4), leap fwd L (ct &).

2 Hop L, touching R in front of L (ct 1), leap fwd R (ct &), hop R, touching L in front of R (ct 2), leap fwd R (ct &), lift R knee in front (ct 3), hold (ct &).

3 Dancing in place: Step R (ct 4), step L (ct &), step R (ct 1), slap L in front of R (ct &), step L (ct 2), slap R in front of L (ct &), step R in place (ct 3), quickly step L next to R (ct uh), quickly step R in place (ct &), step L slightly swd to L (ct 4), stamp R beside L (ct &).

4 Jump in place, spread ft apart (ct 1), click ankles together in air (ct &), land on L, thrusting R fwd in air (ct 2), slap R in front of L (ct &).

IV. Back Out and in Place

1 Moving bwd out of cir: Step R (ct 1), step L (ct &), step R (ct 2), stamp L beside R (ct &), step L (ct 3), step R (ct &), step L (ct 4), stamp R beside L (ct &).

2 Repeat action of meas 1, continuing bwd.

3 Dancing in place: Stamp R in front of L, twisting body to L so that R instep is at L toe (ct 1), stamp R beside L while facing fwd again (ct &), hop on L, bringing R in back (ct 2), touch ball of R across in back of L (ct &), hop on L (ct 3), slap R fwd in front of L (ct &), hop on L (ct 4), slap R diag to R (ct &).

4 Step R in place (ct 1), quickly step L next to R (ct uh), quickly step R in place (ct &), step L slightly to L (ct 2), stamp R beside L (ct &), jump to both ft apart in place (ct 3), click ankles together in air (ct &), land on L, thrusting R fwd in air (ct 4), slap R in front of L (ct &).

Repeat action of fig I through fig IV of Part Two.

HORA FETELOR

Hora Fetelor (HOH-rah FEH-tehl-lohr) is a woman's line dance from the Calafat region of Oltenia. Alexandru David learned it while dancing with the Romanian State Ballet. The dance is *not* restricted to women.

Record: "Gypsy Camp," GC 5201, side 1, band 3

Formation: Mixed lines of dancers. Joined hands held at shldr level, elbows bent and held down (W pos). Face slightly R of ctr, wt on L.

Steps and Styling: Style throughout is lyrical, smooth, graceful.

Two-step: Step fwd on R (ct 1); close L to R (ct 2); step fwd on R (ct 3); hold (ct 4). Repeat of step begins with L ft.

Lift: Rise on ball of supporting ft and then lower heel. Free ft leaves floor slightly but has no other movement.

Meter 4/4   Pattern

Meas

No intro

I. Two-Steps and Lift

1 With shldrs facing almost ctr, hips turned twd LOD, move in LOD with a Two-step, begin R (cts 1, 2, 3); hold (ct 4).

2 Continue in LOD with a Two-step, beginning L ft (cts 1, 2, 3); hold (ct 4).

3 Face LOD, step R fwd (ct 1); lilt on R (ct 2); step L in place (ct 3); close R to L (ct 4).

4 Step L fwd (ct 1); hold (ct 2); turning to face ctr, close R to L (ct 3); hold (ct 4).

5–8 Repeat action of meas 1–4 (fig I), reversing ftwk and direction.

9–16 Repeat action of meas 1–8 (fig I).

II. Turns, to Ctr and Back, Grapevine

1 Face ctr, step R across L (ct 1); lilt on L (ct 4).

2 Release hands, do a full 3 step turn to R (CW) moving in LOD, step R, L, R (cts 1, 2, 3); lilt on R (ct 4).

3–4 Repeat action of meas 1–2 (fig II), reversing ftwk and direction, but on ct of meas 4, step R beside L. End facing ctr.

5 Two slow steps twd ctr, L (cts 1, 2); R (cts 3, 4).

6 Four small steps bkwd with a slight up-down-up-down action, stepping L, R, L, R (cts 1, 2, 3, 4). Then step R on ct 4 in a small leap in preparation for following grapevine.

7 Grapevine moving LOD: Step L in front of R (ct 1); step R to R (ct 2); step L behind R (ct 3); step R to R (ct 4).

8   Step L slightly in front of R (ct 1); stamp R beside L twice, no wt (cts 2, 3); hold (ct 4).

9–16   Repeat action of meas 1–8 (fig II).

III. Two-Steps and Lift

1–8   Repeat action of fig I, meas 1–8, only.

IV. Turns, to Ctr and Back, Grapevine

1–16   Repeat action of fig II, meas 1–16.

INVÎRTITA DE LA SIBIU

Invîrtita de la Sibiu (in-vehr-TEE-tah deh lah see-BYOO) comes from Sibiu, a town in southern Transylvania. It was introduced by Eugenia Popescu-Judetz. The Invîrtita is a turning dance usually done in couples, but Madame. Popescu-Judetz claims that the young people in that area also like to do this dance in small circles consisting of two to four couples.

Record: "Romanian Folk Dances," Folkraft F-LP 33, side A, band 9

Formation: 1. Cpls in random arrangement about room. Ptrs are facing in shoulder-waist pos.
2. Small circles of 2 to 4 cpls, hands joined in a Back Basket Hold (arms pass behind back of adjacent dancers to clasp hands with second dancer on either side). Joined hands are high (rib cage area) on neighbor's back. All face ctr of small circle.

Steps and Styling: Heel Lift: With wt on designated ft, lift heel off floor. This could be called a modified hop. Description same for M and W.

Meter 2/4   Pattern

Meas

     No intro

I. Side Steps

1   Moving in own CCW circle, step on R to R side (ct 1); step L next to R (ct 2); step on R to R side (ct &).

2   Continuing, step L next to R (ct 1); step on R to R side (ct &); step L next to R, no wt (ct 2).

3–4   Repeat action of meas 1–2, but reverse direction and ftwk.

5–8   Repeat action of meas 1–4.

II. Crossing Steps

1   Moving in own CCW circle, step on R to R side (ct 1); step on L in front of R (ct 2); small step on R to R side (ct &).

2   Continuing, step on L in front of R (ct 1); small step on R to R side (ct &); step on L in front of R (ct 2); small step on R to R side (ct &).

3–4   Repeat action of meas 1–2 (fig II), but reverse direction and ftwk.

5–8   Repeat action of meas 1–4 (fig II).

III. Turning Steps

If dancing in cpls, make 4 CCW turns during meas 1–8. Adjust shoulder-waist pos by moving a little to own R (L hips are closer together but not adjacent). M may put R hand on W L upper arm. If dancing in small circles, turn body to face a little L of LOD. Because of more people, it will not be possible to make 4 CCW turns. After the first 2 walking steps all steps are small.

1–8   Dance pattern cuts across the meas; for clarity's sake it is described in 16 cts (8 × 2). All movement is CCW (LOD). Walk R, L (cts 1, 2). Heel lift on L (ct 3). Step R (ct &); L, bending knee a little (ct 4). Heel lift on L (ct 5). Step R (ct &); L (ct 6); R (ct &); L, bending knee a little (ct 7).
Repeat action of meas 3–7 (cts 8–12). Heel lift on L (ct 13). Step R (ct &); L, bending knee a little (ct 14). Heel lift on L (ct 15). Step R (ct &); L (ct 16); R (ct &). When dancing in cpls, make 1 CCW turn on cts 1–4. Make 2 more turns on cts 5–12. Make the 4th turn on cts 13–16.

9–16   Repeat action of meas 1–8 (fig III), but reverse direction, pos, and ftwk. If dancing in cpls, make 4 CW turns. Repeat dance two more times. On very last turn CW omit cts 15, &, 16, &. Instead, step on L (ct 15) and hold.

RUSTEMUL

Rustemul (roo-STEH-mool) is from the region of Muntenia, in southern Romania. It was learned by Mihai David while dancing with the Romanian State Folk Dance Ensemble.

Record: "Gypsy Camp" (LP) GC 5201, "The Lark," (10″ LP) FLDR, side 1, band 5; "Lark," (45 rpm) 3708-B.

Formation: Lines of dancers facing ctr of circle, hands in "V" pos.

Steps and Styling: Hop, Step, Leap. Ftwk is light and fast. Hands swing bkwd (ct 1) and fwd (ct 4) throughout the dance, except during fig II, meas 3–6.

Meter 6/8   Pattern

Meas

1–4   Intro: on ct 6 of meas 4 hop on L, raising bent R knee fwd.

I. In Place

1 Step to R on R with bent knee, arms swinging bkwd (cts 1, 2). Step on L across in front of R (ct 3). Step on R in place, arms swinging fwd (cts 4, 5). Hop on R, raising bent L knee fwd (ct 6).

2 Repeat action of meas 1 with opp ftwk.

3 Step to R on R with bent knee, arms swinging bkwd (cts 1, 2). Step on L across in front of R (ct 3). Step on R in place, arms swinging fwd (cts 4, 5). Step on L to L (ct 6).

4 Step on R in place, arms swinging bkwd (cts 1, 2). Step on L across in front of R (ct 3). Step on R in place, swinging arms fwd (cts 4, 5). Hop on R, raising bent L knee fwd (ct 6).

5-8 Repeat action of meas 1-4, but reverse ftwk and direction.

II. Diag in and out of Ctr

1-2 Repeat action of fig I, meas 1-2, but end by leaping onto R on ct 6 of meas 2, with L knee raised and very bent. Hold arms in low handhold.

3 Step on L across in front of R (cts 1, 2). Moving diag R twd ctr, step on R close behind L (ct 3). Step on L fwd (cts 4, 5). Hop on L with R knee raised and very bent (ct 6).

4 Step on R across in front of L, traveling on L diag twd ctr (cts 1, 2). Step on L close behind R (ct 3). Step R fwd (cts 4-6).

5 Stamp on L with wt into ctr, turning to face LOD (cts 1-3). Step on R, traveling sdwd out of ctr (cts 4, 5). Step on L beside R (ct 6).

6 Step on R to R (cts 1, 2). Step on L beside R (ct 3). Step on R to R (cts 4, 5). Hop on R, turning to face ctr, L knee raised and bent (ct 6).

7-8 Repeat action of fig I, meas 1-2, but reverse ftwk and direction.

9-16 Repeat action of meas 1-8 (fig II), but reverse ftwk and direction. On last hop on L, turn to face LOD.

III. Travel in Lod and RLOD

1 Step on R in LOD, arms swinging bkwd (cts 1, 2). Hop on R with L knee slightly bent (ct 3). Step on L in LOD, arms swinging fwd (cts 4, 5). Hop on L with R knee slightly bent (ct 6).

2 Repeat action of meas 1 (fig III).

3-4 Facing ctr, repeat action of fig I, meas 1-2.

5 Step on R behind L (cts 1, 2). Hop on R (ct 3). Step on L behind R (cts 4, 5). Hop on L, raising bent R knee fwd (ct 6). Arms continue to swing.

6 Repeat action of meas 1, (fig I).

7-12 Repeat action of meas 1-6 (fig III), but reverse direction and ftwk. Travel in RLOD.
  To finish dance repeat to end of music.

1-8 Fig I
1-16 Fig II
1-8 Fig I
1-12 Fig III

SÎRBA PE LOC

This sîrba (SIR-bah) is done "pe loc" (peh LOHK), which means "in place." It comes from the Muntenia region of southern Romania. Alexandru David learned the dance from the Romanian folk dance ensemble Perinița.

Record: "Gypsy Camp," (LP), GC 5201

Formation: Medium length lines of mixed M and W facing ctr with hands on neighbors' shoulders in "T" pos

Meter 4/4 Pattern

Meas

1-8 Intro: no action

I. Sîrba

1 Step swd R (ct 1), step L behind R (ct 2), step swd R, extending straight L leg fwd and down (ct 3), small hop on R, pulling L heel sharply toward R instep and bending L knee (ct 4).

2 Reverse action of meas 1 to L with opp ftwk.

3-16 Repeat action of meas 1-2 seven more times.

II. Fall

1 Step swd R (ct 1), step L behind R (ct 2), step swd R (ct 3), step onto ball of L ft across in front of R, raising on ball of R at same time so that wt is evenly distributed (ct 4).

2 Fall onto L across in front of R with a sharp stamping action and raising R in back (ct 1), step R behind L (ct 2), step swd L (ct 3), step onto ball of R ft across in front of L, raising on ball of L at same time so that wt is evenly distributed (ct 4).

3 Reverse action of meas 2 to the R with opp ftwk.

4-7 Repeat action of meas 2-3 two more times.

8 Repeat action of cts 1, 2, 3 of meas 2 (cts 1, 2, 3), hop on L (ct 4).

III. Clicks

1 Step R in place (ct 1), hop on R, clicking L heel to R (ct 2), step L in place (ct 3), hop on L, clicking R heel to L (ct 4).

2 Step swd R (ct 1), step L behind R (ct 2),

step swd R (ct 3), hop on R, clicking L heel to R (ct 4).

3–4   Reverse action of meas 1–2 with opp ftwk.

5–16   Repeat action of meas 1–4 three more times.

IV. Clicks and Stamps

1   Step R in place (ct 1), hop on R, clicking L heel to R (ct 2), step L in place (ct 3), stamp R next to L, no wt (ct 4).

2   Step swd R (ct 1), step L behind R (ct 2), step swd R (ct 3), hop on R, clicking L heel to R (ct 4).

3–4   Reverse action of meas 1–2 with opp ftwk.

5–16   Repeat action of meas 1–4 three more times. Repeat entire dance from beginning.

Note: For clicks, M circle leg out to side with a larger movement than W, who are more restrained.

Brigham Young University Dancers. Photo by Van W. Frazier

RUSSIA AND THE UKRAINE

Russian and Ukrainian Folk Dancing

by Vincent Evanchuk

In terms of its history, size, and complexity, Russia is a world all its own. It is a vast, sprawling land straddling all of Asia and half of Europe. Commonly known as Russia, it is more correctly called the Union of Soviet Socialist Republics. It is a country spanning more than 8.5 million square miles, in which there is a feeling of remoteness and endless expanse.

Between the Ural Mountains and the Pacific Ocean, Siberia is traversed by nine major rivers. The rivers flow through the virgin forests of the Taiga into the frozen tundra and on to the Arctic Ocean, and to Tatar Strait. Unfenced fields and pastures of western Russia stretch to the distant horizon—and far beyond—across the rich, rolling plains or steppes of the Ukraine to the Black Sea in the south, and across the endless forests and swamps to the Gulf of Finland and the Barents Sea in the north.

Some 241.7 million people live in the cities and villages of the U.S.S.R. Their customs and dances are as diverse as the conglomeration of peoples who speak a hundred languages and dialects and whose racial and cultural origins stem from a score of civilizations, from ancient Greece to Genghis Khan's Mongolia.

A turbulent history has resulted in a many-faceted population made up of Russians, Ukrainians, Belorussians, Uzbeks, Tatars, Kazakhs, Azerbaijanians, Armenians, Georgians, Lithuanians, Moldavians, and 113 other ethnic groups. Interest in dance and music has been strong in this country throughout its history. There has been a great emphasis on ballet since the days of Catherine the Great in the eighteenth century. In conjunction with the present emphasis in the Soviet Union on physical fitness, even preschool childrens7 are taught folk dancing in state nurseries. Ballroom dancing is popular, and in homes during evening parties children, parents, and guests sometimes folk dance.

These dances, classified as Russian dances, are from Great Russia, a geographical area in Central Russia. The Russian folk dances basically have no fixed patterns. The pattern is left to the inspiration and ability of the dancers and reflects regional styling and characteristics. The typical dance form, however, is a circle. Exhibition groups performing Russian dances around the world are semi- or entirely professional ensembles that present choreographed dances based on cultural and political selections.

The earliest eyewitness account describing Ukrainian dances, according to the *Ukrainian Encyclopedia* [ed. Vlodymyr Kubijovyč (University of Toronto Press, 1963)], was by K. J. Hildebrandt, covering the years 1656–57. He reported on a series of women's dances he had seen.

Ukrainian life has greatly changed since that time. Some dances presented in this section are still being done regularly as part of a way of life, while others belong to the past and are presently being done as historical pieces. It should be emphasized that both forms of presentation are considered valid and are important for the continuation of Ukrainian dance.

Ukrainian dance forms include women's dances, men's dances, and couple dances, all of which tend to follow and display in movement the melodic pattern of the music.

Years ago, most Ukrainians were healthy, hard-working farmers. Dancing usually took place during important rites of passage, such as a wedding or baptism. Furthermore, the sight of people dancing after a hard week's work in the fields and around the farm underscored the major social function of dance.

Today, in Ukrainian communities all over the world, the life-style has obviously changed. The public dance hall, or church hall, has moved the family celebration away from the home. Dancing now takes place at almost any time. This has given rise not only to changes in dances but to new forms, including such interesting titles as "Kolomeyka Twist!" In recent years, dance groups performing Ukrainian dance in theaters have appeared, and have become a vital element in the continuation of the form.

All Ukrainian folk dances, both new and old, still retain the wild and happy characteristics they have had since ancient times, making them a pleasure to research and a glory to dance.

Some of the Russian and Ukrainian dances brought to this country by performing groups, or introduced by immigrants and researchers, have become popular with international folk dancers.

(Vincent Evanchuk was born in the Ukrainian quarter of Winnipeg, Canada. He began dancing at the age of three and moved to the United States when he was twelve years old. He danced professionally with the Santa Monica Ballet and has done dance research in Canada and the Ukraine. Although folk dancing is his hobby, he has conducted seminars and workshops for many Canadian and American folk dance groups and acts as choreographer for the Duquesne University Tamburitzans for their Ukrainian, Russian, and Georgian dances.

Evanchuk's educational background includes a bachelor's degree in electrical engineering and master's degrees in systems engineering and nuclear engineering. At present he is Missions Operation and Engineering Manager at the Jet Propulsion Laboratory of the California Institute of Technology.

Robin, Evanchuk's wife, shares his interest in folk dancing. She has a bachelor's degree in theater arts and a master's in folklore and mythology. Her special field is American dance, including dances of the colonial period, the Shakers, the Cajuns, and Texas dances.)

RUSSIAN AND UKRAINIAN FOLK DANCES

ALEXANDROVSKA

Alexandrovska (ah-lex-ahn-DROHV-skah) is an old Russian ballroom dance of unknown origin.

Record: Kismet 129 or Imperial 1025; any slow Russian waltz with eight-measure phrases.

Formation: Couples; partners facing with both hands joined and raised sideward shoulder high.

Steps: Waltz, Step-Close. Steps described for M; W uses the counterpart hand or foot.

Meter 3/4   Pattern

Meas

I. Back-to-back (man facing LOD, moving toward center)

1   Starting with outside foot (man's L, woman's R) step sideward (ct 1) close inside foot to outside (ct 2, 3).

2   Step to side with outside foot (ct 1), release forward hands (man's L, woman's R), swing other joined hands forward, bringing partners into back-to-back position (ct 2, 3). On the turn, pivot on outside foot, swinging inside hands forward; join other hands shoulder high.

3   Still back to back, step forward with inside foot (ct 1), close outside foot to inside (ct 2, 3).

4   Step forward with inside foot again (ct 1), pause, drawing foot almost to close (ct 2, 3).

5–8   Still back to back, repeat above in opposite direction.

Note: On meas 6 the joined forward hands are swung backward, bringing partners face-to-face.

9–16   Repeat steps described for meas 1–8, fig I.

II. Women Turn

1–4   Position: Partners facing, inside hands joined, outside on hips, woman turns under man's raised R arm. Man: step sdwd L (ct 1), close R (ct 2, 3). Repeat three times, pausing on last measure without closing R to L. If preferred, man may waltz forward for 4 meas. Woman: Meas 1—step sideward R (ct 1), close L (ct 2, 3). Meas 2—with same step make a complete turn to R under joined hands. Repeat this step.

5–8   Same as for meas 1–4 in opposite direction.

9–16   Repeat steps described for meas 1–8, fig II.

III. Skating Waltz (hands joined in skating pos)

1   Waltz forward.

2   With one waltz step, face in opposite direction, turning in toward each other.

3–4   Waltz backward for one meas, then step R (ct

1), raise (slightly) and point L (ct 2, 3).

5–8   Repeat action for meas 1–4 in opposite direction, ending by pointing with R.

9–16   Repeat steps described for meas 1–8, fig III.

IV. Couple Waltz (closed pos)

1   Step with outside foot (ct 1), close (ct 2, 3).

2   Step with outside foot (ct 1), pause, drawing foot almost to close (ct 2, 3).

3–4   Same in reverse direction.

5–8   Turning and progressing forward with four waltz steps.

9–16   Repeat steps described for meas 1–8, fig IV.

HOPAK

Hopak (HOH-pahk) is a Ukrainian folk dance performed by men. It is often used in ballets as a solo or ensemble dance. When danced as an ensemble there are two parts: the couple dance and the men's solo. The solo displays the man's agility and is danced to please the ladies. As the men dance they may exclaim, "hup, hup." The pattern that follows was arranged by Henry "Buzz" Glass utilizing typical Ukrainian patterns for group participation.

Records: Kismet A 106, Columbia 20346F, Victor V-21123 A, Kismet LP

Formation: Cpls in circle formation, Varsouvienne pos

Steps and Styling: Pas de Basque, Touch-Extend, Russian Polka Step, Buzz Step, Lunge-Cut, Push-Away, Toe-Heel-Touch-Kick Step, Prysiadka. Fists are positioned on hips unless otherwise stated.

Meter 2/4   Pattern

Meas

Intro: Kismet A 106 and Kismet LP have no intro.

I. Pas de Basque

1–16   In Varsouvienne pos, move fwd (LOD) with alternate pas de basque steps, L, R. Posture erect, chest lifted, leaning slightly bkwd with wt over heels. M accentuates leap of pas de basque, W is reserved.

II. Touch Extend

1–2   Varsouvienne pos. Hop on R and touch L toe beside R (ct 1); hop again on R and extend L fwd, straightening knee sharply (ct 2). Move fwd with 3 light running steps, L, R, L (cts 1, &, 2).

3–16   Repeat action of meas 1–2 (fig II) 7 times, alternating ftwk (8 times in all).

III. Russian Polka

1–16   Varsouvienne pos. Begin L. Move fwd (LOD) with 16 Russian polka steps: 1 light leap, close

to the floor, 2 running steps. The step is smooth, with ft close to floor. The first step of each polka is accented, long, smooth, and a reaching step danced on the balls of the ft. Cpls sway slightly from side to side as they move fwd. (Step on L on last ct and in preparation for next fig.)

IV. Buzz-Step Turn

1–16   Release hands and turn individually to own R (CW). R arm is extended, with gaze twd palm of hand. L fist on hip. Dance 15 buzz steps turning R (CW). Stamp L as R fist returns to hip on ct 16. Change hands and reverse turn and stamp, turning L (CCW). (Step on R on last ct and in preparation for next fig.)

V. Lunge-Cut

1–16   In Varsouvienne pos lunge fwd L, knee slightly bent, L shoulder leading (ct 1); cut R to L, straightening L knee and extending L very close to floor (ct 2). Move fwd with 3 running steps L, R, L (cts 1, &, 2). Change shoulder lead on 1st step, repeat lunge-cut step, alternating ftwk 7 times. (Step on L on last ct and in preparation for next fig.)

VI. Buzz-Step Turn with Partner

1–16   On preliminary (ct &), last meas of fig V, step L in order to turn CW. Ptrs begin with R hip adjacent, R arms around ptr's waist, L arms extended outward from shoulder, about 45° from head. Begin R. Turn with 15 buzz steps and stamp R. Change pos to L hips adjacent and beginning L, repeat buzz-turn and stamp CCW. Finish in single circle facing ptr, M R and W L shoulder twd ctr of circle.

VII. Push Away

1–16   R arms extended overhead, about 45° from the head, palm turned inward, L fist on hip, head turned away from extended arm (focus on ptr). Move away from ptr with 14 push-stamps and 3 stamps (L, R, L). On the 3 stamps the fists are on the hips. Repeat push steps and 3 stamps, moving L and back to ptr, but with R arm extended again as above. Push steps: Step R flat sdwd (ct 1); push down and sdwd L with ball of L as L is flicked outward, heel lifted and L knee bent (ct &). Repeat action for ct 2 &, etc. The action is down-up.

VIII. Toe-Heel-Touch-Kick

1–16   Ptrs face, M inside and W outside of circle. Touch R toe in inverted pos, at the same time hop on L and turn R hips twd ptr (ct 1); hop again on L, turning L hips twd ptr, and replace R toe with R heel (ct &); hop L and touch

R toe in front of L (ct 2); hop L and extend R leg fwd sharply, straightening R knee (ct &). Small leap onto R, touching L toe in inverted pos to repeat action of meas 1 & 2 & (fig VIII) 7 times, alternating ftwk.

IX. Improvised Steps

While W improvises with pas de basque steps, back skipping steps, or toe-heel-touch-kick steps, M demonstrates his masculine vigor with prysiadka steps (see Lexicon). As M begins his final prysiadka, the W may turn in place with a buzz turn.

Note: The improvised pattern may be cut in half by substituting the buzz turn with ptr pattern (fig VI) for the last 8 meas, or the entire improvised pattern may be eliminated and the buzz turn with ptr (fig VI) substituted. This turn may also be danced with the back of the R shoulder adjacent pos.

KATHERINE

This is a Ukrainian couple dance composed by Vince Evanchuk and dedicated to his daughter, Katherine. It is a composed dance using the traditional steps and styling of the Poltava region, located in the northeastern Ukraine.

Record: Express 160-A

Steps and Styling: Scissor Kick, Pas de Basque, Prysiadkom, Pereskok, Syncopated Step

Meas	Cts	
1	1	*Kolesenya (Scissor Kick)* Leap lightly onto L, while raising R straight fwd about 6 inches above the floor.
	2	Leap lightly onto R while raising L straight fwd.
		Presoovenyam (Syncopated Step)
1	1	Step to R onto R ft.
	2	Bring L heel to R ankle.
2	1	Step to L onto L ft.
	2	Bring R heel to L ankle.
3–4		Same as meas 1–2.
		Note: Double time for meas 5–8.
5	1	Step to R onto R ft.
	&	Bring L heel to R ankle.
	2	Step to L onto L ft.
	&	Bring R heel to L ankle.
6–8		Repeat meas 5.
		Pereskok z Prysiadkom—Man's Step
1	1	Leap onto R ft, crossing R in front of L, at same time L ft crosses up and behind R calf.

2		Hop on R as L is lifted and straightened diag to L side.
2	1	Drop into a full squat.
	2	Raise up to full standing pos, weight on both ft.
		Pereskok—Woman's Step
1		Same as meas 1 of "Pereskok z Prysiadkom."
2		Pas de Basque in place.
		Pas de Basque (P.D.B.) Leap fwd on R ft. Step fwd L ft. Close R ft to L ft.

Meter 2/4   Pattern

Meas

Figure I
1–4   Introduction
5–8   Scissor kick moving away from ptr, raising arms to sides, shoulder height (7 scissor kicks, close R to L on last ct).

Figure II
1–8   Syncopated step moving twd ptr, arms coming fwd, waist high (4 slow, 8 fast).

Figure III
1–8   Join hands with ptr. R hip to R hip, raise hands to shoulder height with elbows up. Both M and W R arms are straight while L arms are bent and in front of own chest. Turning CW do 8 P.D.B., on 8th P.D.B. reverse pos.
9–16   L hip to L hip do 8 P.D.B. turning CCW.
17–20 Scissor kick (fig I, meas 5–8).

Figure IV
W hands on waist, fingers fwd, thumb back. M arms raised shoulder height.
1–2   M Pereskok z Prysiadkom, W waits.
3–4   W Pereskok, M waits.
5–8   Repeat meas 1–4.
9–16   Moving fwd slowly with P.D.B., alternately thrust arms fwd on ct 2. Arms are waist high relative to ft (i.e., when P.D.B. starts on R ft, the R arm is thrust fwd) (8 P.D.B.).
17–20 Ptrs join hands shoulder high and form a circle with their arms. P.D.B. and rock arms, alternately raising M R, W L arms, then M L and W R (4 times).

Figure V
With hands still joined and in the same relative pos as in fig III, both ptrs bring their L hand (still holding ptr R) behind their own head so that their ptr's R arm is now resting on the R shoulder.

1–8   Turning CW, do 8 P.D.B., on 8th P.D.B. reverse pos.

9–16   In reverse pos do 8 P.D.B. turning CCW.

17–20   Scissor kick (fig I, meas 5–8).

Figure VI

1–8   Repeat fig IV, meas 1–8.

9–16   Repeat fig II, meas 1–8.

17–20   Scissor kick (fig I, meas 5–8). On meas 20, ct & extend L heel fwd on floor and end in an open arm pos.

KOROBUSHKA

According to Michael Herman, Korobushka (koh-ROH-bush-kah) was first presented in the United States by a group of Russian immigrants soon after the close of World War I.

Records: Kismet 106, Kismet KA-1; Tikva T-105; Folkraft 1170; Imperial 1022; National 4523; World of Fun M 108; World of Fun LP 3; Folk Dancer 1059; Stinson 8001

Formation: Ptrs face each other (M back to ctr of circle, W face ctr). Joined hands extended between them at comfortable height.

Steps and Styling: Schottische, Hungarian Break Step, Three-Step turn.

Meter 2/4   Pattern

Meas

Intro (no. of meas depends on record selected)

I. Schottische

1–2   Beginning M L, W R, take one schottische away from ctr of circle; M move fwd, W bwd.

3–4   Repeat action of meas 1, reversing direction and ftwk (M move bwd, W fwd).

5–6   Repeat action of meas 1–2.

7–8   Execute Hungarian break step in place. M hop on L, W on R. Release hands.

II. Three-step Turn

M with elbows bent and arms extended away from chest, hands clasped on inside forearms just above bend in elbows, W with fists on hips, elbows held slightly fwd.

1–2   Make one 3-step turn to own R (cts 1, 2, 1); clap own hands to own R side, arms held about shoulder high (ct 2).

3–4   Repeat action of meas 1–2 (fig II), reversing direction and ftwk. Both start L and clap hands to L.

5–6   Face ptr, join R hands. Free hand in fist on hip. Both beginning R, take one two-step balance twd each other (cts 1 & 2); beginning L, take one two-step balance away (cts 1 & 2).

7–8   With 4 walking steps (R, L, R, L) ptrs change

places. W make CCW turn under joined hands, end with back to ctr; M cross to outside of circle, making ½ turn CW toward and facing W.

9–10   Repeat action of meas 1–2 (fig II): three-step turn to R, W on inside of circle, M on outside.

11–12   Repeat action of meas 3–4 (fig II): three-step turn to L.

13–14   Repeat action of meas 5–8 (fig II) with own ptr. To make dance progressive, on meas 11–12 (fig II), take three-step turn to L in place and face new ptr. Repeat meas 5–8 (fig II) with new ptr.

POLYANKA

Polyanka (pohl-YAHN-kah) was arranged by Sergei Temoff.

Record: "Polyanka," Kismet No. 129, Album 3.

Formation: Double circle, W facing in, M facing out. Lines about 6 feet apart. M stand at ease, wt on L ft, R heel slightly off floor, fists placed on hips. W has hands on hips.

Steps and Styling: Russian Polka, Push, Stamp, Scuff, Cut, Brush, Prysiadka, Double Heel, Buzz Turn, Walk, Jump, Leap, Hop, Toe-Slide, Toe-Toe-Kick Step.

Brigham Young University Dancers. Photo by Van W. Frazier

Meter 2/4   Pattern

Meas SLOW PART
No intro

I. Russian Polka (W)

1 W: Beginning R, W move twd M with exaggerated polka step. Step fwd on heel, toe up (ct 1); close L in back of R and take wt on L (ct &); step fwd R (ct 2); hold (ct &).

2 Repeat action of meas 1, beginning L.

3 Repeat action of meas 1, beginning R.

4 Turn L shoulder twd ptr, stamp L (ct 1); hold (ct &); stamp R (ct 2), hold (ct &). On each polka step the corresponding arm sweeps high in an arc overhead, opp shoulder slightly twd ptr, opp hand with knuckles on hip.

Push and Stamp (W)

5–6 W: face CCW and move away from ptr with 3 push steps. Step away from ptr on R and simultaneously push directly fwd twd ptr with L (ct 1), L toe extended; bring L to arch of R and take wt on L (ct &). Repeat push step twice (cts 2, &, 1); do not close L ft to R arch but stamp lightly on L (ct &); stamp lightly on R (ct 2); hold (ct &); make ½ turn CCW to face in opp direction (R shoulder to ptr). The arm pos changes with ½ turn CCW, L arm arched high overhead, R shoulder turned to ptr, R hand on hip. On push step W turn slightly fwd to face ptr, pointing pushing toe directly twd him.

7–8 Repeat action of meas 5–6, beginning L. L arm arched high overhead, R shoulder turned to ptr, R hand on R hip.

M Heel Stamp

9–16 With fists on hips, stamp R heel, leaving toe on floor in place. Straighten knee (ct 1); bend both knees slightly and lift R heel (ct &). Continue heel stamps through phrase, always stamping on strong beat of music.

II. Brush, Two-Step, Turn

M and W: During following action both have L arm arched high, R hand on hip.

1 Both brush R ft diag fwd across L (ct 1); brush R ft diag bkwd (ct 2); kick R ft fwd, turning diag to R; bend knee and slightly scuff L heel fwd (ct &).

2–4 Beginning R, do 3 two-steps. While performing two-steps, form individual circles to R, arms at slight angle, elbow level, palms up. Passing L shoulders with ptr, circle facing ptr and bring hands to hips on ct 2 of meas 4.

5–8 Repeat action of meas 1–4 (fig II) beginning L, R arm arched high; pass R shoulders on 3 two-steps.

III. M and W Solo

1 M: Face ptr. Prysiadka: squat with straight back, knees out in wide inverted "V"; hands fall between knees (ct 1), straighten knees and extend L leg diag to L (heel on floor, toe up); R arm is held in high arc overhead, L arm to side just below shoulder level. Look twd L hand, which has palm up (ct 2).

2 Beginning R, repeat action of meas 1.

3–4 With fists on hips, describe small circle turning CW while taking double heel steps, beginning R (cts 1, &, 2, &, 1, &, 2), stamp lightly on L (ct &). Double heel steps: Scuff R heel and quickly step on R ft.

5–8 Repeat action of meas 1–4 on opp ft.

1 W: L hand on hip, R arm sweeps across to L and back into high arc overhead. Beginning R, take one Russian polka bkwd (cts 1, &, 2, &); turn L shoulder slightly twd ptr.

2 Step L back of R, placing hand on heart (ct 1) and point R ft fwd; bow to ptr. R arm sweeps up in an arc from heart twd R ft (ct 2). This step is executed in an exaggerated, slow tempo.

3–4 W move twd ptr with 4 cut steps, R toe leading (L ft replaces R on cut) (cts 1, &, 2, &). Cut step is executed on numerical ct. Hold arms out to side (palms down), slightly below shoulder level. Rotate arms bkwd and fwd, turning palms up on each numerical ct of the music and down on the "&" ct (cts 1, &, 2, &).

5–8 Repeat action of meas 1–4 (fig III), except at end do only 3 cut steps and stamp R, L (cts &, 2, hold &). Finish with wt on L ft, R hand joined high with ptr's R, L hand on hip.

FAST PART

IV. Russian Polka, Cut, Skip Steps
Ptrs join R hands, L fists on hips.

1–4 Beginning R, W move out of circle, making 2 complete CW turns with 4 polka steps as M follows with 4 polka steps.

5–8 W returns to place with 8 quick cut steps, R ft fwd, while M takes 8 Russian skip steps bkwd. Russian skip step: Step R ft directly behind L ft, displacing L (ct 1), hop on R (ct &), step L ft behind R (ct 2), hop on L (ct &).

9–16 Repeat action of meas 1–8 (fig IV).

V. Push Step, Jump Turn Step, Prysiadka
Ptrs face in double circle, M back to ctr.

1–4 Beginning L, but with wt on R, ptrs move to own R with 8 push steps.

5 W: Make one CW turn in place with jump steps. Jump step: Leap lightly onto L ft and extend R heel diag fwd, toe up (ct 1), change

quickly by leaping onto R and extend L heel fwd, touching floor (ct 2).

6–8   W: Repeat action of meas 5 three more times (8 jumps in all).

5–8   M: simultaneously execute 4 quick prysiadkom in place, turning CW. Prysiadka: Squat with straight back, both hands between knees (ct 1), raise and straighten knees, sliding heels out into a wide inverted "V" (ct 2). Keep wt on heels (ct &). At the same time, open arms low to side, palms up.

9–12 Moving to own L, return to orig place with 8 push steps.

13–16 Begin R with wt on L. W repeat jump step turning CCW, while M execute 4 prysiadkom turning CCW. On push step, M and W stretch arms out to side at shoulder level. W flutter hands, M hold hands still, palms fwd. On jump step W turn with hands high overhead, continuing flutter motion. Finish facing about 4 feet apart.

VI. Russian Polka and Dos-à-Dos

1–2   Beginning R, dance 2 Russian polka steps fwd twd ptr.

3–4   Move bkwd to place with 2 Russian polka steps.

5–8   With 8 gliding walk steps, move fwd, pass R shoulders with ptr and return to place, passing L shoulders.

9–16 Repeat action of meas 1–8 (fig VI), except that ptrs pass L shoulders first.

VII. Turn Away, Jump, Elbow Hook

Ptrs face, inside hands joined (M R, W L); progress CCW in circle.

1–2   Make one complete turn away from ptr with two polka steps; sweep joined hands down and fwd on first polka step. Break on second polka step and rejoin inside hands before beginning next meas.

3–6   Repeat action of meas 1–2 (fig VII) twice.

7–8   Face ptr. Both jump diag R on both ft, L hips adjacent on ct 1, jump back to place on ct 2. Repeat jump diag L (ct 1), jump back to place (ct 2). Hands hang loosely at sides.

9–16 Join R elbows, L arm held in a high arc. Beginning R, turn CW with 8 Russian polka steps. Lean away from ptr on turn and end facing each other.

17–24 Repeat action of meas 1–8, (fig VII).

25–32 Repeat action of meas 9–16 (fig VII). Hook L elbows and begin polka step on L ft with R arm high. At end of each polka step the ft flies up in back in a saucy manner.

VIII. Leap, Buzz, Hop-Turn

1–2   Ptrs face, M back to ctr. With L shoulder to ptr, both leap lightly diag fwd R on R (ct 1), close L to R (ct &), change wt to R (ct 2), hold (ct &). Leap back to place on L (ct 1), close R to L (ct &), change wt to L (ct 2), hold (ct &). M: thrust arms down and slightly fwd, palms fwd (meas 1), then back to pos low on hips with fists (hands closed) thumb pointing bkwd (meas 2). W: bend slightly bkwd on this step, thrusting hands high, upward and fwd, palms up (meas 1), return hands to hips (meas 2).

3–4   M with both hands remaining low on hip, W with R arm held high, L hand on hip, make one solo turn CW in place with 4 buzz steps (cts 1, &, 2, &, 1, &, 2, &).

5–8   Repeat action of meas 1–4 (fig VIII), beginning L, with R shoulder twd ptr and finish facing each other.

9–16 Step fwd R so that hips are adjacent, R arm around ptr's waist, L hand held high. Take 16 hops on R, 2 hops to each meas; extend L leg back, knee straight. W must end turn in orig pos.

17–32 Repeat action of meas 1–16 (fig VIII) beginning L. Hop on L with L hips adjacent and R arm high.

IX. Polka, Prysiadka in Star

1–4   M: In groups of 6, take 4 polka steps (L, R, L, R), casting off to L to form L-hand star. Arms are outstretched at shoulder level, palms up.

5–8   In L-hand star pos, prysiadka 4 times, kicking R ft diag fwd. Both arms remain outstretched in star.

9–12 Break from star formation. Beginning L, take 4 polka steps (L, R, L, R) to orig pos to face ptr. Keep both arms outstretched when returning to pos.

Toe-Heel Slide, Kick

W: Arms are folded and held at shoulder level throughout entire figure.

1–4   Beginning with ft together, turn toes out to R (ct 1), slide heels to R (ct 2). Repeat toe-heel slide 3 times.

5   Hop on L, touch R toe to R side (one foot from L toe, with R toe turned down, heel up (ct 1). Hop again on L, touch R toe in front of L toe, R knee turned out (ct 2).

6   Hop again on L and kick R diag fwd (ct 1), step R beside L (ct 2).

7–8   Repeat action of meas 5–6 (fig IX), beginning L.

9–12 Repeat action of meas 1–4 (fig IX), moving to L. Return to orig pos to face ptr.

X. Polka, Skip

1–4 Ptrs take shoulder-waist pos. With 4 polka steps turn CW and travel CCW. Complete polka in single circle, W facing ptr, R hands joined high, L hands on hips.

5–8 Beginning R, take 4 polka steps in LOD (CCW) as W makes 2 turns CW under raised joined hands. M stamps ft on first ct as he follows W.

9–11 L hands joined in front, R hand at W R waist, make one complete turn CW with 6 skipping steps. W skip bkwd, M fwd.

12 Keeping L hands joined, M turn W to R. Released R hands go into high arc as ptrs pose, M back to ctr, W facing him.

RUSSIAN PEASANT DANCE

This dance was arranged by Sergei Temoff.

Record: "Russian Peasant Dance," National 4001; "Shining Moon," Victor 25-0030A

Formation: Cpls in a circle, ptrs facing, M back to ctr. Free fists on hips unless otherwise stated. W, hands on hips, may carry handkerchief to use during W solo.

Steps and Styling: Russian Polka, Pas de Basque, Walk, Three Step Turn, Push Step, Slide, Pivot, Hop, Run, Hungarian Turn Pos, Varsouvienne Pos.

Prysiadka: Squat on heels with hands down between knees (cts 1, 2); rise to astride pos with wt on heels, toes pointing up, open arms sdwd about waist level (cts 1, 2).

Prysiadka with Pivot Turn: Squat on heels with hands down between knees (cts 1, 2). Rise to astride pos, wt on R ft, L heel extended diag fwd, toe up, R arm arched high, L hand extended sdwd (cts 1, 2). Step on L (ct 1), pivot turn CCW (ct 2); step R (ct 1), hold (ct 2). Repeat step, reversing ftwk and pivot turn.

Russian Skip (2 to a meas): Step R directly behind L, displacing L (cts 1, &); hop R (ct ah), step L behind R, displacing R (cts 2, &), hop L (ct ah) (same timing as regular skip). Keep knees turned out.

Hop-Tap (CW turn): Hop R and at the same time tap L ft on floor (ct 1), hop R and at the same time raise L ft off floor, knee bent, ft under body (ct 2). Reverse ftwk for CCW turn.

Toe-Toe-Kick Step: Hop L, touch R toe to R side, toe turned down, heel up, knee turned in (ct 1); hop L, touch R toe in same spot, heel up, knee turned out (ct 2). Hop L, kick R ft diag fwd, leg

straight (ct 1), step R to L (ct 2). Repeat step, reversing ftwk.

Jump-Tap: Handkerchief may be held in R hand. Jump on L, making ¼ turn CCW, at the same time tap R toe on floor in front of L toe (both arms come down in front of body) (ct 1); hop L, raise R knee, knee out, toe down, and make ¼ CW turn (R arm swings high to R side) (ct 2). Repeat step, reversing ftwk, direction of turn, and arm.

Step-Slap: Step fwd on R heel, toe pointed up (ct 1), lower toe to floor with a slap, take wt on R (ct 2). Repeat step, reversing ftwk.

Meter 2/4   Pattern

Meas

1–16 Intro: watch ptr with interest

I. Away, Together

1–4 Both bend fwd from hips; on ct 1 of each meas clap own hands in front and at the same time stamp R ft on floor slightly fwd (4 times in all).

5–8 Dance 8 Russian skip steps bkwd away from ptr; M fists on hips. W start with hands on hips, gradually extend hands twd ptr, palms up, arms rounded.

9–12 Repeat action of meas 1–4.

13–16 Both begin R. With 2 Russian polka steps and 3 stamps, R, L, R, move twd ptr. Place R arm around ptr's waist, L arm arched high, R hips adjacent (Hungarian turn pos).

II. Hop-Tap

1–8 Dance 8 hop-tap steps turning CW in place.

9–16 Reverse ftwk and direction and repeat action of meas 1–8 (fig II). Finish sequence with ptrs facing, M back to ctr.

III. Reaching, W Around M

Arms extended sdwd, palms down, lending arm slightly above shoulder level, trailing arm slightly below shoulder level.

1–2 Beginning M L and W R, place heel sdwd twd LOD, knees straight (ct 1), bend knees slightly (ct 2); straighten knees (ct 1); lower toe to floor, taking wt and turn ½ (M CCW, W CW) to finish back-to-back (ct 2).

3–4 Repeat action of meas 1–2 (fig III), reversing ftwk and turns. Finish face-to-face.

Note: Arms are lowered as ptrs turn on ct 2 of meas 2 and 4.

5–8 Repeat action of meas 1–4 (fig III). Join inside hands (M R, W L).

9–16 M: L fist on hip, kneels on L knee and remains in this pos as he leads W twice around him

Illinois State University Dancers. Photo by Nelson R. Smith

15–16 Walk R, L (RLOD) (cts 1–2), stamp R (ct 1), hold (ct 2). On the two walking steps M arms gradually extend fwd; on the stamp, open twd ptr with a strong gesture.

9–10 W: move sdwd (RLOD) with 4 push steps, L arm across front of chest, R arched high. On ct & of 4th push step, turn ½ CW to face outside of circle, back to ptr; reverse arm pos.

11–12 With 4 push steps and ½ turn CW, W continue moving sdwd R (RLOD). Change arm pos on turn (face ptr).

13–14 Repeat action of meas 9–10 (fig V).

15–16 Walk R, L, turning ½ CW to face ptr (cts 1–2), stamp R (ct 1), hold (ct 2).

Note: W turn is always CW, trailing arm is always high. On the 2 walking steps, arms gradually extend fwd; on the stamp open twd ptr with a strong gesture.

CCW. On ct 2, meas 16, M rises and takes ptr in varsouvienne pos, both facing LOD (CCW).

9 W: hold skirt with R hand, step fwd L bending knee (ct 1), sweep R ft in a half circle CCW, step R beside L (ct 2).

10–16 Repeat action of meas 9 (fig III) 7 times (8 in all). Finish on outside of circle, facing LOD, in varsouvienne pos with ptr.

IV. Pas de Basque, Elbow Hook

1–8 Both begin R. Dance 8 pas de basque steps fwd in LOD (CCW).

9–12 Hook R elbows, L arm arched high, lean away from ptr. Both begin R and walk 8 steps CW in place.

13–16 Repeat action of meas 9–12 (fig IV), reversing ftwk and direction. Finish sequence in a double circle, ptrs side by side. Both move RLOD throughout following figure.

V. Three-Step Turn, Push Step

1–2 Both begin R. With 3 steps R, L, R, make one complete CW turn sdwd to R (cts 1, 2, 1), swing L across R (ct 2).
Note: Remain side by side on turn. Arms hang loosely at sides on turn; clap own hands out to R side on ct 2, meas 2.

3–4 Repeat action of meas 1–2 (fig V), reversing ftwk and direction (3-step turn CCW).

5–6 Repeat action of meas 1–2 (fig V) (3-step turn CW).

7–8 Repeat action of meas 3–4 (fig V) (3-step turn CCW). Omit swing on last ct, face ptr, M back to ctr. W take wt on R.

9–14 M: fists on hips, move sdwd (RLOD) with 12 push steps.

VI. Away, Together, Skipping Turn

1–2 Both begin R. Dance 4 Russian skip steps bkwd, away from ptr. Begin sequence with hands on hips, gradually extend them fwd twd ptr. M may keep fists on hips.

3–4 Both begin R. Move fwd with 2 Russian polka steps to finish with R hips adjacent. Place R arm around ptr's waist, join L hands above heads.

5–6 With 4 walking steps (R, L, R, L), cpl turns once CW in place.

7–8 M: step in place R, L, R, L.
W: turn ½ CW under joined L hands. Finish sequence side by side, M R arm in back of W, with R hands joined on her R waist, joined L hands extended fwd.

9–14 Both begin R. Dance 12 skip steps turning CW. M move fwd, W bwd. Finish sequence M back to ctr.

15–16 M steps in place R, L, R, L as he turns W CW under joined L hands to face him.

VII. M Solo (Prysiadka)

1–8 M: perform 2 prysiadkom with pivot turn steps alternating ftwk, hand movements, and turn.

9–12 M: perform 2 prysiadkom.

13–15 M: fold arms in front of chest; begin R and dance 6 Russian skip steps bkwd in a small CW circle. Finish sequence back to ctr.

16 M: stamp R, open arms twd ptr (ct 1), hold (ct 2).

1–16 W: place R elbow in L palm, R hand near chin, R forefinger on cheek as they watch ptr solo. On ct 1 of each meas, W tap toe on floor and tap cheek with R forefinger.

VIII. W Solo (Jump-Tap)

1–8 M: clap hands and stamp R on ct 1 of each meas while watching W solo.

1–8 W: dance 8 jump-tap steps moving bkwd away from ptr.

9–10 Both begin R. Move fwd with 2 Russian polka steps. If handkerchief is used, W hold each end in both hands and twist it in front about eye level.

11–12 M: with 2 Russian polka steps turns CCW to follow W twd ctr.
W: dances 2 Russian polka steps, continuing twd ctr as she passes M on his R.

13–14 Both continue twd ctr with 2 Russian polka steps.

15–16 Both walk fwd R, L (cts 1, 2), stamp R (ct 1), hold (ct 2). W tuck handkerchief in belt and form circle by joining hands. M join hands to form an outside circle.

IX. Circle

1–4 With 4 Russian polka steps, M begin L and circle CW while W begin R and circle CCW, M face RLOD, W LOD.

5–8 All face ctr, continue with 7 sliding steps and stamp (M L, W R) on meas 8 (ct 2).

9–16 Repeat action of meas 1–8 (fig IX), reversing ftwk and direction. Finish sequence with W in front of M and slightly to his R, join R hands above W head, L on own hip, both facing ctr.

X. Enlarge Circle

1–2 Both begin R and move fwd with 3 small walking steps (R, L, R), tap L with a slight bend of knees.

3–4 Both begin L and move bkwd with 3 longer walking steps (R, L, R) to enlarge circle; tap R with slight bend of knees.

5–8 Repeat action of meas 1–4 (fig X).

9–10 M: step in place and assist W to turn once CW under joined R hands.
W: step R, L, R (cts 1, 2, 1); both stamp L (ct 2), W no wt.

11–12 Repeat action of meas 9–10 (fig X), W reversing ftwk and direction.

13–16 Repeat action of meas 9–12 (fig X). On last turn CW, W finish facing ptr, back to ctr.

XI. Stamp and Pivot Around Ptr

1–2 Both stamp R diag fwd across L (in semicrouch pos) and clap own hands in front (cts 1, 2), stamp R to R side, opening both arms sdwd (cts 1, 2).

3–4 Both pivot CCW (cts 1, 2), step R in place facing ptr (cts 1, 2)

5–8 Repeat action of meas 1–4 (fig XI).

9–12 M fold arms in front of chest, W place hands on hips. With 4 step slap steps move fwd, passing R shoulders.

13–15 With 4 jump-hop steps, move around ptr, passing L shoulders, and return to place.

16 Step L to R (ct 1), hold (ct 2). Ptrs face, W inside with back to ctr.

XII. Step-Swing, Step-Hop

Ptrs move together in LOD.

1–2 M: step fwd R (begin CW turn on ct 1), hop R and swing L ft across R (ct 2); step-hop L, swing R across L, completing turn (cts 1, 2). Arms follow swinging ft.

3–4 Beginning R, move fwd in LOD with 3 walking steps (R, L, R) (cts 1, 2, 1), turn ½ CCW, stamp L twd RLOD (ct 2). Open arms in strong gesture on stamp.

1–4 W dance same sequence with opp ftwk and turn.

5–8 Repeat action of meas 1–4 (fig XII), moving RLOD, reversing ftwk and turn. M begin L, W R.

9–12 M dance 2 prysiadkom. W dance 2 toe-toe-kick steps.

13–16 Hook R elbows, L arm arched high; with 8 quick walking steps (1 step to a ct) turn CW in place. Finish sequence with W on M R, both facing ctr.

XIII. Single Circle, Couple Turn

1–16 All join hands in single circle and, without backing out, move in LOD with 32 running steps.

17–31 Ptrs assume Hungarian turn pos, turn CW in place with small running steps. Finish sequence with M on inside of circle, back to ctr; release ptr.

32 Join inside hands (M R, W L). M turn W CW under joined hands to end in pose, outside hands arched high.

TSIGANOCHKA

Tsiganochka (tsee-GAH-nohch-kah) is a favorite ballroom dance of various Russian-American groups throughout the country. it is also called the Russian Two-Step or Karapiet.

Record: Folk Dancer 1058; "Two-Step," Kismet 101-A; Folkraft 1169; Kismet K-A1

Formation: Double circle, cpls in closed pos, M back to ctr. Both look twd LOD (CCW).

Steps and Styling: Walk, Pas de Basque, Two-Step. When hands are free, place on hips with closed fist. This dance should be done in a rather sober and dignified manner, as contrasted with the more exuberant Russian dances.

Meter 4/4   Pattern

Meas

I. Touch, Walk

1   With wt on inside ft, touch M L, W R toe fwd (ct 1), hold (ct 2); touch M L, W R toe bwd and slightly swd (ct 3), hold (ct 4).

2   Beginning M L, W R, walk 3 steps fwd in LOD (cts 1, 2, 3); close M R, W L ft (no wt), and without changing pos face RLOD (ct 4). Raise joined hands (M L, W R) in arc at rear and keep this pos while moving RLOD.

3–4   Beginning with touch of M R, W L toe, repeat action of meas 1–2, moving in RLOD (CW). Finish facing ptr, release hold, and join inside hands at shoulder height with elbows bent, outside hands on hips.

II. Pas de Basque, Turn

Move in LOD (CCW) throughout this fig.

1   Pas de basque to M L, W R, turning away from ptr (cts 1 & 2); pas de basque to M R, W L, turning twd ptr (cts 3 & 4). Joined hands move easily fwd and back at shoulder level during this action.

2   Release ptr and, progressing in LOD, turn outward (M CCW, W CW) with 4 steps (M L, R, L, R; W R, L, R, L).

3–4   Repeat action of meas 1–2 (fig II).

III. Walk, Two-Step

1   Join inside hands at shoulder height and walk fwd 3 (M L, R, L; W R, L, R); stamp M R, W L heel (no wt) beside supporting ft, turning inwd to face opp direction (RLOD). Keep same hands joined.

2   Beginning M R, W L, repeat action of meas 1 (fig III), moving RLOD. Finish facing ptr. Repeat action of fig II, meas 1. Take closed pos and, beginning M L, W R, turn CW progressing LOD (CCW) with 2 quick two-steps (cts 1 & 2, 3 & 4). Repeat dance from the beginning.

SCANDINAVIA (DENMARK, FINLAND, NORWAY, SWEDEN)

Scandinavian (Danish, Finnish, Norwegian, Swedish) Folk Dancing

by Sharron Deny

The Scandinavian countries include Norway, Sweden, Denmark and Finland. Historically, it is well known that parts of present-day Norway and Sweden were inhabited by nomadic, seafaring people known as the Vikings. They were skilled boatbuilders and seamen who traveled over quite a large area of the globe, raiding, exploring, and trading in areas as far away as the southern parts of Europe, into the Mediterranean, and even over to America. Denmark appears to have been settled by both migrations from the Norwegian and Swedish Vikings, as well as from other Teutonic peoples who pushed northward up into Denmark. The people of Finland are believed to have migrated eastward, crossing the Gulf of Finland. The ethnic origin of the Finns is different from that of the other Scandinavians; they are more closely related to the Magyars of Hungary.

The governments of Norway, Sweden, and Denmark were centralized at an early date, and there was quite a bit of trading back and forth among the countries according to which was in power. At one point Denmark ruled parts of Norway and Sweden, and at another Sweden ruled over Norway, Denmark, Finland, and part of Russia. During the seventeenth century, Sweden ruled Finland, but as a result of the war between Sweden and Russia in 1808–9, Finland was annexed by Russia. Until 1899 Finland was under the protection of the Russian czars, but it was accorded the status of a grand duchy. At that time there was an attempt to impose the Russian language and law upon the people of Finland, which resulted in a revolt and a return to its status prior to 1899. In 1910 a period of Russian domination began again in Finland, continuing until the end of World War I. In 1917 Finland demanded independence and was formally granted it by Russia in 1920. During World War I Norway remained neutral, hoping to do the same in World War II, but she was invaded by Germany. Denmark was also invaded by Germany during World War II and remained under its control until 1945.

Kopachka Dancers

Sweden remained neutral during both world wars. Finland took no active part in World War I, but during World War II she was attacked by land, sea, and air by the Russians, thus losing some of her most valuable territory.

The early pagan cultures of Scandinavia included dance as a part of their rituals and ceremonies of worship. There are historical references to sword dances, dances performed during funeral ceremonies, and ancient chain dances done in circles or rings to the singing of songs. These ancient rituals were slowly replaced by various cultural influences. The conversion to Catholicism occurred during the eleventh and twelfth centuries. In the sixteenth century the Lutheran Church supplanted the Catholic Church. Neither Church encouraged the continuation of the ancient rituals, dance, or music.

Industrialization and the subsequent disappearance of village life as a result of urbanization also played a very large role in the decline of the old celebrations. As the wealthy class and royal courts grew, many dance influences were brought to Scandinavia from the courts of European countries situated farther south, particularly the British Isles, France, and Poland. As young men traveled about during the wars or sought their fortunes, they brought back new styles of dress and new dance patterns from other areas of Europe. By the eighteenth and nineteenth centuries, all but a few of the ancient rituals had been replaced by court dances among the wealthier classes and folk dances done by the peasants.

The themes of the dances performed today include: occupational skills; flirtations or coquetry; some showing off or display of skill and strength by the men, in contrast to demure, feminine behavior by the women; circle and line dances, usually done to singing; many couple dances, which usually include much turning or spinning; and many set or figure dances, which are also performed in couples. Often the steps in the

figure dances are relatively simple, but the patterns of the whole group are quite complicated. The set formations include the square, longways, and circular group formations; of course, many dances are done with free couples scattered about the floor. The steps used include walking, running, hopping, skipping, sliding, jumping, galloping. There are such dance patterns as the waltz, polka, mazurka, buzz step, reel step, schottische, and polka. Continuing influences affecting the dances in each of these Scandinavian countries have historically been the same as those affecting much of the rest of the world since the 1900s, including the advent of movies, television, and records. Each Scandinavian country has incorporated the social dances of the time—like the charleston, fox trot, and tango—leading up to the rock 'n' roll and disco dances of today. It is not unusual to attend an evening of dance in which contemporary rock music is played, interspersed with a hambo, polka, waltz, or schottische.

NORWEGIAN DANCE

Dance in Norway can be divided into: (1) the song dance; (2) the village or regional dance, including some of the older social dances; and (3) the set or figure dances. The song dances, a very old form of dance in Norway, are done using simple steps, with the dancers in line formation holding hands while many verses of narrative songs or ballads are sung. Most of these song dances are no longer done in Norway. However, on the Faeroe Islands, which were settled by many Norwegians, the song dances have been preserved; dances sung to ballads containing many verses are still done. The songs serve as the musical accompaniment to the dance; actually, the major focus of the dance is on the singing of the song. The songs relate heroic, romantic, or dramatic stories, with trolls, giants, kings, or knights being frequent subjects. Since the early 1900s, song dances have been reintroduced to Norway from the Faeroe Islands. Today, song dances are being done by Norwegian folk dance teachers to more recent popular ballads.

The regional or village dances are performed locally and vary from village to village. Most are couple dances probably introduced into Norway in the latter half of the eighteenth century, but they have developed unique styling and patterns that are typically Norwegian. They are done in a free and spontaneous manner, with the man leading the pattern of the steps and selecting the order and number of repetitions of steps to be done. The partners may dance very close together, utilizing a variety of couple dance positions, or they may separate and dance small solo parts, with the man often showing off a little bit while the lady turns or spins very demurely. The most popular of these dances are the pols, the springar (running), the gangar (walking), the vossarul, and many local variants of the polka, mazurka, snoa, reinlendar and vals.

The springar is a very popular dance. Various districts in Norway have their own adaptations of the springar; in Gudbrandsdal the springar is called the springleik. The step patterns of the springar may be in 2/4, 3/4, or 4/4. There are variations of the patterns within the dance, the man and the woman often performing different steps to the same music.

The pols is another couple dance which is done to 3/4 meter. Pols dances arrived in Norway around 1600. Many local variations of the pols can be found in Østerdal, Trøndelag, Nord-Noreg and Nordmøre, with the largest number of variations being found in the Røros area. The pols dances usually have a simple pattern of steps that change from one pattern to the next, at the man's discretion. Usually there are steps to move forward, to turn both clockwise and counterclockwise while progressing forward, and sometimes individual steps done by the man and woman while they are dancing apart from each other.

The gangar is found primarily in two districts of Norway, Telemark and Setesdal. It is a slow, stately dance composed of many changing patterns involving turning and change of directions as the couple progresses around the floor. The foot patterns include walking steps, two-steps and pivot steps, and other fancier steps done by the man to show off. The vossarul is a combination of walking steps, pivot steps, and two-steps, done, for the most part, in a closed position with the couple pivoting clockwise and two-stepping counterclockwise as it progresses around the floor. The polka, mazurka, snoa, reinlendar (schottische), or vals may all be danced in an evening's dance program, depending upon the particular region of Norway.

A man's solo dance called the halling is a very popular dance from Setesdal. In this dance, the man shows off his dancing skills and strength, using many complicated steps, high kicks, deep knee bends, and leaps.

Stoughton Norwegian Dancers. Photo by Wendt Studio

Some arm movements used in the dance have been compared to the arm movements used in some sword dances in the British Isles. At the end of the dance, the man kicks a hat off the end of a long stick or broom held for him throughout the dance by a girl standing on a chair. Sometimes this dance may be done as a contest, with several men competing. Each male dancer takes a turn at performing acrobatic feats or stunts demonstrating his strength and agility while dancing; the others watch in an informal circle. Then each dancer takes a turn at kicking the hat off the stick, trying to be the most graceful while kicking the highest.

The musical instruments used to accompany these village dances include: the hardanger fiddle (with an extra set of sympathetic strings), mainly found in western Norway; the ordinary violin, which predominates in the eastern and northern Districts; and the langleik, an old-fashioned stringed instrument played with the right hand plucking the strings and the left hand playing the melody. Other folk instruments such as the Jew's harp, the willow pipe, and the ram's horn (played like a trumpet or a clarinet) have also been used to accompany dances. Of course, modern instruments such as the clarinet, string bass, guitar, and accordion are used today in folk dance orchestras, along with the violin, hardanger fiddle, and sometimes the langleik.

The third group of dances found in Norway are done in figures. They tend to be dances from other countries that were modified or given a Norwegian character. Many of these dances were introduced around the early 1800s from the courts of France, Spain, and Scotland. Naturally, many figure dances have since been composed in Norway. Generally, these figure dances, or turdansar, are accompanied by the hardanger fiddle, although folk dance orchestras have begun to include two or three additional instruments.

Today in Norway there is a very high degree of active participation in Norwegian song, music, and dance. Numerous national competitions in dance and music attract many Norwegian participants, large Norwegian audiences, and foreign tourists. There has also been a revival of interest in national folk costumes. (Information about costumes may be obtained by writing to the Husfliden in the specific part of Norway where the costume originates.) In Norway, the Norges Ungdomslag (Youth League of Norway) is in charge of the development of folk dance. There are many member-clubs scattered throughout Norway, whose participants are estimated to number about twenty thousand.

SWEDISH DANCE

Dance in Sweden can generally be divided into approximately the same classifications as dance in Norway. These include: (1) the song dance and the långdans; (2) the village dance, including some of the older social dances like the waltz, polka, schottische, and mazurka; and (3) the figure dance. The långdans and the song dance are the oldest forms of dance in Sweden; they are still done today on special holidays and during family celebrations. The långdans is a line dance that is variously done through the rooms of a house and then around the Christmas tree, outside in a snakelike fashion, or around the Midsummer pole in the dance area. The steps for the långdans consist of light running or soft walking steps; the dancers hold on to each other in a line with a simple handhold. Musical accompaniment for a långdans is often provided by a fiddle, but it can also consist of humming or singing "la la."

Song dances are usually done at special times of the year in connection with special holidays—Christmas or Midsummer, for example. The songs, which are sung by the dancers, may contain directions about the dance, or they may be about a boy looking for a girl, or vice versa. The subjects of the songs are often pantomimed in the dance. Often the dancers will be in a ring until partners find each other, at which time they will dance in pairs or in small groups of couples. Many of these ring dances have become part of the choreography for the various folk dances or figure dances whose importance in Swedish dancing during the latter part of the nineteenth century continues right up to the present.

The most frequently performed dance in the villages over the past three hundred years has been some local variation of the polska. The polska has several parts to it. The first part usually contains slow walking steps, which then change into many variations on couples turning or pivoting. During the turning steps, the men's and women's steps are usually different but very interrelated. The polska is found throughout the various provinces of Sweden, the many local variations relating to a specific region. The old polskas were danced in one spot on the floor, but the newer polskas are danced with couples progressing around the room counterclockwise. Today the polska is enjoying a revival of interest among Swedish folk dancers. Several dance teachers are still actively doing research on the polska forms remembered by the elderly inhabitants of the middle and northern areas of Sweden.

One of the most well-known dances of Scandinavia is the hambo, which is a polska. It is done in many parts of Scandinavia, with very little variation from region to region, so that the dance is no longer a regional dance.

The vals, the schottis, the polka and the mazurka were introduced into Sweden and have become a very integral part of Swedish village dances. It is thought that the introduction of the vals might have been responsible for the addition of the counterclockwise progression of couples around the floor in the polska. In some villages these additional dances were danced at the time they were introduced, but in many cases only the rhythm of the newer dances was adopted. In some villages the older forms of the polska were often fitted to the new dance rhythms of the vals, the polka, or the schottis, with little change in the actual dance steps other than the accommodation necessary to fit the steps to the new rhythm. In Kall, the same dance is done in a polska rhythm, a polka rhythm, a schottis rhythm, and a vals rhythm. In each of these dances there are variations in the way the couple begins the dance, in the couple holding positions, and in the transition steps into the "Bakmes" or backwards-turning steps (counterclockwise turning while progressing counterclockwise around the room).

The figure dances were brought to Sweden primarily through the efforts of the nobility, although the farmers or peasants soon adopted many of these dances, adapting and stylizing them into Swedish dance forms. They elaborated on the quadrille and enriched existing movements through the introduction of steps and patterns from older village and song dances. The figure dances use various formations, such as the quadrille, longways sets, various circular patterns, and many combinations of these patterns. The quadrille dances were especially popular in the southern part of Sweden; in many instances they are very similar to the Danish quadrilles. The patterns of movement usually involve choruses and verses. During the choruses, first the head couples and then the side couples take turns leading. During the verses, the whole set usually dances, followed by the ladies, then the men, and then the whole set again. Sometimes the vals, mazurka, schottis or other dance steps were used as a part of the quadrille.

The galopp and the polonaise, or grand march, are other dance forms that have played an important role in Swedish folk dance. The galopp, a very vigorous dance, was often included as a figure in other more complicated dances, but it could also be used as a dance in itself. The grand march was most frequently used by the upper classes, since it was a slow and rather courtly dance. However, it is now often used to begin an evening of folk dancing by a folk dance club; moreover, it is often combined with a långdans, a galopp, and a polka to create a suite of dances.

Dance masters in Sweden during the latter part of the 1800s and the early 1900s composed suites of dances often loosely derived from song dances or polskas. These dances were choreographed for presentation on the stage; they later became the "folk dances" performed by the folk dance clubs of today. Included in these folk dances are some of the best known quadrilles danced by the upper and lower classes. Even though folk dancing consists primarily of figure dances, village or peasant dances are becoming a very popular part of the folk dance club repertoire too. There are even a few groups in Sweden who specialize in village dances and have very little acquaintance with folk dances. There are many outdoor dance arenas in Sweden that present various kinds of dance programs for the public. Programs might include the gammaldans (oldtime dances) such as the vals, the hambo, schottis, polka, and mazurka (done without regional variation), or even dances like the fox trot, the tango, and other Latin dances. The dance evening might also consist of more contemporary dances like rock 'n' roll, with a few older dances like the vals and hambo included.

Music accompanying Swedish folk dancing most often is provided by fiddles. These are usually played in groups, with the fiddling "dialect" being so distinct that there is a great variation in the music played in the different provinces. In some regions of Sweden the key fiddle (nyckelharpa) or the wooden shoe fiddle (tråskofiol, a fiddle made out of a wooden shoe) are utilized, usually accompanying other fiddles or vice versa. Other instruments used to play songs and sometimes dance tunes in the old days included willow whistles and flutes, cow horns, and clarinets. More and more accordions are being utilized to play folk dance music; a contemporary folk dance orchestra may also include various modern instruments accompanying the accordion, such as the bass and guitar (with electronic amplification, of course). But the right instrument for village dances—such as polskas—would almost always be just fiddles, played according to the regional dialect from whence the dance and the music originate.

A revival of interest in Swedish peasant culture occurred as a result of the establishment of the Nordiska Museet and Skansen (a folk park and zoo in Stockholm), which was also aided by the establishment of a society, Friends of Swedish Folk Dance (Svenska Folkdansens Vänner) and a folk dance and music team (Folkvisedanslag) that arranged performances of Swedish folk dances at Skansen. National dress, music, and dance have been of continuing interest to societies formed to preserve local history. Handicraft societies (Hemslöjd) for the various provinces have been very active in the preservation of old or traditional ways of dress and methods of weaving and sewing. Folk parks have been established and many of the old buildings (log houses) and rural "peculiarities" in the various regions have been preserved by local societies. The Swedish Youth Circle for Local Culture (Svenska Ungdomsringen för Bygedekultur) is the central organization to which many dance clubs in Sweden belong.

FINNISH DANCE

Finland has been marked by the influence of the Swedes, the Russians, the Poles, the Germans, and the Lithuanians. For this reason most of their dances are similar in form and pattern to the seventeenth, eighteenth, and nineteenth-century social dances from these countries, although these dance patterns have been molded and stylized by the Finns into personal expressions of their own dance culture.

During the twelfth century young girls did chain dances and sang ballads or epic poems, as in the other Scandinavian countries. Later both men and women danced in these chain or line dances. This eventually led to the development of couple dances or pair dances, which often started with the whole group dancing together. Girls still sing songs and do dances called piiri leiki that are done to singing.

Because of so many external influences affecting her dance tradition the most Finnish dance elements still preserved are found in the Karelian lake and forest areas, which are very remote. These dances are usually danced to singing or humming, and are often imitative of things found in nature, including such animals as seals, for example. Some dances pantomime work movements such as reaping, making coffee, or different farm activities. Several more modern dances include elements of courting or making fun of people. In these dances the movements often clearly pantomime the intended meaning. Many of the best known dances used to be performed at weddings.

As was previously mentioned, many Finnish folk dances of today were the ballroom dances of yesterday. The nobility and rich middle class imported these fashionable dances from many countries. As they went out of fashion, they were adapted and changed to suit the tastes of the peasants. Many have been preserved and are still danced today. Many of the dances bear the names of the countries from whence they came: Anglaise, Française, or Pas d'Espagne. The polka first came into Finland as a couple ballroom dance and was subsequently introduced into the countryside. The polska was also introduced into Finland, where it is now performed in a variety of forms in ¾ meter. Pol-

skas are often done as couple dances, but they can be done as a figure dance by four or more couples standing in a circle or square. The polska was used in an evening's dance program as an introductory dance until the waltz was introduced. The waltz became so popular that it supplanted the polska as an introductory dance and pushed it to the end of the program, changing it to the "parting polska."

On the western side of Finland there is a very great Swedish cultural influence. Even the street signs are written in both Finnish and Swedish in some sections. With the advent of Swedish rule, the Church of Sweden suppressed most of the ancient rituals. Thus, when dancing was introduced by Swedish immigrants there was little left of Finland's original dance culture. The national dress of the western section of Finland is very Swedish in appearance. On the eastern side of Finland there has been a decided Russian influence in the dancing style. The musical accompaniment and dynamic accents closely resemble those of Russia. Also, in many of the dances the men perform hard stunts or feats of skill that display their strength and agility, as is typical in Russian dance.

Steps used in Finnish dancing include walking, running, skipping, sliding, jumping, the waltz, the polka, the mazurka, the varsouvienne, the buzz step, and the polkette. The polkette is a very characteristic and frequently used dance pattern in Finnish dance; most Americans associate it with what they call the Polish polka. Most dances have two or four couples dancing together; there is usually lots of teasing among couples. Many of the dances are in the quadrille or square formation; the head couples and the side couples take turns performing. Often in the music a single note is repeated several times in succession. This element also appears in the dance in such movements as the tapping of the toe or tiny jumps repeated by the dancers, or groups of dancers, one after another. There are also longways dances for eight couples and quadrille dances for eight couples that involve much crisscrossing.

The main festivals in the spring are centered around Easter. In the fall there is a Kalevala Day, when selections from the "Kalevala Book" (book of heroes) are read. Of course, there is also Christmas. Midsummer, or the summer solstice festival, observed on St. John the Baptist's day, is also celebrated. In some areas of Finland bonfires are lit and circle and couple dancing lasts all night. In other areas of Finland a Midsummer pole is decorated with garlands of greenery and flowers and encircled by dancers.

The musical accompaniment to Finnish folk dances is usually provided by the fiddle and clarinet, but the accordion, too, has become quite popular. The national instrument of Finland is the kantele. This instrument is laid on a table, like a zither, but the strings are plucked. In recent years, the kantele has enjoyed new popularity as a folk instrument, and in some instances the number of strings has been increased from the original five to thirty strings. There are many organizations in Finland that have helped to promote the continuation of Finnish folk dancing. The Museum of Seurasaari and Suomalaisen Kansantanssin Ystävät, both in Helsinki, have been influential in continuing folk dance traditions. As in the other Scandinavian countries, there has been a resurgence of interest in Finnish folk culture, including folk dancing, national dress, folk music, and the folk arts.

DANISH DANCE

Generally speaking, the development of dance in Denmark followed the development of dance in the other Scandinavian countries—with one advantage (or disadvantage, depending upon how you look at it). The Danes were closer to the people of Germany and Holland and the courts of Europe. They were among the first Scandinavians to feel the influence of developments in dance that affected the loss of their early dance rituals. Because of its position at the crossroads of Europe, both commercially as well as culturally, Denmark received artistic trends, cultural developments, and changes in fashion from the neighboring European countries and passed them along to the other Baltic countries. This, however, made it more difficult for Denmark to keep a firm hold on its own folk culture for a longer period, especially as far as folk dance and music are concerned. The Danes adopted Catholicism. Then the Protestant Reformation placed the Lutheran Church in power, which was another negative factor in the continuation of the folk dance. Denmark was greatly affected by the Industrial Revolution. The court dances of the eighteenth and nineteenth centuries did not have a difficult time replacing the ancient rituals.

The Danes have a seemingly limitless supply of fun dances. Although they are composed of essentially the same steps and figures, each dance has a spirit and life of its own. The steps used include English or reel steps, buzz step, walking, hopping, skipping, galloping, sliding, a smooth and a hopping polka, waltz, and mazurka. The stamp is often used at the beginning of a chain, at the end of a dance, or even at the beginning of many phrases during a dance. This stamp is frequently done with the whole body being lowered during the stamp or bending forward with the stamp. This movement is accentuated by the flying tassels on the men's caps, which move forward with every bend of the body. The pivot steps are also executed in a uniquely Danish manner: The steps are usually quite small, the knees are quite straight, and the upper halves of the couple's bodies lean away from each other in order to pivot fast enough to complete the turn. (A Norwegian would use springy knees with lots of flex in them, while a Swede would probably keep the body more parallel and his knees would bend with less spring than the Norwegian.)

Danish dance formations include the contra, the square, and several variations of couples in a circle facing into the center or counterclockwise around the room. As many of the Danish dances are done in sets, there is quite a bit of contact between all members of the set while dancing; eye contact is very important and little bowings of the head occur when the dancers pass each other in a chain or move in and out of the circle. The dancers almost always look and act like they are really having a good time. They dance for the fun of it; they are neither as serious as the Swedes nor as individualistic as the Norwegians. Sometimes there are unison chants that accompany some of the dances, and it is very common to hear lots of whoops and shouts from the dancers to underscore the good time they are having.

Danish music differs from other Scandinavian music in that the Danes have a greater written record of their musical inheritance and are far less dependent on an oral tradition. However, the many variations of the same melody in different parts of the country give evidence that the writing down of the melody took place as a result of hearing it sung or played. Musicians recorded the melodies because there were too many to remember. There are many more melodies than there are dance descriptions. Instruments in a typical old-time Danish country orchestra would include a small group of strings and a clarinet. Usually Danish music sounds faster than that of Norway and Sweden; there is less use of the ¾ meter and more use of ⁶⁄₈, for the feeling of the two heavy beats on counts one and four. The bass notes are most often strongly emphasized, more than in Swedish or Norwegian music. (However, in newer Norwegian and Swedish folk dance records there appears to be a greater use of bass note rhythms.) In Denmark the accordion was relied on heavily for dance music. There is a popular Danish folk dance record which includes a banjo playing right along with the other folk instruments.

Danish national dress developed differently in remote and isolated areas. The dress for each region was quite distinct. There has been an increasing interest in folk dress. In 1929 a Danish Folk Dancers Association (Landsföreningens Formand) was formed; by 1976 there were at least fifteen thousand members. They sponsor courses for leaders and dancers and have lots of meetings for interested participants. The Danish have a unique system of folk schools where many age-old traditions, crafts, gymnastic exercises, and dances are passed on or taught to people who have graduated from high school. In America these folk schools often reach out to the younger youth in an effort to teach them their folk and cultural heritage. (Sharron Kerr Deny, a native Californian, graduated from the University of California at Santa Barbara with a bachelor's and a master's degree in physical education and dance; while at the University of Southern California she earned a doctorate in physical education and dance. Her experience includes international folk dancing, with a strong interest in Scandinavian dances. She has been a member of the Swedish Folk Dance Club of Los Angeles since 1970. She and her husband, Armand, have studied dance in Sweden. They are teachers for Skandia South in Los Angeles. Sharron has been a physical education and folk dance teacher in the schools for approximately twelve years.)

SCANDINAVIAN FOLK DANCES

ÅTTA MAN ENGEL

Åtta Man Engel (OHT-tah mahn ENG-el), a dance for four couples, in square formation, comes from the western part of Finland. Since the people of that area speak Swedish, it is proper to use the Swedish title rather than the Finnish Kahdeksan Hengen Enkeliska (KAH-dek-san HENG-en EN-kel-is-kah). The dance was introduced by Susanna Daley of Helsinki, Finland.
Record: Suomen Nuorison Liitto, side A, band 5
Formation: Cpls in a square facing ctr, M behind ptr, hands joined with ptr in slide pos. Cpl 1 stands with backs to music or head of hall; cpl 2 faces cpl 1; cpl 3 stands to L of cpl 1; cpl 4 stands to R of cpl 1. Cpls 1 and 2 are head cpls; cpls 3 and 4 are side cpls.
Steps and Styling:
Slide pos (W in front): M offers his hands by extending them fwd on either side of W so that his palms are parallel to W body at rib-cage level. W takes hold of M hands with her palms resting on the back of the M hands and W fingers bent up across his palms. M curls his fingers over the W fingers. W places the joined hands at her sides as high as is comfortable on the rib cage. Also done with M in front holding W hands high on his rib cage.
Sliding step (2 to a meas): Moving to R side, step on R with a smooth, gliding step (cts 1, &); close L to R (ct ah); repeat exactly (cts 2, ah). To change direction, take no wt on last closing of L ft to R. To move to L side, start with L ft.

Buzz step (2 to a meas): To circle CW or turn CW with a ptr, push off from ball of L ft on upbeat of preceding meas (ct &); step on full R ft, bending knees (ct 1); repeat exactly (cts &, 2). To circle CCW or turn CCW with a ptr, push off from ball of R ft on upbeat (ct &); step on full L ft, bending knees (ct 1); repeat exactly (cts &, 2).
CW Spin pos: Place R hand on ptr's R shldr, arms well extended and inside of elbows adj; join L hands with ptr about waist level. Turn with buzz steps, stepping onto full R ft on ct 1.
CCW Spin pos: Place L hand on ptr's L shldr, arms well extended and inside of elbows adj; join R hands with ptr about waist level. Turn with buzz steps, stepping onto full L ft on ct 1.
Basket: Make 1 large circle facing ctr. M join hands with adj M; W join hands with adj W. When circling CW (to L) L arms are under neighbor's R arms. When circling CCW (to R) R arms are under neighbor's L arms.
Jump (1 to a ct): Spring from one or both ft and land on both ft.

Meter 2/4   Pattern

Meas
2   Intro: no action

I. Slides and Buzz Turns

1–16   Head cpls—sliding steps: Dance 8 short sliding steps to own R (meas 1–4). Dance 8 long sliding steps to own L, passing through own place and continuing out to L side to match distance traveled to R side (meas 5–8). Dance 8 long sliding steps to own R, ending in about the same place as in meas 4 (meas 9–12). Dance 8 short sliding steps to own L to end in orig place (meas 13–16).

Side cpls—buzz turns: W 2 and M 4 (pass ptr to the R) beg R ft, walk 4 steps to meet in the middle of set and take CW spin pos (R hands on R shldrs) (meas 1–2). Turn CW with 12 buzz steps (meas 3–8). End facing own place. W 3 and M 4 pass by L shldr (keep L hands joined long enough to give help), beg L ft, walk 4 steps to meet own ptr and take CCW spin pos (L hands on L shldrs) (meas 9–10). W 4 and M 3 are inactive during meas 1–10. Turn CCW with 12 buzz steps (meas 11–16). Finish in orig slide pos (W in front).

1–16   Head cpls: Dance buzz turns with W 1 and M 2 active. End in slide pos but with M in front.

Side cpls: Dance sliding steps with W in front.

1–16   Head cpls: Dance sliding steps with M in front.

Side cpls: Dance buzz turns with W 4 and M 3 active. End in slide pos but with M in front.

Odin Scandinavian Dancers

1-16 Head cpls: Dance buzz turns with W 2 and M 1 active.
Side cpls: Dance sliding steps with M in front. At end all should be ready to start a grand right and left.

II. Grand Right and Left; Grand Left and Right

1-12 Give R hand to ptr and beg R ft, walk 24 steps in a grand R and L to meet ptr a second time (orig place).

13-16 With ptr take CW spin pos (R hands on R shldrs) and turn with 8 buzz steps. End with M facing RLOD and W facing LOD.

1-12 Beg L ft and L hand with ptr, walk 24 steps in a grand L and R to meet ptr a second time (orig place).

13-16 With ptr take CCW spin pos (L hands on L shldrs) and turn with 8 buzz steps. End in orig place facing ctr, with W to R of ptr, ready to form a basket.

III. Baskets CW and CCW

1-6 All form a basket with L arms under, facing a little L of ctr. Beg R ft, circle CW (L) with 12 walking steps. Stamp on last 2 steps.

7-12 Continue to circle CW with 12 buzz steps.

1-6 Release hands and facing ctr, jump 3 times in place, clapping own hands on each jump. Re-form basket with R arms under, facing a little R of ctr. Beg R ft, circle CCW (R) with 9 walking steps. Stamp on last 2 steps.

7-12 Continue to circle CCW with 12 buzz steps.

1-6 Release hands and do jumps and claps as before. Re-form basket with L arms under. Beg L ft, circle CW (L) with 9 walking steps. Stamp on last 2 steps.

7-12 Continue to circle CW with 12 buzz steps.

1-6 Release hands and do jumps and claps as before. Re-form basket with R arms under. Beg R ft, circle CCW (R) with 9 walking steps. Stamp on last 2 steps.

7-12 Continue to circle CCW (R) with 11 buzz steps. Keeping hands joined, end facing ctr with one jump.

BITTE MAND i KNIBE

Bitte Mand i Knibe (Little Man in a Fix) is reported to have originated in the vicinity of Randers, Jutland. It has enjoyed widespread popularity not only in Denmark but in other lands as well.

Record: Victor 20449-A; Folk Dancer 1054

Formation: Two couples dancing together. Facing in opposite directions, the men hook L elbows. Men have R arms around their partner's waists; ladies have their L hands resting on their partner's R shoulders. Free hands on hips. M & W may join R hands and place them at W R waist.

Steps: Running step, Tyrolian waltz step, waltz step

Meter 3/4   Pattern

Meas

I. Running

1–8   Couples run fwd 24 steps in CCW circle. Slight accent on lst ct of each meas.

1–8   With no pause, M join L hands, as each takes his partner's L hand in his R. M make an arch with their L arms. W both run through arch, passing in front of their respective partners. W turn L about to face each other and join their R hands above those of the M. With arms crossed, continue to run CCW.

II. Waltzing

9–12   Couples break apart, each M holding partner's L hand in his R. Balance 4 times with Tyrolian waltz step (fwd, bwd, fwd, bwd).

13–16   Taking closed waltz position, couples proceed at random about the floor with 4 waltz steps. (Variation: the two couples may revolve about each other in a small CCW circle, keeping close together; M may take opp W for waltz).

9–16   Repeat action of fig II.

Each couple then seeks a new couple with whom to repeat the entire pattern. An odd number of couples will add to the interest of the dance, for with each repetition there is always one "little man in a fix" without a partner couple. (Variation: When couples have revolved around each other in a closed waltz, they repeat the dance over and over with the same couple.)

DØLA MASURKA

Learned in Gudbrandsdal, Norway, by Ingvar Sodal.

Record: RCA (LP) NES65, side 2, band 1, or any mazurka from Gudbrandsdal.

Formation: Couples in a circle moving LOD. Closed shoulder-waist pos. M back to ctr, W facing ctr.

Steps: Masurka, pols turn

Meter 3/4   Pattern

Meas   *Sideways Masurka Steps:*

1   Moving LOD, step M L and W R (ct 1), step M R to L and W L to R (ct &), step M L,

W R, moving LOD but somewhat shorter step than on ct 1 (ct 2), close M R to L and W L to R with a soft dip. Transfer all weight onto M R and W L so that the leading ft is ready for next step (ct 3).

2–7   Continue this step until end of musical phrase. *Note:* Although cpls have shoulder-waist pos during this step, they may face slightly fwd in LOD but not so much that R ft crosses over L on ct 3.

8   Take 3 steps in place, M L, R, L, W R, L, R while making ½ turn CCW.

9–15   Continue sideways masurka steps as in 1–7, but with opposite ftwk. M now faces ctr.

16   Take 3 steps in place, M R, L, R, W L, R, L while making ½ turn CW.

Pols Turn, Man's Step:

17   Step L and pivot CW (ct 1), continue pivot on L while closing R to L in a trailing motion (ct &), close R to L and put wt on both ft (ct 2), step R, leading LOD with a springy motion (sometimes leading to a backward kick with L ft). This completes the turn, which should have an even rotation.

Pols Turn, Woman's Step:

17   Step R and turn CW (ct 1), step L continue CW turn (ct &), step R continue CW turn (ct 2), step L completing the turn (ct 3).

18–24   Continue the pols turn until end of musical phrase.

Repeat meas 1–24 until end of music.

Note: The dance is somewhat freestyle and the various figures may be alternated freely and any number of meas used for each part.

FAMILIE SEKSTUR

Learned by Gordon Tracie. It is often known as "Danish Family Circle."

Record: Danish "Family Circle," Linden 703-B, Tanz E P 58402.

Formation: Cpls in single circle facing ctr, W to R of M. Hands joined at shoulder height, elbows bent V-shaped so that dancers are fairly close together.

Steps: Side-buzz, walking, buzz turn (Danish waltz pos, grand R and L)

Meter 6/8   Pattern

Meas

4   Intro

I. Circle to Left with Side Buzz Step

1–8   In circle formation, all facing ctr, dance to L (CW) with 16 side-buzz steps. Side-buzz steps: Face ctr, step R across in front of L, with slight dip and with toe pointing twd ctr (ct 1), draw

L directly back of R (ct 2), take wt on ball of L (ct 3). There are 2 buzz steps per meas. Steps should be small and light. Keep elbows bent, face ctr, and lean slightly bwd. This step is the "Introduction" and is not repeated.

II. Walk In and Out

9–10 Beginning R, all walk twd ctr with 4 steps (2 steps per meas), gradually raising arms to full height. On last step give a slight "compliment" or nod of head.

11–12 Walk bwd 4 steps to original circle, lowering joined hands to shoulder height and "complimenting" ptr on last step.

13–16 Repeat action of fig II, meas 9–12.

III. Grand Chain

17–24 Facing ptr, join R hands at shoulder height (elbow downward) and walk around circle (2 steps per meas) with grand R and L. M move CCW, W CW. Keep hands at shoulder height. Count aloud (preferably in Danish) for each person met (beginning with *own* original ptr), retaining #7 as new ptr.

IV. Swing Partner

1–8 In closed Danish waltz pos M L and W R joined and extended at arm's length straight out from shoulder (W stands to R of M), swing new ptr CW with 16 buzz steps. End with ptr on M R, all hands rejoined to form single circle. Repeat dance starting with fig II. The sequence is as follows: swing ptr; into ctr and out; grand chain. Only the first time through the side buzz step is danced instead of a ptr swing.

FEIAR MED VALS

Record: TD-3 Norsk Grammofonkompani A/S, Oslo, Norway, or Aqua Viking V 300 B

Formation: Couple dance, any number of couples, free hand on hip, thumb forward

Steps: Waltz, two-step, Hamborgarpols pivot

Hamborgarpols pivot: This is a distinctive turning step falling between a ball-of-foot pivot and a step-hop.

ct 1: Step on the whole ft, with knee bent ct &. Lift heel from floor and straighten knee a bit to raise the body, while turning on ball of ft.

ct 2: Repeat above motion with other ft.

ct &: Finish above motion with other ft.

There are thus *two* distinct motions on each meas. A smooth "bounce" is maintained, the knees flexing lightly, never completely straight.

Sequence: 1. Waltz
　　　　　 2. Feiar (sweeper): two-step fwd and back, with stamping
　　　　　 3. Hamborgarpols pivot and lift

Meter 3/4   Pattern

Intro: 4 meas

1. Closed shoulder-waist pos. 15 waltz steps LOD. M starts on L ft. On 16th meas, cpl stops, facing each other, inside hands joined at shoulder level, held out to M R.

2. Start on outside ft. 3 open two-steps LOD, face to face with arms projected back, back-to-back with arms projected fwd, and face-to-face with arms back again. Release handhold. Join opp hands while turning ½ around (M CW, W CCW), stamping on both steps.

Repeat the 3 open two-steps etc. in opp direction, starting with outside ft (W L, M R), ending with 2 stamps on last meas, facing RLOD.

3. In shoulder-waist pos, M dances a two-step (L, close, L) more or less in place, but turning to his L (CCW), with stamp on last beat, while bringing W over in front of him, W dancing a longer two-step (R, close, R). Closed shoulder-waist pos, and repeat above step in opp direction (CW). Starting on opp ft and with stamp on 1st beat. Cont turning CW with 2 two-steps, no stamp, but with a trace of a hop on last beat of each meas. Pivot CW with 6 Hamborgarpols pivot steps. Final meas M lifts W from his L to his R side.

Pause during pick-up notes. Repeat entire dance.

FJÄSKERN

Fjäskern (F-YESS-kohrn) is a circle mixer folk dance from southern Sweden.

Source: Learned in Sweden by Gordon E. Tracie and is described in *Samkväms & Gillesdanser* published by Svenska Ungdomsringen för Bygdekultur, Stockholm.

Record: Aqua Viking 200

Formation: Cpls in double circle, M on inside, W on outside, beg facing LOD. Open hand pos, joined at shoulder level. Free hands *always* on hips, fingers fwd.

Steps and Styling: Walking, running, and kicking steps. Ftwk is the same for M and W. Throughout entire dance there is a simple L-R alternation of the ft without stopping. The dance is done in a sprightly manner and with humor.

Meter 4/4   Pattern

Meas

I. Circle Fwd and Back

1–4 Inside hands joined, beg on L ft, cpls move fwd in LOD 16 steps. (For the 1st two sequences, walking steps will be used during fig I; succeeding sequences will be running steps.)

1–4 Turning around individually, twd ptr, other hands are joined, and cpls move back in opp direction in similar manner for 16 steps.

II. Kick and Exchange Places

5 Facing ptr squarely, M on inside, W on outside of circle, both hands on own hips, cpls dance 4 kicking steps, beg with wt on L ft (kicking out with R ft).

6 With handclap on 1st beat, ptrs change places with 4 running steps, moving about CW while facing each other (as if hands were joined).

7–8 Repeat action of fig II, meas 5–6 to return to own place.

5–8 Repeat action of fig II, meas 5–8.
Repeat dance from beginning.

HAMBO

The hambo is a favorite wherever it is danced. It is probably the most common folk dance still extant dating back to the nineteenth century. Its popularity in Sweden and the characteristics it has acquired since its adoption many years ago have placed it foremost on the list of beautiful Swedish dances. Its earlier history is rooted in the dances of other countries.

Record: "Styrman Karlssons," Victor 26-1046; "Tip Top Hambo," Imperial 1036; Harmony 30 (intro.)

Source: Learned at Naas Institute, Floda, Sweden, by Lucile Czarnowski.

Formation: Couples in open position. W L hand is on M R shoulder, his R arm is around her waist, outside hands are on hips.

Steps: Dal step, hambo polska

Meter 3/4   Pattern

Meas

I. Dal Steps and Light Running Steps Fwd

1–2 Both starting with outside ft, 2 dal steps fwd.

3 3 light running steps fwd (cts 1, 2, 3).

4 Partners facing, take shoulder-waist position. M steps toward partner with stamp R (cts 1, 2) and shifts wt back on L (ct 3). W steps twd partner with L ft, with slight bend of L knee (cts 1, 2) and shifts wt back onto R ft (ct 3).

II. Hambo Polska Turning Continuously CW

5 M steps twd partner with a stamp R (ct 1); steps back on L (ct 2); touches R toe beside the L ft as he pivots on L (ct 3); gives W a slight lift on cts 2 and 3. Simultaneously W steps twd partner with L ft, slightly bending the L knee (ct 1); touches R toe behind L ft for balance (ct 2); leaps onto R ft (ct 3). This gives a soft down-up motion to her turns.

6–7 Continue with 2 more hambo polska steps.

8 Open dance position is resumed as both step on inside ft (ct 1); both take 2 quick steps in place (outside ft, inside ft) (ct 3).

Note: Expert dancers sometimes omit the transition step described for meas 4 of step I and go immediately into the turning hambo polska. Four hambo polska steps would then be danced in all.

INNHERREDSPOLS

Record: RCA FEP-14

Formation: Couple dance, any number of couples LOD CCW

Steps: Springar steps (as described below), left ft pols steps

Sequence: 1. Springar steps, open pos fwd
2. Closed pos turn CW, left ft pols step

Meter 3/4   Pattern

1. Fwd Springar Step:

ct 1: Small jump on both ft, ft approx 12 inches apart. M leading with L ft, W leading with R ft (face-to-face pos).

ct 2: M R ft up to L.
W L ft up to R.
(face-to-face pos)

ct 3: M L ft fwd LOD.
W R ft fwd LOD.
Both turn slightly outward.
Next step the same, except on opposite ft, and ct 1 starts in back-to-back pos.
Arms: Inside hands joined and inside arms extended back in face-to-face pos. Outside hand on hip, thumb fwd.
Next step in back-to-back pos, inside arms swinging fwd while turning in and out on every other step.
Repeat this figure for one or two meas (4 or 8 steps).

2. Left Ft Pols Step CW in Closed Pos:

ct 1: M L ft, W both ft, keeping wt on L while taking closed pos (small dip for W).

ct 2: M both ft with a small dip, W R ft.

ct 3: M R ft, W L.
Start into closed pos on ct 1. M R arm around W waist, M L around W right shoulder. W left hand on M R shoulder, W R hand high on M back, arm under M L arm. Make an even number of turns (4 or 8) according to the phrasing in the music.

LIRPPU-LARPPU

Lirppu-Larppu (LIRP-poo-LARP-poo) is a couple dance from Kimito, near Turku, in southwest Finland. The dance was introduced by Susanna Daley of Helsinki, Finland.

Record: Suomen Nuorison Liitto, side A, band 1

Formation: Cpls are in a double circle with ptrs facing. M back is to ctr and hands are down at sides.

Steps and Styling:

Step lift (2/4 meter): Step slightly L on L (ct 1); lift L heel as you cross R leg in front of L with R knee bent (ct 2). Knees are crossed but calf and foot hang straight down.

Polska (3/4 meter): Step fwd on L (ct 1); close R to L (ct &); step fwd on L (ct 2); leap fwd on R, kicking L heel up behind (ct 3). Step repeats exactly. Step is also done beg R.

Cross-back pos.

Ftwk for M and W is same throughout dance.

Meter 2/4, 3/4   Pattern

Meas

2 meas Intro: no action

I. Step Lift

1–4   Beg L, dance 4 step lifts in place.

5–6   Moving twd ptr's L side, step fwd L, R (cts 1, 2). Step fwd on L, bending knee and lifting R behind (ct 1); step bkwd on R (ct 2).

7–8   Change places, moving CW around ptr and staying face-to-face. Step fwd L, R, L, close R to L, taking wt. (M is now on outside of circle.)

9–16 Repeat action of meas 1–7. On meas 16 assume cross-back pos, R hips adjacent.

II. Polska

1–6   Dance 6 polska steps, beg L, and turning CW as a cpl approx 2½ times to finish with M on outside of circle.

7–8   Release hands and step L, R, L, turning ¼ to R to face ptr (meas 7). Clap own hands (ct 1); assume cross-back hold, L hips adjacent (ct 2, 3).

9–15 Repeat action of meas 1–7 (fig II), but turn CCW and beg polska with R ft. On meas 15 step R, L, R, turning ¼ to L in own place to face ptr (M on inside of circle).

16   Clap own hands (ct 1); hold (ct 2, 3).
      Repeat entire dance once (2 times in all).

PARISARPOLKA

Parisarpolka (pah-REE-sahr-POHL-kah), Parisian polka, is a traditional couple dance done throughout Norway. It is believed to be the ancestor of the Scandi-navian polka (or Seattle polka in the Pacific Northwest), which is popular in many parts of the United States. It was probably brought to America by Norwegian immigrants during the last century.

Record: "Ola Bakar," Triola TNLP 38 (33⅓), side B, band 2; "Norsk Parisarpolka," RCA LPM 9910 (33⅓), side 1, band 6; "Norsk Parisarpolka," RCA LPM 9810 (33⅓); "Pariserpolka," Harmoni TD-2 (45), side 2, band 1; "Parisarpolka," Viking V 301a (45).

Formation: Cpls in a circle facing CCW with W to M R. Ptrs face slightly twd each other with inside hands joined and held at shoulder level. Outside hands hang freely or are on hips with thumbs fwd, fingers back.

Steps and Styling: Walk (with springy down-up motion), two-step, pivot (with down-up motion), three-step turn, shoulder-waist pos. Dance in a relaxed style, with steps springy but controlled. Look at ptr. M and W are on opp ft throughout dance.

Meter 2/4   Pattern

Meas

4   Intro: no action

I. Forward and Back (inside hands joined)

1–2   Beginning with M L, W R, dance 3 springy walking steps fwd in LOD, then turning to face ptr, M close R to L ft (no wt), W close L to R ft (no wt). Free ft may be touched either beside or across supporting ft.

3–4   Without releasing hands, turn to face RLOD and repeat action of meas 1–2 (fig I) reversing ftwk.

5–6   With inside hands still joined, dance 2 two-steps fwd in LOD beginning M L, W R. Dance slightly face-to-face and back-to-back, keeping eye contact.

7–8   Facing ptr, place R hand on ptr's back at lower rib cage. W place L hand on back of M R shoulder (W L arm is over M R arm) and M place L hand on W back at the shoulder blade (M L arm is over W R arm). In this pos, beginning M L, W R, dance 4 springy pivot steps, making 2 CW turns and prog CCW. (Alternate pos = shoulder-waist).

9–16 Repeat action of meas 1–8 (fig I).

II. Turn Away (no hands joined)

1–2   Beginning M L, W R, dance 1 three-step turn in LOD (M turn CCW, W CW) with springy walking steps, letting arms swing freely. Facing ptr, M touch toe of R ft next to L (W do opp) as you snap fingers, clap hands, or raise arms high.

3–4   Moving in RLOD, repeat action of meas 1–2

(fig II) but with opp ftwk and direction of turns.

5–6 Without joining hands, repeat action of fig I, meas 5–6 (2 two-steps)

7–8 Repeat action of fig I, meas 7–8 (cpl turn).

9–16 Repeat action of meas 1–8 (fig II).

III. Dishrag Turn (two hands joined)

1–2 Facing ptr (M back to ctr), join both hands straight across. Lifting arms fwd and moving in LOD, make a complete turn under both arms (dishrag), repeating ftwk of fig II, meas 1–2.

3–4 Lifting trailing arms and moving in RLOD, repeat action of meas 1–2 (fig III) reversing ftwk and direction of turns.

5–6 With both hands joined and held close together (forearms vertical) at chest level, repeat action of fig I, meas 5–6 (2 two-steps).

7–8 Repeat action of fig I, meas 7–8 (cpl turn).

9–16 Repeat action of meas 1–8 (fig III).

IV. M Forward, W Backward

1–2 With M facing LOD and W to his R facing RLOD, join both hands at shoulder level with R arms outstretched in front of ptr. In this pos repeat action of fig I, meas 1–2, with W walking bkwd.

3–4 Without releasing hands, M raise R hand high and turn ½ CW while W turns ½ CCW to finish with M facing RLOD and W to his L facing LOD, with W L arm outstretched in front of M chest and M L arm behind W waist. In this pos repeat the action of fig I, meas 3–4, with W walking bkwd.

5–6 Releasing M L and W R hand, M dance 2 two-steps fwd in LOD while W turns CW twice (under joined arms) with 4 pivot steps.

7–8 Repeat action of fig I, meas 7–8 (cpl turn).

9–16 Repeat action of meas 1–8 (fig IV).

V. W Turn (one hand joined)

1–2 With inside hands joined (M R, W L), M repeat action of fig I, meas 1–2, while W turns once CW under joined hands, repeating ftwk of fig II, meas 1–2.

3–4 Without releasing hands and moving in RLOD, M repeat action of fig I, meas 3–4, while W turns once CCW under joined hands, repeating ftwk of fig II, meas 3–4.
Variation: M may dance bkwd in RLOD.

5–6 Repeat action of fig IV, meas 5–6 (2 two-steps).

7–8 Repeat action of fig I, meas 7–8 (cpl turn).

9–16 Repeat action of meas 1–8 (fig V).

Note: A customary way of dancing this dance in Norway is to repeat the first figure at the conclusion to "tone down" the dance for a more dignified ending. This will depend on the recording used. With the RCA records, the dance is gone through one time plus the repeat of fig I. With the Harmoni and Viking records, you may dance figs I–V, then repeat figs I–V plus fig I. Thus, fig I is danced twice in a row in the middle of the dance. Another variation that is very popular now is for cpls to enter into the dance at the beginning of any 8 meas phrase and begin with fig I and dance the sequence as written, in which case all cpls are not dancing the same figure at the same time.

SLÄNGPOLSKA FRÅN SKÅNE

This dance is one of the older types of polska, dating from the eighteenth century. It's lively! It was presented by Per and Margareta Jennische.

Record: "Slängpolska from Skåne," Viking SMF-200

Formation:
  1. Partners facing each other with a low double handhold.
  2. Equilateral position when the couple is turning CW; reversed equilateral position when couple is turning CW.

Steps:
  Clockwise: outside foot = L. Step forward with L (1-&), forward with R (2), place L foot close to R heel (&), and step forward with R (3-&).
  Counterclockwise: outside foot = R. Same steps as above with opposite footwork.

Meter 3/4   Pattern

Meas

1–8 Start with position (1) and turn CW, *taking small steps.* The partners lean away from each other but keep their feet close together. On measure 8 they drop hands and both the man and the woman make one turn CCW separately, taking one step per beat (L-R-L). On the last two beats of the measure they clap their hands, once per beat, and the steps are emphasized. Take position (1) again and turn in the opposite direction (CCW); the R foot is now free to start the step. This time the turn on measure 8 is done CW, stepping R-L-R.

9–16 Partners take position (2) and turn CW. The individual turn on measure 16 is done as above for measure 8. The couple then turns CCW, with partners again turning separately on measure 16.

The dance is repeated from the beginning.

"SWEDISH" MASQUERADE

Record: His Master's Voice B2711; Sonart 304; Folk
  Dancer 1019; Folkraft 1097

Formation: Couples in double circle formation facing
  counterclockwise, M inside of circle, R arm linked
  with partner's L arm.

Steps: Walking (four to a measure); Tyrolian waltz
  (one to a measure); Tyroler hopsa step; hopsa step;
  waltz

Meter 4/4, 3/4, 2/4   Pattern

Meas

4/4   *I. Promenade*
1–4   Starting with outside feet, partners take 16
           walking steps counterclockwise; turn toward
           each other to face in opposite direction on the
           last 2 steps.
5–8   Repeat action of meas 1–4 in opposite direction
           (clockwise).

3/4   *II. Tyrolian Waltz*
9–12   Facing counterclockwise with inside hands
           joined (M L hand at L armhole of vest; W R
           hand on hip), dance 4 Tyrolian waltz steps in
           line of direction.
           Tyrolian waltz as taught by Signe Bertelsen
           of Denmark: Step swd, away from partner (ct
           1), step with inside ft in front of outside ft,
           rising on toes (ct 2), close with outside ft (ct
           3); joined hands swing slightly fwd. Repeat ac-
           tion, starting with inside ft, arms swing slightly
           bwd. Move forward on (ct 2).
13–16   In closed waltz position dance 4 waltz steps
           turning CW and progressing CCW.
9–16   Repeat action of meas 9–16.

2/4   *III. Tyroler Hopsa and Hopsa Steps*
17–20   With inside hands joined, dance 4 Tyroler
           hopsa steps, starting with outside ft and moving
           counterclockwise.
21–24   In closed dance position, continue in same di-
           rection with 4 hopsa steps, turning CW with
           partner.
17–24   Repeat action of meas 17–24.

TO TING

The name of this dance means "two things" and
was learned from Carl Hansen.

Record: Folk Dancer 1018, Sonart 303

Formation: Cpls, facing CCW, inside hands joined
  at about shoulder height; outside hands free, or W
  hand on hip and M thumb in armhole of vest.

Steps: Tyroler waltz, walk, pivot

Meter 3/4, 2/4   Pattern

Meas
3/4   Intro
upbeat

           I. Tyroler Waltz
1–4   Beginning M L, W R, dance fwd (LOD) away
           from ptr, twd ptr, away, and twd ptr with 4
           Tyroler waltz steps.
           Assume waltz grasp: M puts R arm around
           W waist and grasps her R hand with his L,
           keeping it extended at shoulder height. W
           places her L hand on back of M R shoulder.
5–8   With 4 waltz steps turn CW while progressing
           CCW.
1–8   Repeat action of meas 1–8.

2/4   *II. Walk and Pivot*
9–10   Release joined hands (M L, W R) and in open
           pos walk fwd 4 steps (LOD).
11–12   Assume shoulder-waist pos and turn CW with
           4 pivot steps, continuing LOD.
13–16   Repeat action of meas 9–12.

TO TUR

Record: Imperial 1038; Kismet 135; Folk Dancer
  1021.

Formation: Single circle of cpls, W to R of ptr, all
  facing ctr, hands joined at shoulder height

Steps: Walking, two-step, grand right and left

Meter 2/4   Pattern

Meas
1–4   Intro: no action

           I. Circle Left, Circle Right
1–8   Beginning L, all circle CW with 8 two-steps.
1–8   Beginning L, all circle CCW with 8 two-steps.

           II. Center and Back
9   Cpls in closed pos facing ctr of circle dance a
           two-step twd ctr, starting M L, W R.
10   Continue twd ctr of circle with 2 walking steps
           (M-R L, W-L R).
11–12   Repeat action of meas 9–10 (fig II), moving
           bwd twd outside of circle without changing pos
           and still facing ctr of circle. M start R, W L.
13–16   With 4 two-steps, starting M L and W R, cpls
           progress CCW around circle while turning CW.
9–16   Repeat action of meas 9–16 (fig II).

           III. Grand Right and Left
1–8   Ptrs face and, offering R hands to each other,
           do a grand R and L with two-steps.
1–8   Continue grand R and L, assuming closed pos
           with person met at end of this phrase. The
           grand R and L is done with 16 two-steps.
           Note: Each dancer who finishes this figure with-

out a ptr should go to ctr of circle to find a new one.

IV. Center and Back
9–16 Repeat action of fig II, meas 9–16 and meas 9–16 repeated.
9–16 Repeat action of figs I, II, III, IV, I and II.

VOSSARULL

This dance is from the town of Voss in Vestlandet, Norway. The rull is one of the five types of Norwegian folk dances.

Record: NKG TD 7, RCA FEP 11.
Formation: Couple dance; any number of couples; open and closed pos as described
Steps: Walking step, pivot, two-step
Sequence: 1. Walking fwd, LOD
2. Pivot
3. Two-steps CCW (any number)
Repeat 2–3

Meter 4/4   Pattern

1. Walking LOD, open pos, M R arm around W waist. W L hand on M shoulder, other hand swinging freely. Springy walk, opp ftwk, start each step with heel on floor as in a natural walk. Each step has a slight springy dip.

2. Closed pos: Face to face, close. M R arm around W waist, M L hand holding W skirt gently out to side (not up). W R hand high on M back under M L arm. W L hand on M R shoulder.
Start pivot on M L and W R ft. Step is symmetrical. R ft always between partner's feet, starting with heel on floor, twist CW and pivot on ball of ft. Slight dip on beginning of step. L ft step same.
Note: Place L ft close to partner's R on the outside. Pivot is completely smooth and well balanced. Make any number of turns.

3. To break up the pivot, assume open pos and walk fwd, as described at beginning of dance, or keep closed pos and make any number of two-steps CCW and CW.

SCOTLAND

Scottish Country Dancing

by Betty Casey

Scottish country dancing has been popular in Scotland for many generations. To preserve a part of their national heritage, in 1923 two Scottish women, the late Miss Jean Milligan of Glasgow and Mrs. Stewart of Fasnacloich, began laying the groundwork for the Royal Scottish Country Dance Society [RSCDS]. Their purpose was to preserve and promote traditional Scottish country dancing, which had not previously been recorded extensively.

Fifty years later, RSCDS had more than fifteen thousand members in branches and affiliated clubs worldwide. The Jubilee Ball, a gala affair held in Edinburgh to celebrate this accomplishment, was attended by Queen Elizabeth, a patron of the Society, and other members of the royal family.

The dances, beloved by all classes of people, were handed down orally from generation to generation. The longways form of the dances, traditionally British, is found in all four countries—England, Scotland, Wales, Ireland—as well as on the Isle of Man. The Scots added the distinctive Strathspey step to Scottish country dance. Developed primarily in the region of Atholl and Strathspey, it is similar to the graceful galliard of the previous century. Although country dancing became less popular during the nineteenth century among the elite, it became increasingly popular at weddings and fairs in Scotland. The precise steps, methods of presentation, and special formations give the dances a definitive and distinctive Scottish style. Scottish technique and presentation are French in character, based as they are on the days of the Auld

Alliance and a time when the mercenary armies of France were largely Scottish. With its elegance and carefully detailed steps, the styling is closely allied to the French court dances from which both Highland and Scottish country dancing derived their form.

Under Miss Milligan's guidance, members of the RSCDS research and publish instructions and alternate names for the traditional dances in booklets and in a textbook called *Won't You Join the Dance?* (The Royal Scottish Dance Society, 12 Coates Crescent, Edinburgh, Scotland EH3 7AF).

A rigorous and detailed training and examination period is required for those who would become certified RSCDS instructors. Each Society or branch (i.e., in America) must have a qualified teacher. Every two years an examiner is sent from Scotland to verify proper credentials for new leaders. To become a candidate for RSCDS, the would-be teacher must have been a branch member in good standing for a year and must be proficient in performing the dances. He or she must undergo twenty to thirty hours of practice teaching under a tutor, usually a senior teacher, before taking the test for a preliminary certificate. If the examiner feels the candidate shows potential as a teacher of country dancing, this certificate is awarded. It entitles the holder to conduct classes under the supervision of a fully certified teacher. After two or more years of practice teaching and another twenty to thirty hours of tutoring, the candidate takes another examination to qualify for a full certificate.

The San Francisco RSCDS branch is more or less typical of some one hundred branches scattered worldwide. It has some two hundred members. In 1971 Dr. Milligan herself was their examiner. In 1973, during an all-day affair, Miss Mina Corson gave certificates for two full and six preliminary teachers, bringing their total to twelve full and seven preliminary accredited instructors.

There are other accredited RSCDS instructors scattered about the United States, with a varying number of branch societies in operation. These societies are completely separate entities from international folk dance groups.

In a letter addressed to me, Miss M. M. Gibson, secretary for Dr. Milligan, former president of RSCDS, wrote, "I have consulted Dr. Milligan, who does not approve of Scottish Country Dancing being included in Folk Dancing publications. Our Scottish Country Dancing derived its origins from the Court rather than folk dancing."

Yet the dances are so enjoyable and so closely related to other set dances originating in England that some have been incorporated on a limited scale into IFD programs. In much the same manner, the term *folk dance,* as it is loosely used in the United States,

includes Russian ballroom dances and French court quadrilles.

The steps and music for Scottish country dancing are called reels, jigs, and strathspeys. Steps done to reels (4/4 meter) and jigs (6/8 meter) are called reel steps. Those done to strathspeys (4/4 meter) are called strathspey steps. The styling is light, precise, and done with cordial teamwork. Following are samples of Scottish dances as done in various sections of the United States.

SCOTTISH COUNTRY DANCES

THE DOUBLE SIXSOME
The Double Sixsome, a dance for six couples, was devised by Mary Brandon.

Record: "Double Sixsome," Pasadena Teachers Choice #2-52575 A; "Double Sixsome," Express 45. The tunes used are "Bert McCroskie" and "Walking on the Moon."

Formation: 6 couples in longways formation. Beginning at the top, couples are numbered from 1 to 6, with the bottom couples 4, 5, and 6 crossed over to the wrong side of the dance.

Steps and Styling: Skip change of step, slip step, set, bow and curtsy, allemande, hands across, rights and lefts

Meter 2/4   Pattern

Meas

Chord Intro: M bow, W curtsy to ptr.

I. Forward and Back: Around Ptr

1–4   All 6 W with hands joined in 2 lines of 3 people dance fwd twd M with 2 skip change of step and then bkwd to place with 2 skip change of step. M stand in place.

5–8   With 4 skip change of step all M dance fwd and CW around ptr, passing R shldr with her and finishing facing her with both hands joined and stretched just slightly out to the sides.

II. Sideward Slides

9–16   Cpls 1, 2, 3 move down the dance with 8 slip steps and back up again with 8 slip steps. Simultaneously, cpls 4, 5, 6 move up the dance with 8 slip steps and down again with 8 slip steps. M pass back to back. Finish with all cpls in allemande (varsouvienne) pos, cpls 1, 2, 3 facing up and cpls 4, 5, 6 facing down the dance.

III. Three Couple Allemande

17–24   Using skip change of step throughout, cpls 1, 2, 3 dance an allemande, with cpl 3 moving between cpls 1 and 2 during meas 19–20. Simultaneously, cpls 4, 5, 6 dance an allemande, with cpl 4 moving between cpls 5 and 6 (meas 19–20). Finish in order from the top: 2, 3, 1, 6, 4, 5.

IV. Hands Across

25–32 Cpls 1 and 6 dance R hands across in the middle with 4 skip change of step. Reverse and dance L hands across with 4 skip change of step. All others stand in place.

V. Rights and Lefts

Cpls 2 and 3, and likewise cpls 4 and 5, dance rights and lefts with 8 skip change of step. Cpls 1 and 6 stand in place.

VI. Cross and Between at Own End

41–46 Using skip change of step throughout, cpl 1 with L hands joined dance up the ctr. Using joined hands to help pull by before releasing them, cross above cpl 3 (W in front of M), dance out between cpls 2 and 3 and then up and around cpl 2. Cpl 1 join nearer hands and dance down the ctr. Simultaneously, cpl 6 with L hands joined dance down the ctr, cross below cpl 4, dance between cpls 4 and 5, down and around cpl 5, and then dance up.

47–48 Cpls 1 and 6 meet in the middle. M 1 and W 6, and likewise W 1 and M 6, join both hands and turn 1/2 CW with 2 skip change of step. On last ct release hands and turn individually halfway around twd ptr (M CCW, W CW), so that M 1 and W 1 continue to face down, while W 6 and M 6 face up the dance.

VII. Cross and Between at Opposite End

49–56 Repeat action of fig VI with cpl 6 dancing the action of cpl 1 and with cpl 1 dancing the action of cpl 6. Finish with cpl 1 in 3rd place and cpl 6 in 4th place.

VIII. Set Twice and Turn Partner

57–64 All join hands in 2 long lines on each side and set twice to ptr. Turn ptr with R hands once CW with 4 skip change of step, finishing back in place.

Repeat dance twice more, finishing in orig place.

Chord M bow, W curtsy to ptr.

THE GARY STRATHSPEY

This recent dance was composed by James B. Cosh of Glasgow and was introduced by C. Stewart Smith.

Record: "The Gary Strathspey," Fontana TFE 17376

Formation: 4 cpls in longways formation

Steps and Styling: Strathspey step, strathspey setting step, Highland schottische step, side step (4/4 meter), reel of four. The body is kept facing fwd and erect but not stiff. The chest is high; arms are held loosely at sides. (W may hold skirt.) All dancing is done on toes, with knees well turned out. Ptrs dance with each other, communicating by means of tension in the arms and by looking at one another. When inactive, stand in place with heels together and toes apart.

Note: Strathspey steps always start R and are used throughout the dance unless otherwise stated. Action is smooth and continuous.

Meter 4/4   Pattern

Meas

Chord Intro: M bow, W curtsy to ptr.

I. Rights and Lefts

Cpl 1 with cpl 2 and cpl 3 with cpl 4 dance R and L halfway around as follows:

1–2 Ptrs change places across the set, giving R hands in passing.

3–4 M with M, W with W change places, moving up and down the dance, giving L hands in passing. M 1 and M 3, W 2 and W 4 finish by turning CCW in twd L arm to face ctr of the dance.

5–8 Cpl 1 with cpl 4 (ctr cpls) dance R and L halfway around by changing places with ptr (R hand) and changing places up and down the dance (L hand) as before.

II. Circles and Lead Up

9–10 Cpl 2 with cpl 4, cpl 1 with cpl 3 join hands in a circle of four dancers and circle ½ CW. Release hands and finish with cpl 4 in top pos, cpl 1 in bottom pos, M and W on wrong side.

11–12 Ctr cpls 2 and 3 turn individually CCW to join hands and circle ½ CCW.

13–16 Joining R hands, cpl 1 (W to M L) lead up the middle of the dance to the top (original place but on wrong side), turning away from ptr (M ½ CW, W ½ CCW), to finish facing down the dance. During meas 15–16 cpls 2, 3, 4 take 1 side-step, moving down 1 place. On last ct finish so that cpl 1 faces cpl 4 and cpl 3 faces cpl 2 up and down the dance, all on the wrong side.

III. Highland Schottische and Grand Chain

17–20 All dance Highland schottische step R and L.

21–24 Dancers give R hands to person they are facing and dance a grand chain (grand R & L) halfway around the set, passing one person for each Strathspey step.

IV. Reels of Four

25–32 After completing the grand chain halfway around, meet the next person to pass by R shoulders and continue dancing reels of four on own side of the dance. At end of reel, face ptr to repeat the dance from beginning with a new top cpl (cpl 2, cpl 3, then cpl 4) until all cpls are back in original places.

Chord M bow, W curtsy to ptr.

HIGHLAND QUADRILLE

Source: Millie von Konsky

Record: Beltona 2338, or any good Scottish reel

Formation: 4 cpls in quadrille formation, W on M right.

Meter 2/4   Pattern

I. Circle

All join hands in a circle, advance 3 steps into the center and hold on count 4, swinging joined hands forward and back. Return to place with 4 steps. Repeat all.

II. Chassé

Cpls 1 and 3 in ballroom pos exchange places sliding (M passing back to back). Continue the slide back to place (couples completing a circle)—16 cts.

III. Ladies Visit

W 1 and 3, starting on R, advance 3 steps to meet. Joining R hands, holding skirt with L, balance back on L on ct 4. Passing R shoulders, continue to opposite M 4 steps, taking ballroom pos and buzz swing 8. Repeat all.

All 4 couples repeat fig I.

Cpls 2 and 4 perform fig II.

W 2 and 4 perform fig III.

Note: While cpls 1 and 3 perform figs II and III, cpls 2 and 4 remain inactive, except during buzz step, at which time all cpls are active. On ct 4 of fig I dancers are known to exclaim "hoot" as they raise hands.

MAIRI'S WEDDING

The tune for Mairi's Wedding (MAH-ree) is an old and traditional one. The dance is approximately twenty years old. It was presented by C. Stewart Smith.

Record: "Step We Gaily," Mercury Me 1203 or PMC 1122 or 3007, side 1, band 1; "Scottish Dance Time," vol. III, Clansmen Records, QC-10, side 2, band 1; "The Gates of Edinburgh," Cal 114, side 1, band 4; "Scottish Country Dances No. 2," Fontana TFE 17048, side 1, band 1.

Formation: 4 cpls in longways formation

Steps and Styling: Skip change of step, slip step, cast, corners, reel of 4. Reel of 3 (8 meas): A dance figure for 3 people in a line, ctr dancer facing out and

outside dancers facing in. All 3 people are active and describe on the floor the pattern of a fig of 8 consisting of 2 loops, one loop made CW and the other CCW. All 3 dancers go around the fig of 8 in the same direction as in "follow the leader." In a L shoulder reel of 3 the ctr dancer (#1) always begins curving CCW to pass L shoulders with the dancer he is facing (#2), who also curves CCW, while the remaining dancer (#3) curves CW. Dancer 2 cuts through the ctr before dancer 3. Each half loop takes approximately 2 meas. At the end of meas 4 dancers 2 and 3 will have changed places, and dancer 1 will have returned to the middle. At the end of meas 8 dancers will be back in original places. Use skip change of step throughout this dance unless otherwise stated, always starting R (with preliminary hop L).

Meter 2/4   Pattern

Meas

Chord Intro: M bow, W curtsy to ptr.

I. R Hand Turn, Cast and L Hand Turn

1–4   With R hands joined, cpl 1 turns once CW and casts down one place on own side. Cpl 2 moves up during meas 3–4.

5–8   With L hands joined, cpl 1 turns once CCW and a little more to finish back to back in the ctr facing 1st corners.

II. Half Reels of 4

9–12   Cpl 1 dances half reel of 4 with 1st corners (the corners changing places).

13–16   Passing L shoulders in the ctr, cpl 1 dances a half reel of 4 with 2nd corners (corners changing places).

17–20   Passing L shoulders again, cpl 1 dances half reel of 4 with 1st corners (who are now on opp side and return to original place with this half reel).

21–24   Passing L shoulders, cpl 1 dances half reel of 4 with 2nd corners (who are on opp side and return to original place).

III. Reel of 3 Across

25–32   W 1 dances reel of 3 with cpl 2, beginning by passing L shoulders with M 2, while M 1 dances reel of 3 with cpl 3, beginning L shoulders to W 3. Cpl 1 finishes in 2nd place.

IV. Circle L and R

33–36   Cpls 2, 1, and 3 join hands and circle L (CW) with 8 slip steps.

37–40   Reverse and circle R (CCW) with 8 slip steps. Cpl 1 repeats dance in 2nd place. During last fig take 8 small slip steps when circling L so as not to go too far, and circle R with 6 larger slip steps to return to place. On last 2 slip steps

cpl 1 releases hands and slides to the bottom on the outside, as cpls 3 and 4 slide up one place on the inside. Cpls 2, 3, and 4 then repeat the dance twice, each in turn.

Chord M bow, W curtsy to ptr.

POLHARROW BURN

This reel is a relatively new Scottish country dance. It was devised by Hugh Foss and was presented by C. Stewart Smith.

Record: Calclan 002A; Pasadena Recorders, Teacher's Choice, side 1, band 2

Formation: 5 cpls in longways formation

Steps and Styling:

Skip change of step: Hop L, lifting R fwd with toe pointing down, knee turned out (ct ah), step fwd R (ct 1), closing step L behind R, L instep close to R heel (ct &), step fwd R (ct 2). Bring L leg fwd, passing through with a straight knee for the next step, which begins with a preliminary hop R. Move up (meas 2): Described for M; W dance counterpart. Step L diag fwd L (ct 1), step R across in front of L (ct 2), step L diag bkwd L (ct 1), close R to L (ct 2).

Cast off (or down): A movement down behind the line to a designated place. To dance it, always make

a CCW turn on M side and a CW turn on W side. If the movement is down behind own Line, make an individual turn outward (the long way). If the movement involves a crossing to opp side and then casting down, make a regular turn (the short way). Figure of eight (8 meas): A pattern basically formed by 3 persons, only 1 of whom is active, the other 2 standing in place. Active dancer loops in one direction (either CW or CCW) around one inactive person (4 meas) and then in other direction around other inactive person (4 meas). If one cpl dances individually around another cpl, then there are really 2 separate figures of 8 being formed—one by the active W and another by the active M. This is the case in this dance, except that only a half figure of 8 is done.

Corners: The 2 dancers that the active person faces when back-to-back with ptr in the ctr, M facing W line and W facing M line. 1st corner is to your R and 2nd corner is to your L.

Use Skip change of step throughout dance and always start R (with preliminary hop L) unless otherwise stated.

Meter 2/2 (cut time)   Pattern

Meas

Chord Intro: M bow, W curtsy to ptr.

I. Cross, Cast and Half Figure of Eight

1–4 Cpls 1 and 3, giving R hands to ptr in passing, cross over and cast off one place to finish in 2nd and 4th place, respectively.

5–8 Cpl 1 dances a half figure of 8 around cpl 2, W 1 crossing in front of ptr to loop CW around W 2 as M 1 loops CCW around M 2. Finish back in 2nd place on own side. Cpl 3 dances similarly around cpl 4. Cpls 2 and 4 move up (meas 7–8).

II. Turn and Chase

9–16 Cpls 1 and 3 join R hands with ptrs and turn once CW (4 meas). Join L hands and turn CCW once and a little more to finish back-to-back in the ctr, facing 1st corners (4 meas). Simultaneously cpls 2 and 5 (the end cpls), giving R hands in passing, cross over to ptr place, and W 2 and M 5 only turn ½ CW to finish facing ptr (2 meas) and "chase" or follow ptr ½ CW around outside to finish at other end of set on own side. Cpl 2 finishs at bottom and cpl 5 at top (6 meas). Throughout entire fig II cpl 4 stands inactive in place.

III. Three Half Reels of Four; Turn and Cast

17–20 Cpls 1 and 3 dance a half reel of 4 with 1st corner.

21–24 Passing ptr L shoulders in the ctr and moving

CCW around the set, cpls 1 and 3 dance a 2nd half reel of 4 with 2nd corners.

25–28 Again passing ptr L shoulder in the ctr and continuing in a CCW direction, cpls 1 and 3 dance a 3rd half reel of 4, starting with person who is now in ptr orig 1st corner pos.

During the 3 half reels of 4, once they get started, cpls 2 and 5 move without stopping from one end of line to other, describing a "V" pattern on floor. Cpl 4 immediately starts to go from middle to end of set diag fwd to R, waiting there for 4 meas and then returning to middle.

29–32 Cpls 1 and 3 turn ptr by L hand once around and cast off one place on own side, finishing in 3rd and 5th place, respectively. Cpls 4 and 5 move up (meas 31–32).

Repeat dance from beginning, with new top cpl and cpl 1 active again in 3rd place. Dance is gone through a total of 5 times.

Chord M bow, W curtsy to ptr.

POSTIE'S JIG

This jig for four couples was devised by Roy Clowes and was presented by Diane Childers.

Record: Caledonian Ball BSLP 1048; Jigtime EMI Waverly SZ—LP 2122, side 1, band 1.

Formation: Four cpls in longway formation

Steps and Styling:

Skip change of step: Hop on L, lifting R fwd with toe pointing down, knee turned out (ct 6 of preceding meas). Step fwd on R (ct 1), closing step behind R, L instep to R heel (ct 3); step fwd R (ct 4), bringing L leg fwd passing through with a straight knee, hop on R (ct 6). Step alternates. Used throughout the dance unless otherwise stated.

Pas de basque: Leap onto R, knee and toe turned out (ct 1); step on ball of L beside R with heel to R instep and L toe turned out (ct 3); step on R extending L diag fwd L, toe pointing down an inch or two off floor, knee straight and turned out (ct 4). Next step begins with leap onto L.

Half figure of eight (4 meas): Moving diag fwd, W cross in front of ptr to dance around inactive M, while M crosses behind ptr to dance around inactive W.

Move up (2 meas): Described for M, W dance counterpart. M step diag fwd L (ct 1), step R across in front of L (ct 4); step diag bkwd L (ct 1), close R to L (ct 4).

Move down: Reverse ftwk of move up.

Always start R unless otherwise indicated.

Meter 6/8   Pattern

Meas

Chord Intro: M bow, W curtsy to ptr.

I. Set and Cast

1–2 Cpls 1 and 4 set to ptr with two pas de basque steps.

3–4 Cpl 1 casts down the outside into 2nd place as cpl 4 casts up on the outside into 3rd place. Cpl 2 moves up, cpl 3 moves down.

5–8 Cpl 1 dances one half figure of 8 around cpl 2, while cpl 4 dances one half figure of 8 around cpl 3. Finish facing ptr on opp side of dance, cpl 1 in 2nd place, cpl 4 in 3rd place.

II. Arches and Turns

9–10 W 1 and W 4 join inside hands, M 1 and M 4 join inside hands to make an arch; M and W change places with W going under the arch.

11–12 W 1 and W 2, with L hands joined, turn ¾ CCW, as W 4 and W 3 with R hands joined turn ¾ CW. Simultaneously, M 1 and M 2, with R hands joined, turn ¾ CW, and M 4 and M 3, with L hands joined, turn ¾ CCW. Finish with cpl 1 at top in ctr facing down, W to M L, and cpl 4 at bottom facing up, W to M R, cpls 2 and 3 in place, facing in.

13–16 Repeat action of meas 9–12 (fig II), with cpl 4 making arch. Turn corners with nearest hands to finish with M and W on own sides, cpl 1 in 3rd place, cpl 4 in 2nd place.

17–24 Repeat action of meas 9–16 with M arching. Turn respective corners ¾ with nearest hands. Cpl 1 arches and changes places with cpl 4, then turns respective corners ¾. End with cpl 4 in 3rd place and cpl 1 in 2nd place on opp sides of dance. Cpls 2 and 3 end in place at top and bottom of set.

III. Half Right and Left, and Turns

Cpls 1 and 4 dance half R and L as follows:

25–26 Ptrs change places across dance, giving R hands in passing.

27–28 W with W, M with M change places, moving up and down dance, giving L hands in passing.

29–32 Cpls 1 and 4 turn ptr once around with R hands joined.

Repeat entire dance three more times with new active cpls each time.

Chord M bow, W curtsy to ptr.

THIRTEEN-FOURTEEN (1314)

Thirteen-Fourteen is a medley of strathspeys and reels, first performed in Stirling on June 24, 1967, to commemorate the battle of Bannockburn, which was fought in the year 1314. The dance was composed by John Drury of Aberdeen, Scotland, and was introduced by C. Stewart Smith.

Record: Calclan CC-1-45; Waverly ELP 154, side 2, band 1.

Formation: Four cpls in a square (W at M R), cpl 1 with back to music, other cpls numbered CCW around square. Free hands at sides or W may hold skirt down at sides.

Steps and Styling: Strathspey step, strathspey setting step, skip change of step, buzz, pas de basque, slip step. Set (2 meas): Strathspey setting step R and L during Strathspey (4/4 meter). Pas de basque R and L during reel (2/4 meter). Ftwk is same for both M and W; all figures start R unless otherwise

stated. Handshake hold is used whenever M turns W and joined hands are held at shoulder height.

Meter 4/4, 2/4   Pattern

Meas

STRATHSPEY

4/4

Chord Intro: M bow, W curtsy to ptr.

I. Reel of Four in the Circle

1–8   Pass first person (ptr) by R shoulder, next person by L shoulder, third person by R shoulder and turn ½ CW; repeat reel, returning to place, and turn CW to finish in own place facing ptr.

II. Promenade

Head cpls (promenade and star)

1–2   Cpls 1 and 3 turn ptr by R hand (M making ½ turn, W full turn CW) to finish with W on inside, both facing CW in promenade pos.

3–4   Cpls 1 and 3 promenade (CW) between side cpls (cpl 1 between cpl 4, cpl 3 between cpl 2) while side cpls are setting.

5–6   Cpl 1 turns around (CW) into 3rd cpl's place, while 3rd cpl turns into 1st cpl's place.

7–8   Cpls 1 and 3 release ptrs L and star R into orig place.

9–16   Cpls 1 and 3 dance action described for side cpls (meas 1–8, fig II).

Side cpls (turn and set)

W 2 and W 4 both turn individually ¾ CW into ctr to finish back-to-back facing out. Simultaneously, M 2 and M 4 turn ¾ CW to outside of square to finish facing ptr.

Side cpls (cpls 2 and 4) set to ptr.

M 2 and M 4 turn ¾ CW into ptr's orig place, while W 2 and W 4 turn ¾ CW into M orig place. Finish facing ptr.

Cpls 2 and 4 turn ptr by R hand halfway round to finish in own place.

Cpls 2 and 4 dance action described for head cpls (meas 1–8, fig II).

III. Circle and Set

1–4   All join hands at shoulder height and circle L (CW).

5–8   Circle R (CCW).

9–12   All set to ptr and turn ptr by R hand.

13–16   All set to corner and turn corner by L hand to finish in own place, with M facing in and W facing out of square (R shoulder twd ptr).

IV. Schiehallion Reel

1–2   All M move (CCW) inside square, diag R, to pos of R-hand W, to finish facing out of square while all W dance small circle CW to finish in ptr's place, facing in. (M and new W finish with R shoulders adjacent.)

3–4   All W move inside square diag R (CCW) to finish in next W place, facing out, while all M dance small circle CW to finish in M place

facing in. (Original ptrs now have R shoulders adjacent).

5–16   Repeat action of meas 1–4 (fig IV) three more times to finish in own place.

V. Turns

1–8   All turn ptr by R hand, corner by L, ptr by R, corner by L. Finish facing ptr. Clap on last ct of meas 8.

2/4   REEL

1–8   Repeat action of fig I, using skip change of step

1–16   Repeat action of fig II, promenade and star with skip.

Change of step: individual turns with pas de basque steps; set with pas de basque steps; and turn ptr with skip change of step.

1–8   Repeat action of fig III, meas 1–8, using 8 slip

steps L and 8 slip steps R.

9–12 All set to ptr with pas de basque steps and turn ptr by the R with 2 skip change of steps.

13–16 All set to corner with pas de basque steps and turn corner by L with 2 skip change of steps. Finish in own place, M facing in, W facing out of square, R shoulders adjacent.

1–16 Repeat action of meas 1–16 (fig IV) (Schiehallion Reel) using skip change of step.

1–8 All turn ptr by the R arm (elbow grip) with 16 buzz steps (no knee bend, up on toes). W free hand at side, M free hand up.

Chord M bow, W curtsy.

TRIP TO BAVARIA

This reel is a modern Scottish country dance. It was devised by a Scottish country dance exhibition team while touring Bavaria and was presented by C. Stewart Smith.

Record: Robin Hood RH 001A (33⅓ rpm), band 1; "Scottish Dances," (Jimmy Blair), side 1, band 6; "Military Two-Step," Pasadena Recorders, "Teacher's Choice," side 1A, band 6.

Formation: 4 cpls in longways formation

Steps and Styling: Hands across, skip change of step, set. Use skip change of step throughout dance unless otherwise stated.

Meter 2/4   Pattern

Meas

4   Intro: M bow, W curtsy to ptr.

I. Cross Over and Hands Across

1–2   Cpls 1 and 4, giving R hands in passing, cross over to opp side. Simultaneously cpls 2 and 3 dance 4 hands across halfway around in a R-hand wheel. (W 2 and M 3 hands on top.)

3–4   All give L hands in passing on corners of set as cpls 1 and 4 move twd ctr to prepare for R hands across and cpls 2 and 3 move out of ctr to finish in 4th and 1st place, respectively, on wrong side (M on W side, W on M side) facing ptr across set.

5–8   Repeat action of meas 1–4, with cpls 2 and 3 dancing action of cpls 1 and 4, and cpls 1 and 4 dancing action of cpls 2 and 3.

9–16   Repeat action of meas 1–8 to finish back in orig place. At end of meas 16, M 1 and 3 and W 2 and 4 make "polite" (long) turns.

II. Set and Cross Over; Forward and Back

17–18   Cpls 1 and 2 face each other diag across and set to opp (M 1 and W 2, and W 1 to M 2).

19–20   Cpl 1 crosses over (W in front of M) and dances down to 2nd place, finishing on wrong side.

Cpl 2 faces up set and dances up into 1st place.

21–24   Cpls 1 and 3 repeat action of meas 17–20 (fig II) with M 1 setting to M 3 and W 1 to W 3. Finish with cpl 1 in 3rd place and cpl 3 in 2nd place.

25–28   Cpls 1 and 4 repeat action of meas 17–20 (fig II) to finish with cpl 1 in 4th place on the wrong side and cpl 4 in 3rd place.

29–30   All join hands on sides to form lines of 4 facing across and dance fwd twd opp line. Cpl 1 joins both hands with ptr to turn ½ CW in ctr (meas 30).

31–32   Cpls 2, 3, 4, and 1, with hands joined on sides, dance bkwd to place.

Repeat dance from beginning with new top cpl. Dance is gone through a total of 4 times.

Chord M bow, W curtsy to ptr.

WHITE HEATHER JIG

This dance, only ten or so years old, was presented by C. Stewart Smith. It was originally danced on a Scottish television program.

Record: Parlophone R-5086 (45); Parlophone PMC 1214, side 1, band 4; Waverly ELP-117, side 2, band 1.

Formation: 4 cpls in longways formation

Steps: Skip change of step throughout. Always begin R.

Meter 6/8   Pattern

Meas

Chord Intro: M bow, W curtsy to ptr.

I. Turn Partner and Cast

1–4   Cpl 1 turns R hands once around (2 meas) and casts off behind cpl 2 as cpl 2 moves up (2 meas).

5–8   Cpl 1 turns with L hands once around, gradually moving up to finish back-to-back in ctr between cpl 2 (M 1 face W 2, W 1 face M 2).

II. Reel of 4 Across

1–8   Cpls 1 and 2 dance a reel of 4 across dance. As cpl 1 finishes L shoulders in the middle, end back-to-back in ctr facing 1st corners.

III. Turn Corner and Partner

1–8   Cpl 1 turns 1st corners with R hands (2 meas), ptr with L hands (2 meas), 2nd corners with R hands (2 meas), and ptr with L hands (2 meas), and finish back-to-back in ctr between cpl 3 (M 1 face W 3 and W 1 face M 3).

IV. Reel of 4 Across

1–8   Cpls 1 and 3 dance a reel of 4 across dance.

At end of reel cpl 3 has moved into 2nd place. Cpl 1 does not pass L shoulders in middle the last time, but finishes facing ptr in ctr.

V. Turn Partner, Cast, and Turn Partner

1–4   Cpl 1 turns with L hands once around (2 meas) and casts off behind cpl 4 as cpl 4 moves up (2 meas).

5–8   Cpl 1 turns with R hands once around. Repeat dance from beginning, with cpls 2, 3, 4 active in turn.

Chord M bow, W curtsy to ptr.

TURKEY

Turkish Folk Dancing

by Süheyla (Kate McGowan)

"Kolay gelsin" (May whatever you are doing come easily)

Turks love their Turkish music: songs, ancient and modern, with wailing cries of *aman, aman* (mercy); the intricate dance rhythms of the large two-headed drum, together with the shrill, excited flute; the epic songs of minstrels, accompanied by the lutelike, long-necked saz. One story claims that Mustafa Kemal Atatürk, in creating a Republic of Turkey during the 1920s and trying to modernize it, forbade the playing of Turkish music over the radio. Hero though he was, this act was too much of a blow to Turkish hearts. Protests and an uproar followed—and the ban was lifted. Nowadays around noon one can walk up the street of old furniture dealers, through the fish market, or down a hill lined with apartment houses and hear the song from beginning to end because each radio is turned up full volume. The ancient songs and rhythms are in the air both afternoons and evenings: in the parks, where a drum and flute player attract a crowd, hoping to gain a few lira for supper; in the summer streets, when gypsies reappear with their tambourines and dancing bears; or emerging from the many casinos or tea gardens. On a more serious level, music emanates from the large halls where student groups gather to learn and preserve Anatolian folk dances.

Turkey is primarily an agricultural country, a developing nation in international terms. Her peasants continue to plant and harvest, herd their sheep and goats, and spin and weave as they have for centuries. In Anatolian villages peasant lore is also preserved, passing from generation to generation; no self-conscious "society" is needed to keep it alive.

Life in Turkey's large cities—Ankara, Istanbul, and Izmir (formerly Smyrna)—is acquiring the polish, taste for convenience, gadgetry, and hurry and tension common in most large cities. Modern, for example, are the traffic jams lasting all the daylight hours, involving thousands of big cars on streets too narrow and twisted to contain them. Modern, too, are the Eczaneler (drugstores) offering drugs and cosmetics galore, boutiques offering the very latest in Paris fashions (copies) in brilliant colors for both men and women. Plastics have found a prominent place here too: they are used for some kitchen utensils; plastic flowers decorate the taxis and horses' halters; and plastic shoes are very popular. Material newness is not the whole story: Istanbul now has a symphony orchestra and a delightful opera company, while Ankara is the home of the national ballet troupe. Though the fine arts cannot be called avant-garde, more and more galleries are exhibiting both the fine arts of present-day Turkey and the crafts and methods used in ancient times.

A rash of new restaurants and nightclubs has lead to the creation of something new: performing musicians and singers. In pursuit of the cosmopolitan, many Turkish entertainers have become expert mimics of Western song styles and jazz; they can sing without a trace of a Turkish accent in several foreign languages. Still, this is Turkey and each show, no matter how Western, includes at least one belly dancer.

Modernity has spread rather tentatively across the city; it is obvious enough, but it is not the only way of life. The old ways and values are at the core of daily routine. From the city's hundreds of mosques muezzins intone the call to prayer five times daily. The old ways are sometimes reflected in rather subtle ways not obvious to the tourist. Within the city, hamals (load bearers) do the work that camels or donkeys do in the countryside, carrying everything on their backs, from loads of printing paper or a refrigerator to the huge baskets full of fresh bread delivered twice daily from the bakeries. Among the many street hawkers is a fellow who shouts "kalayci, kalayci." He takes the household's copper pots and re-tins them. Copper pots are in common use and must always have a good layer of tin on them (untinned copper is poisonous). These trades and many others like them continue because they still have a useful place in the society. The same is true of folk music and dances: They are still useful and meaningful to the Turks.

A variety of dance traditions exist in Turkey. They can broadly be defined as religious, professional hired entertainment, and folk dances.

Religious. Islam at its most orthodox is a rigid, austere religion maintaining a continuing but futile struggle against music and dance. Various monastic dervish orders used a sort of dancing as one form of meditation or litany. Some orders were calm, even secretive, while others were more obviously fanatic and self-castigating. However, when the government was secularized and a republic was formed, these monastic orders were regarded as undesirable and their public religious rites were outlawed in 1926.

The Mevlevi (whirling dervishes) is probably the most widely known order. It was founded by the poet and mystic Mevlâna Celalettin Rumi in Konya, a town in central Anatolia that was once the capital of the Seljuk Turks. Dressed in long, very full white robes and tall conical hats, the dervish bows to his leader and receives his blessing. Arms crossed at his chest, hands clasping his shoulders, head bent down, he slowly starts to turn. Gradually the turn becomes a rapid pivot—and a rotation around the hall—the arms extend horizontally, usually with right palm upward and left palm downward. Symbolically these positions mean that they receive the influence from heaven and pass it to the world below. The robes open fully to swirl and ripple in circles. The whirling symbolizes the cyclical nature of the seasons as well as celestial motion. Since December 1954, the Mevlevi have given a performance once a year on the anniversary of the death of Mevlâna. The performance draws fervent crowds and suggests that Moslem Turks are not entirely at home in a secular state.

Professional hired entertainment. Cengi are professional dancing boys and girls. Belly dancing, or what is known in Turkey today as *çiftetelli,* is all that remains of a very popular entertainment in the taverns and sarays of Istanbul. Until fairly recently there was a quarter called Sulukule, haphazardly built against the ancient Byzantine city walls. This shanty village was destroyed by the government in 1966, shortly after this author had spent an evening there watching this improvised dancing. Scattered were its Gypsy inhabitants. It was here and in the nightclubs that one saw a suggestion of an entertainment long viewed by the Turks with delight but also with an inescapable sense of immortality. Originally these dancers were organized in guilds *(kollar)* largely consisting of various minority groups—Gypsies, Greeks, Armenians, Jews. The guilds were composed of thousands of trained boys who danced as long as they could hide their whiskers and keep their youthful beauty. Their dances are described as hilarious, obscene, or excellent mimicry. And the boys themselves as mischievous, clever, even lords of misrule, and as having elegant charms.

Perhaps there were fewer dancing girls, but they were no less popular, with their swaying bodies and quivering shoulders and hips. All of these dancers were regarded as degraded persons, tantamount to jesters and fools. Nevertheless, their popularity led to so much destruction, shouting, sword drawing, and quarreling—especially among the Janissaries (the Sultan's army) that in the early nineteenth century Sultan Mahmut II forbade their performances. Many dancers fled to Egypt, where their music was written down and kept alive.

Folk dances. Turkish village dancers preserve with precision dances whose essential meaning has either been forgotten or has never been understood. Anatolian dances bear traces of ancient rites belonging to civilizations extant long before the arrival of the Turkic peoples. Other influences come from their central Asian Turkic heritage, and later from the countries included in the empire. Of course, the meaning of most dances is quite clear and is still an integral part of peasant traditions.

In the Hittite Museum in Ankara there is a stone relief depicting Hittite dancers and musicians. What the movements of the dance were we cannot know, but one instrument shown is the long-necked saz, so popular in Anatolia today; another dancer, holding clappers over his head, assumes the pose of Turkish dancing girls today. Tall conical hats worn by Hittites are still worn by some people of that area, being similar to those of the dervishes as well. Traces of ancient fertility rites, or stories of gods representing the earth, the harvest, or the hunt are depicted in some dances. One relates the tale of a man in a fatal fight with an enemy, later brought back to life by a medicine man. Another describes how a girl, abducted from her mother, was later reunited with her. Each embodies fertility concepts of ancient times. The symbolic importance of the deer and the mirror were both recorded by the Hittites and later by the Byzantines. A deer dance became popular in the Ottoman palaces of the seventeenth and eighteenth centuries. The deer was worshiped as a symbol of virility; when it was sacrificed, it was done in the same spirit as a bull sacrifice—to gain its powers. Hittite dancers wore deerskins, horns, and little mirrors for eyes—the latter intended to ward off evil spirits. People in villages in that area still turn their mirrors to the wall when someone dies.

Şamans were the medicine men of the Turkic tribes. Their duties were to heal, exorcise evil spirits, and entertain by singing, dancing, and reciting poetry. The Şaman most frequently used a drum (davūl) in his bouts with evil spirits. A large group of peasant dancers still use this drum; the drummer may whirl around without missing a beat, then kneel suddenly while another dancer leaps on the drum.

One dance whose origins are unknown but that is still widely done is called Sin-sin. Perhaps it was a

Aman Dancers

death and resurrection or a moon dance. Whatever it may have meant, it is said to be very powerful and mysterious to watch. Men form a ring around a fire at night; one dancer is in the center, his left fist held against his chest, his right hand held over his hip to the back. He circles backward to the left and after a while another dancer enters the ring and forces him to leave by striking his right bicep, always with the left hand. He leaves, another dancer enters, and this pattern is repeated many times. The tempo quickens until the dancers are fleeing backward, even leaping over the fire.

Altogether there are hundreds of dances that are still well known in Turkey today. The subject matter is generally related to nature or to the events of daily life. Animal mimicry, the cycles of nature, the tale of the weaver, the baker, the planter, or the expertise of the warrior with sword and knife and, last but not least, the relationships between men and women—all are enacted in dance to reconfirm the peasant experience.

Characteristic folk dances, costumes, and music. Strict regional classifications of dances are not possible. The elements that characterize various groups of dances may be found here and there. But grouping can only be done in a general way.

Bar: chain dances in which one steps very lightly and precisely on the ball of the foot, with the body in an upright position. Many dances of this type are from the Kars region. They seem to be related to dances of the Caucasus in that the women glide and move their hands most gracefully; the men, in soft leather boots, dance on their toes and do other acrobatic steps.

Halay: line dances in which the tempo changes from slow to very quick. Complicated rhythms are accentuated by clapping and music is provided mainly by the davul and zurná, oboelike instruments.

Horon: Black Sea dances of the Laz (Moslems originally from Georgia); line dances in which the body is tense, arms held high, but with limp hands; trembling, sudden movements, and springs make these some of the most dramatic dances. The movements represent the trembling, shimmying movements of fish in the sea.

Kaşık (spoon) oyunu: very rhythmical mixed dances in which each person holds two wooden spoons in each hand, clacking them like castanets.

Nanay: line dances in which dancers are linked by little fingers; the tempo is set by slow songs and the refrain is "nanay-nay-nanay-nay."

Zeybek: a solo dance in which the deliberate steps, outstretched arms, and slow kneeling turns are supposed to be solemn and heroic.

Percussion instruments predominate among the musical instruments used. Tambourines, finger cymbals, spoons, various drums—all are popular. The davūl, mentioned earlier, is most important and is usually accompanied by the zurnā, an oboelike instrument with a sustained shrill sound. Horon dances are done to the music of the kemençe, a three-stringed instrument that is also well known in the Balkans. A primitive bagpipe called a tulum was once used in the Northeast of Turkey, but it has now been replaced by the accordion, a "foreign" instrument.

Each province in Anatolia has its traditional costume, but varied and vivid colors seem to be the general rule. As part of their daily attire, women are no longer veiled; they wear long head scarves like shawls and long skirts or baggy pants. To see them from a distance working in the fields is like seeing a rainbow. In the cities the peasant women are distinguished not only by their long skirts and the perpetual head scarf but by their vibrant colors—usually several at once. Bright cotton prints are now used to make the skirts and baggy pants (şalvar), but the older costumes were often striped and were made of fine silks and satins. Sometimes women wear a little pillbox hat with a scarf draped over it; chains of coins may hang about the face and throat. A woman's hair was not shown. Men wear a white shirt with a bolero, which is often heavily embroidered. The trousers are tight below the knee and have baggy folds from the waist to the knee. Around the waist a multicolored cummerbund is worn, often with a dagger or sword thrust into it.

As in all peasant societies, the main occasions for dancing are celebrations of birth, circumcision, marriage, or perhaps some remnant of a pagan rite. For example, çayda çira, from Elazig, was a henna-staining ceremony. It was a sacred dance in which a little plate with a lighted candle placed on it was held in each hand; it was presumably done to ward off the evil eye. Today henna is still used as a cosmetic; one often sees an old woman with bright orange-pink hair or a young man with his fingertips tinted orange.

I have tried to illustrate the living quality of folk dances in Anatolia. But young Turks of the cities who are better educated and who live in a more modern way have a growing sense of national pride. They seem to want to seek out what is *Turkish* and to de-emphasize what was empire.

(For additional information about Kate McGowan's dance background, see the essay entitled "Danse Orientale" in the section on the Orient.)

TURKISH FOLK DANCES

The Turkish dances that follow are from Bora Özkök's personal collection and are used here with permission. Bora Özkök has a degree in architecture from the University of California at Berkeley. While attending Berkeley, he was selected from among nominees representing five hundred institutions as one of the outstanding Middle East students of the year. He has been an olympic swimmer and an All-American soccer player. He plays many wind and string instruments and has taught the dances of his native Turkey since 1970. This teaching takes him to many countries and to major folk dance camps in the United States. Özkök has done primary dance research in the course of his many return trips to Turkey and takes pride in sharing these dances with international folk dancers.

Bora Özkök

ALI PAŞA

Ali Paşa (AL-ee pash-a) is a dance from western Turkey. The song is about a local hero named Ali Paşa. The steps are authentic but have been arranged by Bora Özkök to fit the available music.

Record: BOZ-OK 102, side 1, band 1

Formation: Mixed lines, little fingers joined and held at shoulder level. Both ends of the lines hold handkerchiefs in free hands.

Steps and Styling: Walk, grapevine, stamp. The dance

is counted QQQS—1, 2, 3, *4*. The dance may be done with or without calls, but if it is done with calls, it should be called in order: 1, 2, 3, 1, 2, 3, etc. When called, the pattern change should come at the beginning of every second phrase: 1, 9, 17, 25, 33, etc. The dance may either be called by number—1(Bir), 2(Iki), 3(Üç)—or simply by calling "geç, geç" (getch, getch), which means "change, change."

Meter 5/4   Pattern

Meas

I. Bir (beer)

1   Facing and moving in LOD, walk R, L, R (cts 1, 2, 3); keeping wt on R, point L toe fwd (ct *4*).

2   Still facing LOD, but moving bkwd, walk L, R, L (cts 1, 2, 3); keeping wt on L, do a small stamp on R beside L (ct *4*).

3–4   Repeat action of meas 1–2, except move into ctr of circle and back to place instead of moving in LOD and back to place.

5–8   Repeat action of meas 1–4.

II. Iki (icky): Grapevine

1   Facing ctr and moving in LOD, step R to R (ct 1), step L behind R (ct 2), step R to R (ct 3), step L in front of R (ct *4*).

2   Repeat action of meas 1 (fig II), except on ct *4* close L to R, keeping wt on R.

3–4   Repeat action of meas 1–2 (fig II) with opp ftwk and in RLOD.

5–8   Repeat action of meas 1–4 (fig II).

III. Üç (ooch)

1   Facing ctr with wt on L, cross R in front of L, touching R toe beside L (ct 1); hold (ct 2); step R to R (ct 3); slight stamp L beside R, take wt on L (ct *4*).

2   Repeat action of meas 1 (fig III).

3   Still facing ctr, step fwd on R (ct 1); step bkwd in place on L (ct 2); step R beside L (ct 3); with wt on R, extend L leg fwd and touch L toe (ct *4*).

4   Facing ctr, step bkwd on L (ct 1); step R beside L (ct 2); step fwd on L (ct 3); stamp R beside L, no wt (ct *4*).

5–8   Repeat action of meas 1–4 (fig III).

DELİLO (DAY-lee-loe)

This dance, whose name means "crazy guy," is from the province of Elazig in central eastern Anatolia. It was learned by Bora Özkök from Güneş Ataç in Istanbul in 1970.

Record: BOZ-OK 101, side 1, band 2

Formation: Mixed line, hands at shoulder height, little fingers connected; ends of line holding handkerchief in free hand.

Steps and Styling: Begin at the beginning of any 8-measure phrase. It is suggested that the introductory figure be danced for 8 measures, after which the leader calls the figures in any order.

Meter 2/4   Pattern

Meas   Intro. Figure

1   Facing ctr, point and touch R foot fwd (ct 1), hold (ct 2).

2   Point and touch R foot toward R side (ct 1), hold (ct 2). Hands move up and down as follows: down (ct 1), up (ct &), down (ct 2), up (ct &).

Figure I

1   Moving fwd and facing ctr, step R (ct 1), step L, bringing it behind R (ct 2). Body leans slightly fwd on ct 1 and slightly bwd on ct 2.

2   Repeat meas 1.

3   Step R (ct 1), lift L leg high in front of R leg, pointing toes down (ct 2).

4   Touch L in front of R (ct 1), lift L leg high, knee bent (ct 2).

5   Moving bwd, step L (ct 1), lift R leg high, knee bent (ct 2).

6   Repeat meas 5, opp ftwk.

7   Step L (ct 1), lift R leg high in front of L leg, pointing toes down (ct 2).

8   Touch R in front of L (ct 1), lift R leg high, knee bent (ct 2).

Figure II

1   Moving fwd at 45° angle to R, step R (ct 1), lift L leg high behind R leg, L knee bent and L foot touching R calf, head turned R and looking up (ct 2).

2   Repeat meas 1, opp ftwk.

3–8   Repeat meas 3–8, fig I.

Figure III

1   Jump on both feet, body turned 45° angle to R (ct 1), hop on R, lifting L leg high in front, L knee bent (ct 2).

2   Repeat meas 1, opp ftwk.

3   Repeat meas 1.

4   Touch L in front of R (ct 1), hop on R lifting L leg, L knee bent (ct 2).

5–8   Repeat meas 1–4, moving straight bwd and using opp ftwk.

Figure IV

1–4   Repeat meas 1–4, fig III, but moving fwd, turning one complete turn CW while doing meas

1–2 and clapping on the first beat of each measure (4 claps in all).

5–8   Repeat meas 1–4 with opp ftwk and moving bwd and turning CCW.

DOKUZLU

A circle dance whose title means "the one with nine." Both men and women participate.

Record: FLDT-1, side B, band 4; BO2-OK 101, side 2, band 1.

Formation: Line with arms on shoulders

Meter 2/4   Pattern

Meas   Intro
Long introduction in the music; then tap the L ft in front twice to the beats of the drum.

Figure I: Jump-Lift-Front-Side

1   Jump on both feet (ct 1), hop on L ft, lifting R leg underneath (ct 2).

2   Hop on L ft, extending R ft forward (ct 1), hop again, extending R ft to side (ct 2).

3–4   Repeat measures 1–2, reversing footwork.

5–8   Do measures 1–4 five more times (6 in all). (The sixth jump is a transition to begin the next step.)

Figure II: Grapevine

1   Step to R on R ft, bending body slightly forward (ct 1), step on L ft behind R ft, leaning back slightly (ct 2).

2   Step to R on R ft again, leaning slightly forward (ct 1), step on L ft in front of R ft, straightening body (ct 2).

3–8   Repeat measures 1–2 three more times (4 in all).

Figure III: Squat-Kicks

1   Jump and squat down on both feet, knees apart (ct 1), jump back up on L ft, extending R ft forward, moving to the L (ct 2).

2–4   Do meas 1 three more times (4 in all).

Jasna Planina Folk Ensemble

Figure IV: Two-steps

1–3 Do 3 two-steps forward starting with R ft.

4–5 Keeping weight on R ft, tap L toe twice with the beats of the drum, keeping L heel on floor.

6–8 Do 3 two-steps moving backward, starting with L ft.

Figure V: Jump-lifts

1 Jump on both feet (ct 1), lift L leg high, across in front R leg (ct 2).

2 Repeat meas 1, reversing footwork.

3–6 Do measures 1–2 two more times (6 jumps in all).

Repeat the dance from the beginning (no intro). At the end, fig V is done for only 4 measures, and the dance ends with a step slightly to the R on R ft (ct 1), and slap L ft in front, bending body forward (ct 2).

IŞTE HENDEK

Işte Hendek (EESH-teh HEN-dek), a dance from eastern Turkey, was learned by Bora Özkök from the University of Istanbul Ethnic Dancers in 1970. This dance was introduced by Özkök.

Record: BOZ-OK 101, side 1, band 1

Formation: Mixed lines, hands clenched, arms straight down at sides, bodies touching. Short lines (no more than ten dancers).

Steps and Styling: Walk, hop, bounce. Raise heels off floor, wt on balls of ft (upbeat, ct ah), lower heels to floor (ct 2). Repeat action (ct ah, &). The leader calls the steps, usually in order. Each line should be very tight and straight so that it can move as a single unit. With hands clenched, tight and down, everyone should apply pressure to his own hands, against his own body at all times in order to retain close body contact.

Meter 2/4   Pattern

Meas

I. Bir (beer)

1 Facing and moving in LOD, step R (ct 1), step L (ct 2), pivot on L to face ctr (ct &).

2 Step fwd on R (ct 1), bend L knee and place L ft behind R calf while bending body bkwd and up sharply (ct 2).

3 Still facing ctr, but moving bkwd with small steps, step L (ct 1), step R (ct 2).

4 Step L beside R, bend knees and lean body bkwd (ct 1), straighten and bounce quickly on both ft (cts 2, &).

II. Iki (icky)

1 Repeat action of fig I, meas 1.

2 Hopping twice on L, swing a stiff R leg in front

of L to finish facing ctr (cts 1, &); step on R (ct 2); bend L knee and place L ft behind R calf while bending body bkwd and up sharply (ct &).

3–4 Repeat action of fig I, meas 3–4.

III. Üç (ooch)

1 Repeat action of fig I, meas 1.

2 Step fwd on R (ct 1); bend body slightly fwd and chug bkwd on R—bend and lift L leg slightly bkwd (ct 2).

3–4 Repeat action of fig I, meas 3–4.

IV. Dört (dirt)

1 Repeat action of fig I, meas 1.

2 Hopping twice on L, swing a stiff R leg in front of L to finish facing ctr (cts 1, &); step on R (ct 2); bend body slightly fwd and chug bkwd on R—bend and lift L leg slightly bkwd (ct &).

3–4 Repeat action of fig I, meas 3–4.

KEÇIKO

(KETCH-ee-koe), which means "beautiful girl," was introduced by Bora Özkök.

Source: Keçiko. This dance, from central eastern Turkey (Elazig), was learned by Bora Özkök from the University of Istanbul Ethnic Dancers in 1970. It is a dance of the Kurds, a tribal minority living in eastern Turkey who speak a language of Assyrian origin yet have adapted to the Turkish way of life.

Record: BOZ-OK-104, side 2, band 1

Formation: Mixed lines, shldr hold, arms kept straight. Ends of line hold handkerchief in free hands.

Meter 2/4   Pattern

Meas Intro

1 Facing in LOD, step R (ct 1), step L (ct 2).

2 Step R next to L while keeping L toe on floor and bending and pushing L knee fwd, then straightening it (cts 1 &), keeping wt on R, again do a knee push with L knee (cts 2 &).

3 Shift wt and push R knee fwd and straighten (cts 1 &), repeat (cts 2 &).

Upon the order "haydi" from the leader, the line moves to face RLOD by doing the entire step once in place, that is, without fwd movement, while turning in the three measures to face RLOD. Having changed direction, the step is then done, same ftwk, moving RLOD until the leader changes direction back to LOD in the same manner. Before starting fig I the line must be moving in LOD.

Figure I

1 Moving in LOD, hop L, at the same time bring-

ing R foot across and slightly to the left of L, step R, step L (cts 1 & 2).

2 Jump on both feet, landing facing RLOD (ct 1), shift wt to R and bounce twice quickly on both feet (cts 2 &).

3 Still facing RLOD, dip in place on both ft (ct 1), hop in place on L while twisting body to face LOD and bending R knee and placing R foot, toes pointed down, behind and touching L knee (ct 2).

Figure II

This figure has two transitional steps, the first moving fwd, the second bwd. The step is danced in this manner:

> forward transition
> figure II
> backward transition
> figure II

Forward Transition

1 Moving fwd, hop L, step R, step L (cts 1 & 2).

2 Jump on both feet (ct 1), lift L, extending L heel fwd (ct 2).

3 Touch L heel fwd and to the right of R (ct 1), scissors-fashion, bring L back next to R while kicking R fwd and across L (ct 2).

Figure II

1 Wt on L, touch R heel fwd and to the left of L (ct 1), touch R heel directly fwd (ct 2).

2 Stomp in place on both ft (ct 1), hop in place on R while lifting L in front (ct 2).

3 Cross and touch L heel in front of and to the right of R (ct 1), scissors-fashion, bring L back to place while kicking R fwd and to the left of L (ct 2). Repeat meas 1, fig II.

Backward Transition

1–3 Repeat fwd transition, except move bwd with a hop-step-step in meas 1 instead of fwd.

YAYLALAR

Source: A circle or line dance learned from Hamit Çelimli in Istanbul in 1977. The dance is from Elazig and is done throughout Turkey. It represents the happy atmosphere of a village wedding. The tune is also well known.

Record: Horon 104, side I, #2

Formation: Men and women in a line or circle, standing very close together, so that their arms are straight down and touching their neighbors' arms, L shoulders in front of R shoulders. Fingers should be gently interlocked. Tension is maintained in the line by pressing one's own arms close to oneself.

Meter 2/4   Pattern

Meas Intro

The introductory movement, getting ready for the dance, is done while the zurna is played. Start dance with the drum. With bodies close, feet tog (fig 1), press R hand down and raise L hand as you lean to the R (fig 2), reverse hand pressure and lean to L (fig 3).

Basic Step

1 Step R to R.

2 Lean fwd slightly and step L across R.

3 Step R in place, turning body slightly L.

4 Point L toe fwd L.

5 Step L in place, turning body slightly R.

6 Point R toe fwd R.

Repeat until end of singing and start of zurna solo.

Turning Step

1 Leader calls "haydi" or "hoppa" and everyone releases handhold but stays close together. Hold hands about shldr ht and step R, starting to turn to R, and clap hands.

2 Step L, completing turn, and clap hands.

3 Step R in place, turning body slightly L, and clap.

4 Point L toe fwd L and clap.

5 Step L in place, turning body slightly R, and clap.

6 Point R toe fwd R and clap.

Repeat turning step three times (4 in all) until singing starts, at which point you resume close handhold and start dance over. It is important that the dancers stay close together during the turning step.

THE UNITED STATES

Some of the dances brought over by the early settlers of this country—like their languages, recipes, and dreams—have changed so much that they are now identified as American. Among them are square, round (couple), and contra dancing.

Square dancing, contra dancing, and round dancing are practiced and organized both as separate and as combined entities, yet a limited number of these dances are integrated into international folk dance programs.

Under separate headings, the background and a sampling of each type is presented. Descriptions of the movements and steps, as well as illustrations of the formations, may be found in the Lexicon.

Brigham Young University Dancers

Contra Dancing

by Don Armstrong

The American contra dance was long considered to be primarily a dance of the New England area. Perhaps the main reason for this is that the New England area continued to use and enjoy contras as part of their dancing programs while other areas did not, thus preserving the contra dance form. Now, however, contras are being enjoyed by ever-increasing numbers of dancers throughout the world.

The contra, which came to this country from the British Isles, was danced in all thirteen of the original colonies. But what about before that time? By referring mainly to documented information and not theorizing too much, we find that contras stemmed from three major sources prior to about 1850 or so. They were definitely influenced by the English "longways for as many as will," the Irish "cross road dance," and the Scottish "reel."

It would surely seem that there is an association between these forms and the ancient fertility rites or religious dances, the Greek and Egyptian procession-als, or even war dances depicting battle lines. English history proves that contras were definitely the rage in England in the seventeenth century and were danced

as well as supported and encouraged by the royal family as early as the sixteenth century. The first edition of John Playford's *The English-Dancing Master* appeared in 1650, with the eighteenth and last edition appearing in 1728. At this time over 700 individual dances have been set down in written form. The Scots and the Irish were dancing then, too, but unfortunately neither were as inclined or as proficient as the English to put their dances into readily understandable written form. Without question, all three groups contributed to the dance that was brought over with the colonial settlers; the English with their highly developed long-ways dances, the Scottish with their beautiful techniques and exactness of steps, and the Irish with their combination of love of dance and their great, lively, enthusiastic music.

The contra was preserved and further developed mainly in New England simply because it was there that most of the settlers who were of English, Scottish, or Irish descent had chosen to reside. They merely continued to enjoy their own dances and wisely permitted them to be modified to suit the changing environment and style of living. During the past one hundred years or so, for example, contras were further influenced by the arrival in New England of French Canadians, who brought with them both their love for the long eight- or sixteen-beat swings and their excellent fiddlers and musicians, with their happy, toe-tapping tunes.

A contra is literally a dance of opposition. It is usually performed by many couples, standing face-to-face, line facing line, in long lines running the length of the hall, so that the *head* of the set is at the caller's end of the hall. The caller can then look *down* the lines. At one time or another—usually back in school—everyone has either danced or watched the Virginia reel. This is just one of many contra forms.

The nine contras selected for inclusion are all very useful and enjoyable dances, ranging from very easy to slightly more complex. Different contra formations are included, as well as dances best enjoyed to reels, jigs, hornpipes, and waltzes. Some of the dances have been popular for well over a century, while others date from the current generation of dancers. Some are obvious descendants of earlier dances. Footnotes call attention to some of these historical links, but the important point is that contras enjoyed today still retain ties with their traditional antecedents.

(This material is presented primarily as a reference tool rather than as a teaching method. Much of the material is condensed from that found in Don Armstrong's *The Caller/Teacher Manual for Contras* (published in 1973 by The American Square Dance Society, 462 N. Robertson Blvd., Los Angeles, Calif., 90048) and is here used with permission. In many instances,

Don Armstrong

recordings are available on 45 rpm records with both an instrumental side and a called side; these records were produced by the Lloyd Shaw Foundation, Educational Mailings Division, 1480 Hoyt, Lakewood, Colorado, 80215. Ralph Page's fine book *Heritage Dances of Early America* (1976) is also available from the Lloyd Shaw Foundation.)

(Donald [Don] Armstrong was among the very first group of traveling callers. He has called or conducted workshops in forty-seven states, six Canadian provinces, England, Scotland, Germany, France, Switzerland, Spain, Portugal, Morocco, South Africa, Rhodesia, Kenya, Iran, Pakistan, Japan, Australia, New Zealand, Chile, Argentina, Panama, Costa Rica, and several of the Caribbean Islands. He has recorded for Windsor, Folk Dancer, Pairs & Squares, Sets In Order, Grenn, MacGregor, and the Lloyd Shaw recording company. He is an active member, teacher, and director of the Lloyd Shaw Foundation and has made many TV appearances throughout the United States and Canada. He regularly serves on the teaching staff, offering short courses and seminars for both undergraduate and graduate credit. He has taught at the University of Florida, Emory University, Southern Mississippi University, the University of Minnesota, Pennsylvania State University, the University of Albuquerque, Colorado State University, the University of Tampa, Central Michigan University, and the University of New Mexico. Armstrong has contributed articles to such nationally recognized dance or recreation publications as *Square Dancing,* the publication of the American Square Dance Society. He wrote *The*

Caller/Teacher Manual for Contras, which was published by the Lloyd Shaw Foundation. Mr. Armstrong is a member of the Square Dance Hall of Fame and was one of the founding members of Callerlab, the International Association of Square Dance Callers. He is regarded as a keen researcher and an exceptionally talented teacher. His contributions to dance in America are both considerable and significant.)

Format

The contra dances as written show the ACTUAL PROMPTS, and WHEN and HOW to say them. The prompter/teacher can actually read the words while practicing by simply counting in time with the music, waiting during each beat where a dash (–) is shown, then saying the words of the prompt as they appear. To assist metering the syllables to fit the available musical beats, the syllable that is accented by each beat is *italicized.* For example: WITH THE *ONE* BE-*LOW DO* SA *DO.* The prompter is thus giving the prompts in advance of the action of the dancers.

CONTRA DANCES

BICENTENNIAL REEL

Ted Sannella introduced this dance in New England and, in doing so, was totally in keeping with the introduction of new dances to commemorate historic events, victories, and other celebrations. Many traditional contras were first presented in this fashion.

Record: Any well-phrased 64-count reel

Formation: Contra lines, 1, 3, 5, etc., couples active and crossed over

To prompt this dance:

Intro	– – – –,	With *cou*ple be*low right*-hand *star*
1–8	– – – –,	Just the *la*dies *do* sa *do*
9–16	– – – –,	Same four circle left
17–24	– – – –,	All *swing* your *part*ner
25–32	– – – –,	Face down down in *twos*
33–40	– –	*Wheel* turn, – – back to *place*
41–48	– –	*Ac*tives cast *off,* others wheel *turn circle* left *half* *
49–56	– –	*Pass* thru, – – do sa *do*

As the dancers learn the figure, less prompting is necessary. For example:

57–64	– – – –,	– – *Right*-hand *star*
1–8	– – – –,	– – *La*dies do sa *do*
9–16	– – – –,	– – *Circle left*
17–24	– – – –,	– – – *Swing*

* Caller indicates CROSS OVER every second and alternate sequence throughout the dance.

25–32 – – – –, – – *Down* in *twos*
33–40 – – – *Wheel,* – – – *back*
41–48 – – *Cast* and *wheel,* – – *circle half*
49–56 – – *Pass thru,* – – *do* sa *do*

Note: The progression action of "Actives cast off while others wheel turn" was originated by Don Armstrong and was found first in a dance called Roadrunner. Contras using this action, and following it with a "Circle four to the left" are incorporating a smooth and flowing action within the traditional choreographic structure.

BROKEN SIXPENCE

Although not a traditional contra, this dance has the style of a dance from the last century. It is truly an international favorite.
Source: Don Armstrong
Record: Shaw 155
Formation: Contra lines, 1, 3, 5, etc., couples active and crossed over.

To prompt this dance:
Intro   – – – –, With the *one* be*low* you *do* sa *do*
  1–8   – – – –, Now *just* the *men* you *do* sa *do*
  9–16   – – – –, Now *just* the *la*dies *do* sa *do*
17–24   – – – –, *Ac*tive *couples swing* in the *mid*dle
25–32   – – – –, *Down* the *center four* in *line*
33–40   – – – –, *Turn* alone come *back* to *place*
41–48   – – – –, *Bend* the *line* and *circle four*
49–56   – – – –, *Star* by the *left* the *oth*er *way back* *

As the dancers learn the figure, less prompting is necessary. For example:
57–64   – – – –, – – *Do* sa do be*low*
  1–8   – – – –, – – *Men* do sa *do*
  9–16   – – – –, – – *La*dies do sa *do*
17–24   – – – –, – – *Actives swing*
25–32   – – – –, – – *Down* in *fours*
33–40   – – – –, – – *Back* to *place*
41–48   – – – –, – – *Circle four*
49–56   – – – –, – – *Star left*

CAMP RUSSEL JIG

This contra was first danced at the Spring Folk Dance Camp held at Camp Russel in Oglebay Park, Wheeling, West Virginia, and spread from there throughout Ohio, Pennsylvania, New York, and the Midwestern States.
Source: Don Armstrong

* Caller indicates CROSS OVER every second and alternate sequence throughout the dance.

Record: Any well-phrased 64-count jig
Formation: Contra lines, 1, 3, 5, etc., couples active and crossed over.
Note: Progression occurs twice in each sequence of this dance.·

To prompt this dance:
Intro   – – – –, *All get set* for the *heel* and *toe*
  1–8   (*Heel toe out* –, *heel toe in* –) (cadence calls not prompts)
  9–16   (*Heel toe out* –, *heel toe*) do sa do
17–24   – – – –, *Pass* them *by* and *swing* the *next* (1st progression)
25–32   – – – –, *Put* her on the *right* and *circle four* (2nd progression)
33–40   – – – –, *Those four right* and left *thru*
41–48   – – – –, – –*Right* and left *back* *
49–56   – – – –, *Same four left*-hand *star*

As the dancers learn the figure, less prompting is necessary. For example:
57–64   – – – –, – – *Heel* and *toe*
  1–8   – – – –, – – – *A*gain
  9–16   – – – –, – – – Do sa *do*
17–24   – – – –, – – Pass *by* and *swing*
25–32   – – – –, – – *Circle four*
33–40   – – – –, – – *Right* and left *thru*
41–48   – – – –, – – – *Back*
49–57   – – – –, – – *Left*-hand *star*

Heel, toe, out; Heel, toe, in: Actives face the couple below (down the set), as the inactives face them (up the set), join both hands, start with the foot on the outside of the set, move away from the center with a "heel and toe, and step, close, step," then with the other foot toward the center with the same action.

DUMBARTON DRUMS

This dance was researched by Dorothy Stott Shaw, the wife of Dr. Lloyd Shaw, in whose honor the Lloyd Shaw Foundation was founded.
Record: Shaw 172
Formation: Lines of four facing lines of four, in columns, with the line nearest the caller (head of hall) having its backs to the caller. An even number of lines is not required since the lines progress toward the next facing them each time the dance is repeated. Partners are not required since each line may be composed of any grouping of dancers; however, where the dancers attend as couples the line should consist of two couples in a line facing two couples in a line.

* Caller indicates CROSS OVER *every* sequence during the dance.

Intro – – – –, *With* the *mu*sic *for*ward and *back*
 1–8   – – – –, Right *couple* in *front sash*ay *over*
 9–16 – – – –, *With* the *mu*sic *for*ward and *back*
17–24 – – – –, Right *couple* in *front sash*ay *back*
25–32 – – – –, *With* the *opp*osites *right*-hand *star*
33–40 – – – –, *Same four left*-hand *star*
41–48 – – – –, *Back* to *lines* then *for*ward and *back*
49–56 – – – –, *Arch* to the *head dive* to the *foot*

As the dancers learn the figure, less prompting is necessary. For example:
57–64 – – – –, *Bow—for*ward and *back*
 1–8   – – – –, – – – Sa*shay*
 9–16 – – – –, – – *For*ward and *back*
17–24 – – – –, – – – Sa*shay*
25–32 – – – –, – – – *Star*
33–40 – – – –, – – – Re*verse*
41–48 – – – –, – *Lines for*ward and *back*
49–56 – – – –, – – *Arch* and *under*

Arch to the head, Dive to the foot: Each half of each line facing the head of the hall (i.e., facing the caller) makes an arch with near hands joined. Each half of each line facing the foot of the hall (backs to caller) joins near hands and, as both lines move forward, dives under the arch. Each line continues forward, without turning, to face a new line of four to start the dance again. Many groups progress thru *two* lines, by either "pass thru two lines," or "dip & dive thru two lines" going under one and over the next. When the lines find themselves facing a wall instead of another line, the dancers then turn to face the column by turning as a couple (wheel turn).

KITCHEN HORNPIPE

In addition to the fact that it is an excellent, enjoyable contra, this dance is included here for two additional reasons. First, it incorporates the traditional "balance and swing" and, second, it is an excellent dance with which to introduce the "triple" formation wherein the 1st, 4th, 7th, etc., couples are active.
Source: Ralph Page
Record: Shaw 1008 or any well-phrased 64-count hornpipe or reel.
Formation: Contra lines, 1, 4, 7, etc., couples active and crossed over.

Intro – – – –, With the *one* be*low bal*ance and *swing*
 1–8   – – – –, – – – –
 9–16 – – – –, *Put* her on *right* and *circle six*
17–24 – – – –, – – *Full a*round
25–32 – – – –, With the *couple* a*bove right*-hand *star*
33–40 – – – –, With the *couple* be*low left*-hand *star*

41–48 – – – –, With the *couple* a*bove right* and left *thru*
49–56 – – – –, *With* the *mu*sic *right* and lef. *back* *

As the dancers learn the figure, less prompting is necessary. For example:
57–64 – – – –, With the *one* be*low bal*ance and *swing*
 1–8   – – – –, – – – –
 9–16 – – – –, – – *Cir*cle *six*
17–24 – – – –, – – – –
25–32 – – – –, A*bove—right*-hand *star*
33–40 – – – –, Be*low—left*-hand *star*
41–48 – – – –, A*bove—right* and left *thru*
49–56 – – – –, – – – *Back*

LONESOME SHEPHERD

This dance is obviously marked by traditional influences. When Ralph Page researched the Doubtful Shepherd (containing almost the same patterns), he said, "This dance is based on five old-time country dances, i.e.: 'What a Beau Your Granny Was' in Saltador Manuscript, 1807; Otsego Manuscript, 1808. The 'Doubtful Shepherd' in Merrill Manuscript, Pejepscot, Maine, 1795; Muzzy Manuscript, Plainfield, Vermont, 1795. 'Half Moon,' Otsego Manuscript. 'L'Allegrant,' Otsego Manuscript. 'Memory,' Otsego Manuscript."
Source: Jack McKay
Record: Shaw 1009
Formation: Contra lines, 1, 4, 7, etc., couples active and crossed over.

Intro – – – –, *Active men* lead *girls* around *op*posites
 1–8   – – – –, – – – –
 9–16 – – – –, *Active la*dies lead *men* around *op*posites
17–24 – – – –, – – – –
25–32 – – – –, *Active couple down* in *twos*
33–40 – – – –, *Turn alone* come *back* to *place*
41–48 – – *Cast off*, with them *right* and left *thru*
49–56 – – – –, *With* the *mu*sic *right* and left *back* *

As the dancers learn the figure, less prompting is necessary. For example:
57–64 – – – –, – – *Men lead*
 1–8   – – – –, – – – –
 9–16 – – – –, – – *La*dies *lead*
17–24 – – – –, – – – –
25–32 – – – –, – – *Actives down*
33–40 – – – –, – *Turn—back*
41–48 – – *Cast off*, – – *right* and left *thru*
49–56 – – – –, – – – *Back*

* Caller indicates CROSS OVER every *third* sequence throughout the dance.

Note: This dance was popularized by Jack McKay, but whether he actually wrote the dance is not known by this author. It is an excellent dance to introduce dancers to triples, being both very easily understood and fun to dance. The suggested record is most pleasant, but the caller should also use other available music; for example, some of the happy, lilting music recorded for English, Scottish, and Irish country dancing.

PETRONELLA

Petronella clearly links the American contra to its Scottish ancestor. The Scottish folk dance of the same name is danced in Scottish style and follows the same pattern, except that the dancers turn first and then balance. Even the music is the same.
Record: Title tune only (several records available)
Formation: Contra lines, 1, 3, 5, etc., couples active but not crossed over.

Intro – – – –, *Actives balance turn quarter right*
 1–8 – – – –, *Balance again turn quarter right*
 9–16 – – – –, *Balance again turn quarter right*
17–24 – – – –, *Balance again turn quarter right*
25–32 – – – –, *Active couples go down the center*
33–40 – – – –, *Turn alone come back to place*
41–48 – – *Cast off*, – – *right and left thru*
49–56 – – – –, *With the music right and left back* *

As the dancers learn the figure, less prompting is necessary. For example:
57–64 – – – –, *Actives balance and turn*
 1–8 – – – –, – – – *Again*
 9–16 – – – –, – – – *Again*
17–24 – – – –, – – – *Again*
25–32 – – – –, – – – *Down*
33–40 – – – –, – – – *Back*
41–48 – – *Cast off*, – – *right and left thru*
49–56 – – – –, – – – *Back*

Actives balance turn one quarter right: Starting with right foot, actives balance right and left (step-swing, pas de basque, etc.), and, in four steps, roll right-face into center of set to end with man facing up, lady facing down, about the same distance apart from each other as when they were in lines, partners facing.
Balance again turn one quarter right: Repeat above ending in partner's original place. Men in ladies' line, ladies in men's line.
Balance again turn one quarter right: Repeat above ending with man facing down, lady facing up, in center of set.

Balance again turn one quarter right: Repeat above ending in original places.

THE MARKET LASS

This beautiful dance, researched by Ralph Page and recorded by the Lloyd Shaw Foundation, is included in Page's fine book *Heritage Dances of Early America.* Mr. Page found it in a book entitled *A New Collection of Country Dances,* by John Burbank, which was printed in Brookfield, Massachusetts, in 1799.
Record: Shaw LS 1008
Formation: Contra lines, 1, 4, 7, etc., couples active but not crossed over.

To prompt this dance:
Intro – – – –, *Actives roll out* and *down the outside*
 1–8 – – – –, *Below two couples* and *cross the set*
 9–16 – *Pass one take both couples forward six and back*
17–24 – – – –, *Right hand to partner turn three quarters*
25–32 – – – –, – *Forward six and back*
33–40 – – – –, *Right hand to partner turn three quarters*
41–48 – – – –, *With the couple above right and left through*
49–56 – – – –, – – *Right and left back.* *

As the dancers learn the figure, less prompting is necessary. For example:
57–64 – – – –, – – *Down the outside*
 1–8 – – – –, – – – –
 9–16 – – – –, – – *Forward six*
17–24 – – – –, – – *Turn three quarters*
25–32 – – – –, – – *Forward six*
33–40 – – – –, – – *Turn three quarters*
41–48 – – – –, – – *Right and left thru*
49–56 – – – –, – – – *Back*

YUCCA JIG

The yucca is a desert plant found in the southwestern United States. This dance was written and first called at the University of New Mexico at Albuquerque.
Source: Don Armstrong
Record: Shaw 196
Formation: Contra lines, 1, 3, 5, etc., couples active and crossed over.

* Caller indicates ON AT THE HEAD every second and alternate sequence throughout the dance.

* Caller indicates ON AT THE HEAD every *third* sequence throughout the dance.

Intro ----, With the *couple* be*low left*-hand *star*
1-8 ----, *Same four star right*
9-16 ----, *Ac*tive *couples down* the *cen*ter
17-24 ----, Be*low* two then *up* the out*side*
25-32 ----, *Ac*tives *do sa do* in the *mid*dle
33-40 ----, With the *one* be*low swing*
41-48 ----, *Put* her on *right* and *half* prome*nade*
49-56 ----, *With* the *music right* and left *thru* *

As the dancers learn the figure, less prompting is necessary. For example:
57-64 ----, -- Be*low* star *left*
1-8 ----, -- *Star right*
9-16 ----, -- *Ac*tives *down*
17-24 ----, -- *Up* the out*side*
25-32 ----, -- *Ac*tives do *sa do*
33-40 ----, -- *Corner swing*
41-48 ----, -- *Half* prome*nade*
49-56 ----, -- *Right* and left *thru*

Round Dancing

by Henry (Buzz) Glass

Round dancing has also been called "couple" or "folk" dancing. Usually done by couples, rounds are characterized by a set routine danced 'round the floor to a particular tune in simultaneous movements following "cues" or directions given by a leader. Some of the rounds, known as mixers, include an exchange of partners in the choreography.

Rounds became popular in the early days of this country as "breathers," providing short respites between squares and contras. They usually included the varsouvienne, schottisches, waltzes, minuets, and polkas of foreign origin. The use of the term *round* has gained in popularity since Dr. Lloyd Shaw published *The Round Dance Book* in 1948.

Along with the upsurge of interest in square dancing during the fifties, interest in rounds began to accelerate and has now developed into a separate program. Dancers and teachers who became bored with the available dances began satisfying their creative urges with the choreography of thousands of rounds set to almost every imaginable rhythm, from rhumba to ragtime. Dances choreographed in America and set to tunes with a foreign flavor, such as the Mexican Waltz, are ethnic hybrids. Certain round dances, both traditional

* Caller indicates CROSS OVER every second and alternate sequence throughout the dance.

and contemporary, are often included on international folk dance programs. The selection of particular rounds to be danced seems to be determined by the personal preference of the folk dance leader or the availability of appropriate recorded music. In many instances, long after a record has become obsolete and the one in the record case is scratched, favorites are programed, or requested, and danced by international folk dancers. A selection from folk dance rounds is included here. Some of the ethnic hybrids are presented under the heading of the particular country with which the music is associated.

After having combed through my library, I discovered some interesting facts apropos of round dancing. *How and What to Dance,* by Geoffrey D'Egville (London: Arthur Pearson, 1919), contains a section called "Round Dances" that includes the following: Waltz, Hesitation, Boston, the Polka, Two-Step, One-Step, Jazz Step, Tango, Highland Schottische, Maxina, Veleta, Barn Dance. *Dancing Made Easy,* by Charles J. Coll (New York: Ed J. Clode, 1919), lists a program as follows: Waltz, Plain Waltz, Polka, Schottische, Polka Quadrille, Redowa, Schottische, Mazurka, Waltz, Varsouvienne, Heel and Toe Polka. He speaks of the Foxtrot (still the heart of round dance) as "a stately and fascinating dance and one that will endure a long time."

Good Morning, by Mr. and Mrs. Henry Ford (Dearborn Publishing Co., 1926), uses the term *round dancing,* so one may speculate that the term has existed for many years. Under the heading "Round Dances" the following are listed: Badger Gavotte, Duchess, The (Gaop) Galop, Polka, Mazurka, Heel and Toe Polka, Seaside Polka, Rye Waltz, Military Schottische, Three-Step, Varsouvienne, Veleta. *Old Time Ballroom Dances,* by Alice Jameyson (1941), is a treasured book. Alice was a fellow member of the first Folk Dance Federation of California research committee and an old and experienced dancer. She speaks of the "Old-fashioned dances of San Ramon and Livermore," which included: Military Two-Step, Gavotte, Schottische, Oxford, Trilby, Berlin, Heel and Toe Polka, Spanish Waltz, Spanish Circle Waltz, Varsouvienne, Rheinlander. *Dance A While,* by Jane Harris, Anne Pittman, and Maryls Waller, states that by the eighteenth century there were couple dances progressing around the room. Frank and Carolyn Hamilton deserve credit and recognition for their *Introduction to American Round Dancing* (1953) and *American Round Dancing* (1956).

I can remember Lucile Czarnowski having some early programs (in California) that included waltzes, polkas, two-steps, and schottisches. Some of the first round dances we did were Laces and Graces, Moon Winks, Rye Waltz, Herr Schmidt, Trilby, and Black

Brigham Young University Dancers

Hawk Waltz. These are well covered in Shaw's *The Round Dance Book*. In the 1940s Herb Greggerson (from El Paso, Texas) taught Californians the Texas Schottische and La Varsouviana as he danced them with his charming wife, Pauline. Also, when Lloyd Shaw started making his national dance tours with his Cheyenne Mountain Dancers from Colorado Springs, this influenced us in our choice of round dances. Their round dances were particularly enhanced by the great style and verve of the dancers. I taught at the Asilomar Square Dance Institute in California in the 1940s, where I met Larry Eisenberg, who taught me a Texas Schottische. I renamed it the Oklahoma Mixer at a (Folk Dance Federation of California) research committee meeting and it has traveled throughout the world under this name. In the 1950s I was invited to Los Angeles by Bob Osgood, editor of *Sets in Order,* to teach Blue Pacific, which I choreographed.

Early on in southern California round dancing started to take off with excellent stylized dances and good teachers. *Roundancer Up To Date,* by Ginger Osgood (1952), included Always, Arizona Waltz, Blue Skirt Waltz, Chinese Toddle, Harvest Moon Mixer, Kentucky Waltz, Mary Lou, Peek A Boo, Old Soft Shoe, Shadow Waltz, Slow Poke, Syncopated Clock, Waltz Delight, Waltz of the West, and Wedding of The Painted Doll. Ginger's book *Round 'n' Round*

also included Butterflies, Waltz Mixer, Candlelight Waltz, Pacific Grove, Connie Jean, Darling Waltz, Diane, Do Sa Do Mixer, Hayloft Schottische, Hula Blues Mixer, Jambalaya, Juanita Waltz, Mission Waltz, Monterey Waltz, Missouri Waltz (mine on Windsor), and Teton Mountain Stomp (soon done by all folk dancers). Ginger also wrote *Today's Round Dances* (1951), which contained Alice Blue Gown, All-American Promenade (a folk dancer's favorite), Beautiful Ohio, Blue Pacific Waltz and Capistrano Waltz. Also included were Chicken Reel, Down the Lane, Irish Waltz, Music Box Waltz, Nola, Stumbling, Swanee River, Sweetheart Waltz, and Tea for Two. The Third Man Theme and the Tennessee Waltz were favorites with folk dancers as well as round dancers. Note the great number of waltzes that were done! In California we composed our own round dance that went to Texas. It was Gypsy Wine and you'll find it in an early edition of *Dance A While*.

Actually, Corrido, considered a folk dance, was really a compilation of social dance patterns. During the war years, I saw Avis Landis teach a group of nationals (Mexicans) in West Oakland. I invited Avis to join the research committee, which she became a member of. This was how Corrido was born. The fellows, who didn't know that much about Mexican folk dance, were doing a number of combinations of social and ranchera steps that they knew. These were put together in a pattern to fit the record of Corrido. Some of the early dances of the Folk Dance Federation of California can be found in some editions of *Dance A While*. For example, we did the Canadian Barn Dance, Glow Worm, Shortcake, Tuxedo (Junction), Jessie Polka, Two-Step, and Cotton-Eyed Joe. The latter was a big hit (a simplified version still is).

After the round dance scene left the old cotillion dances and the old timers behind, the mixture was still kind of folksy. In Arizona, during the late 1940s, I met Dia and Harry Trygg. I have a copy of a little book they did which is a collector's item. I brought back Tennessee Wigwalk, which was their dance, and their English Polka, which was actually Mexican style to Jesucita, and their Varsouviana for Three.

I can remember when square dancing broke away from folk dancing and followed a separate path. The same thing happened with round dancing in regard to square dancing. Soon they developed their own workshops and get-togethers. Typical of the American culture pattern, the round dance became smoother and better; it is now established in its own right. Since I had worked for the Arthur Murray studios as a ballroom dance teacher, I knew the social dance field. I noticed that the round dance teacher was a hybrid, with a definitive style and an approach that was unique. Now they are leaning toward the cha cha, tango, swing, and rock. The still-popular Hot Lips has the feeling of the Lindy. This is also seen in other round dances. There is a great use of ballroom steps and style; the round dancers even go so far as to embrace the English international style. The two-step or foxtrot is quite popular in different combinations and the waltz now shares the limelight with many other dances. Who would have thought that these dancers would do Latins? At one time it was verboten and could only be sneaked in by hiding the steps in the title. Now the biggest item is a cha cha, like in Folsom Prison Blues, but it is done in round dance style. Many years ago I composed a Polka Con Cha Cha, but it was too early. At one time my Cha Vidrio, which I composed upon returning from Mexico, was done nationally. Today, at square dance clubs round dances are cued like square dances. These dances are called square dancer's rounds.

Even some fad dances crept into the round dance movement. For example, different dancers across the nation did Amos Moses, Pata Pata, and others. My friend Jerry Helt of Ohio came up with a winner in Jiffy Mixer, which is an American standard but is not done by round dancers today. We have lost some of our gracious older dances, which would be beautiful with new orchestrations, but many of the round dances are found on folk dance programs.

(Henry [Buzz] Glass started folk dancing during the thirties and was a charter member of the original Chang's International Folk Dancers. As the first president and founder of the Folk Dance Federation of California, he planned their first festival, which was held at Lodi in 1942.

He studied Spanish-Mexican and modern dancing at the University of Southern California and took lessons from José Limón and Katherine Dunham. In 1954–55, under a Ford Foundation fellowship, Glass studied dance and culture in Mexico and later recorded some Mexican folk dances on his own label, Los Amigos.

His teaching experience includes social dancing for the Arthur Murray studios, folk dancing for eleven years at the University of California at Berkeley, and extension work for more than ten other universities in California. This dedicated professional holds workshops on the college and university level and has done them for CAHPER and AAHPER. For thirteen years he has chaired a physical education workshop for elementary school teachers, which is still continuing.

Active in both square and round dancing, Glass became a round dance composer. Several of his dances have become national favorites, including Blue Pacific Waltz, Beautiful Ohio, Missouri Waltz, Skater's Waltz, and Pretty Girl Dressed in Blue. These early rounds were pressed by Windsor. Later he released dances on the Grenn and Educational Activities labels. He also contributed to Frank Hamilton's early book (1953) on round dancing entitled *Introduction to American Round Dancing*. Blue Pacific was honored by the American Square Dance Society in 1977.

Glass has completed twenty-three widely used educational and movement exploration albums and is active in the field of movement education, presenting workshops nationally. This subject involves a movement approach to reading and language. His compositions incorporate material from the culture and dances of black people and material relevant to the children of the inner city.)

ROUND DANCES

BEAUTIFUL OHIO WALTZ
Source: Composed by Henry (Buzz) Glass
Record: "Beautiful Ohio," Columbia 35617
Formation: Couples in closed position (ballroom), M back to center.
Steps: Walk, step close, hesitation step, waltz, open waltz

Meter 3/4   Pattern

Meas

Intro: Partners sway fwd and back in place during introduction.

I. Walk, W Turns and Step Close

1–2 In closed position, walk fwd, counterclockwise 3 steps (M L, R, L and W R, L, R). On last step (M L and W R) pivot inwardly to face clockwise. Retaining closed position, repeat 3 walking steps clockwise (M R, L, R and W L, R, L). On last step (M R and W L) pivot inwardly to face each other. End with M weight on R, L toe pointed sideward, W weight on L, R toe pointed sideward.

3 W makes a three-step turn R (clockwise) under joined forward hands (M L and W R), M takes 1 step close to L.

4 M takes 1 step close to R, W takes 1 step close to L.

5–8 Repeat action of fig I, meas 1–4.

II. Hesitation and Box Waltz

1–4 In closed position, M back to center, dancers execute 2 hesitation waltz patterns turning L counterclockwise, making ½ turn in all. Hesitation Waltz Pattern: M steps fwd on L, taking weight (ct 1), swings R ft fwd past L, pointing toe down (ct 2), hold (ct 3). Step back on R (ct 1), making ¼ turn L, step L beside R (ct 2), step R in place (ct 3). W does same on opposite ft.
Repeat hesitation waltz pattern (meas 3–4), completing another ¼ turn to L. Finish with M facing center.

5–8 Beginning with M stepping fwd L and W bwd R, take 4 box waltz steps in place, making a ¾ turn to L to end with M facing counterclockwise in line of direction.

III. Side Car Waltz, Break Step, and Walk Around
In closed position, couples move fwd diagonally counterclockwise (M fwd and W bwd) as follows:

1 With L hips adjacent, M steps fwd on L (ct 1), steps fwd on R (ct 2), close L to R (ct 3). W steps bwd on R (ct 1), steps bwd on L (ct 2), closes R to L (ct 3).
Note: On ct 3 partners pivot so that R hips are adjacent.

2 Repeat action of meas 1 with R hips adjacent, beginning M R and W L, and pivoting on ct 3 so that L hips are adjacent. Both take a break step as follows:

3 M steps fwd L (ct 1), steps in place R (ct 2),

steps back on L (ct 3) very slightly in back of R ft.
Note: As M takes weight on L on ct 3, he allows displaced R ft to point fwd.
W steps bwd on R (ct 1), steps L beside R (ct 2), taking weight on L, steps fwd on R (ct 3).
Note: On ct 1 L hips are almost adjacent, on ct 2 partners face, and on ct 3 R hips are adjacent.

4 M and W move fwd around each other (clockwise), completing one turn with 3 steps (R hips adjacent) M R, L, R and W L, R, L.

5–8 Repeat action of fig III, meas 1–4.

IV. Open Waltz and Walk Around

1–2 Facing counterclockwise and with inside hands joined, M L hand over hip pocket, W holding skirt with R, take one waltz step moving fwd, slightly back-to-back, and take another waltz step moving fwd face-to-face. M starts on L ft and W on R. On second waltz step M starts R and W L.
Note: On these two waltz steps dancers move away and toward each other in a diamondlike pattern, allowing joined hands to swing fwd and then back.

3–4 Assume closed position, R hips adjacent. M and W walk around each other with 6 small steps, completing only one turn. M walks L, R, L, R, L, R and W walks R, L, R, L, R, L.

5–8 Repeat action of fig IV, meas 1–4.
Repeat dance three times in all.
Note: On final step the action is as follows: Repeat walk, W turns, and step close once through as in meas 1–4, fig I. Again repeat walk step and W turns. Following three-step turn, W curtsies by stepping back on L ft and bending L knee. M, while turning W, step closes R to L, changes and takes W's R hand in his R, steps back on L to end in bow.

BLACK HAWK WALTZ
Record: Folk Dancer MH 3022; Folkraft 1046; MacGregor 309; Imperial 1006 A. (*Note:* 2nd section or B music is played first; 1st section or A music is played last. Other sections may be used as B, but fig II is always danced to A music.)
Formation: Couples in ballroom position, M facing CCW around room
Steps: Waltz, waltz balance

Meter 3/4   Pattern

Meas

Directions given for M; W does counterpart.

1–4   Intro: Dancers stand in place, holding position.

I. Waltz Balance and Turn (B music)

1–2   Beginning L, waltz balance fwd, then bwd R.

3–4   Beginning L, take 2 waltz steps, turning CCW.

5–16   Repeat action of meas 1–4, fig I, three more times and finish with M facing CCW.

II. Cross Step with Point (B music)
This is danced with low reaching steps, allowing the hip to swing easily.

1–2   Step L across in front of R (ct 1, 2, 3), then step R across in front of L (ct 1, 2, 3).

3–4   Step L across in front of R (ct 1); step sdwd R with R ft (ct 2); step L across in back of R (ct 3); point sdwd R with R (ct 1); hold (cts 2, 3).

5–6   Step R across in front of L (ct 1, 2, 3), then step L across in front of R (ct 1, 2, 3).

7–8   Step R across in front of L (ct 1); step sdwd L with L ft (ct 2); step R across in back of L (ct 3); point sdwd L with L ft (ct 1); hold (cts 2, 3).

9–16   Repeat action of meas 1–8, fig II.
Repeat dance from beginning.

BLUE PACIFIC WALTZ

Source: Composed by Henry (Buzz) Glass

Record: Windsor 7609-A

Formation: Couples, partners almost facing, in open position, joined inside hands extended backward. M L hand over hip pocket, W holding skirt with free R hand. Line of direction is CCW.

Steps: Waltz, balance, step-swing, waltz, twinkle step

Meter 3/4   Pattern

Meas

Intro: Balance Forward and Back

4   Swinging joined inside hands forward, step forward on outside ft, M L and W R (ct 1), place R beside L, retaining weight on L (ct 2), hold with weight on L (ct 3). W do same on opposite ft.
Swinging joined inside hands backward, step back on R, taking weight (ct 1), place L beside R, retaining weight on R (ct 2), hold with weight on R (ct 3). Meas 1–2. W do same on opposite ft.
Repeat action of meas 1–2 with balance forward and back.

I. (a) Step-Swing and Change Places

1   Almost facing forward side by side, take a step-swing on the outside ft. M steps on L and swings R across L (cts 1, 2, 3). W steps on

R and swings L across R (cts 1, 2, 3). Joined extended arms swing forward, following body sway on step-swings.

2   Giving the W a lead by sweeping joined hands backward, dancers release hands to change places with the following action: M makes one continuous R turn by moving sideward R in back of W, making a half turn R on R foot (ct 1) and completes turn stepping on L (cts 2, 3). At the same time W makes one continuous L turn by moving in front of M to change places with a half turn on L foot (ct 1), completes turn stepping on R (cts 2, 3).

3–4   In opposite places rejoin inside hands and repeat action of meas 1–2. W step L and swing R, and M step R and swing L. Repeat crossing as described above, the M making one turn L, starting on L, and the W making one turn R, starting on R.

(b) Step-Swing and Waltz

5   With partners directly facing, swing joined inside hands forward, M R and W L, at the same time taking a step-swing. M steps L and swings R across L. W steps R and swings L across R (cts 1, 2, 3).

6   Change hands, joining M L and W R, and take a step-swing slightly facing in a CW direction. M steps R and swings L across R. W steps L and swings R across L (cts 1, 2, 3).

7–8   Assuming closed dance position, dancers take a R turning waltz, making one turn in two waltz patterns. M waltzes L, R, L and R, L, R. W waltzes R, L, R and L, R, L (cts 1–6).

9–16   Repeat action of meas 1–8, fig I (a) and (b).

II. (a) Hesitation, Twinkle Step
Dancers take semiclosed dance position and face forward in line of direction.

1   Step forward on outside ft, M L and W R, swing inside ft, M R and W L, extending forward with toe pointing downward (cts 1, 2, 3). Continue with a twinkle waltz pattern as follows:

2   Step forward on the raised inside ft, M R and W L (ct 1). Step forward M L beside R and W forward R beside L (ct 2), turning to face partner. Step in place, M on R and W on L (ct 3), at the same time turning to face CW.

3   Repeat twinkle step moving CW as follows: M steps forward with L and W R (ct 1), M steps forward R beside L and W L beside R (ct 2), M steps L beside R and W R beside L, with dancers ending facing CCW (ct 3).

4   In semiclosed position, M steps forward with R (ct 1), closes L to R (weight on R) (ct 2),

and holds (ct 3). W steps forward on L (ct 1), closes R to L (weight on L) (ct 2), and holds (ct 3).

5–12 Repeat meas 1–4 three times in all.

(b) Walk Around

13–16 M steps forward on L, swinging extended R forward (cts 1, 2, 3). Placing R in front of L (hook step) (ct 1), M turns L, taking weight on R (cts 2, 3). At end of hook step, M feet are parallel. M facing LOD.

W steps forward on R, swinging extended L forward (cts 1, 2, 3). As M does the hook step, he leads W in front of him CCW, W taking 1 waltz pattern L, R, L (cts 1, 2, 3). W ends facing partner, W back to LOD. Complete figure with two L turning waltz patterns, making almost one turn. M waltzes L, R, L and R, L, R and W waltzes R, L, R and L, R, L (cts 1–6).

At end of waltz, M again has back almost to center, W almost facing center, ready to repeat dance. Repeat dance 4 times.

Ending

1–2 M steps sideward L facing partner (cts 1, 2, 3), closes R to L, at the same time bowing (cts 1, 2, 3).

W steps sideward R facing partner (cts 1, 2, 3), places L in back of R, and does a curtsy (cts 1, 2, 3). W R and M L hands joined.

COTTON-EYED JOE

Cotton-eyed Joe is truly a dance of the folk. In the Southwest it has as many variants as the old folk song to which it is danced.

Record: Imperial 1045, 6045; Folkraft 1124, 1470, 1035; KIK-R 202.

Formation: Cpls anywhere on the floor, in closed pos, M back to ctr

Steps and Styling: Polka (without hop), heel-toe polka, push step

Meter 2/4   Pattern

Meas

Intro: Length may vary, depending upon record used.

I. Heel-toe Polka and Turn Away

1–2 Dance one heel-toe polka step to M L and W R (LOD).

3–4 Without changing hand pos, so that M L and W R arms are extended twd rear (LOD), dance one heel-toe polka to M R and W L (RLOD).

5–8 Release hands. Turn away from ptr and describe a small individual circle (M CCW, W

CW) with 4 polka steps. Finish facing ptr, M back to ctr.

II. Push and Polka

1–2 M with thumbs in belt, W holding skirt, dance 4 push steps twd M L and W R (LOD). Keep ft close to floor.

3–4 Dance 4 push steps in opp direction (RLOD).

5–8 Take closed pos and beginning M L and W R, dance 4 polka steps turning CW and progressing in LOD.

Repeat dance from beginning.

Variation:

Formation: Dancers in side-by-side lines facing LOD (any number in each line)

Meas

1–2 Hop L, kick R fwd; repeat.

3–4 Step R, L, R (moving slightly bwd).

5–6 Hop R, kick L fwd; repeat.

7–8 Step L, R, L (moving slightly bwd).

9–16 Repeat meas 1–8 above.

17–32 Beg L, take 8 two-steps fwd.

Repeat dance from beginning.

OKLAHOMA MIXER

Record: "Dude Ranch Schottische," Sarg 183-45; "Rustic Schottische," Folkraft 1035; "Starlight Schottische," Columbia 37332; "Rustic Schottische," Coral 965517; "Schottische," MacGregor 5003 and National 4535.

Formation: Cpls in double circle, in varsouvienne position, and facing LOD.

Steps and Styling: Two-step; heel-toe. Walking steps are done with a slight swagger.

Meter 4/4   Pattern

Meas

I. Two-step and Walk

1–2 In varsouvienne pos, cpls dance 1 two-step diag fwd L, starting with L ft (cts 1, 2, 3), hold (ct 4), and 1 two-step diag fwd R, starting R (cts 1, 2, 3), hold (ct 4).

3–4 Moving directly fwd, cpls take 4 walking steps L, R, L, R (2 steps per meas).

II. Heel and Toe and Progress

5 Keeping same pos, both M and W place L heel diag fwd L (ct 1), hold (ct 2); place L toe on floor directly behind R ft (ct 3), hold (ct 4).

6 Dropping R hands, W cross to L in front of M with 3 walking steps L, R, L (cts 1, 2, 3), hold (ct 4), to end on inside of circle at L side of M, and facing RLOD (CW). At same time M steps in place L, R, L (cts 1, 2, 3), hold (ct 4).

7   Starting R, both repeat action of meas 5.

8   W takes 3 steps R, L, R (cts 1, 2, 3), hold (ct 4), twd R side of next M (behind present ptr). At same time, W extends R hand to take R hand of new ptr and, turning slightly to L, reaches L hand back to assume varsouvienne pos. M takes 3 steps R, L, R (cts 1, 2, 3), hold (ct 4), moving slightly fwd, extending R hand fwd to new ptr and leading her into varsouvienne pos.

Repeat dance from beginning.

SALTY DOG RAG

Record: Decca 27981; Black Mountain 1008; MCA 81745

Position: Couples, side by side facing LOD, with promenade crossed hands grasp

Pattern

Meas

1–2   Side, behind, side, brush. Side, behind, side, brush. Grapevine to R, then grapevine to L. Step R to side, L behind R, step R to side, brush L across R. Repeat in opposite direction.

3–4   Walk 2, 3, 4.

Four slow walking steps forward, starting with R foot.

5–8   Repeat above.

9–10   Cross, 2, 3, Brush. Roll, 2, 3, Brush.

Release R hands but retain L hands, gent does a grapevine to R and brushes L over R; lady crosses to inside toward center of hall in three running steps and brushes L over R. Then, starting with L foot, *both* make a L face turn (roll) in three fast steps, the gent passing RLOD from his lady, ending in facing pos holding R hands, gents back to center of hall.

11–12   Star Around 2, 3, 4.

In R-hand star pos strut around partner in four slow steps, rejoin L hands.

13–16   Repeat 9–12 above, ending in promenade pos.

TETON MOUNTAIN STOMP

Source: Composed by Doc & Winnie Alumbaugh

Record: Windsor 4615 (45 rpm)

Position: Partners in closed dance position, M facing LOD

Steps and Styling: Opposite footwork throughout for M and W; steps described are for M.

Pattern

Meas

1–4   Side, close; side, stomp; side, close; side, stomp.

Step to L side twd center on L foot, close R foot to L; step again to L side on L foot, stomp R foot beside L but leave weight on L ft; repeat action, starting on R foot and moving away from center.

5–8   Side, stomp; side, stomp; walk, two; three, four.

Step to L side twd center on L foot, stomp R foot beside L; step to R side away from center on R foot and stomp L foot beside R; in "banjo" position with R hips adjacent, M takes four walking steps fwd in LOD, L R L R, while W takes four steps bwd in LOD, starting R foot, R L R L.

9–12   Change, and walk; three, four; change, and progress; three, four.

Partners change to "sidecar" position with L hips adjacent by each making R face ½ turn in place, M remaining on inside and facing RLOD and W remaining on outside and facing LOD. M walks four steps bwd in LOD, L R L R, while W walks four steps fwd in LOD, R L R L. Partners change back to "banjo" position with R hips adjacent by each making a L face ½ turn, then immediately release each other and M walks fwd four steps in LOD, L R L R, to meet *second* W approaching him, while W walks fwd four steps in RLOD, R L R L, to meet *second* M approaching her.

13–16   Two step; two step; pivot, two; three, four.

New partners take closed dance position and do two turning two-steps, starting M L foot and making one complete R face turn while progressing in LOD; then do four pivot steps, starting M L foot, to make one complete R face turn and ending with M facing in LOD, ready to repeat dance.

Repeat entire dance for a total of eleven times.

Note: If preferred, a "buzz" type square dance swing may be substituted for the two-steps and pivots during meas 13–16, taking eight steps during the swing and making sure that swing ends with M facing in LOD.

Square Dancing

by Betty Casey

The square dance is a lively, traditional American folk dance enjoyed by Americans young and old since pioneer days. There is a wide difference between pioneer and modern styles of square dancing, but, old style or new, it is set against a variety of rhythmic tunes

Brigham Young University Dancers with director Mary Bee Jensen at the microphone.

usually ranging from fiddled old-time hoedowns to popular songs. Recorded music is commonly used for square dancing. Squares are usually danced by sets or squares made up of four couples whose movements are directed by a caller. The step is a swift gliding walk.

Early Appalachian Mountain squares may be done in either a square formation or in big circles consisting of any number of couples. These dances were introduced from England during colonial days. The Country Dance and Song Society and some other groups have revived these dances and incorporated them in their programs, complete with early styling.

The caller chants, says, or sings the square dance calls. The movement patterns range from simple to complicated geometric designs, including lines, stars, circles, squares, and cloverleafs. Dancers familiar with the language of square dancing, dancer designations, and individual movements can perform a wide variety of patterns. This is the essence of square dancing.

The American square dance is different from other folk dances. It is the only folk dance that is always directed by a caller, who exercises his prerogative to extemporaneously choose patterns from known basic movements and terminology, or even to make up new patterns consisting of original combinations of movements for the dancers to follow. Since square dance movements have no set patterns, within the four couple/caller format new movements and calls are constantly evolving.

The square dance is uniquely American. Vibrant strands of Americana woven into the dance calls reflect historical developments and the background of the American way of life—from homespun to wash-and-wear. The format, many of the folk dance movements, and the terminology incorporated into the square dance were brought by early emigrants from other countries to the United States. Borrowed bits from such foreign dances as French quadrilles, Irish jigs, English reels, and Spanish fandangos have blended with American folkways and customs to create the square dance.

When, after a period of comparative inactivity, the folk dance craze burst upon the scene in the early and middle forties, square dancing was an integral part of the movement. Interest really mounted during the World War II years, when transportation was limited and there was a need for recreation closer to home. Dances from all cultures were done, including American square and round dances as well as those of other nationalities.

In those days square dancers were folk dancers—there was no difference. Squares became very popular and soon many clubs began to specialize in them. Publications dealing exclusively with square dancing made their appearance. Gradually, the folk and square dance movements drifted apart until a complete separation occurred.

The California-based magazine *Let's Dance* originally contained much square dance material, including lists of records, a caller-of-the-month, the latest in square dance clothing, and other square dance material. In fact, until 1965 *Let's Dance* described itself as the "Magazine of Folk and Square Dancing" on the cover. *Folk Dance Scene*, the Southern California Federation magazine, still devotes a section to square dancing. The Federation often includes squares in its teacher-training programs.

Squares continue to be an important part of the folk dance movement. Although many clubs do no squares at all, most folk dancers do some of the simpler movements and a few clubs even specialize in them. Squares continue to be included as an integral part of festival programs.

(Portions of the preceding material were excerpted with permission from this author's *The Complete Book of Square Dancing (and Round Dancing)*, published by Doubleday & Company, Inc.)

Betty Casey

Square Dances

SQUARE DANCE CALLS

The two types of square dance calls are "patter" calls and "singing" calls. Patter calls consist of free-form choreography of selected movements extemporaneously chosen by an experienced caller. The patter calls given here are arranged to present smooth-flowing patterns. They may be called to any good hoedown or rhythmic music. Singing calls are made up of movements choreographed into set patterns to fit a particular tune, with the calls replacing some of the words to the song. Usually they are made up of a break (chorus) and a figure (verse) arranged in this order: break, figure (twice), break, figure (twice), break. Singing-call records are usually 45s, with the voice and music on one side and the instrumental only on the flip side. (For an explanation of square dance terms see the Lexicon of Folk Dance Definitions in Section VIII.)

PATTER CALLS

Record: Any good hoedown or tune with an even rhythm at about 128–32 beats per minute.

Call 1
Join hands circle left
U-turn back single file
When you get home
Swing your own

Call 2
Allemande left, do sa do partner
Men star left, star promenade
Inside out, outside in
Men turn back on the outside track
Swing your partner, promenade

Call 3
Allemande left, promenade
Heads wheel around to a line of four
Right and left through
Cross trail to corner
Allemande left, promenade partner

Call 4
Allemande left in Alamo style
Right to partner, balance
Turn half with the right, balance again
Half with the left, balance once more
Turn half with the right, balance there
Half with the left, swing your own
Promenade

Call 5

Circle left, rollaway with a half sashay
Allemande left and allemande thar
Go right and left (hold on)
(Men) form a (backward) star
Shoot that star, go right and left
Make a new star, back it up boys
Slip the clutch, left allemande
Promenade

Call 6

Sides face, grand square

One, two, three, turn
One, two, three, turn
One, two, three, turn
One, two, three, reverse

One, two, three, turn
One, two, three, turn
One, two, three, turn
One, two, three, swing

Call 7

Heads promenade, halfway around you go
Come down the middle and pass thru
Separate go round one into the middle
Square thru four hands around and then
Separate go round two down the middle again
Cross trail thru and find the corner
Left allemande, promenade partner

Call 8

Heads go forward and back
Pass thru, U-turn back, star thru
Right and left thru the outside two
Dive thru, star thru
Right and left thru across the way
Rollaway a half sashay and star thru
Right and left thru the outside two
Dive thru, star thru
Right and left thru, cross trail
Left allemande
Grand right and left, promenade partner

Call 9

One and three lead right, circle up four
Make a line go forward eight and back
Pass thru, bend the line
Go forward and back, right and left thru
Two ladies chain across, chain 'em back
Same couples forward up and back
Pass thru, bend the line
Go forward and back, right and left thru
Join hands and circle left
Allemande left, promenade partner

Call 10

One and three square thru
Make it four hands around
Count four hands
Right and left thru with outside two
Half square thru two hands
Bend the line, right and left thru
Half square thru
U-turn back and box the gnat
Right and left thru turn the girl around
Square thru three quarters
Allemande left, promenade partner

Call 11

All around the left-hand lady
Seesaw pretty little taw
Four men star by the right
And home you go
Partner left a do paso, her by the left
Corner by the right
Partner by the left hand round full turn
All four ladies chain, chain four girls
Across the set, chain 'em back
Same old way you turn the girl
Then join hands and circle to the left
Circle left go round the land why then
Left allemande, promenade partner

Call 12

Heads star thru, California twirl
Do sa do with the outside two
Back up look 'em in the eye
Square thru four hands, count four
When you're facing out, bend the line
Forward up to the middle and back
Pass thru, bend the line
Do a right and left thru
Turn the girl around
Square thru four hands, count to four I'll tell you
    when
Do a U-turn back and box the gnat
Right and left thru the other way back
Inside arch and dive thru
Square thru three hands around the land
Allemande left, promenade partner

SINGING CALLS

AUCTIONEER (Called)

Dance and calls by Marshall Flippo
Record: BS-9001-B
Intro, Break, Ending

Now join up hands gotta make that ring, circle to the left like everything
Then reverse trail the other way back home, face the corner
Do an allemande left that corner girl, do a do sa do walk around your own
Then all four gents star by the left you know
Well get back home do sa do, you walk around that Jane
Swing that girl then promenade that ring
He said, "Oh my, it's do or die, I've got to learn that auction cry
Gotta make my mark and be an auctioneer."

Figure:
Now the head two couples pass thru, separate and get around two
Go all the way back home and swing your man
Same two couples make a right-hand star, go once around from where you are
And go to the corner and do a left allemande, come on home
Do a do sa do walk around your own, same little girl you swing
Swing that gal and promenade that ring
Twenty-five dollar bid, now thirty dollar thirty, will you give me thirty
Make it thirty, bid in form of thirty dollar
Will you give me thirty, who'll make a thirty dollar bid

EL PASO CITY
Dance and calls by Ernie Kinney
Record: Hi-Hat 471
Opener, Break, Ending

(circle left) From thirty thousand feet above
I see El Paso City there below . . .
Left allemande your corner . . .
Come back, do sa do, men star left now
Star promenade her . . . by the Rio Grande
Men back out, left allemande
Come back and then you promenade
Felina back home to old El Paso . . .

Figure:
All four ladies chain across
You turn and chain 'em right back home again . . .
Put the ladies back to back
Men you promenade around the outside track
Do paso . . . by the Rio Grande
Swing your corner round and round
Promenade the Rio Grande, and
You will go back home to old El Paso . . .
Tag: Go back home to El Paso

FIRST THING EVERY MORNING (called)
Dance and calls by Marshall Flippo
Record: BS-9001-A
Intro, Break, Ending

Join hands and circle go round that ring now
Go all the way till you get back home, face the corner
Do an allemande left with the corner, get back do a do sa do
Now swing your partner, then face that corner girl
Do an allemande left, pull the partner by
Grand right and left the ring, go in and out and promenade and sing
The very first thing every morning, and the last thing every night

Figure:
Four gents star right go round to the corner
Do an allemande left that corner girl, come on home do a do sa do
Then all four ladies into the middle circle round the ring
Go once around, do sa do that Jane
Face your corner, do an allemande left, come back and swing your own
Swing the gal and promenade back home
The very first thing every morning, and the last thing every night

JOSÉ
Dance and calls by C. O. Guest
Record: KALOX K-1031
Opener, Break, Ending

Join your hands and form a ring you circle left I sing
All the way around you go you get back home and then
Allemande left that corner girl, right hand swing your own
Señor star left its once around you roam
Box the gnat and the corner allemande
Swing your señorita then promenade the land
Sing hasta la vista, hasta la vista José done and gone
Singing Ah Yii Ah Yii and how he'd carry on

Figure:
Señoritas promenade go inside of the ring
Home you go and swing señor you swing
Allemande left that corner lady turn a right hand round your own
Señor star by the left its once around you roam
Home you go and do sa do and then the corner swing
Swing that señorita then promenade the ring
Sing hasta la vista, hasta la vista José done and gone

Singing Ah Yii Ah Yii and how he'd carry on
Sequence:
Opener, figure twice, break, figure twice, ending

SMILE AWAY EACH RAINY DAY
Dance and calls by Joe Lewis
Record: KALOX K-1182
Opener, Break, Ending

Four ladies promenade inside the ring
Come home and your partner swing
Join your hands and circle left around the town
Allemande left and everybody gonna weave around
Keep in mind the clouds are silverlined
Do sa do and promenade away
Let love light the sky up, tell the clouds to dry up
Smile away each rainy day

Figure:
Heads (sides) square thru four hands around
With the out sides right-hand star
Heads (sides) make a left-hand star in the middle of
    town
Corners do a right and left thru, turn that pretty little
    girl around
Dive thru and square thru, let's make it three
Gonna swing my corner and take her home with me
Make light of trouble, even though you're seeing it
    double
Smile away each rainy day
Sequence:
Figure twice for heads, break, figure twice for sides,
    ending

YUGOSLAVIA

Yugoslavian Folk Dancing

by Dick Oakes

Yugoslavia, one of the five Balkan countries, is physiographically and ethnically a most complex country. A rough terrain isolating segments of the population and years of conquest and occupation by many nations have interwoven scattered remnants of culture into the underlying native folkways. These factors are reflected in the diversity and complexity of its folk dances.

Seen from a passing satellite, Yugoslavia would appear to be a tangled network of densely wooded, inhos-

Duquesne University Tamburitzans

pitable mountains pocked with boulder-strewn valleys. Its mountains, which are bordered by other Balkan countries, fall away to a broken coastline washed by the Adriatic Sea.

Five South Slav peoples make up the Yugoslav population: Serbians, Croatians, Slovenians, Macedonians, and Montenegrins. "Yug" is the Slav word for "south," so the literal meaning of Yugoslavia is "land of the South Slavs." Linguistically, the national groups are closely related through four main languages, but historical and cultural differences have been the cause of tensions and rivalries. Diversity within a fundamental unity is a major theme of Yugoslavian history.

The principal centers of population are in the fertile lowlands and along the maritime frontage of the Adriatic Sea. On the Croatian coastal regions and in Dalmatia, next to the dazzling blue of the Adriatic Sea where tourists swarm today, life a mere decade ago was a nightmare due to chronic afflictions visited on Yugoslavia as well as other Balkan lands by invaders. There are now great universities in the large cities, whereas once the Yugoslavians were deprived by conquerors of the right to an education.

In the period of decline of the Roman Empire, great migrations took place, resulting in ethnic mixtures. Then darkness fell over a large part of the South Slav land when the Turks began a five-hundred-year siege by defeating its strongest state, Serbia, in 1389. Despite the fact that one of the first printing presses in the world was established there in 1494, the Turkish invasion brought to a halt the rapid development of the

South Slav civilization, which at that time had developed an advanced literature. The people were subjugated and were prevented from publicly using their language and literature and developing their culture. Though the fierce resistance of the Yugoslavs continued throughout those many years of Turkish domination, the long rule of the Ottoman Empire is evidenced by the mosques and palaces that may still be seen in certain areas of the country.

Others besides the Turks coveted the rich lands of the South Slavs, however, and for centuries the Republic of Venice (later Italy) sought a foothold on the Dalmatian coast. The Austrians and Hungarians came to take what they felt was their share of the spoils. The struggle for independence reached its climax during the last 150 years, which saw 28 separate rebellions. Intellectual ferment, political struggle, and internal strife plagued the country between World War I and II. Hard-fought battles against invading Nazi forces during World War II ended in 1945 with the establishment of the Federal People's Republic of Yugoslavia, composed of six republics: Slovenia, Croatia, Bosnia-Herzegovina, Montenegro, Serbia, and Macedonia.

Yugoslav folk art is rooted in rich cultures dating from the eleventh to the fourteenth centuries, between the time of the fall of the Byzantine Empire and the onslaught of the destructive Ottoman Empire of the Middle Ages. Solely permitted to express their feelings orally, Yugoslavians recited or sang them to the accompaniment of local instruments. Folk stories were transmitted from father to son and were given expression in ballads and music, elaborate embroidery, intricate wood carving, and a rich dance tradition. These highly developed folk arts, which are of more than mere ethnographic interest, have been preserved in the recent past.

Of these folk art forms, none is livelier than the enormously variegated Yugoslav dances. These include not only kolos ("circle dances") but also a number of other dances, such as heroic dances, children's dances, and community dances.

The kolos can be divided into two groups: ritual dances, which have all but disappeared, and a secular group of dances. In the latter group, happy, lively dances predominate, a fact that is in keeping with the spirit of the Yugoslav peoples. These dances often stress bravery and endurance. Apart from these, there are humorous, mimicking dances in which animals are imitated; sentimental dances; dances that mark the beginning or end of a social gathering; and erotic dances. The humorous dances, besides being happy, may also strike out at such undesirable traits as laxness and dishonesty. In some dances the elements of mimicry assume the character of a small play in which the words of the accompanying songs describe the action performed in the dances.

In addition to countless dances expressing joyous feelings, there are also sentimental and romantic ones. Among the latter, those from Macedonia are especially lovely. The emotional musical accompaniment may signify longing for the homeland, while the drooping heads of the dancers may express a staggering under the burden of a yoke. In some parts of the country it is the custom for women to mourn their dead in kolos. Erotic feelings are implied in the majority of couple dances, but they allude to love and longing in a discreet way.

Yugoslav dance rhythms are nearly as varied as the dances themselves. The standard Western 2-beat rhythm is found in such dances as U Šest from Serbia, Slavonsko Kolo from Croatia, and Belasičko Oro from Macedonia, while Biserka from Serbia reflects the 3-beat rhythm popular at elegant balls at the turn of the century. Other rhythms are also possible, combining "quick" beats of two counts each and "slow" beats of three counts each. For example, Tino Mori utilizes a 7-count slow-quick-quick (3-2-2 = 7) rhythm while Čamče has a 7-count quick-quick-slow (2-2-3 = 7) rhythm. More complicated rhythms are evident in Četiri U Krst (3-2-3 = 8), Čučuk (2-2-2-3 = 9), Fatiše Kolo (2-3-2-2 = 9), Ovčepolsko Oro (2-2-3-2-2 = 11), and Postupano (2-2-2-3-2-2 = 13). There are even examples of combined or alternating rhythms in such dances as Ergensko Oro (2-3-2-2 = 9 + 2-3-2-2-2-2 = 13) and Pop Marinko (2-2-2-3 = 9 + 3-3-2-3 = 11).

Duquesne University Tamburitzans

It is often awkward to give English equivalents to the many different kolo steps, but because some steps occur frequently, especially in dances of the same area, we can recognize a few of the more common denominators that are significant in the repertoire of the kolo dancer. In addition to steps—which often have a quick bend of the knee between them in series—and hops—which are more like simple lifts of the heel, with the free foot staying very near to or on the floor—some basic combinations of these with which the kolo dancer rapidly becomes familiar include step-hop and hop-step-step. There are also running threes (a series of three running steps), unsyncopated threes (steps danced on three even counts), and syncopated threes (three steps in which the first is held longer than the other two). This last step may be done very fast with a shaking of the body, as in the Croatian Drmeš. A grapevine step, consisting of crossing in front and in back (or vice versa), is popular in Serbian dancing. One particular step combination, commonly called the basic kolo step, probably evolved from a simple sideward step-close-step pattern. It combines a sideward hop-step-step and a step-hop in a two-measure phrase. It is easy to predict that with further embellishment and improvisation on these component steps, new material will be researched and presented for years to come.

Of the regional styling of Yugoslav dance it can generally be said that the body is held proudly erect, the knees are slightly flexed, and the footwork is usually small and kept close to the floor. While the men's steps are often flashy and vigorous, the women's steps are usually more restrained. A man always leads the kolo in Yugoslavia and may start a dance with only one or two more dancers, who may later be joined by others.

The handholds used in Yugoslav dancing are many. Besides the couple dance positions, which include the varsouvienne, shoulder-waist, and closed ballroom, the greatest variety occurs in the kolos. Basket holds, both front and back, are prominent in the north; low or "V" handholds are widespread in central Yugoslavia; and belt holds, shoulder holds, and joined hands held at shoulder level in "W" handholds may be found in the south. These handholds are not, of course, limited to just the areas mentioned. In addition, little finger holds, middle finger holds, and an escort hold are known.

In the last twenty-five years, kolos have become more and more popular with folk dancers all over the United States and Canada. Not only have folk dancers in general accepted them as belonging on the list of dances to be learned and danced often; second-generation Yugoslavs have also taken a much greater interest in kolo dancing. Both groups enjoy these dances at their parties and celebrations and both try to learn them correctly. Whether at ethnic gatherings, folk dance festivals, or civic celebrations, these dances usually headline a program of exhibition dances.

In order to feed this growing interest and introduce dancers to the joie de vivre of the Yugoslav people, many teachers of Yugoslav dances have appeared on the U.S. and Canadian folk dance scene. Notable among these in the formative years of U.S. kolo dancing were Vyts Beliajus, Michel Cartier, Dick Crum, John Filcich, Michael and Mary Ann Herman, and Anatol Joukowsky. A significant impact in the field of folk dancing was later made by Pece Atanasovski, Dennis Boxell, Martin Koenig, Atanas Kolarovski, George Tomov, and Rubi Vučeta. More recently, Bora Gajicki, Elsie Ivancich-Dunin, Anthony Shay, Bob Liebman, and Ron Wixman have continued to bring Yugoslav dancing to the folk dance public. While this list is by no means complete, it illustrates that interest in Yugoslav dance in the United States has been steadily on the upswing—for without that interest there would not have been such a demand for so many specialty teachers.

And what of the future of Yugoslav dancing in the United States? The hope is that the Kolo Maniac and Balkan Freak labels will become things of the past as the "hotshots" place less importance on collecting yet more *dances* and begin to experience the inner joy of Yugoslav *dancing*.

(Dick Oakes represents the product and the essence of international folk dancing in the United States. A versatile, professional teacher-performer-dancer, he is proficient in a wide spectrum of folk dances. His interest in folk dance was sparked when he was still a young sailor stationed in San Diego. Since then he has studied with top international teachers, performed with professional dance groups (including the famed Aman Folk Dance Ensemble), and has taught at camps, seminars, and universities and colleges in

Dick Oakes

nearly a hundred cities across the continental United States, in Canada, and in Hawaii.

Stage and television performances have included dances from Romania, Bulgaria, Croatia, Hungary, Bavaria, Poland, Russia, Serbia, The Ukraine, Turkey, Lithuania, and the United States. A popular folk dance specialist with a large collection of records and background material, his expertise also encompasses Greek, Macedonian, Scandinavian, and other dances.

Among his leadership roles, Dick Oakes served as codirector of Holiday Camp, held various offices in folk dance clubs and the Folk Dance Federation of California, South, and has been a member of the Federation's Research and Standardization Committee.)

YUGOSLAVIAN FOLK DANCES

BAVNO ORO

Bavno Oro (BAHV-no OH-roh), meaning "slow dance," is from Macedonia. In the early fifties Boris Karlov recorded his arrangement of the Macedonian folk song "Snosti Sakav Da Ti Dojdam" under this name. This version of the dance was introduced by

Dennis Boxell under the original title of Makedonska Bavno Oro. Another version has been taught by Anatol Joukowsky.

The slow part of the dance is in a 7/8 slow-quick-quick rhythm that changes to a 7/16 quick-quick-slow rhythm during the fast part after a 3/16 slow (1-beat) measure. These seven-count rhythms are known among Balkan music and dance specialists as the "Macedonian seven" (Makedonska sedmorka).

Record: Xopo (45 rpm) X-301; Nama (LP) 1001

Formation: Open line of M and W with M at front of line and W at other end, hands joined at shldr level and held slightly fwd, end dancers' free hands on hip or waving a handkerchief. The last M and the first W hold a handkerchief between them.

Meter 7/8, 7/16   Pattern

Meas

No Intro

I. Side-cross and Lift (25 meas)

1 Facing slightly to R, step swd R (ct 1), step L across in front of R (ct 4), hold (ct 6).
   Note: In many areas of U.S. this step has been modified and resembles the traditional Lesnoto step: Step swd R (ct 1), slight bounce on R with L knee slightly raised in front of (ct 4), step L across in front of R (ct 6).

2 Facing ctr, step swd R (ct 1), slight bounce on R, M raising bent L knee high in front of R with L ft in front of R leg, W raising L low in front of R (ct 4), slight bounce on R with L remaining in same pos as before (ct 6).

3 Reverse action of meas 2 to L with opp ftwk.

4–24 Repeat action of meas 1–3 seven more times.

25 Repeat action of meas 1.

II. Heel Touch and Dip (17 meas)

1 Facing ctr, slight step swd R, bending R knee slightly (ct 1), lightly tap L heel fwd and slightly diag to L (ct 4), lightly tap L heel directly fwd and parallel to R (ct 6).

2 Step L next to R, bending L knee slightly (ct 1), lightly tap R heel fwd and slightly diag to R (ct 4), step slightly swd R (ct 6).

3 Facing slightly to R, step L across in front of R, bending L knee in a "dip" (ct 1), facing ctr, step swd R (ct 4), step L across in back of R (ct 6).

4–15 Repeat action of meas 1–3 four more times.

16 Repeat action of meas 1.

17 Facing ctr, step L in place, bending L knee slightly (ct 1), lightly tap R heel fwd and slightly diag to R (ct 4), lightly tap R heel fwd (ct 6).

III. Side-cross and Lift (24 meas)

1–24 Repeat action of fig I, meas 1–24. (Note that there is no meas 25 this time.)

IV. Heel Touch and Dip (15 meas)

1–15 Repeat action of fig II, meas 1–15.

Note: Fig IV is followed by a single beat corresponding to the first "slow" beat, or ct 1, upon which dancers leap swd R, bending knee and thrusting L ft fwd as a transition into fig V (ct 1).

V. Side-behind and Thrust (29 meas)

1 Facing ctr, step swd L (ct 1), step R across in back of L (ct 3), fall swd L, bending L knee and thrusting R fwd (ct 5).

2 Step swd R (ct 1), step L across in back of R (ct 3), quick light step swd R (ct 4), step L across in front of R, bending L knee in a "dip" (ct 5).

3 Step swd R (ct 1), step L across in back of R (ct 3), fall swd R, bending R knee and thrusting L fwd (ct 5).

4–27 Repeat action of meas 1–3 nine more times.

28–29 Repeat action of meas 1–2.

BELASIČKO ORO

Belasičko Oro (bell-ah-SEECH-koh OH-roh) is a line dance that comes from the town of Strumica in Macedonia. It is named after a nearby mountain called Belasiča. The footwork is influenced by the rocky terrain, the dance being done by the shepherds in the area. It was introduced by Atanas Kolarovski.

Record: Festival Records (45 rpm) FM-4005A; Voyager Records (LP) VRLP 402, side 2, band 1; "Dances of Yugoslavia," (LP) WRS 768, side 2, band 2

Formation: Broken circle, leader at R end, hands joined and held down. Originally M and W did not join hands, holding a handkerchief between them. Today usually only the leader holds a handkerchief in his hand and uses it to signal a change from one dance pattern to the next.

Steps and Styling: Walk; run; step-close. Body is held erect but relaxed. The bouncy character of the steps is reflected throughout the body. When directions say to step on heel, this does not mean that toes point in the air. Ball of foot is on, or close to, floor, but heel bears weight.

Meter 2/4   Pattern

Meas   No Intro

I. Step-Pattern One

1 Facing slightly to R of ctr, and moving in LOD,

step on R heel (ct 1). Close L to R, taking wt (L instep to R heel), knees bent and apart (ct 2).

2 Step on R heel in LOD (ct 1), close L to R (ct &); step on R heel in LOD (ct 2), bend R knee (ct &).

3 Still moving in LOD, repeat action of meas 2, but with opp ftwk.

4 Turning to face ctr, step on R to R (ct 1), bend R knee (ct &). Lift L leg in front of R, knee bent, at same time straightening R knee (ct 2); bend R knee (ct &).

5–8 Repeat action of meas 1–4, but with opp ftwk and moving in RLOD.

II. Step-Pattern Two

1 Facing ctr, raise joined hands to shoulder height, elbows bent, and step to R on R heel (ct 1); step on L across in back of R, bending L knee (ct 2).

2 Step to R on R heel (ct 1), step on L across in back of R (ct &) (same as meas 1, fig II, but twice as fast). Step to R on R (ct 2), lift L leg, knee bent, beside R (ct &) (R knee bends during this small, low lift).

3 Step L beside R, lifting R leg, knee bent, beside L (ct 1). Raise and lower L heel as lower leg is extended fwd a little (ct 2).

4 Repeat action of meas 3, fig II, but with opp ftwk.

5–8 Repeat action of meas 1–4, fig II, but with opp ftwk and moving in RLOD.

III. Step-Pattern III

1 Bringing hands down and turning to face LOD, step fwd R (ct 1). Bring L leg to R so that L ankle is behind R calf, L knee turned out. At same time R knee bends and body leans fwd from hips (ct 2).

2 Turn quickly to face RLOD and step fwd (RLOD) L, R, L (ct 1, &, 2), hold (&).

3 Still moving in RLOD, step fwd R (ct 1). Raise L leg (knee bent) in front of R (ct 2) as R heel is raised and lowered.

4 With body bent fwd from hips in crouching pos, move fwd RLOD with 3 small running steps, L, R, L (cts 1, &, 2), hold (ct &). Turn to face ctr on last step L in preparation for either a repeat of Step-Pattern III or to move into Step-Pattern IV.

IV. Step-Pattern IV

1 Facing ctr and with joined hands held down, step fwd R (twd ctr) in front of L, lifting L leg off floor in back of R and bending body slightly fwd from hips (ct 1). Step on L behind R, bringing body to erect position and raising

joined hands to shoulder height (ct 2).

2 Step on R beside L (ct 1). Raise L leg, knee bent, in front of R (ct 2). (*Note:* no heel lift here.)

3 Bend R knee, at same time turn R knee out to L (ct 1). Straighten R knee, return L knee to position as in meas 2, fig IV (ct 2).

4 Still facing ctr, step L, R, L in place (cts 1, &, 2), hold (ct &).

DRMEŠ IZ ZDENČINE

Drmeš iz Zdenčine (DER-mesh eez ZDEHN-chee-neh), a Croatian dance meaning "shaking dance from Zdencine," was learned in Yugoslavia by Dick Crum.

Record: Folk Dancer (45 rpm) MH 3030; Folkraft (45 rpm) 45-1500

Formation: A small closed circle of dancers, preferably not more than 10 people. Use back-basket-hold throughout.

Steps and Styling: Time step (2 per meas): Stamp entire R, slightly bending knee (ct 1); momentarily take wt on entire L, knee straight (ct &); repeat action (ct 2, &).

Shaking step (move very slightly to L): With R a bit fwd from place, step R, but do not take L from floor (ct 1); shake whole body vertically once without raising any part of ft from floor (ct &); shift wt onto L in place (ct 2); shake again (ct &). During this step, keep body very erect.

Step-hop step (traveling step): To move L, face diag L, step R with accent (ct 1); pause (ct &); hop R (ct 2); step L (ct &). Keep ft underneath body. To move R, face diag R and use opp ftwk.

Meter 2/4 Pattern

Meas No Intro

I. Time Steps and Shaking

1–7 With 14 time steps move gradually to L (CW).
8 Lightly stamp R, L.
9–15 With 7 shaking steps move gradually to L (CW).
16 Stamp R, L.

II. Revolving

1–8 With 8 step-hop steps turn circle to L (CW) rapidly.
9 Still facing L, stamp R in place (ct 1); pivot CW on R to face R (ct 2).
10–11 Facing R, stamp L in place (ct 1); hold (ct 2); stamp R in place (ct 1); hold (ct 2).
12–15 Beginning L, with 4 step-hop steps turn circle to R (CCW) rapidly.
16 Step-hop L, turning ¼ L to face ctr and repeat dance from beginning.

GLAMOČ

Glamoč (GLAH-moch) originated in the Glamočko Polje, or plains (valley) of Galmoč, in Bosnia. It is a "silent dance," meaning that there is no instrumental accompaniment and therefore it is considered silent ("gluho njemo"). There are many such "silent dances" performed throughout the Dinara Planina (Dinaric Alps) region, which includes parts of the republics of Croatia, Bosnia-Hercegovina, and Montenegro. Glamoč was introduced by Elsie Dunin, who learned the dance in Yugoslavia in 1957.

A caller improvises the sequence and may continue the dance as long as he wishes. After the call, each figure is continued until the next call, with the exception of the figure "Vrati," which is done once with each call during the "Hajde" figure. The basic "Hajde" (meaning "come along") is usually called between each of the other figures. The dance begins with a slow tempo which gradually increases. The *leader* dictates tempo.

Record: Being a "silent dance," there is no musical accompaniment.

Formation: Closed circle (kolo) of mixed M and W, hands joined and held forward at shoulder level with elbows bent. Bodies are held quite erect and feet are placed a shoulder width apart and parallel. The dance begins when absolute silence reigns. A leader *(kolovođa)* calls the figure changes.

Meter 3/4, 5/4, 6/4, 6/8, 8/4 Pattern

Meas *I. I (ee)* "And" which signals "begin"

Leader begins arm movement slowly to L and R, first straightening L arm to L while bending R arm across chest, then straightening R arm to R while bending L arm across chest. Head does not follow arm movement but faces toward ctr of cir. Next call is usually made after leader is satisfied that all dancers are ready and as arms are moving to the R.

(6/4) *II. Kreni Kolo* (KREH-nee KOH-loh): "Turn the Circle"

Arms stay at shoulder level and during the two walk steps R arm is straightened to the R and L arm is bent across the chest. Arms then move in opposition during pivots.

1 Facing and moving to the L, step L.
2 Step R.
3–4 Step L, pivoting to face diag R (R stays in place while wt is maintained on L).
5–6 Shift wt onto R, pivoting to face to the L (L stays in place while wt is maintained on R). Repeat action of cts 1–6 until next figure is called.

(3/4) *III. Hajde* (HAEE-deh): "Come Along" (basic step)

Joined hands held down in "V" pos.

1	Facing and moving to the L, step L.
&	Step R.
2	Step L.
&	Hop on L, swinging R up in front.
3	Step R.
&	Hop on R, swinging L leg up in front.

If tempo becomes faster, leave out hops. Remember, the caller dictates tempo.

Repeat action of cts 1–3 until next figure is called.

(3/4) *IV. Jedan U Kolo* (YEH-dahn oo KOH-loh): "One in the Circle"

Joined hands held down in "V" pos.

1	Facing and moving to the L, step L.
&	Step R.
2	Step L.
&	Face twd ctr.
3	Stamp R twd ctr with bent knee taking wt, arms slightly fwd.
&	Hold pos.

Repeat action of cts 1–3 until next figure is called.

(5/4) *V. Dva U Kolo* (DVAH oo KOH-loh): "Two in the Circle"

Joined hands held down in "V" pos.

1–3	Repeat action of cts 1–3, fig IV.
4	Shift wt back onto L raising R.
5	Stamp R twd ctr again with bent knee taking wt, arms fwd.

Repeat action of cts 1–5 until next figure is called.

(8/4) *VI. Tri U Kolo* (TREE oo KOH-loh) "Three in the Circle"

Joined hands held down in "V" pos.

Men:

1–3	Repeat action of cts 1–3, fig IV.
4–7	R knee only leans to L, R, L, R.
8	R ft cuts sharply back, displacing L as L comes up to cross behind R ankle.

Women:

1	Step L.
&	Close R to L pivoting to face ctr.
2–8	Heels move L, R, L, R, L, R, L (seven times) while toes stay in place. (The heels barely come off floor and knees bend slightly when heels come down.)

Repeat action of cts 1–8 until next figure is called.

(3/4) *VII. Vrati* (VRAH-tee) "Turn back"

This call is usually made on the first count of a basic "Hajde" figure. Joined hands held down in "V" pos.

1	Facing and moving to the L, step L.
&	Step R.
2	Step L.
&	Pivot ½ turn CW, releasing hands but keeping L hand in front.
3	Stamp R, taking wt and resuming handhold.
&	Hold pos.

Resume "Hajde" figure until next figure is called. Circle is now moving CCW and does so until another "Vrati" figure is called.

(6/8) *VIII. Puza* (POO-zah): "Crawl"

Joined hands held down in "V" pos.

1	Facing and moving to the L, step L.
2	Step R.
3 & 4	Step L R L in place.
5 & 6	Step R L R in place.

Repeat action of cts 1–8 until next figure is called.

(6/8) *IX. Sa Ruke* (SAH roo-keh): "With Hands"

1	Facing ctr, hands in original formation pos and shaking vigorously, step L in place.
2	Step R in place.
3 & 4	Step L R L in place.
5 & 6	Step R L R in place.

X. Stoj (stoee): "Stop"

1	All dancers freeze instantly into original formation pos.

Dance may continue if leader so desires or it may end there; leader may also put in several false stops. For instance, if a dancer errs in "Vrati," leader may advance to the poor performer and say something like, "Ti, ne valja" ("you, no good"), causing that dancer to leave the circle. Or another leader may begin the kolo again. Should a leader feel that the dance has continued for a sufficient amount of time, he can stop the kolo and call out, "Dosta" (DOH-stah) ("Enough") and the dance is ended. The above items represent only a portion of the figures that may be done.

SAVILA SE BELA LOZA

Savila Se Bela Loza (SAH-vee-lah seh BEH-lah LOH-zah), a dance from Šumadija, Serbia, means "A Grapevine Entwined with Itself." It was presented by Dick Crum and Dennis Boxell.

Record: Folkraft (45 rpm) 1496. This record should be slowed; Festival Records (7″ EP) KF-109

Formation: Open circle of dancers, hands joined and held low at sides.

Steps and Styling: Run

Schottische: Face ctr, step swd to R (ct 1), cross L in front (ct 2), step swd R (ct 1), hop R and lift L ft (ct 2). The step should be small and bouncy and executed with flexible knees. Moving to L, reverse ftwk.

Double hops: Face ctr, hop L (ct 1), small step to R on R (ct &), step L next to R (ct 2); small step to R on R (ct 1), hop on R (ct 2). Start next step with hop on R and move slightly to L.

Body is held erect, hands relaxed. The running step is easy and smooth.

Meter 2/4   Pattern

Meas

No Intro

I. Running

1-9   Beginning R, with 18 small running steps, move LOD (CCW).

10   Step R, hop R and turn to face RLOD (cts 1–2).

11-20   Repeat action of meas 1–10 (fig I); reverse direction and ftwk.

II. Double Hops or Schottische

1-12   Dancers may do either double hops or schottische (three times each way). Each dancer does not necessarily have to be dancing the same figure.

Variation of fig I:

1-10   Repeat action of fig I (meas 1–10). M on R end of line may start winding up by leading line in CCW direction until 10–15 persons form small (not tight) circle.

11-20   Person at L end of line repeats maneuver of fig I (meas 1–10) traveling CW to form similar circle. As person at L end of line executes this maneuver, line on R unwinds and straightens. Repeat action of meas 1–12 (fig II) (either double hop or schottische) facing ctr. Dancers on L end of line may not be unwound. On third repetition M leading line may choose not to "wind up." Person on L end of line *never* leads variation.

ŠETNJA

Šetnja (SHET-nyah), meaning "walking," was introduced by Dick Crum. He learned it from Miodrag Vuković, a folk dancer from Belgrade, in 1954 and also observed it at many gatherings in Šumadija, Serbia. In Šumadija, located in the central part of Serbia, Šetnja is a time-honored traditional dance with a definite place in the program. When a young man arrives at the field or churchyard where festivities are taking place, he seeks out one of the many gypsy musicians

who have come to town for the day, pays him a certain amount of money to play for him, and then proceeds to gather his friends one by one on his left side. The dance they ordinarily do is Šetnja. They meander about the whole dancing area gathering up people. When a large enough circle is formed, the dance is speeded up, ended, and U Šest Koraka generally follows.

Record: Festival Records (45 rpm) F-4816; Folkraft (45 rpm) 1490x45; Folk Dancer (45 rpm) MH-3029

Formation: Open circle. During slow (beginning) part of dance an "escort" hold is used as follows: Leader at R end of line holds vest with R hand and hooks L thumb in belt at L side. Other dancers join in, grasping or hooking on to R neighbor's bent L elbow, keeping own L elbow bent, and placing L fist on own hip or thumb in belt. When music speeds up and faster variant begins, dancers join hands down at sides.

Steps and Styling: Walk: This step is done with a gentle flex of knees on each beat of music.

Hop: In fig II this flex becomes a definite hop.

Keep upper part of body erect.

Meter 2/4   Pattern

Meas

No Intro

I. Walking

1   Facing R and moving to R (LOD), step on R (ct 1); step L (ct 2).

2   Continuing in LOD, step R (ct 1); step L (ct &); step R (ct 2); pause and turn to face ctr (ct &).

3   Moving bwd and away from ctr, step with L ft behind R heel (ct 1); step R behind L heel (ct 2).

4   Step bwd *very slightly* with L (ct 1); close R beside L (ct &); step L in LOD (ct 2); pause (ct &).

Repeat action of meas 1–4 until music accelerates.

II. Hopping (danced when music speeds up) When music accelerates, join hands and hold low at sides. Add hops to steps described above as follows:

1   Facing R and moving to R (LOD), step R (ct 1); hop R (ct &); step L (ct 2); hop L (ct &).

2   Continuing in LOD, step R (ct 1); step L (ct &); step R (ct 2); hop on R while turning to face ctr (ct &).

SUKAČICA

Sukačica (SOO-kah-chee-tsah), a Croatian couple dance from the Prigorje area north of Zagreb, was learned from the Croatian Folk Ensemble LADO by Rubi Vučeta. Sukačica refers to a girl from the Prigorje area and was danced at weddings.

Record: "Sukačko Kolo," Festival Records (45 rpm) FM-4002B; Mediterranean (45 rpm) 4002B

Formation: Couples facing in any direction, side by side, with W to M R, inside hands joined and held down in "V" pos, outside hands flat on hips with fingers fwd and thumb back. Ftwk is same for M and W unless otherwise noted.

Meter 2/4   Pattern

Meas   Intro: 8 meas

I. Away-Together

Note: Step is written for M; W do opp ftwk.

1   Turning away from each other, step on L with flex of knee and, swinging joined hands fwd (ct 1), bounce on both feet (ct 2), bounce on both feet, taking wt on L (ct &).

2   Repeat action of meas 1 with opp ftwk, swinging joined hands bwd on ct 1.

3–12   Repeat action of meas 1–2 five more times. M take wt on L and ct & of final meas 12 in preparation for fig II.

II. Turns

Note: The hop in this fig should be done in place as a pivot with the R ft to provide momentum for turning.

Formation is shoulder-waist pos, with partners facing squarely twd each other, knees bent. There is almost no up and down motion during turning.

1   Turning CW, step on R across in front of L, with toe angled to R (ct 1). Lift on R (modified hop) (ct 2). Step swd on L around ptr (ct &).

2–16   Repeat action of meas 1 fifteen more times.

III. Side-to-Side

Note: Flex and stiffen knees with each step for a shaking (drmeš) effect.

Formation is side by side, with W to M R, inside hands joined, both hands of each ptr held up and slightly fwd at shoulder height in "W" pos. Hands move L and R with ftwk with "windshield wiper" action. Take no wt on last ct.

1   Step swd L to L (ct 1). Close and take wt on R next to L (ct 2).

2–3   Repeat action of meas 1 two more times, with wt remaining on L on ct 2 of meas 3.

4–6   Repeat action of meas 1–3 with opp ftwk to R.

7–12   Repeat action of meas 1–6.

IV. Turns

1–16   Repeat action of fig II.
Repeat entire dance from beginning.

TINO MORI

Tino Mori (TEE-noh MOH-ree), a dance from Macedonia, was introduced by Atanas Kolarovski. Tino is a girl's name.

Record: Folkraft (45 rpm) 1557x45; Festival Records (7″ EP) KF-109.

Formation: Broken circle moving in LOD, leader at R end. Hands joined about shldr height and slightly fwd. Face diag R of LOD.

Rhythm and Styling: Since 3 beats can be felt in each meas, each meas will be counted in three. Mood of dance is flowing, smooth, and lyrical.

Meter 7/8, 3/8, 2/8   Pattern

Meas

Intro

1–16   No action is necessary, but if leader wishes he may walk the line in LOD, taking 2 steps to a meas (cts 1, 2–3). Joined hands are down during walking. On meas 16 leader pauses and joined hands are raised into pos.

I. Long Sequence

1   Step fwd on R in LOD (ct 1); lift L leg, knee slightly bent, across in front of R while raising and lowering R heel (cts 2–3).

2   Step fwd on L in LOD (ct 1); quickly close R to L (ct ah); step fwd on L in LOD (cts 2–3). These steps feel like a two-step.

3   Repeat action of meas 1.

4   Step fwd on L in LOD (ct 1); while raising and lowering L heel, turn to face slightly L of ctr, R ft next to L ankle (cts 2–3). Body is bent slightly fwd.

5   Continuing in LOD, step bwd R (ct 1), step bwd L (cts 2–3).

6   Turning to face slightly R in LOD, step fwd R (ct 1); while raising and lowering R heel, lift L leg, slightly bent, across in front of R (cts 2–3).

7   Step on L in LOD (ct 1); quickly close R to L (ct ah); turning to face ctr, step on L (cts 2–3). Do not make a sharp turn.

8   Facing ctr, step fwd R in front of L, bending R knee (ct 1); step back onto L (cts 2–3).

9   Step bwd onto R (ct 1); while raising and lowering R heel, lift L leg, slightly bent, across in front of R (cts 2–3).

10   Repeat action of meas 7 twd ctr, keeping steps small.

11–12   Repeat action of meas 8–9.
13   Step swd L on L, keeping R ft in place (ct 1); bend and straighten L knee slightly (cts 2–3). Do not bend from side to side; keep body erect with wt over supporting ft.
14   Shift wt onto R ft, leaving L in place (ct 1); bend and straighten R knee slightly (cts 2–3).
15   Repeat action of meas 14, but shift wt onto L ft.
16   Shift wt onto R ft, leaving L in place (ct 1); shift wt onto L ft, leaving R in place (cts 2–3).
17–32   Repeat action of meas 1–16 (long sequence).

II. Short Sequence

1–11   Repeat action of fig I, meas 1–11 (long sequence).
12   Step bwd on R (ct 1); step L beside R (cts 2–3).
        Repeat dance as written (2 long sequences and 1 short sequence) and finish with 1 long sequence. At end of dance, on retard of music, dancers may pose by placing R toe (heel up) across in front of L toe.

U ŠEST

U Šest (oo SHEST) is short for U Šest Koraka, meaning "in six steps." According to Dick Crum, noted Balkan dance researcher, the Serbian definition of a step *(korak)* is "a shift of wt onto a given foot *plus* whatever follow-up movement of the other foot." The step pattern described here as "sedam," along with its accompanying "syncopated threes," is the basis for the naming of this dance type. U Šest is the single most popular kolo in Serbia.

Record: Nama 1 (LP) 1001; Nama 2 (LP) 1002; Monitor (LP) MFS-702; Folkraft (45 rpm) 1497; Folkraft (45 rpm) 1547; or any other U Šest music.

Formation: Open cir or line of mixed M and W with leader at R end, hands joined and held down in "V" pos, or linked arm in arm in "escort" pos, or (especially when danced only by M) on neighbors' shldrs in "T" pos. End dancers may place free hand at small of back, hold lapel of vest or coat, or even put it in a trouser pocket.

Steps and Styling: Styling varies considerably from dancer to dancer—from the easy, relaxed, soft rolling walk of the elderly or the tired to the highly energetic leaping and bouncing of the young or the "hotshots." In Serbia this dance is freely improvised by each dancer within the symmetrical pattern of 4 meas to the R and 4 meas to the L, using his arms as flexible shock absorbers. The selected steps described may therefore be danced in any order and for any number of repetitions, depending upon the whim of each dancer. For ease in teaching, it may be helpful to the dancers to first dance each figure in the order given, both to the R and to the L, two times before going on to the next, adding the combinations given later as proficiency is gained. Syncopated threes: Turning to face slightly L, step slightly swd R with the heel slightly turned out and bending knee slightly (ct 1), hold (ct &), step L next to R (ct 2), step R next to L (ct &). Repeat in next meas, using opp ftwk. (*Note:* Syncopated threes may also be danced with bounces on cts 2, &.)

Meter 2/4   Pattern

Meas

I. Kokonješte (or Hajde!)

1   Facing slightly and moving R, step R (ct 1), bend R knee slightly (ct &), step L across in front of R (ct 2), bend knee slightly (ct &).
2   Turning to face slightly L of ctr, step slightly swd R with heel slightly turned out (ct 1), bend knee slightly (ct &), touch L heel next to R instep (ct 2), bend knee slightly (ct &).
3   Repeat action of meas 2 to L with opp ftwk.
4   Repeat action of meas 2.
5–8   For repeat of fig, dance kokonješte to L with opp ftwk.

II. Čuješ

1   Facing slightly and moving R, step R, bending knee slightly (ct 1), low hop R (ct 2), step L across in front of R (ct &).
2–4   Dance 3 syncopated threes in place.
5–8   For repeat of fig, dance čuješ to L with opp ftwk.

III. Četiri

1   Step swd R (ct 1), step L across in back of R (ct &), step swd R (ct 2), step L across in back of R (ct &).
2–4   Dance 3 syncopated threes in place.
5–8   For repeat of fig, dance četiri to L with opp ftwk.

IV. Tri Skoči

1   Step swd R, bending knee slightly and at same time bringing L heel to R instep (ct 1), hop R (ct 2), step L across in back of R (ct &).
2–3   Repeat action of meas 1 two more times.
4   Dance 1 syncopated three in place.
5–8   For repeat of fig, dance tri skoči to L with opp ftwk.

V. Sedam (U Šest!)

1   Step swd R (ct 1), step L across in back of R (ct &), step swd R (ct 2), step L across in back of R (ct &).

2   Step swd R (ct 1), step L across in back of R (ct &), step swd R, bending knee slightly (ct 2), hold (ct &).

3–4   Dance 2 syncopated threes, beg L.

5–8   For repeat of fig, dance sedam to L with opp ftwk.

There are many other steps available to the native dancer. Since this is still a "living" dance form, its variations are constantly evolving and changing. For instance, the following combinations may be made from the above steps to further enhance the dance:

čuješ-skoči-čuješ plus 1 syncopated three
skoči-čuješ-skoči plus 1 syncopated three
četiri-škoci-škoči plus 1 syncopated three
skoči-skoči-četiri plus 1 syncopated three

Lexicon of Folk Dance Definitions

A folk dancer's vocabulary includes words and symbols having special meanings—terms, abbreviations, steps, formations, and positions. The lexicon provides definitions for a selected group of terms and symbols used throughout this book. Specialized styling instructions and steps used only in specific dances are described in the notes accompanying each dance description.

For the sake of convenience, certain categories of information have been grouped together in the Lexicon under a single heading. These include: Abbreviations; Dance Formations (illustrated); and Social Dance Positions. For the sake of conciseness, appropriate abbreviations have also been used in the definitions to describe dance steps, patterns, and movements.

Abbreviations

&	and (used only for counts)
adj	adjacent
B	in back of (RXB, right foot crosses in back of left foot)
beg	begin, begins, beginning
bk	back
bkwd, bwd	backward
CCW	counterclockwise
cir	circle
COH	center of hall
cont	continue
cpl(s)	couple(s)
ct(s)	count(s) or beat(s) of a measure of music
ctr	center of hall, circle, or line
CW	clockwise
diag	diagonally
dir	direction
dn, dnwd	down, downward
F	in front of (LXF, left foot crosses in front of right)
fig(s)	dance figure(s)
ft	foot, feet
ftwk	footwork
fwd	forward
H	hand
hold	keep foot in place
ht, hgt	height
in	toward center of hall (COH)
L	left (side, direction, foot, arm, hand)

LOD	line of dance direction (CCW)
L^R	either L or R
M	man('s), men('s)
meas	measure of music
no. (#)	number
O	symbol for woman in a formation
opp	opposite
orig	original
out	away from center of hall (COH)
PDB	pas de basque
pl	place
pos	position
pt	point (toe down or up)
ptr(s)	partner(s)
Q	quick
R	right (side, direction, foot, arm, hand)
R^L	either R or L
RLOD	reverse line of dance direction (CW)
S	slow
sdwd, swd	sideward
shldr	shoulder
□	symbol for man in a formation
step	combination of dance movements usually designated by a specific name such as schottische step (step-step-step-hop); also single step.
tch	touch (usually applies to one toe, heel, or foot)
tn	turn
tog	together
twd	toward
uh, ah	a "pick up" beat or a short note before the first beat of a measure
W	woman('s), women('s)
wall	away from center of hall (COH)
wt	weight
X	cross (usually one ft in front or behind the other)
×	symbol for man in a formation
Yem	Yemenite

A

above Next couple(s) up the set from the actives.

accent Emphasis of music beat or dance step.

acknowledge Side-by-side ptrs facing same dir, W to R of M, inside hands joined, both step diag bwd on outside ft away from ptr (ct 1), tch toe of inside ft diag fwd (ct 2), step fwd to orig pos on inside ft (ct 3), pt outside ft diag fwd (ct 4).

active dancers   Those involved at the moment in performing action of dance.

actives   Dancers initiating a contra movement.

alamo style   A circle formation with alternate dancers facing opp dir, hands joined, palm to palm, fingers pointing up with elbows bent.

all around left-hand lady/see saw taw   Corners turn CW around each other with R shoulders adjacent/ then partners turn CCW around each other with L shoulders adjacent.

allemande left, right

1. *square dance*   A L forearm CCW swing with square dance corner, ending facing opp from orig dir with backs to each other. R forearm CW swing as above.

2. *contra*   A L (CCW) or R (CW) hand turn between two dancers, sometimes using a pigeon wing pos.

allemande thar   From a square formation, ptrs turn to face each other, R hand pull by with ptrs, join L forearms with next dancer and turn CCW to pos with M backing in a R-hand star and W dancing fwd on the outside.

alone   Used in a contra prompt to direct single dancer action.

alternate duple   A contra formation with actives (1st, 3rd, 5th, etc.) crossed over.

andalgo (AHN-dahl-goh)   See *csárdás.*

arch   Two people raise indicated joined hands (R, L, both) into an arch slightly higher than their heads.

arch to the head   Couples facing head of longways set form an arch.

arm swing (turn)   Two dancers with R^L forearms (or hands) joined turn CW^{CCW} around each other.

arming   See *elbow hook position.*

around one, two, three   Active dancer passes beside, behind, and to the other side of one, two, or three stationary dancers as directed.

astride position   Feet spread apart sdwd, legs straight.

atole (ah-TOH-lay)   See *borracho.*

away and together   Two dancers move apart and back together.

B

back hold position   Ptrs face opp dir with R sides adj, R arms extended behind each other's backs, L arms behind own backs, L hands joined with ptrs R. See photo.

back with the left   Reverse dir faced by turning around from a R-hand star to a L-hand star.

balance   There are three common types of balance steps:

1. *square dance balance*   Step fwd L^R (ct 1), touch

Back hold position

R^L next to L^R (ct 2), step bwd R^L (ct 3), touch L^R next to R^L (ct 4).

2. *two-step balance*   Step L^R (ct 1), step R^L beside L^R, rising on balls of both ft (ct &), lower heels (ct 2, &).

3. *waltz balance*   Same as two-step balance (cts 1, 2, 3).

(See also *Yemenite step.*)

ball change   Step R^L (ct 1), step on ball of L^R next to R^L (ct &), step R^L in place (ct 2).

ballroom dance   See *social dance.*

banjo position   See *social dance positions.*

barn dance step   See *schottische.*

barrel hold position   Side-by-side dancers face same dir, join hands with adj dancers (R-hand palm up

Barrel hold position

under L palm down), hands extended fwd at shoulder height. See photo.

basket position Side-by-side dancers (any number) face same dir.

1. *front basket* Arms extended to each side (waist high) and hands clasped in front of adjacent dancers with next person beyond them, R hands to L hands, R arms crossing under L arms if dance moves predominantly to R, L hands cross under if to L. See photo.

Front basket

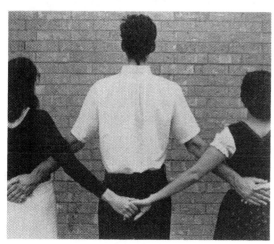

Back basket

2. *back basket* Same position except arms crossed in back of adjacent dancers. See photo.

below The next couple(s) down a longways set from the actives.

belt hold position Side-by-side dancers facing same dir hook fingers (up to base of thumb, over top of belt and downward) in adjacent dancer's belt at front of hip, usually with R arms behind L. See photo.

Belt hold position

bend Same as flex.

bend the line Dancers in a line separate (break) the line into two equal lines, then dance into pos with new lines facing.

bleking step (BLEH-king) Danced in place by either two people facing each other, with both hands joined in uncrossed pos, or by any number of people with hands joined in a circle. All begin with same ft. With a low leap onto R^L extend L^R heel fwd, touching floor (or ft flat on floor) (ct 1), with a low leap reverse pos of ft (ct 2).

bokazo (BOH-kah-zoh) (also called *Hungarian breakstep*) The following are just two among many variations of this step.

1. Hop L^R, pointing R^L toe fwd, heel slightly turned in (ct 1); hop L^R, placing R^L beside L^R with heels of both ft turned out (ct &); bring heels together with sharp clicking movement (ct 2).

2. M: With wt on balls of both ft, click heels together three times (cts 1, &, 2), lower heels to floor (ct &). W: With wt on ball of R^L, hop R^L, pointing L^R toe fwd touching floor (ct 1); leap L^R in place, pointing R^L toe fwd touching floor (ct &); bring R^L to L^R and click heels together (ct 2); hold on balls of both ft (ct &).

borracho (boh-RRAH-choh) Step diag fwd R^L with accent R^L shoulder leading (ct 1), step L^R on ball of ft behind R^L (ct 2), step fwd R^L (ct 3).

bottom Foot of a contra set.

bounce Quickly raise and lower one or both heels from the floor (ct 1). Usually accompanied by a slight knee bend. See *hop*.

bow (also called *honor*) To bend slightly at waist toward person indicated.

bow and curtsy Danced with ptrs making eye contact. M bow from waist, back straight, arms held easily near body. W step R^L (small step) fwd or swd, touch toe of L^R in back of R^L, and bend both knees; back straight; may flare skirt at sides. Both return to standing pos.

box step See *two-step, waltz.*

box the gnat/swat the flea M and W facing each other make an arch with R hands joined; W backs under arch as M dances past her back and they exchange places/same action using L hands.

break-step (also called *Hungarian break-step*). See *bokazo.*

broken circle Same as open circle. See DANCE FORMATIONS *(illustrated).*

brush With wt on one ft, lightly whisk ball or toe of other ft across floor in dir indicated.

butterfly position Partners face each other, extend arms sdwd about shoulder level, palms facing fwd and touching. See photo.

Butterfly position

buzz step (also called *vrtanje*) There are two common types of buzz steps:
1. *Two dancers* in side-by-side pos—sidecar, banjo, or shldr-waist. With outside of adjacent ft near each other and shldrs leaning away from ptr, step fwd

R^L, bending knee and turning toe to R^L (ct 1), step on ball of L^R beside and slightly fwd of R^L (ct &). Repeat while swinging each other around.
2. *Circle* of dancers with hands joined. Step R^L across in front of L^R, bending knees (ct 1), step swd L^R on ball of ft (ct &).

C

California twirl (also called *frontier whirl*) Side-by-side partners facing same dir (W to R of M) join inside hands and make an arch, face toward each other, walk fwd (W tn CCW under arch, M tn CW in back of W) to exchange places and face opposite from orig dir (W to R of M).

caller The person who calls out the movements to be danced in a square dance.

camel step
1. Step fwd R^L, bending knee (ct 1), rise onto balls of both ft with L^R remaining in place, straightening knees (ct &), transfer wt to L^R, keeping knees straight and bending fwd at hips with a straight back (ct 2), transfer wt fwd over R^L, bending knees (ct 3), step fwd L^R, straightening knees and bringing body to an erect pos (ct 4).
2. Step fwd R^L, bending knee (ct 1), step on ball of L^R beside R^L (ct 2), step R^L, leading with bent knee (ct 3), rise onto ball of R^L (ct 4).

canter Step R^L (ct 1), hold (ct 2), quickly close L^R to R^L (ct 3).

cast Dancers turn outward from set or partner and move to designated place.
1. *cast down* Move down set number of places indicated.
2. *cast off* Move down set one place.
3. *cast through* Pass through with dancers across set.
4. *cast up* Move up set one or more places.

catch step See *two-step.*

četiri (CHEH-tihree) (also called *moravac*) Step swd R^L (ct 1), step L^R across in back of R^L (ct &), step swd R^L (ct 2), step L^R across in back of R^L (ct &).

change hands Change grasp from one hand to other hand.

change step See *two-step.*

chase step See *chassé.*

chassé (shah-SAY) Step swd L^R (ct 1), hold (ct &, 2), quickly close R^L to L^R (ct &).

cherkassiya See *tcherkessia.*

chiapanecas (cheeah-pah-NAY-kahs)
Meas 1: Step fwd L^R (ct 1), hop L^R (ct 2), step R^L in front of L^R (ct 3).
Meas 2: Step L^R in place (ct 1), hop L^R (ct 2), step R^L in back of L^R (ct 3).
Meas 3: Step L^R in place (ct 1), hop L^R (ct 2), step R^L in front of L^R (ct 3).

Meas 4: Run L^R, R^L, L^R (cts 1, 2, 3) in dir indicated.

chotis (CHOH-tis) Same as running *schottische*.

chug An abrupt movement on one or both ft in dir indicated; similar to hop, but without raising supporting ft from floor.

cifra (SEEF-rah) There are several variations of cifra steps, of which this is just one: Leap lightly onto ball of R^L (ct 1), step on ball of L^R beside R^L (ct &), step on ball of R^L beside L^R (ct 2). See *pas de basque*.

circassia See *tcherkessia*.

circle A formation with dancers in a ring. See DANCE FORMATIONS (*illustrated*).

circle (break) to a line Dancers, with hands joined in a circle, break at L side of lead dancer ("lead gent" in square dancing) and straighten circle into a line.

circle L, R Dancers in a closed or open (broken) circle move CW or CCW, with hands positioned as indicated. Square dancers join hands at waist level, M palm up, W palm down.

clasp To grasp.

click step (also called *hołubiec*) Hop L^R, raising R^L swd from floor, usually with straight knee; while both ft are off floor, strike heels or edges of ft together (ct 1).

clog step (also called *shuffle*) Here is one among several combinations: Brush R^L fwd, tapping toe as it is extended (ct 1), tap toe in same place as R^L begins to return bwd (ct &), step R^L beside or fwd of L^R (ct 2).

close After a preceding step L^R has separated the ft, step R^L with free ft next to L^R as indicated, taking wt.

closed circle A complete, unbroken circle.

closed position See *social dance positions*.

coffee grinder See *prysiadka*.

column A line of dancers facing same dir, one behind the other.

common step combinations
1. hop-step, hop-step-step, hop-step-step-step.
2. step-bend.
3. step-brush, step-brush-hop.
4. step-close.
5. step-hop, step-hop-step, step-step-hop, step-step-step-hop.
6. step-kick.
7. step-lift.
8. step-stamp, step-stamp-stamp.
9. step-swing.
10. step-touch.

contra A dance performed by two lines or columns of dancers.

contra corners Usually inactive dancers diag R and diag L across a longways set from active dancer(s).

contra set Four or more couples in a double column, or two files, W to R of M. See *social dance positions*.

corner
1. The person adjacent to a dancer on the side opposite from the dancer's partner.
2. Usually the one below for M in longways alternate formations. W's corner is above.

corté (kor-TAY) See *dip*.

counterpart Corresponding action (step, hand movement) with opp ft or hand.

country dance step A smooth walking (or shuffling) step danced with body relaxed.

couple A M and a W dancing as ptrs.

couple star position See *star positions*.

couple wheel around A side-by-side couple facing same dir reverses dir by making CCW spot turn as a unit.

courtesy position (also called *promenade position* and *skaters position*) Side-by-side ptrs face same dir, W to R of M, W R hand at side waist, palm bwd, or R hand flaring skirt at side. M L hand held palm up at waist level and R arm around back of W, hand on her waist or joined with her hand (if held at waist). W L hand extended in front of M to rest in M L palm down. See photo.

Courtesy position

courtesy turn A couple in courtesy pos makes a CCW turn as a unit.

cross Change to other side of ptr, W usually passing in front of M.

cross back hold position Ptrs face same dir side by side, with M R arm and W L arm crossed in bk and around each other's waists, M R hand in W R (held palm out) on her hip, W L in M L (palm out) on his hip. See photo.

Cross back hold position

cross over   Change to opposite line in a set.

cross over at head, foot
1. A previously inactive couple exchanges places at head of set to become active.
2. A previously active couple exchanges places at foot of set to become inactive.

cross step turn   Step R^L across in front of and next to L^R, with outsides of ft together (ct 1), pivot on balls of both ft, turning CCW^{CW} (ct 2), lower both heels (ct 3).

cross trail through (thru)   Two facing couples pass through, then the individuals in each couple exchange places, the one on the R crossing in front.

csárdás (CHAR-dahsh)   There are two basic csárdás steps:
1. *ingo* (EEN-goh) or *single csárdás:* Step swd R^L (ct 1), touch L^R beside R^L (ct 2).
2. *andalgo* (AHN-dahl-goh) or *double csárdás:* Step swd R^L (ct 1), close L^R to R^L (ct &), step swd R^L (ct 2), touch L^R beside R^L (ct &).
Vibrating (quivering or slight flexing) knee action accompanies each step and there is a slight sway in dir of movement. When knees are straightened on ct, it is called "up-beat" csárdás; when knees are bent on ct, it is known as "down-beat" csárdás.

cue(s)   Word(s) spoken in conjunction with music to direct dancer in patterns to be performed.

čujuš (CHOO-yesh)   Step swd R^L (ct 1), hold (ct &), hop R^L (ct 2), step L^R slightly across in front of R^L (ct &).

curtsy   See *bow and curtsy.*

cut step   A quick displacement of one ft by the other. Step on R^L (ct 1), quickly bring L^R to R^L, displacing it (ct 2).

czardas   See *csárdás.*

Czechoslovakian polka   See *polka.*

D

dal step (DAHL)   Step fwd L^R (ct 1), slightly bend supporting L^R knee (ct 2). Swing extended R^L leg across in front of L^R, straightening supporting leg (ct 3).

dance formation(s)   Specific arrangement of dancers on the floor in relation to each other and to the walls and center of the dance area.

DANCE FORMATIONS (*illustrated*)

dance position(s)   Placement and arrangement of body parts for a particular step or dance, and in relation to partner(s), if any.

DANCE POSITIONS (*illustrated*)   See individual dance positions.

dead at the head   A temporarily inactive couple facing out at the head of a contra set.

debka jump (DEB-kah)   Spring into the air and land with ft together, toes pointing to L^R, hips twisted to L^R (ct 1); repeat, facing ctr or to R^L, as indicated. May also be danced on one ft.

dip (also called *corté*)   Step bwd (fwd) L^R, taking full wt with knee bent (ct 1). Other leg remains extended at knee and ankle, forming straight line from hip, toe remaining in contact with floor.

dive through   Two couples (W to R of M) with inside hands joined face each other. Active couple goes under as arch made by other couple moves over them. In square dancing, couple facing out automatically does a *California twirl,* which leaves both couples facing in same direction, one behind the other.

dive to the foot   Couples facing foot of a longways set duck under arch formed by couples arching to head.

do sa do (doh sah DOH)   Facing dancers dance fwd diag L and in one continuous movement loop completely around each other, passing R shoulders, back to back, L shoulders, ending in original position.

double circle   One circle within another. See DANCE FORMATIONS (*illustrated*).

double progression   Two progressions down or up.

double steps   Four light, springy steps.

down   Toward foot of a longways set.

Legend: ▶ Woman, ▶ Man, ●—● Hands Joined,

* Caller or Prompter

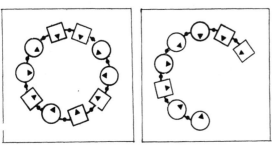

Single circle, all facing center *Broken circle*

Single circle, all facing LOD (CCW)

Partners in single circle, facing center, W to M R

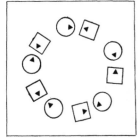
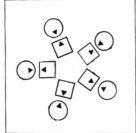
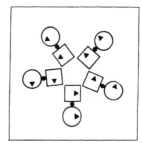
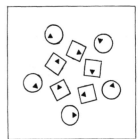

Single circle, partners facing, M facing LOD (CCW), W facing RLOD (CW)

Double circle, partners facing, M back to center

Double circle, couples facing LOD (CCW), W on outside

Double circle, M facing RLOD (CW), W facing LOD (CCW)

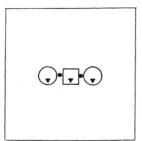

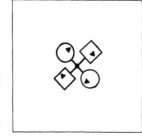

Line, all side by side, facing same direction

Set of three in a line, side by side

Set of three in a circle

Right-hand star

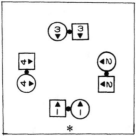
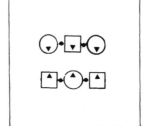
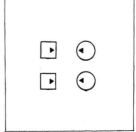

Sicilian circle, sets of two couples, couples facing

Set of four couples, square, quadrille, with caller

Sets of three, facing

Set of two couples, partners facing

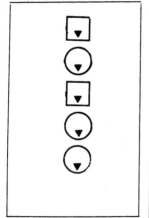

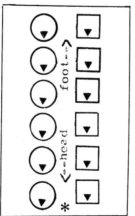

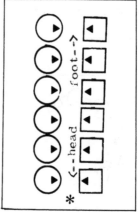

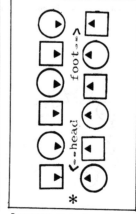

Single column or file

*Longways or contra set,
couples facing head
(prompter)*

*Longways or contra set,
partners facing*

*Longways or contra set,
actives (cpls 1, 3, 5) crossed
over*

down in twos, threes, fours Lines of 2, 3, or 4 move toward foot of a longways set.

down the inside Dancers move down set between lines.

down the outside Dancers move down set outside lines.

draw

1. *2/4 time* After a preceding step L^R (ct 1), bring R^L along floor, closing it to L^R (ct 2).

2. *3/4 time* After a preceding step L^R (ct 1), bring R^L slowly twd R^L (ct 2), close R^L to L^R (ct 3).

drmeš (DER-mesh) Here is just one among many drmeš step variations:

Meas 1: Step R^L (ct 1), hop R^L (ct &), step L^R (ct 2), hop L^R (ct &).

Meas 2: Step R^L (ct 1), step L^R (ct &), step R^L (ct 2), hop R^L (ct &).

Drmeš steps are danced with ft close to floor, knees relaxed, with a vibration or shaking of entire body.

E

elbow hook position (also called *arming*)

1. Ptrs face opp dir, hook bent R or L elbows dnwd.

2. Side-by-side dancers face same dir, hook elbows with adjacent dancers. See photo.

elbow swing Dancers hook bent R^L elbows and turn CW^{CCW} around each other.

English running step A light, bouncy (but dignified) half-walking, half-running step.

escort position

1. *couple* Side by side and facing same dir. W to R of M. M holding R arm near body, with elbow bent at R angle. W hooks L hand through M bent elbow.

Elbow hook (arming) position

2. *line* Side-by-side dancers facing same dir; dancers bend L elbow at R angle, with L hand on own hip, hook R hand through adjacent elbow, resting hand on forearm. See photo.

espunti (ehs-POON-tee) Start with ft together, toes turned out. Pivoting on ball of R^L and heel of L, move R^L heel swd to R^L as L^R toe is pointed inward toward R^L (ct 1); lower R^L heel, taking wt on it and ball of L^R; pivoting on ball of L^R and heel of R^L, move L^R heel swd R and toe of R^L swd R, lowering heel to end in original pos (cts 2, 3).

ethnic dance A dance of a specific national group distinguished by particular customs, physical characteristics, or language.

Escort position

F

face to face/back to back Side-by-side ptrs, with inside hands joined, turn diag in to face twd each other; then, still holding hands, turn diag away with backs twd each other. Steps vary as described.

farandole (FAR-uhn-dohl) Usually a non-ptr line or circle of dancers winding and unwinding in spiral or serpentine patterns.

figures Recognizable sequences of step patterns, positions, and group movements forming patterns common to many dances.

flex knee (also called *plié*) A bending of knee, usually followed by straightening of knee.

fling See *kick*.

folk dance A dance originating among the common people of a district or country.

folk dance camp Any folk dance event spanning more than one day may be called a camp, whether it is held in a hotel, on a college campus, or at a campground.

foot of set The place in contra set farthest from head.

forearm grasp With R to R or L to L, two dancers lightly grasp forearms.

formation(s) See DANCE FORMATIONS *(illustrated)*.

forward and back Dance fwd and back to place.

four-hand star position See *star position*.

free foot, leg, hand, arm The ft or leg without wt or being otherwise involved; the hand or arm not joined or otherwise involved.

frontier whirl See *California twirl*.

full turn To turn completely around.

G

gallop (galop) A small leap followed by a quicker closing step in uneven rhythm. The knees are lifted higher than in a slide. The same ft always leads in a series of gallops.

glide A smooth walking step done by lightly sliding ball of advancing ft along floor.

grand chain See *grand right and left*.

grand right and left Partners (W to R of M if couples) in a square or circle formation tn to face each other, join R hands as if shaking hands, pull by R shoulder to R shoulder, release hands, join L hands with next person met, pull by L shoulder to L shoulder and release hands. Repeat as directed.

grand square A precise 32-count routine danced by four cpls in square formation. The routine is divided into 4-step sequences. In advance, side (head) cpls turn to face partners.

Sequences:

1 *Head cpls* walk fwd 4 steps to ctr of square, turning on 4th step to face ptr; at same time *side cpls* back away from each other 4 steps twd outside corners of square, turning on 4th step to face original opposites (ct 1, 2, 3, turn).

2 *Head cpls* back up 4 steps (side by side with opposites), turning on 4th step to become side cpls in side pos; at same time original *side cpls* walk 4 steps fwd to meet in head pos and turn to face ctr to become *head cpls* (ct 5, 6, 7, turn).

3,4 New *head cpls* and new *side cpls* repeat sequences 1 and 2, except that they stop in place without turning on ct 16 (ct 9, 10, 11, turn) (ct 13, 14, 15, don't turn).

5–8 *Heads* and *sides* reverse direction traveled in sequences 1–4 (ct 17, 18, 19, turn) (ct 21, 22, 23, turn) (ct 25, 26, 27, turn) (ct 29, 30, 31, 32).

grapevine (also called *mayim step, vine*) A series of swd steps with a slight turning of body as legs are crossed alternately in back and in front. May start first across in back, across in front, or to side, depending on particular dance description. The following is a common sequence: Step swd L^R (ct 1), step R^L across in back of L^R (ct 2), step swd L^R (ct 3), step R^L across in front of L^R (ct 4).

H

hajde (**'ajde**) (AY-deh) Any number of step patterns are given this catchall term meaning "let's go." For a popular one, see *kokonješte*.

half sashay Partners exchange places sdwd, W passing in front; or, with inside hands joined, W turns to face partner, they join free hands, release the others, and W opens to place at M L side (rollaway).

hambo polska (HAHM-boh POHL-skah) (also called *hambo turn*) A full CW turn in one 3-beat meas danced by cpls in shoulder-waist or polska pos. Steps are similar for M and W except they are done at different times, something like singing a round. M steps (or stamps, taking wt) R with knee bent as W steps L with knee bent (ct 1), M steps L as W touches R toe next to L heel (ct 2), M touches R next to L as W steps R (ct 3).

hambo turn See *hambo polska*.

harmonica step Step L^R across in front of R^L (ct 1), step R^L bwd (ct &), step fwd L^R (ct 2), hop L^R (ct &).

head of hall Designated end of dance area, usually one where caller, prompter, or music is located.

head of set The end of a longways set nearest prompter, caller, or music.

heads Couples 1 and 3 in square dancing.

heel and toe step Touch R^L heel diag fwd, touch R^L toe next to or in front of L^R.

heel cifra (TSEE-frah) See *pas de basque*.

heel pas de basque See *pas de basque*.

heel squat See *prysiadka*.

heel touch With wt on R^L, knee slightly bent, touch heel of L^R swd or fwd with toe pointed up.

hey A figure of eight for three people. Described in detail for individual dances.

Highland fling step See *Highland schottische step*.

Highland schottische step

Meas 1: Hop L^R, extending R^L swd, touching pointed toe to floor (ct 1); hop L^R, raising R^L in back of L^R and pressing side of pointed ft to back of calf (ct 2); hop L^R, extending R^L swd, touching pointed toe to floor (ct 3); hop L^R, raising pointed R^R ft in front of L^R leg, with bent knee turned out (ct 4).

Meas 2: Dance one strathspey setting step R^R. See *strathspey setting step*.

hold To clasp or grasp with hand(s), as indicated.

hołubiec (hoh-WOO-byets) See *click step*.

home position Original position.

honor See *bow*.

hop There are two types of hopping steps:

1. *Spring from floor* on one ft and land *on same ft.*

2. *Low hop (lift, bounce)* With wt on one ft, briefly raise and lower heel of same ft without taking ball of ft from floor. Often referred to simply as "hop" and sometimes as "lift" or "bounce." Amount of energy expended determines actual difference, depending on dance or dancer's style.

hopsa (HOHP-sah) There are three common types of hopsa steps:

1. *hopsa* A turning step danced by cpls in closed or shoulder-waist pos. Spring briefly onto R^L (ct uh), close L^R to R^L (ct 1), step R^L, bending knee slightly (ct 2).

2. *single Tyrolean hopsa* Step L^R (ct 1), swing R^L across in front of L^R (ct 2).

3. *double Tyrolean hopsa* A fwd step danced by ptrs side by side, W to M R, inside hands joined. Opp ftwk. Spring briefly onto R^L (ct uh), step fwd L^R, swinging joined hands fwd and turning slightly away from ptr (ct 1), step fwd R^L, swinging joined hands bwd and turning slightly toward ptr (ct 2).

hora step The step takes 1½ meas; 2 hora steps require a 3-meas phrase.

Meas 1: Step swd R^L (ct 1), step L^R across in back of R^L (ct &), step fwd R^L (ct 2), swing L^R leg across in front of R^L (ct &).

Meas 2: Step swd L^R (ct 1), swing R^L leg across in front of L^R (ct &).

hornpipe step Hop L^R and raise R^L in front of L^R (ct 1), step R^L next to L^R (ct 2), step L^R (ct 3), step R^L (ct 4). Danced lightly on balls of ft, with body held erect, knees turned out, and toes pointed when raised.

hub backs out, rim goes in See *inside out, outside in*.

Hungarian break-step One of the bokazo steps. See *bokazo*.

Hungarian turn (also called *Russian turn*) Ptrs in Hungarian turn pos turn CCW^{CW} with buzz steps or hop-step-steps.

Hungarian turn position (also called *Russian turn position*) Ptrs face opp dir, R^L hips adjacent, each R^L arm around other's waist in front, free arms held sdwd and upward. See photo.

Hungarian turn position

I

inactive dancers Those not involved momentarily in performing action of dance.

inactives Dancers not designated as actives.

ingo (EEN-goh) See *csárdás*.

in place At approximately same place where previous step on same ft was taken.

inside
1. Place within a set.
2. Center position(s) in a line.

inside foot, hand Foot or hand nearest ptr when standing in side-by-side pos.

inside out, outside in Changes a star promenade to reverse, or vice versa, by "insides" backing out of center and "outsides" dancing fwd to center.

itik-itik step (EE-TEEK)
Meas 1: With wt on R^L, slide ball of L^R diag fwd (ct 1), slide ball of L^R back to R^L with heels together or with L^R heel next to R^L instep (ct &). Repeat (cts 2, &).
Meas 2: Repeat cts 1, & of meas 1 (cts 1, &), slide ball of L^R diag fwd and take wt (ct 2). Supporting ft bounces slightly in time with music.

J

jarabe step (hah-RAH-bay) Small step fwd on heel of R^L (ct 1), step on ball of L^R near R^L heel (ct 2), step on ball of R^L next to L^R (ct 3).

jig step Dancing with knees turned out, step L^R in back of and displacing R^L while extending R^L diag fwd (ct 1), hop L^R (ct &), step R^L in back of L^R heel (ct 2), hop R^L (ct &).

jump Spring from one or both ft and *land on both ft*.

K

kick A vigorous thrust with free ft up and out in dir described, with toe up or extended and knee bent or straight, as indicated.

kis harang (KEESH haw-rawng) A smooth movement resembling swing of a pendulum. With wt on L^R and R^L leg extended slightly out to side, close R^L to and displace L^R with a *cut-step* (ct 1), step L^R next to R^L (ct &), step R^L next to L^R, swinging L^R leg swd to L (ct 2), hold (ct &).

knocker step Hop R^L, raising L^R knee in front (ct &), stamp L^R next to R^L *taking wt* (ct 1), stamp R^L next to L^R *taking wt* (ct 2).

kokonješte (koh-kohn-YESH-teh)
Meas 1: Step R^L (ct 1), step L^R across in front of R^L (ct 2).
Meas 2: Small step R^L (ct 1), touch L^R next to R^L (ct 2).
Meas 3: Small step fwd L^R (ct 1), touch R^L next to L^R (ct 2).

Meas 4: Small step sdw R^L (ct 1), touch L^R next to R^L (ct 2).

kolo (KOH-loh) The name by which certain dances performed in a circle are known.

kolo step.
Meas 1: Hop L^R (ct 1), step R^L (ct &), step L^R (ct 2), hold (ct &).
Meas 2: Step R^L (ct 1), hop R^L (ct 2).

L

ladies chain May be danced by two facing couples or four couples in square formation. Designated W turn CW in a R-hand star to opposite M and courtesy turn with him (them).

ladies to center back to back From a square formation the W step fwd and turn around to face out.

ländler (laendler) See *waltz*.

ländler (laendler) position See *shoulder blade–shoulder blade position*.

lead couple Active couple.

lead foot The foot in advance of the other in a step pattern.

lead to the right Designated dancer(s) dance to a position facing dancer(s) at their R side(s).

leap Spring from the floor on one ft and *land on other ft*.

leap waltz See *waltz*.

left-face turn Turn counterclockwise (CCW).

left-hand lady Corner woman.

leg circling See *prysiadka*.

lift The following three meanings are possible, depending on context:
1. A low hop (see *hop*).
2. To raise a leg, knee, ft, hand, or arm in indicated dir.
3. To raise body up on ball of indicated ft for specified length of time.
4. To elevate ptr from floor.

limp step A walking step accented by a heavier step and bending of same knee on one side.

line Dancers side by side in straight formation. See DANCE FORMATIONS *(illustrated)*.

little finger hold position With arms usually in "W" pos and little fingers held out to sides, each dancer hooks little finger of dancer to R from underneath and behind. See photo.

longways A type of dance using a two-line or column formation. See DANCE FORMATIONS *(illustrated)*.

low hop See *hop*.

lunge Step diag fwd L^R, bending knee (ct 1), cutstep R^L fwd, displacing L^R (ct 2). Often followed by three steps L^R, R^L, L^R.

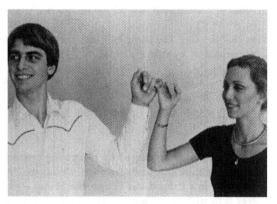

Little finger hold position

M

mayim step (mah-YEEM) See *grapevine*.

mazurka step (mah-ZOOR-kah) Glide step fwd R^L (ct 1); close L^R to R^L (ct 2), hop L^R, raising bent R knee fwd (ct 3).

mescolanza A formation of four (2 couples) facing four others.

meter Rhythm in music established by divisions into measures or bars having uniform numbers of beats of a designated note value.

mince Dance tiny steps with heels raised.

minuet

Meas 1: Step fwd L^R (ct 1, 2, 3).

Meas 2: Touch pointed R^L toe fwd (ct 1), hold (ct 2, 3).

moravac (MOH-rah-vahts) See *četiri*.

move down Move toward foot of set.

move up Move toward head of set.

movement(s) Body or group action involved in a particular dance.

N

national dance Refers to type of folk dance performed most widely throughout a given country.

neheimer step (NEE-hai-mer)

Meas 1: Hop L^R, touching R^L toe swd with toe and knee turned inward (ct 1); hop L^R, touching R^L toe next to L^R with toe and knee turned slightly outward (ct &); hop L^R, touching R^L heel next to ball of L^R with ft parallel (ct 2); hop L^R, touching toe of R^L next to ball of L^R (ct &).

Meas 2: Step R^L, L^R, R^L, taking wt on both ft on third step (cts 1 & 2), bounce on both ft if step is to be repeated with opp ftwk or hold if it is not (ct &).

O

ocean wave Four dancers in a line facing alternate directions with inside hands joined.

one-step Stepping evenly on alternate feet.

open circle A partial (broken) circle formation. See DANCE FORMATIONS *(illustrated)*.

open couple position Ptrs face same dir side by side, W to R of M, inside hands (M R palm up, W L palm down) joined, free hands down at sides. W may flair skirt with free hand. See photo.

Open couple position

opposite A person or couple being faced at a given time.

outside

1. A designated place in the area outside a set.
2. Outer positions in a line.

outside foot, hand The foot or hand farthest from partner when in side-by-side pos.

P

pack-saddle hold Each dancer (usually 4 men in square dancing) in star formation grasps wrist of person immediately in front. See photo.

parallel tortiller See *tortiller step*.

Pack-saddle hold

partner One member of a couple dancing as a one-unit entity.

pas de basque [PDB] (pah de BAHSK) The following are just three among many variations:

1. *pas de basque* Dancing lightly with body held erect, low leap swd L^R (ct 1), step briefly on ball of R^L in front of L^R (ct &), step L^R in place (ct 2).

2. *cifra* (SEE-frah) Leap lightly onto ball of R^L (ct 1), step on ball of L^R next to R^L (ct &), step on ball of R^L next to L^R (ct 2).

3. *heel cifra* (heel pas de basque) Same as cifra except that step is taken with heel on ct &.

paseo step (pah-SAY-oh) Slow, walking steps.

paso doble See *two-step*.

pass thru Opposites dance fwd, pass R shldrs, and stop with backs twd each other.

patter call(s) See *square dance call(s)*.

pattern An arrangement of recurring and varied steps, positions, and movements comprising a dance.

pesah step (PEH-sah) Step R^L (ct 1), bend knee (ct &), straighten knee (ct 2).

phrase A short, distinct passage of music, usually 2, 4, or 8 measures.

pigeon wing position A position with two joined hands, R^L fingers pointed up at shoulder height, elbows down near body. See photo.

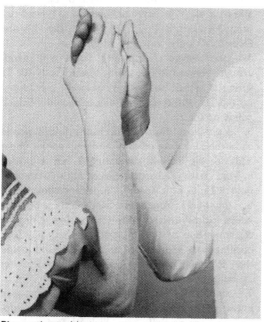

Pigeon wing position

pirouette (peer-oo-WET) The following is just one among many forms: Beginning with R^L crossed in front of and next to the side of L^R, with wt on both ft, turn CCW (CW) one full turn without ap-

preciable wt transfer, ending with ft crossed L^R in front of R^L. See *cross step turn*.

pivot Can have two meanings:

1. Turning CW or CCW on ball of one or both ft.

2. A buzz step turn by ptrs.

place To put ft or hand in indicated pos. Also, the original spot on floor from which a movement or dance began or begins.

plié (plee-AY) See *flex knee*.

point With wt on one ft, touch toe of free ft to floor in indicated dir.

polka A light, springy step with several variations:

1. *basic polka* Hop R^L (ct &), step L^R (ct 1), step R^L next to L^R (ct &), step L^R (ct 2). *Czechoslovakian, Russian, or Texas polka.* Same as basic polka except hop is omitted.

2. *heel-toe polka* Hop R^L, touching L^R heel diag fwd, toe up (ct 1); hop R^L, touching L^R toe bwd near L^R heel (ct 2); follow with basic polka.

3. *Polish polka* Quick hop L^R, touching R^L slightly fwd (ct uh), bounce on both heels as wt shifts predominantly onto R^L (ct 1), bounce on both heels as wt shifts predominantly on L^R (ct &), shifting full wt fwd onto R^L (ct 2).

4. *running polka* Run L^R, R^L, L^R, bending knee on final step (cts 1, &, 2), hold (ct &).

pols (POHLS) See *polska*.

polska (POHLS-kah) Ptrs make full turn on each three-beat meas. There are many other variations. See *hambo polska*.

polska position Ptrs face each other, stand slightly to L with R ft between ptr's ft, M R arm in front around to W L shoulder blade and L hand supports W R arm just above elbow. W L hand on M R shoulder and R hand grasps M L shoulder, or arm just above elbow. See photo.

pousette (poo-SET)

1. A movement designed as a method of progression for a couple.

2. *roundabout pousette* A movement in which two couples move around each other to finish in original positions. Detailed directions are provided for specific dances.

progression An entire sequence of a contra, ending with dancers in new positions.

promenade half, three-quarters Couples or singles dance in LOD (CCW). For square dancing, halfway refers to opposite side of square; three-quarters designates ¾ around square.

promenade position (also called *courtesy position* or *skaters position*) See *side-cross hold position* (for square dance).

promenade step The following are just three among several variations:

Polska position

1. *jig* (6/8 time)   Hop on L^R (ct 6), step R^L (ct 1), step on L^R (ct 2), step on R^L (ct 3).
2. *reel* (2/4 time)   Leap onto R^L (ct 1), step on L^R (ct 2), step on R^L (ct 3).
3. *square dance*   A smooth, gliding walk.

prompter   The person announcing contra movements.

prysiadka (Russian: pree-SYAD-kah; Ukrainian: PRIH-shid-ka)   Squatting steps performed only by men in Russia and the Ukraine. Hand pos described for Russian dances. In Ukrainian dances, hands usually remain held out wide to sides with palms up. Except as indicated, squat is on balls of ft, with knees turned out and well fwd, back straight and held vertically without leaning fwd. The following are just a few of the many types of prysiadkas. (For other steps not mentioned, see specific dance descriptions.)

1. *coffee grinder (leg circling)*   Squat with hands flat on floor and R^L leg extended swd. Remaining in this pos, swing R^L leg fwd and around in a complete cir, touching edge of ft on floor, raising each hand briefly as leg passes under. As proficiency is gained, dancer will want to keep active ft slightly above and not touching floor. With further proficiency, dancer may want to do step on spread fingertips or even one-handed if there is enough control.

2. *duck walk*   These steps remain low to floor. They may be classed as schupaks (see below), but they have a style of their own. The following are two types:

   a.   Remaining in squat pos and *keeping knees together*, arms crossed over chest, flick R^L heel up and out to side. Alternate by kicking L^R up and out to side. Step may move slightly in direction desired or in place.

   b.   Remaining in squat pos and *keeping knees together*, arms crossed over chest, swing R^L in large arc outward from back to front, sliding edge of boot along floor. Alternate by making arc with L^R. When proficient, dancer will try to keep active ft slightly above and not touching floor. Step usually travels fwd but may be done in place.

3. *schupak squat-kicks* (SCHOO-pahk)   Squat with arms folded across chest (or out to sides) and *remaining in squat pos,* alternately kick R^L ft fwd with slightly bent knees, toes extended. When done slowly, heel or sole of boot may be slapped fwd on floor on offbeat, or kicking ft may be slapped by hand on same side. Dancer may move in one dir or the other with squat kicks; or dancer may alternate sides in any combination, a typical one being 3 kicks L^R, R^L, L^R; 2 kicks R^L, then L^R, and kicks to R^L only, moving swd off floor.

4. *squat-astride (heel squat)*   Squat with hands crossed between knees, palms toward body (ct 1), spring to astride pos with wt on heels, toes turned up and out, and open arms wide at shoulder height, palms up (ct 2).

5. *squat-cross*   Squat with hands folded across chest (ct 1), spring off floor, crossing ankles under body (ct &). Repeat, alternating ft that is crossed in front. With proficiency, dancer will want to clear floor with as little space as necessary above floor.

6. *squat-heel*   Squat with hands crossed between knees, palms toward body (ct 1), slowly rise (ct &), small hop L^R (ct uh), touch R^L heel diag fwd, opening arms wide, palms up, with L^R hand higher than R^L hand and body bent slightly twd R^L (ct 2), hold (ct &).

7. *squat-kick*   Squat with hands crossed between knees, palms toward body (ct 1), hop L^R with supporting knee partially bent, kick R^L fwd with toe extended, and open arms wide at shoulder height, palms up (ct &). May also be danced swd with kicks to side.

8. *squat-kick-cross-kick*   Squat with hands crossed between knees, palms toward body (ct 1),

hop L^R with supporting knee partially bent, kick R^L swd but low toward floor, with toe extended, and open arms wide at shoulder height, palms up (ct &), step R^L across in front of L^R, bending knee and raising very bent and turned out L^R knee swd to L^R (ct 2), straightening supporting leg, extend L^R straight out to side (ct &).

9. *squat-scissor kicks* Squat with hands crossed between knees, palms toward body (ct 1), hop L^R, kicking extended R^L fwd low and open arms wide, palms up (ct &), leap R^L, kicking extended L^R fwd at greater height than before (ct 2), leap L^R, kicking extended R^L even higher than before (ct &).

10. *squat-toe-heel* Squat with hands crossed between knees, palms toward body (ct 1), hop L^R, touching R^L toe swd to floor, heel raised outward, hips twisted slightly to L^R, and open arms wide, palms up, with L^R hand higher than R^L hand and body bent slightly twd R^L (ct 2), touch R^L heel swd, toe up, twisting hips twd ctr (ct &).

pull by Two dancers briefly join R^L hands, passing R^L shoulders.

push step Step swd L^R with a quick lunging movement, pushing away with a small flick from ball of R^L (ct 1), step on ball of R next to L^R (ct &).

Q

quadrille

1. A square dance of French origin performed by four couples.

2. A square formed by four couples.

quebrado (keh-BRAH-doh) Step R^L, leaving free ft in place and rolling it onto outer edge, without putting wt on it, in a "broken ankle" movement.

R

random formation Dancers anywhere within the dancing area.

rant step Dancing with vigor, hop L^R (ct &), touch R^L toe (or heel) to floor (ct 1), hop L^R (ct &), small leap R^L in place (ct 2). Similar to polka step.

reel for four A straight hey for four people. See *hey*.

reel step With knees turned out, hop R^L, swinging L^R fwd, swd, and around to back of R^L (ct &), step L^R in back of R^L, displacing L^R fwd (ct 1).

reel the set A couple alternates one-arm turns with each other and with each of the other couples in a set.

rida (REE-dah) A buzz step qualified by which ft leads and how the steps are accented by bending. If the ft are separated on the first ct, it is termed *open rida*, whereas if closed or crossed on the first ct, it is termed *closed rida*. When wt is taken on a straight leg on first ct, step may be called *upbeat rida*; if it is taken on a bent leg on first ct, step

may be called *downbeat rida*. The most common combinations are "upbeat, open rida" and "downbeat, closed rida," although a downbeat, closed rida is possible.

right and left through Two couples, facing each other, join R hands with opposite dancers, pull by, and courtesy turn with ptr to face opp from orig dir. For Scottish dances and contras, hands are not always joined.

right-face turn Turn clockwise (CW).

rock Dance in a rocking motion without shifting wt completely to either ft. Step fwd L^R (ct 1), step bwd (or in place) R^L (ct 2). If rock is continued, center of wt remains between ft. First step R^L may also be across in front of L^R. See specific dance descriptions.

rollaway with a half sashay See *half sashay*.

round dance Choreographed dances performed simultaneously by couples following each other in a circular pattern LOD or RLOD.

run (running steps) A series of fast-paced alternating steps in even rhythm in which transfer of weight occurs in midair, with momentary loss of contact with floor, usually in fast tempo.

Russian polka See *polka*.

Russian turn See *Hungarian turn*.

Russian turn position See *Hungarian turn position*.

S

Scandinavian closed position Same as closed pos, but with elbows raised sdwd to shoulder height. See *social dance positions*.

schottische (SHAH-tish)

1. Name of a dance.

2. Name of a dance pattern, as follows: Step L^R (ct 1), step R^L (ct 2), step L^R (ct 3), hop L^R (ct 4). A running schottische leaves off hop.

scissor kick Alternating steps or leaps with simultaneous kicks fwd with free ft.

scrape To drag foot along floor.

sedam (SEH-dahm) (also called *u šest koraka*)

Meas 1: Step swd R^L (ct 1), step L^R across in back of R^L (ct &), step swd R^L (ct 2), step L across in back of R^L (ct &).

Meas 2: Step swd R^L (ct 1), step L^R across in back of R^L (ct &), step swd R^L (ct 2), hold (ct &).

see saw taw See *all around left-hand lady*.

separate Partners turn away from each other.

set A given number and formation of people for a particular dance. See DANCE FORMATIONS *(illustrated)*.

set of three Three dancers in a line or circle. See DANCE FORMATIONS *(illustrated)*.

sevens and threes

1. *jig* 6/8 (one sidestep or 1 seven and break)
Hop on L^R, R^L ft raised in front (ct 1), step swd
R^L (ct 2), step L^R in back of R^L (ct 3), step swd
R^L (ct 4), step on L^R in back of R^L (ct 5), step
swd R^L (ct 6), step L^R in back of R^L (ct 7).

2. *reel* 2/4 (one sidestep or 1 seven and 2 threes)
Leap lightly L^R in back of R^L (ct 1), step swd R^L
(ct 2), step L^R in back of R^L (ct 3), step swd R^L
(ct 4). Step L^R in back of R^L (ct 5), step swd R^L
(ct 6), step L^R in back of R^L (ct 7).
Leap lightly R^L in back of L^R (ct 1), step L^R in
place (ct 2), step R^L in place (ct 3).
break
Hop on L^R in place, R^L ft raised in front, hop L^R
in place, step back on R^L, hop on R^L and end with
4 steps in place, L^R, R^L, L^R, R^L.

shoot the star From allemande thar star position,
M release right hand, turn CCW with L hand to
exchange places.

shoulder blade–shoulder blade position (also called
Ländler [Laendler] position) Ptrs face each other,
place arms around ptr's rib cage and rest hands
on ptr's shoulder blades, W arms above M. See
photo.

Shoulder hold position ("T")

shoulder hold position (also called "T" position)
Side-by-side dancers face same dir, arms extended
sdwd, hands resting lightly on near (or sometimes
far) shoulders of adjacent dancers. See photo.

shoulder-waist position Ptrs face each other, arms
extended, W hands on M shoulders, M hands
around and at back of W waist. See photo.

Shoulder blade–shoulder blade position

Shoulder-waist position

shuffle An easy, smooth one-step in even rhythm, keeping light contact with floor, weight on balls of feet.

Sicilian circle A double circle with couples (W to R of M) facing alternately LOD and RLOD.

sidecar See *social dance positions.*

side-cross hold position (also called *promenade position* and *skaters position*) Side-by-side ptrs face same dir, R hands in handshake grasp, L hands joined (below R) M palm up, W palm down. See photo.

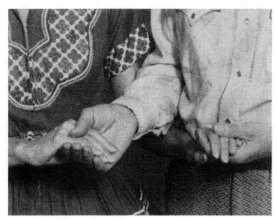

Side-cross hold position

side step Takes two meas:
Meas 1: Step diag fwd L^R (ct 1), step R^L across in front of L^R (ct 2).
Meas 2: Step diag bwd L^R (ct 1), step R^L next to L^R (ct 2).

sides Couples two and four in square dance formation.

siding A courtesy movement danced while maintaining eye contact with ptr. Dance fwd 3 steps and turn on 4 in a CCW arc, exchanging places with ptr, turn ½ CCW and repeat, dancing in a CW arc back to place.

singing call(s) See *square dance call(s).*

single circle See *circle* and DANCE FORMATIONS *(illustrated).*

skaters position Same as *side-cross hold (promenade) position* or *courtesy position.*

skip A hop and step on same ft in uneven rhythm, with quick ct being hop and slow ct being step.

skoči (SKOH-chee) Step swd R^L, quickly bringing L^R to R^L, heel to heel, ankle or instep, and bending supporting knee slightly (ct 1), hold (ct &), hop R^L, bringing L around in tight arc in back of R^L in preparation for next step (ct 2), step L^R across in back of, but very close to or even wrapping around, R^L (ct &). Three skoči steps done together are called "tri skoči."

slide (slide-close) A chassé danced with glide steps, keeping balls of ft in contact with floor.

slide step Usually in uneven rhythm (long-short). Same foot maintains lead and is displaced by following foot in a cut-step (close).

slip step Step swd L^R on ball of ft with knees turned out (ct 1), hold (ct &), close R^L heel to L^R heel with knees turned out (ct 2).

slip the clutch From allemande thar star position, release hands, all dance fwd (M CW, W CCW) to join L hands with next person met (usually followed by allemande left).

social dance A kind of dance in which a male and a female assume a given position and dance as partners.

social dance positions
1. *closed* Ptrs face each other. M R arm around W waist, with hand on W lower R rib cage, L hand extended sdwd, elbow curved, about chest high with palm up. W L hand on M R shoulder, with R palm down in M L hand. See photo.

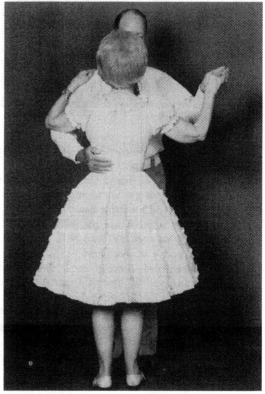

Closed position

2. *banjo* Ptrs in loosened social dance pos with R hips adjacent. See photo.

Banjo position

Sidecar position

3. *Sidecar* Ptrs in loosened social dance pos with left hips adjacent. See photo
4. *half open* Side-by-side social dance pos with M L and W R hands not joined and held at sides. W may flair skirt with outside hand. See photo.
5. *semiclosed* Social dance pos with grasp adjusted to allow an open "V" twd M L and W R. See photo. L and W R. See photo.
6. *reverse semiclosed* Same as semi-closed pos but adjusted to an open "V" twd M L and W R. See photo.
7. *Scandinavian* Same as closed pos except M R and W L arms held at shoulder height, with M L and W R elbows extended, arms straight.
soldado (sol-DAH-doh) With ptrs in closed pos, M back to ctr of cir, dance 4 gliding steps twd ctr and 4 gliding steps diag away from ctr to M L.
split the ring See *split two.*
split two Active dancer(s) pass between a couple.
square A four-sided formation, or set, outlined by four pairs (couples) of dancers, one pair facing in from each side. Square dance couples consist of a M with a W at his side. Couples are numbered 1,

Half-open position

Semiclosed position

Reverse semiclosed position

2, 3, 4 CCW, beginning with couple facing away from music or caller. See DANCE FORMATIONS *(illustrated)*.

square dance A traditional American dance done by four couples, one couple on each side of a square formation, with movements directed by a caller. (See "Square Dancing" essay in this book.)

square dance call(s) Directions chanted or sung by a caller for movements to be performed in a square dance. There are two kinds of calls:

1. Patter calls are composed of an extemporaneous selection of movements chosen by caller;

2. Singing calls are made up of specific movements parodied in a set form to a song or tune.

square dance couple position W to R of M in side-cross hold pos.

square dance step Variations include:

1. modern: a smooth one-step;
2. early: a two-step;
3. clogging: see *clog step*.

square dance swing See *swing*.

square through (½, ¾, full) A four-part routine danced by two facing couples and used as a whole or in segments designated by number of handclasps, pull bys, and precise quarter turns completed. Opposites pull by R hand and make a quarter turn to face ptrs; ptrs pull by L hand (two-hand or ½) and make a quarter turn to again face opposites; opposites pull by R hand (three-hand or ¾) and make a quarter turn to face ptr; ptrs pull by R hand (four-hand or full).

square your sets Take places in four couple square formations.

squat To (almost) sit on the heels, knees bent, feet supporting wt.

stamp To strike floor with ft or heel, usually without wt. When done with wt, it is usually indicated. See *stomp*.

star With R^L hands extended sdwd, two or more dancers join hands as indicated. Movement may be CW, CCW, fwd, or bwd. See *star positions*.

star positions

1. *two-hand* Two dancers side by side face opp dir, R^L sides adjacent, elbows bent, hands joined palm to palm at shoulder height, fingers pointing up. See photo.

2. *four-hand* Four dancers with R^L sides adjacent, hands touching in pack-saddle hold or opp hands joined in handshake with elbows straight. See photo. (Handshake not shown.)

star promenade and **reverse** Danced by couples, W to R of M, with inside arms around each other's waists. M form a L-hand pack-saddle star, all dance CCW (see photo). For reverse, W form R-hand star, all dance CW.

Two-hand star position

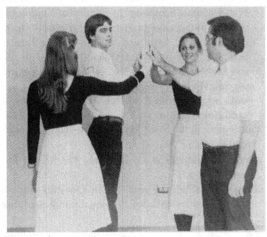

Four-hand star position

Star promenade position

star through   M and W, facing each other, make an arch with his R and her L hands; W dances fwd under arch and turns ¼ L (CCW) while M dances behind her and turns ¼ R (CW), to become a side-by-side couple.

step
1. Movement taken in any dir or in place by transferring wt from one ft to other.
2. Short form of *step pattern*.

step hop   A combination of a step and a hop in even rhythm.

step pattern   A combination of basic foot steps and movements that are known by a specific name (e.g., schottische: step-step-step-hop).

stomp   A stamp with wt, or taking wt; used infrequently.

strathspey (STRATH-spey) **rocking step**
Meas 1:   With knees turned out, step diag fwd R^L on ball of ft (ct 1), hop R^L, bringing pointed L^R toe behind R^L ankle (ct 2), step L^R back in place (ct 3), hop L^R (ct 4).
Meas 2:   Step R^L in back of L^R (ct 1), step swd L^R (ct 2), step R^L in front of L^R (ct 3), hop R^L (ct 4).

strathspey setting step   Step swd R^L, knee turned out (ct 1), close L^R behind R^L, L^R instep to R^L heel (ct 2), step R^L sdwd (ct 3), hop R^L and bring L^R up behind R^L ankle, L^R knee turned out and toe pointing down (ct 4).

strathspey traveling step   Step fwd on ball of R^L (ct 1), close L^R instep to R^L heel (ct 2), step fwd on ball of R^L, bending supporting knee slightly (ct 3), hop R^L, bringing pointed L^R fwd close to floor, with knee turned out and toe pointed down (ct 4).

strut   A series of walking steps with exaggerated knee bends on the offbeat.

supporting foot   Ft bearing wt.

swat the flea   See *box the gnat*.

swing   The following are just two among many meanings:
1. *swing leg or ft*   With wt on one ft, extend free leg or ft in indicated dir with a sweeping motion.
2. *square dance swing*   Ptrs in banjo pos walk, buzz, or two-step smoothly around each other. M stops when facing proper dir for next movement (or figure) and W turns R to face same dir at his side. See photo.

swing partner   Ptrs in closed social pos, banjo, sidecar, two-hand, or Hungarian turn pos walk, buzz, two-step, or skip step around each other.

symbols   See *abbreviations*.

T

taconazo (tah-koh-NAH-zoh)   See *zapateado*.

take weight   Shift wt onto free ft.

Square dance swing position

tandem position Two couples standing one behind the other and facing same direction, inside hands joined with ptrs, outside hands joined with person of other couple either directly behind or directly in front.

tap With wt on one ft, strike floor lightly with toe or heel of free ft (usually without transferring wt).

taw Square dance term for M partner.

tcherkessia step (chair-keh-SEE-yah) There are two variations:

1. *tcherkessia* Step or leap fwd R^L (ct 1), step bwd L^R (ct &), step bwd R^L (ct 2), step fwd L^R (ct &).

2. *double tcherkessia* Step R^L across in front of L^R (ct 1), step bwd L^R (ct &), step swd R^L (ct 2), step L^R across in front of R^L (ct &), step bwd R^L (ct 3), step swd L^R (ct &). Step takes 6 cts.

tempo The rate of speed at which music is played or a dance moves.

Texas polka See *polka*.

threes (also called triplets) The following are two versions:

1. *threes* Step R^L (ct 1), step L^R next to R (ct &), step R^L next to L^R (ct 2), hold (ct &).

2. *syncopated threes* Step R^L (ct 1), hold (ct &), step L^R next to R (ct 2), step R^L next to L^R (ct &).

three-step turn A complete turn CW or CCW with three steps.

time Tempo, duration, meter, and rhythm; also, a general term encompassing many concepts.

tinikling step (TIH-nih-kling)

Meas 1: Hop L^R (ct 1), leap R^L between poles (ct 2), step L^R between poles (ct 3).

Meas 2: Leap R^L outside poles (ct 1), leap L^R between poles (ct 2), step R^L between poles (ct 3).

tortiller step (tor-ti-YAY)

1. *double tortiller* With wt bwd on heels of both ft together, pivot toes swd R^L (ct 1, 2), shift wt fwd to balls of ft and pivot heels to R^L (ct 3).

2. *single tortiller* Dance same movements as above on one ft.

touch Place toe, heel, or ft, without taking wt on floor, in place indicated.

tour A German word denoting a section of a musical or dance composition.

"T" position Same as shoulder hold position.

trailing foot Foot used in a follow-up step.

tramp Step with emphasis.

trembling heel-walk Step fwd on R^L heel with toe turned up and knees straight (ct 1), roll wt fwd onto ball of R^L, bending knees (ct &), rise onto ball of R^L, striking L^R heel to floor, toes up, knees straight (ct 2), roll wt fwd onto ball of L^R, bending knees (ct &).

triplets See *threes*.

turn To move in a circular pattern (e.g., to turn R, CW, L, CCW, back, in, out, around) either individually, in a single circle, as ptrs in a cpl pos, or as otherwise indicated.

turn back, U-turn back Turn around individually to reverse direction.

turn single Turn alone in a small circle with four light, springy steps.

twinkle Step with free foot across, in front, or in back of and beyond supporting foot.

twirl A turn made by one dancer under an arch made by one of his own hands joined with the hand of another dancer. See photo.

Twirl

twizzle step Turning to face slightly L^R from orig dir, and with a preceding quick, low hop ("lift") on L^R, take a very small step slightly diag bwd onto R^L, with wt briefly on both ft, with L^R somewhat fwd, toe turned out, with L^R heel close to instep or ball of R^L ft. May be followed with same action in opp dir or by a series of small leaping steps swd to L^R (e.g., swd L^R, R^L across in back of L^R, swd L^R, R^L across in back of L^R).

two-hand hold position

1. *uncrossed* Ptrs face each other, hands joined R to L, M palm up, W palm down. See photo.

2. *crossed* Hands are joined R to R, L to L in handshake pos. See photo.

U

uncrossed Actives not crossed over to other line in a contra set.

up Toward head of longways set.

"U" position Side-by-side dancers join hands with adjacent dancers, raise joined hands above heads. See photo.

up the center Move up set between lines.

up the outside Move up set outside lines.

up the set Toward head of set.

u šest (u šest koraka) (oo SHEST KOH-rah-kah) See *sedam.*

Uncrossed two-hand hold position

Crossed two-hand hold position

two-step (also called catch step, change step, paso doble)

1. *basic two-step* Step L^R (ct 1), close R^L to L^R (ct &), step L^R (ct 2), hold (ct &).

2. *box two-step* Step to the four corners of a square in two meas.

Meas 1: Step sdwd L^R (ct 1), close R^L to L^R (ct &), step fwd L (ct 2), hold (ct &).

Meas 2: Step sdwd R^L (ct 1), close L^R to R^L (ct &), step bwd R^L (ct 2), hold (ct &).

Tyrolean hopsa See *hopsa.*

V

vals See *waltz.*

valseado (vahl-say-AH-doh) See *waltz.*

varsouvienne (vahr-soo-ve-EHN), **varsouvianna** (vahr-soo-vee-AN-ah) **position** Side-by-side ptrs face same dir, W to R of M, W both hold arms up at sides, hands shoulder height, palms fwd. M reaches L hand across his chest to join his L palm to W L palm, R arm around W shoulders to join M R to W R hand. See photo.

varsouvienne, varsouvianna step The following are

"U" position

Varsouvienne position

just two among many variations usually danced in varsouvienne pos:

1. *Long phrase*

Meas 1: Touch pointed toe of L^R in front of R^L with knee bent, bending body slightly fwd (ct 1), glide fwd L^R (ct 2), step fwd R (ct 3).

Meas 2–3: Repeat meas 1 twice.

Meas 4: Step L^R (ct 1), point R^L diag fwd to R^L (ct 2, 3).

Meas 5–8: Repeat action of meas 1–4 with opp ftwk.

2. *Short phrase*

Meas 1: Touch pointed toe of L^R in front of R^L with knee bent, bending body slightly fwd (ct 1), step L^R (ct 2), step R^L (ct 3).

Meas 2: Step L^R (ct 1), point R^L toe diag fwd to R^L touching floor (ct 2), hold (ct 3).

Meas 3–8: Repeat meas 1–2 three times with alternating ftwk.

vine (also called *mayim step*) See *grapevine*.

"V" position Side-by-side dancers (any number) face same direction, hands joined with adjacent dancers, arms held down. See photo.

vrtanje(ver-TAHN-yeh) See *buzz step*.

W

walk (walking steps) An alternate transfer of weight from one foot to the other in even rhythm. In a dance walk toes and ball of foot touch floor first, foot glides forward, shifting weight to entire foot while pushing off from back foot in a smooth, sustained movement.

"V" position

waltz (also called *vals*) Has many variations as well
as stylistic differences. See specific dance descriptions. The following are several versions:
1. *basic waltz* Three smooth, even steps. May be
danced in any dir or turning. Step L^R (ct 1), step
R^L (ct 2), close L^R to R^L (ct 3).
2. *box waltz*
Meas 1: Stepping to the four corners of a square,
step fwd L^R (ct 1), step diag fwd R^L (ct 2), close
L^R to R^L (ct 3).
Meas 2: Step bwd R^L (ct 1), step diag bwd L^R
(ct 2), close R^L to L^R (ct 3).
3. *leap waltz* Leap R^L, raising bent knee high (ct
1), small step L^R (ct 2), small step R^L (ct 3).
4. *native "waltz"* A two-step danced to a three-
beat meas.
5. *running waltz* Three small steps per meas,
with slight accent on first ct.
6. *waltz balance* See *balance*.
weave the ring Same as grand right and left but
danced without joining hands.
wheel around A side-by-side pair of dancers turns
CCW as a unit to reverse direction.
window position
1. *little window* Ptrs side by side, R^L sides adjacent, R^L hands joined above shldrs, L^R hands joined
through arch made by R^L hands. See photo.

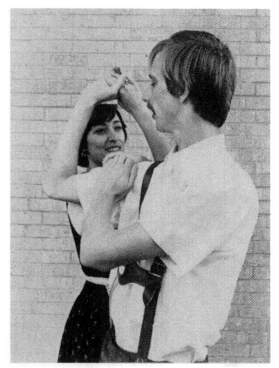

Little window position

Big window position

"W" position

Wrap position

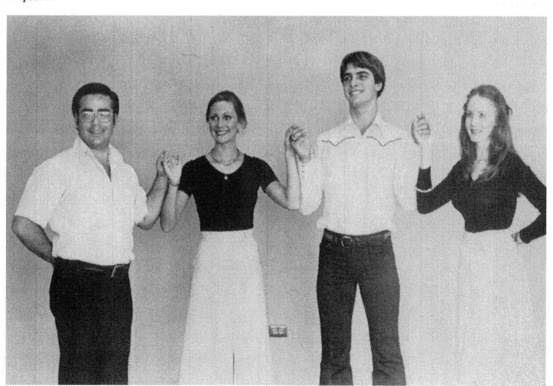

2. *big window* M R^L arm extended across in bk of W, W R across in front of her, W holds M R^L hand on her L^R hip, L^R hands joined in large arch (window) above heads. See specific dance descriptions for movements preceding this position. See photo.

"W" position Side-by-side dancers face same dir and join hands with adjacent dancers at shoulder height, elbows bent, usually with R palm up, L palm down. See photo.

wrap position

1. *one hand* Side-by-side ptrs facing same dir join inside hands (M R/W L). W makes a full L turn (keeping free R hand up and ending with joined arms wrapped around her. Free hands (W R/M L) may then be joined in front.

2. *two hand* Ptrs in two-hand uncrossed pos make an arch. W makes L^R-face turn (CCW-CW) under arch into curve of M R^L arm as hands are lowered to her waist. See photo.

Y
Yemenite step

1. *Yemenite L(R)* Step swd L^R, bending knee (ct 1), step on ball of R^L near and to back of L^R (ct &), step L^R across in front of R^L (ct 2).

2. *Yemenite fwd* Step fwd R^L, bending knee (ct 1), step fwd on ball of L^R (ct &), step fwd R (ct 2).

Z
zapateado (tsah-pah-tay-AH-doh) Rhythmic ft patterns that involve tapping heel work and brushing steps. See specific dance descriptions.

Select Bibliography

BOOKS

American Square Dancing Through the Years, 1776–1976. National Square Dance Convention Booklet, 1976.

Angeles, Alura Flores de. *The Mexican Dances of Alura Flores de Angeles*, comp. Ron Houston, forthcoming.

Beliajus, Finadar Vytautas. *Dance and Be Merry*, vol. 1 (1940), vol. 2 (1942). Evanston, Ill.: Clayton F. Summy. *Merrily Dance*, Cooperative Recreation Service, 1947.

Berk, Fred. *Ha-Rikud: The Jewish Dance*, 1972; *Chasidic Dance Book*, 1975. New York: American Zionist Youth Foundation/Union of American Hebrew Congregations.

Berquist, Nils. *Swedish Folk Dances*. New York: A. S. Barnes, 1928.

Bidstrup, Georg and Marguerite. *Folk Dances* (lithographed). Asheville, N.C.: Stephens Press, 1952.

Burchenal, Elizabeth. *Dances of the People*, 1913; *Folk Dances of Finland*, 1915; *Folk Dances and Singing Games*, 1933. New York: G. Schirmer.

Casey, Betty. *The Complete Book of Square Dancing (and Round Dancing)*. Garden City, N.Y.: Doubleday, 1976.

Chapru, Doleta. *A Festival of the English May*. Dodgeville, Wisc.: Inkwell Printers, 1977.

Clemson Area Citizens Education Center. *Recreation, Folk Games, and Party Mixers* (booklet, mimeographed). Clemson, S.C., 1955.

Cooperative Recreation Service. *Handy Country Dance Book*. Delaware, Ohio, n.d.

Culic, Dmitar. *Guide Jugoslavia*. Beograd: Izdavacki zavod Jugoslavia, 1967.

de Mille, Agnes. *The Book of the Dance*. New York: Golden Press, 1963.

Duggan, Ann; Schlottman, Jeannette; and Rutledge, Abbie. *Folk Dances of Scandinavia*. New York: A. S. Barnes, 1948.

Dunsing, Gretel and Paul. *A Collection of the Description of Folk Dances*, 1976; *Second Collection of Dance Descriptions*, 1976; *Third Collection of Dance Descriptions*, 1977 (mimeographed); *Dance Lightly* (booklet). Delaware, Ohio: Cooperative Recreation Service, 1946.

Eisenberg, Larry. *The World of Fun Series*. El Cerrito, Calif.: Methodist Radio and Film Commission, 1951.

Ellfeldt, Lois. *Folk Dance*. Dubuque, Iowa: Wm. C. Brown, 1969.

Fajardo, Libertad V. *See the World in Dances*, 1967; *Visayan Folk Dances*. Manila. Vol. 1, 1966; Vol. 2, 1974; Vol. 3, 1975.

Farwell, Jane. *Folk Dances for Fun*. Delaware, Ohio: Rural Recreation Service, n.d.

Folk Dance Directory, P.O. Box 500, Midwood Station, Brooklyn, N.Y. 11230.

Folk Dance Federation of California, Inc. *Folk Dances from Far and Near* (mimeographed). Vol. A-1, 1953; Vol. A-2, 1962; Vol. B-1, 1953; Vol. B-2, 1965; Vol. C-1, 1960; *Steps and Styling* (mimeographed); *Teacher-Training Program* (mimeographed), 1977. Alameda County School Department.

Folklore Village Farm. *Folk Dances and Music* (booklets). Dodgeville, Wisc.: Folklore Village Farm, vol. 1, 1975; vol. 2, 1976.

Ford, Mr. and Mrs. Henry. "Good Morning," 4th ed. Dearborn, Michigan, 1943.

Gadd, May. *Country Dances of Today*. New York: Country Dance Society of America, 1951.

Gault, Marian and Ned. *100 and 1 More Easy Folk Dances*. Privately printed, 1977.

Gilbert, Cecile. *International Folk Dance at a Glance*. Minneapolis, Minn.: Burgess, 1974, 1979.

Gurzau, Elba Farabegoli. *Folk Dances, Costumes and Customs of Italy*. Newark, N.J.: Folkraft Press, 1964.

Harris, Jane A.; Pitman, Anne; and Waller, Marlys S. *Dance a While*, 4th ed. Minneapolis, Minn.: Burgess, 1968.

Heikel, Yngvar, and Collan, Anni. *Dances of Finland*. London: Max Parrish, 1948.

Herman, Michael. *Folk Dances for All*. New York: Barnes & Noble, 1954.

Holden, Rickey, and Vouras, Mary. *Greek Folk Dances*. Newark, N.J.: Folkraft Press, 1965.

Howard, Carole. "Four Biographies of Women" (academic field study). Central Michigan University, 1977.

Jensen, Mary Bee and Clayne R. *Folk Dancing*.

Provo, Utah: Brigham Young Univ. Press, 1973.

Joukowsky, Anatol M. *The Teaching of Ethnic Dance.* New York: J. Lowell Pratt, 1965.

Kraus, Richard. *Folk Dancing.* New York: Macmillan, 1962.

Lawson, Joan. *European Folk Dance.* London: Sir Isaac Pitman and Sons, 1953.

Lidster, Miriam D., and Tamburini, Dorothy H. *Folk Dance Progressions.* Belmont, Calif.: Wadsworth, 1965.

Milligan, Jean C., comp. *101 Scottish Country Dances,* 1956; *99 More Scottish Country Dances,* 1963. Glasgow & London: Collins.

Mynatt, Constance, and Kaiman, Bernard D. *Folk Dancing for Students and Teachers.* Dubuque, Iowa: Wm. C. Brown, 1968; 2nd ed. 1975.

National Dance Association of the American Alliance for Health, Physical Education, Recreation and Dance. *Focus on Dance, VIII: Dance Heritage.* Washington, D.C.: AAPHERD Publications, 1977.

Nevell, Richard A. *A Time to Dance.* New York: St. Martin's Press, 1977.

People's Folk Dance Directory, P.O. Box 8575, Austin, Texas 78712.

P[hysical] E[ducation] Teachers. *The Folk Dance Book.* New York: Crampton, 1909.

Reek, Jeanne; Seamonson, Kay; and Ralph, Shirley. *Folk Dance and Lore of Norway.* Madison, Wisc.: Wisconsin House, 1971.

Sachs, Curt. *World History of the Dance* (trans. Bessie Shönberg). New York: W. W. Norton, 1937.

Salven, Erik. *Dances of Sweden.* New York: Chanticleer Press, 1949.

Scandinavian Folk Dances and Tunes, comp. Bob Werner, Dodgeville, Wisc.: Folklore Village Farm, 1977.

Seeman, Kenneth. "Traditional Dance in Sweden," *Let's Dance* 31, no. 6 (July-Aug. 1974): 4–7; "History and Development of Traditional Dance in Sweden," *Let's Dance* 35, no. 6 (July-Aug. 1978): 9–12.

Shaw, Lloyd. *Cowboy Dances,* 1939; *The Round Dance Book,* 1948. Caldwell, Idaho: Caxton Printers.

Silver, Judy. "Dancing in the Midnight Sun," *Folk Dance Scene* 14, no. 2 (April 1978): 9–11.

Tolentino, Francisca Reyes (Aquino). *Philippine National Dances.* New York: Silver Burdett, 1946.

Tolman, Beth, and Page, Ralph. *The Country Dance Book.* A. S. Barnes, 1937; rpt. Brattleboro, Vt.: The Stephen Greene Press, 1976.

Wakefield, Eleanor Ely. *Folk Dancing in America.* New York: J. Lowell Pratt, 1966.

PERIODICALS

American Square Dance (monthly)
Stan Burdick
Box 788
Sandusky, Ohio 44870

Country Dance and Song (annual)
Country Dance and Song Society
Joan Carr
505 Eighth Avenue, Rm. 2500
New York, N.Y. 10014

The Folk Dancer (Published by Mary Ann and Michael Herman; now out of print)

Folk Dance Scene (monthly except August; mimeographed)
Paul Pritchard
13250 Ida Avenue
Los Angeles, Calif. 90066

Folk Dance Scene (mimeographed)
Vonnie Brown
4431 Blecker Drive
Baton Rouge, La. 70809

Let's Dance, A Magazine of International Folk Dancing (monthly)
Folk Dance Federation of California, Inc.
1275 "A" Street, Rm. 111
Hayward, Calif. 94541

Mixed Pickles (Folk Dance Association's monthly newspaper; now out of print)
Ray LaBarbera
P.O. Box 500, Midwood Station
Brooklyn, N.Y. 11230

Northern Junket (traditional dance magazine published ten times a year)
Ralph Page
117 Washington Street
Keene, New Hampshire 03431

Northwest Folk Dancer, Inc.
Art Brooks
10707 North Park North
Seattle, Wash. 93133

Rosin the Bow (out of print) (July 1952), IV, no. 8.

Square Dancing (monthly)
Bob Osgood
462 North Robertson Boulevard
Los Angeles, Calif. 90048

Viltis (folklore magazine published six times a year)
Vyts Beliajus
Box 1226
Denver, Colo. 80201

INDEX

781574411188
93.319 CAS
asey, Betty, 1916-
nternational folk dancing U.S.A

**NEW YORK MILLS PUBLIC
LIBRARY**
399 Main St.
New York Mills, NY 13417
(315) 736-5391

DISCARD

New York Mills Public Library
0001200978946

CPSIA information can be obtained
at www.ICGtesting.com
Printed in the USA
LVHW061911110523
746711LV00007BA/284

9 781574 4111